SEVENTH EDITION

Constitutional Law *and the* Criminal Justice System

J. SCOTT HARR, J.D.
Concordia University, Saint Paul

KÄREN M. HESS, Ph.D.
Normandale Community College

CHRISTINE H. ORTHMANN, M.S.
Orthmann Writing and Research

JONATHON KINGSBURY, J.D.
Lieutenant, Minneapolis (MN) Police Department

CENGAGE Learning

Australia • Brazil • Canada • Mexico • Singapore • United Kingdom • United States

CENGAGE Learning

Constitutional Law and the Criminal Justice System, Seventh Edition

Christine H. Orthmann, Jonathon Kingsbury, Kären M. Hess, J. Scott Harr

Product Director: Marta Lee-Perriard

Product Team Manager: Carolyn Henderson-Meier

Content Developer: Katie Seibel

Product Assistant: Timothy Kappler

Marketing Manager: Mark Linton

Art and Cover Direction, Production Management, and Composition: Lumina Datamatics, Inc.

Manufacturing Planner: Judy Inouye

Cover Image: Tetra Images/Getty Images; iStock/giftlegacy; Lisa S./Shutterstock.com; Billion Photos/Shutterstock.com

Unless otherwise noted all items © Cengage Learning®

© 2018, 2015 Cengage Learning

ALL RIGHTS RESERVED. No part of this work covered by the copyright herein may be reproduced or distributed in any form or by any means, except as permitted by U.S. copyright law, without the prior written permission of the copyright owner.

> For product information and technology assistance, contact us at
> **Cengage Learning Customer & Sales Support, 1-800-354-9706.**
> For permission to use material from this text or product, submit all requests online at **www.cengage.com/permissions.**
> Further permissions questions can be e-mailed to
> **permissionrequest@cengage.com.**

Library of Congress Control Number: 2016955572

Student Edition:
ISBN: 978-1-305-96646-8

Loose-leaf Edition:
ISBN: 978-1-305-96653-6

Cengage Learning
20 Channel Center Street
Boston, MA 02210
USA

Cengage Learning is a leading provider of customized learning solutions with employees residing in nearly 40 different countries and sales in more than 125 countries around the world. Find your local representative at **www.cengage.com.**

To learn more about Cengage Learning Solutions, visit **www.cengage.com.**

Purchase any of our products at your local college store or at our preferred online store **www.cengagebrain.com.**

Printed at CLDPC, USA, 02-22

Brief Contents

1. A Historical Overview 3
2. An Overview of the U.S. Legal System 29
3. The U.S. Supreme Court: The Final Word 58
4. Equal Protection under the Law: Balancing Individual, State, and Federal Rights 79
5. The First Amendment: Basic Freedoms 126
6. The Second Amendment: The Gun Control Controversy 174
7. The Fourth Amendment: An Overview of Constitutional Searches and Seizures 203
8. Conducting Constitutional Seizures 246
9. Conducting Constitutional Searches 286
10. The Fifth Amendment: Obtaining Information Legally 345
11. The Sixth Amendment: Right to Counsel and a Fair Trial 392
12. The Eighth Amendment: Bail, Fines, and Punishment 427
13. The Remaining Amendments and a Return to the Constitution 455

Epilogue 473

Appendix A The U.S. Constitution and Amendments 476
Appendix B Reading Legal Citations 489
Appendix C Briefs of *Marbury* and *Miranda* 490
Appendix D Citating a Case 492
Appendix E Legal Research 493

Glossary 497
Case Index 506
Authors Index 510
Subject Index 512

Contents

About the Authors xv

Preface xvii

Acknowledgments xxiii

SECTION I A Foundation for Understanding Constitutional Law

Prologue 1

1 A Historical Overview 3

Introduction 4
Where It All Began 5
Development of the United States of America 6
  Colonial Dissension Grows 7
  The First Continental Congress 8
  The Revolution Begins 9
  The Second Continental Congress 10
The Declaration of Independence 10
  What It Cost the Signers 10
  The Articles of Confederation 11
The Constitution Takes Shape 12
  The Influence of the Magna Carta 12
  The 1787 Constitutional Convention of Delegates 13
  The Issue of Slavery 15
  Drafting the Constitution 15
The Constitution of the United States: An Overview 16
  Article 1: The Legislative Branch 16
  Article 2: The Executive Branch 17
  Article 3: The Judicial Branch 18
  Article 4: Other Provisions 19
  Article 5: The Amendment Process 19
  Article 6: The Constitution as the Supreme Law 19
  The Signing of the Constitution 19
  Ratification 20
The Bill of Rights: A Balance Is Struck 21
  The Bill of Rights: An Overview 22
  A Living Law 25
A Nearly Timeless Document 26
Summary 27
Discussion Questions 28
References 28
Cases Cited 28

2 An Overview of the U.S. Legal System 29

Introduction 31
Theories About and Purpose of the Legal System 31
   Purpose of Law: Consensus Theory versus Conflict Theory 31
   The Purpose of the Criminal Justice System:
      Crime Control versus Due Process 32
   The Challenge: Balancing Individual and Societal Rights 34
Definition and Development of the Law 35
   Evolution of Common Law and Stare Decisis 35
   The Continuing Need for Law 36
Categorizing Law 37
   Who? (Jurisdiction) 37
   How? (Procedural) 38
   What? (Criminal or Civil) 38
Researching the Law 40
   Sources of Information about the Law 40
   Reading Legal Citations 41
   Reading Case Law 41
   Briefing a Case 42
   Citing 43
The Court System 44
   The State Court System 45
   The Federal Court System 47
   Officers of the Court 49
   An Adversarial Judicial System 49
   Doctrines Governing What Cases Will Be Heard 50
The Components of the U.S. Legal System: The Big Picture 51
   The Juvenile Justice System 52
   The Changing Face of American Criminal Justice and
      Constitutional Law 53
U.S. Criminal Justice Beyond Our Borders 53
Summary 56
Discussion Questions 56
References 57
Cases Cited 57

3 The U.S. Supreme Court: The Final Word 58

Introduction 59
Authority for the Supreme Court 60
Jurisdiction of the Supreme Court 61
Judicial Review 63
   Controversy Over and Alternatives to Judicial Review 65
   Certiorari: Deciding Which Cases to Hear 65
The Supreme Court Justices 67
   Politics and the Supreme Court 68
   The Current Supreme Court 69
Traditions and Procedures 73
   Opinions 74

Interpretations 75
Where Supreme Court Decisions May Be Found 75
The Power of the Supreme Court 76
Summary 77
Discussion Questions 77
References 77
Cases Cited 78

SECTION II The Guarantees of the Constitution: Civil Rights and Civil Liberties

4 Equal Protection under the Law: Balancing Individual, State, and Federal Rights 79

Introduction 80
The Thirteenth Amendment 81
The Fourteenth Amendment 82
Due Process 83
   Enumerated Rights and Incorporation 84
   Procedural Due Process 86
   Substantive Due Process 87
   Due Process and Privacy Rights 90
Discrimination versus Prejudice 92
The Roots of Racial Discrimination 93
The Struggle for Equality 94
   The Rise of Affirmative Action Programs 95
   Reverse Discrimination 98
   Racial and Gender Equality in the Twenty-First Century 100
   Other Forms of Discrimination 101
   The Immigration Issue 104
Equal Protection in the Criminal Justice System 110
   Discrimination in Law Enforcement 111
   Discrimination in the Courts 114
   Discrimination in Corrections 116
A Check on Federal Power 118
   Federalism Revisited 119
   The Public Safety Employer-Employee Cooperation Act of 2009 119
Summary 122
Discussion Questions 122
References 123
Cases Cited 124

5 The First Amendment: Basic Freedoms 126

Introduction 127
Freedom of Religion 129
   The Establishment Clause 130
   The Free Exercise Clause 134
   Interpretations 138

Freedom of Speech 138
   Pure Speech 139
   Symbolic Expression 140
   Protected versus Unprotected Speech—
     Determining Boundaries 145
   Restrictions on Freedom of Speech 152
   First Amendment Expression Rights of Public Employees 156
   Freedom of Speech, the Internet, and Technology 159
   The Right to Record 160
Freedom of the Press 161
   Balancing Freedom of the Press with the Right to a
     Fair Trial 163
   The Effect of Media Coverage on Criminal Investigations 164
The Right to Peaceful Assembly 164
Freedom of Association 166
First Amendment Rights of Prisoners 168
Summary 171
Discussion Questions 171
References 172
Cases Cited 172

6 The Second Amendment: The Gun Control Controversy 174

Introduction 175
Historical Background 176
The Debate: Interpreting the Second Amendment 176
   Modern-Day Militias in the United States 177
   Balancing Individual and States' Rights 177
Case Law Regarding the Second Amendment 178
   A Shift in Interpretation: The Heller Decision 179
   Incorporation of the Second Amendment 180
Variation in State and Local Gun Laws 182
   Concealed Carry Laws 183
   Castle Laws 184
   Restrictions on Types of Firearms 186
Federal Regulation and the Second Amendment 186
   The Brady Act 188
   The Violent Crime Control and Law Enforcement
     Act of 1994 190
   The Law Enforcement Officers Safety Act 193
   Other Proposed Federal Legislation 193
Guns, Crime, and Violence 194
The Current Gun Control Debate 196
   In Opposition to Gun Control 197
   In Support of Gun Control 197
   Gun Control as a Political Issue 197
Finding Common Ground—Is a Compromise Possible? 198
Summary 200

Discussion Questions 200
References 201
Cases Cited 202

SECTION III — The Fourth Amendment: Governing Constitutional Searches and Seizures

7 The Fourth Amendment: An Overview of Constitutional Searches and Seizures 203

Introduction 205
The Importance of the Fourth Amendment to Law Enforcement 207
Who Is Regulated by the Fourth Amendment? 208
The Clauses of the Fourth Amendment 212
  Two Interpretations 212
  Reasonableness 213
  Probable Cause 214
  Sources of Probable Cause 215
Search and Arrest Warrants 219
  Knock-and-Announce Rule 220
  Special Conditions 221
  Executing the Warrant 222
The Continuum of Contacts 222
The Law of Stop and Frisk 225
  Basic Definitions 225
  Terry v. Ohio 227
Consequences of Fourth Amendment Violations 229
  The Exclusionary Rule 229
  Exceptions to the Exclusionary Rule 234
  Internal Sanctions, Civil Liability, and Criminal Liability 239
A Final Consideration: When State Law Conflicts with Constitutional Law 241
Summary 243
Discussion Questions 243
References 244
Cases Cited 244

8 Conducting Constitutional Seizures 246

Introduction 247
Intensity and Scope of a Seizure: Stop and Arrest Compared 248
Investigatory Stops 249
  Establishing Reasonable Suspicion 250
  Length of the Stop 254
  Protective Actions during Stops 256
  The Controversy over Pedestrian Stops 256
  Traffic Stops 257

Roadblocks and Checkpoints 261
Stops at International Borders 262
Arrests: An Overview 264
When Arrests May Be Lawfully Made 264
Where Arrests May Be Made 266
The Community Caretaking Doctrine 267
An Arrest or Not? De Facto Arrests 267
Pursuit 268
Use of Force 270
What Is Reasonable Force? 271
Use of Less-Lethal Force 275
The Use of TASERs 276
Use of Deadly Force 278
Putting It All Together 280
Citizen's Arrest 281
Immunity from Arrest 282
Summary 283
Discussion Questions 283
References 284
Cases Cited 284

9 Conducting Constitutional Searches 286

Introduction 287
Tenets of Fourth Amendment Search Analysis 288
The Scope of Searches 290
Searches with a Warrant 291
Executing the Warrant 293
The Knock-and-Announce Rule Revisited 293
Detention during a Search 294
Conducting the Search 295
Searches without a Warrant 296
Searches with Consent 297
Frisks 301
Plain Feel and Plain Touch 302
Plain View Evidence 303
Searches Incident to Lawful Arrest 305
The Automobile Exception 311
Exigent Circumstances 315
Open Fields, Abandoned Property, and Public Places 319
Border Searches 323
Special Needs Searches 325
Administrative Searches 326
Public School Searches 326
Jail, Prison, Probation, and Parole Searches 327
Searches of Public Employee Work Areas 331
Electronic Surveillance, Privacy Interests, and the Fourth Amendment 333
The Electronic Communications Privacy Act 335
Balancing Security Concerns with Privacy Interests 338

Contents **xi**

Summary 341
Discussion Questions 342
References 342
Cases Cited 343

SECTION IV Due Process: The Fifth, Sixth, and Eighth Amendments

10 The Fifth Amendment: Obtaining Information Legally 345

Introduction 346
Government's Need to Know 347
The Right Against Compelled Self-Incrimination 348
Due Process of Law 350
The Fifth Amendment and Confessions 351
   Voluntariness of Confessions 352
   A Standard for Voluntariness 354
   False Confessions 357
Miranda v. Arizona 357
   The Case 358
   The Miranda *Warning* 358
   The Wording 359
   Premature Miranda *Warnings* 360
   When the Miranda *Warning Must Be Given* 361
   Waiving and Invoking the Rights 365
   Beachheading or "Question First" 370
   Miranda *Survives a Challenge—Dickerson v. United States* 372
   Miranda, *The Right against Self-Incrimination, and Impeached Testimony* 373
   Miranda *Issues Continue* 373
   When Miranda *Warnings Generally Are Not Required* 374
   The Public Safety Exception 375
   Consequences of a Miranda *Violation* 375
   Fifth Amendment Miranda *Implications of Using Informants* 376
Entrapment 377
Other Rights Guaranteed by the Fifth Amendment 378
   The Right to a Grand Jury 379
   Double Jeopardy 380
   Just Compensation 382
Fifth Amendment and Corrections 384
USA PATRIOT Act 385
   Elements of the USA PATRIOT Act 385
   The Renewal of the USA PATRIOT Act 387
Summary 389
Discussion Questions 389
References 390
Cases Cited 390

11 The Sixth Amendment: Right to Counsel and a Fair Trial 392

Introduction 393
The Seven Discrete Clauses of the Sixth Amendment 394
    Speedy and Public Trial 394
    An Impartial Jury 396
    Where the Trial Is Held 401
    Being Informed of the Accusation 402
    The Right to Confront Witnesses 402
    Compulsory Process 404
    Right to Counsel 404
Right to Counsel at Critical Stages of Criminal Proceedings 408
    Critical Stages during the Criminal Investigation 409
    Rights during Identification 411
    Critical Stages at Hearings, Trials, and Appeals 415
The Presumption of Effective Counsel 420
Waiver of Sixth Amendment Right to Legal Counsel 421
The Right to Act as One's Own Counsel 421
Juveniles and the Sixth Amendment 423
The Sixth Amendment and Corrections 423
Summary 424
Discussion Questions 424
References 425
Cases Cited 425

12 The Eighth Amendment: Bail, Fines, and Punishment 427

Introduction 428
A Brief History of Punishment 429
Bail 430
    The Evolution of Legislation and Case Law on Bail 430
    The Bail Reform Act of 1966 430
    The Bail Reform Act of 1984 431
Fines 433
    Asset Forfeiture and the Prohibition against Excessive Fines 433
Cruel and Unusual Punishment 435
    Punishment Options 437
    Physical Forms of Punishment 438
Capital Punishment 440
    Is Capital Punishment Cruel and Unusual? 440
    Are Lengthy Delays in Execution Cruel and Unusual? 443
    Who Can Be Executed? 443
    Appeals 445
    Costs of the Death Penalty 446
    Juries and Capital Punishment Cases 446
    Continuing Controversy 447

The Eighth Amendment and Corrections   448
  Conditions of Confinement and Deliberate Indifference   449
  Use of Force and Good Faith   450
  Other Correctional Issues and the Eighth Amendment   451
Summary   452
Discussion Questions   452
References   453
Cases Cited   453

SECTION V   Coming Full Circle

13   The Remaining Amendments and a Return to the Constitution   455

Introduction   456
The Remaining Amendments to the Bill of Rights   457
  The Third Amendment   457
  The Seventh Amendment   457
  The Ninth Amendment   458
  The Tenth Amendment   460
Amendments Beyond the Bill of Rights   463
  The Eleventh Amendment (1795)   463
  The Thirteenth Amendment (1865)   463
  The Fourteenth Amendment (1868)   464
  Amendments Related to Elections and Structure of Congress   465
  Voting Rights   466
  Taxes   468
  Prohibition   468
Attempts at Other Amendments   468
The Process of Amending the Constitution   470
Summary   471
Discussion Questions   471
References   471
Cases Cited   471

Epilogue   473

Appendixes
  A. The U.S. Constitution and Amendments   476
  B. Reading Legal Citations   489
  C. Briefs of *Marbury* and *Miranda*   490
  D. Citating a Case   492
  E. Legal Research   493

Glossary   497

Case Index   506

Authors Index   510

Subject Index   512

About the Authors

This text is dedicated to J. Scott Harr (1953–2008), the original lead author of this text whose 30-year career embodied true commitment to the law and allegiance to the U.S. Constitution. Scott was a recipient of the Warren E. Burger Award, given in honor of the former Chief Justice of the U.S. Supreme Court, and a member of the U.S. Supreme Court bar, placing him among attorneys permitted to practice before the Supreme Court. As a police officer, police chief, attorney, and educator in criminal justice, Scott Harr's passion for and belief in the law was inspirational to his students, colleagues, and the communities in which he served. He is deeply missed.

KÄREN MATISON HESS, PH.D., (d. 2010) wrote extensively in law enforcement and criminal justice, gaining a respected reputation for the consistent pedagogical style around which she structured each textbook. She developed the original edition of *Constitutional Law and the Criminal Justice System* with Scott Harr and carried it through four successful revisions; much of her work and influence remains unchanged in this new edition.

Other texts Hess authored or co-authored for Cengage Publishing are *Careers in Criminal Justice and Related Fields: From Internship to Promotion*; *Community Policing: Partnerships for Problem Solving*; *Criminal Investigation*; *Introduction to Law Enforcement and Criminal Justice*; *Introduction to Private Security*; *Management and Supervision in Law Enforcement*; *Juvenile Justice*; and *Police Operations*.

Dr. Hess held a Ph.D. in English and in instructional design from the University of Minnesota and was a nationally recognized educator. She was an instructor in the English department at Normandale Community College (Bloomington, Minnesota), a frequent instructor for report writing workshops and seminars for law enforcement agencies around the country, and President of the Institute for Professional Development. In 2006, Hess was honored by the University of Minnesota College of Education and Human Development at the school's 100-year anniversary as one of 100 alumni who have made a significant contribution to education and human development.

CHRISTINE HESS ORTHMANN holds an M.S. in criminal justice from the University of Cincinnati and has been writing about and researching various aspects of criminal justice for more than 20 years. Orthmann is a co-author of numerous Cengage texts, including *Community Policing: Partnerships for Problem Solving*; *Criminal Investigation*; *Introduction to Law Enforcement and Criminal Justice*; *Juvenile Justice*; *Management and Supervision in Law Enforcement*; and *Police Operations: Theory and Practice*. She is also a major contributor to *Introduction to Private Security* and *Careers in Criminal Justice and Related Fields: From Internship to Promotion*.

Orthmann is a member of the Academy of Criminal Justice Sciences, the American Society of Criminology, the Text and Academic Authors Association, and the National Criminal Justice Honor Society (Alpha Phi Sigma). She is a former reserve officer with the Rosemount (Minnesota) Police Department.

JONATHON KINGSBURY, J.D., has been with the Minneapolis (Minnesota) Police Department since 1995. Most of his career has been spent in uniform, both as a patrol officer and a supervisor. In addition to his time in uniform, he has experience as a department physical fitness instructor, defense tactics coordinator, field training officer, SWAT team supervisor, and in-service trainer. Lt. Kingsbury received a B.A. from the University of Minnesota and a J.D. from Hamline University School of Law, graduating magna cum laude. He has taught college courses in report writing and criminal procedure, and has acted as a law enforcement consultant in the areas of use of force and search and seizure. He is a member of several organizations, including the Minnesota State Bar Association, the International Law Enforcement Educators and Trainers Association, and the National Tactical Officers Association.

Preface

Constitutional Law and the Criminal Justice System was written with the criminal justice student in mind. We developed a natural progression to help students build their knowledge of the Constitution and how it directs law enforcement procedures and practices. Plain language is preferred to legalese. Court opinions are important, and students have opportunities in this text to learn how to read them, and even to read and brief some. Mastering the basic concepts of constitutional law is only the beginning, however; U.S. law is unique in that it can, and does, change to meet the changing needs of the society it serves. Thus, an important part of the knowledge students will acquire through this text and course is how to keep current with this exciting and evolving area of law.

Organization of the Text

Section I provides a foundation for understanding constitutional law beginning with a historical overview of how the Constitution came to be (Chapter 1). This is followed by an overview of our country's legal system (Chapter 2) and an examination of the Supreme Court of the United States as the final word on any legal issues (Chapter 3).

Section II focuses on the guarantees of the Constitution to citizens: their civil rights and civil liberties. The discussion first focuses on equal protection under the law and efforts to balance individual, state, and federal rights (Chapter 4). The focus then shifts to the basic freedoms guaranteed by the First Amendment (Chapter 5). This section concludes with a discussion of the gun control controversy arising from the Second Amendment (Chapter 6).

Section III describes in depth the constitutional amendment that governs searches and seizures—the Fourth Amendment. It begins with an overview of constitutional searches and seizures as required by the Fourth Amendment (Chapter 7). A detailed look at conducting constitutional seizures is presented next (Chapter 8), followed by an equally detailed look at conducting constitutional searches (Chapter 9).

Section IV examines the three other amendments particularly crucial to those in the criminal justice profession as they apply to citizens' due process rights. The section first discusses due process and obtaining information legally as required by the Fifth Amendment (Chapter 10), followed by citizens' right to counsel and a fair trial as required by the Sixth Amendment (Chapter 11). The section concludes with a discussion of bail, fines, and punishment as regulated by the Eighth Amendment (Chapter 12).

The final section of the text, Section V, provides a discussion of the remaining amendments and how additional amendments might come to be in the future (Chapter 13).

How to Use This Text

Constitutional Law and the Criminal Justice System is a carefully structured learning experience. The more actively you participate in it, the greater your learning will be. You will learn and remember more if you first familiarize yourself with the total scope of the subject. Read and think about the table of contents, which provides an outline of the many facets of constitutional law. Then follow these steps for *quadruple-strength learning* as you study each chapter:

1. Read the Learning Objectives (LOs) at the beginning of the chapter. Assess your current knowledge of the subject of each objective. Examine any preconceptions you may hold. Look at the key terms, and watch for them when they are used.
2. Read the chapter while underlining, highlighting, or taking notes—whatever is your preferred study method. Pay special attention to all highlighted information, which represents the chapter-opening LOs and reinforces the key concepts in the chapter:

> **LO 1** *Article 3 of the U.S. Constitution established the authority for a federal judiciary. The Federal Judiciary Act of 1789 established the first Supreme Court, and although the number of justices has varied, nine has remained the agreed-upon number since 1869.*

Also, pay special attention to all the words in boldface type and their corresponding definitions. The key terms and their definitions appear in the margin the first time they are used:

judicial review the power of a court to analyze decisions of other government entities and lower courts

3. When you have finished reading the chapter, read the summary—your third exposure to the chapter's key information. Then return to the beginning of the chapter and quiz yourself. Can you respond to all of the learning objectives? Can you define the key terms?
4. Finally, read the Discussion Questions at the end of the chapter and be prepared to contribute to a class discussion of the ideas presented in the chapter.

By following these steps, you will learn more information, understand it more fully, and remember it longer.

Note: The material selected to highlight using the quadruple-strength learning instructional design includes only the chapter's key concepts. Although this information is certainly important in that it provides a structural foundation for understanding the topic(s) discussed, you cannot simply glance over the highlighted boxes that correspond to each Learning Objective and the summary and expect to master the chapter. You are also responsible for reading and understanding the material that surrounds these basics—the "meat" around the bones, so to speak.

New to This Edition

The seventh edition of *Constitutional Law and the Criminal Justice System* has been completely updated with the most recent Supreme Court decisions and references available. Each chapter has been revised and updated as follows:

- **Chapter 1: A Historical Overview**   Streamlined discussion to reduce redundancies; added a new key term (*confederation*); added a new Myth/Fact box.
- **Chapter 2: An Overview of the U.S. Legal System**   Added a new key term (*collective conscience*); changed the term *Shepardizing* to *citing* to reflect contemporary terminology; updated the section discussing Shepardizing to reflect the fact that many citing methods exist now, all under the original idea of Shephard; added information about codifying law for historical context; added a new Myth/Fact box; updated statistics on court caseloads and juvenile cases.
- **Chapter 3: The U.S. Supreme Court: The Final Word**   Reorganized chapter content for improved presentation and reduced the number of first-level headings; added a new Myth/Fact Box; updated caseload statistics and public opinion data; added an explanation of the *in forma pauperis* docket; added a discussion about the current vacancy left by Scalia; added a comment about judicial interpretation; added a new "In the News" article.
- **Chapter 4: Equal Protection under the Law: Balancing Individual, State, and Federal Rights**   Added several new key terms (*implicit bias, procedural justice*), as well as accompanying discussions about implicit bias and procedural justice; added a new Constitutional Law in Action box pertaining to enumerated versus unenumerated rights; updated the decisions for *Schuette* (2014) and *Fisher* (2016); added discussions for several new cases (*EEOC v. Abercrombie and Fitch*, 2015; *City and County of San Francisco v. Sheehan*, 2015); added a quote by Senator Hubert Humphrey regarding affirmative action; added Case in Brief boxes for ten cases (*Brown v. Board of Education*, 1954; *Regents of the University of California v. Bakke*, 1978; *Schuette v. Coalition to Defend Affirmative Action*, 2014; *Ricci v. Destefano*, 2009; *EEOC v. Abercrombie and Fitch*, 2015; *City and County of San Francisco v. Sheehan*, 2015; *United States v. Windsor*, 2013; *Obergefell v. Hodges*, 2015; *Strauder v. West Virginia*, 1880; and *Wolff v. McDonnell*, 1974); updated information pertaining to public opinion on illegal immigration; added a new table comparing Secure Communities to PEP; included a few sentences on Obama's executive order and the November 2014 memo by the DHS Secretary; added a few paragraphs on *United States v. Texas* (2016) and the ruling that blocks Obama's immigration executive action; included mention of new training to help officers identify and control implicit bias; added a new "In the News" article.
- **Chapter 5: The First Amendment: Basic Freedoms**   Added new key term (*pure speech*) and reorganized the "Freedom of Speech" section to introduce the reader to the concept of *pure speech*; included discussions of six new cases (*Marsh v. Chambers*, 1983; *Town of Greece v. Galloway*, 2014; *Holt v. Hobbs*, 2015; *Burwell v. Hobby Lobby*, 2014; *McCullen v. Coakley*, 2014; and *Lane v. Franks*, 2014); added Case in Brief boxes for eight cases (*Everson v. Board of Education*, 1947; *Agostini v. Felton*, 1997; *Town of Greece v. Galloway*, 2014; *Burwell v. Hobby Lobby*, 2014; *Holt v. Hobbs*, 2015; *Reed v. Town of Gilbert*, 2015; *United States v. Stevens*, 2010;

and *Lane v. Franks*, 2014); added a brief explanation of separationist versus nonpreferentialist theory in the discussion of freedom of religion; expanded the discussion of the RFRA to include mention of the separation of powers issue (Congress v. Judiciary) and to provide a segue into two recent decisions: *Holt v. Hobbs* (2015) (RLUIPA) and *Burwell v. Hobby Lobby* (2014) (RFRA); added a new "In the News" article.

- **Chapter 6: The Second Amendment: The Gun Control Controversy** Updated statistics throughout; added a new "In the News" article; added discussions and Case in Brief boxes for *Caetano v. Massachusetts* (2016) and *Abramski v. United States* (2014); added a discussion of the cases for *Peruta v. County of San Diego* (2016) and *Moore v. Madigan* (7th Circuit, 2012) to demonstrate the inconsistent rulings at the circuit court level for concealed carry; included a mention of the NICS Improvement Amendments Act of 2007 (NIAA), recent changes that allow submission of mental health information (HIPPA rules) to NICS, and a push to have Social Security Administration (SSA) records submitted for people who are receiving disability payments for mental health problems as ways to improve quality of background checks; updated data on active anti-government groups in the United States; added information about terrorist watch lists and the NICS; added a new "In the News" article.

- **Chapter 7: The Fourth Amendment: An Overview of Constitutional Searches and Seizures** Added several new key terms (*consent decree, memorandum of agreement [MOA]*); added a new Constitutional Law in Action box dealing with probable cause; added considerable discussion of *Utah v. Strieff* (2016) and the attenuation doctrine; added Case in Brief boxes for *Florida v. Harris* (2013) and *U.S. v. Leon*; included a short discussion on writs of assistance/general warrants and four relevant cases; added discussion of *U.S. v. Tapley* to provide a more recent case example illustrating who is regulated by the government; added a quote by Justice Scalia in *City of Los Angeles v. Patel* (2015) regarding reasonableness of searches; clarified *privacy* in context of First Amendment versus Fourth Amendment; revised the *Spinelli* case discussion for clarity and accuracy; revised the definition of *reasonable suspicion* for clarity; added a brief discussion on consent decrees and memorandums of agreement (MOAs); revised a Constitutional Law in Action box to focus on an identity theft ring.

- **Chapter 8: Conducting Constitutional Seizures** Added new discussions and Case in Brief boxes for *Heien v. North Carolina* (2014), *Navarette v. California* (2014), and *Rodriguez v. United States* (2014); added a discussion of *Alabama v. White* (1990) and anonymous tips; streamlined the discussion of the *Harris v. Commonwealth* case; added a short discussion on *Steagald v. United States* (1981); included a paragraph on force needing to be *intentional* to come under Fourth Amendment regulation; added a few sentences regarding the current debate on use-of-force continuums; added a paragraph on de-escalation in use of force; included a case discussion on Tasers (*Armstrong v. Village of Pinehurst*, 2016); added a discussion and accompanying table on how a person's status (free, pre-trail detainee, convicted) affects how the use of force will be evaluated by the court and the test used; added a use of force discussion regarding *Kingsley v. Hendrickson* (2015); streamlined overall chapter organization by moving the *Hastings* case to the "Use of Force" section and moving the "Knock and Announce Rule Revisited" section to Chapter 9.

- **Chapter 9: Conducting Constitutional Searches**   Added new discussions and Case in Brief boxes for *Fernandez v. California* (2014), *Birchfield v. North Dakota* (2016), and *Riley v. California* (2014); added a Case in Brief box for *Horton v. California* (1990); expanded the discussion on search incident to arrest to include *Riley v. California* and *Birchfield v. North Dakota*; expanded the "hot pursuit" discussion to include coverage of *Stanton v. Sims* (2013) and *United States v. Santana* (1976); included a brief discussion of *Grady v. North Carolina* (2015); updated and reorganized the section on electronic surveillance and the Fourth Amendment; added a bullet point for *In Re: Application for Telephone Information Needed for a Criminal Investigation* (2015); added a new "In the News" article.
- **Chapter 10: The Fifth Amendment: Obtaining Information Legally**   Added several new key terms (*eminent domain, rebut*); added a discussion of *Salinas v. Texas* (2013) and the need to actively invoke the right to remain silent versus mere silence; expanded the discussion of *Garrity* and *Gardner* and added a Case in Brief box for *Garrity*; added a discussion and a new Case in Brief box for *Kansas v. Cheever* (2013); added mention of *Estelle v. Smith* (1981), which deals with compelled self-incrimination; added a mention of *Martinez v. Illinois* (2014), which deals with double jeopardy; included a discussion of the Blockburger test used in double jeopardy issues; added a discussion of *Evans v. Michigan* (2013) dealing with double jeopardy; expanded the discussion of just compensation to include the Takings Clause, and to include mentions of several cases (*Horne v. Department of Agriculture*, 2015; *Loretto v. Teleprompter Manhattan CATV Corp.*, 1982; *Lucas v. South Carolina Coastal Council*, 1992; *Pennsylvania Coal Co. v. Mahon*, 1922; *Penn Central Transportation Co. v. New York City*, 1977; and *Kelo v. New London*, 2005); added Case in Brief box for *Kelo v. New London*; added a new Constitutional Law in Action box dealing with the Takings Clause; added a new "In the News" article.
- **Chapter 11: The Sixth Amendment: Right to Counsel and a Fair Trial**   Added several new key terms (*prima facie, testimonial statement*); added new case discussions for *Betterman v. United States* (2016), *Strunk v. United States* (1973), *Lewis v. United States* (1996), *Ohio v. Clark* (2015), and *Kuhlman v. Wilson* (1986); added a Case in Brief box for *Ohio v. Clark*; clarified the jury nullification discussion; expanded the discussion of the *Batson* challenge to explain what is required; included a new Constitutional Law in Action box to illustrate *Batson* challenges; added a new "In the News" article.
- **Chapter 12: The Eighth Amendment: Bail, Fines, and Punishment**   Updated Table 12.1; added mentions of these cases: *Schilb v. Kuebel* (1971), *Montgomery v. Louisiana* (2015), *Glossip v. Gross* (2015); *Hall v. Florida* (2014); *Apprendi v. New Jersey* (2000); and *Hurst v. Florida* (2016); reorganized the section on Corrections to include a discussion on the use of force and Eighth Amendment claims of cruel and unusual punishment (*Hudson v. McMillian*, 1992).
- **Chapter 13: The Remaining Amendments and a Return to the Constitution**   Added a new key term (*disenfranchise*); added mentions of these cases: *Wesberry v. Sanders* (1964), *Brown v. Thomson* (1983), and *Evenwel v. Abbott* (2016); added detail to the section on the Fifteenth Amendment; added a discussion on "one person, one vote"; expanded the discussion on the Twenty-Seventh Amendment; added a brief section explaining how an amendment gets passed; added a new Constitutional Law in Action box.

Ancillaries

For the Instructor

Online Instructor's Manual. The Instructor's Manual contains a variety of resources to aid instructors in preparing and presenting text material in a manner that meets their personal preferences and course needs. For each chapter, it includes learning objectives, key terms, a detailed chapter outline and summary, lesson plans, discussion topics, student activities, and media tools.

Online Test Bank. Updated by Keith Bell of West Liberty University, the Test Bank contains multiple-choice, true/false, completion, and essay questions to challenge your students and assess their learning. It is tagged to the learning objectives that appear in the main text, references to the section in the main text where the answers can be found, and Bloom's taxonomy. Finally, each question in the test bank has been carefully reviewed by experienced criminal justice instructors for quality, accuracy, and content coverage.

Cengage Learning Testing Powered by Cognero. The Test Bank also is available through Cognero, a flexible, online system that allows you to author, edit, and manage test bank content as well as create multiple test versions in an instant. You can deliver tests from your school's learning management system, your classroom, or wherever you want.

Online PowerPoints. Helping you make your lectures more engaging while effectively reaching your visually oriented students, these handy Microsoft PowerPoint® slides outline the chapters of the main text in a classroom-ready presentation. The PowerPoint® slides prove concept coverage using images, figures, and tables directly from the textbook.

For the Student

MindTap for Constitutional Law and the Criminal Justice System. With MindTap™ Criminal Justice for *Constitutional Law and the Criminal Justice System*, you have the tools you need to better manage your limited time, with the ability to complete assignments whenever and wherever you are ready to learn. Course material that is specially customized for you by your instructor in a proven, easy-to-use interface keeps you engaged and active in the course. MindTap helps you achieve better grades today by cultivating a true understanding of course concepts, and includes a mobile app to keep you on track. With a wide array of course-specific tools and apps—from note-taking to flashcards—you can feel confident that MindTap is a worthwhile and valuable investment in your education.

You will stay engaged with MindTap's career scenarios and remain motivated by information that shows where you stand at all times—both individually and compared to the highest performers in class. MindTap eliminates the guesswork, focusing on what's most important with a learning path designed specifically by your instructor and for your Constitutional Law course. Master the most important information with built-in study tools such as visual chapter summaries and integrated learning objectives that will help you stay organized and use your time efficiently.

Acknowledgments

The authors would like to thank the reviewers of this edition for their insightful feedback and constructive suggestions: Dennis Masino, Briarcliffe College; Peter Phipps, Brookline College; James Sangiorgio, Briarcliffe College; Pamela Seay, Florida Gulf Coast University; Michael Teague, Keiser University; Duane Tomokins, Community College of Vermont; and Dean H. Wyks, Atlantic Cape Community College.

We would also like to thank the reviewers of previous editions: Brent Catchings, Southern Union State Community College; Mitch Chamlin, University of Cincinnati; Bob Diotalevi, Florida Gulf Coast University; Karen Dowell, LeMoyne-Owen College; Wayne Durkee, Durham Technical Community College; Omobolanle Ene-Korubo, Miles College; Laura Woods Fidelie, Midwestern State University; Shane Gleason, Southern Illinois University; Melissa Harrell, Bainbridge College; Richard Heinzman, Amridge University; Jill Jasperson, Utah Valley State College; Morris Jenkins, University of Toledo; Charles Johnson, University of Maine at Presque Isle; Mark Jones, Atlantic Cape Community College; Bill Kitchens, University of Louisiana–Monroe; Jeff Kleeger, Florida Gulf Coast University; Deborah Klein, College of DuPage; Wayne Logan, SUNY–Albany; Jerry Maynard, Cuyahoga Community College; Donna McIntyre, Ogeechee Technical College; Milo Miller, Southeast Missouri State University; Richard Pacelle, Georgia Southern University; Russ J. Pomrenke, Gwinnett Technical College; Linda Rawls, Esq., Davenport University; Leanna Rossi, Western New Mexico University; Vincent Russo, City Colleges of Chicago; James Sanderson, Robeson Community College; Joseph G. Sandoval, Metropolitan State College of Denver; Pamella Seay, Florida Gulf Coast University; Caryl Lynn Segal, University of Texas–Arlington; Gene Straughan, Lewis and Clark State College; Robert Wiggins, Cedarville University; Denise R. Womer, Southwest Florida College; and John Wyant, Illinois Central College.

The authors also wish to thank Carolyn Henderson-Meier, product team manager; Katie Seibel, content developer; Carly Belcher, intellectual property project manager; Timothy Kappler, product assistant; Sharib Asrar, project manager at Lumina Datamatics; and Kristina Mose-Lisbon, art director at Lumina Datamatics.

Prologue

Constitutional law—no other subject guides our daily lives as does the Constitution of the United States. Each of us can go about our business in a fairly predictable, safe way because of the guarantees and personal freedoms ensured by our Constitution. And yet how many Americans know much about it? Most have never read it. Few have studied it. Even fewer have taken the time to contemplate the implications of this incredible document—one many have died for.

Walk into any law library and the sheer volume of material is overwhelming. Yet to remain law, every one of these books must balance ever so delicately on one other, much smaller, document—the U.S. Constitution. This is a heavy burden for the Constitution to bear, yet it has done so admirably for more than two centuries. And all you have to do to see that it continues to do so is to maintain an awareness of current events. The U.S. living law changes before your eyes.

When the document was drafted in 1787, it was never meant to be an all-inclusive compendium of legal answers. It was intended as a basic framework within which all other law must remain. It is so powerful a document that any laws people try to impose on it that do not meet its tenets are simply void. However, the difficulties faced by Rosa Parks and other American heroes who have stood up for their constitutional rights remind us that the process is not quite that easy.

Those drafting the Constitution had a timeless vision. They knew society would change, as would its needs. They realized they could never foresee all the issues their country would confront (and what issues there are!). But the framers of our Constitution successfully developed the charters that established our unique U.S. legal system. The basic organizational structure is created so no one person, royalty or dictator, shall ever have total rule, and so that a handful of precious basic rights are ensured. This is what the U.S. Constitution is about. It is really quite simple. So why does a course in constitutional law strike fear in the hearts of students of all ages? Because anything that has worked so well for so many, for so long, must have some built-in complexity. And it does—interpretation.

Myriad forces affect interpretation of the Constitution: the era, societal norms, and politics. Indeed, constitutional interpretation is political, explaining why Presidents want to exercise the powerful right to appoint justices to the U.S. Supreme Court. This text addresses the awesome power the Court has in being the final arbiter of which laws are constitutional and which are not. In this role, the Supreme Court becomes the ultimate maker of law. In the famous case of *Marbury v. Madison* (1803), the Court considered whether it had the authority to review laws passed by the Congress—and the Court declared that it did. Some argue that by doing so, the U.S. Supreme Court has become the de facto ultimate lawmaking body in our country. For this reason, it has become important for political leaders to have justices on the bench whose ideologies are in accord with theirs. Politics does play a real part in interpreting laws.

The Constitution works because those who wrote it more than 200 years ago provided only basic tenets, leaving open the challenge of interpreting them as they relate to current issues. For example, free speech issues are decidedly different today than two centuries ago—but the basic idea remains. The Fourth, Fifth, and Sixth Amendments still guide government investigations, but such matters as the use of sophisticated electronic eavesdropping and computer equipment have now become an issue.

How people interpret the Constitution can cause confusion. For all who are certain how the Constitution should be read (in their favor, of course), others are just as certain it should be interpreted differently. Today's issues of abortion, gun control, and the environment beg for interpretation, flip-flopping back and forth, up and down, through our legal system, always searching for a final interpretation. Most often, the U.S. Supreme Court, as the final arbiter of law, tells us what that interpretation is—until the Court itself makes a change or until another case with a slightly different twist than previous cases is decided differently.

Before you look ahead, it is important to take time to reflect on the past. History seems to be an accurate predictor of the future because it has a unique way of repeating itself. Yet history is often overlooked. That is why this text starts with a brief, but important, review of what led to the U.S. Constitution, re-establishing the foundation on which the subsequent information neatly rests, and making the study of the Constitution logical, perhaps even enjoyable. This point is reinforced by two statues positioned at the rear exit of the National Archives in Washington, DC. Most visitors would never see these imposing statues unless they went out the wrong door. Those who do may stop, look around to get their bearings, and note the crucial advice emblazoned on one statue: "What Is Past Is Prologue."

CHAPTER 1

A Historical Overview

Give me liberty, or give me death!

—Patrick Henry

What is past is prologue.

Section I A Foundation for Understanding Constitutional Law

Learning Objectives

LO1 *Identify the three main groups that coexisted in 1775 in the land that would become the United States of America and which of these groups U.S. history tends to ignore.*

LO2 *Know when, where, and why the First Continental Congress and the Second Continental Congress convened and what each resulted in.*

LO3 *Name the document that formally severed the American colonies' ties with Great Britain and know when this document was signed.*

LO4 *Clarify what the primary purpose of the Constitution is and how it is achieved.*

LO5 *Describe how the balance of power was established.*

LO6 *Summarize what the Bill of Rights is and why it was included with the Constitution.*

LO7 *Pinpoint the glaring omission in the Constitution and Bill of Rights that contradicted the Declaration of Independence.*

Key Terms

amendments	Federalists	Patriot
anti-Federalists	Great Compromise	pluralism
confederation	law	ratify
constitution	Loyalist	supremacy clause
constitutionalism	minutemen	

Introduction

It has been said that the best way to know where you are going is to look where you have been. As discussed in the introduction to this section, constitutional law can become complicated. Any endeavor becomes easier, however, if a firm base is established from which to proceed. Although you might think a historical review is unnecessary, or that you took a wrong turn when opening a constitutional law text to begin reading about the colonists, you should gain some important insights.

This chapter begins with a discussion of the roots of the U.S. Constitution and contributions from the past. This is followed by an examination of how the United States of America developed, including a discussion of the American Revolution and the signing of the Declaration of Independence. Then the move toward the Constitution is described, followed by an overview of the Constitution itself and the balance struck through the addition of the Bill of Rights. The chapter concludes with an assessment of how the Constitution and Bill of Rights, as examples of living law, are nearly timeless documents.

Chapter 1 A Historical Overview   **5**

Where It All Began

A **constitution** is a system of basic laws and principles that establish the nature, functions, and limits of a government or other institution. The U.S. Constitution (always written with a capital "C") is youthful, which makes it all the more impressive. Consider other nations that rely on many more centuries, even thousands of years, of tradition and law that have been fine-tuned to serve them. And although the U.S. Constitution may be young, the history that influenced it can be traced back to when people first began forming groups throughout the world.

Every group has rules, and rules that become laws are an element of every society. **Law** is a body of rules promulgated (established) to support the norms of a society, enforced through legal means (i.e., punishment). The laws that the framers of the U.S. Constitution were familiar with helped form what would become the new law of the new country.

Representatives from every culture that has come to the United States, regardless of when they arrived or where they came from, share in the historical development of our country and legal system. It is the common thread that binds all who have come here—the desire for something better—that makes U.S. law so unique in serving the pluralistic society that created it. **Pluralism** refers to a society in which numerous distinct ethnic, religious, or cultural groups coexist within one nation, each contributing to the society as a whole.

Pluralism existed in the New World long before the colonists "discovered" America. Before the colonization of the United States, the American Indian tribes had their distinct territories, languages, and cultures. But when the colonists arrived and began taking over the land occupied by the American Indians (a population also called Native Americans), the American Indians began to band together in self-defense.

The colonists came from various countries and were of different religions and cultures. Initially they settled in specific areas and maintained their original culture, for example, the Pennsylvania Dutch. A pluralistic society challenged the colonists to exercise tolerance and respect for the opinions, customs, traditions, and lifestyles of others. Cultural and ethnic diversity enriched early American life and strengthened the emerging nation. The following list shows the ethnic population of the colonies in 1775 by percentage:

constitution a system of basic laws and principles that establish the nature, functions, and limits of a government or other institution

law a body of rules promulgated (established) to support the norms of a society, enforced through legal means (i.e., punishment)

pluralism a society in which numerous distinct ethnic, religious, or cultural groups coexist within one nation, each contributing to the society as a whole

48.7	English
20.0	African (slaves)
7.8	Scots-Irish
6.9	German
6.6	Scottish
2.7	Dutch
1.4	French
0.6	Swedish
5.3	Other

Source: Armento et al., 1991, p. 49.

Interestingly, the American Indians are absent from this chart because they were not considered part of the colonies. Also of interest is the 20 percent African population, who were slaves brought to this country primarily to work on Southern plantations. In many Southern states, slaves outnumbered colonists. For example, in 1720, South Carolina's population was 30 percent white and 70 percent black (Simmons, 1976). Concerned about the dangers the oppressed slaves could create, some of the first new laws colonists wrote were slave laws. Most Southern colonies established a special code of laws to regulate the slaves and established special enforcement officers, known as slave patrols, to ensure that these laws were obeyed.

LO1 *In 1775, three large groups coexisted in the land that would become the United States of America: the American Indians, the African slaves, and the colonists. American Indians and African Americans are not often given the recognition they are due, but these groups played an important part in the development of the United States.*

The history of the United States has generally focused on only the colonists, and the colonists with the most wealth and power—white, male property holders—are credited with creating the basic structure of our country.

Over time, interaction, and eventually assimilation, occurred among the colonists, commonly referred to as a "melting pot" because several different nationalities combined into what was known as "the American colonist." Such assimilation was encouraged by the vast, apparently unlimited resources available, as well as by the struggle for survival. Colonists faced the threat of foreign countries wishing to control them, the dangers posed by the American Indians they were displacing, and the often-rebellious slaves in the South. Therefore, it was natural that they should band together.

Colonies developed and organized in unique ways. The emerging nation saw different priorities and different norms. Some colonies banded together for security in ways not unlike modern businesses. Massachusetts Bay and Virginia, for example, entered into business-like agreements, or charters, establishing cooperative government. Other colonists entered into compacts with primarily religious purposes that established how they chose to govern themselves, as was the case with the Plymouth, Rhode Island, Connecticut, and New Haven colonies.

Regardless of how unique the states were allowed—in fact, encouraged and demanded—to be, it was undeniable that benefits remained in working together rather than separately. A fragmented beginning was developing into a single nation. The terms *liberty* and *limited government* were ideals that compelled all that was necessary for establishing a new country. But what did these terms mean, and how could a new country be effectively governed for the good of all while ensuring individual liberty and limited government? The task was daunting, but the promise of what could be was highly motivating.

Levy and Mahoney (1987, p. 35) explain how this new country was forging the law to come: "To keep government limited—that is, to remain a constitutional society, Americans took sovereignty away from government and lodged it with the people . . . with separation of powers. Because the people, rather than government at any level, must be sovereign, they can delegate some powers to their state governments and others to a national government."

Development of the United States of America

The land that now composes North America has always held an attraction. As long ago as 30,000 B.C.E., people began traversing the continent to seek something that held the promise of more than they had. And whether the motivations for these incredible journeys were as basic as food or as complicated as a search for political and religious freedoms, people came hoping for something better.

After its "discovery," America became viewed as an attractive area for expansion by the world powers. Spain, France, and England, as well as other countries, saw great importance in adding the "New World" to their growing empires. This desire for existing nations to make America a part of their government planted the tiny seed of what was to grow into independence. Just as American Indians had seen their freedom threatened by the colonists and the African American slaves had been stripped of their freedom, the colonists realized their freedom was in jeopardy from abroad and vowed to not sit idly by while those asserting power attempted to coerce them into submission. When the colonies were confronted with attempts, primarily by Great Britain, Spain, and France, to consume and control the New World, resistance grew, exemplifying the spirit associated with the United States.

Colonial Dissension Grows

As the colonies' populations began to grow, so did serious differences between those who saw themselves as free, independent colonies and those who wanted a foreign flag flying over them. As existing empires positioned themselves politically and militarily to expand their boundaries into the New World, conflict was inevitable.

In 1750, French troops began arriving from Canada, building forts and laying claim to land that American Indians were occupying and that England was eyeing. A showdown eventually occurred in 1754, when British leaders ordered the Virginia governor to forcibly repel the French. George Washington and about 150 colonists marched against the French in what became known in North America as the French and Indian War (1754–1763). This competition between the British and the French was part of a larger, general European conflict—the Seven Years' War. By 1763, after the French and Indian War, French resistance was defeated, and the Treaty of Paris resulted in France losing most of the land it had claimed in America. But British problems were far from resolved.

Great Britain confronted two significant problems, the first being continued westward settlement by the colonists. This was problematic for Great Britain because the American Indian tribes fought to protect their land from the colonists, and the British army was unable to protect the isolated frontier settlements. For example, nearly 2,000 colonial men, women, and children died during Pontiac's Rebellion (Divine, Breen, Fredrickson, & Williams, 1991). In December 1763, British and colonial troops finally crushed the American Indians' defense of their territory. When King George III learned of the fighting, he issued the Proclamation of 1763, closing the western frontier to colonial settlement and placing it under military rule. Settlers already there were ordered to leave.

The second major problem facing Great Britain was the huge debt resulting from English military action to expand the empire. The British Parliament felt the colonists should share this debt. The colonies resisted the restrictions to westward settlement and to paying for Great Britain's war debts. Significant leaders began emerging—George Washington, Benjamin Franklin, Paul Revere, and Thomas Jefferson—leaders who had found strength in cooperating to resist the French and who now redirected their resistance toward Parliament's efforts to control America.

Spurred on by its belief that the American colonies should share in the expenses incurred, Parliament passed the Stamp Act in 1765, requiring stamps to be purchased and placed on legal documents such as marriage licenses and wills, as well as several commodities, including playing cards, dice, newspapers, and calendars. Further resentment grew when, in 1765, Parliament passed the Quartering Act, which required colonists to feed and shelter the 10,000 British troops in America.

Protests against the increasing British attempts to rule the colonies intensified, but demands that Parliament repeal these laws were rejected—objections to the Quartering Act later found their way into the Third Amendment to the U.S. Constitution. In addition, when the king's troops marched out of Boston on their way to Lexington and Concord, they were searching for munitions—hence the wording of the Second Amendment to the U.S. Constitution.

In 1766, the Stamp Act was finally repealed but was replaced by other taxes on commodities the colonists needed to import from England. New York resisted the Quartering Act, and Parliament again found itself trying to rule from abroad, which was not working well. Dissension increased, as did tensions between the colonists and the British soldiers sent to enforce Parliament's demands.

Finally, in 1770, after 4,000 armed British troops had come to Boston from Nova Scotia and Ireland, colonists began taunting British soldiers and throwing snowballs and ice at them. The soldiers fired on these colonists in what became known as the Boston Massacre. Attempting to quell the volatile situation, Parliament eventually repealed most of the taxes and duties, except those on tea. For both sides, this remaining tax was a symbol of British rule over the colonies. In December 1773, disguised as American Indians, colonists boarded three British ships in Boston Harbor and dumped the cargos of tea overboard. This event, known as the Boston Tea Party, represented the colonists' unwillingness to pay taxes without representation.

As a result of the tea dumping, Parliament passed several laws in retaliation for such an open act of defiance, including the following:

- Town meetings were restricted to one a year.
- The king was required to appoint people to the governmental court rather than have them elected.
- The Quartering Act was expanded, requiring soldiers to be housed in private homes and buildings (which seemed like spying to the colonists).
- British officials accused of crimes in the colonies were permitted to be tried in England, away from angry American colonists.

Again the colonists were not complacent. They met to address the situation.

The First Continental Congress

In September 1774, 55 delegates from 12 colonies met in Philadelphia to address their mounting complaints against Great Britain. At this First Continental Congress, such leaders as Samuel Adams and Patrick Henry resolved to resist British rule and agreed on three important actions. First, they adopted a set of resolutions defining the rights, liberties, and immunities of the colonists and listing actions of the British government that violated these rights. Second, they drew up an address to King George III and another to the citizens of Britain, presenting American grievances and calling for a restoration of American rights. Third, they called for each community to establish a boycott committee to prevent colonists from buying British goods until the Congress's demands were met. In general, someone who bought British goods was branded a **Loyalist** or Tory. One who supported the boycott was called a **Patriot** or rebel.

By the beginning of 1775, the colonies were actively preparing for what many saw would be an inevitable confrontation with the British. **Minutemen**, the name given to the colonial soldiers, were drilled and equipped to respond at a minute's notice to protect American lives, property, and rights. In March 1775, Patrick Henry delivered his famous plea for freedom:

> Sir, we have done everything that could be done to avert the storm which is now coming on. We have petitioned; we have remonstrated; we have supplicated; we have prostrated ourselves before the throne and have implored its interposition to arrest the tyrannical hands of the Ministry and Parliament. Our petitions have been slighted; our remonstrances have produced additional violence and insult; our supplications have been disregarded; and we have been spurned, with contempt, from the foot of the throne. In vain, after these things, may we indulge the fond hope of peace and reconciliation.
>
> There is no longer any room for hope. If we wish to be free; if we mean to preserve inviolate those inestimable privileges for which we have been so long contending; if we mean, not basely to abandon the noble struggle in which we have been so long engaged, and which we have pledged ourselves never to abandon, until the glorious object of our contest shall be obtained; we must fight! I repeat it, sir, we must fight!! . . . It is vain, sir, to extenuate the matter. Gentlemen may cry, peace, peace; but there is no peace. The war is actually begun! The next gale that sweeps from the north will bring to our ears the clash of resounding arms! Our brethren are already in the field! Why stand we here idle? What is it that gentlemen wish? What would they have? Is life so dear or peace so sweet as to be purchased at the price of chains and slavery?
>
> Forbid it, Almighty God—I know not what course others may take, but as for me, give me liberty, or give me death! (Brown & Bass, 1990, p. 140)

Loyalist a colonist who did not support the boycott of British goods in the colonies and who still paid allegiance to the British monarchy

Patriot a colonist who supported the boycott of British goods in the colonies and who owed allegiance to America rather than to the British monarchy

minutemen colonial soldiers

The Revolution Begins

The American Revolution was led, financed, and designed by and for those with social and economic power. Ironically, some African American slaves joined the fight for freedom. With tensions at their flash point, minutemen in Lexington and Concord were alerted by William Dawes, Paul Revere, and other midnight riders that the British soldiers were coming.

On April 19, 1775, the waiting minutemen in Lexington saw the British Redcoats approaching. Shots were exchanged, and the British killed eight Americans that morning and then moved on to Concord. The battles at Lexington and Concord strengthened the colonists' resolve and prompted them to meet again to determine how to proceed.

> **LO2** The First Continental Congress, which convened in September 1774, resulted in the first written agreement among the colonies to stand together in resistance against Britain. The Second Continental Congress, which met for the first time in May 1775, established the Continental Army and named George Washington its commander. This Congress made plans to raise money and buy supplies for the new army and to seek support from other countries by opening diplomatic relations with them.

The Second Continental Congress

In May 1775, the Second Continental Congress convened in Philadelphia, with many of the same delegates from the First Continental Congress in attendance.

The colonists were now prepared for all-out war with the British.

George III denounced the American leaders as "rebels" and ordered the British military to suppress the disobedience and punish the authors of the "treacherous" resolves. The ensuing battles of Ticonderoga, Bunker Hill, Trenton, and Saratoga, among others, showed the American people's commitment to fight for what they held so dear—their independence. As the war continued, prospects for reconciliation with Great Britain dimmed.

In May, the Congress instructed each colony to form a government of its own, assuming the powers of independent states. The movement for a break with Great Britain spread upward from the colonies to the Continental Congress, with the desire for independence firmly resolved.

The Declaration of Independence

In July 1776, after arduous debate, delegates at the Second Continental Congress voted unanimously in favor of American independence. Thomas Jefferson was selected to coordinate writing the formal announcement, which would become known as the Declaration of Independence. It listed the complaints the people had against Britain and justification for declaring independence.

> **LO3** On July 4, 1776, the 56 men of the Continental Congress signed the American Declaration of Independence, which formally severed ties with Great Britain.

The entire text of the Declaration of Independence can be found on the National Archives website (www.archives.gov). However, it is important to highlight here the important sections of this historic work. First, the opening paragraph explains why the Declaration was issued, that is, the compelling necessity for the colonists to break their political ties with Great Britain. The second paragraph, the crucial statement of the purposes of government, declares that a government's right to rule is based on permission from the people who are governed. Third, charges against the British king were reviewed in a long list that enumerated how the king's government had denied the American colonists their rights. Fourth, the Declaration describes the colonists' attempts to obtain justice and the British lack of response. Fifth, the last paragraph proclaimed independence and listed actions the new United States of America could take as a country.

> **MYTH**
> The Declaration of Independence states that ours should be a government "of the people, by the people, for the people."
>
> **FACT**
> This phrase comes from President Abraham Lincoln's Gettysburg Address, delivered 87 years after the signing of the Declaration of Independence.

What It Cost the Signers

The men who signed the Declaration were the elite of their colonies, men of wealth and social standing. They were, indeed, risking all. To sign the Declaration of Independence was an act of treason—punishable by death. Because it was so dangerous to publicly accuse their king, the names of the signers were kept secret for six months. Although most of the 56 signers survived the war and many went on to illustrious careers—including two presidents, as well as vice presidents, senators, and governors—not all were so fortunate.

Nine of the 56 signers died during the American Revolution, never tasting independence. Five were captured by the British. Eighteen had their great estates looted or burned by the British. Carter Braxton of Virginia, an aristocrat who invested heavily in shipping, had most of his ships captured by the British navy and his estates ruined. He became a pauper. Richard Stockton, a New Jersey Supreme Court judge, was betrayed by his Loyalist neighbors, dragged from his bed and imprisoned, brutally beaten, and starved. His estate was devastated. Although he was released in 1777, his health was ruined, and he died within five years, leaving his family to live on charity. John Hart, the speaker of the New Jersey Assembly, was forced to flee in 1776 at the age of 65 from the bedside of his dying wife. He hid in forests and caves while the British destroyed his home, fields, and mill, and took his 13 children. When he returned, his wife was dead, his children missing, and his estate destroyed. He never saw his children again and died, shattered, in 1779 (Jacoby, 2000).

Indeed, Americans owe much to those 56 signers of the Declaration of Independence. Because of their commitment to liberty, the colonists were able to move forward in establishing the foundation for their new, free country.

The Articles of Confederation

The Second Continental Congress acted to declare independence for America and set about determining how government should be developed. Richard Henry Lee, the delegate who made the resolution for America to be independent, encouraged a **confederation** of independent states, or a union in which each state maintained sovereignty.

The 13 states were cherishing their independence and resisted agreeing to a single government of any kind. The tension over whether to secede from Great Britain in the first place, both for fear of the Crown's power and fear of the unknown, was replaced with a new tension. Once the break was made, might not a new government be even worse? Could any single government meet their needs? The colonists' solution was a confederation of independent states. In 1777, the delegates to the Second Continental Congress drafted the Articles of Confederation, creating a governmental model for this new country. The Articles of Confederation formally pledged the states to "a firm league of friendship," and "a perpetual union" created for "their common defense, the security of their liberties," and their "mutual and general welfare."

These articles were important because after they were approved in 1781, the duties of government were divided among the states and the central government. During the eight years that America operated under them, great strides were made toward unifying a group of states that had, by their own desire, become separate. And although the inadequacies of this document eventually led to the Constitution itself, the Articles of Confederation were an important stepping-stone. The articles established a congress to conduct the necessary tasks of a central government, including waging war and making peace, controlling trade with the Indians, organizing a mail service, and borrowing money.

Reflection on the reasons for the events that led up to this point can easily explain why this preliminary attempt to establish a federal government left

confederation a union of independent states, in which each state maintains sovereignty

MYTH
The Articles of Confederation mentioned establishing a confederation of only the 13 original colonies.

FACT
Article XI of the Articles of Confederation mentions allowing Canada to join and receive all of the same benefits as each state if it agreed to the confederation. No other colony was able to become part of the confederation unless nine states agreed to the admission.

Congress with much weaker powers than would eventually be established. *The founders feared a concentrated, centralized political power.* Therefore, Congress was *not* empowered to:

- Regulate trade—internally or externally.
- Levy taxes. They could ask but could not compel.
- Draft soldiers. Again, they could ask but could not compel.
- Establish a court system.
- Regulate money.

Nevertheless, Benjamin Franklin commented, "Americans are on the right road to improvement [with the Articles of Confederation], for we are making experiments." George Washington, however, cautioned that the articles did not have the necessary strength to run a new country, and as the confederation stood, it was little more than the "shadow without the substance."

The colonists were faced with the formidable task of governing themselves and holding together their agreed-upon union. Disputes arose within and between colonies, but they could no longer look to England for resolution. Loyalists, who had opposed the revolution, called for re-establishing a monarchy for America. Others called for a military dictatorship. The need for some sort of strong leadership became more apparent as complaints against state governments grew in number and strength.

In some states, such as Massachusetts, the right to vote was restricted to property owners and taxpayers. Creditors could sue debtors and take property away from farmers who could not pay what they owed. In 1786, a band of debt-burdened farmers in Massachusetts, led by Captain Daniel Shays, attempted to shut down the courts through armed force in what became known as "Shays' Rebellion." Although the state government was eventually able to overcome the rebellion and restore order, they could not ignore the strong public support surrounding the uprising and, because of that, did nothing to punish Shays or anyone else involved in the popular revolt (Beard & Beard, 1968). Shays' Rebellion reflects the impact individuals had in forging the shape of their government and was one of the most important, if not the most important, catalysts in bringing about the Constitution (Woodard, 2006).

The Constitution Takes Shape

It can be difficult to grasp all that lies behind the Constitution unless one keeps in mind the underlying reason for the Constitution, that is, to provide a system of government that would prevent one individual from having complete power. Understandably, such a system would, out of necessity, have complexities built in to achieve such a lofty goal, but the basic reasoning is simple.

The Influence of the Magna Carta

The U.S. Constitution has important ties to what is perhaps the most important instrument of English government—the Magna Carta. This document, which King John was forced to sign on June 12, 1215, established the supremacy of the law over the ruler and guaranteed English feudal barons individual rights and "due process of law," including trial by jury. To this day, the British have never operated their government under a centralized "constitution." Rather, they work under tradition, and at the heart of that tradition is the historic Magna Carta.

Those who came to America in 1620 and their descendants ultimately rejected, via the Revolutionary War, rule under the British Crown and what it had come to symbolize. However, they continued to believe in the principles contained in the Magna Carta, which was a precedent for democratic government and individual rights and the foundation for requiring rulers to uphold the law.

The colonists recognized that a document such as the Magna Carta provided a stable framework from which to start. First, the Magna Carta was a step away from total rule by a single individual. Second, it had a fairly long history of success by the time the New World began to receive visitors from abroad seeking to colonize. And finally, it provided some security in that not everything needed to start from scratch.

For some 20 years, the British Magna Carta significantly influenced the development of other documents drafted in response to colonists' ever-growing desires for fairer treatment by their government. The revision of the Articles of Confederation was one such example. The Articles of Confederation had established "a firm league of friendship" between the states. However, they were inadequate as the foundation for effective government because they lacked a balance of power between the states and the central government. In September 1786, near the time of Shays' Rebellion, the Annapolis Convention occurred; only five states sent delegates. The goal of this convention was to modify the Articles of Confederation to alleviate some of the economic troubles resulting from the lack of a strong central government. The delegates who attended wrote a report to congress, urging another convention be convened. The sentiment that change was needed was steadily growing, and in 1787, the Congress of the Confederation finally called for a convention of delegates from the original states to meet in Philadelphia to revise the Articles of Confederation.

The 1787 Constitutional Convention of Delegates

In May 1787, delegates to the Constitutional Convention met at Independence Hall in Philadelphia. George Washington was elected to preside over the meetings. The public was not permitted in the meetings so the delegates could speak more freely.

Arduous debate occurred during this Constitutional Convention. The delegates decided how many votes each state would have and that a new document was preferable to merely amending the Articles of Confederation. The challenge of drafting the Constitution began.

The summer of 1787 was one of record heat, and because of the standard dress of the day, the framers worked for only a few hours in the mornings. Afternoons were filled with much camaraderie and imbibing of favorite beverages. Bearing in mind the combined difficulties of communication and travel, the willingness and persistence of the delegates who gathered to shape what was to become the Constitution speaks directly to their need for such a tool. For without it, even the most revered and capable politicians and leaders of the time would have been doomed to failure. Instead, the most incredible chapter of U.S. history was slowly being opened.

Issues that became prominent during the convention included the economy and representation, as well as the structure and powers of Congress (the legislative branch), of the executive branch, and of the judicial system. What was sought was an array of checks and balances that would allow the system to work, while achieving the primary goal of limiting power to any individual or section of the government.

The delegates at the Constitutional Convention, who came from varied backgrounds, rose to the challenge. Individual power was never their objective, but rather societal cohesiveness and democratic power to achieve "one nation, with liberty and justice for all." The delegates who would help make the Constitution came that year with differing views but all were advocates of **constitutionalism**. That is, they believed in a government in which power is distributed and limited by a system of laws that must be obeyed by those who rule. According to that principle, constitutions are a system of fundamental laws and principles that prescribe the nature, functions, and limits of a government or other body. Constitutions are distinguished from ordinary acts of legislation in that they are drafted by special assemblages and ratified by special conventions chosen by the people. A constitution is supreme law, not to be annulled by legislation. Constitutionalism is one of the most original, distinctive contributions of the American system of government.

constitutionalism a belief in a government in which power is distributed and limited by a system of laws that must be obeyed by those who rule

LO4 *The purpose of the Constitution was to establish a central government authorized to deal directly with individuals rather than states and to incorporate a system of checks and balances that would preserve the fundamental concepts contained in the Magna Carta, that is, to limit the power of the government.*

Like those who wrote the Articles of Confederation, the framers of the Constitution recognized that the people are the power. The delegates to the First Continental Congress in Philadelphia had been selected by the people of the colonies, not by existing colonial governments. Likewise, the delegates to the Constitutional Convention represented the people.

All states except Rhode Island were represented at the Constitutional Convention, which met at the State House in Philadelphia from May 25 to September 15, 1787. The 55 delegates included many of the most influential men in the country. Eight had signed the Declaration of Independence, seven were governors of their states, and 39 were congressmen. More than half were college graduates, and at least one-third were lawyers. Most held prominent positions in the Revolutionary War, and all were highly respected property owners.

Although unanimously elected president, George Washington took a limited but effective role in the deliberations. Despite some talk of the larger states getting more votes than the smaller states, the convention followed the procedures used to develop the Articles of Confederation, giving each state one vote, with seven states constituting a quorum. Any vote could be reconsidered during the convention, and many were. The convention was also governed by a rule of secrecy, requiring that nothing said during the deliberations be printed, published, or otherwise communicated without permission. Such secrecy was vital to unbiased discussion and to prevent rumors and misconceptions. The official journal to the convention was closed until 1819.

The convention first debated the Virginia resolution, calling for a national government with a bicameral legislature, an executive, and a judiciary branch.

The smaller states, however, backed the New Jersey Plan, calling for only modest revisions in the Articles of Confederation. In addition, the larger states supported representation proportional to a state's population, whereas the smaller states wanted one or two votes per state. A threatened deadlock was averted by the **Great Compromise,** which gave each state an equal vote in the Senate and a proportionate vote in the House.

Great Compromise the agreement reached in drafting the U.S. Constitution that gave each state an equal vote in the Senate and a proportionate vote in the House

The delegates also had differing philosophies regarding how the leaders of the new government should be chosen. For example, Alexander Hamilton did not believe that the general populous could be trusted to select the leaders of the country. Charles Pinckney, on the other hand, believed the opposite: that the people could, in fact, be trusted to make important decisions.

Finally, after lengthy debate, the delegates also decided to strengthen the central government and to clearly define federal powers. All other powers were entrusted to the individual states and to the people. Specifically, the country was to be governed by a president to be chosen by electors in each state, a national judiciary and a two-chamber legislature. The House of Representatives was to be popularly elected. The Senate, however, which shared certain executive powers with the president, was to be chosen by individual state legislatures. Under the Great Compromise between the large and small states, representation in the House was to be proportional to a state's population; in the Senate each state was to have two votes. The national plan for government agreed to by the convention delegates clearly separated the powers of the three branches of government and created a system of checks and balances among these three branches, as well as between the federal and state governments and the people both were to serve.

The Issue of Slavery

The issue of slavery was omitted during the constitutional debates. Although none of the framers knew whether this radical document would be ratified, they knew it would have zero chance of getting Southern ratification if it dealt with the slavery issue. At the time, slavery was on its way out in many states. Some plantation owners in the South had their doubts about slavery as well. It was not until Eli Whitney's invention of the cotton gin six years later that the demand for slaves greatly increased. As Thomas Jefferson said, "Slavery is like holding a wolf by its ears. You don't like it, but you're afraid to let it go." The Tenth Amendment, by default, left the slavery issue up to each state. The omission of slavery from the Constitution, and indirectly the failure to compromise, would lead to civil war.

Drafting the Constitution

After all issues had been debated and agreement reached, a committee was formed to draft the Constitution based on those agreements. On Tuesday, August 7, 1787, a draft Constitution was ready for a clause-by-clause review (Armento, Nash, Salter, & Wixson, 1991). After four months, what had developed is nothing short of amazing. The material was old, connected back to the Magna Carta, but it was new—with some rather brilliant concepts. It was the brainchild of a relatively select few, but if it were to work, it had to be accepted by all. The task was monumental:

> In the Constitution that emerged from these deliberations, the concept of government by consent of the governed formed the basic principle; accountability was the watchword. The rights of the people were to be protected by diffusing power among rival interests. (Mitchell, 1986, pp. 1–2)

The final document was put before the Convention on September 17. Following are the provisions of the articles contained in the final draft of the Constitution.

The Constitution of the United States: An Overview

Descriptions of the debates that forged the Constitution during the summer of 1787 in Philadelphia are fascinating, and this is certainly worthwhile reading for those who wish to pursue it further. The following condensation describes the results of those debates—the articles contained in the final draft of the Constitution (Lieberman, 1976, pp. 33–41).

The Constitution is both a structure for government and a set of principles, that is, a method for making law and a law itself. Of all the principles in this 7,000-word document, the single most important principle is that the government has been delegated its powers by the people. The government is not superior to them; its powers come only from them.

The first three articles of the Constitution establish the legislative, executive, and judicial branches of government and the country's system of checks and balances. It is interesting to note that Articles 1 through 3 go in descending order of power, with the power designated by Article 1 being greater than that in Article 2, which is greater than that presented in Article 3. The government's accountability to the people follows the same trend, in that the more power a branch has, the greater its accountability to the people.

Article 1: The Legislative Branch

Article 1 establishes the legislature: "All legislative Powers herein granted shall be vested in a Congress of the United States." This legislature may pass laws, but it has no power to enforce or interpret them. This article contains the Great Compromise. Congress has two chambers, a Senate and the House of Representatives, each acting as a check against the other. Senators are chosen by each state's legislature, with each state having two senators, and each senator having one vote. (Senators are no longer chosen by state legislatures.)

Laws of the United States—in the form of bills—may originate in either house. The sole exception is that only the House of Representatives may first consider "bills for raising revenue." The cry "no taxation without representation" was still strong among the delegates. Thus, only the popular body, the house representing the people, was given the power to initiate taxes.

All bills must clear three hurdles before they can become laws. They first must pass each house in identical form and then meet the approval of the president.

The president has the power to veto, but Congress, in turn, can override that veto if each house, by a two-thirds vote, chooses to do so.

Section 8 of Article 1 grants specific powers to Congress, including coining money and establishing post offices, as well as the power to:

- Lay and collect taxes.
- Borrow money on the credit of the United States.
- Regulate international and interstate commerce.
- Naturalize foreign-born citizens.
- Raise and govern the military forces.
- Declare war.

In what has come to be known as the "elastic clause," Congress also was given the power "to make all Laws which shall be necessary and proper for carrying into execution the foregoing Powers, and all other Powers vested by this Constitution in the Government of the United States, or in any Department or Officer thereof." In other words, Congress was granted an enormous potential reserve of power to do what was "necessary and proper" to pass laws for the nation. For the first time, the new Congress could do what the old Congress could not: enact laws that directly affected the people.

The Supreme Court addressed the necessary and proper clause in *McCulloch v. Maryland* (1819), establishing the authority of the federal government to address national issues. Historically, the clause caused considerable debate because of concern that it was too open-ended and could lead to excessive federal authority. However, the need to permit Congress to make necessary laws and carry out their enumerated powers was acknowledged in *McCulloch v. Maryland*, and reinforced in *Kinsella v. Singleton* (1960). In this later case, the clause was not considered a grant of federal power, but a declaration that Congress does possess the means needed to carry out its authority as set forth in the Constitution to run the country by enacting laws that are necessary and proper.

Article 1 is just one building block of our national government. Like the other articles and the Bill of Rights, none are exclusive and, in fact, all work together to prevent any one branch of government from having excessive or exclusive power. Although Congress is a powerful element of American law, it remains but one component required to lawfully interact with the others.

Article 2: The Executive Branch

The office of president was created to carry out the law; to provide a commander in chief of the military forces; to carry out the nation's foreign policy, including entering into treaties with other nations; and to appoint the ambassadors, judges, and officials needed for the government to function. The president is chosen through a complex system that uses "electors," selected by procedures that vary from state to state. The number of electors equals each state's number of senators and representatives in Congress. Therefore, it is possible for a president to be elected without receiving a majority of the popular votes. Whether an electoral college is needed is a continuing controversy.

As a check against the president's power, many of the president's most significant actions must be approved by the Senate. For example, treaties require a two-thirds Senate vote. Judges and appointed executive officials need a majority Senate vote to be confirmed. In addition, the president must report periodically to Congress on the state of the Union and may recommend laws Congress should enact. The president's most important duty is phrased, characteristically, in general language requiring that the president "shall take care that the laws be faithfully executed."

Like the other articles and elements of our legal system, the presidency is not immune from limitations. Nowhere are absolute rights or privileges guaranteed because of the ever-present tension between the people's rights and the government's needs. Individuals do not have boundless freedoms, and their government does not have boundless power, including the presidency. Although the president has great power, it is not absolute. A president can be impeached or removed from office. Although two presidents have been impeached (Andrew Johnson and Bill Clinton), none have actually been removed from office. No public figure can completely escape public or private accountability, as evidenced by the Supreme Court permitting the sexual harassment suit by Paula Jones to proceed (*Clinton v. Jones*, 1997).

> **MYTH**
> Those who fought for independence intended for the Constitution to protect my right to do whatever I like. After all, "It's a Free Country!"
>
> **FACT**
> The Constitution protects many civil rights but never declares that individuals are free to do whatever they wish.

Article 3: The Judicial Branch

The third article completes the national government structure, vesting judicial power in the U.S. Supreme Court, as discussed in depth in Chapter 3. Congress is also empowered to create lower courts. Federal court judges are appointed by the president and hold office for life.

As a check against judicial power, Congress is authorized to regulate the courts' dockets by deciding what kinds of cases the Supreme Court may hear on appeal. This power of Congress to regulate the courts' jurisdiction further illustrates how each branch of government is given significant power to affect the others. Congress enacts laws, but the president may veto them, and the courts may interpret them.

Federal versus State Power The fact that powers not specifically delegated to the federal government were reserved for the states and the people has been a big issue. Many court cases and policy debates revolve around that issue. Slavery, segregation, education, transportation, and environmental concerns, such as migrating waterfowl versus nonmigratory birds and the like, are all issues that at one time or another have inspired debate on the role of the federal government versus that of state government.

> **LO5** *The balance of power was established vertically through the separation of power between the federal government and the states and laterally through the three branches of government with its system of checks and balances.*

Checks and Balances The Constitution established an effective system of checks and balances on the power of any one of the three branches of government. The president has veto power, but Congress can override with two-thirds majority vote. The president nominates Supreme Court Justices, but the legislative branch confirms or denies the nomination. The president is commander in chief, but the legislative branch declares war and pays for it.

Article 4: Other Provisions

Article 4 contains a variety of provisions, some taken over from the Articles of Confederation, further describing the creation of the federal union. The article also deals with criminal extradition, formation of new states, and Congress's power to govern in territorial lands not yet states.

Article 5: The Amendment Process

Article 5 dictates how the Constitution may be amended. An amendment must first be approved by a two-thirds vote in each house of Congress. It is then submitted to the states for ratification, requiring the approval of three-fourths of the states to pass the amendment. The people may also begin the amendment process if the legislatures of two-thirds of the states call for a constitutional convention. This article was extremely important in allowing the Bill of Rights to be added to the Constitution, as discussed shortly.

Article 6: The Constitution as the Supreme Law

The second section of Article 6 contains the famous supremacy clause:

> The Constitution and the Laws of the United States which shall be made in Pursuance thereof; and all Treaties made, or which shall be made, under the Authority of the United States, shall be the supreme Law of the Land; and the Judges in every State shall be bound thereby, any Thing in the Constitution or Laws of any State to the Contrary notwithstanding.

Here, in a stroke, was the solution to the problem of dual sovereignty of the federal and state governments. It was denied. In matters over which the Constitution grants the federal government authority, the states must concede.

Thus, through the **supremacy clause**, the Constitution declared itself the supreme law of the land. This clause also did something else momentous: It permitted the Supreme Court to become the ultimate decision maker in whether laws and actions of the government circumvent the Constitution and to invalidate them if they do so. This article also requires the allegiance of every federal and state official to the Constitution.

supremacy clause
Constitutional doctrine that federal law will reign when there is conflicting state law (U.S. Const. Art. VI, Paragraph 2)

The Signing of the Constitution

Once the overall format was agreed on, the next step was to seek approval of the document by the delegates. After hearing the debate over the final version of the Constitution, Benjamin Franklin, on Saturday, September 15, 1787, eloquently urged the convention to respect the spirit of compromise:

> I confess that there are several parts of this Constitution which I do not at present approve. But I am not sure I shall ever approve them. For having lived long, I have experienced many instances of being obliged by better information or fuller consideration, to change opinions even on important subjects, which I once thought right, but found to be otherwise ... I consent, Sir, to this Constitution because I expect no better and because I am not sure that it is not the best. (Lieberman, 1987, p. 447)

Franklin urged, "Every member of the Convention who may still have objections to it [the Constitution], would, with me, on this occasion doubt a little of his own infallibility, and . . . put his name to this instrument." He moved that the Constitution be approved unanimously and signed by those states present. The delegates voted to accept the Constitution, and the following Monday, it was ready to be signed.

Forty-two of the 55 delegates were present on September 17, 1787, to sign the U.S. Constitution in Philadelphia, with only three members refusing to sign, including George Mason, who cited the lack of a bill of rights as a remaining concern. He proposed adding a bill of rights, but other delegates argued that the individual states' declarations of rights would sufficiently protect individual liberties. They voted against adding a bill of rights. James Madison was quoted (The Records of the Federal Convention of 1787):

> Whilst the last members were signing it, Doctor Franklin looking towards the President's chair, at the back of which a rising sun happened to be painted, observed to a few members near him, that painters had found it difficult to distinguish in their art a rising from a setting sun. I have, said he, often in the course of the session . . . looked at that [sun] behind the President without being able to tell whether it was rising or setting. But now at length I have the happiness to know that it is a rising and not a setting sun. (Armento et al., 1991, p. 133)

The delegates agreed that the Constitution should next be submitted to special conventions of the states for ratification.

Ratification

ratify approve a constitutional amendment

Federalists colonists who favored a strong federal government

anti-Federalists colonists who opposed a strong federal government

Although the delegates to the Constitutional Convention had agreed to the makeup of the Constitution, each state had to approve, or **ratify**, it. Delaware was the first state to do so. New Hampshire cast the decisive vote, but ratification was not a sure thing. Many people had grave reservations. Although they were all supportive of the Constitution, the dispute tended to be more about how strong or weak the central government should be. **Federalists,** who favored a strong central government, were greatly challenged by **anti-Federalists,** who favored a weaker central government.

Political leaders such as Alexander Hamilton, James Madison, and John Jay wrote powerful essays in a newspaper called *The Federalist Papers*, which encouraged the ratification of the Constitution and the formation of a strong national government. The anti-Federalists, however, feared such a strong federal government; what would assure the country that this attempt would not fail, too? Further, they were reluctant to ratify the Constitution without a bill of rights to guarantee individual liberties.

The anti-Federalists were not successful in blocking the final ratification of the Constitution, but they did raise awareness regarding the need for a bill of rights. Because the Constitution primarily addressed the formation of a government with limited and distributed powers, a bill of rights to protect individuals was not considered necessary.

After the Philadelphia convention, most of those who drafted the Constitution could not understand why a bill of rights was such an issue for many states. They believed the Constitution could stand on its own. Nonetheless, most Federalists were willing to compromise on this issue to ratify the Constitution and establish a new government. Fearing defeat in the Massachusetts ratifying convention, Federalist leaders sought support by drafting a list of **amendments,** additions to improve the Constitution. They enlisted John Hancock, the most popular man in Massachusetts, to present these amendments to the state convention. The proposed amendments made the Constitution acceptable to many who had opposed ratification.

amendments changes to a constitution or bylaws

The compromising strategy of the Massachusetts Federalists turned the tide of ratification. As other states debated ratification, they also insisted on amendments that would guarantee individual rights. The Bill of Rights became part of the Constitution in 1791 by the addition of ten amendments designed to ensure that the national government would not interfere with individual liberties. By December 15, 1791, the states had ratified 10 of the 12 proposed amendments to the Constitution, and the United States had a Bill of Rights. Figure 1.1 illustrates the timeline of events occurring in the United States and elsewhere between the 1620 landing of the Mayflower and the 1791 ratification of the Bill of Rights.

The Bill of Rights: A Balance Is Struck

The framers of the Constitution sought to balance the powers of the legislative, executive, and judicial branches of government. The proposed amendments aimed at balancing the rights of the states and of individual citizens against the powers of the central government. In December 1791, the 13 states passed the ten amendments that constitute the Bill of Rights. Proof of how well the Constitution would work was seen by the fact that it could, as a single document, embrace the additions that those it was drafted to serve determined necessary. Thomas Jefferson's comment on this process was of great significance: "The example of changing a Constitution by assembling the wise men of the State instead of assembling armies."

The Bill of Rights is intriguing because, whereas the Constitution is general, the amendments are specific. However, even these directives have offered enough room for interpretation to keep a steady flow of constitutional cases before courts at all levels.

The Bill of Rights continues as an outgrowth of the Magna Carta. The English, including those who left to establish the United States, found that documenting their laws reduced the likelihood of abuse, misunderstanding, or being forgotten. Because the charters and compacts of the colonies were all different, the benefits of some uniformity in a national set of laws made sense.

LO6 *In 1791, ten amendments, known as the Bill of Rights, were added to the Constitution to ensure the individual rights of American citizens.*

It was illogical for civil liberties to be safe from an overly strong federal government, only to be abused by the states. And it made even less sense for some states to have a version of a bill of rights and others to have none. James Wilson of Pennsylvania suggested, "An imperfect bill of rights was worse than none at all because the omission of some rights might justify their infringement by implying an unintended grant of government power" (Levy, 1999, p. 21).

Americans were becoming more comfortable with a clearly established, written law. Documented agreements worked. Recognizing that certain rights were so important to the country to ensure that no government, state or federal, could infringe on them, the Bill of Rights was finally agreed on. To this day, amendments are not taken lightly, and adding or deleting amendments is extremely difficult.

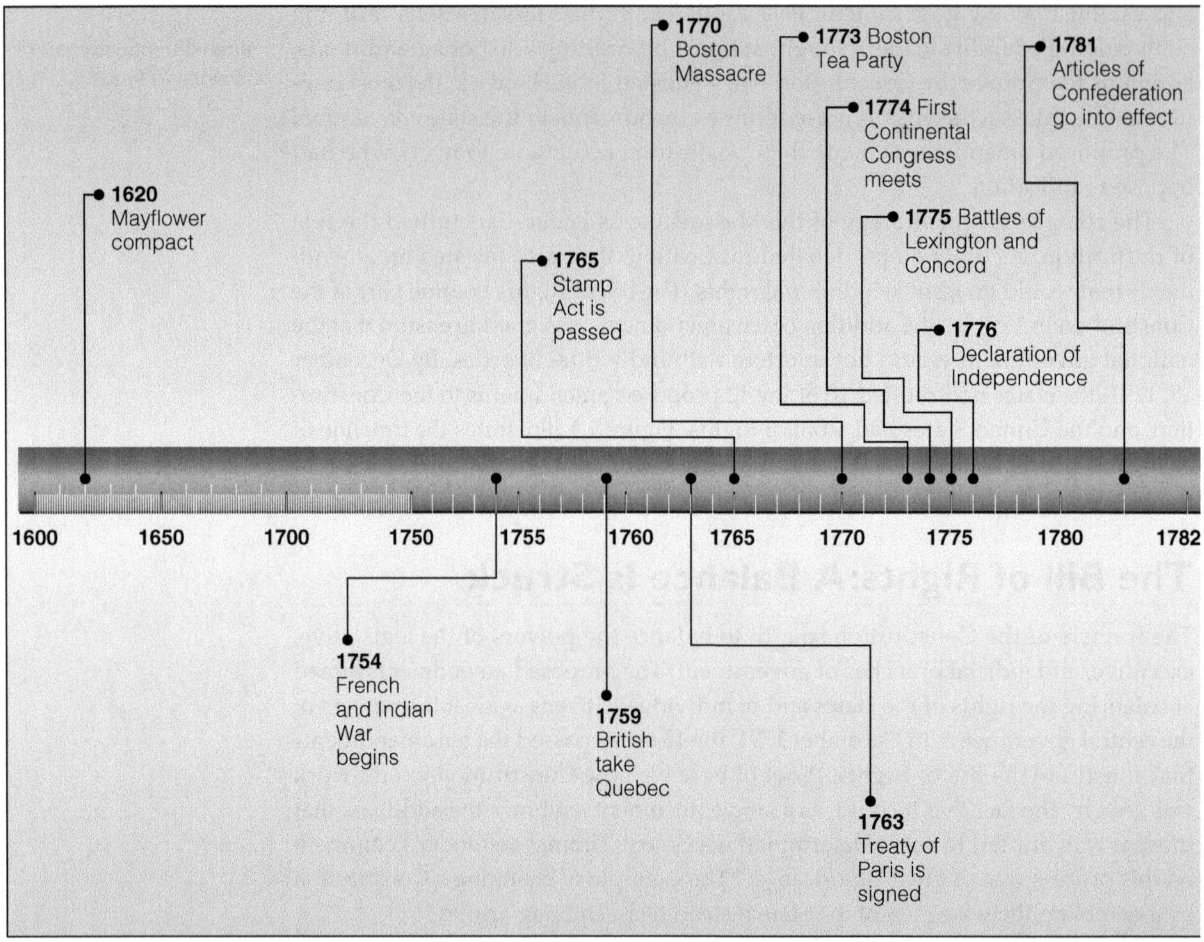

Figure 1.1 Timeline of Events

Had the Constitution been ratified without a bill of rights, it would have taken several years for those protections to be passed. By taking the form of amendments, these provisions became an integral part of the Constitution that many had argued be included originally. As noted by Supreme Court Chief Justice Warren E. Burger during the Constitution's bicentennial (Armento et al., 1991, p. 26):

> The Founders, conscious of the risks of abuse of power, created a system of liberty with order and placed the Bill of Rights as a harness on government to protect people from misuse of the powers. The evils of tyranny even today fall on most of the world's people and remind us of what life would be like without our respect for human dignity and freedom. We must never forget what our strength was meant to serve and what made that strength possible—the Constitution and the Bill of Rights as they stand today.

The Bill of Rights: An Overview

Sections II, III, and IV of this text focus on the Bill of Rights, as well as additional amendments made to the Constitution. Most laws and controversies deal with these amendments. The following brief introduction to each of the first ten amendments provides an overview on which later discussions can be based.

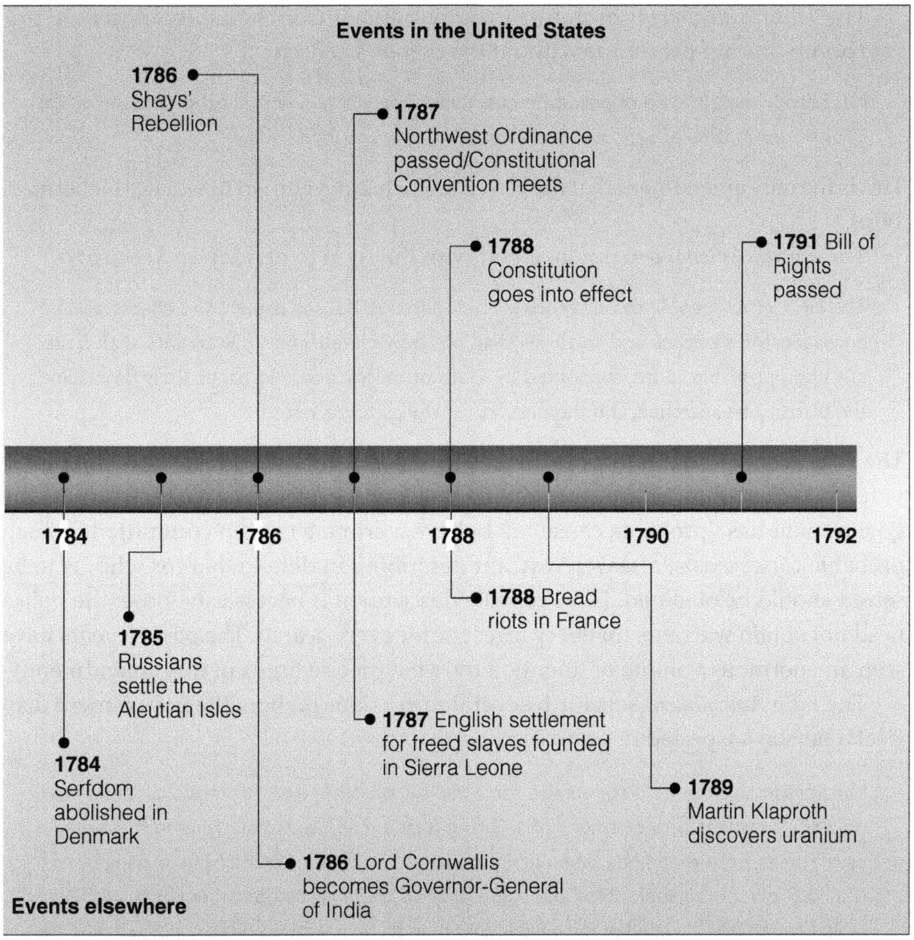

Events in the United States

- **1786** Shays' Rebellion
- **1787** Northwest Ordinance passed/Constitutional Convention meets
- **1788** Constitution goes into effect
- **1791** Bill of Rights passed

1784 — 1786 — 1788 — 1790 — 1792

Events elsewhere

- **1784** Serfdom abolished in Denmark
- **1785** Russians settle the Aleutian Isles
- **1786** Lord Cornwallis becomes Governor-General of India
- **1787** English settlement for freed slaves founded in Sierra Leone
- **1788** Bread riots in France
- **1789** Martin Klaproth discovers uranium

Figure 1.1 (*Continued*)

The *First Amendment* lists important individual liberties, including freedom of religion, speech, and the press:

> Congress shall make no law respecting an establishment of religion, or prohibiting the free exercise thereof; or abridging the freedom of speech, or of the press, or the right of the people peaceably to assemble, and to petition the Government for a redress of grievances.

These freedoms are so basic to the American way of life that they are sometimes referred to as "First Amendment rights."

The *Second Amendment* preserves the right of the people "to keep and bear arms":

> A well-regulated Militia being necessary to the security of a free State, the right of the people to keep and bear Arms, shall not be infringed.

The courts have ruled that this is not an absolute right. Laws prohibiting private paramilitary associations and carrying concealed weapons have been upheld.

MYTH
The U.S. government is a democracy.

FACT
The Constitution established the U.S. government as a republic, not a democracy. In fact, the word *democracy* appears nowhere in the Constitution. Article IV, Section 4 of the Constitution states, in part: "The United States shall guarantee to every State in this Union a Republican Form of Government. . . ." A democracy functions under majority rule (mob rule) and lacks legal safeguards protecting the rights of individuals in the minority. Because the framers of the Constitution feared democratic rule and how it allowed the omnipotent majority to trample on the rights of the minority, they created a republic—a representative government rule by law (the Constitution)—recognizing the inalienable rights of *all* individuals, not just those of the majority. *Think about words in the Pledge of Allegiance and what you are vowing to uphold.*

The *Third Amendment* prohibits the government from housing soldiers in private homes during peacetime without the owner's consent:

> No Soldier shall, in time of peace, be quartered in any house without the consent of the Owner, nor in time of war but in a manner to be prescribed by law.

This is the only amendment that the government has never tried to violate (Lieberman, 1976).

The *Fourth Amendment* is concerned with the right to privacy and security:

> The right of the people to be secure in their persons, houses, papers, and effects, against unreasonable searches and seizures, shall not be violated, and no Warrants shall issue, but upon probable cause, supported by Oath or affirmation, and particularly describing the place to be searched, and the persons or things to be seized.

The Fourth Amendment forbids the government or its agents from searching individuals, their homes, or their personal possessions or from seizing them unless the government has "probable cause" to believe a crime has been committed. If such probable cause exists, a search warrant describing in detail what (or who) is to be seized should be obtained. (This capsule description is necessarily loose: the police need not obtain warrants for every arrest or for every search. The past 15 years have seen an enormous volume of litigation over the precise limits of this amendment.)

The *Fifth Amendment* sets forth several restrictions on how the government may treat a person suspected of a crime:

> No person shall be held to answer for a capital, or otherwise infamous crime, unless on a presentment or indictment of a Grand Jury, except in cases arising in the land or naval forces, or in the Militia, when in actual service, in time of War or public danger; nor shall any person be subject for the same offence to be twice put in jeopardy of life or limb; nor shall be compelled in any criminal case to be a witness against himself; nor be deprived of life, liberty, or property, without due process of law; nor shall private property be taken for public use, without just compensation.

The Fifth Amendment establishes the need for a grand jury indictment for felony cases. It prohibits double jeopardy, meaning a person acquitted by a jury of a crime may not be retried for the same offense. It prohibits the government from forcing a person to testify against himself; hence the expression "pleading the Fifth." It also contains the famous due process clause: "nor shall any person . . . be deprived of life, liberty, or property without due process of law."

The *Sixth Amendment* describes the requirements for a fair trial:

> In all criminal prosecutions, the accused shall enjoy the right to a speedy and public trial, by an impartial jury of the State and district wherein the crime shall have been committed, which district shall have been previously ascertained by law, and to be informed of the nature and cause of the accusation; to be confronted with the witnesses against him; to have compulsory process for obtaining witnesses in his favor, and to have the Assistance of Counsel for his defense.

The trial must be convened speedily and must be public. The accused is entitled to an impartial jury in the community where the crime occurred and must be advised of the crimes being charged. Accused individuals must also be allowed to cross-examine witnesses who testify against them. In addition, they can compel witnesses who will testify in their favor to come to court. Finally, they have the right to be represented by a lawyer.

The *Seventh Amendment* preserves the right to trial by jury in common law cases "where the value in controversy shall exceed twenty dollars":

> In Suits at common law, where the value in controversy shall exceed twenty dollars, the right of trial by a jury shall be preserved, and no fact tried by a jury, shall be otherwise re-examined in any Court of the United States, than according to the rules of the common law.

This amendment is one of the few clauses in the Constitution that includes a figure that has lost meaning over the years. By law today, federal courts cannot hear cases where the contested value is less than $10,000, unless a federal law is involved. The amendment also forbids courts to re-examine facts found by juries, except as the common law permits.

The *Eighth Amendment* prohibits excessive bail, excessive fines, and cruel and unusual punishment:

> Excessive bail shall not be required, nor excessive fines imposed, nor cruel and unusual punishments inflicted.

This is the amendment that opponents of capital punishment most frequently cite.

The *Ninth Amendment* answered the objections of those who thought that naming some rights but not all might result in the government's claiming more power than was intended:

> The enumeration in the Constitution, of certain rights, shall not be construed to deny or disparage others retained by the people.

The *Tenth Amendment* further underscores the framers' intent to reserve certain powers to the states and to the people:

> The powers not delegated to the United States by the Constitution, nor prohibited by it to the States, are reserved to the States respectively, or to the people.

This amendment establishes no rights nor takes any away. It is a reminder that the government is for the people, not the reverse.

The U.S. Constitution and its amendments are provided in Appendix A.

> **MYTH**
> The guarantees of "Life, Liberty, and the Pursuit of Happiness" are Constitutional rights.
>
> **FACT**
> This phrase is stated in the Declaration of Independence, not the Constitution. However, the Fifth Amendment does guarantee Constitutional protection to "life, liberty, or property," stating the government cannot deprive anyone of these things without due process of law.

A Living Law

The inclusion of the Bill of Rights stands as an example of how the U.S. Constitution lives. It is neither unchangeable nor unresponsive. It is not merely a piece of paper locked away in a vault in Washington, DC. The framers took a lot of good ideas referenced previously and, with the political skill of compromise, developed a workable form of government that continues to this day. It was designed to grow, develop, and be redefined if necessary to best serve the people's needs. Study of the amendments and how they have been interpreted since their inception makes it obvious that the Constitution is a living document that grows with the citizens it was written to protect.

A Nearly Timeless Document

The final draft of the Constitution established a broad framework for the new American government. However, it did contain one critical error; it did not abolish slavery:

> Those who detested slavery reconciled themselves to this grievous and glaring flaw that contradicted the Declaration of Independence at its most solemn point—that all men are created equal—by assuming that slavery would in time vanish naturally. But it would not go away so easily. The compromise that saved the Union could not be peacefully eliminated, and the amendments that would make the Constitution true to itself could come about only after the bloodiest war in American history (Lieberman, 1976, p. 49).

Although nearly timeless, the Constitution reflects the will and values of the people who originally drafted it and those charged with maintaining it. For example, whereas the Constitution as originally ratified did not prevent slavery and other discriminations, the ability of our law to be amended (in this case by the Fourteenth Amendment) speaks volumes about the American spirit to learn, even from its own mistakes.

For more than 200 years, the Constitution has been flexible enough to meet the nation's changing needs without extensive formal revision. Although the framers of the Constitution would find many modern governmental practices quite foreign, the basic system continues to operate as they planned. Recognizing the importance of ensuring in practice the division of power, Madison suggested this could best be done "by so contriving the interior structure of the government as that its several constituent parts may, by their mutual relations, be the means of keeping each other in their proper places."

L07 *The Constitution and Bill of Rights failed to abolish slavery.*

The Declaration of Independence, which established the United States as an independent nation; the Constitution, which established its form of government; and the Bill of Rights have been carefully preserved and are housed in the Rotunda for the Charters of Freedom at the National Archives in Washington, DC. These valuable documents are contained in ballistically resistant casements and displayed under armed guard.

Summary

From the beginning, the colonists sought structure and collaboration. Law is a body of rules promulgated (established) to support the norms of that society, enforced through legal means (i.e., punishment). The U.S. Constitution was written to serve the needs of a pluralistic society. *Pluralism* refers to a society in which numerous distinct ethnic, religious, or cultural groups coexist within one nation, each contributing to the society as a whole.

The history of the Constitution is rooted in the colonists' desire for freedom from foreign rule. The colonists resisted increased taxes because they felt it was taxation without representation. The Boston Tea Party, in which colonists boarded British ships and threw their cargos of tea in the harbor, represented the colonists' unwillingness to pay taxes without representation.

As tension between the British and the colonists increased, the First Continental Congress was called and resulted in the first written agreement among the colonies to stand together in resistance to Great Britain. The British retaliated by sending more troops to quell the "rebels." In 1775, the Second Continental Congress established the Continental Army and named George Washington as its commander. On July 4, 1776, the president of the Congress signed the American Declaration of Independence, which formally severed ties with Great Britain.

The Congress also drafted the Articles of Confederation, which formally pledged the states to "a firm league of friendship," and "a perpetual union" created for "their common defense, the security of their liberties," and their "mutual and general welfare." This loose governmental structure proved unsatisfactory and resulted in the colonists seeking a stronger central government—one established by the Constitution.

The U.S. Constitution was greatly influenced by the Magna Carta, which established the supremacy of the law over the ruler and guaranteed English feudal barons individual rights and "due process of law," including trial by jury. Americans continued to believe in the principles contained in the Magna Carta, which was a precedent for democratic government and individual rights and the foundation for requiring rulers to uphold the law. The Magna Carta greatly influenced the writers of the U.S. Constitution.

The purpose of the Constitution was to establish a central government authorized to deal directly with individuals rather than states and to incorporate a system of checks and balances that would preserve the fundamental concepts contained in the Magna Carta, that is, to limit the power of the government. The first three articles of the Constitution establish the legislative, executive, and judicial branches of government and the country's system of checks and balances. The balance of power was established vertically through the separation of power between the federal government and the states and laterally through the three branches of government with its system of checks and balances. In the supremacy clause, the Constitution declared itself the supreme law of the land.

The U.S. Constitution was signed in Philadelphia on September 17, 1787. The next step was for the individual states to ratify it. The Federalists favored a strong central government. They were greatly challenged by the anti-Federalists, who favored a weaker central government. Some states opposed the Constitution because it did not contain a bill of rights. In an important compromise, ten amendments, known as the Bill of Rights, were added to the Constitution in 1791 to ensure the individual rights of American citizens. The Constitution and Bill of Rights had one serious shortcoming: They failed to abolish slavery. The Declaration of Independence, the U.S. Constitution, and the Bill of Rights are housed in the Rotunda for the Charters of Freedom at the National Archives in Washington, DC.

Discussion Questions

1. Few people could live together and not have laws. Why?
2. Does pluralism have any negative aspects? Why have some fought so hard against the concept in the United States?
3. Do demonstrations such as the Boston Tea Party have any effect? Are they positive or negative?
4. What factors make it amazing that any organization among the colonies was successful?
5. Were the Articles of Confederation a wasted effort or were they needed?
6. What do you think about the Constitutional Convention being closed to the public? Was this necessary?
7. Why is the Constitution called a living document? Give examples.
8. What do you think the anti-Federalists were really afraid of?
9. Why should the Bill of Rights *not* have been left up to each state to develop on its own?
10. If the U.S. Constitution works so well, why do all countries not adopt it?

References

Armento, B.J.; Nash, G.B.; Salter, C.L.; & Wixson, K.K. (1991). *A More Perfect Union*. Boston: Houghton Mifflin Company.

Beard, C.A., & Beard, M.R. (1968). *The Beards' New Basic History of the United States*. Garden City, NY: Doubleday & Company, Inc.

Brown, R.C., & Bass, H.J. (1990). *One Flag, One Land*. Morristown, NJ: Silver Burdett and Ginn.

Divine, R.A.; Breen, T.H.; Fredrickson, G.M.; & Williams, R.H. (1991). *America: The People and the Dream*. Glenview, IL: Scott, Foresman and Company.

Jacoby, J. (2000, July 4). "56 Who Pledged Their Lives, Fortunes, Sacred Honor." *Boston Globe*. Reprinted in (Minneapolis/St. Paul) *Star Tribune*, July 4, 2000, p. A11.

Levy, L.W. (1999). *Origins of the Bill of Rights*. New Haven, CT: Yale University Press.

Levy, L.W., & Mahoney, D.J., eds. (1987). *The Framing and Ratification of the Constitution*. New York: Macmillan Publishing Company.

Lieberman, J.K. (1976). *Milestones!* St. Paul, MN: West Publishing Company.

Lieberman, J.K. (1987). *The Enduring Constitution: A Bicentennial Perspective*. St. Paul, MN: West Publishing Company.

Mitchell, R. (1986). *CQ's Guide to the U.S. Constitution: History, Text, Glossary, Index*. Washington, DC: Congressional Quarterly, Inc.

Simmons, R.C. (1976). *The American Colonies*. New York: D. McKay Company.

Woodard, D. (2006). Personal communication with author.

Cases Cited

Clinton v. Jones, 520 U.S. 681 (1997)
Kinsella v. Singleton, 361 U.S. 234 (1960)
McCulloch v. Maryland, 17 U.S. (4 Wheat.) 316 (1819)

CHAPTER 2

An Overview of the U.S. Legal System

The law must be stable, but it must not stand still.

—Roscoe Pound

The United States is a country of laws. Citizens have not only a right but also a responsibility to be active participants in the U.S. legal system.

Learning Objectives

LO1 *Compare and contrast the two prominent theories about the underlying purpose of law.*

LO2 *Show similarities and differences between two competing value systems (models) often identified when discussing the purpose of the criminal justice process.*

LO3 *Explain what the basic purpose of the U.S. legal system is.*

LO4 *Recognize how common law began, what it is based on, and what it is synonymous with.*

LO5 *Understand the difference between a crime and a tort.*

LO6 *Name the components of a legal opinion.*

LO7 *Describe the levels on which the judicial system operates and what main functions are served by courts.*

LO8 *Identify the officers of the court.*

LO9 *Summarize the three doctrines that govern whether a case will be heard in court.*

Key Terms

adversarial judicial system	consensus theory	petition for certiorari
affirm	Crime Control Model	procedural law
amicus briefs	crimes	promulgate
appellate jurisdiction	dicta	remand
brief	dissenting opinion	reverse
caption	Due Process Model	ripeness doctrine
case law	exclusive jurisdiction	social contract
citing	general jurisdiction	standing
codified law	holding	*stare decisis*
collective conscience	jurisdiction	status offenses
common law	legal citation	statutory law
comparative law	limited jurisdiction	string cites
concurrent jurisdiction	mootness	substantive law
concurring opinion	ordinances	tort
conflict theory	original jurisdiction	vacate
	penal codes	venue

Introduction

This chapter describes the U.S. legal system and how it operates. Through understanding *how* it operates comes an appreciation of the crucial role the U.S. Constitution plays in achieving the primary goals of the framers of the Constitution—liberty, freedom, and fairness.

The chapter begins with a discussion of the theories about and purpose of the U.S. legal system and a definition of law and how it has developed throughout the centuries. This is followed by a description of categories of law—often overlapping—found in the U.S. legal system and how to research the law when you need more information about a legal case or concept. Next is a discussion of the U.S. court system and the officers of the court. The chapter concludes with an explanation of the adversarial nature of the judicial system, a discussion of the various components of the U.S. legal system, and a look at the emerging influence of U.S. law beyond our borders.

Theories About and Purpose of the Legal System

Futurist Joel Barker defines a *paradigm* as a boundary or parameter that outlines a rule and is based on experience. Sociologist Max Weber contends that the primary purpose of law is to regulate human interactions—to support social function. Combining these two views leads to the concept that a society's legal paradigm defines the behavioral boundaries of that culture.

As law evolves, different theories emerge to explain its development. People want to know not only *what* the law is but also *why* it exists as such. One theory is natural law, which suggests people should not create law in conflict with the natural order. Legal positivists suggest law is strictly a response to what is occurring at the moment. Many other theories fill volumes that can be explored independently.

To present a solid base from which to develop an understanding of law and its development, this text focuses on the basic premise that throughout history law has regulated human interactions for different reasons: to protect society's interests, to deter antisocial behavior, to enforce moral beliefs, to uphold individual rights, to support those in power, and to punish lawbreakers or seek retribution for wrongdoing.

Purpose of Law: Consensus Theory versus Conflict Theory

Although many theories exist, two different views address the underlying purpose of the law: consensus theory and conflict theory.

Consensus theory holds that individuals in a society agree on basic values and on what is inherently right and wrong. Laws express these values. Consensus theory dates back at least to Plato and Aristotle. Society, in general, agrees on what is right and wrong and makes laws to prohibit deviant behavior. Consensus theory was expanded on by French historian-philosopher Montesquieu (1689–1755). His philosophy focused on the **social contract** whereby free, independent individuals agree to form a society and to give up a portion of their individual freedom

consensus theory holds that individuals in a society agree on basic values, on what is inherently right and wrong, and that laws express these values

social contract a philosophy proposed by French historian-philosopher Montesquieu, whereby free, independent individuals agree to form a society and to give up a portion of their individual freedom to benefit the security of the group

to benefit the security of the group. Later, Émile Durkheim (1858–1917) described social solidarity as the shared values of a society, its **collective conscience**. The Durkheimian perspective saw punishment as revenge and a means to restore and solidify the social order.

A second prominent theory regarding the underlying purpose of the law, conflict theory, is not as humanitarian. **Conflict theory** holds that laws are established to keep the dominant class in power. (Recall that the framers of our Constitution were socially, politically, and economically powerful men in the New World.) The roots of this theory are found in Karl Marx (1818–1883) and Friedrich Engels' (1820–1895) *Manifesto of the Communist Party* (1848):

> The history of all hitherto existing society is the history of class struggles. Freeman and slave, patrician and plebeian, lord and serf, guild-master and journeyman, in a word, oppressor and oppressed stood in constant opposition to one another, carried on an interrupted, now hidden, now open fight, a fight that each time ended in either a revolutionary reconstruction of society at large, or in the common ruin of the contending classes.

Rather than regarding punishment as a way to provide social solidarity, Marx regarded punishment as a way to control the lower class and preserve the power of the upper class. This rationale has its roots in the Middle Ages, the Renaissance, the Reformation, and into the nineteenth century. During those times, society was divided into a small ruling class, a somewhat larger class of artisans, and a much larger class of peasants. Harsh laws kept the "rabble" under control.

Conflict theory is used by some sociologists and criminologists to explain how laws protect the interests and values of the dominant groups in a society:

collective conscience social solidarity fostered by the shared values of a society

conflict theory holds that laws are established to keep the dominant class in power, in contrast to the consensus theory

LO1 *Two prominent theories about the underlying purpose of the law are consensus theory and conflict theory. Consensus theory holds that laws express societal values regarding what is right and wrong and are created to prohibit deviant behavior. Conflict theory, in contrast, holds that laws are established to keep the dominant class in power.*

> Conflict theory holds that the administration of criminal justice reflects the unequal distribution of power in society. The more powerful groups use the criminal justice system to maintain their dominant position and to repress groups or social movements that threaten their position.... Conflict theory explains the overrepresentation of racial and ethnic minorities in the criminal justice system in several ways...."[S]treet crimes" that are predominantly committed by the poor and disproportionately by racial and ethnic minorities are the target of more vigorous enforcement efforts than are those crimes committed by the rich.... [The result is] the overrepresentation of racial and ethnic minorities among people arrested, convicted, and imprisoned. (Walker, Spohn, & DeLone, 2012, pp. 118–119)

The Purpose of the Criminal Justice System: Crime Control versus Due Process

Just as there are competing views on the purpose of law in our society, so too are there various views as to the purpose of our criminal justice system. Herbert Packer (1968) has offered a robust explanation of the Crime Control Model and the Due Process Model, two competing value systems underlying the administrative purposes of the criminal process.

Under Packer's paradigm, the operational value of "crime control" exists at one end of a spectrum and "due process" at the other end. The two extremes are meant to illustrate the tension between competing interests in the criminal justice system: the government's ability to maintain an orderly society (crime control) and the individual's right to freedom and protection (due process). In reality, the actual criminal justice system operates somewhere between these two extremes because it seeks to balance its duty to both society and the individuals who comprise our population. The prevailing political and social climates are two factors that influence where on the spectrum the system currently operates. Throughout our country's history, as sociopolitical climates have shifted, the criminal justice system has responded by moving one way or the other to favor efforts aimed at either more crime control or greater due process.

The **Crime Control Model** emphasizes the "repression of criminal conduct" and holds that the most important function of the criminal justice system is to bring criminal behavior under tight control (Packer, 1968, p. 158). This model requires efficiency of operation, meaning the criminal justice system must be capable of processing a high number of cases relatively quickly.

To achieve this goal, police powers to investigate and control crime must be high, and "technicalities" that limit police power should be reduced or eliminated. Under this model, the early part of the criminal justice process—the stages at which the police and prosecutors become involved—is the most crucial. As "gatekeepers" to the criminal justice system, the police are presumed to be sufficiently accurate and reliable in their fact-finding investigations to the point that once the "right" person is identified and arrested, the remaining steps in determining guilt and sanctioning the guilty (trial, conviction, disposition) are more or less just a matter of "going through the motions." The Crime Control Model dictates that the criminal justice system operate under a mechanism Packer refers to as the "presumption of guilt," meaning if someone is arrested and prosecuted, they are probably guilty (Packer, 1968).

Packer compares the Crime Control Model of criminal justice to an assembly-line conveyor belt, in which cases must be continuously pushed through the system for the process to operate successfully (i.e., efficiently). As such, this model places a premium on speed, informality, uniformity, and finality. Appeals are to be minimized, again based on the presumption that those whose cases go to trial are probably guilty, and allowing an appeal to set a guilty person free because of a technicality thwarts justice. The Crime Control Model concedes the possibility, indeed the *probability*, that mistakes will be made and that some innocent people might get caught up in the system. This allowance for error is made tolerable by the prevailing philosophy that it is better to cast a wide net and make sure the guilty are caught and punished, even if a few innocents are captured in the net as well, because crime control is the ultimate goal.

The **Due Process Model,** in contrast, emphasizes the rights of the individual and requires that the criminal justice system and its processes for enforcing the law be fair. This model rests on the presumption of innocence and holds that individual rights are not to be sacrificed for the sake of efficiency.

Packer makes it clear that the due process ideology is not the converse of crime control. Although the repression of crime remains an important goal under this model, it cannot come at the expense of sacrificing individual rights. On the due process end of the spectrum, it is believed that the fact-finding abilities of the police and prosecutors are prone to error. For example, error might be caused by

Crime Control Model
emphasizes the "repression of criminal conduct" and holds that the most important function of the criminal justice system is to bring criminal behavior under tight control as efficiently as possible

Due Process Model
emphasizes the rights of the individual, rests on the presumption of innocence, and holds that individual rights are not to be sacrificed for the sake of efficiency

LO2 *Two competing value systems underlying the administrative purposes of the criminal process are the Crime Control Model and the Due Process Model. The Crime Control Model emphasizes efficiency and uniformity, rests on the presumption of guilt, and takes an assembly line approach to justice. The Due Process Model, in contrast, emphasizes that individual rights are not to be sacrificed for the sake of efficiency, rests on the presumption of innocence, and takes an obstacle course approach to justice.*

police bias, coercion, or witness unreliability. "Facts" suggesting a suspect's guilt may be exaggerated or entirely wrong, and because of the enormous stakes involved for the suspect—the coercive power of the state to deprive the accused individual of their freedom and, possibly, end their life—the criminal justice system's foremost purpose is to prevent or eliminate mistakes that lead to wrongful conviction.

Packer likens the Due Process Model to an obstacle course, with sufficient "formidable impediments" and hurdles the criminal justice system must clear to push a case further along (1968, p.163). Guilt of a suspect must be determined in a formal, adversarial setting where adequate safeguards are in place to protect the accused. Due process focuses on legal guilt, which can only be determined by an impartial court and only after ensuring all procedural rules have been followed. This means despite factual guilt (crime control), a person cannot be held legally guilty of a crime unless the rules of criminal procedure are followed (due process). If the Constitution is violated, which is a serious breach of a safeguard, a person cannot be convicted.

Packer (1968, p. 153) cautions: "These models are not labels Is and Ought, nor are they to be taken in that sense. Rather, they represent an attempt to abstract two separate value systems that compete for priority in the operation of the criminal process."

The Challenge: Balancing Individual and Societal Rights

Chapter 1 discussed the challenge facing the framers of the Constitution to balance the rights of individuals against the rights of society. Recollections of the tyranny of British rulers prompted the framers of the Constitution to build in many safeguards against any such tyranny in the United States. Nonetheless, to avoid anarchy, a country of laws had to be established. Consider this challenge: to meet the needs of the individual and the government—a strong, but not excessive, system of law and order.

Achieving a workable system that balances the rights and needs of individuals as well as those of the society being served is no small task. In fact, many have died here, and continue to die in other countries, fighting for a system of government that provides the freedoms U.S. citizens now enjoy.

Some argue that in striving to balance individual and societal rights and needs, the system itself has become so complicated that justice is compromised. Although the Constitution appears complex, the many laws subsequently enacted to maintain the balance have created the massively intricate body of law. To those not educated in the law, it might appear that legal loopholes abound, when in reality the crucial balance is struck through the passage of new laws and the continual evolution of existing laws.

LO3 *The basic purpose of the U.S. legal system is to ensure fairness in balancing individual and societal rights and needs, while preventing excessive government power.*

Because the Constitution is meant to be basic, it is, by itself, easy to begin to understand. Students of the Constitution need to grasp the "bigger picture" before looking at the developments that have occurred in the past 200 years. Details can get in the way of understanding the system and how it works.

Definition and Development of the Law

Laws are rules with the power of the government behind them. In the United States, these rules are created by legislative bodies empowered by the people to pass laws. The term **promulgate** means to make law through such legal process. These laws reflect what the citizenry holds important, and they support the norms of society by enforcing its rules through legal consequences that are in accordance with the tenets of the Constitution.

promulgate to make law through a legal process

The development of societal rules began the first time people congregated. When people are together, a norm is established so individuals know what is expected of them relative to the group as a whole. Whether via de facto rules, which naturally develop, or de jure results, which are promulgated, some order must arise to prevent chaos. Law generally evolves through four phases:

1. People come together seeking collective security, to collectively gather food, and to satisfy other mutual needs.
2. They discover that they need rules to maintain order and their sense of security.
3. Inevitably some individuals break the rules.
4. Consequences are established for breaking the rules.

Of great influence on the U.S. legal system was early Roman law dealing with basic rules related to economic, religious, and family life contained in the Twelve Tables, written about 450 B.C.E. These rules were based on tradition and a quest for fairness. Another important period in Roman history was the rule of Emperor Justinian I (ruled A.D. 527–565). His Justinian Code distinguished public and private laws and influenced legal thought throughout the Middle Ages.

Evolution of Common Law and *Stare Decisis*

Another significant influence on the development of the U.S. legal system was the system of common law that evolved in England during the Middle Ages. Rather than smaller groups of people relying completely on local custom to determine their rules or law, royal judges traveling through the territories began to apply a broader or national norm as cases were decided. In essence, the law became more common throughout the country.

L04 *Common law* began as early English judge-made law, based on customs and traditions that were followed throughout the country. As a term in U.S. law, it is synonymous with *case law*. This system of common law is the basis for U.S. law, in which the decisions made in past cases are routinely examined when new cases are considered.

Although initially unwritten, the decisions of the cases heard became the basis for how subsequent cases were decided. If a current case was similar enough to a preceding case, the current case was decided on the basis of the ruling in the previous case. Eventually the cases were written down, and by 1300, recorded decisions were serving as precedent, making it easier to maintain the continuity of the developing legal system. This development was important because the people wanted predictability and stability in the law. A body of written common law allowed people to "know where they stood" and be able to better predict the consequences of their actions.

common law early English judge-made law based on custom and tradition; a legal system that, as in the United States, decides present cases on past decisions

As English Parliament took over the role of promulgating law, the role of common law courts changed. For example, offenses that once were considered personal wrongs, such as murder, rape, and burglary, were redefined by English judges as crimes against the state because such transgressions disrupted the security of the

case law common law approach, so named because it is based on previous cases; as a term in U.S. law, it is synonymous with *common law*

entire community, not just the individual victimized. These redefinitions also made offenders subject to state control and punishment.

U.S. common law also took on the role of interpreting and defining existing law, building on itself to forge new law. And although common law still has the capacity to create law as well as interpret it, it also depends heavily on predictability through precedent. Courts continue to rely on prior cases—directly, by implication or conceptually—to maintain continuity. This continuity results in current cases being decided in ways that relate to existing law (from past cases) and provides the U.S. system of law development a stronger, more predictable basis on which to determine future cases. This common law doctrine is termed *stare decisis*, a Latin term that literally means "let the decision stand," and it requires that precedent set in one case shall be followed in all cases having the same or similar circumstances, thus ensuring consistency in the law.

Although this doctrine has its roots in early English law, the court in *Moore v. City of Albany* (1885) set forth, "When a court has once laid down a principle of law as applicable to a certain state of facts, it will adhere to that principle and apply it to all future cases where facts are substantially the same." When a legal principle has been determined by a higher court, lower courts must apply it to all later cases containing the same or similar facts. Of course, one side will argue that the facts are the same and, as such, *stare decisis* dictates that a certain ruling prevail. The other side will assert that the facts are not exactly the same, and so a different result should be reached. The doctrine of *stare decisis* does not, however, prevent the law from growing, changing, or even reconsidering itself in matters from which undesirable law results.

stare decisis a common law doctrine requiring that precedent set in one case shall be followed in all cases having the same or similar circumstances, thus ensuring consistency in the law; Latin for "let the decision stand"

The Continuing Need for Law

People need laws to know what behavior is socially and legally acceptable and to be able to deal consequences to those who do not follow the law. In any society laws should—must—be obeyed for the good of all. In a sense, obedience to the law is voluntary. At least in countries that enjoy freedom, people are permitted to carry on with life's activities, for the most part, as each sees fit. People obey traffic laws because they should. They pay taxes because they should. However, people have freedom to decide, including the decision to not obey laws.

A critical issue arises when those making and enforcing the law act outside the law. Remember, the purpose of the Constitution remains to limit government power. The law itself controls government by restricting how and when government can and cannot interfere with citizens' lives. The Latin phrase *nulla poena sine lege* translates to "no punishment without law." Similarly, *nullum crimen sine lege* means "no crime without law."

Because the needs of any group change as that group itself changes, effective law should be flexible enough to respond to those changing needs, as introduced in Chapter 1. Human nature dictates that different needs are perceived at different times. For example, laws against witchcraft in colonial America are now perceived as unnecessary and inappropriate, as are laws permitting slavery or prohibiting women to vote. Similarly, laws pertaining to the use of drugs have changed as societal norms have changed, as evidenced by laws dealing with certain uses of marijuana (deemed less serious than a decade ago) or the increasing strictness of laws dealing with driving under the influence. The constitutional amendments dealing with prohibition provide a concrete example of how law can advance and retreat as needs and expectations change.

Constitutional amendments are not easily or frequently added or removed. It takes two-thirds of each house of Congress, or conventions called by two-thirds of the state legislatures, to propose constitutional amendments. For an amendment to be ratified, three-fourths of the state legislatures or special conventions must agree. More than 7,000 amendments have been proposed in Congress, with only 33 of those passed and submitted to the states, where more fell short of the requisite vote.

When amendments are passed, they reflect true societal changes. Since the Bill of Rights was ratified in 1791, 17 amendments have been successfully ratified. Those considered most influential came after the Civil War:

- The Thirteenth Amendment (ratified in 1865) abolished slavery.
- The Fourteenth Amendment (1868) prevented the states from denying former slaves equal protection and due process of law.
- The Fifteenth Amendment (1870) ensured the right to vote regardless of race.
- The Nineteenth Amendment (1920) extended the right to vote to women.
- The Twenty-First Amendment (1933) repealed prohibition, which was ratified as the Eighteenth Amendment in 1919.

As you develop an understanding of what modern law is and how it developed from the needs of the earliest gatherings of people, it becomes obvious why it has reached its level of complexity. With more than 323 million people in the United States,[1] and with the importance we place on pluralism, our needs are varied. A legal system that responds to such societal diversity and technological change becomes, out of necessity, complex. One of the complexities is that various categories of law exist, often overlapping in an effort to respond to society's changing needs.

Categorizing Law

Different aspects of the law interact in ways that may appear confusing at first. For clarity, go back to the basics: What is the purpose of law? To limit government power and to provide societal guidelines. Why is there so much law? To strive for justice and due process in a growing and increasingly complex society with many different viewpoints. To further clarify, it helps to categorize the law by asking: *Who? How?* and *What?*

Who? (Jurisdiction)

This question is actually twofold: *Who makes the law?* and *Who does the law affect?*

Who makes the law is whichever group has **jurisdiction**, or authority, to promulgate that law. It might be a legislative body, such as the elected or appointed members of the city council, county board, and state or federal legislatures. Or it could be a court that makes decisions through case law or common law. Who the law affects are the people over which the law-making group has jurisdiction.

jurisdiction the authority of a legislative body to establish a law, the authority of a particular court to hear certain types of cases, or the authority a law has over a specific group of people

---
[1] According to the U.S. Census Bureau U.S. Population clock, an estimated 323,675,250 people were living in the United States on June 1, 2016.

statutory law law set forth by legislatures or governing bodies having jurisdiction to make such law

codified law law specifically set forth in organized, structured codes such as the U.S. criminal code, state statutes, or local ordinances

ordinances laws or codes established at the local level, that is, the municipal or county level

Statutory law is promulgated by legislatures or governing bodies. Statutory law can also be referred to as **codified law** because it is set forth in organized, structured codes such as the U.S. Criminal Code or the criminal code of a specific state.

Local jurisdictions, such as county or municipal levels, also enact their own specific codes, often referred to as **ordinances**. Codes and statutes have been woven together with common law principles to make the legal system we have today. Of crucial importance is the fact that no statutory law, regardless of the level of jurisdiction, can violate the Constitution.

The mid to late 1800s saw a move toward codifying the law, and one of the most well known is the "Field Code," written by David Dudley Field. Field's goal was to simplify the law, and his code contained not only a set of standardized criminal and civil procedures but also uniform criminal statutes. The Field Code was adopted by New York and served as a model for other states, mostly those in the western United States. Other codes were authored by Jeremy Bentham in England and Edward Livingston in the United States.

A group need not be elected to have authority to promulgate law. Legislative bodies have the authority to appoint administrative groups to make rules that have the power of law. The reason administrative agencies may do so is twofold. First, legislative groups do not have time to address every issue that arises. Second, they often lack the knowledge to adequately address every issue that arises. So they appoint people who have the time and expertise. Examples of administrative agencies include federal regulatory agencies such as the Food and Drug Administration. Examples of state agencies include the fire marshal's office or the state police licensing board. Other examples include county, city, or other local groups, such as a metropolitan council, health department, or even a park board.

Remember that courts make law through their holdings that act as rules because of *stare decisis*. Whatever they have decided becomes the law and is relied on in subsequent cases. The fact that courts are making law, but for the most part are not elected to do so as are legislators, stirs debate. This is especially the case at the Supreme Court level and is why the ability of a president to appoint justices is so powerful.

How? (Procedural)

substantive law establishes rules and regulations, as in traffic law

procedural law how the law is to be enforced, for example, how and when police can stop people

Rules and regulations (like traffic law) are established by **substantive law**. How the law is to be enforced is embodied in **procedural law.** For example, how and when police can stop people is governed by procedural law. The effects of substantive law being enforced in violation of law (i.e., by illegal procedure) can result in serious consequences for the government. For example, the exclusionary rule (discussed in Chapter 7) prohibits evidence obtained in violation of a person's constitutional rights to be used in court, no matter how incriminating. This is why it is crucial for criminal justice professionals to know the law and know when it changes.

What? (Criminal or Civil)

This question asks whether the wrong considered is a *public* wrong or a *private* wrong. In other words, who is the victim? The answer affects several critical factors.

Criminal law considers society the victim because whenever a crime is committed, the act disrupts the community. Although one or possibly more than one victim is identifiable, if the community's security is upset, *all* community members are considered victims. Society's welfare has been violated. This is why the caption (name) of a criminal case is the government, representing the people, versus the defendant (e.g., *United States v. Smith, State of Maine v. Jones*). Wrongs that disrupt the status quo of the community are called **crimes,** and criminal laws are found in each state's **penal codes.**

If a dispute involves only individuals and affects only them, it is considered a civil case, and the wrong is called a **tort.** These cases are captioned with the name of the aggrieved party bringing the legal action, generally referred to as the plaintiff, versus the individual accused of causing the harm, generally referred to as the defendant. Although there may be more than one plaintiff, as in the case of a class-action lawsuit, civil cases involve individuals, and the government usually is not involved.

A drunk driver causing a crash, for example, could be guilty of the crime of driving under the influence, as well as be held civilly liable for the injuries caused to others by the tort committed. This example also helps explain other differences between crimes and torts, including the burden of proof required and the desired outcome.

In a criminal action, the government must prove its case *beyond a reasonable doubt*, which one could view as to a 99 percent degree of certainty. It does not mean without *any* doubt because few decisions in life can be made with no doubts. This is the same standard applied to any of life's major decisions—marriage, having children, divorce, taking a new job, or undergoing surgery. Facts are gathered, decisions reached, and action taken. The government is required to meet this high standard in proving its case because the consequences for the accused are so significant, including imprisonment or the ultimate sentence imposed, the death penalty. The system seeks to ensure, to the highest degree possible, that the government is right when the ultimate goal of the criminal justice system is punishment.

In a civil action, the plaintiffs have only to prove their case by a *preponderance of the evidence*, which means "more likely than not," or to any level of certainty greater than 50 percent. This lower burden of proof exists in the civil arena for several reasons, a primary one being that the defendants do not face the same monumental loss of freedom as they do if they are found "guilty" in criminal court. Because the goal of the civil system is to right the wrong by making the victim or plaintiff "whole" again, civil damages are usually limited to financial awards or injunctions to return the plaintiff to where they were to begin with, for example, paying on a broken contract, removing a fence on someone else's land, or paying to compensate for a wrongful injury. The civil system also acknowledges that individuals have limited resources compared with the government and likely could not afford the experts often used during a criminal investigation, so their use would not be warranted.

To return to the drunk-driving example, whereas the driver could be charged criminally because of the disruption caused to the community, the person injured in the crash could also sue civilly to recoup medical costs and compensate for injuries

crimes acts defined by federal or state statute or local ordinance that are punishable; wrongs against the government and the people it serves

penal codes criminal codes or laws

tort civil wrong by one individual against another, with the remedy most often being either an order by the court for particular action or compensation

> **LO5** *Civil laws deal with wrongs against individuals—called torts. Criminal laws deal with wrongs against society—called crimes. An act may be both a tort and a crime.*

sustained. One decision does not depend on the other. In the infamous O. J. Simpson case, the defendant was acquitted on the criminal charges because the government could not prove its case beyond a reasonable doubt, but the plaintiffs in the civil case were successful in proving their case by a preponderance of the evidence.

A final note, as with the different standards regarding burden of proof, civil and criminal trials are governed by different procedural rules. Although the rules in both areas were developed to promote efficiency and predictability and to protect individual rights, the emphasis differs between the two types of trials based on the nature of risk to the accused. In a civil trial, the defendant's money and reputation are at risk, and the federal courts are bound by the Federal Rules of Civil Procedure, which articulate such things as how a lawsuit must be initiated, under what conditions depositions can be taken, or how a claim can be dismissed before trial as a matter of law.

In a criminal trial, however, the stakes are much greater for the individual, who may lose their freedom or even their life as the result of a conviction. Thus, in criminal trials there is a heavier emphasis on procedures that protect the defendant. We usually think of criminal procedure as the law surrounding the Fourth, Fifth, Sixth, and Eighth Amendments. And with such constitutional limits in mind, criminal procedural rules have been developed to address such things as the time of day a search warrant may be served, who may be present during a grand jury hearing, or how to schedule a pretrial conference.

Researching the Law

Criminal justice professionals, including police officers, are expected to know the law and when it changes. And it *will* change throughout your education and your career. Knowing how to research the law is an important skill that enables you to find answers to legal questions and, perhaps more important, to better understand the judicial system. Although some departments have legal departments or city attorneys who try to keep officers updated through regular training, many agencies do not. Thus, the responsibility falls to the individual officers.

Basic legal research skills are as important as any of the more traditional job-related skills. As a student of the law and as a criminal justice practitioner, you are more likely to be looking for legal basics than for the detailed information found in legal briefs. Criminal justice professionals are not expected to be legal scholars or expert researchers after this short introduction, but it will be a stepping-stone for efforts to find and understand U.S. laws.

Sources of Information about the Law

The most authoritative information source about the law is primary information—the actual cases and the opinions handed down. Sources of primary information for legal research include the U.S. Constitution, the constitutions of the 50 states, the statutes of the U.S. Congress and the statutes of the 50 state legislatures, as well as appellate court decisions of the federal and state courts. However, for the non-lawyer, it is usually easier to understand secondary information sources, which select, evaluate, analyze, and synthesize data contained in primary information sources. Among the important secondary information sources for legal research are periodicals, treatises/texts, encyclopedias, and dictionaries. These secondary information sources usually can be found in a general library or online.

A helpful general resource is a *Guide to Law Online*, prepared by the Library of Congress Public Services Division (www.loc.gov/law/help/guide.php). Other useful sources of information include the U.S. Supreme Court's official website (www.supremecourt.gov/) and www.oyez.org/, which offers audio recordings of oral arguments, access to full written opinions, breakdowns of how justices voted in cases, and biographies, as well as a Google map feature to show the location of the case in question. Finally, CourtListener.com provides oral arguments from the federal courts and opinions from state and federal courts, and is updated regularly.

An important note about the reliability of sources: Wikipedia and even lesser respected sites are *never* considered reliable sources for academic purposes. These sites should not be used to research the law, nor should they ever be referenced in academic papers.

With this overview of the sources of information available to research a case, consider next how to read a legal citation once it is found.

> **MYTH**
> The Internet is a great source of reliable information to be used in legal research.
>
> **FACT**
> Yes and no. The Internet does provide access to a wealth of information and is easily searchable. However, not all web sources are created equal. You must know the source you are citing and be able to show reliability. Propriety sources are generally accepted because they are subject to peer review and the material is able to be cross-referenced. Free resources are often not subject to the same scrutiny, and the veracity of their content is often questionable. This is not to say that all free resources are unreliable. Some are legitimate for research purposes, and much depends on the original source of the information.

Reading Legal Citations

Case citation is important to understand when researching the law or, for that matter, even writing a paper. Citations show the student exactly where to find an important point, right down to the page, and let the reader know immediately if the case is relevant to the problem they are researching.

A **legal citation** is a standardized way of referring to a specific element in the law. It has three basic parts: a volume number, an abbreviation for the title, and a page or section number. Legal citations are usually followed by the date. For example, the official cite for the *Miranda* case is *Miranda v. Arizona*, 384 U.S. 436 (1966). Sometimes additional cites will be given. These are called **string cites** or parallel citations. The additional cites show where the case could be found in other commercial reporting services. A string cite for this case would be *Miranda v. Arizona*, 384 U.S. 436, 86 S.Ct. 1602, 16 L.Ed.2d 694 (1966). A more detailed explanation of how to read legal citations and string cites is provided in Appendix B.

Locating provisions of federal and state constitutions does not present a problem. When it comes to case law, however, the situation is different. Millions of judicial opinions have been written in the United States, with thousands more published each year.

legal citation a standardized way of referring to a specific element in the law

string cites additional legal citations showing where a case may be found in commercial reporting services

Reading Case Law

You may find yourself challenged with attempting to read actual case law at some time. It is helpful to become familiar with some basic concepts and terminology you will encounter. To begin, the **caption** (title of the case) tells who is involved. It may be the government against a criminal defendant (*State of Washington v. Smith*), or it may be two individuals disputing an issue (*Anderson v. Smith*). The caption (title) is always italicized.

The parties to the action may be identified by different titles (defendant, plaintiff, petitioner, respondent), depending on the nature of the case. The particular

caption the title of a case setting forth the parties involved

> **MYTH**
> Appellate courts serve to recheck the factual issues of a case, allow witnesses not previously heard to testify, and use a second jury to verify that the trial court jury reached the right verdict.
>
> **FACT**
> Only trial courts determine the factual issues of a case. An appellate court does not try factual issues, nor does it allow new evidence to be presented or witnesses to testify. It does not use a jury to reach its decision. An appellate court reviews the trial court record as well as briefs prepared by both the prosecution and defense, and it may allow brief oral arguments from both sides, after which it determines whether sufficient evidence exists to support the findings of the trial court and whether the trial court followed the rules of criminal procedure.

holding the rule of law applied to the particular facts of the case and the actual decision

affirm agree with a lower court's decision

reverse overturn the decision of a lower court

remand return a case to the lower court for further action

vacate set aside or annul a case

concurring opinion one written by a justice who agrees with the holding, but who gives additional or different reasons for voting with the majority

dissenting opinion written by a justice who disagrees with the holding and voted against the majority

brief an outline of a legal case that contains the case name and citation, a summary of key facts, the legal issues involved, the court's decision, the reasons for that decision, and any separate opinions or dissents

court and level of legal action (whether it is an appeal, etc.) will determine whose name comes first in the caption. This is usually clarified within the first part of the case.

Most cases start in the trial court. The trial court has two basic responsibilities: to find out what happened and to determine which legal rules should be used in deciding the case. The trial court makes its decision on the basis of facts presented by the lawyers representing both parties (or by the individuals themselves if not represented by legal counsel), using the legal rules the judge determines are appropriate to apply to this case. The party that does not emerge victorious may appeal to a higher court on any number of issues. However, only legal issues will be reviewed on appeal because new evidence is not permitted. In fact, appeals are considered only by the appellate judges reviewing written and oral arguments from the parties, along with case transcripts and opinions issued by the previous judge involved. (Not all cases produce opinions, particularly at the trial court level.)

Although many issues may be presented in one case, they may not all be addressed by the court deciding the case. Whether to save time or perhaps even to avoid other issues within a case, a court may choose to answer only one issue in its opinion, leaving the others for future cases.

Court decisions are recorded as opinions, which include more than simply a statement of who won the court case. Opinions describe what the dispute was about, which legal rules were applied to the case, and what the court decided and why. The **holding** of a case is the rule of law applied to the particular facts of the case and the actual decision. A court may **affirm** (support), **reverse** (overturn), or **remand** (return the case to the lower court). It may also **vacate** (set aside or annul) a case. An opinion may be written by one member of the court, or there may be many concurring and dissenting opinions. A **concurring opinion** is one written by a justice who agrees with the holding, but who gives additional or different reasons for voting with the majority. A **dissenting opinion** is written by a justice who disagrees with the holding and voted against the majority. Some landmark cases have eight or nine opinions.

Three skills are required to read case law. First, you must think in reverse. The opinion provides the result of the deliberations. You must isolate what the dispute involved, what the trial court decided, how it proceeded, and what happened on appeal.

This is a critical first step because knowing what the legal issue is will help identify what facts are important in that case. Understanding these facts within the context of the law helps the researcher read the case with purpose.

Second, you must untangle the interplay of the basic components of a judicial opinion. Each affects the others in a process that goes back and forth and around in what may appear to be circles. Third, not all the elements of the judicial opinion may be included. You must infer them from the decisions made.

Briefing a Case

Once you locate a case, you will want to make some notes to help you decipher it. Because cases are usually rather long, the best way to do this is to outline, or **brief**, the case. Most case briefs contain the case name and citation, a summary of key facts, the legal issues involved, the court's decision, the reasons for that decision, and any separate opinions or dissents.

Traditionally, law is taught through case law. This is an arduous process by which issues and rules are dissected from court opinions. This discipline is necessary for those intending to become lawyers because case analysis is the cornerstone of understanding how and why cases are decided as they are and why the law in any particular area developed as it did.

LO6 *A legal opinion usually contains (1) a description of the facts, (2) a statement of the legal issues presented, (3) the relevant rules of law, (4) the holding, and (5) the policies and reasons that support the holding.*

Case law, also known as common law, depends on comparing one case with others. As difficult as the case analysis approach to learning law is, it definitely has its place. However, this complex approach can hinder understanding the basics of constitutional law as they apply to criminal justice—the focus of this text.

You should, however, know what a case opinion looks like, as well as how a brief of that case might be used to analyze the issues and rules drawn from it. Opinions also provide judges with an opportunity to express thoughts on issues not essential to the court's decision, looking at facts or issues other than those needed to determine the case. These are called **dicta** and are not binding on future courts. A dictum is a means for the majority to address other issues beyond the facts before them. Consequently, an opinion holds a great deal of information to be scrutinized.

dicta statements by a court that do not deal with the main issue in the case or an additional discussion by the court

Two famous, relevant cases illustrate opinions and the briefs that might be written from them. *Marbury v. Madison* (1803) was selected because it is the pivotal case of constitutional law granting the Supreme Court authority to review legislation to determine whether it is constitutional—and thus legal. *Miranda v. Arizona* (1966) was selected because it is perhaps one of the most famous constitutional law cases in criminal justice. The complete opinions for these two cases may be found online. Appendix C provides the briefs for these two cases.

A great deal more could be addressed regarding the legal process and how to decipher legal cases and their resulting opinions. However, this text was not intended to address these specific issues. The goal in this section is to provide the basic information to seek out the law as needed. One last skill is needed by those performing actual legal research: going beyond the case itself to determine if it is still a precedent or if it has been overturned or expanded—a process known as *citing*.

Citing

After a case has been researched, the current status of the case should be determined because relying on a case that has been overturned or otherwise rendered invalid could prove disastrous. **Citing** a case involves using references that track cases so legal researchers can easily determine whether the original holding has been changed through any appeals.

citing using resources and references that track cases so legal researchers can easily determine whether the original holding has been changed through any appeals

Previous editions of this text referred to this process as *Shepardizing*, a term that came from a legal service started by Frank Shepard (1848–1902), who published *Shephard's Citations*, which were lists of all of the authorities citing a specific case, statute, or other legal authority. In 1996, Shepard's was bought by LexisNexis (a subsidiary of Reed Elsevier). In 1999, LexisNexis released an online version of *Shepard's Citations* to provide a more efficient, faster, and current resource for legal research. Today, the more common term used to refer to such a resource is *citator*, because other methods now exist, all based on the original idea of Shepard. Lexis still Shepardizes; WestLaw has a citator called KeyCite.

Citing cases is almost the exclusive domain of attorneys and their clerks. It is improbable that criminal justice practitioners such as law enforcement officers will actually perform this step in the legal research process; however, it is important to know the procedure and the term. Appendix D provides an example of a page from Shepard's to illustrate the complexity of the process and the amount of detail that can be obtained. For those readers desiring additional information on researching the law, Appendix E provides information relating to computerized legal research, a list of URLs to access criminal justice sources online, and step-by-step guidance on researching a law of interest.

The Court System

Recall that Article 3 of the U.S. Constitution established the federal judicial system: "The judicial Power of the United States shall be vested in one Supreme Court, and in such inferior courts as the Congress may from time to time ordain and establish." In addition, the congresses of the individual states have established state supreme courts and inferior courts.

The types of cases a court can hear depend on its jurisdiction. The term *jurisdiction* refers to:

- The authority of a legislative body to establish a law or a court to hear a case.
- The authority a law has over a specific group of people.

original jurisdiction courts authorized to hear cases first, try them and render decisions

appellate jurisdiction courts authorized to review cases and to either affirm or reverse the actions of a lower court

general jurisdiction courts having the ability to hear a wide range of cases

limited jurisdiction restriction of the types of cases a particular court might hear

exclusive jurisdiction courts that can hear only specific cases

concurrent jurisdiction two or more courts authorized to hear a specific type of case

venue the geographic area in which a specific case may come to trial, and the area from which the jury is selected

Three levels of jurisdiction exist: federal, state, and local. In addition, jurisdiction can be original or appellate. **Original jurisdiction** describes a court authorized to hear cases first, try them, and render decisions. Such courts are often called trial courts. **Appellate jurisdiction** describes a court authorized to review cases and to either affirm or reverse the actions of a lower court.

Courts may also have general or limited jurisdiction. As the names imply, courts with **general jurisdiction** may hear a wide range of cases; those of **limited jurisdiction** hear a much narrower range of cases. Further, courts may have exclusive or concurrent jurisdiction. **Exclusive jurisdiction** applies to courts that can hear only specific cases. **Concurrent jurisdiction** refers to two or more courts authorized to hear a specific type of case.

Finally, jurisdiction may refer to a geographical area. A more precise term to describe the geographic area in which a case may be heard is **venue,** the place a specific case may come to trial and the area from which the jury is selected.

Just as the U.S. Constitution established the federal court system, state constitutions establish their own court systems with many variations from state to state. At either tier, three levels of courts function: a lower level or trial court, an appellate court, and a court of last resort, or supreme court, as illustrated in Figure 2.1.

The U.S. legal system was designed to provide individuals with a fair and just trial conducted under fair rules of procedure in an atmosphere of objectivity. These levels exist to ensure that if either side thinks procedural rules were violated, that side can appeal the case to a higher court. This appellate court can uphold the lower court's finding, order a new trial, or overturn, reverse, or dismiss the charge.

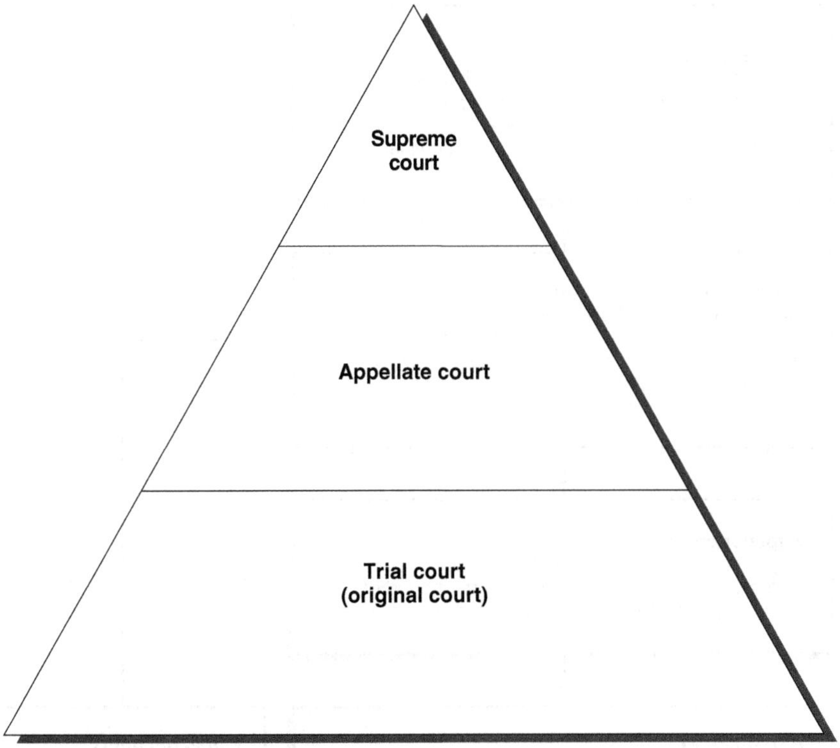

```
        /\
       /  \
      / Supreme \
     /  court    \
    /─────────────\
   /               \
  /   Appellate     \
 /      court        \
/─────────────────────\
/                       \
/      Trial court       \
/     (original court)    \
/_____\
```

Figure 2.1 Levels in the State and Federal Court System

The State Court System

Individual states establish a variety of lower courts with a variety of names. Figure 2.2 illustrates the state court system. The Court Statistics Project (CSP) reports that more than 96 million cases were filed in the courts of our 50 states, the District of Columbia, and the Territory of Puerto Rico in calendar year 2012 (LaFountain, Schauffler, Strickland, Holt, & Lewis, 2014). The majority of cases (51.9%) involved traffic offenses, 19.3 percent were criminal cases, 17.9 percent were civil cases, 5.2 percent involved domestic relations, and the remaining 1.7 percent were juvenile cases.

LO7 *The U.S. judicial system is two-tiered, consisting of state and federal court systems. Each includes specific levels of courts. The courts' two main functions are to settle controversies between parties and to decide the rules of law that apply in the specific case.*

Lower Courts Lower courts include municipal courts, inferior courts of limited jurisdiction, and county courts. Municipal courts hear ordinance violations, minor criminal cases, traffic cases, and sometimes more major cases. Their authority is usually limited to the city or county in which the court is located.

Inferior courts of limited jurisdiction include probate courts, family courts, police courts, justice of the peace courts, and traffic courts. A few states still have police courts, courts that try misdemeanor offenses and conduct preliminary examinations to decide whether evidence is sufficient to bring the case to trial in a higher-level court. Some states have established these inferior courts of limited jurisdiction to eliminate the expense and inconvenience of traveling to a county or district court.

MYTH
The majority of criminal cases filed go to court and are decided by a trial.

FACT
Few criminal cases actually make it to trial. The vast majority of criminal convictions—as much as 90 percent by some estimates—are the result of plea bargaining.

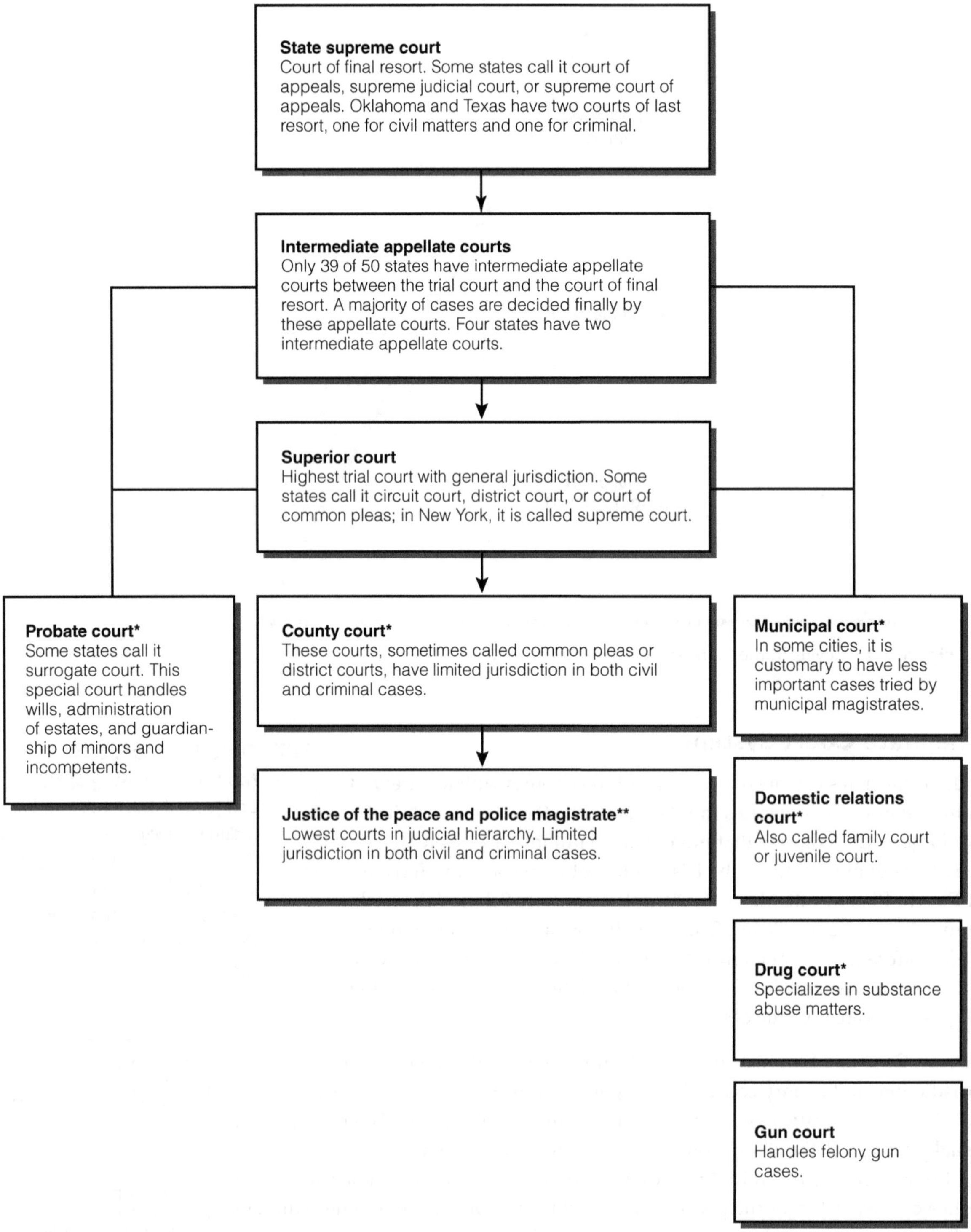

State supreme court
Court of final resort. Some states call it court of appeals, supreme judicial court, or supreme court of appeals. Oklahoma and Texas have two courts of last resort, one for civil matters and one for criminal.

Intermediate appellate courts
Only 39 of 50 states have intermediate appellate courts between the trial court and the court of final resort. A majority of cases are decided finally by these appellate courts. Four states have two intermediate appellate courts.

Superior court
Highest trial court with general jurisdiction. Some states call it circuit court, district court, or court of common pleas; in New York, it is called supreme court.

Probate court*
Some states call it surrogate court. This special court handles wills, administration of estates, and guardianship of minors and incompetents.

County court*
These courts, sometimes called common pleas or district courts, have limited jurisdiction in both civil and criminal cases.

Municipal court*
In some cities, it is customary to have less important cases tried by municipal magistrates.

Justice of the peace and police magistrate**
Lowest courts in judicial hierarchy. Limited jurisdiction in both civil and criminal cases.

Domestic relations court*
Also called family court or juvenile court.

Drug court*
Specializes in substance abuse matters.

Gun court
Handles felony gun cases.

Figure 2.2 State Judicial System

*Courts of special jurisdiction such as probate, family, or juvenile courts, and the so-called inferior courts such as common pleas or municipal courts, may be separate courts or part of the trial court of general jurisdiction.

**Justices of the peace do not exist in all states. Where they do exist, their jurisdictions vary greatly from state to state. Note: In California all justice courts are municipal courts.

Source: SIEGEL/SENNA. *Introduction to Criminal Justice* (with CD-ROM and InfoTrac®), 10E. © 2005 Wadsworth, a part of Cengage Learning, Inc. Reproduced by permission. www.cengage.com/permissions. Adapted from American Bar Association, *Law and the Courts*. Chicago: American Bar Association, 1974, p. 20.

County courts often have exclusive jurisdiction over misdemeanor cases and civil cases involving a limited amount of money. In some states, county courts are also probate courts and juvenile courts. Some states have combined various courts under the umbrella of the county courts.

Superior courts are the highest trial courts with general jurisdiction. More than 3,000 such courts exist in the United States. This is where most felony cases enter the system. Some states call them district courts, circuit courts, or courts of common plea. These courts may have an appellate department to hear and decide appeals from the municipal courts.

Intermediate Appellate Courts These courts were created in several states to reduce the caseloads of state supreme courts. Appealed cases generally go to the intermediate appellate court first.

State Supreme Courts State supreme courts are the highest courts in a state and are generally called supreme courts, although some states call them courts of appeals. These courts are given their power by the individual state constitutions, generally oversee the intermediate appellate courts, and have few areas of original jurisdiction. If someone petitions the supreme court to review the decision of an appeals court, this is called a **petition for certiorari**. A lower court must abide by the decision of a higher court.

petition for certiorari
request that the Supreme Court or a state supreme court review the decision of a lower court

The Federal Court System

The federal court system consists of a number of specialized courts, a number of district courts with general jurisdiction, 12 circuit courts of appeals, and the U.S. Supreme Court (Figure 2.3).

Special U.S. Courts Congress has created several specialized courts that seldom involve the criminal justice system. They include the Court of Military Appeals, the Court of Claims, the Court of Customs and Patent Appeals, the Customs Court, and the Tax Court.

U.S. District Courts The district courts are trial courts with general, original federal jurisdiction that try both civil and criminal cases, the vast majority of which are civil cases. Each state has at least one district court. Some large states have four. The total number of district courts is 94 (92 in the states, 1 in the District of Columbia, and 1 in Puerto Rico).

U.S. Courts of Appeals Like the intermediate appellate courts at the state level, the U.S. Courts of Appeals were created to ease the caseload of the Supreme Court. The 94 district courts are organized into 12 regional circuits, each of which has a U.S. Court of Appeals. A thirteenth court at this level is the Court of Appeals for the Federal Circuit, which has nationwide jurisdiction for special appeals. These courts have jurisdiction over final decisions of federal district courts. They are the courts of last resort in most federal cases.

The U.S. Supreme Court The U.S. Supreme Court is the ultimate court of appeal. Its chief function is as an appellate court. It receives petitions for certiorari from more than 6,000 cases a year but usually accepts fewer than 10 percent

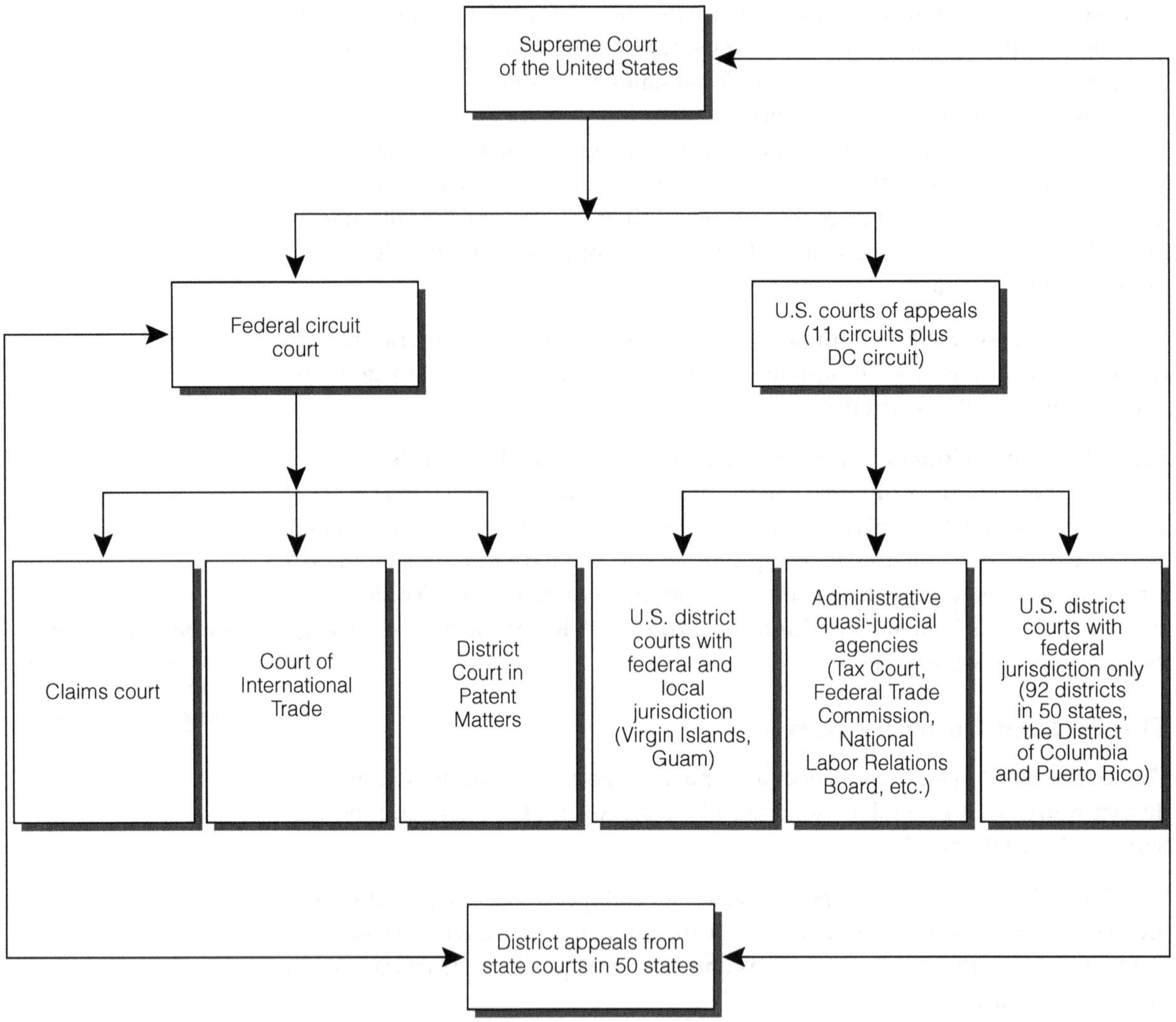

Figure 2.3 Federal Judicial System

Source: SIEGEL/SENNA. *Introduction to Criminal Justice* (with CD-ROM and InfoTrac®), 10E. © 2005 Wadsworth, a part of Cengage Learning, Inc. Reproduced by permission. www.cengage.com/permissions. Adapted from American Bar Association, *Law and the Courts*. Chicago: American Bar Association, 1974, p. 20.

for review. More than a third of the cases received are from state supreme courts. The Supreme Court is restricted by an act of Congress to hear only certain types of appeals from federal appeals courts and state supreme courts. Basically, the cases must involve a federal or state statute alleged to be unconstitutional. There is no right to have a case heard by the Supreme Court. It hears only cases of extreme national importance to set important policy.

The Supreme Court has dealt with such controversial issues as abortion and school prayer. Bills have been introduced in Congress to prevent the Supreme Court from ruling on such "moral" issues, leaving it up to the individual states. The Supreme Court is the only court empowered to handle lawsuits between two states. Because of its extreme importance in shaping the country's laws, the next chapter is devoted to the Supreme Court.

Officers of the Court

The legal system does not consist simply of buildings. It is about people. It is there to serve people and does so through those who play important and varied roles in the system. Those whose jobs are to carry out the administration of law are called officers of the court, and this assemblage of professionals is commonly referred to as the courtroom work group.

Judges, sometimes called justices or magistrates, are elected in some states and appointed in others. Judges preside over trials and hearings and render decisions. They also oversee the selection of juries and instruct them during jury cases.

Lawyers represent one side or the other. In a civil case, the plaintiff's lawyer represents the party bringing suit. In a criminal case, the prosecutor represents the state. The lawyer representing the accused or answering party is the defense attorney. The lawyers prepare and present their clients' cases to a judge and sometimes to a jury.

Clerks of court schedule cases, officially record all business conducted by the court, and receive and file all official documents related to a case, for example, summons and complaints. Sheriffs and marshals serve summons and other court documents and enforce court orders. Sheriffs function at the state level and marshals at the federal level. Bailiffs are responsible for keeping the courtroom proceedings orderly and dignified and for protecting everyone in the courtroom.

> **LO8** *The officers of the court are judges, lawyers, clerks of court, sheriffs, marshals, and bailiffs.*

> **MYTH**
> The judge is the only "courtroom actor" who can dispose of cases.
>
> **FACT**
> The prosecutor often functions in a judicial capacity and is authorized to negotiate guilty pleas before a case goes to trial.

An Adversarial Judicial System

After a person is charged with an offense, civil or criminal, sides are drawn—*accuser v. accused*. The accusing side has the burden of proof to establish guilt. The defendant is presumed innocent until this has been accomplished. It is expected that each side will assert their positions vehemently, not only so that their situation will be resolved but also so that truth will prevail. This is accomplished by having both sides provide the strongest legal response possible, a concept difficult to appreciate by those who lack understanding of the law. For example, a question frequently asked of defense lawyers is: "How can you defend someone accused of such a horrible crime?" The answer is that even the accused has a right to legal representation as aggressive as the law allows. It could be a matter of life and death.

The legal system established in the United States is termed an **adversarial judicial system** because only in an actual conflict will a judicial body hear the case. Theoretically, courts will not entertain "what if" questions. Actual people must have reached an impasse and require a binding decision by a court. In practice, however, the court has frequently relaxed this barrier, finding exceptions to it and applying it inconsistently. The abortion case *Roe v. Wade* (1973), for example, was decided long after the petitioner's pregnancy had terminated and the controversy ended.

As designed, however, the system places one side against the other, whether the government against a private party or individual against individual. Although problems are encouraged to be settled out of court, the system is prepared to be accessed when necessary.

The overall legal system is organized to provide parties to a case the most accessible tribunal. For example, a matter involving a local building code dispute is best

> **MYTH**
> The victim, by filing charges against a defendant, is granted considerable say in how a criminal case will be prosecuted.
>
> **FACT**
> In our adversarial justice system, a crime is considered an offense against the state, and therefore it is the state, through the prosecutor's office, that gets to determine if and how a case will be prosecuted. In criminal matters, it is the government versus the defendant, and the actual crime victim is only a witness. Even in domestic violence cases, the trend is to prosecute without a cooperating victim.

adversarial judicial system a legal system, such as that of the United States, that places one party against another to resolve a legal issue, stipulating that only in an actual conflict will a judicial body hear the case

taken up by a municipal board of adjustments and appeals or the city council. The violation of a state statute, however, is best dealt with by a state court.

All levels of jurisdiction have avenues of appeal so that matters may be heard by another body of decision makers. This system provides a degree of checks and balances and removes the element of personal involvement sometimes present at the local level.

Doctrines Governing What Cases Will Be Heard

LO9 Three important doctrines govern whether a case will be heard by the court: standing, mootness, and ripeness.

In recognition of the fact that not every dispute warrants the attention and resources of the court, guidelines have been established to govern which cases the court will hear.

Standing To bring a case or to argue a legal issue in court, one must have **standing,** meaning an actual interest in the matter of dispute. It is not permissible for just anyone to bring a legal action unless they are actually a party to the matter intended to be adjudicated. Someone must have been legally wronged or accused of the wrongdoing to be involved in a legal case. For example, in *Minnesota v. Carter* (1998) the defendant had gone to the apartment of a third party for the sole purpose of packaging cocaine. An officer, acting on a tip, went to the building and, looking through a gap in the blind of the apartment window, observed Carter packaging cocaine. A warrant was obtained, the apartment was searched, and the defendant was arrested. The defense attorney moved to suppress the cocaine and other evidence seized from the apartment, arguing that the officer's initial observation through the window was an unreasonable search violating Carter's Fourth Amendment rights. The trial court held that because Carter was not an overnight guest, he was not entitled to Fourth Amendment protection. The State Court of Appeals held that Carter did not have "standing" to object to the officer's actions. The State Supreme Court, however, reversed and held that the defendant did have "standing" to claim Fourth Amendment protection because he had a legitimate expectation of privacy. Finally, the case came before the Supreme Court, which reversed and remanded the case, ruling that Carter had no expectation of privacy, and thus, no standing to contest the alleged Fourth Amendment violation because he was in the apartment for only two hours, had never been there before, and was there for the sole purpose of packaging cocaine.

The state courts' analysis of respondents' expectation of privacy under the "standing" doctrine was expressly rejected in *Rakas v. Illinois* (1978). To claim Fourth Amendment protection, a defendant must demonstrate that he or she personally has an expectation of privacy in the place searched and that this expectation is reasonable.

standing having an actual interest in the matter of dispute

amicus brief a "friend of the court" brief submitted by a person not a party to the action but interested in the outcome

People who are not a party to the action may still have an interest and are permitted to submit an **amicus** ("friends of the court") **brief** arguing their perspective. However, these are only considered at the pleasure of the court and as merely thoughts of a nonparty.

mootness exists when the issues that gave rise to a case have either been resolved or have otherwise disappeared

Mootness When the issues that gave rise to a case have either been resolved or have otherwise disappeared so that a court decision would have no practical effect, **mootness** exists. An example of a case dismissed for mootness is one in which a group of students and their parents filed suit challenging the inclusion of two prayers and a hymn during a 1991 public high school graduation ceremony as unconstitutional. Although the federal district court rejected the challenge, the circuit court of appeals declared the practice unconstitutional under the Establishment Clause of the First Amendment. However, the Supreme Court remanded the case, instructing the court of appeals to dismiss it as moot because the students who filed the suit had already graduated. A court can use the mootness doctrine to avoid considering controversial constitutional issues.

Ripeness When a case comes to court too soon, the **ripeness doctrine** is invoked. This doctrine prevents the court from getting prematurely involved in a case that may eventually be resolved through other means. For example, in *National Park Hospitality Association v. Department of the Interior* (2003), park concessioners challenged a rule made by the National Park Service that made a prior congressional act inapplicable to contract disputes. However, because the concessioners were challenging the rule before an actual contract dispute had arisen, the Supreme Court said the case was not yet ripe for a decision.

> **ripeness doctrine** invoked when a case comes to court too soon, preventing the court from getting prematurely involved in a case that may eventually resolve through other means

Ripeness may be an issue in disputes between Congress and the president, as was the case when President Jimmy Carter terminated diplomatic recognition of Taiwan as the legitimate government of China. In *Goldwater v. Carter* (1979) the Supreme Court found the case to be unripe because Congress had not yet actually objected. In his concurring opinion, Justice Lewis Powell stated that courts should decline on the grounds of ripeness to decide "issues affecting the allocation of power between the President and Congress until the political branches reach a constitutional impasse." A similar situation existed when Congress attempted to stop President George W. Bush from invading Iraq before he had actually done so.

The Components of the U.S. Legal System: The Big Picture

Just as a complicated engine is made of many individual parts, the legal system has many components that must work together to produce the desired result. Thus far, this chapter has focused on the courts because this is where constitutional issues are decided. However, the courts are only one component of the U.S. system of justice, both at the adult and juvenile levels. The Constitution also directly affects what happens before a case comes to court (law enforcement actions) and after the court renders a decision (correctional officer actions).

Law enforcement officers, as the gatekeepers of the criminal justice system, must be thoroughly versed in the Fourth Amendment's guarantee of the right to be free from unreasonable search and seizure. The Constitution applies to the police officer who wants to search the interior of a car stopped for a traffic violation as well as to searches conducted within the walls of a prison by a correctional officer.

Furthermore, these same constitutional constraints apply to nonsworn police, community service officers and animal control personnel, fire and building inspectors, community corrections workers (probation and parole officers), food and drug inspectors, and postal inspectors. The number of jobs in the governmental system is huge, and all those working in them are regulated by the Constitution. Finally, those constraints apply to all who work within the juvenile justice system as well, to which the discussion will now briefly turn.

The Juvenile Justice System

More than 100 years ago, a separate juvenile justice system was created in the United States through the passage of the Illinois Juvenile Court Act of 1899. Soon thereafter, every state had designated a separate court system in which to handle cases involving youth. Reformers, believing that the punitive focus of the adult system was not in the "best interest of the child," sought to establish a court whose purpose was to rehabilitate youthful offenders rather than punish them. Initially youths coming before the juvenile court had no due process rights whatsoever. But as the juvenile court evolved, so too did youths' rights. The result today is a juvenile justice system that closely parallels the adult (criminal) justice system and that handled an estimated 1,058,500 delinquency cases in 2013 (Hockenberry & Puzzanchera, 2015).

A particular distinction in how society seeks to regulate youthful behavior is seen in the establishment of **status offenses,** conduct prohibited by law simply because the person engaging in the behavior is a minor (usually younger than 18). Examples of such offenses include smoking cigarettes, drinking alcohol, running away from home, and truancy. In 2013, juvenile courts petitioned and formally disposed of an estimated 109,000 status offense cases, a 13 percent decrease since 1995 (Hockenberry & Puzzanchera, 2015).

Beginning in 1980, a trend emerged to "get tough" on juvenile offenders, especially those committing more serious crimes. Many states implemented legislative provisions to allow juveniles to be tried in criminal courts, thus increasing sentencing options by juvenile courts and reducing juvenile court confidentiality.

The juvenile justice system has the same three components as the criminal justice system: law enforcement, courts, and corrections.

Law Enforcement Many police departments have a separate juvenile division or at least a few juvenile officers. Many other departments have no such specialists, and all officers are responsible for both juvenile and adult offenders. The terminology usually differs, however. Juveniles are *taken into custody*; adults are *arrested*. Juveniles are accused of *delinquent acts*; adults are accused of *crimes*. Juveniles are directed to appear in court by a *petition*; adults are directed to appear in court by an *information* or *indictment*. Juveniles and adults may be kept in custody before appearing in court to protect the public or ensure their court appearance. In the case of juveniles, this is called *detention*; adults are *jailed*. Adults usually have a right to bail; juveniles do not in most states.

Courts Juvenile court proceedings are less formal and may be private; adult proceedings are more formal and public. Juvenile identifying information is usually not released to the press; adult information is released. Juveniles have no constitutional right to a jury trial, but adults do (some states, however, have extended this right to juveniles). Both systems require proof beyond a reasonable doubt and the right to be represented by an attorney, and both allow appeals to a higher court.

MYTH
Juveniles are becoming more violent and criminally dangerous.

FACT
Juvenile violent crime peaked in 1994 and has been declining steadily since, with the prediction of a wave of juvenile super-predators never reaching fruition.

status offenses offenses deemed to be illegal when committed by juveniles because of their age, which are not unlawful for adults, such as smoking, drinking, and curfew violations

The initial appearance before a juvenile judge is called a *conference*; before a criminal judge it is called a *preliminary hearing*. In juvenile court, the *adjudication hearing* parallels the adult *trial*. Juvenile court proceedings are quasi-civil and may be confidential; criminal court proceedings are open.

During a juvenile hearing, a youth may be adjudicated *delinquent*; in the adult court, the defendant is declared a *criminal*. In either court, if a guilty decision is rendered, a hearing to determine the outcome is held. In juvenile court, this is the *dispositional hearing*; in adult court, it is the *sentencing hearing*. In either system, the disposition or sentence cannot be cruel or unusual.

Although controversy has always surrounded the death penalty, the controversy increases about whether it should be applied to juveniles. In the landmark case of *Roper v. Simmons* (2005) the execution of minors was held to violate the Eighth Amendment prohibition against "cruel and unusual punishment," and the Supreme Court ruled it unconstitutional to impose capital punishment for crime committed by a defendant who was younger than age 18 at the time of the offense.

Corrections As noted, juvenile and adult correctional facilities are to be separated. Available juvenile sentences typically span the full range of correctional options, from fines and restitution, to probation and intermediate sanctions, to incarceration in a juvenile detention facility. Juveniles released from custody receive *aftercare*; adults receive *parole* or *probation*.

The Changing Face of American Criminal Justice and Constitutional Law

This brief overview of the criminal and juvenile justice systems has been provided to stress the importance of the Constitution at every juncture within these systems. Whatever the role of government agents, their power is limited by the constraints of the Constitution. This should never be viewed as a hindrance or something negative. Rather, this provides the government, and those it serves, with clear guidelines that maintain the purpose the framers of the Constitution had in mind more than two centuries ago. This system of reserved power benefits all concerned.

The Constitution is not just about history and theory. It applies to every criminal justice practitioner. Each is expected to understand constitutional rights and to apply them in any number of situations, including many that have not previously arisen. Actually, U.S. constitutional law is being challenged in numerous unprecedented ways because technology and travel make crossing international borders an everyday event for millions around the world. Returning to a concept introduced previously—that U.S. law is living and ever evolving—this chapter concludes with a look at how the blurring of jurisdictional boundaries affects constitutional law.

U.S. Criminal Justice Beyond Our Borders

Legal traditions and laws in the United States have a high degree of similarity and uniformity because of their closeness to the values and beliefs of those who formed our nation. The fact that the Constitution applies to the states also helps create a level of consistency in the law (the "floor," so to speak). But our nation does not exist in isolation, and people have come together in a variety of ways, including business deals, migration, wars, and other conflicts, all of which have led to an interaction of legal concepts, each influencing the other.

As the entire world continues to become closer for reasons that include electronic communication, the Internet, and ease of travel, people find themselves increasingly interested in laws different from their own. The study of **comparative law** is just that, comparing and contrasting laws to expand understanding of law and legal theory. It is fascinating to delve into the historical development of legal systems and compare them with ours, finding some are quite similar and some vastly different.

Even more relevant to the study of the U.S. Constitution and criminal justice system is the impact of our Constitution and the laws of other nations when Americans are called to provide services in foreign lands. Because the Constitution serves as the primary roadmap for U.S. law enforcement, primarily involving U.S. citizens, entirely different rules, regulations, policies, and procedures are considered when foreign governments are involved. It is not as simple as having U.S. law enforcement officials conduct their official duties the same elsewhere as they do at home.

Without more powers, any foreign official may be restricted to lawfully gathering data with no more authority than any other citizen or visitor would have. Cooperative agencies such as the International Criminal Police Organization (INTERPOL) serve as clearing houses but cannot summarily grant expanded police powers. The U.S. National Central Bureau of Interpol, the Interpol unit in the United States, operates in Washington, DC, and directly involves multiple federal agencies and cooperates with foreign police entities. According to the U.S. Department of Justice (2014):

> INTERPOL Washington, the United States National Central Bureau, serves as the designated representative to the INTERPOL on behalf of the Attorney General. INTERPOL Washington is the official U.S. point of contact in INTERPOL's worldwide, police-to-police communications and criminal intelligence network. A component of the U.S. Department of Justice (DOJ), INTERPOL Washington is co-managed by the U.S. Department of Homeland Security (DHS) pursuant to a Memorandum of Understanding that ensures a continuing commitment to the guidance and oversight of the organization and reinforces its role in effectively sharing and exchanging international criminal investigative and humanitarian assistance information.
>
> INTERPOL Washington operates 24/7/365 and supports more than 18,000 local, state, federal, and tribal law enforcement agencies in the United States as well as their foreign counterparts that seek assistance in criminal investigations that extend beyond their national borders.
>
> INTERPOL Washington's mission is to coordinate U.S. law enforcement actions and responses, ensuring that they are consistent with U.S. interests and law, as well as INTERPOL policies, procedures, and regulations. This includes strict adherence to Article 3 of the INTERPOL Constitution, which expressly forbids the Organization to "...undertake any intervention or activities of a political, military, religious, or racial character."

The authority by which U.S. law enforcement may act in any official capacity in a foreign country is the result of compacts, treaties, or other formal arrangements with those nations. Times of war bring additional rules regulating what is and is

---

comparative law
comparing and contrasting laws to expand understanding of law and legal theory

not permissible. Recently, the complexities of incorporating such laws as promulgated by the Geneva Convention and Uniform Code of Military Justice have been scrutinized regarding such issues as the treatment of military prisoners at the Abu Ghraib prison in Iraq. The increased practice of combining military and private security during wartime has expanded the complexities of rules that apply during global conflict.

Because the Constitution is considered the basis of U.S. law and that which is considered just, those pursuing further studies of comparative, military, and law enforcement on foreign soil are best served by developing an initial understanding of the U.S. Constitution.

Summary

In the United States, two prominent theories about the underlying purpose of law are consensus theory and conflict theory. Consensus theory holds that laws express societal values regarding what is right and wrong and are created to prohibit deviant behavior. Conflict theory, in contrast, holds that laws are established to keep the dominant class in power.

Two competing value systems underlying the administrative purposes of the criminal process are the Crime Control Model and the Due Process Model. The Crime Control Model emphasizes efficiency and uniformity, rests on the presumption of guilt, and takes an assembly line approach to justice. The Due Process Model, in contrast, emphasizes that individual rights are not to be sacrificed for the sake of efficiency, rests on the presumption of innocence, and takes an obstacle course approach to justice.

The basic purpose of the U.S. legal system is to ensure fairness in balancing individual and societal rights and needs, while preventing excessive government power. This balance between individual and societal rights and needs is represented by the scales of justice.

Our legal system has its roots in the common law of England, the early English judge-made law based on custom and tradition and followed throughout the country. In U.S. law, common law is synonymous with case law. *Stare decisis* is a common law doctrine requiring that precedent set in one case shall be followed in all cases having the same or similar circumstances, thus ensuring consistency in the law. The Constitution ensures individual rights by limiting government power. And although the law, in fairness, must be consistent, it is also flexible. U.S. law is considered a living law because it can change along with society.

In addition to common law, the legal system also relies on statutory (codified) law, which is promulgated by legislatures or governing bodies. The U.S. legal system categorizes offenses into two specific areas: civil and criminal. Civil laws deal with personal matters and wrongs against individuals—called *torts*. Criminal laws deal with wrongs against society—called *crimes*. An act may be both a tort and a crime.

A *legal citation* is a standardized way of referring to a specific element in the law. It has three basic parts: a volume number, an abbreviation for the title, and a page or section number. A legal opinion usually contains (1) a description of the facts, (2) a statement of the legal issues presented, (3) the relevant rules of law, (4) the holding, and (5) the policies and reasons that support the holding. Most case briefs contain the case name and citation, a summary of key facts, the legal issues involved, the court's decision, the reasons for that decision, and any separate opinions or dissents.

When civil or criminal laws are broken, the courts' two main functions are to settle controversies between parties and to decide the rules of law that apply in specific cases. The U.S. judicial system is two-tiered, consisting of state and federal court systems. Each tier includes specific levels of courts. The officers of the court are judges, lawyers, clerks of court, sheriffs, marshals, and bailiffs. Three important doctrines govern whether a case will be heard by the court: standing, mootness, and ripeness.

Discussion Questions

1. Could a country such as the United States function without a federal constitution? Would it be possible for each state to merely abide by its own constitution?
2. Why should the Constitution not include an overall criminal code specifying crimes and punishments that could apply throughout the United States?
3. Why is society considered the victim of a crime rather than the individual victimized?
4. Why must the legal system provide an appeal procedure?
5. Can you develop an argument against *stare decisis*?
6. Why should courts not be permitted to argue "what if" questions?

7. Which underlying theory about the purpose of law do you feel makes most sense—consensus or conflict theory?
8. If the basic purpose of the U.S. legal system is to ensure fairness in balancing individual and societal rights and needs, is that end best served by an adversarial system in which the person with the best lawyer often comes out on top? Does this system of justice provide equal access to people of different socioeconomic classes?
9. Which operational end of the spectrum do you think our current criminal justice system is positioned closer to: due process or crime control? Why?
10. What problems could arise for any law enforcement professional not keeping up with the law?

References

Hockenberry, S., & Puzzanchera, C. (2015). *Juvenile Court Statistics 2013*. Pittsburgh, PA: National Center for Juvenile Justice.

LaFountain, R.; Schauffler, R.; Strickland, S.; Holt, K.; & Lewis, K. (2014). *Examining the Work of State Courts: An Overview of 2012 State Trial Court Caseloads*. Williamsburg, VA: National Center for State Courts.

Marx, K., & Engels, F. (1848). *Manifesto of the Communist Party*. London.

Packer, H.L. (1968). *The Limits of Criminal Sanction*. Stanford, CA: Stanford University Press.

United States Department of Justice. (2014, June 30). "About INTERPOL Washington." Washington, DC: Author. Retrieved June 19, 2016 from https://www.justice.gov/interpol-washington/about-interpol-washington

Walker, S.; Spohn, C.; & DeLone, M. (2012). *The Color of Justice: Race, Ethnicity, and Crime in America*, 5th ed. Belmont, CA: Wadsworth Publishing Company.

Cases Cited

Goldwater v. Carter, 444 U.S. 996 (1979)
Marbury v. Madison, 5 U.S. (1 Cranch) 137 (1803)
Minnesota v. Carter, 525 U.S. 83 (1998)
Miranda v. Arizona, 384 U.S. 436 (1966)
Moore v. City of Albany, 98 N.Y. 396 (1885)
National Park Hospitality Association v. Department of the Interior, 538 U.S. 803 (2003)
Rakas v. Illinois, 439 U.S. 128 (1978)
Roe v. Wade, 410 U.S. 113 (1973)
Roper v. Simmons, 543 U.S. 551 (2005)

CHAPTER 3

The U.S. Supreme Court:
The Final Word

The principle is that ours is a government of laws, not of men, and that we submit ourselves to rulers only if under rules.

—Justice Robert H. Jackson
Youngstown Sheet & Tube Co. v. Sawyer (1952)

Despite its role as a coequal branch of government, the Supreme Court did not have its own building until 1935, its 146th year of existence. In laying the cornerstone for the building on October 13, 1932, Chief Justice Charles Evans Hughes expressed the importance of the Supreme Court in the American justice system when he stated, "The Republic endures and this is the symbol of its faith."

Learning Objectives

LO1 *Understand the authority under which the Supreme Court operates.*

LO2 *Explain the jurisdiction of the Supreme Court.*

LO3 *Describe the significance of* Marbury v. Madison *(1803).*

LO4 *Identify the significance of* Martin v. Hunter's Lessee *(1816).*

LO5 *Determine how long a Supreme Court appointment lasts and the justification behind this length of tenure.*

LO6 *Summarize how Supreme Court terms are structured and who is permitted to observe sessions.*

Key Terms

certiorari	liberal	sittings
conservative	opinion	strict construction
judicial review	recesses	

Introduction

The U.S. Supreme Court is uniquely American, and like U.S. law itself, its roots extend to the history of why the framers of the Constitution—representing those who came to this country in search of freedom, due process, and the possibilities of a better life—created the United States. Visitors to our nation's capitol may be overwhelmed with symbols of the hope, dreams, and challenges of creating a new government two centuries ago. Two statues outside the National Archives in Washington proclaim *Study the Past* and *What Is Past Is Prologue.*

This chapter has been included not because many of us will ever find ourselves appearing before the Supreme Court, but because what occurs there affects each of us daily. Unfortunately, many Americans take this for granted. Criminal justice professionals cannot. The history of the Supreme Court, including those who make it up, combines with its role as defined by the Constitution to create this uniquely effective overseer of the legal system. Therefore, it is imperative that those studying law, and particularly constitutional law, have a working knowledge and understanding of the role the Supreme Court and the Justices appointed to it play in the continuing saga of the country's living law.

In the final analysis, the Supreme Court is about people. It is about nominees and those appointed to it. It is about the individuals named in cases that gain infamy by having been involved in something that turns out to have broadly reaching effects and those whose seldom-heard stories changed the course of history.

Table 3.1 Public Opinion of the Supreme Court

	"Very favorable opinion"	"Mostly favorable opinion"	"Mostly unfavorable opinion"	"Very unfavorable opinion"	"Can't rate"
1987	13%	63%	15%	2%	7%
1997	13%	64%	12%	6%	5%
2007	18%	54%	14%	3%	9%
2013	7%	45%	21%	10%	15%

Source: Adapted from *Sourcebook of Criminal Justice Statistics Online* (2013).

Table 3.2 Public Confidence in the Supreme Court

	Great deal	Fair amount	Not very much	None at all	Don't know/refused
1974	17%	54%	20%	5%	5%
1997	19%	52%	22%	5%	2%
2007	15%	54%	23%	6%	1%
2012	41%	53%	27%	4%	2%

Source: Adapted from *Sourcebook of Criminal Justice Statistics Online* (2012).

> **MYTH**
> The Constitution dictates that the Supreme Court consist of nine justices.
>
> **FACT**
> The Constitution does not enumerate the size of the Court, only that there shall *be* a Supreme Court and that the number of justices shall be determined by Congress. The first Judiciary Act, passed in 1789, set the number of Justices at six, one Chief Justice and five Associates. Over the years Congress has passed various acts to change this number, fluctuating from a low of five to a high of ten. The Judiciary Act of 1869 fixed the number of justices at nine, and no subsequent change to the number of justices has occurred.

And it is about each person affected by the cases the Court hears and those they elect not to hear. Every U.S. citizen is affected by all the Supreme Court does.

For the past 30 years the public has expressed a generally favorable opinion of the Supreme Court (*Sourcebook of Criminal Justice Statistics Online*, 2013). However, favorable ratings have declined considerably in recent years, as shown in Table 3.1.

Polls show that the public's confidence in the Court has remained relatively stable and high during the same timeframe, as shown in Table 3.2 (*Sourcebook of Criminal Justice Statistics Online*, 2012).

In addition to influencing every U.S. citizen, the Supreme Court has had a profound influence on criminal justice and on law enforcement in particular: "Over the past 50 years, the U.S. Supreme Court has molded law enforcement from a seat-of-the-pants job to a highly standardized profession" (Spector, 2003, p. 16). Literally hundreds of Supreme Court cases, many of which are discussed in this text, have helped lay the foundation for practically every action today's police officers take.

This chapter begins with a discussion of how the U.S. Supreme Court gets its authority and its jurisdiction and the powerful influence it has through judicial review and the ability to grant certiorari. Next the makeup of the Supreme Court is discussed, including a general discussion of Supreme Court Justices and a more specific look at the composition of the present-day court. This is followed by a discussion of the political nature of and public attitudes toward the Supreme Court. The chapter concludes with a description of some of the Court's traditions and procedures, where its decisions may be found, and a final look at the power wielded by the highest court in this country.

Authority for the Supreme Court

The law that emanates from the Supreme Court is the law of the land, and no other judicial or political body can overrule decisions it makes. Because U.S. law is a living law, conceivably the Supreme Court could overrule itself, which it has, in fact, done.

The constitutional establishment of authority for a federal judiciary is found in Article 3. The Constitution itself is a rather brief document, intended to set forth the framework of the new government rather than to provide lengthy specifics that others would find themselves having the responsibility of developing. It should not surprise—or trouble—us that this article is brief and to the point as well. Article 3 of the U.S. Constitution ordains:

LO1 *Article 3 of the U.S. Constitution established the authority for a federal judiciary. The Federal Judiciary Act of 1789 established the first Supreme Court, and although the number of justices has varied, nine has remained the agreed-upon number since 1869.*

> The judicial Power of the United States shall be vested in one supreme Court, and in such inferior Courts as the Congress may from time to time ordain and establish.

Jurisdiction of the Supreme Court

Section 2 of Article 3 of the Constitution defines the jurisdiction (or boundaries) of the Supreme Court:

> Section 2. The judicial Power shall extend to all Cases, in Law and Equity, arising under this Constitution, the Laws of the United States, and Treaties made, or which shall be made, under their Authority;—to all Cases affecting Ambassadors, other public Ministers and Consuls;—to all Cases of admiralty and maritime Jurisdiction;—to Controversies to which the United States shall be a Party;—to Controversies between two or more States;—between a State and Citizens of another State;—between Citizens of different States;—between Citizens of the same State claiming Lands under Grants of different States, and between a State, or the Citizens thereof, and foreign States, Citizens or Subjects.
>
> In all Cases affecting Ambassadors, other public Ministers and Consuls, and those in which a State shall be Party, the supreme Court shall have original Jurisdiction. In all the other Cases before mentioned, the supreme Court shall have appellate Jurisdiction, both as to Law and Fact, with such Exceptions, and under such Regulations as the Congress shall make.

The Supreme Court has jurisdiction over two general types of cases: cases that reach it on appeal and cases over which it has original jurisdiction, meaning the case actually starts at the Supreme Court. Whether a case begins in the state or federal system, the path to appeal a case to the Supreme Court is the same, as shown in Figure 3.1.

Because the framers of the Constitution did not want any individual or body to have excessive authority, the Supreme Court has only specific authority itself. It may hear appeals from lower state and federal courts on issues that involve interpretation of either federal law or the applicability of the Constitution to the subject at hand. The Supreme Court can also hear appeals on cases dealing with treaties the United States has entered into, admiralty and maritime cases, or those involving certain public officials and political entities.

It should not be assumed, however, that the Supreme Court and inferior (lower) federal courts have carte blanche to do whatever they want. In the post–Civil War case *Ex parte McCardle* (1868), Congress reserved the right to limit the jurisdiction of federal courts, including the Supreme Court. This does not mean that Congress, or

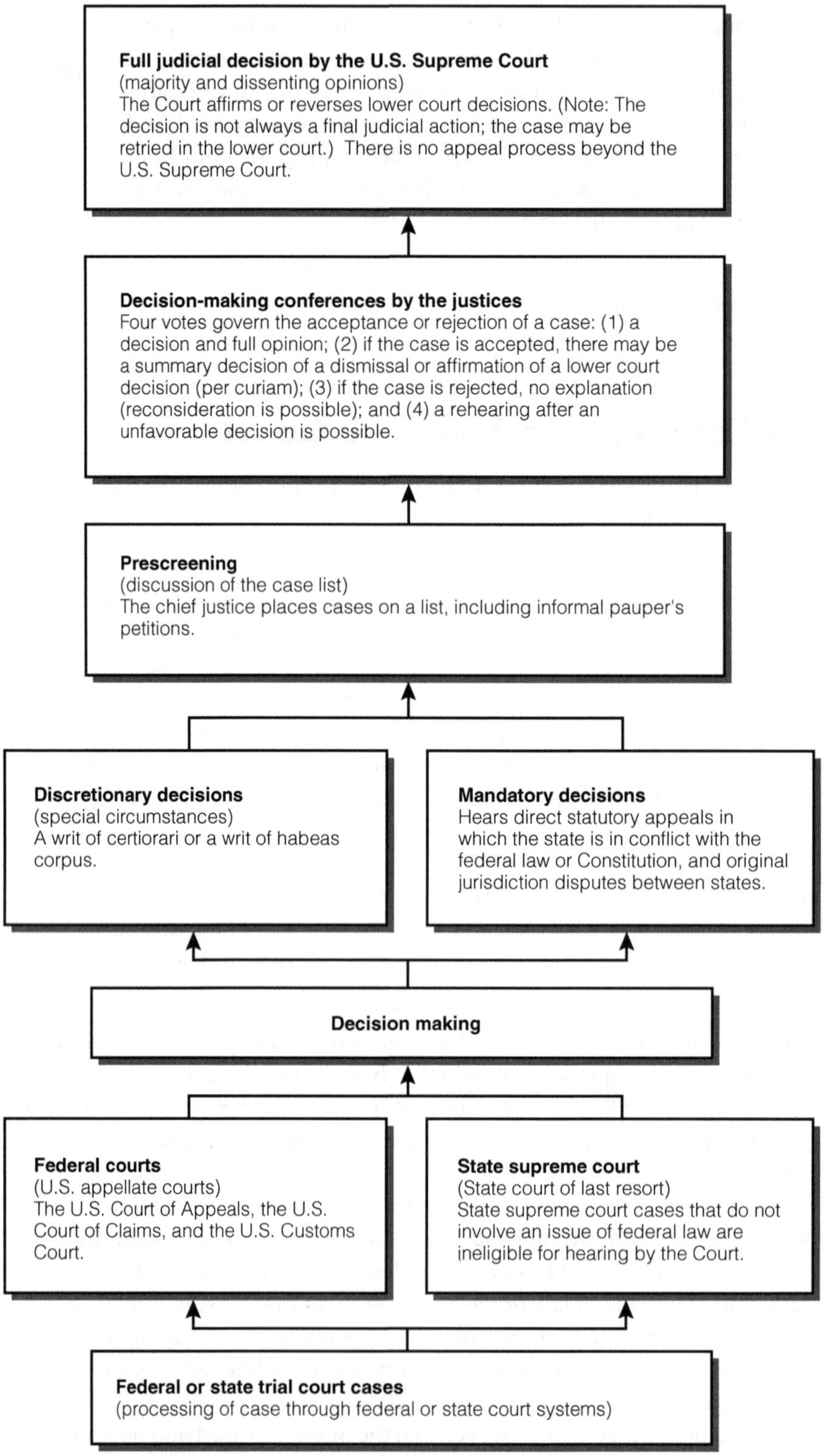

62 Section I A Foundation for Understanding Constitutional Law

Full judicial decision by the U.S. Supreme Court
(majority and dissenting opinions)
The Court affirms or reverses lower court decisions. (Note: The decision is not always a final judicial action; the case may be retried in the lower court.) There is no appeal process beyond the U.S. Supreme Court.

Decision-making conferences by the justices
Four votes govern the acceptance or rejection of a case: (1) a decision and full opinion; (2) if the case is accepted, there may be a summary decision of a dismissal or affirmation of a lower court decision (per curiam); (3) if the case is rejected, no explanation (reconsideration is possible); and (4) a rehearing after an unfavorable decision is possible.

Prescreening
(discussion of the case list)
The chief justice places cases on a list, including informal pauper's petitions.

Discretionary decisions
(special circumstances)
A writ of certiorari or a writ of habeas corpus.

Mandatory decisions
Hears direct statutory appeals in which the state is in conflict with the federal law or Constitution, and original jurisdiction disputes between states.

Decision making

Federal courts
(U.S. appellate courts)
The U.S. Court of Appeals, the U.S. Court of Claims, and the U.S. Customs Court.

State supreme court
(State court of last resort)
State supreme court cases that do not involve an issue of federal law are ineligible for hearing by the Court.

Federal or state trial court cases
(processing of case through federal or state court systems)

Figure 3.1 The Path of a Case to the U.S. Supreme Court

Source: SIEGEL. *Introduction to Criminal Justice*, 12E. © 2010 Wadsworth, a part of Cengage Learning, Inc. Reproduced by permission. www.cengage.com/permissions

any legislature, can override the Constitution by promulgating unconstitutional law. It does mean that Congress retains the authority to determine the types of cases these courts can hear, thus affecting their jurisdictional authority.

United States v. Klein (1871) supported the *McCardle* decision when the Supreme Court held that Congress, indeed, retains the power under Article 3 to determine which federal courts may hear certain types of cases. These two cases dealt with what types of appeals could be presented to federal courts. This is an excellent example of the *natural tension* the Constitution creates to prevent any one branch of government from exercising excessive power. These cases show how power with limitations is granted to Congress and the Court to ensure the balance sought by a free society through the Constitution.

The Constitution permits the Supreme Court original jurisdiction in cases dealing with foreign dignitaries or cases involving legal disputes between states, with the rationale that a state court could not remain unbiased if its state was a party to the suit. All other cases the Court considers only on appeal.

As noted by Goebel, "The brevity of the constitutional description left to Congress and the Court itself the task of filling in much of the substance and all of the details of the new judicial system. One early observer commented, 'The convention has only crayoned in the outlines. It is left to Congress to fill up and colour the canvas'" (1971, p. 280). One of the most important ways in which the Court did so was to establish judicial review of laws passed or of cases settled by lower courts.

LO2 *The Supreme Court has original jurisdiction in cases dealing with foreign dignitaries and legal disputes between states. All other cases are considered only on appeal.*

Judicial Review

The Supreme Court has tremendous power through the process of **judicial review**—the power of the Court to analyze decisions of other government entities and lower courts. The doctrine of judicial review allows the courts to pass upon the constitutionality of an action taken by the legislative and executive branches of the government (Ducat, 2010). And as Chief Justice Charles Evans Hughes put it during a speech in 1907 before the Chamber of Commerce in Elmira, New York, "We are under a Constitution, but the Constitution is what the judges say it is." The Supreme Court can decide which laws and lower court decisions are constitutional. Thus, the Supreme Court has effectively created most of its own power and authority through the process of judicial review.

judicial review the power of a court to analyze decisions of other government entities and lower courts

Initially, the Supreme Court did not review state decisions. It is not surprising that lively debate has occurred over just exactly how far the Supreme Court may go in performing its job or what that job actually is. As with other parts of the Constitution, brevity leaves room for much interpretation, debate, and disagreement.

In 1803, the stage was set when the Supreme Court forcefully asserted its right to judicial review in *Marbury v. Madison*, taking advantage of the opportunity to define its own role. William Marbury had been appointed justice of the peace for the District of Columbia in 1801 by President John Adams, just before Adams left office. When Thomas Jefferson became president, his new Secretary of State, James Madison, would not acknowledge Marbury's position. Marbury took the case to the Supreme Court, demanding that the new secretary of state recognize his appointment. (See Appendix C for a brief of the case.)

Although admittedly a complex case, Chief Justice John Marshall recognized the opportunity to definitively state that, indeed, the Supreme Court had the power to declare an act of Congress (in this case, Section 13 of the Judiciary Act passed by Congress in 1789) unconstitutional. Chief Justice Marshall went so far as to say that it was the Supreme Court's responsibility to overturn unconstitutional legislation because of its duty to uphold the Constitution. Chief Justice Marshall forcefully established the Supreme Court's authority as the final interpreter of the Constitution, and his words still ring: "If the courts are to regard the Constitution as superior to any ordinary act of the legislature, the Constitution and not such ordinary act must govern the case to which they apply. . . . It is emphatically the province of the judicial department to say what the law is."

> **LO3** Marbury v. Madison (1803), a case often regarded as the cornerstone of constitutional law in the United States and which highlighted the conflict between judicial review and political democracy, established that the Supreme Court has the authority to nullify and void an act of Congress that violates the Constitution.

In stating that the Constitution is the supreme law of the land and that the justices are required to follow it rather than inconsistent provisions of legislation, the Supreme Court denied Marbury his commission. Some scholars describe *Marbury v. Madison* as the cornerstone of American constitutional law because for the first time the Supreme Court nullified a provision of federal law. Chief Justice Marshall established that judges are authorized to nullify any law that *in their view* violates the Constitution. This case called attention to the conflict between judicial review and political democracy by asking, "Who makes the law—those elected by the people or those sitting on the Supreme Court bench?" The Court's decision was seen as completely opposed to political democracy.

In short, the legal groundwork (precedent) was established authorizing the Supreme Court to maintain a position of the ultimate de facto lawmaker by deciding what legislation is and is not constitutional. Arguably, although Congress could regroup and promulgate additional legislation, the Supreme Court could declare it unconstitutional as well. The Supreme Court does, in fact, have awesome power.

The Supreme Court extended its review authority beyond federal law to state laws through *Fletcher v. Peck* (1810) and again in *Martin v. Hunter's Lessee* (1816), a case that established the power Congress had given the Supreme Court to hear cases involving federal law and constitutional issues. In *Martin*, the Supreme Court determined that it could reverse state court decisions that involved federal legal issues. This case involved a dispute over land ownership. When the Supreme Court heard the case and made a determination, the Virginia state courts refused to follow the Court's decision, arguing that the Supreme Court had no authority to overrule their decision. Again, although the case is complex, the final determination was that the Supreme Court did have the authority to review cases dealing with federal law, even though the case is pending in a state court.

> **LO4** Martin v. Hunter's Lessee (1816) held that the Supreme Court can review and reverse state court decisions and can review pending state cases.

To clarify, Supreme Court Justice Oliver Wendell Holmes asserted that whereas *Marbury v. Madison* gave the Supreme Court the power to declare acts of Congress unconstitutional, it was even more important that, in the case of *Martin v. Hunter's Lessee*, the Supreme Court had the authority and power to review and reverse state court decisions to ensure consistent interpretations of federal law.

Controversy Over and Alternatives to Judicial Review

Opponents of judicial review contend judges have too much power: "The main alternative to judicial review is legislative supremacy, and the question is whether the courts have the power to overrule the decisions of elected legislators. Thus, today, opponents of judicial review call for the courts to give up the power to declare state or federal statutes unconstitutional" (Farber, 2003, p. 417).

Proponents of judicial review, on the other hand, argue there must be some watchdog to maintain the constitutionality of law, even if passed by elected bodies of government: "Essentially, judicial review is an attempt to solve a practical problem: how to keep politicians from violating individual rights or undermining the overall system of government for short-term gains" (Farber, 2003, p. 443).

Admittedly, judicial oversight is not the only option available. The most basic alternative is for judges to simply refuse to overrule a law, albeit unlikely. Alternative means of resolution could keep cases from finding their way to the courtroom. One often suggested alternative is mediation. Other alternatives include subgroups within legislatures to provide self-oversight, leaving an obvious potential conflict of interest. Another alternative is to have legislative bodies assess the actions of others. Some have even proposed an individual, such as the president, be the final arbiter. However, "If Congress is not to be trusted to be the sole judge of its own authority, and if the state governments are eliminated, that leaves only the President as an alternative to judicial review," and even presidential decisions may necessitate judicial oversight (Farber, 2003, p. 441).

The debate is not that there needs to be some form of final say as to what law is constitutional. The debate is over *who* should have that final say. And so, the issues set forth in *Marbury v. Madison* more than two hundred years ago persist. It is important to understand that methods do exist for citizens to voice their displeasure with a court's interpretation of the Constitution and bring about change, thereby limiting the final say. For example, the amendment process is one way to "overrule" a judge's interpretation of the Constitution. Getting an amendment passed is far from easy but has occurred (see the Fourteenth and Twenty-Sixth Amendments in response to Court decisions). The appointment process is a second alternative. Sitting presidents try to fill Supreme Court vacancies with judges who hold political and social views similar to their own, and these justices, in turn, influence changes in legal interpretation to be more consistent with the viewpoints of the president. Public outcry and open debates, however, may cause judges to change or modify their views. The appointment of justices and the shifting political landscape of the Court are discussed later in the chapter.

Certiorari: Deciding Which Cases to Hear

The Supreme Court's decision to review a case is almost entirely discretionary. Rarely are cases heard by the Court simply because there is a right to have them heard. The Supreme Court may review a case if a federal appeals court requests that the Supreme Court "certify" or clarify a legal point. The Court is also obligated to hear certain cases meeting the requirements for an "appeal of right," although these types of cases occur infrequently.

certiorari Latin for "to be informed"

> **MYTH**
> We have the right to be heard in the Supreme Court.
>
> **FACT**
> This statement is not supported by the Constitution, nor by congressional law, nor by the rules of the Supreme Court itself. According to Rule 17 of the Supreme Court (effective June 30, 1980), "[a] review on writ of certiorari is not a matter of right, but of judicial discretion."

> **MYTH**
> Every case that gets escalated to the Supreme Court gets heard or at least commented on.
>
> **FACT**
> The vast majority of cases submitted to the Court for review are denied, with no comments generated.

The vast majority of cases heard by the Supreme Court occur through the writ of **certiorari** (*certiorari* is Latin, meaning "to be informed"), whereby the Court determines which cases are worthy of review on the basis of their national importance.

One of the primary reasons the Supreme Court will choose to hear a case is because it involves conflict among the circuits. The Court wants law to be consistent across the nation, so when two circuits are in conflict, the Court will be more likely to grant certiorari. Another determining factor is whether the legal issue falls into the "cases and controversies" category, meaning the Court will hear only legitimate cases and will not give advisory opinions, unlike some state supreme courts. The Court will also not hear cases involving "political" questions, such as those involving issues that are "textually" committed to another branch of government or those in which there is a lack of "judicially discoverable and manageable standards for resolving the question." Finally, the case must involve federal law, the U.S. Constitution, or somehow otherwise fall within the jurisdiction of the federal courts. In determining which cases to hear, the justices are looking for cases involving matters that directly influence the law and the nation, another example of how powerful this institution is. The justices alone determine on which cases a final decision will be made.

Staff attorneys begin the process of deciding which cases will be heard. A "discuss list" is generated and considered during private meetings of the justices. Any case that does not have at least one justice expressing interest in it is summarily denied. This accounts for the disposition of more than 70 percent of cases submitted. Known as the "Rule of Four," at least four of the nine justices must vote in favor of granting certiorari for a case to be accepted for review. Even then, more than 90 percent of all cases submitted for certiorari are denied.

According to the Supreme Court's official government website (www.supremecourt.gov), the justices' caseload has increased substantially during the last half century. Currently approximately 7,000–8,000 new cases are filed in the Supreme Court each Term, compared to 1,195 new cases in the 1950 Term and 3,940 new cases during the 1975 Term: "Plenary review, with oral arguments by attorneys, is currently granted in about 80 of those cases each Term, and the Court typically disposes of about 100 or more cases without plenary review. The publication of each Term's written opinions, including concurring opinions, dissenting opinions, and orders, can take up thousands of pages. During the drafting process, some opinions may be revised a dozen or more times before they are announced" (Supreme Court of the United States, 2014b).

During the 2014 Term, 7,033 new cases were filed in the Supreme Court. Only 1,545 of these cases, or less than one-quarter (22%), were filed on the paid docket. The majority (5,488) of cases were filed in the Court's *in forma pauperis* docket (Supreme Court of the United States, 2015). *In forma pauperis* is Latin for "in the form of a pauper" and is a filing status indicating that typical court fees have been waived because the petitioner is indigent. A considerable percentage of *in forma pauperis* filings involve prisoners, and research has shown that these cases are significantly less likely to be granted review by the Court than those on the paid docket (Thompson & Wachtell, 2009). During the 2014 Term, 75 cases were argued and 75 were disposed of in 66 signed opinions, compared with 79 cases argued and

77 disposed of in 67 signed opinions during the 2013 Term (Supreme Court of the United States, 2015). The Court also issued eight per curiam decisions during the 2014 Term in cases that were not argued.

The power that goes with granting certiorari is significant but so is not "granting cert," as it is also referred to. Newspapers and online sources of law enforcement often erroneously report that when the Supreme Court denies "cert," it is upholding the state's ruling. For example, when the Supreme Court denied "cert" to hear an appeal from a decision of the Virginia Supreme Court (*Virginia v. Harris*, 2009), several headlines read, "Supreme Court Upholds Ban on Traffic Stops Based on a Caller's Tip." As Rutledge explains, "Under the rules as to what does and what does not constitute a holding of the Supreme Court, the fact that the state court ruling was not acted upon does not mean that the Supreme Court 'upholds' the state's ruling. It means that the Supreme Court is not expressing either *approval* or *disapproval*, and nothing is to be inferred from the denial of review" (2010, p. 64). The Court has time to examine only about 1 percent of the roughly 7,000 cases it is asked to review each year and has repeatedly emphasized that it takes no official position on the remaining 99 percent of cases to which certiorari is denied, including the *Virginia v. Harris* case: "As the Court has repeatedly said, the fact of non-review 'imports no expression of opinion upon the merits of the case,' and no one should assign 'any precedential value' to the fact that a particular ruling of a lower court was not reviewed (*Teague v. Lane* [1989])" (Rutledge, 2010, p. 64).

> **MYTH**
> When the Supreme Court denies certiorari, it is effectively upholding the ruling of the court below it, thus setting precedent.
>
> **FACT**
> When certiorari is denied, the Court is expressing neither *approval* nor *disapproval* of the lower court's ruling—it is simply refusing to consider the case. This has the effect of letting the lower court's ruling stand, but it does not mean the Court agrees with the holding.

The Supreme Court Justices

The Supreme Court has one Chief Justice and eight Associate Justices, nominated by the President of the United States and confirmed by the Senate. Clearly, the framers of the Constitution did not intend for undue influence to be applied to justices serving on the Supreme Court or on any inferior court, as stated in Section 1:

> The Judges, both of the supreme and inferior Courts, shall hold their Offices during good Behavior, and shall, at stated Times, receive for their Services, a Compensation, which shall not be diminished during their Continuance in Office.

No one trying to influence the justices' decisions can ever hold either their jobs or their paychecks over their heads.

Article 2 of the Constitution directs that the president of the United States shall nominate a judge for appointment to the Supreme Court, which the Senate must confirm. Article 2 also directs that federal judges, along with all other government officials, could be removed from their offices "on impeachment for and conviction of, treason, bribery, or other high crimes and misdemeanors."

L05 *A Supreme Court appointment is a lifetime appointment so a justice may not be unduly influenced.*

Impeachment is a complex process whereby the House of Representatives brings forth articles of impeachment and the Senate holds the trial. The process, which cannot be based on anything other than actual misconduct, has resulted in only one Supreme Court Justice being impeached (Samuel Chase in 1804), but because of the political motivations behind it, he was never actually convicted by the Senate. Unless they engage in criminal conduct or obviously unethical actions, federal judges need not worry that their decision might cost them their jobs.

Nominating Supreme Court Justices is a particularly powerful responsibility. Although the president will have no authority over a justice once the justice is appointed, considerable research is conducted before the president recommends an individual. By scrutinizing a judicial candidate's record, a president is likely to predict how someone might lean when deciding certain politically important issues. A conservative president will seek a conservative judge; a liberal president will seek a liberal judge. The power of a president to potentially mold the makeup of the Supreme Court is a most envied political privilege.

Politics and the Supreme Court

It is interesting to listen to laypeople discuss the Supreme Court and try to argue that it is too political or should not be politicized. Comments such as these show a misunderstanding of the Supreme Court. Make no mistake, the Court *is* a political body. The political nature of the Supreme Court is exactly why the Constitution gives the power of appointing justices to the president. The unique twist is that once appointed, justices are beholden to no one and truly are their own people. Although politics may have helped them get the job, that is where party lines end, as illustrated in the preceding discussion.

Since the origin of the Supreme Court in 1790, more than 100 Justices have served. Scholars who study political science data and trends say that nearly every judicial decision can be assigned an ideological value, and these decisions have led to the Justices being informally categorized as conservative, moderate, or liberal. Classifications in the Supreme Court Judicial Database highlight the differences between liberal and conservative judgments. **Liberal** decisions favor criminal defendants and are pro–civil liberties or civil rights claimants, pro-indigents, pro–American Indians, and antigovernment. **Conservative** decisions favor the government's interest in prosecuting and punishing offenders over recognition or expansion of rights for individuals (Smith, 2003).

A president seeks nominees who have political views similar to his or hers and those of his or her party. This is common sense. The president is not likely to appoint justices who have vastly different views. Although ability is a factor in selecting justices, the appointment process, as well as the confirmation process, revolves around the appointee's political views.

The confirmation process is difficult for any potential justice because during this process all questions are allowed, and politics become readily apparent. People may argue that this is not fair; however, the U.S. legal process is not only fair but logical. The president is elected to perform a job that includes appointing Supreme Court Justices who will support the ideals of the president's party. The argument that holds more weight is this: Once appointed, how are the justices held accountable? This argument becomes more of a "greater good" argument: Is it better for the greater good to have justices who cannot be influenced by anyone rather than putting them in a position to have to consider being re-elected?

This system is not without fault. But given the number of justices on the bench and the process used, the system has proved itself to work extremely well, unless you happen to disagree with the justices' politics. The Supreme Court creates

---

liberal decisions that are pro–person accused or convicted of a crime, pro–civil liberties or civil rights claimants, pro–indigents, pro–American Indians, and antigovernment

conservative decisions that favor the government's interest in prosecuting and punishing offenders over recognition or expansion of rights for individuals

---

MYTH
Like Congress and the president, the Supreme Court is politically accountable to the citizens.

FACT
The Supreme Court is not directly politically accountable to the electorate. They cannot be "voted off" the bench because of their political views. One of the primary ways of ensuring that the justices remain insulated from outside political pressure was to grant them lifetime tenure.

policy through the decisions it makes. Issues are carefully considered by the entire Court, and changes to American law are never taken lightly. It is never one justice's decision alone, and although many decisions come down to a 5–4 vote, it can be said that some of the great legal minds in the country have given their best consideration to the decision.

The 1960s saw a liberal Supreme Court under Chief Justice Earl Warren, with a focus on the rights of the accused. The expansion of criminal procedural rights was slowed in the 1970s and 1980s by President Richard M. Nixon's appointments of conservatives Warren Burger and William H. Rehnquist. However, another Nixon appointee, Harry Blackmun, tended to the liberal side. President Gerald R. Ford's single appointee, John Paul Stevens, tended to be moderate to liberal in his views, rather middle of the road, not greatly influencing the direction of the Court.

President Ronald Reagan's three appointments shifted the Court toward a more conservative stance. Sandra Day O'Connor, the first woman to serve on the Court, was seen as moderate to conservative, usually voting to limit prisoners' rights. Antonin Scalia and Anthony Kennedy were both considered very conservative. Also tipping the balance to the conservative side was the appointment of Rehnquist as Chief Justice.

When conservative David Souter was appointed by President George H. W. Bush to replace liberal William Brennan in 1990, the trend continued, with the Court increasingly favoring the state and law enforcement's position over that of criminal defendants. The conservative nature of the Court was further bolstered when the first President Bush appointed Clarence Thomas (yet another conservative) to replace liberal Thurgood Marshall. President Bill Clinton's 1993 appointment of Ruth Bader Ginsburg did little to change the existing "law and order" Court.

President George W. Bush in his second term appointed John Roberts, Jr., to the Court and chose him to replace William Rehnquist as Chief Justice after Rehnquist's death. Interestingly, Roberts was nominated by President George H. W. Bush in 1992, but no vote occurred before President Clinton took office. President George W. Bush succeeded with the appointment in 2005 and appointed Samuel Alito to replace retiring O'Connor. The conservative Rehnquist Court gained a reputation for consistently supporting expanded discretionary authority for state legislatures, prosecutors, police officers, and corrections officials, in sharp contrast to the rights-expanding performance of the Warren Court era (Smith, 2003).

The Current Supreme Court

The views of the current Supreme Court are often guided and constrained by rulings of previous courts. The Warren Court (1953–1969) was liberal by majority, with rulings that generally expanded civil liberties, focused on due process, and tended to reflect empathy toward suspects and defendants who were mistreated by an abusive government. The Burger Court (1969–1986) was also considered liberal, despite the conservative leanings of its Chief Justice. Since 1986, however, the Court's rulings have shifted to reflect a more conservative stance. For example, the majority of the Rehnquist Court (1986–2005) Justices were selected by Republican presidents who emphasized "law and order" crime control policies, and most of the justices appointed to the Rehnquist Court, only one of whom remains on the

Table 3.3 The Current U.S. Supreme Court

	President appointing	Political party	Year nominated	Age at nomination	Born	Years of previous judicial experience	Views	Home state
Anthony Kennedy	Reagan	Republican	1988	51	1936	12	Very conservative	California
Clarence Thomas	George H. W. Bush	Republican	1991	43	1948	1	Conservative	Georgia
Ruth Bader Ginsburg	Clinton	Democrat	1993	60	1933	13	Moderate	New York
Stephen G. Breyer	Clinton	Democrat	1994	56	1938	14	More liberal	Massachusetts
John G. Roberts, Jr.*	George W. Bush	Republican	2005	50	1955	2	Conservative	New York
Samuel Alito	George W. Bush	Republican	2006	56	1950	16	Conservative	New Jersey
Sonia Sotomayor	Barack Obama	Democrat	2009	55	1954	17	Liberal	New York
Elena Kagan	Barack Obama	Democrat	2010	50	1960	0	Uncertain but tends toward liberal	New York

VACANCY left by Antonin Scalia's death on February 13, 2016—Scalia was considered very conservative

*Chief Justice

Source: Adapted from the Supreme Court Historical Society.

bench (Thomas), brought a criminal justice perspective from their experiences as lawyers on the staffs of county prosecutors, state attorney generals, or the U.S. Justice Department (Smith, 2003). The Rehnquist Court will perhaps be primarily remembered for its revival of federalism. This continued with Chief Justice Roberts having been a deputy solicitor general arguing cases for the government and Justice Alito having been a federal attorney. Table 3.3 describes the makeup of the current Supreme Court.

On Saturday, August 7, 2010, Elena Kagan was sworn in as the 112th justice to serve on the Supreme Court, swearing to "administer justice without respect to persons, and do equal right to the poor and to the rich." Kagan joined two other women, Justices Ruth Bader Ginsburg and Sonia Sotomayor, on the Court and was the first Justice appointed since William H. Rehnquist without any experience as a judge (Baker, 2010).

During its first decade, the Roberts Court appears to have moved to the right, becoming the most conservative court since 1937, based on four sets of political science data. It is popularly accepted that Chief Justice Roberts and Justices Scalia, Thomas, and Alito composed the Court's conservative wing. In fact, these 4 justices are considered to be among *the most* conservative of the 45 justices to sit on the Court since 1937 (Liptak, 2010). With the vacancy created by Scalia's passing, there exists an opportunity to lessen, if even slightly, the influence of these conservative views. Justices Sotomayor, Ginsburg, and Breyer are generally held to constitute the Court's liberal wing. Although still relatively new to the Court, early speculation is that Justice Kagan's ideological slant is, at the least, moderately liberal, based on her prior experience in the Clinton administration and her appointment as Solicitor General under the Obama administration. Time will tell how her influence will affect the balance of the Court. Justice Kennedy, generally thought of as a moderate conservative, is considered most likely to be the swing vote that determines the outcome of certain close cases (Robinson, 2010).

Since Roberts is only in his 60s, he is likely to head the Court for a very long tenure. If the Court continues on the course the past five years suggest, it is likely to elaborate further on the scope of the Second Amendment right to bear arms and to curtail affirmative action and protections for people accused of crimes.

And despite the conservative label, their views of constitutional law are quite different and predictable. Two of the newest members of the bench, Chief Justice Roberts and Justice Alito, tend to be cautious in their votes and reluctant to reject the Court's own precedents, ruling in a way to preserve them. Justice Thomas, on the other hand, tends to issue sweeping opinions calling for fundamental changes in constitutional law. Scalia also tended to rule in much the same manner as Thomas. In most of the key cases their reasoning and view of the law has differed, but they have agreed on the outcome in several cases regarding these key constitutional principles—the right to abortion, affirmative action programs, presidential power in connection with the war on terror, and campaign-finance legislation.

The situation surrounding the vacancy left by the sudden passing of Justice Scalia on February 13, 2016, shows just how politically charged the Court is. A long tradition exists to at least nominate a Supreme Court Justice to fill a vacancy in an election year. In fact, "There is *not a single case in American history* in which a president chose *not* to make a Supreme Court nomination to fill a vacancy occurring during the last two years of a presidential term, even for vacancies occurring during the election year itself, even extremely late (or after) the election year" (Wildenthal, 2016, p.16). History shows that nominees who are considered during election years are usually confirmed (Aisch, Keller, Lai, & Yourish, 2016). However, as this text goes to press, Senate Republicans have vowed to block any nomination made by President Obama to fill the vacancy on the High Court before his term in Office ends.

Many expect that the discord between political parties will cause the vacant seat to remain unfilled for a time much longer than has been typical in recent decades. The longest vacancy recorded in a Supreme Court seat was 841 days and occurred in the mid-1840s. Since the 1970s, the average length of a Supreme Court seat vacancy has been just over 55 days (DeSilver, 2016). When Justice Scalia died, 342 days remained in President Obama's second term (Aisch et al., 2016). Figure 3.2 illustrates how the duration of Supreme Court seat vacancies has shortened over the years.

When a new justice is placed on the Supreme Court, speculation abounds as to whether there will be a shift from one side of the political spectrum and whether the junior justice will maintain his or her existing ideological and political leanings. The past decade has seen four new justices, including one who has now become Chief Justice, and history shows that justices' thinking has a tendency to evolve after they are appointed to the Supreme Court (Dwyer, 2009).

Throughout the remainder of the text, cases decided by the current Supreme Court will include which judges concurred with the majority opinion and which dissented.

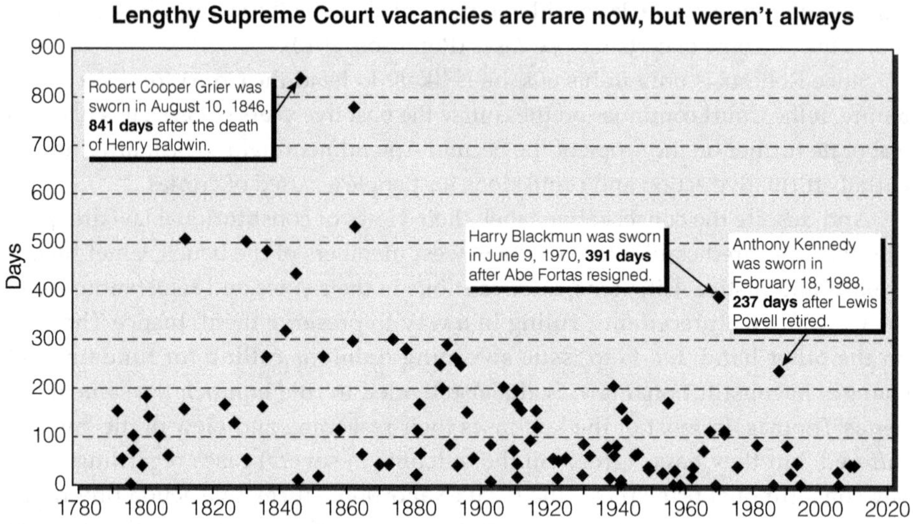

Lengthy Supreme Court vacancies are rare now, but weren't always

- Robert Cooper Grier was sworn in August 10, 1846, **841 days** after the death of Henry Baldwin.
- Harry Blackmun was sworn in June 9, 1970, **391 days** after Abe Fortas resigned.
- Anthony Kennedy was sworn in February 18, 1988, **237 days** after Lewis Powell retired.

Figure 3.2 Supreme Court Seat Vacancies, By Duration

Source: U.S. Senate, "Supreme Court, nominations, present—1789"; Supreme Court "Members of the Supreme Court of the United States"; Pew Research Center calculations. http://www.pewresearch.org/fact-tank/2016/02/26/long-supreme-court-vacancies-used-to-be-more-common/

IN THE NEWS

"Scalia's Death, Senate Inaction Leave Supreme Court in Bind"

By Mark Sherman (*Associated Press*, June 24, 2016)

WASHINGTON (AP)—Justice Antonin Scalia's unexpected death in February and the Senate's refusal to confirm a successor has left the Supreme Court in a bind on several closely divided cases.

Even as some justices have said the short-handed court will continue to get its work done, Justice Ruth Bader Ginsburg has noted, "Eight is not a good number."

The court's 4-4 tie Thursday in a case about President Barack Obama's plan to help millions of immigrants living in the U.S. illegally was the latest illustration of what Ginsburg meant. The justices were unable to resolve a case without Scalia's vote and unwilling to keep the case on hold for an indefinite period because they don't know when a ninth justice will join them.

The high court has been operating with eight justices instead of its full complement of nine since Scalia died. Obama has nominated Judge Merrick Garland to take Scalia's place, but Senate Republicans have refused to hold a hearing or a vote.

Garland wouldn't have been available to take part in this term's cases even if the Senate had acted quickly on his nomination. But the other

(Continued)

justices might have ordered new arguments in some cases in which they split 4 to 4 if they knew Garland would be on the bench by the time the next term begins in October.

Instead, they announced ties Thursday in the immigration case and another dispute involving the authority of tribal courts. The Supreme Court was evenly divided in two earlier cases decided after Scalia's death, including one in which public-sector labor unions staved off a significant defeat over their ability to collect user fees from people who choose not to join the union.

A Supreme Court tie is akin to the court having never heard the case at all, a waste of time and effort. The decision of the lower court remains in place, but no national precedent is established. The high court typically takes cases on important issues of law and policy, and also resolves conflicting rulings from lower courts.

Scalia's absence also appears to have affected the outcome of the court's ruling Thursday in favor of affirmative action.

Justice Anthony Kennedy and three liberal justices would have lacked the votes to issue a surprising affirmation of the use of race as a factor in college admissions if Scalia, long an opponent of race-conscious admissions policies, had been alive.

Justice Elena Kagan also didn't take part in the affirmative action case because she worked on it while serving in the Justice Department.

At worst, for opponents of affirmative action, the case would have ended in a tie and the same outcome, a victory for the University of Texas, but with no opinion from the Supreme Court.

Scalia took part in the affirmative action arguments in December. It is impossible to know how the justices initially voted after the arguments and how Scalia's death might have altered the outcome. The court held onto the case for more than six months, which sometimes is a hint that something changed between the justices' initial vote and the issuance of the decision.

Kennedy had never before voted to uphold a race-based affirmative action policy. He did so Thursday and wrote an opinion that would not have garnered a court majority with Scalia around.

Traditions and Procedures

Although there is certainly definitive authority regarding what the Supreme Court can hear, how the Court conducts its business is based largely on tradition, with respect for the process that has endured, along with the Constitution and the findings of the Supreme Court itself.

Usually each side has 30 minutes to present its arguments, with 22 to 24 cases presented at one sitting. The 10:00 A.M. entrance of the justices into the courtroom is announced by the marshal and is steeped in history and tradition, as described by the Supreme Court itself:

> Those present, at the sound of the gavel, arise and remain standing until the robed Justices are seated following the traditional chant: "The Honorable, the Chief Justice and the Associate Justices of the Supreme Court of the United States. Oyez! Oyez! Oyez! All persons having business before the Honorable, the Supreme Court of the United States, are admonished to draw near and give their attention, for the Court is now sitting. God save the United States and this Honorable Court!" (Supreme Court of the United States, 2014a)

As is customary in American courts, the nine justices are seated by seniority on the Bench. The Chief Justice occupies the center chair, the

LO6 *By federal statute, a term of the Supreme Court always begins on the first Monday in October, continuing until June or July. Terms are made up of* **sittings,** *when cases are heard, and* **recesses,** *during which the Court considers administrative matters at hand and the justices write their opinions. The public is invited to observe the Supreme Court in session, although all Court discussions and decisions occur in private.*

sittings periods during which the Supreme Court hears cases

recesses periods when the Supreme Court does not hear cases but considers administrative matters and writes opinions

senior Associate Justice sits immediately to the Chief's right, the second senior Associate Justice sits immediately to the left of the Chief Justice, and so on, alternating right and left by seniority. Since at least 1800, it has been traditional for justices to wear black robes while in Court.

The exclusion of the public when the Court is discussing and deciding cases has resulted in the Court being one of the most leak-proof organizations in Washington—those who work there abide by this honored tradition. When the Court is in session, the public can observe from the visitors' gallery, and when that is filled, additional visitors are ushered into an area at the rear of the courtroom where people are permitted to sit for as long as 15 minutes before others are allowed the seats. The remaining seats are reserved for lawyers who are admitted to the Supreme Court bar and members of Congress. Also, a chair is always left open for the president, should he or she wish to attend.

Strict protocol is followed, and the air of formality encourages the overall respect the Supreme Court demands and deserves. Although the general traditions of courtesy, civility, and the utmost professionalism result in a subdued atmosphere most of the time, the scene can change when an emotionally charged case is heard or when Americans exert their First Amendment right to speak their mind, often in protest. The abortion issue draws protestors on the anniversary of the *Roe v. Wade* (1973) decision, and when related cases are heard, it can be anticipated that throngs of people on both sides of the issue will be present, as will the media.

During recesses, the justices sit at a large conference table and discuss each case. The most junior justice is required to present his or her view of that particular case first. This allows the most senior justices to control the decisions as the votes come in. The decisions reached are then cast into opinions.

Opinions

opinion a written statement by the court explaining its decision in a given case, usually including the legal issues or points of law involved, a statement of facts, and any precedents on which the decision is based

A written statement by the Court explaining its decision in a given case, usually including the legal issues or points of law involved, a statement of facts, and any precedents on which the decision is based, is called an **opinion**. The Chief Justice assigns the writing of the opinion if he voted with the majority. The Justice may assign the case to himself. If the Chief Justice did not vote with the majority, the most senior justice voting with the majority assigns the writing of the opinion. Any justice is free to write an opinion, even if not assigned to do so. This opinion can be a *concurring opinion* (agreeing with the majority) or a *dissenting opinion* (disagreeing with the majority and the reasons underlying the disagreement).

Concurring opinions, a legal tradition dating back to the 1700s, give justices who did not author the opinion a forum to agree in part, or disagree in part, with what was written. Often, justices will use concurring opinions to address why they agree with the outcome but not with the reasoning. Any opinion issued by a justice has the power to influence others by simple virtue of the fact that a Supreme Court Justice wrote it. These additional opinions might be viewed as "the rest of the story" beyond what the justice writing the majority opinion sets forth, and give readers a glimpse into what other justices were thinking.

Dissenting opinions are included along with the majority opinion to provide the bigger picture and other perspectives. Although including dissenting opinions is a legal tradition dating back to the King's Bench of Great Britain in 1792, there are more purposeful reasons for continuing the practice. Primarily, justices can use the opportunity to assert their opinions in hopes of influencing future decisions. Dissenting opinions may be referred to in briefs written by other lawyers but carry no legal authority.

Interpretations

The justices render decisions, and they interpret the Constitution. The interpretive principles used as the justices deliberate are crucial in accomplishing judicial review.

Judicial interpretation involves many different belief systems, terms, and techniques, the discussion of which extends beyond the scope of this text. A simplified way to break down this complex concept is to divide it into two parts: (1) what sources a judge should employ to interpret the Constitution (e.g., only the text itself, or the text and the original meaning behind it, using history, tradition, and logic), and then (2) what technique to use to interpret the Constitution (e.g., original intent, the text of the Constitution, history and tradition, or social policy).

Strict construction means there is a rigid reading and interpretation of that law. Although there is no formal definition of the term, strict construction would not likely expand the specifically set forth law of the particular statute, particularly in expanding the intent of that law. Others may choose to interpret laws more liberally, often referring to the "spirit of the law" rather than the specific wording of the law.

A justice might interpret the law based on precedent by identifying analogous cases and using the same line of reasoning set forth in a previous opinion to decide a later legal issue. Alternately, a justice might interpret a case based on the text itself or even on how they interpret the *intent* of those who wrote the law or Constitution.

The justices' personal views regarding the civil rights of victims and criminals influence the day-to-day operations of the entire justice system because they shape the meaning of the Constitution. In addition, interpreting the Constitution is inherently subjective, influenced by the long-term political and social pressures of the times.

strict construction a rigid interpretation of a law not likely to expand the specifically set forth law of the particular statute, particularly in expanding the intent of that law

Where Supreme Court Decisions May Be Found

Few people read the full text of Supreme Court decisions, relying instead on the news media for such information. These decisions may be found in newspapers and newscasts and in magazines such as *U.S. News & World Report* and *Time*. In addition, the Public Education Division of the American Bar Association, in cooperation with the Association of American Law Schools and the American Newspaper Publishers Association Foundation, publishes *The Preview of United States Supreme Court Cases*—an annual eight-issue subscription series that provides advance analysis of cases the Court is going to hear during that term. The first seven monthly issues publish from October to April and correspond to the Court's seven argument sessions. The final issue of each year is written after the Court's term closes in June and contains a review of the cases heard during that term. Cases may also be found through Westlaw and Lexis or through free online sources such as Google Scholar, Justia, and CourtListener.

MYTH
The Constitution defines rights of the people.

FACT
No. The Constitution lists the rights of the people and the powers of the government, but it does not define them. Judges, through interpretative techniques, help define the contours of the rights.

The Power of the Supreme Court

The Supreme Court is tremendously powerful. It is so powerful that it has been permitted to actually create much of its own immense authority. In No. 78 of *The Federalist Papers*, Alexander Hamilton referred to the Supreme Court as the "least dangerous" division of the federal government. Yet, in the cases of *Marbury v. Madison* and *Martin v. Hunter's Lessee*, the Supreme Court was permitted to redefine its powers. Who could stop it? Perhaps diabolical in a sense, they are merely carrying out the true intentions of the framers of the Constitution. Who else could practically oversee the Bill of Rights?

It can be interpreted from *The Federalist Papers* that the Supreme Court was assigned to this awesome task. As Hamilton so stated, the interpretation of the Constitution was to become the "proper and peculiar province of the United States Supreme Court." For what other reason would the framers of the Constitution have included a supremacy clause declaring that federal law would outweigh state law?

Any system, including that of the United States, must have a final point. Certainly, many argue that "between here and there" are far too many resting points. For example, there is an effort by many to decrease the number of appeals available to condemned prisoners because of the time and expense involved in the current system. Nonetheless, in the end, the Supreme Court has the definitive say, even if it is by deciding not to hear a particular case.

In many ways, the policies and procedures by which the Supreme Court operates reflect how the U.S. legal system all comes together, quite literally, at the end. It is the appeal of last resort for cases coming before it, reflecting the traditions and complexities of law and the discretion that strongly influences the direction the law takes. Interpretation, application, and review of the law give the Supreme Court tremendous power. However, not even the Court possesses total control over the U.S. legal system. Congress still promulgates law, and the president can still veto. The power of the president to appoint and Congress to endorse the makeup of the Court contributes to how the final picture will be painted.

Summary

Article 3 of the U.S. Constitution established the authority for a federal judiciary. The Federal Judiciary Act of 1789 established the first Supreme Court, and although the number of justices has varied, nine has remained the agreed-on number since 1869.

The Supreme Court has original jurisdiction in cases dealing with foreign dignitaries and legal disputes between states. All other cases are considered only on appeal.

The Supreme Court has effectively created most of its own power and authority through the process of judicial review. Two precedent cases confirmed this power. *Marbury v. Madison* (1803) established that the Supreme Court has the authority to nullify and void an act of Congress that violates the Constitution. *Martin v. Hunter's Lessee* (1816) held that the Supreme Court can review and reverse state court decisions and can review pending state cases.

Because justices decide matters vital to national interest, a Supreme Court appointment is a lifetime appointment so a justice may not be unduly influenced. By federal statute, a term of the Supreme Court always begins on the first Monday in October, continuing until June or July. Terms are made up of sittings, when cases are heard, and recesses, during which the Court considers administrative matters at hand and the justices write their opinions. The public is invited to observe the Supreme Court in session, although all Court discussions and decisions occur in private.

Discussion Questions

1. Should any one court be given the final say? Why or why not?
2. Is there a negative side to appointment for life on the Court? Does this and the inability to lessen a justice's salary really prevent influencing a Supreme Court Justice?
3. Do you think the Supreme Court is a de facto lawmaker? Why or why not?
4. Is it possible for the justices to provide a fair review of a case when they hear about it so briefly from the lawyers arguing it before them?
5. Should the Supreme Court accept so few cases? Does the fact the justices decide this totally in private concern you?
6. Do you think the current Supreme Court is carrying out the desires of the founders of our Constitution?
7. Explain where you see the real power of the Supreme Court. What makes the justices so powerful as individuals and as a group?
8. Do you believe the Supreme Court acted properly in the 2000 presidential election in *Bush v. Gore* (2000)?
9. If you were sitting on the Supreme Court, what sorts of cases would you look for to review?
10. What facts or circumstances might a justice focus on if he or she interpreted the Constitution using precedent as a guiding principle? What about if the justice approached interpretation from the standpoint of the original intent of the authors of the Constitution?

References

Aisch, G.; Keller, J.; Lai, K.K.R.; & Yourish, K. (2016, March 16). "Nominees Considered in Election Years Are Usually Confirmed." *The New York Times*. Retrieved June 25, 2016 from http://www.nytimes.com/interactive/2016/02/15/us/supreme-court-nominations-election-year-scalia.html?_r=1

Baker, P. (2010, August 7). "Kagan Is Sworn In as the Fourth Woman, and 112th Justice, on the Supreme Court." *The New York Times*. Retrieved June 24, 2016 from http://www.nytimes.com/2010/08/08/us/08kagan.html?_r=0

DeSilver, D. (2016, February 26). "Long Supreme Court Vacancies Used To Be More Common." Washington, DC: Pew Research Center. Retrieved June 25, 2016 from http://www.pewresearch.org/fact-tank/2016/02/26/long-supreme-court-vacancies-used-to-be-more-common/

Ducat, C.R. (2010). *Constitutional Interpretation*, 9th ed. Belmont, CA: Wadsworth/Cengage Learning.

Dwyer, T.P. (2009, December 16). "U.S. Supreme Court Year in Review: Cases and Faces from 2009." *PoliceOne.com News*. Retrieved June 24, 2016 from www.policeone.com/investigations/articles/1979268-U-S-Supreme-Court-year-in-review-Cases-and-faces-from-2009/

Farber, D.A. (2003, October). "Judicial Review and Its Alternatives: An American Tale." *Wake Forest Law Review*, Vol. 38, pp. 415–450. Retrieved June 24, 2016 from http://scholarship.law.berkeley.edu/facpubs/906/

Goebel, J., Jr. (1971). *The Oliver Wendell Holmes Devise History of the Supreme Court of the United States, Volume I, Antecedents and Beginnings to 1801*. New York: The Macmillan Publishing Company, Inc.

Liptak, A. (2010, July 24). "Court Under Roberts Is Most Conservative in Decades." *The New York Times*. Retrieved June 25, 2016 from http://www.nytimes.com/2010/07/25/us/25roberts.html

Robinson, R.R. (2010, July 31). "'Still Chastened': Assessing the Scope of Constitutional Change under an 'Obama Court.'" *The Forum*, Vol. 8, Issue 2, Article 3. Retrieved June 25, 2016 from http://papers.ssrn.com/sol3/papers.cfm?abstract_id=1610251

Rutledge, D. (2010, January). "Beware of False Headlines." *Police*, pp. 64–67. Retrieved June 26, 2016 from http://www.policemag.com/channel/patrol/articles/2010/01/beware-of-false-headlines.aspx

Smith, C.E. (2003, May). "The Rehnquist Court and Criminal Justice: An Empirical Assessment." *Journal of Contemporary Criminal Justice*, 19(2), pp. 161–181.

Sourcebook of Criminal Justice Statistics Online. (2012, November). "Table 2.0031.2012: Reported Confidence in the Federal Judicial Branch Including the U.S. Supreme Court." Albany, NY: University of Albany, Hindelang Criminal Justice Research Center. Retrieved June 25, 2016 from http://www.albany.edu/sourcebook/pdf/t200312012.pdf

Sourcebook of Criminal Justice Statistics Online. (2013, March) "Table 2.0006.2013: Respondents Reporting Their Overall Opinion of the U.S. Supreme Court." Albany, NY: University of Albany, Hindelang Criminal Justice Research Center. Retrieved June 25, 2016 from http://www.albany.edu/sourcebook/pdf/t200062013.pdf

Spector, E.B. (2003). "50 Years of Supreme Court Decisions." *Law and Order, Fiftieth Anniversary Issue, 1953–2003*, pp. 16–21.

Supreme Court of the United States. (2014a). "The Court and Its Procedures." Washington, DC: Author. Retrieved June 25, 2016 from http://www.supremecourt.gov/about/procedures.aspx

Supreme Court of the United States. (2014b). "The Justices' Caseload." Washington, DC: Author. Retrieved June 24, 2016 from http://www.supremecourt.gov/about/justicecaseload.aspx

Supreme Court of the United States. (2015). *2015 Year-End Report on the Federal Judiciary*. Washington, DC: Author. Retrieved June 24, 2016 from http://www.supremecourt.gov/publicinfo/year-end/2015year-endreport.pdf

Thompson, D.C., & Wachtell, M.F. (2009, April 13). "An Empirical Analysis of Supreme Court Certiorari Petition Procedures: The Call for Response and the Call for Views of the Solicitor General." *George Mason Law Review*, 16(2), pp. 239–302.

Wildenthal, B.H. (2016, February 20). "Memorandum on Supreme Court Vacancies and Confirmations during Presidential Election Years." San Diego, CA: Thomas Jefferson School of Law Research Paper No. 2735256. Retrieved June 24, 2016 from http://papers.ssrn.com/sol3/papers.cfm?abstract_id=2735256

Cases Cited

Bush v. Gore, 531 U.S. 98 (2000)
Ex parte McCardle, 74 U.S. (7 Wall.) 506 (1868)
Fletcher v. Peck, 10 U.S. (6 Cranch) 87 (1810)
Marbury v. Madison, 5 U.S. (1 Cranch) 137 (1803)
Martin v. Hunter's Lessee, 14 U.S. (1 Wheat.) 304 (1816)

Roe v. Wade, 410 U.S. 113 (1973)
Teague v. Lane, 489 U.S. 288 (1989)
United States v. Klein, 80 U.S. (13 Wall.) 128 (1871)
Virginia v. Harris, 558 U.S. ___ (2009)
Youngstown Sheet & Tube Co. v. Sawyer (1952)

CHAPTER 4

Equal Protection under the Law:
Balancing Individual, State, and Federal Rights

All persons born or naturalized in the United States and subject to the jurisdiction thereof, are citizens of the United States and of the State wherein they reside. No State shall make or enforce any law which shall abridge the privileges or immunities of citizens of the United States; nor shall any State deprive any person of life, liberty, or property, without due process of law; nor deny to any person within its jurisdiction the equal protection of the laws.

—Fourteenth Amendment to the U.S. Constitution

Equal protection under the law is a cornerstone of American justice. Students place a new sticker on the door at the ceremonial opening of a gender neutral bathroom at Nathan Hale High School Tuesday, May 17, 2016, in Seattle. President Obama's directive ordering schools to accommodate transgender students has been controversial in some places but since 2012 Seattle has mandated that transgender students be able to use of the bathrooms and locker rooms of their choice. Nearly half of the district's 15 high schools already have gender neutral bathrooms, and one high school has had a transgender bathroom for 20 years.

Learning Objectives

LO1 *Understand the significance of the Thirteenth Amendment.*

LO2 *Explain the significance of the Fourteenth Amendment.*

LO3 *Describe how enumerated and unenumerated rights differ and the two types of standards used by the Supreme Court to evaluate them.*

LO4 *Clarify how discrimination differs from prejudice.*

LO5 *Grasp the significance of the Supreme Court's ruling in* Plessy v. Ferguson.

LO6 *Summarize the intent of affirmative action programs.*

LO7 *Compare and contrast disparity and discrimination and understand whether either serves as a legitimate basis for decisions in the criminal justice system.*

Key Terms

affirmative action	equal protection of the law	procedural due process
American dream	implicit bias	procedural justice
contextual discrimination	incorporation doctrine	racial profiling
discrimination	Jim Crow laws	reverse discrimination
disparate impact	movant	right
disparate treatment	penumbra	SAR
disparity	preemption	substantive due process
due process	prejudice	summary judgment
due process of law	privilege	unenumerated rights
		zones of privacy

Introduction

What can now be seen as an obvious shortcoming of the Constitution and Bill of Rights was their failure to abolish slavery; however, the Supreme Court's ultimate decision to reverse itself, following ratification of the Thirteenth and Fourteenth Amendments, making slavery illegal, is important for more than the obvious reason. This is an example of our living law at work. Bearing in mind that law supports social norms, as hard as it is to imagine, not everyone objected to slavery at the time the *Dred Scott* case was decided in 1856. Social norms changed, and the Constitution and constitutional interpretations have accommodated them.

In addition, although the Bill of Rights, as originally drafted and ratified, guaranteed American citizens basic freedoms that the federal government could not infringe on, it did not apply to the states, each of which had its own constitution and statutes. To ensure that the states did not deny the basic rights set forth in the Constitution and the Bill of Rights, Congress passed the Fourteenth Amendment. Keep in mind the Constitution was initially drafted to limit power of the federal government, with later amendments extending this limitation to state and local governments as well.

This chapter begins with a brief look at the abolition of slavery through the Thirteenth Amendment and a discussion of the Fourteenth Amendment, which granted slaves citizenship and required that states abide by the federal Constitution and specific provisions in the Bill of Rights. This is followed by a discussion of due process, an explanation of enumerated rights and incorporation, a deeper examination of procedural due process and substantive due process, and a look at due process and privacy rights. Next is an examination of discrimination versus prejudice, the roots of racial discrimination, and the struggle for equality. The issue of equal protection and discrimination within the criminal justice system is also explored. The chapter concludes with a look at how federal powers are checked.

The Thirteenth Amendment

The Civil War resulted from a variety of issues, including differing interpretations of the Constitution stemming from the different norms of a still-developing country. The legal conflict with the emerging Constitution was that although the framers sought to prevent excessive *federal* authority, their desire to give states more authority over their own development resulted in problems the national government simply could not continue to overlook. Among the issues were state banks and money versus national banks and currency, federal aid versus state aid for improving roadways and railways, and freedom versus slavery. During debates involving these issues, two theories as to the nature of the Constitution emerged, articulated during the 1830 Great Debate in the Senate between Robert Hayne of South Carolina and Daniel Webster of Massachusetts.

On the one hand, Hayne asserted that the Union created by the Constitution was merely a compact between sovereign states, a league of independent states, and as such, states may lawfully withdraw from the Union if they so wish. Webster, on the other hand, asserted that the Constitution established an indivisible Union with laws binding on the states, and states could not simply leave the Union.

These issues came to a head when Abraham Lincoln was elected president in 1860. That December, South Carolina passed a resolution to withdraw from the Union. Early in 1861, Florida, Georgia, Alabama, Mississippi, Louisiana, and Texas did the same.

President Lincoln was faced with the task of trying to keep the Union together. He had been elected on a promise to abolish slavery in the territories, but he conceded that under the Constitution, slavery was legal in the states where it had been established. Lincoln tried to assure the Southern states that he had neither the right nor the intent to interrupt their way of life. The Supreme Court had ruled in *Dred Scott v. Sandford* (1856) that a freed slave did not have the right to remain free in a territory where slavery was still legal and that even free blacks, who "had no rights which a White man was bound to respect," could not be citizens of the United States. The Southern states were not convinced, however, and the Civil War ensued (1861–1865).

The Civil War affected this country in ways no other war could. The casualties were enormous—at least 618,000 Americans died, and the resulting divisiveness in the nation was deep, with impacts remaining to this day (Davis, 1988). This war pitted American against American and sometimes brother against brother. It is a prime example of how important societal norms are and again showed the U.S. resolve to stand firm to the principles on which the country was founded, as so eloquently expressed by Lincoln in his Gettysburg Address, which began with this declaration:

> Fourscore and seven years ago our fathers brought forth on this continent a new nation conceived in liberty and dedicated to the proposition that all men are created equal ...

And ended with this promise:

> We here highly resolve that these dead shall not have died in vain, that this nation under God shall have a new birth in freedom, and that government of the people, by the people, for the people shall not perish from the earth.

While debating and passing bills regarding such critical issues in a new country as taxes, tariffs, banking, and conducting war, Congress also sought to deal with the slavery issue. In April 1862, slavery was abolished in the District of Columbia and two months later in all the territories. In the summer of 1862, Lincoln announced that unless the Southern states returned to the Union, he would call for an end to slavery in all rebelling states. In the Emancipation Proclamation, issued January 1, 1863, Lincoln declared free all the slaves in the rebelling states. In effect, this proclamation did little. Those in the South retained their slaves, as did those in slave states that remained loyal to the Union. What the proclamation did, however, was set a national tone that gained momentum toward abolishing slavery.

In January 1864, a resolution to amend the Constitution to abolish slavery throughout the United States was introduced in Congress. After a year of prolonged discussion, the Thirteenth Amendment was approved by the required two-thirds vote in both houses of Congress and ultimately ratified by the states in December 1865:

> Neither slavery nor involuntary servitude ... shall exist within the United States or any place subject to their jurisdiction.

LO1 *The Thirteenth Amendment, ratified in 1865, abolished slavery.*

Although the Thirteenth Amendment abolished slavery in 1865, after the Civil War, many Southern states continued discrimination by passing "Black Codes," which forbade blacks to vote, serve on juries, hold certain jobs, move freely, own firearms, or gather in groups. Racial turbulence ensued, and groups such as the Ku Klux Klan emerged in defiance and bigotry in many communities. To remedy this situation, Congress passed the Fourteenth Amendment, which gave blacks citizenship, a status previously defined only by the states.

The Fourteenth Amendment

The Fourteenth Amendment is a significant addition to the Constitution, and although the amendment has five sections, Section 1 has had the most lasting significance through its creation of three important provisions concerning citizenship, due process, and equal protection.

The first sentence in Section 1 contains the Citizenship Clause and states that "all people born or naturalized in the United States, and subject to the jurisdiction thereof, are citizens of the United States and of the State wherein they reside," a decree that effectively overrode the *Dred Scott* decision (a case discussed later in this chapter). Southern states were required to ratify the Fourteenth Amendment before re-entering the Union.

Citizenship, however, was not the only issue addressed in the Fourteenth Amendment. The more looming concern was that states remained able to infringe on due process and equal protection rights from which the federal government was prohibited. The 1833 land dispute case of *Barron v. Mayor and City Council of Baltimore* illustrates the contradictions caused when different standards are applied to federal and state government. In this case, the plaintiff challenged the constitutionality of Baltimore taking his land for public use and not adequately compensating him, as mandated in the Fifth Amendment. The Supreme Court held that such a case involving local government had no place in federal court because the first ten amendments to the Constitution (the Bill of Rights) were not applicable to state governments. Writing for a unanimous majority, Chief Justice John Marshall's opinion held that each state was permitted to draft its own constitution, and that the federal Constitution was intended as a means to maintain a separation of powers. The Bill of Rights was meant to be a check on the new national government by limiting its control of state laws.

LO2 *The Fourteenth Amendment, ratified in 1868, granted citizenship to all persons born or naturalized in the United States and subject to the jurisdiction thereof. The Fourteenth Amendment also forbid the states to deny their citizens due process of law or equal protection of the law; that is, it made certain provisions of the Bill of Rights applicable to the states.*

However, the Civil War had altered the perception that national and state governments needed to be considered so separately that one could do what the other was prohibited from doing. And as a result, the second sentence of Section 1 of the Fourteenth Amendment extended to the states many of the same limits placed on federal power by promulgating: "No State shall make or enforce any law which shall abridge the privileges or immunities of citizens of the United States; nor shall any State deprive any person of life, liberty, or property, without due process of law; nor deny to any person within its jurisdiction the equal protection of the laws." Through the Due Process Clause and Equal Protection Clause, the Fourteenth Amendment thus sought to prevent both the federal and state governments from infringing on the majority of constitutionally guaranteed rights because abuse at either level could assault the liberties the Constitution sought to protect.

The Fourteenth Amendment prohibits the government *at any level* from unfairly or arbitrarily denying a citizen his or her fundamental and constitutionally protected rights to life, liberty, and property **(due process of law)** and requires that similarly situated people or classes of people be treated in similar ways under the law **(equal protection of the law)**. These rights have been the basis of many modern cases in constitutional law.

due process of law prohibits the government from unfairly or arbitrarily denying a citizen his or her fundamental and constitutionally protected rights to life, liberty, and property

equal protection of the law requires that similarly situated people or classes of people be treated in similar ways under the law

due process provides rules and procedures to ensure fairness to an individual and to prevent arbitrary government actions; the Fifth and Fourteenth Amendments' constitutionally guaranteed right of an accused to hear the charges against him or her and to be heard by the court having jurisdiction over the matter

Due Process

Due process is such an important concept of American law that no precise definition accurately suits it, although the gist of it is quite simple: basic fairness must remain part of the legal process. **Due process** provides rules and procedures to ensure fairness to an individual and to prevent arbitrary government actions, by which discretion left to an individual is removed in favor of an openness through which fundamental individual rights—the rights to life, liberty, and property—are protected.

Due process is further distinguished as *procedural* or *substantive*. **Procedural due process** refers to how laws are applied. Procedural due process applies in both the criminal and the civil arenas and comes into play whenever the government seeks to interfere with a person's liberty or a property interest. A concept related to procedural due process is **procedural justice**, the idea of being treated fairly during a process or procedure. A positive process experience outweighs a positive outcome. For example, someone who receives a speeding ticket will regard the system favorably if he or she thinks that the outcome is arrived at fairly. Procedural justice facilitates positive police contacts, which build public trust and enhance police legitimacy.

Substantive due process, on the other hand, requires that the laws themselves, in substance, be fair—not just how laws are enforced. Laws that unjustly limit a person's freedom or property rights will be found to violate the right to due process. Examples include laws that have permitted segregation and the unjust taking of property by the government. Both types of due process will be discussed in more depth shortly. For now, it is sufficient to note that procedural due process and substantive due process work to ensure to everyone the fairness of law under the Constitution.

The various and specific ways in which the Due Process Clause affects criminal justice will be expanded on throughout the remainder of the text, including how it regulates the activities of law enforcement officers as they strive to balance individual rights and liberties with the needs of society, for example, in the context of confessions and lineups. What is important to comprehend at this point is how the Due Process Clause (1) serves as the vehicle by which specific enumerated rights contained within the Bill of Rights are made applicable to the states (the doctrine of incorporation) and (2) has been applied by the Supreme Court, through its interpretation of the term *liberty*, to develop a series of fundamental rights not specifically enumerated in the Bill of Rights (e.g., the right to privacy).

Enumerated Rights and Incorporation

Following ratification of the Fourteenth Amendment, courts were faced with the task of interpreting the Due Process Clause in ways that applied the fundamental provisions of the Bill of Rights, known as enumerated rights, to the states. This process of interpretation and application is referred to as *incorporation*. The **incorporation doctrine** holds that those provisions of the Bill of Rights that are fundamental to the American legal system are applied to the states through the Due Process Clause of the Fourteenth Amendment, thereby preventing state or local governments from infringing on people's rights when the federal government would not be allowed to. Thought of another way, incorporation sets a minimum standard or a "Constitutional floor," allowing state governments the opportunity to offer more protection to its people, but not less than what the Constitution commands.

Two general theories of incorporation exist: a selective approach and a "total incorporation" approach. The total incorporation theory posits that the Fourteenth

---

procedural due process constitutionally guaranteed rights of fairness in how the law is carried out or applied

procedural justice the idea of being treated fairly during a process or procedure

substantive due process constitutional requirement that laws themselves be fair

incorporation doctrine holds that those provisions of the Bill of Rights that are fundamental to the American legal system are applied to the states through the Due Process Clause of the Fourteenth Amendment, thereby preventing state or local governments from infringing on people's rights when federal government would not be allowed to

Amendment should be interpreted such that the entirety of the Bill of Rights and all of the guarantees and protections therein are applicable to the states under the Due Process Clause. This theory was championed by Justice Hugo Black in *Adamson v. California* (1947) when he wrote in his dissent that the Fourteenth Amendment required "total incorporation" of the Bill of Rights, nothing more or nothing less. This approach provides that the "liberties" applied to the states are those explicit in the Constitution. The total incorporation theory, however, has remained a relatively obscure interpretive stance among Supreme Court justices; the far more prominent theory has been that of selective incorporation.

The ad hoc or selective approach starts with the notion that *if a right is implicit in the concept of ordered liberty*, it is absorbed into the Due Process Clause and is, therefore, applicable to the states. In one of the first incorporation cases, Justice John Marshall Harlan stated, "There are principles of liberty and justice lying at the foundation of our civil and political institutions which no state can violate consistently with that due process of law required by the Fourteenth Amendment in proceedings involving life, liberty or property" (*Plessy v. Ferguson*, 1896). And in *Palko v. Connecticut* (1937), Justice Benjamin Cardozo asserted there were rights "so rooted in the traditions and conscience of our people as to be ranked as fundamental," meaning "essential to justice and the American system of political liberty."

Presently, the test for determining what should be incorporated is based on the premise that if a right is "*fundamental* to the *American* scheme of justice," it should be applied to the states through due process, a standard set forth by the Court in *Duncan v. Louisiana* (1968). In this case, the defendant, Gary Duncan, was driving his car when he noticed two of his cousins involved in a conversation with four boys on the side of the road. Duncan's cousins, who are black, had been recently involved in racial incidents at their school. The four boys with whom they were speaking were white. Duncan stopped his car, got out, and encouraged his cousins to come with him and leave. Just before Duncan and his two cousins got into the car to leave, Duncan touched one of the other boys' elbows. Duncan was later arrested and charged with assault. At trial, the four boys testified that Duncan slapped the white boy, whereas Duncan and his cousins testified that he merely touched the other boy. Duncan, who requested a jury trial and was denied, was found guilty of simple battery by a judge and given a 60-day prison sentence and a $10 fine. The maximum sentence was two years imprisonment and up to a $300 fine.

Duncan appealed, claiming violations of his Fifth and Sixth Amendment rights, and the case reached the Supreme Court, which ruled in favor of appellant Duncan. In their analysis, the Court held that the test for determining whether a right extended by the Fifth and Sixth Amendments with respect to federal criminal proceedings is also protected against state action by the Fourteenth Amendment is to assess whether the right is among the "fundamental principles of liberty and justice which lie at the base of all *our* civil and political institutions." In *Duncan*, the Court noted how "The guarantees of jury trial . . . reflect a profound judgment about the way in which law should be enforced and justice administered." The Court emphasized that the right of a jury trial in serious criminal cases qualifies for protection under the Due Process Clause of the Fourteenth Amendment and must be enforced against the states. The Court explained this through a thorough evaluation of the history surrounding trial by jury and described the evils one is meant to protect against.

CASE IN BRIEF

Duncan v. Louisiana (1968)

ISSUE Is the denial of a jury trial in a state criminal prosecution, where a sentence of up to two years of imprisonment is possible, a violation of the Sixth and Fourteenth Amendments of the U.S. Constitution?

RULING Yes, because the right to a jury trial is "fundamental to the American scheme of justice."

Duncan illustrates the "modern" test of incorporation of an enumerated right, and importantly, prescribes that the incorporated rights apply to the states in the same way that they apply to the federal government.

The differing incorporation theories are, today, largely of historical significance because most of the Bill of Rights has been incorporated. In fact, to answer the question of which rights within the Bill of Rights apply to the states, it is often easier to answer, instead, which do *not*. Of the first eight amendments, only two individual guarantees have not been made applicable to the states by the Supreme Court:

- The Fifth Amendment clause guaranteeing criminal prosecution only on a grand jury indictment.
- The Seventh Amendment guarantee of a jury trial in a civil case.

Previous editions of this text also included the Second Amendment, which guarantees the right to bear arms, among the unincorporated amendments. However, in June 2010, the Supreme Court issued a landmark decision, holding that the right of an individual to keep and bear arms, as protected by the Second Amendment, is incorporated by the Due Process Clause of the Fourteenth Amendment and, as such, applies to the states (*McDonald v. Chicago*, 2010).

Referring to the Court's ruling in *Duncan* and the position that incorporation decisions should consider not what legal traditions exist in Europe or elsewhere in the world but only those prevailing in the United States, Justice Alito stated:

> The Court made it clear that the governing standard is not whether *any* "civilized system [can] be imagined that would not accord the particular protection." Instead, the Court inquired whether a particular Bill of Rights guarantee is fundamental to *our* scheme of ordered liberty and system of justice ... referring to those "fundamental principles of liberty and justice which lie at the base of all *our* civil and political institutions." (*McDonald v. Chicago*, 2010)

The Third Amendment prohibiting the quartering of soldiers in private houses and the Eighth Amendment prohibiting excessive fines have yet to be addressed by the Court.

Before leaving the discussion of incorporation, it is fair to ask why an amendment was not passed that simply applied the Bill of Rights, in its entirety, to the states. The short answer to this immensely complicated political, philosophical, and legal question is that the tremendous changes occurring in the norms of this emerging country had to be given ample time to evolve on their own. Interpreting the Constitution on the basis of societal norms—the essence of a "living law"—is what has allowed the Constitution to remain effective, and this would prove itself as the era of civil rights and liberties continued to emerge.

Procedural Due Process

The Due Process Clauses of the Fifth and Fourteenth Amendments provide procedural safeguards. Procedural due process is required when the government seeks to deprive a person of life, liberty, or property. Procedural due process challenges the fairness of *how* a government action is carried out—the legality of the actual *process*—and not the substantive basis of the law itself.

Central to the discussion of procedural due process is the concept of *interest*; if a legitimate interest is not at stake, procedural due process will not apply. Life, liberty, and property are protected interests, but what, exactly, constitutes these interests? The Court has explained it this way:

> While this Court has not attempted to define with exactness the liberty ... guaranteed [by the Fourteenth Amendment], the term has received much consideration and some of the included things have been definitely stated. Without doubt, it denotes not merely freedom from bodily restraint but also the right of the individual to contract, to engage in any of the common occupations of life, to acquire useful knowledge, to marry, establish a home and bring up children, to worship God according to the dictates of his own conscience, and generally to enjoy those privileges long recognized ... as essential to the orderly pursuit of happiness by free men. (*Meyer v. Nebraska*, 1923)

Liberty interests, which are highly protected, cover a broad spectrum. The Constitution is the source for fundamental liberty interests. Lower-level liberty interests also exist and are government-created by state legislation.

Property interests also require procedural due process but, unlike liberty interests, are not derived from the Constitution, instead being created and defined by state law (*Board of Regents of State Colleges v. Roth*, 1972). Real estate and personal property are examples. Supreme Court decisions have found property interests in welfare benefits, unemployment compensation, and professional licenses. Property interests receive procedural due process protection when the government has made it clear the interest will not be impaired except under certain conditions. To have a property interest in a government-created interest, one "must have more than an abstract need or desire for it" and "have a legitimate claim of entitlement to it" (*Roth*, 1972).

Procedural due process requires a person be given notice of the deprivation and a reasonable opportunity to be heard. Notice requires the conveyance of all necessary information so the person can protect the interest. Depending on the interest at stake, the opportunity to be heard might be as elaborate as a trial or as simple as a chance to respond in writing (*Boddie v. Connecticut*, 1971). To determine how complex a procedure must be, the court will examine (1) the significance of the affected interest, (2) whether additional safeguards would reduce the risk of error, and (3) the public interest in resolving the matter efficiently so as to avoid administrative and fiscal burdens (*Mathews v. Eldridge*, 1976).

Substantive Due Process

The Due Process Clauses of the Fifth and Fourteenth Amendments, in addition to guaranteeing procedural safeguards, also protect substantive rights and require that laws themselves, in substance, be fair. Substantive due process comes into play when a legislature enacts a law that interferes with individual rights because the Supreme Court has interpreted the Due Process Clause as guaranteeing that a person's life, liberty, and property cannot be taken by the government without appropriate justification, regardless of the procedures employed during the taking.

Although substantive due process is a concept related to the textual guarantees of the law, it also operates to protect those characteristics of life, liberty, or property not specifically mentioned in the Constitution. These rights are found in the substance of the "liberty" aspect of the Due Process Clause, as stated by Chief Justice Warren Burger in *Richmond Newspapers Inc v. Virginia* (1980):

> Notwithstanding the appropriate caution against reading into the Constitution rights not explicitly defined, this Court has acknowledged that certain unarticulated rights are implicit in enumerated guarantees. For example, the rights of association and of privacy, the right to be presumed innocent, and the right to be judged by a standard of proof beyond a reasonable doubt in a criminal trial, as well as the right to travel, appear nowhere in the Constitution or Bill of Rights. Yet these important but unarticulated rights have nonetheless been found to share constitutional protection in common with explicit guarantees.... Fundamental rights, even though not expressly guaranteed, have been recognized by the Court as indispensable to the enjoyment of rights explicitly defined.

unenumerated rights rights not specifically listed in the Bill of Rights

Rights not specifically listed or articulated in the Bill of Rights are known as **unenumerated rights.** They are no less important than specified rights but have been left to develop with our society. Among the unenumerated rights the Supreme Court has recognized are the right to privacy, the right to interstate and international travel, the right to vote, and freedom of association.

How these rights are determined and what level of judicial scrutiny should be applied to laws that interfere with them are the main questions associated with substantive due process.

CASE IN BRIEF ▶

Lochner v. New York (1905)

ISSUE Does a New York state law forbidding a baker to work more than 10 hours in a day or 60 hours in a week violate the liberty protected by the Fourteenth Amendment?

RULING Yes. The Supreme Court decided the law is not reasonable and interferes with the right to contract found in the liberty aspect of the Due Process Clause.

Finding the Right to Exist Substantive due process began as a way to protect individual economic rights not textually guaranteed by the Constitution. In *Lochner v. New York* (1905), the Court determined that a freedom to contract existed via the liberty aspect in the Due Process Clause. When the New York legislature enacted a law that limited the number of hours a baker could work, the Court determined that was a violation of due process.

Substantive due process was also employed in areas of civil liberties where there was no specific enumerated right. For example, in *Meyer v. Nebraska* (1923), a case involving a state law that prohibited the teaching of a foreign language to grade school children, the Court simply determined a liberty interest existed in parents' ability to control their children's education.

CASE IN BRIEF ▶

Griswold v. Connecticut (1965)

ISSUE In the case of a married couple, can a state law restrict the counseling of contraceptives without violating the Constitution?

RULING No. A right to privacy is found in the penumbras of the enumerated rights protected by the Constitution. The Connecticut law interferes with that right and is therefore unconstitutional.

penumbra a type of shadow in astronomy with the principle extending to the idea that certain constitutional rights are implied within other constitutional rights

The *Griswold* Approach to Finding Unenumerated Rights The notion that unenumerated rights existed went into a hiatus after the *Meyer* decision but was revived in *Griswold v. Connecticut* (1965), a case involving an 1897 Connecticut law that made it illegal to use, or counsel another to use, contraceptives. The Supreme Court, noting that a "right to privacy" in regard to marriage existed within the Fourteenth Amendment, found the Connecticut law to violate due process. However, rather than simply stating that a right to privacy existed, in *Griswold*, the Court tied this new right to those enumerated in the Constitution. In his opinion, Justice William Douglas explained the Court's rationale:

> The association of people is not mentioned in the Constitution nor in the Bill of Rights. The right to educate a child in a school of the parents' choice—whether public or private or parochial—is also not mentioned. Nor is the right to study any particular subject or any foreign language. Yet the First Amendment has been construed to include certain of those rights.

Douglas expounded on the Court's position by asserting that certain rights and liberties, even though not be specifically stated in the Constitution, exist because "specific guarantees in the Bill of Rights have penumbras, formed by emanations from those guarantees that help give them life and substance" (*Griswold v. Connecticut*, 1965). In astronomy, a **penumbra** is a type of shadow. Douglas used astronomy as an example to show how certain rights in the Bill of Rights have other peripheral rights implied in or along with them. These peripheral rights are important and necessary to protect the specific, enumerated rights.

Through its various opinions in *Griswold*, the Court went on to explain that specific enumerated rights contained within the Constitution—namely guarantees provided within the First, Third, Fourth, Fifth, and Ninth Amendments—and their penumbras converged and overlapped to create **zones of privacy,** which are areas safe from governmental intrusion. In the *Griswold* case, the fact that marital privacy exists within the zones was evident to the Court, with Justice Douglas writing that the intimacy of the marriage relationship involved a "right of privacy older than the Bill of Rights." Consequently, the Connecticut law was struck down as unconstitutional.

Note that now, through *Roe v. Wade* (1973), the Court merely accepts that a "right to privacy" exists in the concept of liberty contained within the Fourteenth Amendment. This privacy right has been extended to many areas, including abortion, marriage, family life, sexual orientation, and the right to refuse medical care. We will return to privacy rights shortly, after finishing our examination of substantive due process and how the Supreme Court has interpreted the concept of *liberty* contained within the Fourteenth Amendment to identify nontextual rights.

Modern Substantive Due Process The penumbras method used by the Court in *Griswold* to identify unenumerated rights via the Due Process Clause has since fallen by the wayside. Now, the Court carefully describes the perceived right and examines the question of whether that right possesses ideals that are "deeply rooted in our history and traditions, or so fundamental to our concept of constitutionally ordered liberty, that they are protected by the Fourteenth Amendment" (*Washington v. Glucksberg*, 1997). If the right meets this standard, it is considered a *fundamental* interest.

When the Court finds that a fundamental liberty interest is at stake, it employs the strict scrutiny test, which looks at the law in question and determines whether it is narrowly tailored to serve a compelling government interest. As such, the onus is on the government to defend the law by showing it is the least burdensome legislation and that the government interest is strong. Textually explicit (enumerated) rights, which are incorporated against the states, are almost always evaluated with strict scrutiny. Nontextual (unenumerated) rights, which exist via the "liberty" guaranteed by the Fourteenth Amendment to protect individuals from state interference, can also be evaluated under strict scrutiny if they are determined to be fundamental (generally those involving civil rights).

If the right is not deemed to be fundamental, the court will apply the rational basis test instead. This approach reverses the burden and places it on the person challenging the law, who must show that it is not rationally related to *any* legitimate governmental goal, regardless of whether the law actually furthers it or not. These rights often lie in the areas of general economic or property liberties and social matters.

---

zones of privacy areas into which the government may not intrude

---

MYTH
The right to privacy is explicitly protected by the Constitution.

FACT
The Constitution does not expressly contain a right to privacy. However, aspects of the Constitution's amendments show a belief that privacy is important and should be protected from the government. For example, the First Amendment protects privacy in the area of freedom of religion; the Fourth Amendment protects an individual's privacy in one's home; and the Fifth Amendment does not allow one to be compelled to testify against him- or herself, showing an interest in protecting personal information. The right to privacy has been developed over many Supreme Court decisions in which the "liberty" guaranteed by the Fourteenth Amendment's Due Process Clause has been interpreted broadly to guarantee a right to privacy.

◀ CASE IN BRIEF

Washington v. Glucksberg (1997)

ISSUE Does a Washington state law prohibiting physician-assisted suicide violate the Due Process Clause because it impermissibly interferes with the liberty interest of a person to choose death over life?

RULING No. The liberty to be assisted in suicide by a physician is not a fundamental right or liberty which is "deeply rooted in this Nation's history and tradition." Although it is an aspect of liberty, it does not deserve high-level scrutiny and must only be rationally related to the state's interests.

> **CASE IN BRIEF** ▶
>
> *Nebbia v. New York* (1934)
>
> **ISSUE** Does a New York law that establishes a minimum milk price violate the Due Process Clause?
>
> **RULING** No. The Supreme Court, in contrast to the previous *Lochner* case, decided that in the area of social and economic legislation, if the law is not arbitrary and has a reasonable relation to promoting public welfare, a state may adopt whatever economic policy it wishes to accomplish its stated purpose and to enforce that policy by legislation adapted to its purpose. The courts are without authority either to declare such a policy or, when it is declared by the legislature, to override it.

Initially the Supreme Court took an active role in the area of economic legislation and highly scrutinized these laws, with early case analysis offering little deference to legislatures in the area of economic liberties, despite the burden being on the government to show justification. Eventually the Court began to view state economic legislation in a different light. During the Great Depression, the Supreme Court decided *Nebbia v. New York* (1934), a case involving a New York law that, in an effort to save farmers, had set a minimum price for milk. In upholding the law, the Court wrote in its opinion:

> With the wisdom of the policy adopted, with the adequacy or practicability of the law enacted to forward it, the courts are both incompetent and unauthorized to deal. The course of decision in this court exhibits a firm adherence to these principles. Times without number we have said that the legislature is primarily the judge of the necessity of such an enactment, that every possible presumption is in favor of its validity, and that though the court may hold views inconsistent with the wisdom of the law, it may not be annulled unless palpably in excess of legislative power.

Thus, the previous high-level scrutiny of economic legislation seen in *Lochner* ceased after *Nebbia*. This important shift in scrutiny signaled the willingness of the Court to give a high level of deference to legislatures on the facts and basis for economic regulation. As long as there was a rational basis for the legislation, the law would stand. The Court would not substitute their social and economic beliefs for that of the legislature.

> **LO3** *Enumerated rights are textually explicit rights incorporated against the states and almost always evaluated with strict scrutiny. Unenumerated rights, in contrast, are not explicitly stated in the Constitution or Bill of Rights but exist via the liberty guaranteed by the Fourteenth Amendment and are considered either fundamental (e.g., civil liberties), thus evaluated under strict scrutiny, or non-fundamental (e.g., economic or property liberties), which are evaluated under a rational basis test.*

The Court, in *United States v. Carolene Products Co.* (1938), emphasized this shift away from high-level scrutiny for economic legislation, with a footnote to the opinion expressing that some liberty interests would come under a higher level of scrutiny. This cemented the direction the Court would take; high-level scrutiny for those laws that infringe on fundamental rights, whereas those laws of an economic nature would only receive a low level of scrutiny.

The Debate The process of identifying liberties or rights that are not specifically written in the Constitution has not occurred without its share of debate. Proponents of the process believe that certain rights need to exist to give the enumerated rights their full force. Also, these liberties and rights are of special concern in that they have a profound impact on an individual. Detractors of the process, however, point to the Constitution as the explicit source of our rights and liberties, contending that the identification of rights not textually enumerated is simply wrong. No matter how the process is described, it nonetheless usurps the power of the legislature and becomes a subjective judicial exercise.

Due Process and Privacy Rights

Since *Griswold*, the issue of privacy rights has expanded in ways the framers of the Constitution and the Bill of Rights could never have foreseen when they promulgated an amendment to protect people's liberty from undue government intrusion.

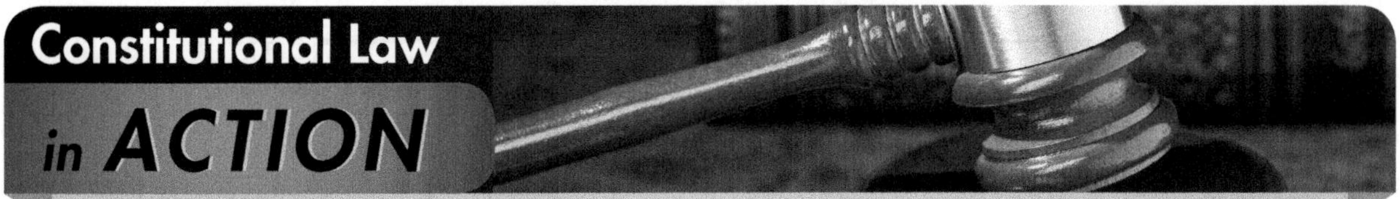

Constitutional Law in ACTION

A state in the United States has changed its driver's license laws, and now the minimum age at which a driver in that state may seek a license is 25 years. Until this point, the minimum age was 16. The state has put forth the argument that young drivers, 16–24 years old, are put in harm's way under the previous law because these immature drivers are ill equipped to handle the dangers and responsibility of driving.

- Is obtaining a driver's license at age 16 a right? If so, is it enumerated or unenumerated? Fundamental or non-fundamental? Why?

- *Assume it is a fundamental right. Which test would a court use to evaluate the constitutionality of the law?*

- *What if the right is determined non-fundamental, and instead affects an economic or property interest? Which test would be used?*

- *What argument would you make to show that the new law is constitutional under a fundamental right? A non-fundamental right?*

Here we will examine two relatively innovative, yet controversial, techniques law enforcement has begun using to be more effective in detecting and solving crime, yet that raise concerns about individual privacy rights: suspicious activity reports and familial DNA testing.

The Nationwide Suspicious Activity Reporting Initiative A suspicious activity report (SAR) is an official documentation of observed behavior that may be indicative of intelligence gathering or preoperational planning related to terrorism, criminal, or other illicit intention. SARs focus on what law enforcement agencies have been doing for years—gathering information regarding behaviors and incidents associated with crime and establishing a process whereby information can be shared to detect and prevent criminal activity, including that associated with domestic and international terrorism, for example, surveillance.

The Nationwide Suspicious Activity Reporting Initiative (NSI) is a collaborative effort among federal, state, local, and tribal government agencies with counterterrorism responsibilities that seeks to establish a unified approach at all levels of government to gather, document, process, analyze, and share information about terrorism-related suspicious activities (Bureau of Justice Assistance, 2009). The NSI makes local SARs available to federal, state, and local law enforcement agencies and to state and major urban area fusion centers. In 2013, the Federal Bureau of Investigation (FBI) and Department of Homeland Security (DHS) took over responsibility for the NSI. The Department of Justice (DOJ) Privacy and Civil Liberties Office also works with the NSI because of the privacy and civil rights implications of the system. Figure 4.1 illustrates the sharing of SAR information.

Although the information entered into the SAR database is vetted, civil rights advocates have questioned the initiative as another instance of "Big Brother."

SAR (suspicious activity report) an official documentation of observed behavior that may be indicative of intelligence gathering or preoperational planning related to terrorism, criminal, or other illicit intention

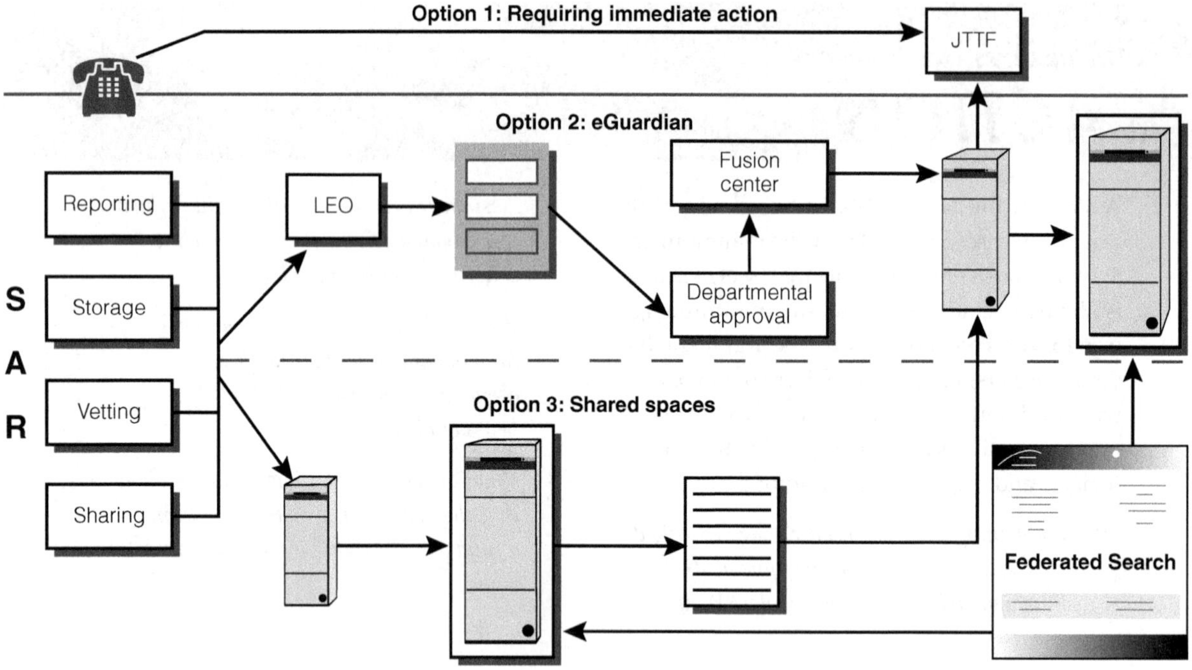

Figure 4.1 Sharing SAR Information

Source: *Nationwide SAR Initiative: Technology Overview.* Washington, DC: Bureau of Justice Assistance, May 2012, p. 2. See URL http://nsi.ncirc.gov/documents/NSI_Technology_Fact_Sheet.pdf.

> **MYTH**
> DNA is only useful if a substantial amount of visible bodily fluid (blood, semen, etc.) is found at a crime scene.
>
> **FACT**
> This may have been true a decade ago, but with improved forensic techniques, a useful amount of DNA material may be found on a discarded cigarette butt or a surface touched by a suspect. Touch DNA, invisible to the naked eye, is genetic material found in skin cells that are left behind when a suspect touches something. A dozen cells are often enough to provide a testable sample.

Familial DNA Database Searches Another relatively recent crime fighting technique is familial DNA analysis. Advances in DNA technology and the development of DNA databases have allowed investigators to search for genetically close matches to help solve crimes committed by relatives of people in the database. Siblings, parents, aunts, uncles, and cousins can be linked to crimes because their relative's DNA closely resembles DNA found at a crime scene. The basic principle is that DNA profiles of people who are related are likely to contain similarities. Familial DNA database searches can lead to the identity of an individual who could be a sibling of the offender or the offender's parent or child. This investigative technique is most commonly used in the United Kingdom. Civil rights groups have strongly opposed this technique as an invasion of privacy.

The preceding examples illustrate the continuing challenge of balancing individual and governmental rights and involve issues that may one day end up before the Supreme Court for a determination of constitutionality. However, one government activity that the Court has continually declared to be unconstitutional is discrimination.

Discrimination versus Prejudice

Most people have some preconceived notions, or prejudices, about specific people or groups of people. This might include members of minority groups and other categories, such as the elderly, teenagers, the disabled, professional athletes, homosexuals, and police officers. According to Moule (2009, p. 322), "Ethnic and racial stereotypes are learned as part of normal socialization and are consistent among many populations and across time." These stereotypes frequently foster unconscious biases, which commonly lead to unintentional racism, "racism that is usually invisible even *and especially* to those who perpetrate it" (Moule, p. 321). This unconscious or *implicit* bias is discussed in greater depth later in the chapter.

In a democratic society, individuals are free to think what they want. People may hold any number of prejudices and are not prohibited by the government from doing so. However, if these thoughts translate into socially unacceptable behaviors, problems arise, sometimes to the point where government is justified in intervening.

L04 Prejudice is an attitude; discrimination is a behavior.

If prejudices are converted into acts, laws punish the actor and protect the victim.

prejudice a negative attitude regarding a person or thing

The Roots of Racial Discrimination

discrimination an action or behavior based on prejudice

Racial discrimination has existed since before the time of colonial America and the Constitution. To people such as George Washington, Alexander Hamilton, and Thomas Jefferson, slavery was an accepted part of life.

Although the Thirteenth Amendment to the Constitution declared slavery illegal, it could not outlaw unequal treatment or change racial attitudes so prominent in Southern states. In 1896, the case of *Plessy v. Ferguson* was brought before the Supreme Court and heightened awareness of racial issues. Homer Plessy had refused to abide by a law that required black people to sit in a separate train car. Plessy, who took a vacant seat in a coach designated to accommodate passengers who were white, was told to move but he refused. He was arrested and charged with violating state law. Plessy, who was seven-eighths Caucasian and one-eighth African blood, and whose mixture of colored blood was not discernable in him, brought suit, arguing that "he was entitled to every right, privilege and immunity secured to citizens of the United States of the white race" and that the law violated his Thirteenth and Fourteenth Amendment rights. The Court ruled against Plessy:

L05 *Plessy v. Ferguson (1896) showed the Court's desire to avoid civil rights issues, declaring discrimination to be outside the realm of the Court.*

> If the two races are to meet upon terms of social equality, it must be the result of . . . a voluntary consent of individuals. . . . Legislation is powerless to eradicate racial instincts . . . and the attempts to do so can only result in accentuating the difficulties of the present situation.

Racial tension mounted as states passed laws to ensure that whites could maintain their privileged status. **Jim Crow laws**, which strictly segregated blacks from whites in schools, restaurants, streetcars, hospitals, and cemeteries, supposedly kept blacks "separate but equal." The compelling question became whether separate could ever really be equal.

The issue of separate but equal was eventually addressed head-on in *Brown v. Board of Education of Topeka* (1954), when a group of black children sought admission to an all-white public school. The plaintiffs claimed they were being denied their constitutional right to equal protection and that the laws of separate but equal were in fact not equal. The Court agreed in *Brown*, holding that separate-but-equal schools were illegal. The momentum of the *Brown* decision prompted further legislation regarding equality and led to one of the greatest civil rights advances in our history, the 1964 Civil Rights Act.

Jim Crow laws laws that strictly segregated blacks from whites in schools, restaurants, streetcars, hospitals, and cemeteries

◀ **CASE IN BRIEF**

Brown v. Board of Education of Topeka (1954)

ISSUE Does segregation in public education violate the Fourteenth Amendment's Equal Protection Clause?

RULING Yes. In the area of public education, "separate but equal" has no place. Separate educational facilities based on race are inherently unequal.

Constitutional Law in ACTION

It is 5 A.M. and you and your partner are responding to a call of a suspicious person near a power plant. The caller, a plant employee, told the dispatcher that there is a Middle Eastern male taking pictures of the power plant guard station and entrances and exits. The caller also explained that the same male had been seen in the area the previous two days at the same time of day.

You arrive and see a minivan parked on the side of the road. You run the out-of-state license plate and notice there is someone sitting in the driver's seat, so you and your partner get out of your squad to go talk to the driver.

He tells you that he is an engineering student with an interest in power plants. You ask him where he goes to school, and he replies that he is not enrolled anywhere right now.

Your partner notices an open notebook on the front seat of the van, with dates, times, and "number of guards" written many times over on the visible page. There is also a laptop computer and several cell phones inside the minivan. In addition, there happens to be a textbook, *Power Plant Architecture*, on the floor in front of the passenger seat.

The driver provides you with an out-of-state driver's license but does not have proof of insurance as required by state law. You issue him a citation for that, write down all of the information you saw, and submit an intelligence report to your department's intelligence unit.

- *Should a person's race, religion, or ethnicity ever be used as a basis for law enforcement action? Why or why not?*

- *Would your answer change based on the severity of the crime being investigated?*

- *Does the level of law enforcement action at issue change your response?*

The Struggle for Equality

Through the tumultuous challenges of racism and segregation during the 1950s and 1960s, the United States continued its struggle with what *equal* really meant. Some chose to embrace equality, whereas others chose to resist any movement toward equality, sometimes to the point of participating in violence, such as that perpetrated by the Ku Klux Klan. But the Supreme Court had spoken, and the tide of public opinion was turning toward a willingness to become a unified country with "equal protection for all."

Racial discrimination has not been the only way segments of U.S. society have been made to feel disenfranchised. Gender discrimination is an issue our law has had to confront as well. As difficult as it is for today's generation to imagine, women were not allowed to vote until 1920, 50 years after discrimination based on race was prohibited by the Fifteenth Amendment. Gender discrimination remained during the 1960s; for example, women often were denied equal pay for equal work. Head-of-household rules granting higher pay applied only to men. Women also often found they would not be promoted, were excluded from certain professions, and were permitted to serve only limited roles in the military. Even educational opportunities were denied to women in some instances.

But, as was the case with people of color who found themselves and their lives limited, eventually laws recognized a changing norm in society. For example, when the federal government brought suit against both Virginia and the Virginia Military Institute (VMI), challenging the male-only admissions policy as a violation of equal protection, the Supreme Court decision in *United States v. Virginia* (1996) held that the exclusion of females from the Institute was unconstitutional (Ducat, 2010).

Other legislation created during this era of expanding civil rights included the Equal Pay Act of 1963, the Civil Rights Act of 1964, the Equal Employment Opportunity Act of 1972, and Title IX of the Education Amendments of 1972, all of which prohibited discrimination based on race, color, religion, sex, or national origin in employment and education in public and private sectors at the federal, state, and local levels.

The Rise of Affirmative Action Programs

Many argued that these antidiscrimination laws were nothing but hollow promises that in reality did little to rid society of discrimination in employment and education opportunities. In response, President Richard M. Nixon's administration formed a coalition to address unequal treatment of minorities and women. The result was affirmative action programs.

LO6 *Affirmative action was created to spread equal opportunity throughout the diverse American population.*

Affirmative action programs, sometimes referred to as ethnic- and gender-preference programs, were designed to cure discrimination in hiring and eliminate past, present, and future discrimination using race, color, sex, and age as deciding criteria. The idea was that minorities and women would no longer be discriminated against in employment and educational opportunities and, in fact, would be given extra consideration to meet goals and quotas. President John F. Kennedy first used the actual phrase *affirmative action* in his 1961 Executive Order 10925 requiring federal contractors to hire applicants without regard to their race, creed, color, or national origin. President Lyndon Johnson's 1965 Executive Order 11246 used the same language. In 1967 Johnson expanded the Executive Order to include affirmative action requirements to benefit women.

affirmative action
programs created to spread equal opportunity throughout the diverse American population

According to Brunner and Rowan (2007), "From the outset, affirmative action was envisioned as a temporary remedy that would end once there was a 'level playing field' for all Americans." Focused on education and jobs, policies required that active measures be taken to make certain that minorities had the same opportunities for promotions, salary increases, career advancement, school admissions, scholarships, and financial aid that had been dominated by white males.

The landmark case in this issue is *Regents of the University of California v. Bakke* (1978), in which the Supreme Court upheld in a 5–4 decision the University of California's use of race as one factor in determining admissions. Alan Bakke, a white male, had twice been denied admission to medical school, even though less-qualified minorities had been admitted. Bakke charged that the university's quota system violated the Equal Protection Clause. In the *Bakke* decision, the Court stated, "Preferring members of any one group for no reason other than race or ethnic origin is discrimination for its own sake. This the Constitution forbids."

CASE IN BRIEF

Regents of the University of California v. Bakke (1978)

ISSUE Did the use of race as a factor to be admitted to the University of California Medical School violate the Equal Protection Clause?

RULING In a complicated decision, the Court ruled that the rigid system in place at the University of California, which used race as an admission factor, violated the Equal Protection Clause. However, the Court upheld the idea that race could be used as an admission factor in higher education and remain constitutional.

The Court reviewed the medical school's racial set-aside program that reserved 16 of 100 seats for members of certain minority groups. The Court's ruling invalidated the program and reversed the state court's injunction against any use of race whatsoever: "The diversity that furthers a compelling state interest encompasses a far broader array of qualifications and characteristics of which racial or ethnic origin is but a single though important element." The following are notable affirmative action cases ruled on by the Supreme Court since *Bakke* (Ducat, 2010, pp. 1171–1172):

- *United Steelworkers of America v. Weber* (1979)—The Court upheld a collective bargaining agreement that voluntarily aimed at overcoming a company's nearly all-white craft workforce by requiring that at least half of the trainees in an in-plant training program be black until the proportion of blacks in the craft workforce matched the proportion of blacks in the local workforce.
- *Fullilove v. Klutznick* (1980)—Congress's enactment of a 10 percent quota of construction contracts to minority businesses was within its authority under either the Commerce Clause or Section 5 of the Fourteenth Amendment.
- *Firefighters Local Union No. 1784 v. Stotts* (1984)—Setting aside least seniority as a basis for laying off workers and substituting race was something not contained in an existing consent decree and was unjustified unless black employees could prove they individually had been victims of discrimination.
- *Wygant v. Jackson Board of Education* (1986)—The preferential protection of minority teachers from layoffs contained in a collective bargaining agreement was unconstitutional.
- *Local 28, Sheet Metal Workers International Association v. EEOC* (1986)—A federal court order imposing a 29 percent non-white membership goal (reflective of the proportion of non-whites in the local workforce) on a union and its apprenticeship committee for discrimination against non-white workers in selection, training, and admission of members to union was upheld.
- *United States v. Paradise* (1987)—A requirement that 50 percent of promotions throughout Alabama state troopers were to go to blacks, if qualified blacks were available, was upheld.

In 1996, state universities in both Texas and California struck down race-based admissions. However, in 2003, in two significant decisions, the Supreme Court again upheld the use of race as one factor in admissions policies. *Gratz v. Bollinger* involved the University of Michigan's undergraduate school, allowing 20 of 100 points for minority status. Citing the *Bakke* decision, the Supreme Court, in a 6–3 vote, upheld the right of universities to consider race in admission procedures to achieve a diverse student body. Argued the same day was *Grutter v. Bollinger*, involving the University of Michigan's law school admission policy, again allowing race to be considered. Although the vote was closer, 5–4, the policy of allowing race to be a factor in admissions was upheld: "The Law School's narrowly tailored use of race in admissions decisions to further a compelling interest in obtaining the educational benefits that flow from a diverse student body is not prohibited by the Equal Protection Clause, Title VI or §1981."

In these two Michigan cases, the Supreme Court ruled that although affirmative action was no longer justified as a means of redressing past oppression and injustice, it did promote a "compelling state interest" in diversity at all levels of society. As Justice Sandra Day O'Connor wrote for the majority, "In order to cultivate a set of leaders with legitimacy in the eyes of the citizenry, it is necessary that the path to leadership be visibly open to talented and qualified individuals of every race and ethnicity" (*Grutter v. Bollinger*, 2003).

Through the decades, this subject has led to intense controversy. Those in favor of affirmative action say this is a necessary policy to ensure that all citizens have access to the **American dream,** the belief that through hard work anyone can have success and ample material possessions. Proponents also believe it helps bring equity to an imbalance in society. Opponents of affirmative action argue that such programs are, themselves, discriminatory.

American dream the belief that through hard work anyone can have success and ample material possessions

In March 2013, the Court granted certiorari to *Schuette v. Coalition to Defend Affirmative Action*, a case that examines whether a state violates the Equal Protection Clause by amending its constitution to prohibit race- and sex-based discrimination or preferential treatment in public university admissions decisions. *Schuette* involves a Michigan law that bans affirmative action in the public college admission process. The Court heard oral arguments in the fall of 2013 and ruled that the ban was constitutional, citing that the case was about whether or not voters may prohibit consideration of racial preferences in governmental decisions (p. 1630 of the case).

◀ CASE IN BRIEF

Schuette v. Coalition to Defend Affirmative Action (2014)

ISSUE Does a state constitutional amendment that prohibits race- and gender-based discrimination and preferential treatment in public education admissions violate the Equal Protection Clause?

RULING No. A plurality of the Court held that a state may prohibit the use of race-based preferences by governmental bodies, particularly those involving school admissions.

The Court has, however, decided *Fisher v. University of Texas at Austin*, a similar affirmative action case challenging whether colleges and universities can continue to apply admissions policies that extend special preference to minority applicants. On June 24, 2013, the Court vacated and remanded *Fisher to the 5th Circuit*, noting that the lower court did not apply strict scrutiny and sending the case back to the appeals court for further review. It was specifically noted that the lower court gave deference to the school's administrators in assessing whether the use of race is a compelling interest, and in fact, the admissions plan is narrowly tailored to meet that interest. "Strict scrutiny does not permit a court to accept a school's assertion that its admissions process uses race in a permissible way without a court giving close analysis to the evidence of how the process works in practice."

Justice Clarence Thomas, in his concurrence, went further than the majority opinion in declaring that the school's admissions program "violates the Equal Protection Clause because the University has not put forward a compelling interest that could possibly justify racial discrimination." Among the several arguments he put forth against affirmative action in higher education admissions, two of Justice Thomas' more interesting arguments were (1) that it is racial discrimination to use race as a factor in higher education admissions and (2) that these programs actually hurt the minority student. Acknowledging that the policy hurts white and Asian applicants by denying them admission, Justice Thomas added that the black and Hispanic students admitted under the program are harmed even more because they are "far less prepared" than white and Asian students who are admitted.

When the appellate court ruled again on Abigail Fisher's claim, upholding the university's admissions process, the case reached the Supreme Court for a second time. In *Fisher II*, the same issue of using race as a factor in the admissions process was questioned. The Court ruled 4–3 that using race as a factor in the admissions process did not violate the Equal Protection Clause, even under the exacting test of strict scrutiny.

The admissions process at issue uses a complex formula that takes into account factors including academic records and SAT scores, as well as numerous other factors such as leadership, extracurricular activities, and "special circumstances," which includes race. These factors are combined and from that, a decision is made on whether an applicant is accepted or not.

In the majority decision, Justice Kennedy wrote that the value of a diverse student body is a compelling government interest, established by prior Court rulings. In accepting this, the Court looked at the benefits that flow from achieving diversity, including preparing "students for an increasingly diverse workforce" and helping to "break down racial stereotypes." The Court noted that the university gave a "reasoned, principled explanation" of why it wanted to pursue these goals. The University was able to show the inability to achieve a diverse student body through any other processes, giving statistical and anecdotal evidence to support its claim. The fact that race is but a small part of the process was significant in determining this, too.

Justice Alito issued a dissent, criticizing the university for not showing compelling enough reasons for why a diverse student body is beneficial, writing, "The University has still not identified with any degree of specificity the interests that its use of race and ethnicity is supposed to serve." In addition, he argued that race is not just a small factor as claimed by the school or the majority. Race, as he noted, "pervades every aspect of UT's admission process," because it is the only holistic factor that appears on the front of every application, making reviewers clearly aware of the applicant's race at every stage of the process.

Justice Thomas, in line with his dissent in *Fisher I*, wrote a short dissent in which he argued that the Equal Protection Clause categorically prohibits the use of race as a consideration in a higher education admissions process. This principle, he explained, does not change even though a theory exists that shows racial discrimination may provide educational benefits.

Importantly, the majority opinion stressed that just because the admissions process is constitutional today, it does not mean that will always be so. "It is the University's ongoing obligation to engage in constant deliberation and continued reflection regarding its admissions policies."

There are currently several lawsuits involving higher education admissions practices that use race as a factor. These include suits against Harvard University and the University of North Carolina.

Reverse Discrimination

Critics of affirmative action policies have contended that civil rights laws cannot remedy the effects of past discrimination. They assert that such policies lead to reverse discrimination because women or racial minorities are to be hired over white males who may be better qualified. **Reverse discrimination** consists of giving preferential treatment in hiring and promoting women and minorities to the detriment of white males.

The question then becomes whether admission to a college on the basis of diversity is simply a nice way of saying the college is going to consider race. Something

reverse discrimination
giving preferential treatment in hiring and promoting to women and minorities to the detriment of white males

must guide the decisions of those who determine who will be hired, fired, or admitted to the college of their choice. The issue of reverse discrimination has separated whites from minorities, men from women, and affirmative action advocates from those who support a strict "merit" principle for admission, employment, and promotion. The majority position has been summarized as a concern that for every deserving minority group member provided a job or promotion through preferential quotas, a deserving and often more qualified nonminority person is thereby deprived of a job or promotion. The courts themselves have been deeply divided over the constitutionality of the reverse discrimination that some believe is implicit in minority quotas and double standards.

Ricci v. Destefano (2009) involved the practice in the city of New Haven, Connecticut, of using objective exams to identify firefighters best qualified for promotion to lieutenant and captain positions. When the results of the exam showed that white candidates had outperformed minority candidates, New Haven became embroiled in public debate. Black firefighters threatened lawsuits if the exam results were certified, and white and Hispanic firefighters threatened to sue if the results were not certified; so the city scrapped the results, a clearly race-based decision (Means & McDonald, 2009). The failure of the city to certify the results lead to a lawsuit by petitioners, white and Hispanic, who passed the exams but were denied a chance at promotions. They claimed discarding the test results discriminated against them based on their race in violation of Title VII of the Civil Rights Act. The defendants responded that had they certified the test results they could face Title VII liability for using a test that had a disparate impact on minority firefighters.

The district court granted summary judgment for the defendants, and the Second Circuit affirmed. A motion for **summary judgment** is a request to the court to review the evidence and, without a trial, reach a decision to dismiss a case against the **movant** (the party making the request) because there is no dispute of material fact that a jury need resolve and because there is legally insufficient evidence to support a verdict in favor of the nonmovant (Scarry, 2008). The Supreme Court, however, reversed and remanded the case, holding that the city's action in discarding the tests violated Title VII.

Title VII prohibits *intentional* acts of employment discrimination based on race, color, religion, sex, and national origin **(disparate treatment)** as well as policies or practices that are not intended to discriminate but, in fact, have a disproportionately negative effect on minorities **(disparate impact)**.

Writing for the 5–4 majority, Justice Anthony Kennedy said, "Fear of litigation alone cannot justify an employer's reliance on race to the detriment of individuals who passed the examinations and qualified for promotions." In dissent, Justice David Souter said a ruling against the city could leave employers in a "damned-if-you-do, damned-if-you-don't situation."

The case drew national attention because Justice Sonia Sotomayor had been a judge on the appellate court that affirmed the city's decision. Means and McDonald (2009, p. 21) point out: "Disparate treatment is relatively easy to recognize, and employers usually manage to avoid it. Ironically, it is this type of discrimination that New Haven ultimately committed in this case."

◀ **CASE IN BRIEF**

Ricci v. Destefano (2009)

ISSUE May a city reject results from a valid civil service exam when the results unintentionally prevent the promotion of minority candidates?

RULING No, but it depends on the facts. Before a city can intentionally discriminate to avoid a "disparate impact" on a protected trait (race, color, religion, national origin), the city must have a "strong basis in evidence" that it will be subject to "disparate impact liability" if it fails to take the discriminatory action. Here, the City of New Haven failed to do so.

summary judgment a request to the court to review the evidence and, without a trial, reach a decision to dismiss a case against the movant because there is no dispute of material fact that a jury need resolve

movant a party making a motion to the court

disparate treatment *intentional* acts of employment discrimination based on race, color, religion, sex, and national origin

disparate impact policies or practices that are not intended to discriminate but, in fact, have a disproportionately negative effect on minorities

CASE IN BRIEF

EEOC v. Abercrombie and Fitch (2015)

ISSUE Can an employer be liable under Title VII for refusing to hire an applicant based on a "religious observance and practice" only if the employer has actual knowledge that a religious accommodation was required and the employer's actual knowledge resulted from direct, explicit notice from the applicant?

RULING Yes. An employer may not make an applicant's religious practice, confirmed or otherwise, a factor in employment decisions. The applicant only needs to show that the need for an accommodation was a motivating factor in not being hired, not that the employer had knowledge of the need for an accommodation.

A recent case discussing disparate treatment is *EEOC v. Abercrombie and Fitch* (2015). In this case retailer Abercrombie and Fitch failed to hire Samantha Elauf, a Muslim who wears a hijab, stating that the wearing of a hijab violated the store's policy on not allowing employees to wear headwear. Elauf wore the hijab at her interview, but did not mention or indicate her need of an accommodation to the store's policy. She was otherwise qualified to be hired. This case discussed whether or not it was a violation of Title VII to fail to hire an applicant only if the employer has direct knowledge of the need for a religious accommodation. Justice Scalia, in the majority opinion, wrote: "Thus, the rule for disparate-treatment claims based on a failure to accommodate a religious practice is straightforward: An employer may not make an applicant's religious practice, confirmed or otherwise, a factor in employment decisions."

The Civil Rights Act, the Fair Housing Act, the Voting Rights Act, as well as other legislation and numerous court decisions have, on paper, outlawed discrimination in this nation. However, generations of attitudes and prejudices cannot be so easily changed. But because laws reflect desired social norms, movement toward equality continues.

Racial and Gender Equality in the Twenty-First Century

Understanding this nation's history helps explain why affirmative action programs first developed. In the 1990s, however, such programs found themselves increasingly challenged as unconstitutional. Today, the tide may again be slowly turning as a new Supreme Court bench emerges, with older justices retiring and new ones being appointed. Although some more recent decisions by the Court have supported affirmative action programs, others are holding them more accountable than in the past. In *Adarand Constructors v. Pena* (1995), an affirmative action program was upheld by only a narrow 5–4 vote. Both Justices Antonin Scalia and Clarence Thomas stated they were against affirmative action. The more recent appointments to the Court will undoubtedly take this issue in one direction or the other, although public sentiment seems to be turning against the concept. For example, the California Civil Rights Initiative (CCRI) forbidding the government to use ethnicity or gender as a criterion for either discriminating against or giving preferential treatment to any individual or group passed unanimously. In 1996, California voters banned affirmative action, as did the University of Texas.

Should affirmative action programs, even though they do treat some differently, continue? Senator Hubert Humphrey, the primary sponsor of the Civil Rights Act of 1964, contradicted the suggestion that the law would demand quotas and preferences based on race: "Title VII prohibits discrimination. In effect, it says that race, religion, and national origin are not to be used as the basis for hiring and firing. Title VII is designed to encourage hiring on the basis of ability and qualifications, not race or religion." But has this truly been the case, or has affirmative action pushed race and religion as a basis for employment? Justice O'Connor's statement in *Adarand Constructors* best states the Court's position now: "The unhappy persistence of both the practice and the lingering effects of racial discrimination against minority groups in this country is an unfortunate reality, and government is not disqualified from acting in response to it."

Other Forms of Discrimination

Religious discrimination has been addressed through various cases, including *Ansonia Board of Education v. Philbrook* (1986).

Discrimination against *people with disabilities* affects criminal justice in a number of ways, including who is hired (or not) and how the system treats those with disabilities. Most efforts to respond to issues of those with disabilities have come through legislation. Congress has responded with Title V of the Rehabilitation Act of 1973 and the Americans with Disabilities Act (ADA) of 1990, both of which seek to remove barriers encountered by those living with disabilities.

Criminal justice agencies have responded to legislation by improving accessibility, such as by installing wheelchair ramps, wider doors, and height-appropriate counters, as well as accommodations for the vision and hearing impaired. As criminal justice agencies seek to have their personnel be more reflective of the communities they serve, they have opened opportunities for employment to those with disabilities. Not everyone has the physical attributes needed to be, for example, a police officer. But those with disabilities can fill many other positions. All that is needed is a respect for the law requiring reasonable accommodations for those with disabilities. In many ways the criminal justice system has been more accommodating to those being arrested than to those who want to be a part of the criminal justice team.

The ADA also states that disabled persons may take part equally in public programs by local, state, or federal government agencies (Title II) but that there is no participation requirement if the person "poses a threat to the health or safety of others." This requires an individual assessment to determine the nature of the risk and whether policies could be modified to lessen the identified risk. The issue of how to respond to calls involving a person with mental illness was at the forefront of *City and County of San Francisco v. Sheehan* (2015). In this case, Sheehan, a woman diagnosed with mental illness, had brandished a knife and was threatening to kill her social worker. The police were called, and two officers entered Sheehan's room, where she grabbed the knife and threatened to kill the officers. The officers left the room, regrouped, and then re-entered in order to take Sheehan into custody. The officers again encountered Sheehan, who was still wielding the knife. After pepper spray failed to gain Sheehan's complaince, the officers shot her multiple times as she continued to advance on them.

Discrimination because of *sexual orientation* is a challenge for the criminal justice system regarding equal protection issues for victims, as well as how gay or lesbian criminal justice professionals are treated by their own agencies. The approach historically used by the American military was a "don't ask/don't tell" policy: Service people were not asked and did not have to tell, but they were discharged if their homosexuality was made public. This policy was held unconstitutional by a U.S. district court, and in September 2011 the policy was officially repealed. However, the criminal justice system has no such policy. Rather, those serving in this field are subject to the same laws pertaining to same-sex relationships but may also find themselves subject to the same discrimination as those who become victims of bias crimes.

◀ **CASE IN BRIEF**

City and County of San Francisco v. Sheehan (2015)

ISSUE Does the ADA require police officers to make accommodations for an armed, violent, and mentally ill person while attempting to take that person into custody?

RULING Unanswered. The Court did not answer this question, and left it open, because San Francisco appeared to have switched arguments as the case developed through the courts. The federal circuits remain divided on whether or not the ADA applies to arrests.

"Towns in Texas, Arizona Are Battlegrounds in Bathroom Debate"

By Paul J. Weber (*Associated Press*, May 26, 2016)

HARROLD, Texas (AP)—An unlikely battleground over whether public schools must allow transgender students to use the bathroom of their choice is taking shape in two tiny towns in Texas and Arizona, neither of which currently enrolls anyone who is transgender.

Eleven states suing the Obama administration claim that a new federal directive about transgender students thrusts "seismic changes" upon 100,000 schools nationwide. But only two districts joined the lawsuit—Harrold, a Texas farming town with 100 students and a 2016 graduating class of four, and the Heber-Overgaard Unified School District northeast of Phoenix, a conservative region where summer homes are popular.

The directive handed down this month says transgender students must be allowed to use bathrooms and locker rooms that match their gender identity. It is a theoretical scenario at best for Harrold and Heber-Overgaard, which together have roughly 550 students.

Kindergarteners and high school students in Harrold share 10 bathrooms in a single brick schoolhouse that is shorter than the football field, where the Harrold Hornets play six-man football because there are not enough players for 11. A few times a day, a train rumbles past the schoolhouse. Superintendent David Thweatt says "hobos" sometimes jump off and wander toward campus. Once, he said, a drifter holed up in a school bus and left a smell that took days to air out.

It's those sorts of strangers, Thweatt says, who could take advantage of bathroom rights for students who are transgender. Even the mere word made him fidget Wednesday while sitting in the teacher's lounge, where Thweatt is used to visiting with reporters. The district previously drew national attention when it encouraged teachers to carry handguns in the classroom.

"I don't agree with the term. Tell me, exactly, where that person fits into?" said Thweatt, 55, who is one of two dozen employees in the district. "If you're just saying, 'I feel like something else,' then that opens the door very widely. It's a slippery slope. What happens when someone says, 'I'm a 35-year-old, but I feel like a 15-year old?' We're going to say what you really are."

Suing the federal government, however, wasn't Harrold's idea.

Thweatt said Texas Attorney General Ken Paxton's office called him May 17, four days after U.S. Attorney General Loretta Lynch announced the directive, and said there was "no room in our schools for discrimination."

Thweatt said he thinks he got the call because someone in Paxton's office knew of him. Legal experts say a more likely reason was strategy: Harrold is near the Texas-Oklahoma border and within the northern Texas federal court district where the lawsuit was filed. The next stop would be the 5th U.S. Circuit Court of Appeals in New Orleans—one of the nation's most conservative benches.

"It's no accident this case was filed in Texas," said Carl Tobias, a law professor at the University of Richmond.

(*Continued*)

The lawsuit asks a judge to declare the directive unlawful, accusing the Obama administration of using powers reserved for Congress and conspiring "to turn workplaces and educational settings across the country into laboratories for a massive social experiment." Other states bringing the challenge are Oklahoma, Alabama, Wisconsin, West Virginia, Tennessee, Maine, Arizona, Louisiana, Utah and Georgia.

Asked why Harrold was chosen to join the lawsuit, Paxton spokesman Marc Rylander would say only that the Texas attorney general's office "engages with many concerned parents and school officials." The White House has declined to comment.

In Arizona, the Heber-Overgaard Unified School District has about 450 students in kindergarten through 12th grade. School officials defended their involvement as a matter of local control and not the socially divisive issue of transgender rights.

Opponents of the directive say school districts could lose federal education dollars if they don't comply, although federal officials have not explicitly made that threat.

Ron Tenney, superintendent of the Arizona district, called the risk of losing government money "kind of disturbing."

Harrold has previously enrolled openly gay students, Thweatt said, proudly adding that they were not bullied.

He said a transgender student would be welcome in the hallways, even though the school board passed a policy this week requiring students to choose the restroom based on their birth certificate. He said the timing was unrelated to the lawsuit filed just two days later.

"We're not mean. We're not awful. As a matter of fact, we can be friendlier and more accommodating than any other place, small schools," Thweatt said. "But our school is not just kids."

—Associated Press Writer Jamie Stengle in Dallas contributed to this report.

Sexual-orientation discrimination and same-sex marriage are issues that continue to garner attention on legislative floors and courtrooms, with changes occurring on both fronts so rapidly that attempts to provide current law are almost immediately outdated. Two such cases were recently argued before the Supreme Court, with decisions on both handed down on the same day. *Hollingsworth v. Perry* (2013) involved challenges to the constitutionality of California's Proposition 8, an amendment to that state's constitution, voted on and passed by popular vote. Proposition 8 stipulated, "Only marriage between a man and a woman is valid or recognized in California." However, the state still allowed "domestic partnerships" that gave same-sex couples the same rights and responsibilities as a heterosexual marriage.

The case began when two same-sex couples challenged Proposition 8 as unconstitutionally violating the Equal Protection Clause by defining marriage so as to exclude a certain class of people. When the state declined to defend the law in court, proponents of Proposition 8 stepped up instead. It was this issue of *standing* that captured the Court's attention—whether those who were defending the law in court had a legal right to do so (recall the discussion on standing in Chapter 2). On June 26, 2013, in a 5–4 decision, the Court vacated and remanded, with Chief Justice John Roberts stating, "We have never before upheld the standing of a private party to defend a state statute when state officials have chosen not to." Because the petitioners (those who were defending Proposition 8) had no legal standing—they were unable to demonstrate invasion or harm of a personal legal interest or that the

> **CASE IN BRIEF**
>
> *United States v. Windsor* (2013)
>
> **ISSUE** Does the Defense of Marriage Act's definition of marriage as being between a man and a woman deprive same-gender couples who are legally married under state law of their rights and violate the Equal Protection Clause?
>
> **RULING** Yes. The definition denies same-gender couples rights under federal law when marriages consisting of a man and a woman receive those rights.

> **CASE IN BRIEF**
>
> *Obergefell v. Hodges* (2015)
>
> **ISSUE** Does the Fourteenth Amendment require a State to license a marriage between two people of the same sex and to recognize a marriage between two people of the same sex when their marriage was lawfully licensed and performed out-of-State?
>
> **RULING** Yes. Marriage is a fundamental right inherent in the liberty of the person. Under the Due Process and Equal Protection Clauses of the Fourteenth Amendment, couples of the same sex may not be deprived of that right and that liberty, and they may exercise the fundamental right to marry.

outcome of the controversy would result in direct personal injury—the intermediate appellate court did not have standing to hear the case either, and their decision held no legal force. The Court's ruling, therefore, sent the case all the way back to the district court where the original decision that ruled Proposition 8 as unconstitutional stands, and where the injunction also stands.

Also decided on June 26, 2013, with similar results, was *United States v. Windsor* (2013), the Defense of Marriage Act (DOMA) case. DOMA was passed in 1996 and defined marriage as the union of one man and one woman for the purposes of federal law. However, in a 5–4 decision, the Court held that DOMA unconstitutionally discriminates against same-sex couples who are legally married according to the laws of the state in which they reside. Recognizing that the authority to regulate and define marriage rests with individual states, and noting that the respondent in this case held legal married status in a state that allowed same-sex couples to marry, the Court ruled that DOMA violates basic due process and equal protection principles and that same-sex couples who are legally married must be treated the same under federal law as married opposite-sex couples.

The Court went further in 2015 when, in *Obergefell v. Hodges*, it struck down state bans on same-sex marriages. The bans were those enacted by state law and voter initiatives, which defined marriage as being between a man and a woman. The Court said that marriage is a fundamental right that cannot be denied to a class of people (i.e., same-sex couples), setting the requirement that same-sex marriages be legally recognized in all 50 states.

Laws pertaining to *immigration* and *residency discrimination* are also currently in the throes of debate and change.

The Immigration Issue

"Give me your tired, your poor, Your huddled masses yearning to breathe free, The wretched refuse of your teeming shore, Send these, the homeless, tempest-tost to me, I lift my lamp beside the golden door!" are the immortal words of poet Emma Lazarus that appear at the base of the Statue of Liberty in New York. These words once reflected a welcoming philosophy of a country developed largely by immigrants.

Today, immigration issues challenge our past beliefs and some would say the future of the United States. After decades of rapid growth and reaching an all-time high of 12.2 million in 2007, the number of unauthorized immigrants in the United States has declined slightly and stabilized in recent years. In 2014 an estimated 11.3 immigrants were in the country illegally (Krogstad & Passel, 2015). These immigrants have become an increasing focus of controversy. The economy, possibly racism, and the September 11, 2001, attack on the United States, carried out by hijackers who entered the country on student or tourist visas, contribute to the changing political climate. Americans recognize the porous borders and lax enforcement of immigration laws as security threats, and in Congress, both parties have pushed for a tougher line.

In April 2006, hundreds of thousands of pro-immigration demonstrators mobilized on the National Mall in Washington, DC, and in scores of cities across the country, in a powerful display of grassroots muscle-flexing that organizers described as a "watershed moment," marking a coming-of-age for Latino political power in the United States. Statements from demonstrators included these: "We decided not to be invisible anymore," and "We deserve to be here. We work hard. We are immigrants, but we are not terrorists."

Courts have faced increasing struggles with constitutional interpretation. The Fifth and Fourteenth Amendments do not just protect *citizens* but use the broader term *persons*. The Supreme Court has stressed the text of the Fourteenth Amendment in striking down a number of state laws that differentiate between residents and nonresidents or between citizens and aliens.

The Supreme Court has held that whether people are considered legal or otherwise, government does not have a legitimate interest in denying certain services. Laws requiring a one-year waiting period before new legal residents could receive welfare benefits were struck down in *Shapiro v. Thompson* (1969). In *Plyler v. Doe* (1982), the Court held that a Texas law denying public education to children of illegal immigrants was unconstitutional. And in *Sugarman v. McDougall* (1973) and *Hampton v. Mow Sun Wong* (1976), the Court held that state and federal laws preventing aliens from being given civil service jobs were illegal.

Beginning around 2007, state legislatures increasingly began passing laws to deal with immigration. Resentment began rising over the increasing problem of illegal immigration and by the stalling of a broad immigration bill in the Senate in June 2007. That bill, the End Racial Profiling Act (ERPA) of 2007, was referred to committee in December 2007 and has remained there without any action. Nationwide, legislatures adopted measures to curb employment of unauthorized immigrants and to make it more difficult for them to obtain state identification documents such as driver's licenses. In October 2007, the Police Executive Research Forum (PERF) surveyed its members and, based on the concern shown over the immigration issue, conducted an "immigration summit" in November 2007, the results of which are published in *Police Chiefs and Sheriffs Speak Out on Local Immigration Enforcement* (PERF, 2008). Of those surveyed, 51 percent reported that the immigrant population in their jurisdiction had increased "substantially," by more than 10 percent (PERF, 2008, p. 8). Despite this growth, 71 percent of respondents said their jurisdiction did not have any policy, law, or mandate concerning enforcing immigration laws by local law enforcement (PERF, 2008, p. 11).

> The immigration issue is not one of those issues that remained hidden and then surfaced suddenly and unexpectedly. The immigration issue is a freight train that has been barrelling down the tracks toward us for some time, whistle blaring. Here's one example of what I mean by that: For more than a year, anyone who has been attending PERF's Town Hall Meetings, where police chiefs and other leaders are invited to speak out on any issue they choose, cannot help but have noticed that the immigration issue spontaneously becomes the hot-button issue whenever there is an open forum of police leaders....
>
> Some chiefs do not believe that local law enforcement agencies should spend much of their limited resources to take on what has essentially been the federal responsibility for illegal immigration enforcement in our communities. And many are concerned that tougher immigration enforcement on the local level will threaten the advances we have made in community policing over the last 20 years.

> Some chiefs and sheriffs point to facts and figures indicating that illegal immigrants commit a sizeable portion of their local crimes, and these police executives think they have no choice but to work as closely as they can with federal authorities to arrest, prosecute, incarcerate and eventually deport these offenders. For these chiefs, immigration enforcement is primarily a matter of local crime control and public safety. (Wexler, 2008, p. iii)

A recent Gallup Poll (May 18–22, 2016) asked the following open-ended question: "Regardless of who wins the election, what single issue or challenge are you most interested in having the next president address when he or she takes office next January?" The number one response was "the economy," followed by "immigration." "Terrorism" was ninth of the list (Gallup, 2016).

Another poll conducted by Rasmussen Reports found higher public support for stricter border control versus granting legal status to immigrants who are already in this country illegally. The majority of poll respondents thought that providing a pathway to citizenship for those who are already in this country illegally would only encourage more illegal immigration, compounding a problem that has persisted due to current U.S. policies and practices that do little to discourage people from illegally entering the country. Nearly three-fourths (72%) of surveyed adults believe the federal government is not being aggressive enough in tracking down and sending home individuals who have overstayed their visas (Rasmussen Reports, 2016).

Although the public clearly has concerns about illegal immigration and wants the "government" to control the borders and deal with the millions of illegal immigrants, the question becomes *How*?

Several challenges face law enforcement agencies in jurisdictions with large immigrant populations, including:

- Large numbers of people who do not speak English well (or at all).
- Immigrants' reluctance to report crime.
- Fear of police.
- Effects of federal law enforcement actions.
- Confusion over whether and to what extent local police enforce immigration laws.
- Misunderstandings based on cultural differences.
- Personal interaction between immigrants and police officers that damage good will and trust (Lysakowski, Pearsall, & Pope, 2009, p. 3).

To meet these challenges, Congress authorized the Illegal Immigration Reform and Immigrant Responsibility Act of 1996, which amended the Immigration and Nationality Act by adding section 287(g).

287(g) Section 287(g) was intended to strengthen immigration enforcement efforts by allowing local law enforcement agencies to partner with the Department of Homeland Security's (DHS) Immigration and Customs Enforcement (ICE) through Memorandums of Agreement (MOAs) authorizing local police to function as immigration officers. The program grew quickly, and by February 2009, 950 law enforcement officers in 23 states had been trained by U.S. ICE agents. The program, however, was widely criticized by civil liberties groups, Hispanic citizens, and congressional auditors with claims that the program promoted racial profiling ("Government's 287(g) Program Criticized in Hearings in House," 2009, pp. 5–7).

Despite efforts to quell critics by standardizing MOAs used to enter into 287(g) partnerships, persistent reports of police and ICE noncompliance gradually led to the scaling back and re-evaluation of the program. At the end of 2012, ICE announced it would not be renewing any of its agreements with state and local law enforcement agencies operating under the 287(g) program. Instead, it would be placing new focus on its Secure Communities initiative.

Secure Communities Secure Communities was a tool that used an already established federal information-sharing partnership between ICE and the FBI to identify "removable aliens" or immigration violators who had been arrested and booked for a criminal offense. Assessment of the program noted its success in facilitating ICE's ability to identify and remove criminal aliens: "Between October 2008 and the end of fiscal year 2011, the number of convicted criminals that ICE removed from the United States increased 89 percent, while the number of other aliens removed dropped by 29 percent. These trends are due in significant part to the implementation and expansion of Secure Communities" (Office of the Director, 2012, p. 18).

Priority Enforcement Program Secure Communities was replaced in July 2015 by the Priority Enforcement Program (PEP) as the result of a November 2014 executive order and DHS Secretary Jeh Johnson's memorandum, which is the heart of the *United States v. Texas* lawsuit (discussed shortly). Table 4.1 compares how Secure Communities and PEP differ.

The 2010 Arizona Immigration Law Backing up a few years before the creation of Secure Communities and its eventual replacement by PEP, citizens in some communities and states were growing increasingly dissatisfied with the way the immigration issue was being handled, with many asserting that the federal government was not doing all they could, and should, to tackle the problem of illegal immigration. This tension came to a head in April 2010, when Arizona passed a law criminalizing illegal immigration. The law, Arizona S.B. 1070, made Arizona the first state to criminalize illegal immigration by defining it as trespassing, spelling out that police may not "solely consider race, color, or national origin" in questioning people about their immigration status (Markon & Kornblut, 2010, p. A03). The law requires officers, while enforcing other laws, to check a person's immigration status if there's a reasonable suspicion that the person is here illegally. It also bans people from blocking traffic when they seek or offer day-labor services on streets and prohibits illegal immigrants from soliciting work in public places.

Despite the seemingly widespread public support for the controversial legislation, in July 2010 the U.S. Justice Department filed a lawsuit challenging the constitutionality of Arizona's new law. Such a lawsuit had been hinted at since May 2010, when then-Attorney General Eric Holder told ABC's *This Week* program he was concerned that "you'll end up in a situation where people are racially profiled, and that could lead to a wedge drawn between certain communities and law enforcement, which leads to the problem of people in those communities not willing to interact with people in law enforcement, not willing to share information, not willing to be witnesses where law enforcement needs them" (CNN Wire Staff, 2010).

Table 4.1 Comparison of Secure Communities and Priority Enforcement Program

Secure Communities	Priority Enforcement Program
Relied on fingerprint-based biometric data submitted during bookings by state and local law enforcement agencies to the FBI for criminal background checks.	Continues to rely on fingerprint-based biometric data submitted during bookings by state and local law enforcement agencies to the FBI for criminal background checks.
Prior to December 21, 2012, the only policy limitations on detainer issuance were that (1) a law enforcement agency (LEA) had exercised its independent authority to arrest the individual and (2) the immigration officer had reason to believe that the individual was subject to ICE detention for removal or removal proceedings. Circumstances under which a detainer could be issued were narrowed by a December 12, 2012 policy memorandum, but still included individuals charged, but not yet convicted, of criminal offenses, in addition to individuals with no criminal history, such as individuals with final orders of removal from an immigration judge. Detainers could also be issued in circumstances in which ICE determined an individual posed a significant risk to national security, border security, or public safety.	A November 20, 2014 memorandum from DHS Secretary Jeh Johnson significantly narrows the category of individuals for whom DHS will seek transfer from LEA custody and prioritizes individuals who pose a threat to public safety. Under PEP, ICE will no longer seek transfer of individuals with civil immigration offenses alone, or those charged, but not convicted of criminal offenses. Instead, ICE will seek transfer where a removable individual has been convicted of specifically enumerated crimes, has intentionally participated in criminal gang activity, or poses a danger to national security.
Requested that LEAs detain an individual beyond his or her scheduled release date.	In many cases, ICE will simply request notification of when an individual who falls within the PEP priorities is to be released—rather than issue a request for detention beyond that point. Under PEP, detainers may only be issued in limited circumstances, when ICE indicates on the form that the individual is both a PEP enforcement priority and that there is probable cause to believe that the subject is removable (such as a final order of removal).
Detainer form **requested** that LEA provide a copy to the individual subject to the detainer.	Detainer form **requires** that LEA provide a copy to the individual subject to the detainer **in order for the request to be effective**.
Request to maintain custody was limited to 48 hours, excluding Saturdays, Sundays, and holidays.	Request to maintain custody is limited to 48 hours. Saturdays, Sundays, and holidays are no longer excluded.
Basis for "reason to believe" the subject was removable, and therefore subject to a request for detention, was not disclosed on the detainer form.	Detainer form requires that the basis for "probable cause" that an individual is removable be indicated: ■ final order of removal; ■ pendency of removal proceedings; ■ biometric match reflecting no lawful status or otherwise removable; or ■ statements by the subject to an immigration officer and/or other reliable evidence.
Some ICE detainers were issued with respect to foreign-born individuals who did not have records or a biometric match in ICE databases without any other additional information.	ICE no longer issues detainers in cases of foreign-born individuals who do not have records or a biometric match in ICE databases, without any other additional information. Detainers must include an indication of probable cause and that the individual is an enforcement priority under PEP.

Source: U.S. Immigration and Customs Enforcement. (n.d.). "How Is PEP Different from Secure Communities?" Washington, DC: Author. Retrieved June 28, 2016 from https://www.ice.gov/pep

preemption federal law supersedes state law; if a state law stands as an obstacle to the purposes, objectives, and execution of the federal law, the Supremacy Clause preempts the state law

The key difference between the federal law and the Arizona law is that the federal government wants to focus on the most dangerous immigrants: gang members, drug traffickers, and threats to national security, leaving alone those law-abiding immigrants without documentation (Christie, 2010). What started as a civil rights issue has become an issue of federal versus states' rights, with the lawsuit contending: "In our constitutional system, the federal government has preeminent authority to regulate immigration matters. This authority derives from the U.S. Constitution and numerous acts of Congress." Thus, at the heart of the matter is the concept of **preemption**, meaning if a state law stands as an obstacle to the purposes, objectives, and execution of the federal law, the Supremacy Clause *preempts* the state law. This may occur even if the state law is generally compatible with federal law. Although it is generally presumed that Congress, acting through federal law, does not intend to interfere with the police powers of a state, under the Supremacy Clause, the Court said in *Gibbons v. Ogden* (1824) that laws made by Congress under the Constitution are superior to state laws that conflict or interfere with the act. Consequently, as specifically noted in the lawsuit (see www.justice.gov/opa/documents/az-complaint.pdf, 2010, pp. 23–24), the federal government has based its suit against Arizona on (1) violation of the Supremacy Clause, (2) preemption under federal law, and (3) violation of the Commerce Clause.

The Arizona law was challenged by the federal government as unconstitutional on the theory that the state was intruding on the federal government's superior power to enforce federal immigration laws, and this is the basis for the Court's decision. On June 25, 2012, the Court voted 5–3 (Kagan recused) in *Arizona v. United States* to invalidate three of the four provisions of S.B. 1070 because they either operated in areas solely controlled by federal policy or they interfered with federal enforcement efforts. Invalidated were the sections:

- making it a crime to be in Arizona without legal papers,
- making it a crime to apply for or get a job in the state,
- allowing police to arrest individuals who had committed crimes that could lead to their deportation.

The Court left intact, but subject to later challenges in lower courts, a provision requiring police to arrest and hold anyone they believe has committed a crime and whom they think is in the country illegally and to hold them until their immigration status could be checked with federal officials.

Immigration Law Continues to Evolve Courts have repeatedly upheld that the regulation of immigration and related enforcement responsibilities are federal matters (Dwyer, 2010). Guidance on this issue is provided by two U.S. Supreme Court decisions. In *United States v. Brignoni-Ponce* (1975) the Court ruled that police officers must have probable cause to arrest individuals for immigration enforcement purposes, and in *De Canas v. Bica* (1976) the Court held that any local statute directed at regulating immigration is a violation of the Supremacy Clause: "State involvement in this area, except as specifically allowed under federal law (such as 287g programs) is preempted by the supremacy clause to the U.S. Constitution. The crux of the judge's decision rests on the burden the law would place on *legal* resident aliens who may be unconstitutionally held as a result of this law" (Dwyer, 2010).

On April 18, 2016 the Supreme Court heard oral arguments in *United States v. Texas* (2016), a case that challenged President Obama's November 20, 2014 executive order and a co-occurring memorandum issued by DHS Secretary Johnson, in which Johnson directed his subordinates to establish a process for considering deferred action for certain aliens who have lived in the United States for five years and who either came here as children or already have children who are U.S. citizens or permanent residents. In *United States v. Texas*, the Court was faced with several questions, one of which was whether the President violated the Constitution by not carrying out federal immigration laws "faithfully," as written in the Take Care Clause. The focus of the case is the 2014 "Deferred Action for Parents of Americans and Lawful Permanent Residents" (DAPA). This program would allow parents of children who are citizens or permanent resident as of November 2014, and have been in the United States themselves since November 2014, to be lawfully present in the country for three years and, during that time, be eligible for benefits, such as Medicare and Social Security.

Texas and 25 other states filed a lawsuit in a Texas Federal District Court to enjoin the DAPA program. The district court ruled in favor of the states, and the 5th Circuit upheld that decision. These rulings by both courts were not based on the constitutional issue of the Take Care Clause but were, instead, based on violation of the Administrative Procedure Act (APA) because DAPA had not been put through the notice and comment process mandated by the APA. In addition the 5th Circuit ruled that the President had exceeded his authority in issuing the executive order. What these rulings mean is that DAPA cannot be instituted anywhere in the nation until a trial on the merits has occurred, unless the Supreme Court overrules the 5th Circuit and blocks the issuance of the temporary order. The Obama administration appealed, seeking a removal of the district court order to allow the program to take affect and be administered until a trial can occur. The Supreme Court affirmed the lower court's ruling in a nine-word *per curiam* opinion, "The judgment is affirmed by an equally divided Court." Thus, the injunction will stay in place until a trial can occur and a ruling is made. The future of this case is uncertain; it may appear before the court again, or it may "die" with a new administration.

An important sidebar from this case is that the Federal District Judge, Judge Hanen, found serious ethical violations by the attorneys for the Justice Department when the case was heard in his courtroom. While the attorneys had been assuring the judge that the government was not taking steps to implement the program while the case was before him, it was later revealed that the attorneys were, in fact, aware that measures were underway to implement the program.

Attitudes change, and so does the law. Where barriers once did not exist, lines have been drawn. As the Court and all of society struggle with how to combine the richness that immigration has contributed to the United States with challenges brought on by changes over the past two centuries, the future cannot help but reflect our past. And this past reflects, in the words of the Pledge of Allegiance, *"one nation . . . with liberty and justice for all."* As this text goes to press, the controversy continues.

Equal Protection in the Criminal Justice System

disparity a difference, but one that does not necessarily involve discrimination

LO7 *Disparity results from differences based on legal factors, such as the seriousness of a crime, an offender's prior criminal record, and whether any aggravating or mitigating circumstances exist. Discrimination results when extralegal factors, such as race, ethnicity, gender, social class, and lifestyle, are used by criminal justice officials as the basis for decisions.*

When examining the question of whether there is discrimination in the criminal justice system, it is important to distinguish discrimination from disparity: **"Disparity** refers to a difference, but one that does not necessarily involve discrimination" (Walker, Spohn, & DeLone, 2012, p. 26). Differences leading to disparity can be explained by *legal factors* related to an individual's actions, including the seriousness of the offence, aggravating or mitigating circumstances, or prior criminal record. *Extralegal factors* include race, ethnicity, gender, social class, and lifestyle, factors that are *not* legitimate bases for decisions by criminal justice officials because these factors do not relate to a person's criminal behavior. Using any of these extralegal factors as the basis for action results in *discrimination*, "differential treatment of groups without reference to an individual's behavior or qualifications" (Walker et al., 2012, p. 27). The degree and prevalence of discriminatory treatment within the criminal justice system can be thought of as existing along a continuum between the extremes of pure justice and systematic discrimination, as illustrated in Figure 4.2.

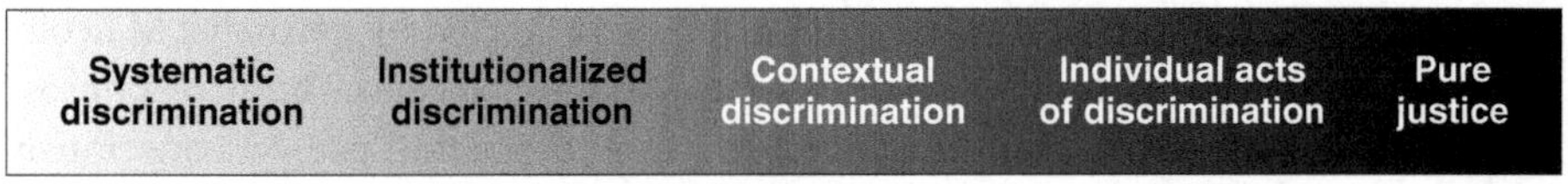

| Systematic discrimination | Institutionalized discrimination | Contextual discrimination | Individual acts of discrimination | Pure justice |

Figure 4.2 Discrimination Disparity Continuum
Source: WALKER, et al. *The Color of Justice: Race, Ethnicity and Crime in America*, 5E, p. 26. © 2012 Wadsworth, a part of Cengage Learning, Inc.

At one extreme is pure justice, describing treatment in which no degree of racial or ethnic discrimination occurs at any point or time in the criminal justice process. At the other extreme is systematic discrimination, in which discrimination is pervasive in every aspect of the criminal justice system. Walker et al. (2012, p. 274) suggest that, based on a review of research, the U.S. criminal justice system falls in the middle on the continuum, characterized by **contextual discrimination**, that is, discrimination that occurs in certain parts of the justice system but not necessarily all parts all the time: "Discrimination . . . is confined to certain types of cases, certain types of settings, and certain types of defendants." Whatever it is called, the fact remains that minorities are disproportionately represented in all three components of the criminal justice system: number of arrests by law enforcement, number of minorities going to court, and number of minorities incarcerated.

contextual discrimination describes a situation in which racial minorities are treated more harshly at some points and in some places in the criminal justice system but no differently than whites at other points and in other places

Of increasing concern is the disproportionate minority contact (DMC) with minority youths in the juvenile justice system. The Juvenile Justice and Delinquency Prevention Act of 2002 provides that if a state fails to address the overrepresentation of minority youths in the juvenile justice system, the Office of Juvenile Justice and Delinquency Prevention (OJJDP) may withhold 20 percent of the state's formula grant allocation for the following year. The Act also expanded the requirement to include disproportionality at all points in the juvenile justice system (Solar & Garry, 2009).

Discrimination in Law Enforcement

Considering the wide amount of discretion granted to police officers, it follows that those in law enforcement may be accused of discrimination, whether on the basis of age, gender, or race. Discretion allows officers to treat different people differently. For example, some officers are harder on minorities, men, or juveniles. This may be seen as discrimination and, in fact, sometimes is. This may also be conscious or unconscious discrimination.

Unconscious or **implicit bias** is the unintentional, subconscious, and automatic sorting and processing of information by the brain which, when combined with a person's history and cultural influences, leads to the formation of associations among groups of people and stereotypes about those groups. These automatic associations influence behavior and can make people respond in biased ways even when they hold no explicit prejudices (National Initiative for Building Community Trust and Justice, 2015). Decades of research in neurology and social and cognitive psychology support the conclusion that all people, even those who are well-intentioned and unequivocally reject bigotry, possess implicit biases based simply on exposure to or insulation from the social world around them.

implicit bias the unintentional, subconscious, and automatic sorting and processing of information by the brain which, when combined with a person's history and cultural influences, leads to the formation of associations among groups of people and stereotypes about those groups

On one level, the human brain operates on an implicit system designed to be "reactive rather than reasoned." This "thinking without thinking" allows for quick generalizations and mental shortcuts, a phenomenon labeled by journalist Malcolm Gladwell as "blink." Biases that are unconscious or implicit cause "blink responses" that influence a person's choices and behaviors without that person consciously thinking or deciding to act a certain way (Fridell, 2011).

Although implicit bias is part of human nature, it is also malleable and can be changed. Training is now being conducted by police departments across the country to educate officers about their own implicit biases, how such biases impact their decisions, and how biased associations can be unlearned and replaced with nonbiased ones. Initiatives to achieve fair and impartial policing (FIP) posit that through training and policy review, officers can be taught how to identify their "blink responses" and pause their decision making long enough to form a reasoned, rather than reactive, response (Dasgupta, 2013). Based on the science of bias, the FIP perspective reflects a new way to approach the issue of biased policing and reveals that it is not, as many argue, caused by widespread racism in policing but is instead a manifestation of subconscious biases that can impact the perceptions and behavior of even well-intentioned people, including police officers (Fridell, 2015).

The most frequently alleged form of discrimination by the police is racial discrimination. Some argue that minority overrepresentation in the criminal justice system begins with law enforcement and the discriminatory attitudes and practices some officers apply toward members of racial and ethnic groups. In fact, officers themselves admit that a citizen's race and socioeconomic status can lead to unequal treatment and even unwarranted physical force by the police. The contention that police single out subjects solely on the basis of the color of their skin frequently leads to allegations of racial profiling. **Racial profiling** can be defined as the practice of relying "to any degree on race, ethnicity, national origin, or religion in selecting which individual to subject to routine or spontaneous investigatory activities or in deciding upon the scope and substance of law enforcement activity following the investigatory procedure" ("Racial Profiling Prohibition Will Be Debated in Congress," 2007, p. 3). Such an event may be called "DWB" (driving while black), "DWA" (driving while Asian), or "DWM" (driving while Mexican). Regardless of the acronym used, the event signals the unethical and illegal practice of racial profiling.

The Equal Protection Clause of the Fourteenth Amendment to the Constitution applies to racial profiling. Race-based enforcement of the law is illegal. However, the exact prevalence of the problem remains unclear because research findings thus far lack consensus on the extensiveness of discrimination in police stops, searches, and arrests. To help present a more complete picture, many agencies now require the collection of additional racial data about drivers and passengers involved in traffic stops.

Several research studies on what appears to be racial profiling have possible explanations for its existence other than discrimination. One study of traffic stops at both the macrolevel (whole department) and microlevel (individual officers) found that both levels confirmed racial *disparity* in the frequency of traffic stops as well as the police treatment (Roh & Robinson, 2009). The likelihood of being subjected to unfavorable police treatment was greater in beats where more blacks or Hispanics resided or more police were deployed. The spatial analysis at the macrolevel found

racial profiling the process of using certain racial characteristics, such as skin color, as indicators of criminal activity

Constitutional Law in ACTION

It was 2 A.M. and Officers Baylor and Breen were on patrol in an area of town where the resident population was predominantly African American. They drove past a parked car occupied by a white male driver and a black female passenger, and Officer Baylor mumbled, "That guy doesn't belong here." However, being white in a black neighborhood is not illegal and certainly is not enough to warrant any immediate action. So the officers decided they would simply stop and observe for a few minutes.

As the officers were turning their squad around, the passenger in the parked car got out and walked away from the vehicle. The driver pulled the car away from the curb but did not turn his headlights on. The officers followed. The driver continued for several blocks before turning on the headlights.

The officers decided to make a traffic stop on the car and driver to see what he was doing in that neighborhood, so they drove up close behind the car and activated their emergency lights. The driver pulled over and parked at the curb.

Officer Breen approached the driver, who immediately blurted out, "You are just stopping me 'cuz I am White!" During that brief moment, Officer Breen recognized a strong odor of marijuana. The driver was later arrested after several kilograms of marijuana were found under the backseat.

The driver later tried to suppress the evidence, claiming there was no reason for the traffic stop other than his race, a claim supported by the fact that the squad camera recorded Officer Baylor's previous statement. The camera also, however, recorded the fact that the driver went several blocks without his headlights on.

- *In your opinion, is the traffic stop constitutional? Why?*
- *What are the objective facts in this scenario?*
- *Should objective facts be given more weight than subjective facts?*

(The legality of traffic stops will be covered in detail in Chapter 8. Keep this scenario in mind.)

---

that the areas with more frequent stops and more adverse stop outcomes were spatially clustered rather than dispersed, and the majority of the clusters spatially coincided with minority residential areas or police resource concentration areas, likely the result of policing "hot spots" (Roh & Robinson, 2009).

Another study used data from a New Jersey Turnpike Speeding Survey and found that black drivers, young drivers, and male drivers were all more likely to speed at high rates (15 mph or more above the speed limit) in 65 mph speed zones than were non-black drivers, older drivers, and female drivers. However, "More research is needed to determine whether traffic stops for Driving While Black are in small part the result of Speeding While Black" (Lundman & Kowalski, 2009, p. 504).

Many criminal justice professionals suggest that a distinction should be made between profiling as a legitimate policing technique and the politically charged term *racial profiling*. Refer to *racially biased policing* instead.

MYTH
Race can never be considered by law enforcement when deciding on a course of action.

FACT
Race is a legitimate and easy way to include or eliminate a person as a suspect quickly. It is a useful tool and exists as one descriptive factor among many, but it may never be used as the sole basis for a police encounter.

It is possible that criminal justice practitioners may encounter allegations of other forms of discrimination as well, sometimes even personally. The Court dealt with *age discrimination* in *Massachusetts Board of Retirement v. Murgia* (1976) by upholding a state law that prohibited uniformed police officers from working beyond the age of 50. The Americans with Disabilities Act of 1990, along with other legislation and case law, seeks to address *disabilities discrimination*.

A developing area of discrimination law affecting police officers deals with pregnancy policies. Acknowledging the importance of recruiting and retaining women to serve in law enforcement, policies are needed that support families and parenting without negatively affecting police operations (Kruger, 2006). The Federal Pregnancy Discrimination Act of 1978 and a series of developing court holdings are cited as sources for this developing area of law.

Discrimination in the Courts

Discrimination also exists in some courts. Even before a defendant appears for trial, discrimination in the jury selection process may negatively affect the outcome of the case.

After the Civil War ended, the Equal Protection Clause of the Fourteenth Amendment was used as a legal tool to abolish statutes excluding African Americans from jury selection. In 1880, the Supreme Court cited the Equal Protection Clause in *Strauder v. West Virginia* (1880) when it struck down a statute explicitly prohibiting African Americans from serving on juries. To get around such rulings and continue excluding racial minorities from jury duty, some states passed new laws requiring all jury members to be landholders or pay real estate taxes. Although such laws appeared race and gender neutral and not overtly discriminating, only white males actually met these criteria.

Not until 1935, in *Norris v. Alabama*, did the Court acknowledge that virtual exclusion of African Americans from juries constituted an equal protection violation. Nonetheless, little effort was made to correct the discrepancies, and African Americans remained noticeably underrepresented on juries, particularly in the South. Even during the civil rights revolution of the 1950s and 1960s, the Supreme Court did not extend its desegregation rulings to the subject of juries. Consequently, in *Swain v. Alabama* (1965), the Court found no equal protection violations in a county where 26 percent of eligible voters were black, yet only 10 to 15 percent of the jury panels were black. The Court denied that such a statistical pattern precluded a fair jury-selection process, stating, "Neither the jury roll nor the venire need be a perfect mirror of the community or accurately reflect the proportionate strength of every identifiable group."

The Court, however, reversed its position in *Batson v. Kentucky* (1986), when it ruled the use of peremptory challenges to deliberately produce a racially unbalanced jury was unconstitutional. In *Batson*, the defendant was African American, and the prosecutor in the first trial used the state's peremptory challenges to remove all four prospective black jurors, leaving an all-white jury that ultimately convicted Batson. The conviction was upheld by the Kentucky Supreme Court, but the U.S. Supreme Court overturned the lower courts' rulings:

> The State's privilege to strike individual jurors through peremptory challenges is subject to the command of the Equal Protection Clause. Although a prosecutor ordinarily is entitled to exercise peremptory challenges "for any reason at all, as long as that reason

CASE IN BRIEF ▶

Strauder v. West Virginia (1880)

ISSUE Does West Virginia's state law that allows only whites to serve on a jury violate the Equal Protection Clause?

ISSUE Yes. Denying a person the ability to participate in the administration of justice solely on the basis of race violates the guarantees of the Fourteenth Amendment.

is related to his view concerning the outcome" of the case to be tried....The Equal Protection Clause forbids the prosecutor to challenge potential jurors solely on account of their race or on the assumption that Black jurors as a group will be unable impartially to consider the State's case against a Black defendant.

The Court extended the *Batson* ruling in *J.E.B. v. Alabama* (1994), when it held that gender, as with race, could not be used as a proxy for juror competence. In this case, the state of Alabama, on behalf of a minor child's mother, filed a complaint for paternity and child support. A jury pool of 36 potential jurors was assembled—12 males and 24 females. Two jurors were removed for cause, and peremptory challenges used by both sides removed 18 more. The result was an all-female jury, who found the petitioner to be the child's father. The father appealed. The Supreme Court upheld the petitioner's challenge, stating, "Equal opportunity to participate in the fair administration of justice is fundamental to our democratic system. It not only furthers the goals of the jury system. It reaffirms the promise of equality under the law—that all citizens, regardless of race, ethnicity, or gender, have the chance to take part directly in our democracy. When persons are excluded from participation in our democratic processes solely because of race or gender, this promise of equality dims, and the integrity of our judicial system is jeopardized." In sum, the Equal Protection Clause prohibits discrimination in jury selection on the basis of race or gender.

Just as discrimination can affect court proceedings before a trial, it can also affect the stage after trial—sentencing. Prosecutorial discretion may also contribute to sentencing disparity. A common tactic used by prosecutors to secure a guilty plea is to offer the defendant a lesser charge. Consequently, the sentence received is based on the charges brought, not necessarily on the act committed.

It should come as no surprise then that great variation exists among the sentences received by offenders convicted of the same offense. In an effort to standardize sentencing and eliminate disparity, many state and federal sentencing guidelines have been established. In 1984, Congress passed the Sentencing Reform Act (SRA), the purpose of which was to achieve honesty, uniformity, and proportionality in sentencing.

Numerous studies have documented sentencing disparities among various races of offenders, with some of the disparity attributed not to the race of the defendant but, rather, to that of the victim. One well-known study found that defendants charged with murdering white victims were 4.3 times as likely to receive a death sentence as were defendants charged with killing blacks (Baldus, Woodworth, & Pulaski, 1990). This result was later used by Warren McClesky, a black man sentenced to death after being convicted of armed robbery and the murder of a white police officer in Georgia. McClesky claimed the state's capital-sentencing process operated to deny him equal protection of the laws in violation of the Fourteenth Amendment. In *McClesky v. Kemp* (1987), however, the Supreme Court found no evidence of such racial discrimination and affirmed the judgments of the lower courts:

> For this claim to prevail, McClesky would have to prove that the Georgia Legislature enacted or maintained the death penalty statute because of an anticipated racially discriminatory effect. In *Gregg v. Georgia* (1976), this Court found that the Georgia capital sentencing system could operate in a fair and neutral manner. There was no evidence then, and there is none now, that the Georgia Legislature enacted the capital punishment statute to further a racially discriminatory purpose.

Eliminating racial discrimination was the major goal of the sentencing guidelines movement that started in the 1970s. Today, according to a study by the National Center for State Courts, such sentencing guidelines have effectively reduced the negative impacts of extralegal factors, such as offender race, gender, and socioeconomic status, on the sentences handed down for criminal offenses (Ostrom, Ostrom, Hanson, & Klieman, 2008).

In July 2010 Congress passed a bill that changed a quarter-century-old law subjecting tens of thousands of blacks to long prison terms for crack cocaine convictions while treating those caught with the powder form of the drug, mainly whites, with far more lenient sentences. The bill modifies a 1986 law passed when crack cocaine use was rampant and considered a particularly violent drug and that allowed a person convicted of crack cocaine possession to receive the same mandatory prison term as someone convicted of possessing 100 times the amount of powder cocaine. The new legislation reduces the 100–1 ratio to about 18–1 and eliminates the 5-year mandatory minimum for the first-time possession of crack.

Senator Patrick Leahy from Vermont praised the vote: "These disproportionate punishments have had a disparate impact on minority communities. This is unjust and runs contrary to our fundamental principles of equal justice under the law." However, Representative Lamar Smith from Texas warned that the legislation "could expose our neighborhoods to the same violence and addiction that caused Congress to act in the first place" because crack cocaine is often associated with a greater degree of violence than other drugs (Frieden, 2010).

Whatever sentencing decisions are made by the courts, the corrections system must then execute. Consequently, any disparity or discrimination generated at the court stage is inherited by corrections.

Discrimination in Corrections

What has been termed the *due process revolution* that emerged during the politically tumultuous 1960s and 1970s affected every area of the law. In addition to the civil rights movement, the plight of groups who had been in many ways ignored by the Bill of Rights—for example, children—gained national attention. The field of corrections changed forever in 1968, when, thanks to television and the media, many Americans had their first look inside prisons. And they were horrified.

The Attica Prison riot, followed by the New Mexico Penitentiary riot and a host of other uprisings in American correctional facilities, shocked the public. The deplorable conditions that spawned much unrest by inmates and the way law enforcement and correctional personnel were treating inmates reversed roles and made the government look like the criminals. Like every other segment of society in the United States during that period, corrections and the prison system were facing vast changes, including the unprecedented granting of rights to prisoners. And with more than 2 million people now incarcerated, prisoners' rights continue to greatly affect the judicial system.

Perhaps because few Americans ever saw what prison life was actually like, and maybe did not care, the plight of inmates was long ignored. However, once Americans learned of the atrocities happening in U.S. correctional institutions, they recognized the need for due process there as well.

It comes as a surprise to many that prisoners have any rights at all. Historically, they had few or none. Once people were remanded to a correctional facility, what happened to them seemed to be of little concern:

> During his term of service in the penitentiary, he is in a state of penal servitude to the State. He has, as a consequence of his crime, not only forfeited his liberty, but all his personal rights except those which the law in its humanity accords him. He is for the time being the slave of the State. He is civiliter mortuus; and his estate, if he has any, is administered like that of a dead man. (*Ruffin v. Commonwealth*, 1871)

The judiciary of that time also believed separation of government prevented them from interfering with executive agencies. From the 1820s through the early 1940s, prison administrators were essentially sovereign, enjoying enormous power and little accountability. In the 1940s, however, the attitude in the United States toward corrections began to change as a move toward rehabilitation, rather than strictly punishment, emerged. In *Ex parte Hull* (1941), one of the formative cases affecting the prisoner's rights movement, the Supreme Court acknowledged that even prisoners had rights and that the previous and routine practice of censoring and discarding prisoners' legal petitions to courts was unconstitutional. The Court also held, not totally dissimilar to the holding in *Marbury v. Madison* (1803), that court officials, not correctional officials, held the decision-making authority regarding what rights prisoners had.

The Court further ruled, in *Cooper v. Pate* (1964), that inmates could sue the warden for depriving them of their constitutional rights under Section 1983 of the U.S. Code, thereby opening the door for inmates to seek legal redress in court. And although there was a brief flurry of frivolous lawsuits filed by prisoners (one inmate claimed his religion forbade him from eating "pungent" foods, such as anything cooked with onions or garlic), and such frivolities still continue, although to a lesser extent, the system sought a balance, reflected in the cases discussed in subsequent chapters.

It is important to differentiate between privileges and rights of inmates, and this is where the public gets confused. A **right** is a legally protected claim, whereas a **privilege** is not necessarily legally protected.

Although there are different theories on what privileges benefit prisoners or prisons (e.g., television may be seen by the public as an unnecessary privilege, whereas corrections officials view it as a way to keep inmates occupied and to prevent moral and behavioral problems resulting from total boredom), these should not be confused with rights all Americans, even those incarcerated, have under the Constitution.

For prisoners, cases based on Fourteenth Amendment rights involve equal protection on the basis of race, gender, and the availability of facilities and services. Correctional facilities are required by the Americans with Disabilities Act (ADA) to provide special accommodations, programming, and services to disabled inmates. The ADA gives inmates with disabilities legal leverage in obtaining special benefits. Not providing adequate services may lead to expensive, time-consuming lawsuits. For example, sign language interpreters are usually required for hearing-impaired inmates.

MYTH
Prisoners, by virtue of their incarceration, relinquish all constitutional rights.

FACT
Although prisoners do not have full constitutional rights, they do retain some, including:

- the Eighth Amendment's protection against cruel and unusual punishment
- the Fourteenth Amendment's due process right to access to court and administrative appeals
- the protection against unequal treatment on the basis of race, sex, and creed, according to the Equal Protection Clause of the Fourteenth Amendment
- limited First Amendment rights to speech and religion

right a legally protected claim

privilege a claim that is not legally protected

CASE IN BRIEF

Wolff v. McDonnell (1974)

ISSUE Are disciplinary hearings in the Nebraska state prison system required to include due process protections?

ISSUE Yes. The Supreme Court held that although prisoners are not entitled to full due process protections, disciplinary proceedings must include (1) written notice to the inmate of the charges, (2) a written statement of evidence, and (3) the opportunity for an inmate to call witnesses and present evidence.

Disciplinary Hearings The Fourteenth Amendment also covers due process rights during disciplinary hearings. *Wolff v. McDonnell* (1974) involved the claim that Nebraska's disciplinary procedures, particularly those relating to loss of good time (credited reduction in time served on a sentence because of an inmate's good behavior, participation in programs, and so on), were unconstitutional. As a result, the Supreme Court determined that disciplinary proceedings differed from criminal prosecutions such that prisoners were not owed the full due process rights to which a defendant on trial is entitled. The minimum requirements specified by the Court concerning disciplinary proceedings included the right to receive advanced written notice of the alleged infraction, to have sufficient time to prepare a defense, to present documentary evidence and to call witnesses on his or her behalf, to seek counsel when the circumstances of the case are complex or if the prisoner is illiterate, to have a written statement of the findings of the disciplinary committee, and to maintain a written record of the proceedings.

Access to Court Access to court is another Fourteenth Amendment right issue. Since *Cooper v. Pate* (1964), a lengthy list of "access-to-court" cases has been generated. The validity of a prisoner's right-to-court access was solidified in *Cruz v. Hauck* (1971), when the court stated, "ready access to court is one of, perhaps *the* most fundamental constitutional right." However, few resources were available to inmates faced with preparing a defense. In *Bounds v. Smith* (1977), the Court ruled that North Carolina must furnish each correctional institution with an adequate law library. Some states have even provided law libraries so extensive as to be envied by attorneys.

In *Johnson v. Avery* (1969), the Supreme Court had ruled it acceptable for inmates to help each other with legal work in case preparation, unless the correctional facility provided other reasonable legal assistance. The libraries allowed an inmate with sufficient interest in learning the law to become a "jailhouse lawyer." Some facilities have avoided the extensive use of jailhouse lawyers by establishing legal-assistance programs staffed by practicing lawyers or law students. More constitutional law affecting corrections is included in subsequent chapters.

A Check on Federal Power

Just as states may exceed their power, so too, can the federal government. An example of this is the Brady Bill or the Brady Handgun Violence Prevention Act, which became law after President Bill Clinton signed it in November 1993. The bill was named after James Brady, the press secretary to President Ronald Reagan who, during the assassination attempt on Reagan, was shot and permanently disabled. Some of the provisions of the bill were later deemed by the Supreme Court to be unconstitutional, for example, the five-day waiting period stipulated by the Act with the National Instant Check System (NICS) allowing for instant background checks.

Another example of the legislature declaring legislation, or portions of legislation, unconstitutional is *United States v. Lopez* (1995), in which the Supreme Court struck down a 1990 federal law aimed at banning firearms in schools, ruling 5–4 that Congress had exceeded its power under the Commerce Clause of the

U.S. Constitution when it enacted the law. The U.S. Court of Appeals for the Fifth Circuit ruled that Congress had exceeded its power in enacting the law, and the Supreme Court agreed.

In another case, *Jones v. United States* (1999), the Supreme Court limited the reach of the federal arson law. Jones was convicted of throwing a Molotov cocktail into the home of his cousin and was sentenced to 35 years in federal prison. Jones appealed, arguing that the federal arson law did not apply to cases like his. The Supreme Court granted certiorari and ruled the law had, in fact, been misapplied. The federal law, as written, applies only to property used in interstate or foreign commerce, not to the arson of an owner-occupied private residence.

Federalism Revisited

Many citizens lament that the country is headed toward more and bigger government. The founding fathers feared big government and built safeguards against it into the Constitution. However, a study by *The Washington Post* found that, in the years since the terrorist attacks of 9/11, the massive web of entities involved in counterterrorism efforts—some 1,271 government organizations and 1,931 private companies, in more than 10,000 locations across the country, working on homeland security and intelligence programs and generating 50,000 intelligence reports a year—has become so unwieldy that it is impossible to determine its effectiveness (Priest & Arkin, 2010). The result is that many reports are routinely ignored. "These are not academic issues; lack of focus, not lack of resources, was at the heart of the Fort Hood shooting that left 13 dead, as well as the Christmas Day bomb attempt thwarted not by the thousands of analysts employed to find lone terrorists but by an alert airline passenger who saw smoke coming from his seatmate" (Priest & Arkin, 2010). Figure 4.3 illustrates the myriad counterterrorism command centers in the Washington area alone.

Another issue currently involving constitutional issues and federal powers, like the immigration issue, is the controversy over S.3194, the Public Safety Employer-Employee Cooperation Act of 2009, and the role of unions in public safety organizations.

The Public Safety Employer-Employee Cooperation Act of 2009

A battle is underway. On one side are local police chiefs and sheriffs who oppose legislation requiring state and local government to give police officers the right to bargain collectively. On the other side are organizations representing rank-and-file officers, including the National Association of Police Organizations (NAPO) and the National Fraternal Order of Police (FOP) who have been working to win passage of such legislation. "Similar bills have been considered by Congress for more than a decade, but law enforcement organizations on both sides of the issue indicated that passage this year is a real possibility—or threat, depending on the point of view" ("House Passes Bill," 2010, p. 3).

The controversial bill, S.3194 (the Public Safety Employer-Employee Cooperation Act of 2009), which began as H.R.413, would authorize the Federal Labor Relations Authority (FLRA) to identify which states do not provide certain

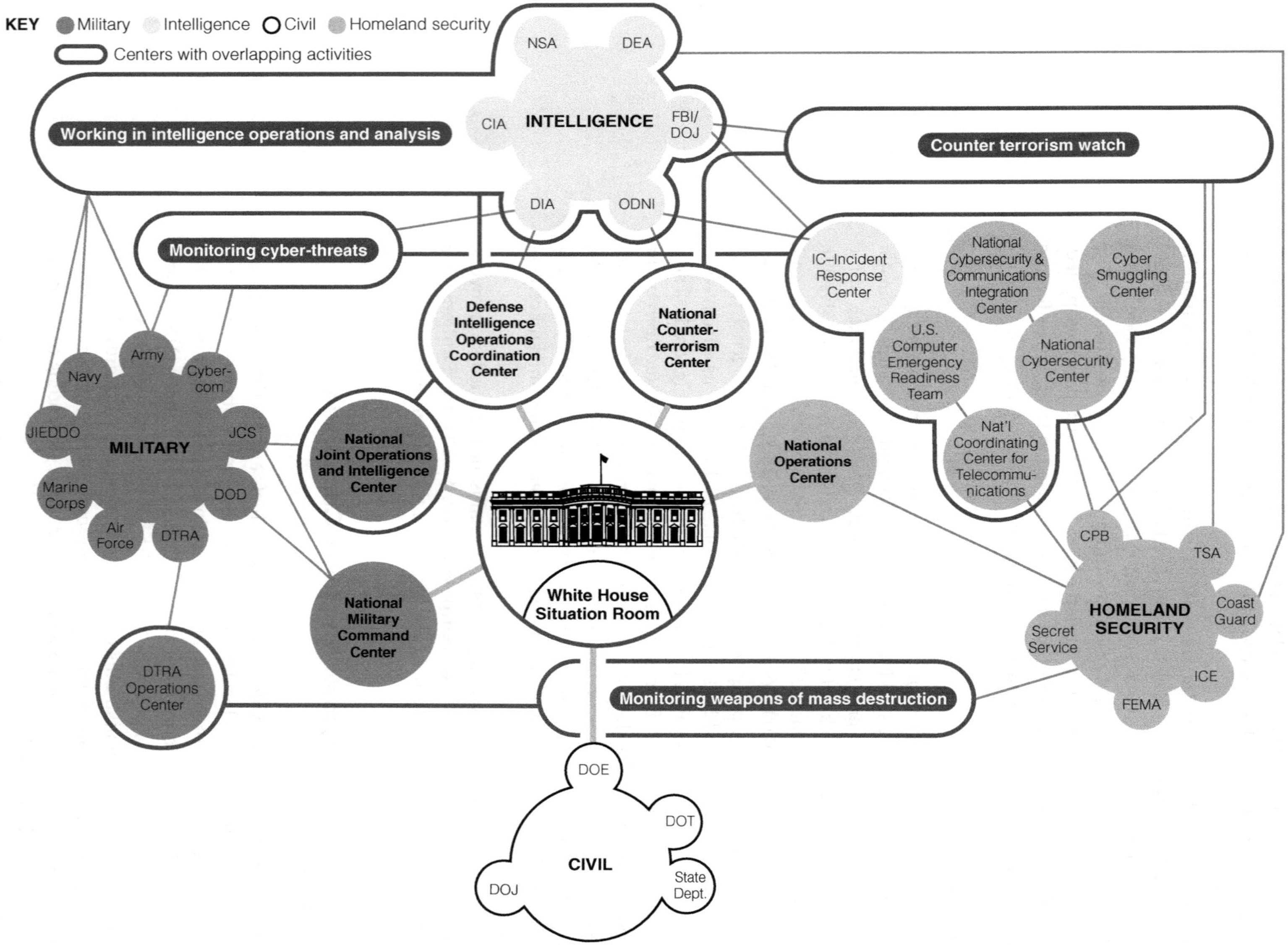

120 Section II The Guarantees of the Constitution: Civil Rights and Civil Liberties

Figure 4.3 A Constellation of Counterterrorism Command Centers in the Washington, DC, Area

Source: Adapted from *The Washington Post* graphic, "A Constellation of Counterterrorism Command Centers in the Washington Area." From article by Dana Priest and William M. Arkin, "Top Secret America. U.S. Security Turns Corporate," *Star Tribune*, July 12, 2010, p. A3. *The Washington Post*. All Rights Reserved.

collective bargaining rights to first responders and then issue regulations establishing those rights. Police chiefs and sheriffs have voiced concern, warning that it would create a "one size fits all straightjacket on law enforcement agencies." Mayors and city council members expressed anger over the federal government moving to take over local officials' job of managing city finances.

In an effort to ensure that the bill would pass, the House attached it to the "must pass" funding bill financing the war effort. The bill passed, and the union declared victory. The Senate, however, rejected the bill 46–51, voting to send their original version of the bill, which does not include the collective bargaining requirement, back to the House. Since April 13, 2010, the bill has sat, without progress, on the Senate Legislative Calendar under General Orders.

This issue, along with many others, will be debated in the months, and possibly years, ahead. How such issues are resolved will have a direct impact on law enforcement and the public it serves.

Summary

To ensure "liberty and justice for all," two additional amendments to the U.S. Constitution were passed. The Thirteenth Amendment, ratified in 1865, abolished slavery. The Fourteenth Amendment, ratified in 1868, granted citizenship to all persons born or naturalized in the United States and subject to the jurisdiction thereof, and forbid states to deny their citizens due process of law or equal protection of the law; that is, it made certain provisions of the Bill of Rights applicable to the states. Procedural due process requires the law to be applied and executed fairly. Substantive due process requires that the laws, themselves, be fair.

The doctrine of incorporation holds that those provisions of the Bill of Rights that are fundamental to the U.S. scheme of justice—enumerated rights— are applied to the states through the Due Process Clause of the Fourteenth Amendment.

Enumerated rights are textually explicit rights incorporated against the states and almost always evaluated with strict scrutiny. Unenumerated rights, in contrast, are not explicitly stated in the Constitution or Bill of Rights but exist via the *liberty* guaranteed by the Fourteenth Amendment and are considered either fundamental (e.g., civil liberties), thus evaluated under strict scrutiny, or non-fundamental (e.g., economic or property liberties), which are evaluated under a rational basis test.

Prejudice is an attitude; discrimination is a behavior. Racial discrimination in the United States has its roots in our nation's history of slavery. The *Dred Scott* decision (1856) ruled that a freed slave did not enjoy the right to remain free in a territory where slavery was still legal. *Plessy v. Ferguson* (1896) showed the Court's desire to avoid civil rights issues, declaring discrimination to be outside the realm of the Court. Jim Crow laws strictly segregated blacks from whites in schools, restaurants, streetcars, hospitals, and cemeteries.

The Court did not directly confront civil rights until the 1950s and 1960s. The Equal Pay Act of 1963, the Civil Rights Act of 1964, the Equal Opportunity Act of 1972, and Title IX of the Education Amendments of 1972 prohibit discrimination based on race, color, religion, sex, or national origin in employment and education in public and private sectors at the federal, state, and local levels. Affirmative action was created to spread equal opportunity throughout the diverse U.S. population.

The Equal Protection Clause of the Fourteenth Amendment to the Constitution applies to racial profiling. Race-based enforcement of the law is illegal. The Equal Protection Clause also prohibits discrimination in jury selection on the basis of race or gender.

A right is a legally protected claim, whereas a privilege is not necessarily legally protected. For prisoners, cases based on Fourteenth Amendment rights involve equal protection on the basis of race, gender, and the availability of facilities and services.

Discussion Questions

1. Why was the Fourteenth Amendment necessary?
2. Why has the entire Bill of Rights not been embraced by the Fourteenth Amendment?
3. What is implicit bias? Are there positive or negative effects, or both, of such bias?
4. Do you think employment quota laws improve fairness or worsen it? For whom?
5. Can it be argued that government has "gone too far" by requiring all people to be treated equally? Can you think of instances in which different people might not be equally able to do a job?
6. Should inmates be allowed to file as many petitions as they please, or should a limit be placed so they would be more selective in bringing up their grievances? Is there a potential for corruption in either scenario?
7. What are your views on the immigration issue?
8. What role do you think the Great Depression played in the Supreme Court changing its level of scrutiny regarding economic legislation?
9. What is "right-to-work" legislation? Does it have the same affect on public employees and private employees?
10. Would you have a procedural due process claim if the state suspended your driver's license? What facts would you need to show this violated due process?

References

Baldus, D.C.; Woodworth, G.; & Pulaski, C.A. (1990). *Equal Justice and the Death Penalty*. Boston: Northeastern University Press.

Brunner, B., & Rowan, B. (2007). "Affirmative Action History: A History and Timeline of Affirmative Action." Information Please Database, 2007. Retrieved July 1, 2016 from www.infoplease.com/spot/affirmative1.html

Bureau of Justice Assistance. (2009). *Nationwide Suspicious Activity Reporting (SAR) Initiative (NSI)*. Washington, DC: Author.

Christie, B. (2010, July 8). "Selective Enforcement at Heart of Arizona Immigration Lawsuit." *Associated Press*. Retrieved July 1, 2016 from http://www.semissourian.com/story/1648015.html

CNN Wire Staff. (2010, May 9). "Holder: Feds May Sue over Arizona Immigration Law." CNN.com. Retrieved July 1, 2016 from http://www.cnn.com/2010/POLITICS/05/09/holder.arizona.immigration/index.html

Dasgupta, N. (2013). "Implicit Attitudes and Beliefs Adapt to Situations: A Decade of Research on the Malleability of Implicit Prejudice, Stereotypes, and the Self-Concept." *Advances in Experimental Social Psychology*, 47, pp. 233–279.

Davis, B. (1988). *The Civil War: Strange and Fascinating Facts*. New York: Random House Value Publishing.

Ducat, C.R. (2010). *Constitutional Interpretation*, 9th ed. Belmont, CA: West/Thomson Learning.

Dwyer, T.P. (2010, July 28). "Understanding the Precedent for Judge Bolton's Ruling on Ariz. 1070." *PoliceOne.com News*. Retrieved July 2, 2016 from www.policeone.com/legal/articles/2147676-Understanding-the-precedent-for-Judge-Boltons-ruling-on-Ariz-1070

Fridell, L. (2011). *Fair and Impartial Policing*. PowerPoint. Retrieved July 1, 2016 from http://www.cops.usdoj.gov/pdf/conference/2011/FairandImpartialPolicing-Fridell.pdf

Fridell, L. (2015). *Fair and Impartial Policing*. Tampa, FL: Fair and Impartial Policing. Retrieved July 1, 2016 from http://static1.squarespace.com/static/54722818e4b0b3ef26cdc085/t/5623ec8ce4b0099ac9caaada/1445194892676/Extended_About+FIP_2015.pdf

Frieden, T. (2010, July 28). "House Passes Bill to Reduce Disparity in Cocaine Penalties." *CNN.com*. Retrieved July 1, 2016 from http://www.cnn.com/2010/POLITICS/07/28/house.drug.penalties/index.html

Gallup. (2016, May 18–22). "Presidential Election 2016: Key Indicators." Washington, DC: Author. Retrieved June 27, 2016 from http://www.gallup.com/poll/189299/presidential-election-2016-key-indicators.aspx?g_source=POLITICS&g_medium=topic&g_campaign=tiles#pcf-top

"Government's 287(g) Program Criticized in Hearings in House." (2009, March 2). *Criminal Justice Newsletter*, pp. 5–7.

"House Passes Bill Requiring Collective Bargaining for State and Local Police, Fire and EMS Workers." (2010, July). *Subject to Debate*, p. 3.

Krogstad, J.M., & Passel, J.S. (2015, November 19). *5 Facts about Illegal Immigration in the U.S.* Washington, DC: Pew Research Center. Retrieved June 28, 2016 from http://www.pewresearch.org/fact-tank/2015/11/19/5-facts-about-illegal-immigration-in-the-u-s/

Kruger, K. (2006, March). "Pregnancy Policy: Law and Philosophy." *The Police Chief*, pp. 10–11.

Lundman, R.J., & Kowalski, B.R. (2009, September). "Speeding while Black? Assessing the Generalizability of Lange et al.'s (2001, 2005) New Jersey Turnpike Speeding Survey Findings." *Justice Quarterly*, 26(3), pp. 504–527.

Lysakowski, M.; Pearsall, A.A., III; & Pope, J. (2009, June). *Policing in New Immigrant Communities*. Washington, DC: Office of Community Oriented Policing.

Markon, J., & Kornblut, A.E. (2010, April 29). "Justice Department Considers Suing Arizona to Block Immigration Law." *The Washington Post*, p. A03.

Means, R., & McDonald, P. (2009, September). "New Haven Firefighters Case . . . 'Reverse' Discrimination: The Final Answer?" *Law and Order*, pp. 18–22.

Moule, J. (2009, January). "Understanding Unconscious Bias and Unintentional Racism." *Phi Delta Kappan*, pp. 321–326.

National Initiative for Building Community Trust and Justice. (2015). *Implicit Bias*. Community-Oriented Trust and Justice Briefs. Washington, DC: Office of Community Oriented Policing Services. Retrieved July 1, 2016 from http://ric-zai-inc.com/Publications/cops-w0793-pub.pdf

Office of the Director. (2012, April 12). *Protecting the Homeland: ICE Response to the Task Force on Secure Communities Findings and Recommendations*. Washington, DC: Department of Homeland Security, Immigration and Customs Enforcement. Retrieved July 1, 2016 from https://www.dhs.gov/sites/default/files/publications/ICE%20Response%20to%20Task%20Force%20on%20Secure%20Communities_0.pdf

Ostrom, B.J.; Ostrom, C.W.; Hanson, R.A.; & Klieman, M. (2008). *Assessing Consistency and Fairness in Sentencing: A Comparative Study in Three States.* Williamsburg, VA: National Center for State Courts.

Police Executive Research Forum. (2008, April). *Police Chiefs and Sheriffs Speak Out on Local Immigration Enforcement.* Washington, DC: Author.

Priest, D., & Arkin, W.M. (2010, July 19). "A Hidden World, Growing Beyond Control." Top Secret America: Washington Post Investigation. *The Washington Post*. Retrieved July 1, 2016 from http://projects.washingtonpost.com/top-secret-america/articles/a-hidden-world-growing-beyond-control/

"Racial Profiling Prohibition Will Be Debated in Congress." (2007, December 17). *Criminal Justice Newsletter*, pp. 3–4.

Rasmussen Reports. (2016, February 23). "Immigration Update: Border Control Still Top Immigration Priority for Most Voters." Asbury Park, NJ: Author. Retrieved June 28, 2016 from http://www.rasmussenreports.com/public_content/politics/current_events/immigration/immigration_update

Roh, S., & Robinson, M. (2009, June). "A Geographic Approach to Racial Profiling." *Police Quarterly*, 12(2), pp. 137–169.

Scarry, L.L. (2008, September). "Cause for an Arrest, or Protected Speech?" *Law Officer*.

Solar, M., & Garry, L.M. (2009, September). *Reducing Disproportionate Minority Contact: Preparation at the Local Level.* Washington, DC: Office of Juvenile Justice and Delinquency Prevention (NCJ 218861).

Walker, S.; Spohn, C.; & DeLone, M. (2012). *The Color of Justice: Race, Ethnicity and Crime in America*, 5th ed. Belmont, CA: Wadsworth/Thomson.

Wexler, C. (2008, April). "Introduction," in *Police Chiefs and Sheriffs Speak Out on Local Immigration Enforcement*. Washington, DC: Police Executive Research Forum. pp. i–iii.

Cases Cited

Adamson v. California, 332 U.S. 46 (1947)
Adarand Constructors v. Pena, 515 U.S. 200 (1995)
Ansonia Board of Education v. Philbrook, 479 U.S. 60 (1986)
Arizona v. United States, 567 U.S. ___ (2012)
Barron v. Baltimore, 32 U.S. (7 Pet.) 243 (1833)
Batson v. Kentucky, 476 U.S. 79 (1986)
Board of Regents of State Colleges v. Roth, 408 U.S. 564 (1972)
Boddie v. Connecticut, 401 U.S. 371, 378 (1971)
Bounds v. Smith, 430 U.S. 817 (1977)
Brown v. Board of Education of Topeka, 347 U.S. 483 (1954)
City and County of San Francisco v. Sheehan (2015)
Cooper v. Pate, 378 U.S. 546 (1964)
Cruz v. Hauck, 404 U.S. 59 (1971)
De Canas v. Bica, 424 U.S. 351 (1976)
Dred Scott v. Sandford, 60 U.S. (19 How.) 393 (1856)
Duncan v. Louisiana, 391 U.S. 145 (1968)
EEOC v. Abercrombie and Fitch (2015)
Ex parte Hull, 312 U.S. 546 (1941)
Firefighters Local Union No. 1784 v. Stotts, 467 U.S. 561 (1984)
Fisher v. University of Texas at Austin, 570 U.S. ___ (2013)
Fisher v. University of Texas at Austin, 579 U.S. ___ (2016)
Fullilove v. Klutznick, 448 U.S. 448 (1980)
Gibbons v. Ogden, 22 U.S. (9 Wheat.) 1 (1824)
Gratz v. Bollinger, 539 U.S. 244 (2003)
Gregg v. Georgia, 428 U.S. 153 (1976)
Griswold v. Connecticut, 381 U.S. 479 (1965)
Grutter v. Bollinger, 539 U.S. 306 (2003)
Hampton v. Mow Sun Wong, 426 U.S. 88 (1976)
Hollingsworth v. Perry, 570 U.S. ___ (2013)
J.E.B. v. Alabama, 511 U.S. 127 (1994)
Johnson v. Avery, 393 U.S. 483 (1969)
Jones v. United States, 527 U.S. 373 (1999)
Local 28, Sheet Metal Workers International Association v. EEOC, 478 U.S. 421 (1986)
Lochner v. New York, 198 U.S. 45 (1905)
Marbury v. Madison, 5 U.S. (1 Cranch) 137 (1803)
Massachusetts Board of Retirement v. Murgia, 427 U.S. 307 (1976)
Mathews v. Eldridge, 424 U.S. 319 (1976)
McClesky v. Kemp, 481 U.S. 279 (1987)
McDonald v. Chicago, 561 U.S. 3025 (2010)
Meyer v. Nebraska, 262 U.S. 390 (1923)
Nebbia v. New York, 291 U.S. 502 (1934)
Norris v. Alabama, 294 U.S. 587 (1935)
Obergefell v. Hodges, 576 U.S. ___ (2015)
Palko v. Connecticut, 302 U.S. 319 (1937)
Plessy v. Ferguson, 163 U.S. 537 (1896)
Plyler v. Doe, 457 U.S. 202 (1982)
Regents of the University of California v. Bakke, 438 U.S. 265 (1978)
Ricci v. DeStefano, 557 U.S. 557 (2009)
Richmond Newspapers Inc v. Virginia, 448 U.S. 555 (1980)
Roe v. Wade, 410 U.S. 113 (1973)
Ruffin v. Commonwealth, 62 Va. (21 Gratt.) 790 (1871)

Schuette v. Coalition to Defend Affirmative Action, Docket No. 12-682 (2013)
Shapiro v. Thompson, 394 U.S. 618 (1969)
Strauder v. West Virginia, 100 U.S. 303 (1880)
Sugarman v. McDougall, 413 U.S. 634 (1973)
Swain v. Alabama, 380 U.S. 202 (1965)
United States v. Brignoni-Ponce, 422 U.S. 873 (1975)
United States v. Carolene Products Co., 304 U.S. 144 (1938)
United States v. Lopez, 514 U.S. 549 (1995)
United States v. Paradise, 480 U.S. 149 (1987)
United States v. Texas, 579 U.S. ___ (2016)
United States v. Virginia, 518 U.S. 515 (1996)
United States v. Windsor, 570 U.S. ___ (2013)
United Steelworkers of America v. Weber, 443 U.S. 193 (1979)
Washington v. Glucksberg, 521 U.S. 702 (1997)
Wolff v. McDonnell, 418 U.S. 539 (1974)
Wygant v. Jackson Board of Education, 476 U.S. 267 (1986)

CHAPTER 5

The First Amendment:
Basic Freedoms

Congress shall make no law respecting an establishment of religion, or prohibiting the free exercise thereof; or abridging the freedom of speech, or of the press, or the right of the people peaceably to assemble, and to petition the Government for a redress of grievances.

—First Amendment to the U.S. Constitution

The freedom to assemble and peacefully protest is a cornerstone not only of the Constitution but of American U.S. ideology. The recent incidents of black men being killed by white police officers has created a volatile situation in many communities throughout the country and placed a severe strain on the relationship between the police and the public they have sworn to protect and serve.

Chapter 5 The First Amendment: Basic Freedoms

Learning Objectives

LO1 List the basic freedoms guaranteed by the First Amendment.

LO2 Identify the freedoms included in religious freedom.

LO3 Understand what freedom of speech guarantees to U.S. citizens.

LO4 Explain the two conditions under which police officers' speech is protected by the First Amendment.

LO5 Know whether citizens have the right to record officers performing their duties in public.

LO6 Grasp what is included in freedom of the press.

LO7 Name the basic freedoms that prison inmates have.

Key Terms

balancing test	Free Exercise Clause	prior restraint
"clear and present danger" test	"imminent lawless action" test	pure speech "rational basis" test
"clear and probable danger" test	judicial activism	strict scrutiny
Establishment Clause	preferred freedoms approach	symbolic speech

Introduction

Americans often know more constitutional law than they think. The media, despite criticisms about reporting, present so much about the law that the general public cannot help but develop a sense of some basic legal tenets. This is certainly the case with the First Amendment.

Differences and difficulties in interpretation have characterized much of the later history of the First Amendment. For example, despite the apparent absolute prohibition in the phrase "Congress shall make no law," Congress has, in fact, passed laws in the public interest many times that restrict freedom of religion, speech, and press. No rights are absolute, so government can regulate them when social interests outweigh those of the individual. Keep in mind that the framers of the Constitution intended to construct only the basic framework of U.S. law. General terms such as *religion*, *speech*, and *press* have generated great debate as U.S. law continues to grow and change.

LO1 The First Amendment prohibits Congress from making any laws that restrict freedom of religion, freedom of speech, freedom of the press, or the right to gather or assemble peaceably and to request the government to respond to complaints from its citizens.

In addition, federal agencies and prosecutors have initiated actions that have resulted in certain limitations on freedom of speech and press. In ruling on the constitutionality of various restrictions on these civil rights, the Supreme Court has at times tended to support either individual rights or society's interests. It sounds simple, but it is not. Private and public interests continue to be at odds and give courts continual opportunities to provide solutions that best serve all involved, including those who will rely on past law to determine future decisions.

Since the early 1950s, the Supreme Court has sought a balanced approach whereby both private and public interests are weighed in each case, as illustrated in Figure 5.1.

The framers of the Constitution intended that it be interpreted. Interpretation plays an important role in constitutional law, and that is why those who drafted the document kept it so fundamental. The basic nature of the Constitution permits courts to continue to interpret law to allow it to grow with society.

This chapter provides an in-depth look at how the First Amendment has been interpreted over the years, beginning with freedom of religion, followed by freedom of speech and freedom of the press. Next the right to peaceful assembly and freedom of association are discussed. The chapter concludes with a look at the First Amendment rights of prisoners.

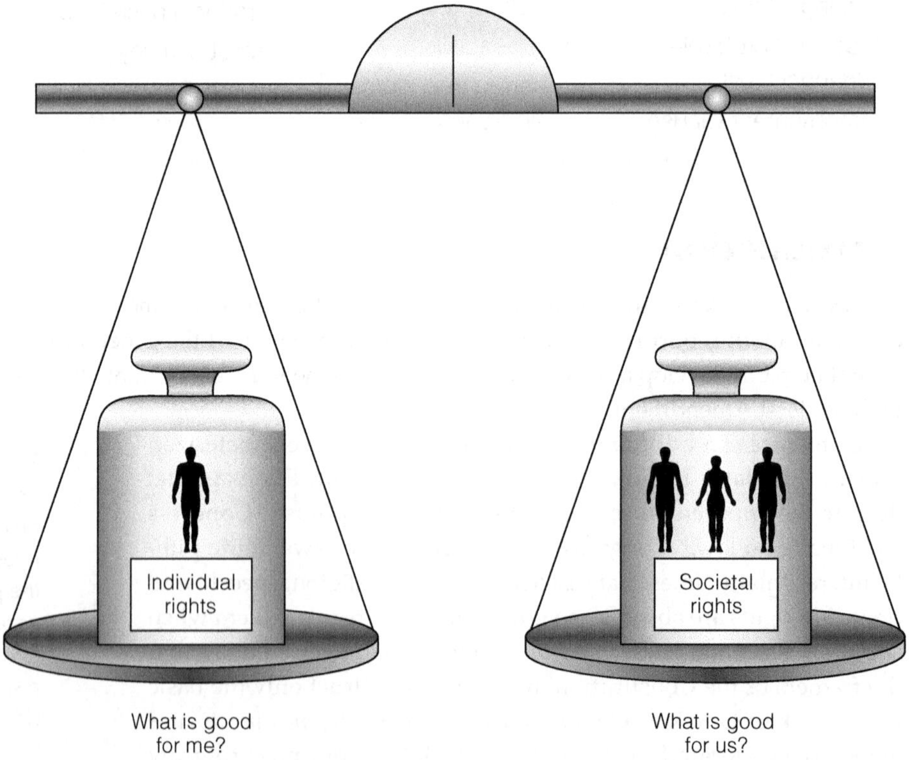

Figure 5.1 Balancing Individual and Societal Rights

Freedom of Religion

Freedom of religion is the first right set forth in the Bill of Rights. The colonists who fled religious persecution cherished their right to worship as they saw fit in their new country. Because religions differed from colony to colony, with Episcopalians predominating in one area, Presbyterians in another, and Congregationalists and Quakers in still others, the founding fathers wanted to guarantee every individual religious freedom.

Laws regarding religion in the newly independent America created a "crazy quilt" (Davis, 2010, p. 87). For example, Massachusetts allowed only Christians to hold public office, and Catholics were required to renounce papal authority to hold public office. New York's constitution banned Catholics from public office. In Maryland, Catholics had full civil rights, but Jews did not. Several states had official, state-supported churches. While some of our new nation's early leaders held tolerant views toward religious diversity, others were not as open-minded and slow to accept or trust those of different faiths. For example, in Massachusetts an anti-Catholic mob burned a convent to the ground, and in Philadelphia anti-Catholic sentiment along with an anti-immigration mood resulted in the Bible Riots of 1844, in which houses were torched, two Catholic churches were destroyed, and at least 20 people were killed (Davis, 2010).

At about the same time, Joseph Smith founded Mormonism and met with the "wrath of the mainstream Protestant majority," who tarred and feathered him, marking the beginning of a long battle between Christian America and Smith's Mormonism. In 1960 Catholic presidential candidate John F. Kennedy made a major speech declaring that his loyalty was to the United States, not the pope, and in 2012 Mormon candidate Mitt Romney addressed the suspicions still directed toward the Church of Jesus Christ of Latter-day Saints. In addition, anti-Semitism has been practiced institutionally and socially for decades (Davis, 2010).

In the United States in the present day, particularly since the terrorist attacks of September 11, 2001, the country is experiencing a deep distrust of Muslims, as attested to by the controversy of building a mosque near the site where the Twin Towers once stood in New York City. However, "America can still be, as Madison perceived the nation in 1785, 'an asylum to the persecuted and oppressed of every nation and religion.' But recognizing that deep religious discord has been part of America's social DNA is a healthy and necessary step" (Davis, 2010, p. 96).

Freedom of religion is a political principle that strives to forbid government constraint on people's choices of beliefs. It requires also that people be free to act on their beliefs.

L02 *Religious freedom includes the freedom to worship, to print instructional material, to train teachers, and to organize schools in which to teach, including religion.*

The concept of separation of church and state is an important legal issue related to freedom of religion. Such a separation is not necessarily present in other parts of the world, and its absence does not necessarily indicate the absence of religious freedom. Many governments attempt to control their society by controlling religion. Some dictatorships have banned certain religions altogether. The United States, however, has always held such basic freedoms in high regard.

To truly separate church and state is challenging. In fact, it cannot be done totally, even if that was the intent. Churches must conform to building and fire codes. Certain behaviors are not accepted anywhere, including churches. Although some separations are obvious, the line can easily become blurred. Ultimately, the government must decide whether a group claiming to be a religion actually is. The First Amendment demands that in making these decisions, the government neither favors nor is hostile toward one religion over others. Government is to remain neutral.

Freedom of religion is commonly discussed in terms of two clauses: the Establishment Clause and the Free Exercise Clause. Students should understand that these clauses overlap at times and that the Supreme Court has shown a reluctance to provide a stable, consistent interpretation of these clauses. To fully understand this area of Constitutional law, it must be looked at from multiple perspectives, as well occur as the chapter progresses.

The Establishment Clause

Establishment Clause clause in the First Amendment that states, "Congress shall make no law respecting an establishment of religion"

The **Establishment Clause** of the First Amendment states, "Congress shall make no law respecting an establishment of religion." That is, Congress cannot create a national church or prescribed religion. The Establishment Clause has been interpreted at various times to mean either that church and state must be kept completely separate or that the government cannot show preference to any particular religion (or to religion over nonreligion).

These two interpretations have resulted in competition between two theories: separationist versus nonpreferentialist. Separationist theory is rooted in the "wall of separation" idea and stresses the fact that government and religion do not mix well. The nonpreferentialist theory, on the other hand, holds that the government is able to provide aid to religion and religious institutions as long as there is no preference for one religion over another, or preference shown to religious versus nonreligious entities. The nonpreferentialist theory rejects the complete separation of church and state.

Emotional disputes have involved litigation over such issues as government assistance to religiously sponsored schools, devotional practices in public schools, and treatment of sectarians, whose religious convictions are not easily accommodated by local law. The cases that follow illustrate how the Supreme Court has struggled with religious issues.

CASE IN BRIEF ▶

Everson v. Board of Education (1947)

ISSUE Does a New Jersey statute, which allowed for the reimbursement of school transportation costs to all parents, even those whose children attend a religious school, violate the Establishment Clause?

RULING No. The First Amendment's Establishment Clause does not prohibit the state from spending tax-raised funds to pay the bus fares of religious school students as a part of a general program under which it pays the fares of students attending public schools.

The Establishment Clause and separation of church and state were made applicable to the states in *Everson v. Board of Education* (1947), in which the Supreme Court held that a state statute allowing reimbursement to parents for money spent to transport their children to parochial schools on the public bus system did not constitute an establishment of religion. The Court explained how bussing, like police and fire protection, are so "separate and so indisputably marked off from the religious function" that for New Jersey to provide these types of services did not violate the First Amendment. Citing the words of Thomas Jefferson—that the clause against the establishment of religion by law was intended to erect a "wall of separation between Church and State"—and noting the reimbursement policy applied to parents of both public and parochial school students, the Court determined the policy did conform to the separationist intent of the clause and likened the statute to general public-welfare legislation. Also in reaching its decision, the

Court looked to world history and early colonies to explain why government and religion do not mix well and should be kept separate. According to the Court, history shows us that the group in power will use religion to maintain political power and suppress other groups, or vice versa, using political power to maintain religious supremacy. This reasoning is at the heart of the separationist theory.

In *Engle v. Vitale* (1962), the Court held that prayer, voluntary or otherwise, conducted in public school classrooms was unconstitutional. This decision was also the holding in *Abington School District v. Schempp* (1963) and *Murray v. Curlett* (1963), two cases heard together, regarding schools that began each day by reading Bible verses. In 1985 in *Wallace v. Jaffree,* the Court held that even a "moment of silence for meditation or voluntary prayer" was being used to encourage religious values and was unconstitutional.

Law challenging the Establishment Clause because of an incidental benefit must meet three standards: it must (1) have a primary secular purpose, (2) have a principle effect that neither advances nor inhibits religion, and (3) not generate excessive entanglement between government and religion, as set forth in *Lemon v. Kurtzman* (1971). In this case, Rhode Island was providing a 15-percent salary supplement to teachers of secular subjects in private schools. The Court invalidated the state's attempt to subsidize costs of parochial school education by ruling that the statutes fostered an excessive entanglement between church and state in violation of the Establishment Clause. The Court's reasoning in this case became known as the *Lemon* test.

Chief Justice Warren E. Burger stressed that programs that provided significant ongoing aid to parochial elementary and secondary schools injected an explosive political issue that caused division along religious lines, effectively guaranteeing yearly public debates and political conflicts. In *Lemon*, the Court found that secular and religious education were so tightly intertwined that to support one without supporting the other would be virtually impossible and that separating the two would involve the state so deeply in the religious institution's administration as to impair its independence, generating an "excessive entanglement" in conflict with a central purpose of the establishment clause.

In 1980, the Court struck down a Kentucky law requiring the posting of the Ten Commandments in all classrooms (*Stone v. Graham*, 1980). The "Equal Access" law of 1984, however, gave students the right to hold religious meetings in public high schools outside class hours.

The *Lemon* test, although still important, is not the only method of evaluating Establishment cases. *Aguilar v. Felton* (1985) began an analytical change by the Court in holding that rather than the specific elements of *Lemon*, the Establishment Clause barred the City of New York from sending public school teachers into parochial schools to provide remedial education to disadvantaged children pursuant to a congressionally mandated program. The intense state monitoring of public employees who teach in religious institutions to ensure they were not including religion necessitated excessive government entanglement with religion, leading the Court to place a permanent injunction on state aid to parochial schools.

However, the Court's decision in *Agostini v. Felton* (1997) took the opposite direction. At issue was a federally funded remedial education program in New

CASE IN BRIEF ▶

Agostini v. Felton (1997)

ISSUE Is the Establishment Clause violated when public school teachers instruct in parochial schools?

RULING No. The Supreme Court overruled its prior decision in *Aguilar v. Felton* (1985). Public school teachers sent into religious schools would not lead to a state-sponsored religion, reversing its earlier view. Only policies which have excessive conflict between church and state will be seen as violating the Establishment Clause.

York City, based on Title I of the Elementary and Secondary Education Act of 1965, aimed at economically disadvantaged and educationally deprived children, most of whom attended parochial schools. Public funds were used to purchase materials and supplies and to pay instructors, including those teaching in the private schools. In *Agostini*, the New York City Board of Education sought relief from the injunction resulting from *Aguilar*, contending that the cost of compliance severely restricted the money available to provide remedial instruction to the students who needed it.

In examining its own seemingly opposing interventions involving the time from *Aguilar* to *Agostini*, the Court acknowledged its *Aguilar* ruling had, in fact, been undercut by subsequent decisions, most notably *Zobrest v. Catalina Foothills School District* (1993), which held that public assistance could be used for an interpreter for a parochial school student. The Court admitted the assumptions on which *Aguilar* had relied, such as excessive entanglement, had no support in more recent rulings.

This area of constitutional analysis continues to challenge both students and judges. While the separationist theory tended to dominate the Court's decisions in early cases, this approach has, in recent years, been moderated and more recent cases have shown a trend toward nonpreferentialism or even a combination of the two. This development makes decisions by the Supreme Court complicated and reveals an inability to show any consistent theoretical approach. Indeed, the Court itself has been unable to define a clear set of rules to determine outcomes of these cases, as illustrated by a series of decisions that garnered national attention from 2003 to 2005. In 2003, Alabama Supreme Court Justice Roy Moore refused to remove a statue of the Ten Commandments from the judicial building and was eventually removed from his position. The statue was put in a storeroom not accessible to the public. Although refusing to grant certiorari, supporters of Judge Moore pointed out that even the U.S. Supreme Court begins each session with the words, "God save the United States and this honorable court."

CASE IN BRIEF ▶

McCreary County v. ACLU (2005)

ISSUE Does displaying the Ten Commandments in county courthouses and public schools violate the First Amendment's Establishment Clause, which prohibits government from passing laws "respecting an establishment of religion"?

RULING Yes. An observer of such displays posted on walls inside public structures would likely have concluded that the government was endorsing religion.

Then in 2004, the Supreme Court granted certiorari to two similar cases that yielded vastly different rulings and illustrated how two competing theories influence the Court's interpretation of the Establishment Clause. *McCreary County v. ACLU* (2005) involved a lawsuit filed by the American Civil Liberties Union (ACLU) against three Kentucky counties for their displays of framed copies of the Ten Commandments on the walls inside courthouses and public schools. The ACLU argued that the displays violated the First Amendment's Establishment Clause, and the Supreme Court agreed.

However, *Van Orden v. Perry* (2005) was a similar case filed in Austin, Texas, in which Thomas Van Orden sued Texas Governor Rick Perry because one of the 21 statues surrounding the capital building was a 6 × 3.5-foot monolith bearing the Ten Commandments. Van Orden felt the monolith violated the Establishment Clause and wanted it removed. A federal district court ruled for the state, and a federal appellate court affirmed. The Supreme Court granted certiorari and affirmed, with Chief Justice William H. Rehnquist stating, "We think it not useful in dealing with the sort of passive monument that Texas has erected on its Capitol grounds. Instead our analysis is driven both by the nature of the monument and by our nation's history. . . . Texas has treated her Capitol grounds monuments as representing the several strands in the state's political and legal history. The inclusion of the Ten Commandments in this group has a dual significance, partaking of both religion and government. We cannot say that Texas' display of this monument violates the Establishment Clause of the First Amendment." Concurring, Justice Clarence Thomas stated, "In no sense does Texas compel petitioner Van Orden to do anything. The only injury to him is that he takes offense in seeing the monument as he passes it."

McCreary and *Van Orden*, which were decided on the same day, illustrate the challenges facing the Court with respect to this area of constitutional law and the necessity to analyze each case based on its unique facts and circumstances. The *McCreary* decision adheres to standards set forth in the *Lemon* test and follows the complete "wall of separation" theory, which insists that the government and religion are kept separate as much as possible. Government neutrality concerning religion is necessary. The Court in *Van Orden*, on the other hand, did not apply the *Lemon* test, instead championing the theory that government and religion need not, and in fact cannot, be completely separated. The Court noted how religion has been involved in government action and traditions for centuries; for example, the House and Senate each have paid chaplains, and the Supreme Court opens its sessions with a prayer.

In *Town of Greece v. Galloway* (2014) the Court had the opportunity to make the law surrounding the Establishment Clause clear but chose not to. As before this decision, no one test or analysis can be said to control the decisions in these cases. *Galloway* was a straightforward Establishment Clause case. In 1999, the town began to open their monthly town meetings with a prayer. No one was denied the opportunity to give the opening prayer; any layperson or clergy of any persuasion was allowed to give a prayer. Two residents complained that Christian themes dominated the views of the opening prayers and eventually sued the town, claiming the prayers preferred Christianity over other religions.

The Court looked to an earlier case that examined prayer given at the beginning of legislative sessions. The ruling in *Marsh v. Chambers* (1983) held that opening a state legislative session with a prayer, paid for from state funds and to a chaplain, did not violate the First Amendment. The Court in *Marsh* held that history supported the conclusion that legislative invocations are compatible with the Establishment Clause, writing, "In light of the unambiguous and unbroken history of more than 200 years, there can be no doubt that the practice of opening legislative sessions with prayer has become part of the fabric of our society." In *Greece*, the Court ruled that the practice used by the town to open their sessions with prayer followed the long line of tradition by both Congress and state legislatures.

The cases demonstrate the struggle between changing norms and constitutional interpretations. The United States was created as a place where all people could worship as they liked. A number of the founders were able to risk what they did because of the courage their faith provided as proudly proclaimed in much of the Constitution's history. Andrew Jackson pointed out, "The First Amendment to our Constitution was designed to avoid these conflicts by avoiding these beginnings" (*West Virginia State Board of Education v. Barnette*, 1943).

◄ **CASE IN BRIEF**

Van Orden v. Perry (2005)

ISSUE Does the Establishment Clause allow a monument inscribed with the Ten Commandments to be displayed on the state capitol grounds?

RULING Yes. The Establishment Clause is not violated simply because a monument has a religious message or promotes a message consistent with religious doctrine.

◄ **CASE IN BRIEF**

Town of Greece v. Galloway (2014)

ISSUE Does a prayer at the beginning of a legislative session violate the Establishment Clause, even if there is no discrimination against specific faiths or prayer content?

RULING No. There is a long-standing tradition of opening legislative sessions with prayer. The opinion explained, "legislative prayer lends gravity to public business, reminds lawmakers to transcend petty differences in pursuit of a higher purpose, and expresses a common aspiration to a just and peaceful society."

The Free Exercise Clause

"Congress shall make no law . . . prohibiting the free exercise [of religion]." So declares the **Free Exercise Clause** of the First Amendment. This clause involves both the freedom to believe and the freedom to act. In *Davis v. Beason* (1890), the Court described the First Amendment free exercise clause:

> The First Amendment was intended to allow everyone under the jurisdiction of the United States to entertain such notions respecting his relations to his Maker and the duties they impose as may be approved by his judgment and conscience, and to exhibit his sentiments in such form of worship as he may think proper, not injurious to the rights of others.

Free Exercise Clause clause in the First Amendment that declares, "Congress shall make no law . . . prohibiting the free exercise [of religion]"

However, the freedom to act is not so protected, a distinction further clarified when the free exercise clause was made applicable to (incorporated in) the states in *Cantwell v. Connecticut* (1940). In this case, three Jehovah's Witnesses were convicted under a statute that forbade the unlicensed soliciting of funds on the representation that they were for religious or charitable purposes. While soliciting in a strongly Catholic neighborhood, the Jehovah's Witnesses had played a phonographic recording that insulted the Christian religion and the Catholic Church in particular, leading to an altercation and a charge of breach of the peace against the Jehovah's Witnesses. Through its ruling, the Court emphasized how religious beliefs cannot be regulated by the government and helped delineate how beliefs and acts differ with regard to First Amendment protection:

CASE IN BRIEF ▶

Cantwell v. Connecticut (1940)

ISSUE Does the Free Exercise Clause protect an individual from state criminal prosecution when the person played a record that is offensive to some because of its religious viewpoint?

RULING Yes. The Free Exercise Clause, being fundamental to the concept of liberty, protects a person's ability to profess religious beliefs, even if others find such statements offensive.

> Freedom of conscience and freedom to adhere to such religious organization or form of worship as the individual may choose cannot be restricted by law. On the other hand, it safeguards the free exercise of the chosen form of religion. Thus, the Amendment embraces two concepts—freedom to believe and freedom to act. The first is an absolute, but, in the nature of things, the second cannot be. Conduct remains subject to regulation for the protection of society. The freedom to act must have appropriate definition to preserve the enforcement of that protection.

The Free Exercise Clause has taken some interesting paths as various issues have been presented to the Court. In *West Virginia State Board of Education v. Barnette* (1943), the Supreme Court held that states could not require children to pledge allegiance to the United States each school day. In his opinion, Justice Robert Jackson said that everyone has a First Amendment right to not pledge allegiance because of the "freedom of thought and belief that is central to all First Amendment freedoms."

In *Lynch v. Donnelly* (1984), a government-subsidized Christmas display of a crèche was found not an advancement or endorsement of religion, and therefore, permitted. In *Wooley v. Maynard* (1977), the Supreme Court held that a state could not punish someone for blacking out the part of his car's license plate that set forth the state's motto, "Live Free or Die," holding that the government is not permitted to compel citizens to advertise government or religious beliefs or to comply with advertising or asserting them.

However, in balancing this assertion, the Court held in *Wooley* that printing "In God We Trust" on money did not violate the Constitution because money is passed among people, and therefore, does not indicate that a particular individual agrees with a religious or governmental belief, like a motto on a license plate might. Also money is transported in such a manner as to not be a public display. These decisions are being made in an effort to strike a fine balance that sometimes seems out of sync with either social norms or other law.

In *Employment Division v. Smith* (1990), the Supreme Court stated, "We have never held that an individual's religious beliefs excuse him from compliance with an otherwise valid law prohibiting conduct that the State is free to regulate." In this case, two Native American drug counselors in Oregon lost their jobs because they used peyote, a hallucinogenic drug, as part of a religious ritual in the Native American church. Some states allowed such a practice, but Oregon did not. The Court decreed, "Because respondents' ingestion of peyote was prohibited under Oregon law, and because that prohibition is constitutional, Oregon may, consistent with the Free Exercise Clause, deny respondents unemployment compensation when their dismissal results from use of the drug."

Additional examples of how this ruling has affected other religious groups include the performance of autopsies despite families' religious beliefs and the requirement that members of the Amish community put orange reflectors on the backs of their buggies. However, when Congress passed and President Bill Clinton signed the Religious Freedom Restoration Act (RFRA) in 1993 and the Religious Land Use and Institutionalized Persons Act (RLUIPA) in 2000—acts intended to provide broad protections for religious freedom—government interference with religious practices was made more difficult.

The RFRA was a direct response to *Smith*, in which the Court's ruling allowed laws that burden religious expression as long as the law was one of general applicability. If the law was not as such, a strict scrutiny test would have been used to evaluate it. The RFRA was enacted to restore the strict scrutiny test to laws that "substantially burden" a person's exercise of religion, even in cases of general applicability. **Strict scrutiny** is the legal standard applied to due-process analysis of fundamental rights, such as freedom of religion, and asks (1) is the law in furtherance of a compelling governmental interest and (2) is the law narrowly tailored to provide the least restrictive means of furthering that compelling governmental interest? The RFRA applied to all federal, state, and local actions, whether occurring before or after the act was passed. Congress based its power to legislate in this area on Section 5 of the Fourteenth Amendment, which states, "The Congress shall have power to enforce, by appropriate legislation, the provisions of this article."

However, in *City of Boerne v. Flores* (1997), the Court explained that Congress had exceeded its authority under Section 5 of the Fourteenth Amendment because the RFRA seemed not to be an enforcement statute but one that instead defined a right, which was the realm of the Judiciary, not Congress. The law was therefore declared inapplicable to state and local governments but remained valid against the federal government. The RFRA was amended in 2003 to state that it applies only to the federal government and its entities.

Congress responded to the Court's *Boerne* decision by enacting the Religious Land Use and Institutionalized Persons Act (RLUIPA) of 2000. This law applies to states and municipalities, but instead of relying on Section 5 of the Fourteenth Amendment, Congress used its authority under the Spending and Commerce Clauses. The statute is applicable to those entities that receive federal funding for

◀ **CASE IN BRIEF**

Employment Division v. Smith (1990)

ISSUE Is the Free Exercise Clause violated by denying unemployment compensation to a person fired for using a substance (peyote) that is banned by state law despite the fact it was used for a religious purpose?

RULING No. Personal religious beliefs do not excuse a person from complying with an otherwise valid law.

strict scrutiny the legal standard applied to due process analysis of fundamental rights, such as freedom of speech, in which the state must establish it has a compelling government interest that justifies and necessitates the law in question and that the law is narrowly tailored to fit that interest; a high standard and difficult to defend

CASE IN BRIEF

Burwell v. Hobby Lobby (2014)

ISSUE Does the Religious Freedom Restoration Act (RFRA) of 1993 prohibit a government mandate that forces closely held corporations to provide certain health insurance coverage for employees that violate sincerely held religious beliefs of the owners?

RULING Yes. Mandating certain insurance coverage that violates the owner's sincerely held religious beliefs imposes a substantial burden. If the government cannot show that the mandate furthers a compelling government interest and is the least restrictive means of doing so, the RFRA is violated, and the mandate is not applicable to the closely held corporations.

the program or activity that is being challenged. The law impacts two areas: land use regulations and religious exercise by institutionalized persons.

In a recent case, *Burwell v. Hobby Lobby* (2014), the Supreme Court struck down the contraception coverage requirement under the Affordable Care Act as it applies to closely held corporations under the protections of the RFRA. Based on the substantial fines a corporation would face for noncompliance, the Court found that mandating insurance coverage that provided contraception, which the owners of Hobby Lobby would not provide because of their religious beliefs, amounted to a substantial burden. And because a substantial burden existed, the government needed to show that it was furthering a compelling government interest and that the mandate was the least restrictive means to achieve that interest. The Court did not decide whether or not the government had a compelling interest. Instead, it focused on the least restrictive means prong and found that other means existed to achieve the government goal. Therefore, the Court ruled, the current means were not the least restrictive.

It is often difficult to tell when a law attempts to regulate religious belief or conduct, but the distinction is important because it changes how the law is scrutinized. Obviously, *belief* regulation is not allowed, but regulation of *conduct* can happen. If the conduct is regulated because of specific religious attachments, that regulation will receive a high level of judicial scrutiny. Such was the case in *Church of Lukumi Babalu Aye v. Hialeah* (1993). In *Lukumi*, a church whose congregants practiced the Santeria religion, which employs animal sacrifice as one of its principal forms of devotion, had leased land in Hialeah, Florida, and announced plans to establish a house of worship and other facilities there. Many local residents became distressed and angry at the prospect of a Santeria church in their community, and the Hialeah city council was pressured to hold an emergency public session to address the matter. The result of the emergency session was the adoption of Resolution 87-66, which noted the "concern" expressed by residents of the city "that certain religions may propose to engage in practices which are inconsistent with public morals, peace or safety," and declared that "[t]he City reiterates its commitment to a prohibition against any and all acts of any and all religious groups which are inconsistent with public morals, peace or safety." At subsequent meetings, the city council approved several other emergency ordinances, including one that incorporated Florida's animal cruelty laws and subjected to criminal punishment "[w]hoever . . . unnecessarily or cruelly . . . kills any animal"; and one that defined "sacrifice" as "to unnecessarily kill . . . an animal in a . . . ritual . . . not for the primary purpose of food consumption," and prohibited the "possess[ion], sacrifice, or slaughter" of an animal if it was killed in "any type of ritual" and there is an intent to use it for food.

The Church petitioners filed suit alleging violation of their rights under the Free Exercise Clause of the First Amendment. Although acknowledging that the city ordinances were not religiously neutral, the District Court ruled in favor of Hialeah, concluding, among other things, that compelling governmental interests in preventing public health risks and cruelty to animals fully justified the absolute prohibition on ritual sacrifice accomplished by the ordinances, and that an exception to that prohibition for religious conduct would unduly interfere with fulfillment of the governmental interest. The Court of Appeals affirmed. However, the Supreme Court granted certiorari and, although acknowledging that such activity may offend some and noting that sport hunting was not regulated by the city ordinance, reversed the lower courts' rulings and struck down the law. The Court stated that because the law was drafted pursuant to the religious group announcing their plan, its intent was to restrict the religious freedom of that specific group and, as such, was unconstitutional. Writing the majority opinion, Justice Anthony Kennedy declared: "Our review confirms that the laws in question were enacted by officials who did not understand, failed to perceive, or chose to ignore the fact that their official actions violated the Nation's essential commitment to religious freedom. The challenged laws had an impermissible object; and in all events, the principle of general applicability was violated because the secular ends asserted in defense of the laws were pursued only with respect to conduct motivated by religious beliefs."

Table 5.1 summarizes conduct not protected by the Freedom of Religion Clause.

Courts have had to balance the requirements of the Free Exercise Clause against society's legal, social, and religious needs. For example, in St. Paul, Minnesota, after a string of bank robberies, thefts, and crimes at a mall, the city implemented an ordinance prohibiting people from hiding their identity "by means of a robe, mask or other disguise." Police used the ordinance as a prevention tactic. However, when officers ticketed a Muslim woman for wearing a veil as part of her religious practice, the result was anger among the local Muslim community. The court ruled the ordinance unconstitutional.

Another area of controversy is court-ordered treatment that includes religion. In a series of cases, the Court has continued to deny certiorari, thus letting stand

CASE IN BRIEF

Church of Lukumi Babalu Aye v. Hialeah (1993)

ISSUE Does a city ordinance that prohibits the ritual sacrificing of animals violate the Free Exercise Clause?

RULING Yes. Under a strict scrutiny analysis the Court determined that the ordinance infringed religious conduct without being justified by a compelling interest and not narrowly tailored to fit that interest. The case record shows that the reason for the ordinance was to "suppress elements of the Santeria worship service."

Table 5.1 Conduct Not Protected by the Freedom of Religion Clause*

Conduct not protected	Case
Multiple marriages in violation of state polygamy laws (crime of bigamy)	*Reynolds v. United States*, U.S. Supreme Court (1879) 98 U.S. 145, 25 L.Ed. 244
Handling poisonous snakes in a public place in violation of state law as part of a religious ceremony	*State v. Massey*, North Carolina Supreme Court (1949) 229 N.C. 734, 51 S.E.2d 179
Requirements at airports, state fairs, and so on that religious, political, and other groups distribute or sell literature only from booths provided for that purpose	*Heffron v. International Society for Krishna Consciousness*, U.S. Supreme Court (1981) 452 U.S. 640, 101 S.Ct. 2559
Violation of child labor laws	*Prince v. Massachusetts*, U.S. Supreme Court (1944) 321 U.S. 158, 64 S.Ct. 438
Air Force officer continued to wear his yarmulke (Jewish skullcap) after repeated orders to remove it. He was dropped from service. Affirmed for Air Force.	*Goldman v. Weinberger*, U.S. Supreme Court (1986) 475 U.S. 503, 106 S.Ct. 1310
Members of the Old Order Amish, who do not use motor vehicles but travel in horse-drawn buggies, would not obey a state law requiring reflecting triangles on the rear of all slow-moving vehicles. Held not exempted from complying with this highway safety law.	*Minnesota v. Hershberger*, U.S. Supreme Court (1990) 495 U.S. 901, 110 S.Ct. 1918, *vacating* 444 N.W.2d 282

*The Freedom of Religion Clause could not be used as a defense for destroying government property [*United States v. Allen*] (760 F.2d 447 [1985]); extortion and blackmail [*United States v. Starks*] (515 F.2d 112 [1975]); racketeering [*United States v. Dickens*] (695 F.2d 765, review denied 460 U.S. 1092 [1983]); refusal to testify before a grand jury [*Smilow v. United States*] (465 F.2d 802; see 409 U.S. 944 [1972]); refusal to be photographed after being arrested [*United States v. Slabaugh*] (848 F.2d 113 [8th Cir. 1988]); putting a logging road through an area sacred to Native American tribes [*Lyng v. Northwest Indian Cemetery Protective Association*] (108 S.Ct. 1319 [1988]); refusal to have children vaccinated [*Jacobson v. Massachusetts*] (25 S.Ct. 358 [1905]); and refusal to participate in the Social Security system [*United States v. Lee*] (102 S.Ct. 1051 [1982]), although in 1988 Congress enacted 26 U.S.C. § 3127, which permits members of certain religious groups, such as the Amish people, to elect to opt out of the employee portion of Social Security taxes.

Source: GARDNER/ANDERSON. *Criminal Law*, 11E. © 2012 Wadsworth, a part of Cengage Learning, Inc.

the previous rulings, in which judicially mandated involvement in Alcoholics Anonymous (AA) or Narcotics Anonymous (NA) was determined to violate the Establishment Clause because of the religious components of 12-step programs that reference God or a higher power. These cases include *Griffin v. Coughlin* (1997), which involved privileges being denied to atheist or agnostic prisoners who refused to participate in AA faith-based treatment, and *Warner v. Orange County Dept. of Probation* (1993), in which the defendant objected to the religious content of mandated AA participation.

Interpretations

What, then, exactly did the authors of the First Amendment Freedom of Religion Clause intend? Did they mean, as Justice Hugo Black argued, that the statement "Congress shall make no law" meant just that, that Congress (and through the Fourteenth Amendment, the states) could not in any way, shape, or form do anything that might breech the "wall of separation?" Did they mean that although government could not prefer one sect over another, it might provide aid to all religions equally?

Some scholars believe the historic record is confused and contradictory. At the core of the problem is one's view of the Constitution and its role in U.S. government. Advocates of what they assert is the original intent believe the framers' vision is as good today as it was 200 years ago. They believe any deviation from that view abandons the ideals that have made this country free and great, that judges should go strictly by what the framers intended, and that any revisions must be made through the amendment process.

On the other side, defenders of **judicial activism** (allowing judges to interpret the Constitution and its amendments) say that amendments are not necessary. Judges should be allowed to interpret the Constitution and its amendments, and if law is changed, that is what the common law system permits. Such defenders believe that for the document to remain true to the framers' intent, the framers' spirit must reach a balance with modern society realities. They suggest the framers set out a series of ideals expressed through powers and limitations and deliberately left details vague so those who came after could apply the ideals to their world.

judicial activism allowing judges to interpret the Constitution and its amendments

Freedom of Speech

The liberty to speak openly without fear of government restraint or punishment for what one says is freedom of speech. Implicit in this freedom is the right to hear others' ideas. Freedom of speech is closely linked to freedom of the press because this freedom includes both the right to speak and the right to be heard. In the United States, both freedoms, commonly called freedom of expression, are protected by the First Amendment.

A generation of Americans witnessed firsthand the influence free speech had during the Vietnam War, the civil rights movement, and elections across the country. The downside may be that a generation of Americans takes such freedom for granted because of its continual

LO3 Freedom of speech and expression include the right to speak and the right to be heard. The First Amendment protects both pure speech and symbolic expression.

existence. Over the decades, court opinions in free speech cases have come from numerous perspectives, including:

- self-governance and the essential role that free speech plays in democratic decision making;
- freedom of speech as the only way to prove things false or true, also known as counter speech, as stated by Justice Oliver Wendell Holmes, Jr., in his dissent in *Abrams v. United States* (1919): "...the best test of truth is the power of the thought to get itself accepted in the competition of the market";
- free speech as promoting autonomy and self-development, for example, through art and literature;
- a simple distrust of government to regulate speech.

Being able to speak out, particularly against the government, remains a cornerstone of freedom in the United States. What free speech is there if not in opposition to those in power? No greater right do we have in this country than that of speaking our minds and being able to hear from others. However, even this right is not absolute, and there is some speech that falls outside the protections of the First Amendment.

Freedom of speech and the constitutional limits to it have been defined in practice by Supreme Court rulings. The First Amendment right to free speech was the first guarantee to be made applicable to the states through incorporation in *Gitlow v. New York* (1925). In *Gitlow*, the Court noted the importance of speech and the press: "For present purposes we may and do assume that freedom of speech and of the press—which are protected by the First Amendment from abridgment by Congress—are among the fundamental personal rights and 'liberties' protected by the due process clause of the Fourteenth Amendment from impairment by the States." Thus, Supreme Court rulings have consistently ruled that speech may not be restricted or prohibited just because some find it offensive. To date, virtually every case involving an arrest for offensive speech, where there is no other "criminal" behavior, has either been dismissed before trial or the person is convicted at trial but has the conviction overturned on appeal (Mayes, 2010).

The following discussion is organized in a way that takes the reader through the typical reasoning process the courts have used to evaluate free speech cases, beginning with the question: Is it speech that is involved? If it is speech, is it speech that is protected or not protected under the First Amendment? If it is protected, what allowable government restrictions might come into play and what tests are used by the courts in terms of content versus conduct?

When analyzing a freedom of speech issue, it is first important to identify if speech is actually involved, because if what is at issue is not speech, the First Amendment protections will not apply. *Speech* is a broad term that includes not only spoken and written words but also nonverbal, expressive conduct that conveys the "speaker's" beliefs, feelings, or intentions.

Pure Speech

When people think of *speech*, they often think of *words* used to convey a message, expressed either verbally or in writing. Verbal and written methods of

pure speech verbal and written methods of communicating or expressing a message

communicating or expressing a message, such as delivering a talk before an audience or authoring a book, are referred to as **pure speech**. The First Amendment protects a person's right to express him- or herself through written and spoken words. In certain, specific cases, however, the government can restrict pure speech. For example, laws pertaining to libel and slander restrict what a person is allowed to write or say that may defame, maliciously misrepresent, or damage the reputation of another.

Symbolic Expression

symbolic speech a form of speech that expresses an idea or emotion without use of words, such as burning one's draft card, bra or flag, or picketing

Black's Law Dictionary (2006) defines **symbolic speech** as "conduct that expresses opinions or thoughts, such as a hunger strike or the wearing of a black armband." Symbolic speech expresses an idea or emotion without the use of words and includes the displaying of a flag or the wearing of certain attire, actions which send a message in a "symbolic" way, as opposed to "pure speech," which is limited to the words necessary to convey the message. Symbolic expression applies to more non-traditional modes of expression, such as architecture or photography, and can also include the act of remaining silent, because in essence, silence can communicate a message.

The nature and context of the "speech" is important in determining what symbolic expression will be given the protection of the First Amendment; that is, was the conduct "sufficiently imbued with elements of communication"? (*Spence v. State of Washington*, 1974). Symbolic acts are included within the protection of the First Amendment. However, the government may regulate or punish symbolic speech, not because of the speech itself but rather because the *conduct* expressing the message is proscribable. Regulation is aimed at the conduct, not the message, which is much easier to restrict.

In Clackamas, Oregon, Robert Ekas filed a federal lawsuit to defend what he says is his First Amendment right to express himself by flipping off police officers. Ekas stated, "I did it because I have the right to do it. We all have that right, and we all need to test it. Otherwise we'll lose it" (Mayes, 2010). Legal experts note, "Even though giving a police officer the finger may be a rude and ill-advised gesture, it is not against the law" (Mayes, 2010).

CASE IN BRIEF ▶

United States v. O'Brien (1968)

ISSUE Is it a violation of Freedom of Speech to punish a person for burning their draft card?

RULING No. The Court ruled that punishing this behavior was constitutional because it was aimed not at the message but, instead, at the conduct used to convey that message. The government had a compelling interest to protect in preserving the draft, and punishing a person for destroying their draft card helped advance the government's interest.

Symbolic speech was the focus in *United States v. O'Brien* (1968), in which the Court considered what actions would be considered constitutionally protected. The case involved draft card burning and was used by the Court to develop a four-part test when it supported the constitutionality of a law prohibiting such burning. Chief Justice Burger stated:

> We cannot accept the view that an apparently limitless variety of conduct can be labeled "speech" whenever the person engaging in the conduct intends thereby to express an idea....A government regulation is sufficiently justified if it is within the constitutional power of the government; if it furthers any important or substantial governmental interest; if the governmental interest is unrelated to the suppression of free expression; and if the incidental restriction on alleged First Amendment freedoms is no greater than is essential to the furtherance of that interest.

In this case, the Court held that the selective service requirement regarding draft cards met these conditions, and the conviction against O'Brien was upheld.

Many symbolic acts, although often highly controversial, fall under First Amendment protection, including flag desecration, cross burning, nude dancing, and the display of yard signs.

Flag Burning Two Supreme Court cases involving symbolic expression demonstrate the centrality of such issues and the danger in assuming easy answers to First Amendment dilemmas. In 1969, after an assassination attempt on a civil rights leader, Sidney Street burned a flag in protest and was arrested for "malicious mischief," a New York law that made acting out verbally or symbolically a crime. The Warren Court did not act on the flag-burning issue in this case, holding only that Street's words were protected speech. The Court suggested, however, that the burning of the flag could be prosecutable, even though it, too, was an act of protest (*Street v. New York*, 1969).

The landmark case in which flag burning as symbolic speech was examined is *Texas v. Johnson* (1989). Gregory Johnson, a demonstrator at the 1984 Republican National Convention in Dallas, unfurled a U.S. flag and set it on fire. While the flag burned, the protesters chanted, "America, the red, white and blue, we spit on you." Johnson was convicted of violating a Texas law prohibiting "the desecration of venerated objects," including the national flag. The Supreme Court ruled, "If there is a bedrock principle underlying the First Amendment, it is that the government may not prohibit the expression of an idea simply because society finds the idea itself offensive or disagreeable." Justice William Brennan, Jr., contended that nothing in the courts' precedents suggests that the state may foster its own view of the flag by prohibiting expressive conduct relative to it. Justice Kennedy concurred, stating, "The ruling [was simply] a pure command of the Constitution. It is poignant and fundamental that the flag perplexes those who hold it in contempt." Four justices dissented, including Chief Justice Rehnquist, who wrote an emotional opinion stressing that millions of Americans have "a mystical reverence" for the flag. Public reaction to the ruling was strong and highly negative.

Members of Congress and political candidates continue to demand constitutional action to overrule the Court; some propose an amendment to the First Amendment to deny flag burning as free speech. In 1989, Congress passed a flag protection act that was short lived; on June 11, 1990, the Supreme Court declared the act unconstitutional as an unwarranted restriction on symbolic expression. This issue remains volatile, and efforts to enact flag desecration amendments have continued.

Cross Burning and Bias or Hate Crimes In 1989, St. Paul, Minnesota, like a number of other cities, passed an ordinance against various forms of expression based on bias or hatred to send a message that crimes against people because of their race or religion would not be tolerated. Several months later, in June 1990, a teenager was arrested under the ordinance and charged with burning a cross at the home of the only black family in a St. Paul neighborhood.

A county district judge initially held the ordinance unconstitutional as a violation of the First Amendment. The Minnesota Supreme Court, however, overturned this decision and upheld the ordinance, maintaining that it could be narrowly interpreted to ban acts of bigotry that arouse anger in others and still protect free speech. The state court said, "Burning a cross in the yard of an African American

◀ **CASE IN BRIEF**

Texas v. Johnson (1989)

ISSUE Is burning the U.S. flag a form of protected speech?

RULING Yes. The State of Texas used the law to restrict the freedom of speech (expression) by punishing a person's message. The law did not meet "most exacting scrutiny" because the interest asserted was not compelling.

family's home is deplorable conduct that the City of St. Paul may without question prohibit. The burning of a cross is itself an unmistakable symbol of violence and hatred based on virulent notions of racial supremacy."

The case was subsequently appealed to the U.S. Supreme Court, which held that the ordinance was unconstitutional (*R.A.V. v. City of St. Paul*, 1992). Justice Antonin Scalia delivered the Court's acceptance of the Minnesota court's narrowing of the ordinance to apply only to so-called fighting words, which Scalia termed *constitutionally proscribable*. Even so, the Court found the ordinance to be unconstitutional on its face because "it prohibits otherwise permitted speech solely on the basis of the subjects the speech addresses." Cross burning and other reprehensible acts, Scalia argued, could be prosecuted under a variety of existing statutes. These means were sufficient for St. Paul to prevent such behavior "without adding the First Amendment to the fire."

Balancing what the Constitution means and what the public wants it to mean at the time is often difficult to effectively accomplish. What the Constitution means to one person is not always what it means to another person. This difference of opinion is why lawsuits occur and why the system is set up to decide which perspective will prevail in a particular case. As the times, politics, and values of the United States change, so do legal arguments, holdings, and precedents. In *Virginia v. Black* (2003), the Supreme Court held that a law banning cross burning as a hate crime itself is unconstitutional because the law presumes hate is the purpose. Without more evidence to prove a hate crime, cross burning is deemed a protected form of speech.

Nude Dancing In 1991, the Supreme Court took up the question of nude dancing as a form of symbolic speech. The case involved nude dancers in the Kitty Cat Lounge in South Bend, Indiana, who were arrested for violating the state's public indecency law. A federal appeals court in Chicago had ruled the dancing was inherently expressive, communicating an emotional message of eroticism and sensuality and that the ban, therefore, violated the First Amendment. Five Supreme Court Justices voted to reverse but were unable to isolate a single reason for the reversal. The essence of the ruling in *Barnes v. Glen Theatre* (1991) was that requiring dancers to wear at least pasties and a g-string did not violate their freedom of speech. It thus gave local prosecutors a new option to restrict totally nude entertainment in their communities.

Civil liberty lawyers, who had feared that the Court might apply a sweeping analysis that could challenge constitutional protection for many forms of artistic expression, were relieved by the Court's relatively narrow approach. Chief Justice Rehnquist for the majority made clear that nude dancing enjoyed some marginal First Amendment protection. However, because of the state's interest in promoting order and morality, nude dancing *could* be prohibited, just as could other forms of public nudity. He observed that the statute's pasties and g-string requirement was a modest imposition and the bare minimum necessary to achieve the state's purpose.

Yard Signs Another area of expression some city ordinances seek to limit is use of yard signs. Many cities prohibit such signs altogether. Other cities have restrictions on the size or number of signs that can be placed in a person's yard or window.

Such restrictions were tested in *City of Ladue v. Gilleo* (1994), a case involving Margaret Gilleo, a resident of an exclusive suburb of St. Louis, Missouri. Gilleo put up an anti-war sign in the second floor window of her home that read "Peace in the Gulf." Ladue's city ordinance prohibits all signs within its boundaries except for real estate signs, road and safety hazards, inspection signs, public transportation markers, and business signs in commercially zoned areas. According to officials, the ordinance is intended to protect the community's aesthetics. Lower courts ruled for Gilleo, saying Ladue was wrong in favoring some signs over others, for example, real estate signs over political protest signs.

The Supreme Court agreed. In June 1994, a unanimous Court ruled that cities may not prohibit residents from putting political or personal signs in their yards. Justice John Paul Stevens, writing for the Court, declared, "A special respect for individual liberty in the home has long been part of our culture and our law. That principle has special resonance when the government seeks to constrain a person's ability to speak there."

The issue of signs came up again in 2015 in the case of *Reed v. Town of Gilbert*. This case involved an ordinance that prohibited outdoor signs without a permit but provided for 23 specific exemptions from the ordinance. One of these exemptions was for "temporary directional signs" to help guide people to religious and charitable events. The ordinance applied limits to these directional signs, including how large the sign could be and how long it could be posted. Clyde Reed, who was the pastor at Good News Community Church, held services at different locations in town due to a lack of a permanent location. The church was cited two times by the town for failing to comply with the ordinance. Pastor Reed challenged the town's ordinance.

The Supreme Court found the ordinance to be content-based, meaning it treated exceptions differently based on the message each sign conveyed. Because of the content-based nature of the ordinance, the Court applied the strict scrutiny test. The town of Gilbert argued that the ordinance was in place to preserve the aesthetic nature of the town and for traffic safety, neither of which the Court found to be a compelling reason. Gilbert allowed unlimited numbers of other types of signs, leading to the same aesthetic problem it claimed temporary directional signs caused. As for the safety issue, the town could not show that temporary directional signs caused more of a traffic safety problem than signs containing other messages.

The fact that some of these cases made their way to any court, especially the Supreme Court, makes one wonder *why*? Often, differing political perspectives are involved or there exists an ongoing issue between a city, for example, and an individual seen as a "troublemaker." Sometimes government officials adhere to a strict interpretation policy and do not anticipate the implications of their actions. Sometimes the government considers the issue to be worthy of the time and expense to pursue. Sometimes the results are not anticipated, with law being promulgated that was not the government's intention. These outcomes illustrate why any government employee needs a working knowledge of constitutional law.

◀ CASE IN BRIEF

Reed v. Town of Gilbert (2015)

ISSUE Does a sign ordinance that restricts the size, location, number, and duration of directional signs violate the Free Speech Clause?

RULING Yes. Because signs under the ordinance were treated differently based on their message, the regulation was content-based. Therefore, strict scrutiny applied. The town's ordinance could not satisfy the test.

"Police Rally as Mayor Says Black Lives Matter Banner Stays"

By Philip Marcelo (*Associated Press*, July 28, 2016)

SOMERVILLE, Mass. (AP)—About 50 police officers and their supporters upset about a Black Lives Matter banner that has been hanging outside City Hall for a year rallied on Thursday to try to pressure the mayor to remove it.

The primarily white opponents of the banner broke into chants of "All lives matter!" and "Take it down!" Many held signs saying "Cops lives matter" and "Support your local police."

Harold MacGilvray, president of a coalition representing 1,500 officers in 26 communities, said a public building like Somerville's City Hall is "no place" for political slogans to be displayed.

The mayor of Somerville, a largely white and historically working-class Boston suburb, had earlier in the day promised not to remove the banner despite complaints from officers across the state.

Mayor Joe Curtatone, a white Democrat, said it's "OK to disagree" and the only way to resolve the impasse is through an "open dialogue" about race.

"That sign is not coming down," he insisted while standing in front of City Hall flanked by the police chief and two deputy chiefs.

The Somerville Police Employees Association was among the unions represented at the opposition rally Thursday evening outside City Hall. Its president, Michael McGrath, said his officers support the "core goal" of the Black Lives Matter movement but believe the banner sends an "exclusionary message" and had become "offensive" to them after this summer's fatal attacks on police in Dallas and in Baton Rouge, Louisiana.

"The banner implies that Somerville police officers are somehow responsible for racially motivated decision-making against minorities," he said.

As the police rally was breaking up, some Black Lives Matter supporters held signs saying "All lives can't matter until black lives matter" or thanking the mayor for his stand.

City resident Roy Pardi, who's white, said some people don't understand what Black Lives Matter means.

"Black Lives Matter doesn't stand for harming police, and it doesn't stand for other people's rights not being considered," he said. "It's just right now we're focusing on black lives. It's pretty basic."

But Jay Colbert, a white local firefighter standing nearby, was unconvinced and said activists were inciting people to take up arms against police.

"Someone hijacked that movement," he said, "and now it's almost synonymous with killing cops."

Curtatone, the son of Italian immigrants and the mayor since 2004, has argued that standing up for minority residents and supporting police aren't "competing interests." He noted the city has hung a banner at police headquarters honoring the officers slain in Dallas and Baton Rouge.

(Continued)

When asked whether he thought it was appropriate to place the Black Lives Matter banner on a government building, he replied: "No one can sit out this conversation. Where this is happening is in cities. This is the grassroots level."

Curtatone hung the 4-foot-by-12-foot banner over City Hall's main entrance in August 2015 at the request of a local Black Lives Matter chapter. He said then it was meant to recognize that "structural racism" exists in society and stressed it wasn't a criticism of his police department.

The police banner hangs over the police headquarters entrance and says, "In honor and remembrance," with an image of the Dallas Police Department badge and a black band across it.

Last week, the city police union called on the mayor to replace the City Hall banner, which says "#BlackLivesMatter," with one that states "All Lives Matter," a phrase some civil rights activists complain diminishes their concerns about the killings of black men and boys at the hands of police.

In response, police Chief David Fallon, who supports keeping the banner over City Hall, chided the union for getting involved in the debate.

Curtatone said opposition to the banner wasn't shared by all police officers. He also said he's "proud" of the response from residents, community leaders, faith-based leaders and activists, and he rejected the notion officers would face reprisals if they attended the opposition rally.

Somerville is a city of more than 80,000 residents that borders Boston and Cambridge and is home to most of Tufts University's campus. It is about 74 percent white, 11 percent Latino, 9 percent Asian and 7 percent black, according to 2010 U.S. Census data.

Protected versus Unprotected Speech—Determining Boundaries

A common practice in free speech cases is to protect even the outer limits of speech, thereby ensuring that the "core" of the freedom is protected. If it is a close call, the Court will most likely rule in favor of protecting the speech. Still, not all speech is protected. Some types of speech have been found to specifically fall outside of the realm of First Amendment protection. What is indecent and what should be restricted as unprotected speech continue to spur differences of opinion in and out of the courtroom, not because the courts are too conservative or necessarily prudish but because society's norms keep changing. What was once considered inappropriate, in poor taste, or even obscene a decade ago can now be heard nightly on prime time television and viewed in movies that younger viewers are permitted to watch. Determining the boundaries between protected and unprotected speech is based on tradition and history, with certain "well-defined and narrowly limited" classes of speech that fall outside the perimeter of constitutional protection.

The focus on history and tradition was emphasized in *United States v. Stevens* (2010) as the rationale for determining what speech is given First Amendment protection. Earlier free speech cases appeared to use a "lack of social value" as the reason for not providing First Amendment protection. The Supreme Court in *Stevens* explained that this "lack of social value" reasoning was only a way of *describing* types of unprotected speech, not the test of what speech is unprotected. In *Stevens*, the Court ruled that federal statute 18 U.S.C. § 48, which criminalized the commercial production, sale, or possession of depictions of cruelty to animals, was an unconstitutional abridgment of First Amendment free speech rights.

CASE IN BRIEF

United States v. Stevens (2010)

ISSUE Are depictions of animal cruelty, as defined in the federal statute, a categorically unprotected free speech?

RULING No. Based upon the Nation's history and tradition, this is not one of the few categories of speech that fall outside the First Amendment. In addition, the statute is substantially overbroad and would punish otherwise legal conduct.

CASE IN BRIEF

United States v. Alvarez (2012)

ISSUE Does a federal law that makes it a crime to lie about receiving military medals or honors violate the First Amendment's guarantee of the right to free speech?

RULING Yes. The Free Speech Clause of the First Amendment protects false statements.

In 2004, Robert Stevens was indicted under 18 U.S.C. § 48 for creating and selling three videotapes, two of which depicted pit bulls engaged in dog fighting. The third tape showed a pit bull attacking a domestic pig as part of the dog's training to catch and kill wild hogs. Although Stevens' criminal prosecution concerned only the three tapes, he had made $20,000 in 2.5 years from selling nearly 700 videos. And although Stevens was not accused of engaging in animal cruelty himself, nor of shooting the footage from which the videos were created, the footage in each video was accompanied by introductions, narration, and commentary by Stevens, as well as literature written by Stevens.

Stevens filed a motion to dismiss the indictment, arguing that the federal statute abridged his right to freedom of speech under the First Amendment. The district court denied his motion in November 2004, and in January 2005, Stevens was convicted by a jury. Stevens appealed, and the Third Circuit vacated his conviction, holding that 18 U.S.C. § 48 did, in fact, violate the First Amendment. The court stated that dog fighting, or the use of dogs to hunt hogs, may be made illegal to protect animals from cruelty. However, the law in question that prohibited the depiction of animal cruelty violated the First Amendment by creating a new category of speech, one not a "long established category of free speech," not protected by the free speech provision of the amendment. Thus, because Section 48 is substantially overbroad, it is invalid under the First Amendment, affirming the Third District Court decision.

United States v. Alvarez (2012), a case that highlights the desire to narrowly define unprotected speech, involved the Stolen Valor Act of 2005 (18 U.S.C. 704(B)), which made it a crime to lie about being awarded military decorations or medals and imposed enhanced penalties for lies involving a Congressional Medal of Honor. In 2007, Xavier Alvarez was charged in the Central District of California with two counts of falsely representing that he had been awarded the Congressional Medal of Honor. Alvarez, who had never served in the armed forces, moved to dismiss on the grounds that the act violated his First Amendment right to free speech. The district court denied the motion to dismiss, and Alvarez pleaded guilty but reserved his right to appeal.

The case ascended to the U.S. Supreme Court, which ruled 6–3 on June 28, 2012, that the government cannot punish people for making false claims about military service or honors and that the First Amendment is written broadly enough to protect intentional untruths as long as they do not serve fraudulent purposes and the person stating such lies is not under oath in a court of law at the time. In writing the Court's opinion, Justice Kennedy stated: "The Nation well knows that one of the costs of the First Amendment is that it protects the speech we detest as well as the speech we embrace. Though few might find respondent's statements anything but contemptible, his right to make those statements is protected by the Constitution's guarantee of freedom of speech and expression. The Stolen Valor Act infringes upon speech protected by the First Amendment."

This opinion illustrates well how many types of speech, even if morally reprehensible, fall within First Amendment protection, meaning the government cannot limit or punish that type of speech. Importantly, the Court notes that "absent from those few categories where the law allows content-based regulation of speech is any general exception to the First Amendment for false statements."

Since *Alvarez*, Congress has worked to revamp the Stolen Valor Act so that it meets the strict scrutiny requirement.

The preceding cases are examples of how the Supreme Court, in its efforts to be judicious about how it determines what does and does not enjoy First Amendment protection, has found certain categories of speech to be protected even when the content is highly offensive or reprehensible to many. Various other Supreme Court rulings have held that the First Amendment provides no protection to obscenity, child pornography, or speech that advocates the use of force to direct, incite, or produce imminent lawless action (Cohen, 2009). The Court has also ruled that the First Amendment does not fully protect speech that may be harmful to children, defamation (libel and slander), commercial speech, speech broadcast on radio and television, and public employees' speech (Cohen, 2009). When cases arise under these circumstances, the issue becomes whether the speech in question meets the definition of the category of unprotected speech.

Fighting Words The Supreme Court defines *fighting words* as those "personally abusive epithets which, when addressed to the ordinary citizen, are, as a matter of common knowledge, inherently likely to provoke violent reaction" (*Cohen v. California*, 1971) or "[words] which by their very utterance inflict injury or tend to incite an immediate breach of the peace" (*Lewis v. City of New Orleans*, 1974). It is important to note that many state courts have held police officers to higher standards and levels of tolerance in cases where officers are on the receiving end of abusive language. The courts' logic has typically been that officers should expect, as part of wearing the uniform, to occasionally encounter citizens who use foul language and insults to express their discontent with the police and that officers, knowing this to be part of the job, are expected to exercise greater restraint in not

Constitutional Law in ACTION

Officer Tollivan is on patrol at 9:30 P.M. when he sees a group of teenagers gathered near a vacant house. Knowing that there has been a problem in the neighborhood with break-ins, he pulls over his squad car and gets out to talk to the group.

As he gets out of the squad car, the group starts to walk away. He calls out, "Hey, can I talk to you?" A girl in the group looks back and replies, "F*ck you, pig!" The girl continues to walk away. Officer Tollivan tells her to stop because she is under arrest for disorderly conduct, citing a state law that prohibits using "offensive, boisterous, obscene, or vulgar language." He places her in handcuffs, puts her in the back of the squad, and brings her to juvenile detention.

- *Does the arrest of the girl punish speech that is protected by the First Amendment?*
- *If this comment were directed at you, how would you feel?*
- *Should an officer have to tolerate this behavior because of the job he holds? Why or why not?*

reacting to such speech (Gardner & Anderson, 2012). However, direct and outright threats to an officer's safety, speech that is likely to incite a surrounding crowd to violent action, or speech that in any way obstructs officers in performing their lawful duty has generally been viewed by the courts as falling outside constitutional protection.

Obscenity   It can be challenging to understand and define the concept of obscenity. However, the courts have developed fairly precise guidelines regarding what legally constitutes obscene material. To qualify as obscene, it must be shown that the work (1) taken as a whole appeals to the prurient (lustful) interest in sex; (2) portrays sexual conduct in a patently offensive way; and (3) taken as a whole does not have a serious literary, artistic, political, or scientific value (*Miller v. California*, 1973).

Inflammatory Speech   When made at the right time and place, inflammatory "pure" speech or symbolic speech can cause violence and other unlawful conduct. But at what point does this inflammatory speech advocate violence or unlawful conduct such that it should lose First Amendment protection? This has been a question the Supreme Court has tried to answer since the early 1900s.

The first specific test of how far government can limit or punish speech occurred with the Espionage Act (1917) passed by Congress during World War I. This act made illegal interference with recruiting or drafting soldiers or any act that adversely affected military morale. The terms used were obviously broad in interpretation. In *Schenck v. United States* (1919), the Court upheld the conviction of a socialist indicted under the Espionage Act on the grounds that freedom of speech is not absolute. When Charles Schenck was charged with espionage for distributing flyers that encouraged young men to resist the draft, his defense asserted such an act of expression was protected speech. Justice Holmes, however, disagreed, stating, "When a nation is at war, many things that might be said in time of peace are such a hindrance to its effort that their utterance will not be endured." This case is an example of when the good of the greater whole outweighs the rights of the individual. Delivering the Court's unanimous opinion, Justice Holmes went on to say:

> The character of every act depends upon the circumstances in which it is done. The most stringent protection of free speech would not protect a man in falsely shouting fire in a theater and causing a panic.... The question in every case is whether the words used are used in such circumstances and are of such a nature as to create a clear and present danger that they will bring about the substantive evils that Congress has a right to prevent.

"clear and present danger" test the test of whether words are so potentially dangerous as to not be protected by the First Amendment

The Court began to apply this **"clear and present danger" test** to subsequent cases involving freedom of speech. Another test of what speech is protected was *Gitlow v. New York* (1925), in which the Court held that "a state in the exercise of its police power may punish those who abuse this freedom by utterances inimical to the public welfare, tending to corrupt public morals, and incite to crime, or disturbing the public peace." Benjamin Gitlow had been indicted under a New York State law that prohibited the advocacy of the overthrow of the government by force or violence. In 1940, Congress enacted the Smith Act, which declared advocating the overthrow of the government by force or violence to be unlawful. Being able to speak against the government has always been recognized as an important right of the people. However, as continuously noted, no right is absolute, and the Court continues to address what is and is not protected speech.

In another speech case, leaders of the Communist Party were convicted under the Smith Act and appealed on the grounds that the Act was unconstitutional. The Court upheld the Act's constitutionality in deciding *Dennis v. United States* (1951), but not on the grounds of the "clear and present danger" doctrine. Instead, the majority adopted a standard put forward by Judge Learned Hand: "Whether the gravity of the 'evil,' discounted by its improbability, justifies such invasion of free speech as is necessary to avoid the danger." This standard has sometimes been called the **"clear and probable danger" test,** the interpretation being that when the government can show that a serious "evil" is at hand, the less probable the "evil" needs to be. In other words, the more serious the speech-advocated evil is, the less demanding the courts will be on the possible occurrence to limit the speech.

In *Brandenburg v. Ohio* (1969), the Court adopted a new test—the **"imminent lawless action" test**. Although government has a justifiable interest in preventing lawless conduct, the mere discussion of such conduct would not necessarily cause imminent lawless action. In *Brandenburg*, the Court created a three-part test that the government must meet if certain communication is not to be protected by the First Amendment: (1) the speaker subjectively intended incitement, (2) in context, the words used were likely to produce imminent, lawless action, and (3) the words used by the speaker objectively encouraged and urged incitement.

This approach, modified by other cases, has been termed the **balancing test,** a position taken by the appellate courts to balance society's need for law and order and for effective law enforcement against the rights of individuals. Indeed, a crucial matter with respect to interpreting the Constitution and understanding the conflicting rights and obligations contained within is the concept of substantive due process—the tension between legitimate state interests (e.g., promoting the public health, welfare, and safety) versus legitimate individual liberty interests (e.g., right to free speech)—and how these interests must be balanced, a theme consistently addressed throughout this text.

Because courts are political institutions and the U.S. legal system is adversarial by design, every case requires a choice between competing social interests. Allowed discretion, judges weigh conflicting social claims, determine each party's rights and obligations, and make choices to distribute benefits and burdens based on the judges' values and attitudes: "This interest-balancing perspective readily translates into judicial self-restraint. When the constitutionality of a law is called into question, judges in a democratic society are duty-bound to respect the balance among interests struck by the statute for the logical reason that, having been passed by a majority of legislators, it presumably satisfies more rather than fewer interests" (Ducat, 2010, pp. 81–82).

When applying the balancing approach to First Amendment free speech cases, the Supreme Court strives to strike a balance between the value of liberty of expression and the demands of ordering a free society. In *Gertz v. Robert Welch, Inc.* (1974), the Court stated, "Under the First Amendment there is no such thing as a false idea . . . however pernicious an opinion may seem, we depend for its correction not on the conscience . . . but on the competition of ideas."

"clear and probable danger" test the test of whether the gravity of the evil discounted by its improbability justifies an invasion of free speech necessary to avoid any danger

"imminent lawless action" test a three-part test that the government must meet if certain communication is not to be protected by the First Amendment: (1) the speaker subjectively intended incitement, (2) in context, the words used were likely to produce imminent, lawless action, and (3) the words used by the speaker objectively encouraged and urged incitement; replaced the "clear and present danger" test

balancing test a position taken by the appellate courts to balance the needs of society for law and order and for effective law enforcement against the privacy rights of individuals

preferred freedoms approach a position that stresses that civil liberties are to take precedence over other constitutional values because they are requisite to a democracy

The **preferred freedoms approach**, a position originally set forth by Justice Harlan F. Stone, has been important in constitutional law since World War II. This approach stresses that civil liberties have a preferred position among other constitutional values because they are requisite to a democracy. Under this concept, the burden lies largely with the government to prove that clear and present danger exists when a freedom is exercised. This concept tends to change the balance sought in judicial decisions, as shown in Figure 5.2.

Some Supreme Court Justices, notably Black and William O. Douglas, have argued that free speech is an absolute right, by definition, and not subject to balancing. Justice Black, in *Konigsberg v. State Bar of California* (1961), stated: "I do not subscribe to that doctrine [the balancing approach] for I believe that the First Amendment's unequivocal command that there shall be no abridgement of the rights of free speech and assembly shows that the men who drafted our Bill of Rights did all the 'balancing' that was to be done in the field."

In opposition to this view and in support of the balancing approach, Justice Harlan, in the same case, wrote, "We reject the view that freedom of speech and association . . . as protected by the First and Fourteenth Amendments, are 'absolutes,' not only in the undoubted sense that where the constitutional protection exists it must prevail, but also in the sense that the scope of that protection must be gathered solely from a literal reading of the First Amendment."

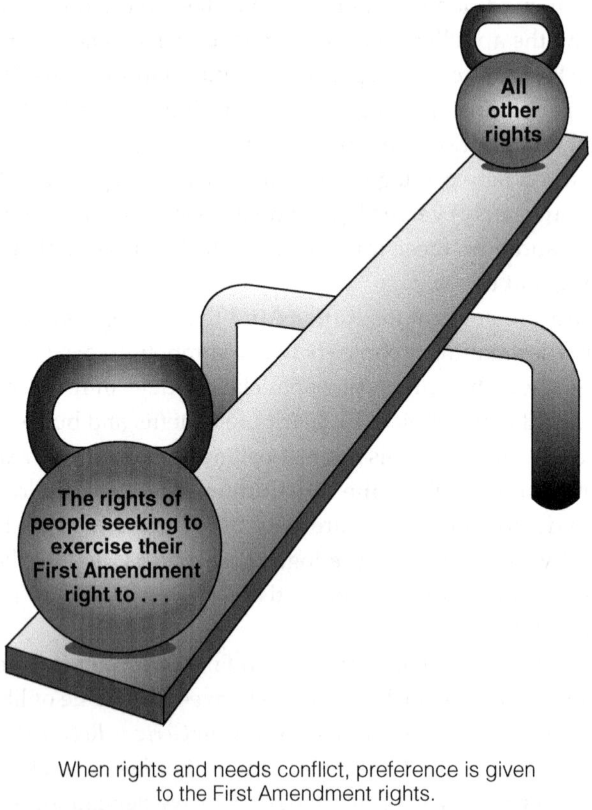

When rights and needs conflict, preference is given to the First Amendment rights.

Figure 5.2 The Preferred Freedoms Approach

The difficulty of the absolute approach to free speech was shown in 1978, when a group of U.S. Nazis sought to hold a rally in Skokie, Illinois. The municipality denied them a permit on the grounds that the Nazi rally would incite hostility in the largely Jewish population, which included many survivors of Nazi concentration camps. Lawyers from the ACLU represented the Nazis, arguing that Skokie laws limiting public demonstrations were unconstitutional. A U.S. Court of Appeals agreed with the ACLU, and the Supreme Court granted certiorari via an application to stay the injunction and ruled, per curium, that the state court must give strict procedural safeguards to a denial of First Amendment rights, which includes immediate appellate review (*National Socialist Party v. Skokie*, 1977). Although many Americans were outraged at the defense of those they considered enemies of free speech, this case illustrated constitutional freedom in action.

Although it's unlawful to shout "fire" in a crowded theater, some messages that may incite panic are actually protected speech. *Fogel v. Collins* (2008) involved a Grass Valley (California) police sergeant who received an anonymous phone call about a parked Volkswagen van that had a message that frightened the caller painted on the back window. The message, printed in block letters said, "I am a *@!%#$ suicide bomber terrorist! Pull me over! Please, I dare ya!" A second message read, "Allah praise the patriot act. . . . *@%#$ Jihad on the First Amendment! P.S. W.O.M.D. on board!" The rest of the van was decorated with slogans and painting, including a U.S. flag, which were not threatening. The investigating sergeant, who determined that the van belonged to 22-year-old Matthew Fogel, took photos of the van but believed the messages to be merely political satire. He called his captain who believed, in contrast, that a criminal act had been committed and ordered the sergeant to treat the matter as a bomb threat.

Although no bomb was found, the officers arrested Fogel and had the van towed. Fogel was charged with "willfully threatening to commit crime" and "use of offensive words in a public place which are inherently likely to provoke an immediate violent reaction." The prosecutor declined to prosecute, and Fogel was released the next day. Fogel then filed a civil lawsuit against the Grass Valley Police Department, the sergeant, the captain, and other officers, alleging they violated his rights under the First, Fourth, and Fourteenth Amendments, as well as for false arrest and assault and battery. The defendants, the police department, and the city filed a motion for summary judgment. The district court found that the police officers could have believed the First Amendment did not protect the message and dismissed the case. Fogel appealed to the Ninth Circuit Court, which found that his messages taken in context were political rhetoric, not directed at anyone in particular, and not a true threat; as such, his "speech" was protected. Political rhetoric criticizing the government is exactly what the First Amendment was intended to protect. Nonetheless, the Ninth Circuit affirmed the district court's granting of summary judgment in favor of the officers based on qualified immunity, reasoning that at the time of the incident, not all police officers would have believed Fogel's speech was protected by the First Amendment.

Given the same set of circumstances, some officers might treat such messages as a real threat whereas others might see it as a political message. A true threat is not protected speech; political hyperbole is. This distinction is what makes First Amendment cases difficult; they are fact-dependent. Facts provide context. Officers must consider the totality of the circumstances and the context in which the message or speech occurs. If the circumstances are as such that a suspect's speech can be considered to constitute a terrorist threat, an officer should err on the side of safety and follow his or her department's policy or protocol for dealing with such threats ("Violent Threats," 2008). Although this ruling applies only to officers in the Ninth Circuit, officers should take note that *Fogel* has set a precedent by ruling that such speech carries First Amendment protection.

Restrictions on Freedom of Speech

Understanding the Constitution requires the awareness that rights are *not* absolute, and this circumstance is the case with freedom of speech. In balancing personal interests and the public good, reasonable limits—that is, when government has a legitimate interest—are placed on where and when things can be said and, occasionally, on what can be said.

Whether symbolic or "pure" speech, the level of protection given to such speech—in other words, the level of government restriction dictating whether the speech is permissible or whether it is punishable—depends on what is being regulated. If the regulation or punishment is aimed at the actual *content* of the message, which regulates the speech based on the idea, topic discussed, or message conveyed, then strict scrutiny is the standard applied. If, on the other hand, the regulation is "*content neutral*," meaning it restricts not the message or the viewpoint, per se, but rather how, when, or where the message can be delivered, then the courts will apply a midlevel analysis or scrutiny. This test examines whether (1) the restriction is justified without reference to the content of the regulated speech, (2) the law is narrowly tailored to serve a significant government interest, and (3) open channels for the communication of the information exist (*Clark v. Community for Creative Non-Violence*, 1984). In some specific areas, the Court has developed a separate test, such as in the area of speech that advocates unlawful conduct.

Restrictions on speech have occurred most often in time of war and national emergency. The Alien and Sedition Acts of 1798 were the first efforts by Congress to specifically limit actual speech. These acts were passed when war with France threatened and the nation's security was considered to be directly affected. They empowered the President to expel "dangerous" aliens and provided for indicting those who should "unlawfully combine or conspire" against the administration by writing or speaking "with intent to defame" the government, the Congress, or the President. Although these laws were never tested in court and expired after several years, what the outcomes *might* have been if tested remain a source of scholarly legal debate.

The importance of freedom of speech was highlighted during the Free Speech Movement of student protesters in the 1960s and 1970s. In the mid-1960s, the University of California, Berkeley, banned political activity on campus. Students wanted to raise money and recruit other students to do civil rights work, but Berkeley officials said they could not. The students rebelled, claiming their First Amendment rights were being denied. The ensuing riot at Berkeley became a catalyst for years of political unrest on the country's college campuses. Ultimately, freedom of speech was established in most colleges and universities.

MYTH
As a free citizen, you may say whatever, whenever, and wherever you want without fear of punishment or restriction from the government.

FACT
Free speech, although a fundamental right, is not absolute. The government may restrict or punish certain speech.

In a 2010 freedom of speech case, *Holder v. Humanitarian Law Project*, the Supreme Court upheld a portion of the USA Patriot Act that makes it a crime to provide "material support" to any group that has been designated by the Attorney General as a "foreign terrorist organization." This case pitted free speech against national security, upholding previous rulings that the government can ban organizations from providing material support to groups designated as terrorist groups, even if the support is in the form of training materials to peacefully resolve conflict.

In this case, two groups designated as terrorist organizations by the Attorney General sought to provide "material support" to the Partiya Karkeren Kurdistan (PKK) and the Liberation Tigers of Tamil Eelam (LTTE), which aim to establish independent states for Kurds in Turkey and Tamils in Sri Lanka, respectively. At issue was whether certain terms found within statute 18 U.S.C. 2339B(a)(1), which prohibits providing certain types of aid to known terrorist organizations, unconstitutionally violate the First and Fifth Amendments by restricting political speech and including overly vague provisions. The Humanitarian Law Project argued a strict scrutiny standard should be applied to the statute because it violates the Fifth Amendment by virtue of its vagueness and infringes on First Amendment rights to expression of political speech and freedom of association (Vernon & Wu, 2010). However, the government maintained that the statute was constitutional, regulating conduct rather than speech, so the statute need only pass intermediate scrutiny.

Although multiple lower court rulings had sided in favor of the Humanitarian Law Project by finding the statute unconstitutionally vague, on June 21, 2010, the Supreme Court held, by a 6–3 vote, that the statute's prohibitions on "expert advice," "training," "service," and "personnel" were not vague, nor did they violate speech or associational rights as applied to the Humanitarian Law Project's intended activities. Chief Justice John Roberts, writing for the majority, reversed the Court of Appeals on the vagueness claims and held that although strict scrutiny apparently applied, even support in the form of intangibles such as human rights training freed up resources that could then be reallocated to the group's terrorist activities, a national security concern sufficient to trump the First Amendment interests of the plaintiffs. Thus, the Court affirmed in part, reversed in part, and remanded. The Court held that the First Amendment does not prevent Congress from barring actions taken to aid terrorist groups simply because the actions may have an expressive component, when it does so based on a reasonable conclusion that the actions are likely to promote the groups' terrorist goals.

The Supreme Court's ruling on this issue will help determine how domestic citizens and organizations interact, if at all, with designated terrorist organizations in the future, as well as whether courts will interpret similar statutory provisions as content-based regulations of speech, or as regulations of conduct that only incidentally affect speech.

Exclusion of groups with political agendas who want to speak at shopping malls is also a controversial area because such malls, although standing on private property, are essentially public places. Since 1968, when the U.S. Supreme Court first said the public had some speech rights in malls, the issue has gone back and forth between civil libertarians and mall owners, with the current trend being that private property owners can restrict speech but not on the public sidewalks around the property.

Snyder v. Phelps (2011) was the highly publicized funeral protest case in which members of Westboro Baptist Church, who were openly critical of the military and its tolerance toward homosexuality, picketed the funeral of deceased Marine Lance Corporal Matthew Snyder. Standing on public land approximately 1,000 feet from where the funeral was being held, the picketers peacefully displayed signs that read, "Thank God for Dead Soldiers," "Fags Doom Nations," "America Is Doomed," and "You're Going to Hell." Snyder's family filed suit against Westboro for defamation, invasion of privacy, and the intentional infliction of emotional distress for displaying such signs at the funeral.

A jury held Westboro liable for millions of dollars in compensatory and punitive damages. Westboro appealed, and although the District Court reduced the punitive damages award, it left the verdict otherwise intact. However, the Fourth Circuit reversed, ruling that Westboro's statements were entitled to protection under the First Amendment because those statements were on matters of public concern, were not provably false, and were expressed solely through hyperbolic rhetoric.

The importance of *Snyder v. Phelps* is that it shows (1) the First Amendment can protect someone from state tort liability for what they have said, (2) matters of "public concern," which are defined as those relating to issues of social, political, or other community concerns, hold a high place in the protected speech area, and (3) how contextual free speech issues are when determining what can and cannot be restricted in reference to "time, place, and manner." An interesting side note: at the time of this opinion, 43 states and the federal government had laws restricting protests at funerals.

A continuing and intensely controversial area surrounds the abortion issue, and antiabortionists' claim that their demonstrations outside abortion clinics are justified, constitutional expressions of free speech. The courts, however, have set limits on such expression. In *Madsen v. Women's Health Center, Inc.* (1994), a state court enjoined Madsen and other antiabortion protesters from blocking or interfering with public access to a Florida abortion clinic and from abusing, intimidating, or touching people who enter or leave the clinic. When the clinic returned to court and argued that protesters were still limiting access to the clinic, even greater restrictions were ordered to provide a larger buffer zone around the clinic and even around the residences of clinic employees.

When Madsen and the other demonstrators challenged the injunction on First Amendment grounds, the Florida Supreme Court upheld the injunction in its entirety. The U.S. Supreme Court, however, granted the protesters' petition for certiorari and found parts of the injunction in violation of the Constitution:

> In sum, we uphold the noise restrictions and the 36-foot buffer zone around the clinic entrances and driveway because they burden no more speech than necessary to eliminate the unlawful conduct targeted by the state court's injunction. We strike down as unconstitutional the 36-foot buffer zone as applied to the private property to the north and west of the clinic, . . . the 300-foot no-approach zone around the clinic, and the 300-foot buffer zone around the residences, because these provisions sweep more broadly than necessary to accomplish the permissible goals of the injunction. Accordingly, the judgment of the Florida Supreme Court is affirmed in part, and reversed in part.

A recent "buffer zone" case made its way to the Supreme Court. *McCullen v. Coakley* (2014) involved a Massachusetts' state law that prohibited knowingly standing on a "public way or sidewalk" within 35 feet of a location that performs abortions. The law was in response to a history of violence and harassment at such places. The Court struck down the statute, and in so doing, noted that in "the traditionally open character of public streets and sidewalks, we have held that the government's ability to restrict speech in such locations is 'very limited.'" In such locations, however, the government is allowed to impose restrictions based on time, manner, and location, as long as the restriction is not based on the message (i.e., the content). These restrictions must still be narrowly tailored to satisfy a significant government interest. The Court found that, despite the law being content-neutral, the burden on free speech was too great and other options existed for achieving the same governmental goal.

Sometimes, multiple freedoms are at issue in a legal dispute, as in the preceding abortion issue, when not only freedom of speech but also freedom to assemble was involved. In another example, *Rosenberger v. Rector and Visitors of the University of Virginia* (1995), both freedom of speech and the Establishment Clause were involved (Ducat, 2010). The University of Virginia, a state school, had a policy of using money from the Student Activity Fund (SAF), derived from mandatory student fees, to pay outside vendors to cover printing costs for a variety of publications produced by student organizations. The university, however, denied authorization for payment of printing costs for "Wide Awake," a newspaper put out by a Christian student group, on the grounds that the payments would implicate the school in promoting a religion.

Rosenberger, a founder of the Christian group, sued the university, arguing that the refusal of payment violated freedom of speech. Both the federal district court and the federal appeals court ruled in favor of the school, concluding that the payment withholding was necessary to comply with the dictates of the Establishment Clause. Rosenberger then petitioned for certiorari, which the Supreme Court granted.

As part of its ruling, the Court declared that no violation of the Establishment Clause occurs when a public university grants access to its facilities, including computer and printing facilities, on a religion-neutral, first-come-first-served basis to a wide spectrum of student groups. Therefore, there is no difference of constitutional significance between a school using its funds to operate a facility where a religious student organization can itself use a computer, printer, or copy machine to generate speech with a religious content or viewpoint and a school paying a third-party contractor to operate the facility on its behalf. In delivering the opinion of the Court, Justice Kennedy stated:

> Government may not regulate speech based on its substantive content or the message it conveys.... In the realm of private speech or expression, government regulation may not favor one speaker over another.... Discrimination against speech because of its message is presumed to be unconstitutional....
>
> There is no Establishment Clause violation in the University's honoring its duties under the Free Speech Clause. The judgment of the Court of Appeals must be, and is, reversed.

First Amendment Expression Rights of Public Employees

Although no citizens, regardless of their work, forfeit their constitutional rights, how these rights are applied can be different, depending on circumstances. For example, how one chooses to dress and groom is considered a matter of personal expression, and the length of a police officer's hair was the subject of litigation in *Kelley v. Johnson* (1976). In this case, Justice Rehnquist held that in an organizational structure that necessitated uniformity, such as that which exists in law enforcement, a requirement on hair length did not violate the officer's constitutional rights because it was not arbitrary and had a "rational connection between the regulation . . . and the promotion of safety of persons and property."

A leading case in freedom of speech of public employees is *Pickering v. Board of Education* (1968), in which a high school teacher's letter to the local newspaper's editor criticizing the allocation of funds between academics and athletics at the local high school led to the teacher's termination. The Supreme Court held that in the absence of proof of a teacher knowingly or recklessly making false statements, the teacher had a right to speak on issues of public importance without being dismissed from his position. An employee's interest as a citizen in making public comment needs to be balanced against the employer's competing interest "in promoting the efficiency of the public services it performs" (*Pickering v. Board of Education*, 1968). As established in *Connick v. Myers* (1983), "Employee speech has to be determined by the content, form and context of a given statement." This balancing test will weigh in favor of the employee when the speech is made *as a citizen*, not an employee, on a matter of public concern. In such cases, the court looks at whether the government employer has an adequate justification for treating the employee differently than a regular citizen, requiring any speech restrictions to be based on the fact that such limitations are needed for the government employer to run an efficient and effective operation.

This balancing inquiry was further addressed in *Garcetti v. Ceballos* (2006), a case in which Ceballos, a supervising deputy district attorney in Los Angeles, became aware of evidence against the defendant that had been obtained through the use of a faulty warrant affidavit. Ceballos brought this information to the attention of his superiors and recommended dismissing the charges, but the prosecutors ignored Ceballos's findings and opted to proceed with the criminal case. This prompted Ceballos to write and submit to the trial court a highly critical dismissal memorandum challenging the submitted evidence. The court, however, rejected Ceballos's challenge.

Ceballos then claimed that, in the weeks and months following this challenge, he was subjected to a series of retaliatory actions by his employer, including reassignment to a less desirable position, transfer to another courthouse, and denial of a promotion. Ceballos filed a lawsuit alleging this retaliation was based on his dismissal memo in violation of his First and Fourteenth Amendment rights, but his claim was rejected by the Court: "The U.S. Supreme Court ruled for the employer by distinguishing the *Pickering* balancing criteria from that here where Ceballos' speech was made pursuant to his official duties, in essence ruling it was speech made as part of his job and not made as a private citizen. The threshold inquiry after *Garcetti* is the extent to which an employee can be said to be speaking in connection with his/her employment" (Dwyer, 2010). Justice Kennedy, writing for the majority stated:

> It is well settled that "a State cannot condition public employment on a basis that infringes the employee's constitutionally protected interest in freedom of expression." The question presented by the instant case is whether the First Amendment protects a government employee from discipline based on speech made pursuant to the employee's official duties.
>
> The Court's decisions, then, have sought both to promote the individual and societal interests that are served when employees speak as citizens on matters of public concern and to respect the needs of government employers attempting to perform their important public functions.
>
> We reject, however, the notion that the First Amendment shields from discipline the expressions employees make pursuant to their professional duties. Our precedents do not support the existence of a constitutional cause of action behind every statement a public employee makes in the course of doing his or her job.
>
> The judgment of the Court of Appeals is reversed, and the case is remanded for proceedings consistent with this opinion. (*Garcetti v. Ceballos*, 2006)

The Court held "that when public employees make statements pursuant to their official duties, the employees are not speaking as citizens for First Amendment purposes, and the Constitution does not insulate their communications from employer discipline." As a result of *Garcetti*, criticism of the "blue wall of silence" and public demand for greater police transparency has hit a "speed bump" because the ruling discourages officers from coming forward with criticism of activities within the department (Dwyer, 2010). Any officer who speaks in public on an employment matter is not protected by the First Amendment. Thus, the rule of *Garcetti* appears to be that an employee is protected only if the speech is unconnected to employment. This rule, however, has recently been clarified.

In *Lane v. Franks* (2014), the Court narrowed the broad interpretation that the lower courts had been giving to the issue of identifying what was official job-duty speech and the connection between the speech and the speaker's official duties. In this case, Lane was hired as the director for a statewide program for underprivileged youth run by a community college. In this capacity, Lane discovered that one employee, who happened also to be a state representative, was being paid but was not showing up for work. Warned that terminating the employee would have negative repercussions, Lane fired the employee anyway. Further investigation into the matter resulted in the employee being federally indicted and ultimately found guilty of theft from a program that received federal funds. Lane was subpoenaed to testify regarding the events that led to the employee's termination and after doing so, was fired by his employer, Franks. Lane sued Franks for violation of his First Amendment rights, claiming his loss of employment was in retaliation for his testimony. Both the District Court and the Eleventh Circuit dismissed the case on the basis of *Garcetti*, ruling that Lane had given the testimony related to his official duties and, therefore, received no protection.

The Supreme Court reversed, finding that *Garcetti* was being interpreted too broadly and explaining that giving testimony under oath was not part of Lane's

◀ **CASE IN BRIEF**

Garcetti v. Ceballos (2006)

ISSUE Does the First Amendment protect the speech made by a government employee pursuant to his or her job?

RULING No. Speech by a government employee will be protected by the First Amendment when the speech is a matter of public concern and made as a citizen, not pursuant to one's job.

◀ **CASE IN BRIEF**

Lane v. Franks (2014)

ISSUE Does a public employee receive First Amendment protection when testimony is given in a trial, and testifying is not part of the employee's regular job duties?

RULING Yes. A public employee's testimony qualifies as citizen speech, not employee speech, when testifying is not part of the employee's regular job duties.

official job duties and was, therefore, speech given as a citizen, not an employee. Justice Sotomayor explained, "In other words, the mere fact that a citizen's speech concerns information acquired by virtue of his public employment does not transform that speech into employee—rather than citizen—speech. The critical question under *Garcetti* is whether the speech at issue is itself ordinarily within the scope of an employee's duties, not whether it merely concerns those duties."

In a concurring opinion, Justice Thomas emphasized the ruling did not address whether the First Amendment would protect testimony of an employee who routinely testified as part of regular job duties. "For some public employees—such as police officers, crime scene technicians, and laboratory analysts—testifying is a routine and critical part of their employment duties."

In *City of San Diego v. Roe* (2004), police officer Roe videotaped himself stripping off an unofficial police uniform and masturbating. He then sold the video on the adults-only section of an online auction site, with his seller profile indicating he was a police officer. When this activity came to the attention of the San Diego Police Department (SDPD), an investigation followed and Roe was ordered to stop, but he did not fully comply, so he was terminated. Roe filed suit, alleging

Constitutional Law in ACTION

Lieutenant Johnston was in charge of the vice unit. Recently, one of his undercover officers acting as a prostitute was solicited by the police chief's brother. The solicitor was arrested, but the charges were later dropped. A local television station made the arrest public. The chief's brother is also a member of the local civilian review board, which investigates allegations of police misconduct.

The lieutenant was upset by the charges being dropped because it is his belief that members of the board should be of the highest moral character and integrity. He also lives in the city and has an interest as a citizen regarding city government. Because of this he attended the next public meeting of the civilian review board, meetings he had attended numerous times in the past and at which he was well known by the regular attendees.

The topic of moral integrity came up during open forum. The lieutenant added to this discussion a rather forceful opinion regarding the chief's brother and his arrest. After the meeting, the lieutenant was approached by the brother and told, "I know who you are, and there will be payback."

The next week the lieutenant was transferred to a much less desirable position, with no reason given for the transfer. The lieutenant filed suit claiming that he was transferred because of his comments at the meeting, and that this violated his right to free speech.

- *Was the lieutenant punished for speaking out at the meeting?*
- *Had the lieutenant not been employed by the city, would he have been punished for the same speech?*
- *Would your opinion change if the lieutenant were in uniform and made his statements as such, rather than as a city resident? Should it matter?*

the department's demand that he stop making and selling the videos, and his subsequent firing because of his refusal to comply, were violations of his First Amendment right to free speech. The case found its way to the Supreme Court, which ruled that although the conduct did not amount to a matter of public concern, it was connected to his employment with the SDPD and that the officer's conduct negatively affected the department's operation and, therefore, was *not* protected by the First Amendment. This case illustrates the fine line public employees walk in matters concerning the First Amendment right to freedom of speech and expression.

> **LO4** As public employees, law enforcement officers' speech is not protected under the First Amendment if it is made while acting in an official job-related capacity.

Freedom of Speech, the Internet, and Technology

A plethora of First Amendment cases have arisen as the Internet continues to make virtually anything available to anyone. The Court began a more definitive review of Internet issues in *Reno v. American Civil Liberties Union* (1997). In this case, the Court struck down a law banning computer-generated or "virtual" child pornography. It acknowledged that in addition to the multifaceted means of disseminating information electronically, much broader community norms had to be considered. Congress responded to the *Reno* decision by promulgating the Child Online Protection Act (COPA) of 1998, which would, in effect, nullify the *Reno* decision. However, in 2008, the Third Circuit affirmed a 2007 district court ruling that COPA does not survive "strict scrutiny" analysis and thus, is an unconstitutional violation of the First Amendment (*American Civil Liberties Union v. Mukasey*, 2008). The following year the Supreme Court denied certiorari (*Mukasey v. American Civil Liberties Union*, 2009), effectively leaving the appellate court ruling to stand.

As is the case with the printed and spoken word, obscenity will continue garnering both legislative and judicial attention, and business communication, privacy issues, and advertising matters will surely be addressed. As the debate continues over what can be virtually made available to whom, in *United States v. American Library Association* (2003), the Court held that Congress could limit funding to libraries that did not filter Internet access to block obscene material and child pornography without violating the First Amendment.

Technology continues to pose new challenges to the law and its interpretation. A case involving technology and restrictions on speech occurred when California attempted to pass a law prohibiting the sale or rental of violent video games to minors (*Brown v. Entertainment Merchant's Association*, 2011). Members of the video game and software industries brought suit against the California governor, Edmund Brown, challenging the constitutionality of the law and arguing that it tread on speech that was shielded by the First Amendment. The Supreme Court agreed, with Justice Scalia delivering the opinion of the Court:

> We have no business passing judgment on the view of the California Legislature that violent video games (or, for that matter, any other forms of speech) corrupt the young or harm their moral development. Our task is only to say whether or not such works constitute a "well-defined and narrowly limited clas[s] of speech, the prevention and punishment of which have never been thought to raise any Constitutional problem," (the answer plainly is no); and if not, whether the regulation of such works is justified

CASE IN BRIEF

Brown v. Entertainment Merchant's Association (2011)

ISSUE Is it constitutional for a state to bar the sale of violent video games to minors?

RULING No. The First Amendment protects video games because, like songs, books, and movies, video games communicate a message. The state law is a content-based restriction on speech and cannot meet the strict scrutiny standard.

by that high degree of necessity we have described as a compelling state interest (it is not). Even where the protection of children is the object, the constitutional limits on governmental action apply.

California's legislation straddles the fence between (1) addressing a serious social problem and (2) helping concerned parents control their children. Both ends are legitimate, but when they affect First Amendment rights they must be pursued by means that are neither seriously under-inclusive nor seriously over-inclusive. See *Church of Lukumi Babalu Aye, Inc. v. Hialeah*. . . . As a means of protecting children from portrayals of violence, the legislation is seriously underinclusive, not only because it excludes portrayals other than video games, but also because it permits a parental or avuncular veto. And as a means of assisting concerned parents it is seriously overinclusive because it abridges the First Amendment rights of young people whose parents (and aunts and uncles) think violent video games are a harmless pastime. And the overbreadth in achieving one goal is not cured by the underbreadth in achieving the other. Legislation such as this, which is neither fish nor fowl, cannot survive strict scrutiny.

The Right to Record

Courts have long ruled that the First Amendment protects the right of citizens to take photographs and videos in public places. However, even more than a decade since the 9/11 terrorist attacks, police officers and security guards view people photographing federal buildings, bridges, and transportation hubs as potential terrorists and attempt to restrict them, often citing authority they do not have. Police and security guards have been called on to be "extra vigilant" and to encourage citizens to do the same. Taking photographs of likely terrorist targets is included in "suspicious behaviors" to watch for.

Police and security often restrict the taking of photographs, despite the public's right to do so. The "disconnect" between policy and practice may be the result of a lack of guidelines about how to balance security concerns with civil liberties (Shin, 2010a). The New York Police Department (NYPD) serves as an example of what an agency might do to close this gap. The NYPD directive on photographs says that photography is "rarely unlawful" and that officers have "no right to demand to see photos or to delete them." The directive allows that although New York is a potential terrorist target, it is also a major tourist destination and "practically all such photography will have no connection to terrorism or unlawful conduct" (Shin, 2010a, p. B02).

Videotaping also raises suspicion. It becomes especially controversial when citizens videotape police officers. Twenty years ago a private citizen videotaped the beating of Rodney King, causing a national uproar. When the four Los Angeles Police Department (LAPD) officers were found not guilty, riots broke out, leaving more than 50 dead and thousands injured. Since then, whether people have the right to videotape police officers has been a topic of debate.

In Maryland, motorcyclist Anthony Graber, wearing a helmet camera, recorded an incident where a plainclothes Maryland state trooper cut him off on an exit ramp and then drew his gun before announcing that he was a law enforcement officer. A week later Graber posted the video recording on YouTube, and the law came down hard on him, charging him with four felony counts, including violating

Maryland's wiretap law. If convicted he could have faced 16 years in prison (Shin, 2010b). Instead the wiretapping charges were dropped and Graber faced only the traffic-related charges.

In another Maryland case, Christopher Sharp used his cell phone to record an incident in which officers with the Baltimore Police Department broke up a fight involving Sharp's friend and arrested her. The officers seized Sharp's phone and deleted the video of the arrest, as well as other videos contained on the device. Sharp sued the Baltimore Police Department claiming officers had violated his First Amendment rights. This lawsuit was eventually settled but garnered national attention and led to the Department of Justice (DOJ) issuing guidance to police departments regarding the First Amendment rights of individuals who video record officers.

> **L05** *Citizens have the First Amendment right to record an officer performing his or her official duties in public.*

Despite citizens having the right to videotape the police, officers also have rights, including the right to due process and to be treated fairly and objectively, through the lens of experience and training, not judged solely by the subjective and selective recording of an event perhaps taken out of context (Slocumb & Roberts, 2010). In addition, officers have the right to order persons to cease activities that are legitimately interfering with law enforcement. However, the level of such interference must be shown to be sufficiently high as to actually obstruct the officer's duties.

Freedom of the Press

Freedom of the press *is* integrally related to freedom of speech because speech is considered not only spoken words but any means of conveying information. As early as 400 B.C.E., the Greek poet Euripides stated, "The tongue is mightier than the blade," and in 1839, Edward Bulwer-Lytton proclaimed, "The pen is mightier than the sword." Thomas Jefferson once stated, "Wherever people are well informed, they can be trusted with their own government." Freedom of the press protects the right to obtain and publish information or opinions without governmental control or fear of punishment.

> **L06** *Freedom of the press applies to all types of printed and broadcast material, including books, newspapers, magazines, pamphlets, films, and radio and television programs.*

Historically, freedom of the press has been attached to the general concept of censorship. In countries with extensive censorship, the right to publish news, information, and opinions is usually tightly restricted. The British government, for example, was able to restrict almost anything that arguably related to the government through use of the Official Secrets Act. Simply, anything the government wished to remain secret, would—period. Under such a law, for example, news of the Three Mile Island nuclear accident in the United States would not have been released had it happened in the United Kingdom. Even in the United States, where censorship is light, the right to publish is not absolute. The constraints on freedom of the press in a free society are controversial and are constantly being redefined by the judiciary.

Governments have restricted the right to publish in two ways: by restraining the press from publishing certain materials prior to the communication occurring and by punishing those who publish matter considered seditious, libelous, or obscene. The first kind of restriction, often called **prior restraint,** is rare in the United States and most other democratic countries. One of the first attacks on prior restraint can

prior restraint a restriction on publishing certain materials prior to a communication occurring

be found in John Milton's essay *Areopagitica* (1644), which was directed against the English licensing and censorship laws enacted in 1534 under Henry VIII. These laws were abolished in England in 1695, but the government was still able to take action on grounds of seditious libel against those who published material, whether true or false, and those who criticized government policies.

In the American colonies, prosecutions of this kind were made more difficult by a jury's decision in *New York v. Zenger* (1735). John Peter Zenger, a New York newspaper publisher, wrote articles critical of the colonial governor. The jury acquitted Zenger on the grounds that his charges were true and, therefore, could not be considered libelous. The Zenger trial is the first case in American law in which truth was asserted as a defense to an action for libel. Although Americans were denied this defense for two centuries following that trial under the common law of many jurisdictions, truth is now a constitutionally protected defense under the First Amendment ("The Trial of John Peter Zenger," n.d.).

This restraint on federal government's interference with freedom of the press was made binding on state governments via incorporation of the Fourteenth Amendment in *Near v. Minnesota* (1931), a case in which the Court ruled that no newspaper could be banned because of its contents, regardless of how scandalous they might be. Still, freedom of the press has frequently been denied in the areas of obscenity and pornography. The courts have, however, had some difficulty delineating appropriate standards of censorship.

For example, in *Roth v. United States* (1957), the Court ruled that obscenity is not a constitutionally protected freedom of speech. The standard to be used, as discussed previously in the chapter, is "whether to the average person, applying contemporary community standards, the dominant theme of the material, taken as a whole, appeals to prurient interest, that is, having a tendency to excite lustful thoughts" (*Miller v. California*, 1973).

Restrictions on the press have often occurred during national emergencies. Censorship during World War I led to the first clear articulation of the limits to freedom of speech with which free press issues are closely tied. During World War II, freedom of the press was greatly curtailed for security reasons, but the press willingly complied with censorship restrictions. Other than in wartime, censorship for national security reasons has been carefully limited.

In 1971, the U.S. government attempted to halt publication of *The Pentagon Papers* on the grounds that it could endanger national security. The Supreme Court ruled (*New York Times v. Sullivan*, 1964) that this case of prior restraint was unconstitutional, citing the *Zenger* trial as relevant. Other cases involving national security have concerned attempts to censor or halt publication of books about the Central Intelligence Agency. In 1983, when U.S. troops invaded Grenada, the press was initially barred from the island. The restrictions later imposed were thought to be unprecedented in U.S. practice and generated much controversy.

Control of the press during the Persian Gulf War (1991) was almost 100 percent. Many criticized the press for accepting conditions that made complete reporting impossible. After the war ended, the accuracy of some press reports was questioned. Constraints on the press are always controversial.

In Minnesota, reporters promised anonymity to a political campaign worker who gave them information. Later, the editors of the papers revealed his name, and he sued them. The Supreme Court ruled in *Cohen v. Cowles Media Company* (1991) that the First Amendment does not give the press a constitutional right to disregard promises that otherwise would be enforced under state law. The case was returned to the Minnesota Supreme Court for reconsideration. Further complicating the issue, several previous decisions appeared to narrow the newspaper reporters' right to withhold information given to them in confidence. In April 1991, a *Washington Post* reporter was held in contempt of court and jailed for refusing to identify a source.

Zenger had established the precedent that truthful statements were not to be considered libelous. The obvious corollary was that damages could be collected for false statements. In *New York Times v. Sullivan*, however, the Supreme Court held that public officials can win damages only if they can show that a statement defaming them was made with actual malice, that is, knowing it was false or recklessly disregarding whether it was false.

Other court rulings have extended the principle to include public figures not in government office, but involved in public controversy. In 1979, the Supreme Court held that a person who involuntarily receives publicity is not necessarily a public figure and, therefore, need not prove that the statements by the press were made with "actual malice" to obtain libel damages (*Hutchinson v. Proxmire*, 1979).

The Supreme Court has also held in *Zurcher v. Stanford Daily* (1978) that newspapers enjoy no special immunity from searches of their premises by police with warrants. In 1980, however, Congress passed a privacy protection act that required the police in most cases to obtain subpoenas for such searches. In 1979, in a controversial effort to curb prejudicial pretrial publicity, the Court ruled (*Gannett v. DePasquale*) that judges can bar the press and the public from criminal proceedings. In other cases, however, the courts have allowed televised proceedings.

The Supreme Court has further ruled that Americans have a free speech right to pass out anonymous political pamphlets (*McIntyre v. Ohio Elections Commission*, 1995). In a 7–2 decision, the Court said, "'Anonymous pamphleteering' has a long and honorable history in this country that extends back to the authors of *Federalist Papers* and is deeply ingrained as the secret ballot. 'Anonymity is a shield from the tyranny of the majority.'"

Balancing Freedom of the Press with the Right to a Fair Trial

A delicate balance exists between the people's right to know, the press' right to publish (First Amendment), and the "public trial" rights of those accused of crimes (Sixth Amendment), as well as the needs of the agencies charged with investigating such crimes (Fourth Amendment). A free press, being vital to the functioning of a democracy, keeps citizens fully informed and able to discharge their civic responsibilities. However, in this country, defendants in criminal cases are guaranteed due process of law and a fair and impartial trial. These guarantees are jeopardized when the media publish detailed information before a defendant is tried.

The question is whether events reported in the press before the trial may unduly influence jurors. In *Sheppard v. Maxwell* (1966), the defendant, Dr. Samuel Sheppard, was accused of brutally murdering his pregnant wife in their home. The pretrial publicity was intensely prejudicial, and Sheppard was convicted of

> **MYTH**
> Virtually no courtroom in the United States allows cameras inside to record the proceedings.
>
> **FACT**
> Every state has adopted rules to allow for cameras in the courtroom. The rules vary from state to state, but coverage (sometimes live feeds) has become more prevalent.

the crime. On appeal, the conviction was overturned, with the Court quoting the Ohio Supreme Court:

> Murder and mystery, society, sex and suspense were combined in this case to such a manner as to intrigue and captivate the public fancy to a degree perhaps unparalleled in recent annals. Throughout the preindictment investigation, the subsequent legal skirmishes and the nine-week trial, circulation-conscious editors catered to the insatiable interest of the American public in the bizarre.... In this atmosphere of a "Roman holiday" for the news media, Sam Sheppard stood trial for his life.

Other high-profile cases include the political, highly publicized trial of Oliver North, the highly publicized 10-day rape trial of William Kennedy Smith, the trial of Mike Tyson for raping a Miss Black America contestant, the trial of O. J. Simpson, and the Casey Anthony murder trial.

The court has a duty to protect those who come before it from undue adverse publicity. Failure to do so may result in a higher court declaring that the trial was unfair and overturning the conviction. In addition, media reports of criminal incidents can hinder police investigations.

The Effect of Media Coverage on Criminal Investigations

In many departments police officers see reporters as enemies who jump at the chance to report law enforcement's mistakes or brutal treatment of citizens. In reality, however, the two fields have much in common: "Both law enforcement agencies and the media are highly visible, powerful institutions. Both professions attract ambitious, strong-minded employees who possess a strong sense of justice and a desire to help others. Both professions are frequently criticized by the public they serve and are highly sensitive to that criticism. The professionals of both can be highly defensive and feel that they are poorly understood by their critics. Both professions are sometimes secretive about their operations and their methods for gathering information. Professionals in both endeavors see themselves as vital to the public welfare" (Garner, 2009, p. 52). Nonetheless, at times reporters' First Amendment rights of freedom of the press can come into conflict with law enforcement's responsibility to investigate crimes without violating a suspect's Sixth Amendment right to a fair trial.

The Right to Peaceful Assembly

Within the First Amendment is the "right of the people peaceably to assemble, and to petition the Government for a redress of grievances." This right is often claimed in conjunction with the right to freedom of speech, as seen in abortion protests. Combined with the Fourth Amendment's guarantee to be free from "unreasonable searches and seizures" people do have an expectation they can gather to interact, speak among themselves, and make their thoughts and ideas known.

The right to assemble does not necessarily require an intent to engage in some specific activity, although when it does, the activity cannot be illegal. In the 1999 case of *Chicago v. Morales*, the Court held that an "anti-loitering" ordinance was unconstitutional because its language was too vague in defining illegal loitering as "to remain in any one place with no apparent purpose." In response to this ruling and with the intent of combating gang activity, Chicago legislators amended the definition to "remaining in any one place under circumstances that would warrant a reasonable person to believe that the purpose or effect of that behavior is to enable a criminal street gang to establish control over identifiable areas, to intimidate others from entering these areas, or to conceal illegal activities." By being more specific, Chicago leaders hope to constitutionally address the city's gang problem without infringing on the rights of others to lawfully assemble.

The right to assemble is an integral part of U.S. culture that allows people to gather and express thoughts and ideas without government interference. Like any other right, however, it is not without limitations. Table 5.2 summarizes several types of property and the types of restrictions that lawfully may be placed on their use for peaceful assembly.

The right to peaceful assembly and, by implication, freedom to petition for redress of grievances was made applicable to the states via incorporation of *DeJonge v. Oregon* (1937). The freedom to petition was the focus of *Duryea v. Guarnieri* (2011), in which police chief Charles Guarnieri had filed a discrimination lawsuit against his employer, the Pennsylvania borough of Duryea, alleging that council members retaliated against him because he had successfully challenged a 2003 decision to fire him. Following Guarnieri's reinstatement as chief in 2005, he alleged that the council had issued 11 new employment directives aimed at placing humiliating restrictions on him, an action, which, in essence, violated his First Amendment right to petition. He further alleged the borough improperly withheld overtime pay from him and had improperly delayed issuing health insurance benefits.

Table 5.2 Types of Public and Quasi-Public Property

Property	Use by public for communicating and demonstrating	Restrictions that may be placed on use
Publicly owned streets, sidewalks, and parks	Such property "has been used for purposes of (public) assembly, communicating thoughts between citizens and discussing public questions."[a]	Reasonable regulations may be imposed to ensure public safety and order (e.g., traffic regulations).
Government buildings, such as courthouses and city halls	Property used for the business of government during business hours is open to the public at these times so that the public may ordinarily come and go as they wish.	Greater restrictions may be imposed to ensure the functioning of government or the regular use of the facilities by the public. They can accommodate only limited expressions of social protest.
Public hospitals, schools, libraries, and so on	Use of these public facilities is ordinarily limited to the specific function for which they are designed.	Because these facilities need more order and tranquility than do other public buildings, they generally have more restrictions concerning use by the public.
Quasi-public facilities, such as shopping centers, stores, and other privately owned buildings or property to which the public has access	Many quasi-public facilities are as extensively used by the public as are public streets, sidewalks, and parks.	Private owners of quasi-public facilities have greater authority to regulate their property than does the government of public streets and parks.
Public property to which access by the public is limited and restricted	Government may limit and restrict in a reasonable manner the access by the public to jails, executive offices (mayor, police chief, and others), and other facilities that must be restricted to permit government to function effectively.	Such restrictions must be made in a reasonable and nondiscriminating manner.

[a] U.S. Supreme Court in *Kunz v. New York*, 340 U.S. 290 (1951).

Source: GARDNER/ANDERSON. *Criminal Law*, 9E. © 2006 Wadsworth, a part of Cengage Learning, Inc.

In district court, a jury found for Guarnieri and awarded him $45,358 in compensatory damages and $52,000 in punitive damages. Duryea appealed to the Third Circuit, which upheld the verdict and ruled that the First Amendment protects public employees in filing grievances concerning any matter, even those of a personal nature. The Supreme Court granted certiorari to determine whether public employees may sue their employers for retaliation, when the alleged reprisal is for the filing of grievances based on private matters rather than issues of public concern. The Court vacated and remanded the lower court order, and the opinion by Justice Kennedy held, "A government employer's allegedly retaliatory actions against an employee do not give rise to liability under the Petition Clause unless the employee's petition relates to a matter of public concern."

Freedom of Association

Closely related to the freedom of assembly is the freedom of association. The right to simply associate with others has been considered to fall under the First Amendment as well as other amendments, although no specific reference occurs anywhere in the Bill of Rights concerning the right of association. This unenumerated but fundamental freedom was extended to the states through *NAACP v. Alabama* (1958) and is evaluated by the courts in one of two contexts. In the first form, the right is evaluated in the context of intimate relationships (e.g., marriage, family) via due process and the right to privacy. The second context is the freedom of individuals to come together in groups, small or large, to engage in activities protected by the First Amendment (such as freedom of speech and expression, freedom to practice their religion).

Wilson v. Swing (1978) was a case involving the First Amendment right of freedom of association, in which a police sergeant was demoted to patrol officer for reasons that included his having an extramarital affair with another officer while off duty. Among the legal issues argued by the officer was that the rule "members and employees shall conduct their private and professional lives in such a manner as to avoid bringing the Department into disrepute" was unconstitutional because it was vague and overbroad. In this case, the Court did not feel the rule was either and held in favor of the employer.

In *Roberts v. United States Jaycees* (1984), the Supreme Court held that the right to freedom of association guaranteed by the First and Fourteenth Amendments did not include the right of a commercial association (the U.S. Jaycees) to deny women admission to the organization because of their gender. In a unanimous vote, the Court emphasized that the state had a compelling interest to eliminate gender discrimination and assure its citizens equal access to publicly available goods and services. In delivering the opinion of the Court, Justice Brennan wrote:

> An individual's freedom to speak, to worship, and to petition the government for the redress of grievances could not be vigorously protected from interference by the State unless a correlative freedom to engage in group effort toward those ends were not also guaranteed....According protection to collective effort on behalf of shared goals is especially important in preserving political and cultural diversity and in shielding dissident

expression from suppression by the majority.... Consequently, we have long understood as implicit in the right to engage in activities protected by the First Amendment a corresponding right to associate with others in pursuit of a wide variety of political, social, economic, educational, religious, and cultural ends.

An interesting side note to *Roberts* is that this case also recognized the right to not associate with someone.

On June 28, 2010, in *Christian Legal Society v. Martinez*, the Supreme Court affirmed and remanded the Ninth Circuit's decision that a public university law school (in this case, the Hastings College of Law in San Francisco, headed by acting Chancellor Leo Martinez) could deny school funding and other benefits to a religious student organization (the Christian Legal Society [CLS]) because the group required its officers and voting members to agree with its core religious viewpoints. The CLS, headquartered outside Washington, DC, is a national network of lawyers guided by their Christian faith, with student chapters at law schools across the country. If members do not sign the CLS's statement of faith, they cannot vote or hold office. CLS members must also sign a statement that they understand that any "sexually immoral lifestyle" is grounds for disqualification, including "all acts of sexual conduct outside of God's design for marriage between one man and woman." Greg Baylor, CLS attorney, argues that the case was not about discrimination but about shared beliefs (O'Brien, 2010).

The Hastings Law School had denied giving student group status to CLS based on the school's "all-comer" policy, under which groups are required to accept anyone into membership, regardless of "status or beliefs" (Belz, 2010). The Supreme Court ruled in favor of the college. Justice Ginsburg wrote in the 5–4 majority opinion that the "all-comer" policy is "reasonable" and constitutional. The holding applies only to the Hastings-style "all comers" policy, which does not exist at any other public university.

This case reached the Supreme Court at a time in the nation's history when our society and law are much more supportive of inclusion than of exclusion (O'Brien, 2010). Antidiscrimination laws that go far beyond what the Constitution might require have sprung up around the country. However, "The First Amendment also guarantees freedom of association, a fundamental right to gather with whomever we choose and collectively express ourselves" (O'Brien, 2010). Again a balance must be sought. Justice Samuel Alito, writing in dissent, stated:

> The Court's treatment of this case is deeply disappointing. The Court does not address the constitutionality of the very different policy that Hastings invoked when it denied CLS's application for registration. Nor does the Court address the constitutionality of the policy that Hastings now purports to follow. And the Court ignores strong evidence that the accept-all-comers policy is not viewpoint neutral because it was announced as a pretext to justify viewpoint discrimination. Brushing aside inconvenient precedent, the Court arms public educational institutions with a handy weapon for suppressing the speech of unpopular groups—groups to which, as Hastings candidly puts it, these institutions "do not wish to lend their name(s)."

CLS will have a chance to raise these points because the Supreme Court remanded the case to the lower court for further consideration.

First Amendment Rights of Prisoners

The last area to consider in the discussion of basic rights is that of the First Amendment rights of prisoners in the correctional system, to which certain rights were extended as a result of the "due process revolution." Using a **"rational basis" test,** the Supreme Court has upheld prison regulations that are, as Justice Sandra Day O'Connor stated in *Turner v. Safley* (1987), "reasonably related to legitimate penological interests." She listed in the opinion four criteria of the "rational basis" test, which continue to be the standard for analyzing First Amendment claims by prisoners and other constitutional claims as well: (1) there must be a rational connection between the regulations and legitimate interest put forward to justify it, (2) alternative means of exercising the right must remain open to prison inmates, (3) the regulations must have only a minimal impact on correctional officers and other inmates, and (4) a less restrictive alternative must not be available.

It is worth briefly explaining here the difference between *rational basis* and *strict scrutiny*, a difference that affects how the Court treats freedom of speech issues involving content control. *Rational basis* means simply that a law or regulation must bear some relationship (i.e., be rationally related) to a legitimate government interest. In other words, as long as there are facts that support the law as furthering a government goal, the law is valid. The burden with rational basis is on the challenging party, and usually the legislation stands. However, when the content of speech is regulated, as opposed to speech in a neutral way, a higher standard must be met for it to be legal when regulated, a standard of review known as *strict scrutiny*, which was introduced previously in the chapter. Recall that with strict scrutiny, the burden shifts to the state to show the law is narrowly tailored to fit a compelling government interest.

Free speech is a right of prisoners, and the burden is on the correctional institution to provide valid reasons for restricting this right. Prisoner correspondence has been the focus of much litigation, often because personal correspondence involves a nonincarcerated person who is protected by the First Amendment. In *Prewitt v. State of Arizona ex rel. Eyman* (1969), the Court justified the screening of inmate mail: "Mail censorship is a concomitant of incarceration, and so long as the censorship does not interfere with the inmate's access to the courts, it is a universally accepted practice."

However, the court's ruling in *Procunier v. Martinez* (1974) restricted the censorship of inmates' mail, holding such practices to be permissible only in the event of a compelling government interest in maintaining security. This decision greatly enhanced prisoners' abilities to communicate with the outside world. In *Turner v. Safley*, the Court upheld a restriction on prisoners from different institutions corresponding because of related gang problems and the potential for escape planning. In *Shaw v. Murphy* (2001), the Supreme Court reiterated that "incarceration does not divest prisoners of all constitutional protections . . . [but] the constitutional rights that prisoners possess are more limited in scope than the constitutional rights held by individuals in society at large." In this case, the Court held that a prisoner's rights are not heightened because the material being read by prison officials happens to be legal advice.

"rational basis" test the standard for analyzing First Amendment claims by prisoners and other constitutional claims as well

---

MYTH
Prisoners have the same First Amendment rights as free citizens.

FACT
Although many of the same rights exist, the particular rights are evaluated differently because of the prison setting.

Hearing is as much a part of free speech as is speaking or writing, and what individuals are allowed to hear and read has always been part of the First Amendment. This right has concerned corrections because of what might be included with other materials sent to prisoners. In *Thornburg v. Abbott* (1989), the Court held that although prisoners had a right to receive some periodicals, these publications did not have the same First Amendment protections as personal mail, and so periodicals deemed detrimental to the institution's security and order could be banned. Using the "clear and present danger" standard, correctional officials are also required to justify any limitations on mail.

In *Beard v. Banks* (2006), Justice Breyer explained, "While imprisonment does not automatically deprive a prisoner of constitutional protections . . . the Constitution sometimes permits greater restriction of such rights in a prison than it would allow elsewhere." Relying on a previous case (*Turner v. Safley*), Breyer further stated, "Under *Turner*, restrictive prison regulations are permissible if they are 'reasonably related to legitimate penological interests.'" In this case, Banks claimed his First Amendment rights were violated by not having free access to nonreligious reading material, but the Court disagreed that "a Pennsylvania prison policy that denies newspapers, magazines and photographs to a group of especially dangerous and recalcitrant inmates violate[s] the First Amendment."

Freedom of religion has also proved challenging for the correctional system. Prisoners have brought an increased number of lawsuits that claim their religious freedoms have been infringed on when the institution limited such areas as access to faith leaders, special dietary options compatible with their faith's requirements, and opportunities to assemble with other prisoners of the same faith to worship. In *Fulwood v. Clemmer* (1962), a federal court ruled that Black Muslims must be recognized as a religion and members be permitted to worship in accordance with their faith. This ruling was also made in the case in *Cruz v. Beto* (1972), which concerned a Buddhist inmate who demanded the right to practice his religion. In such cases, the Court has refused to hold that "different" is synonymous with "clear and present danger."

Disruptive activity in the name of religion, however, has not been permitted. In *O'Lone v. Estate of Shabazz* (1987), the Court refused to force a prison to alter an inmate's work schedule so he could attend certain services, citing the facility's restrictions based on security concerns as "reasonably related to legitimate penological interest." However, reasonable accommodations must be made for prisoners to practice their religious faiths.

An example of the tension within the legal system regarding how far correctional facilities must go to ensure the observance of inmate rights is the Religious Freedom Restoration Act (RFRA), discussed previously. RFRA aimed to protect religious practices from undue governmental restrictions and had broad applications, such as the regulation of hiring and firing decisions based on an employee's religious practices. The result of RFRA for corrections was an avalanche of lawsuits by inmates claiming their behavior was religious and, therefore, protected. Although some of these lawsuits were justified, many others were frivolous and unnecessarily clogged the court system. As explained previously, in *City of Boerne v. Flores* (1997) the Supreme Court declared RFRA's application to the states as unconstitutional. RFRA still applies to the federal government.

> **CASE IN BRIEF**
>
> *Holt v. Hobbs* (2015)
>
> **ISSUE** Does a Department of Corrections policy prohibiting the growth of a one-half inch beard by an inmate who maintains that the beard is a form of religious expression violate the Religious Land Use and Institutionalized Persons Act of 2000?
>
> **RULING** Yes. As long as the expression is based on a sincerely held religious belief, the Department of Corrections must show that the policy promotes a compelling government interest and it is the least restrictive means of doing so.

L07 *Prisoners' rights based on the First Amendment involve censorship of mail, expression within the institution, association within the institution, religion, appearance, and visitation rights.*

In *Shaw v. Murphy* (2001), the Supreme Court ruled that prison inmates do not have heightened protection in their speech when that speech contains legal advice. The Supreme Court remanded the case, reminding the lower court that "because the 'problems of prisons in America are complex and intractable,' and because courts are particularly 'ill equipped' to deal with prison problems, courts have generally deferred to the judgments of prison officials in upholding these regulations against constitutional challenge."

As discussed earlier in the chapter, the Religious Land Use and Institutionalized Persons Act (RLUIPA) was passed in 2000 by Congress to extend religious protection to institutionalized persons. The law applies to state and local governments. A recent case examined a prison's ability to mandate a grooming policy, premised on maintaining prison security, which inhibited a prisoner's right to practice his religion.

In *Holt v. Hobbs* (2015), the Court faced the issue of whether the Arkansas Department of Corrections policy that prohibited an inmate from growing a one-half inch beard, according to his religious beliefs, violated the RLUIPA. The RLUIPA employs a strict scrutiny test on any substantial burden by the government of religious expression, even in the instance of general applicability of the challenged law or policy.

The Department of Corrections argued that the no beard policy furthered the compelling interest of stopping the flow of contraband into the prison, as well as helping in prisoner identification. The Court explained that, although these are important interests, the no beard policy was not the least restrictive means of achieving these goals. The least restrictive standard requires the government to show that no other means of achieving its goal exist. In this case, the Department of Corrections could not show this.

Summary

The First Amendment prohibits Congress from making any laws that restrict freedom of religion, freedom of speech, freedom of the press, or the right to gather or assemble peaceably, and to request the government to respond to complaints from its citizens. However, no rights are absolute, so government can regulate them when social interests outweigh that of the individual.

Religious freedom includes the freedom to worship, to print instructional material, to train teachers, and to organize schools in which to teach, including religion. The establishment clause of the First Amendment states, "Congress shall make no law respecting an establishment of religion." That is, Congress cannot create a national church or prescribed religion. The Free Exercise Clause of the First Amendment declares, "Congress shall make no law . . . prohibiting the free exercise [of religion]."

Freedom of speech and expression include the right to speak and the right to be heard. The First Amendment protects both pure speech and symbolic expression. Congress has passed laws to limit speech that advocates overthrowing the government by force. The "clear and present danger" test was replaced by the "imminent lawless action" test to determine when speech should not be protected by the First Amendment. As public employees, law enforcement officers' speech is not protected under the First Amendment if it is made while acting in an official job-related capacity. Citizens have the First Amendment right to record an officer performing his or her official duties in public.

Freedom of the press applies to all types of printed and broadcast material, including books, newspapers, magazines, pamphlets, films, and radio and television programs.

Prisoners' rights based on the First Amendment involve censorship of mail, expression within the institution, association within the institution, religion, appearance, and visitation rights.

Discussion Questions

1. Is the First Amendment the most important amendment?
2. Is free speech a right that should be absolute?
3. Speaking from a historical perspective, why do you think the framers of the Constitution placed so much importance on the First Amendment?
4. Should the government tolerate people speaking against or criticizing it?
5. Should an amendment to ban burning the U.S. flag be passed?
6. Imagine you are an attorney asked to defend nude dancing as an act of expression that should be allowed in a small town bar. What would you say to represent your client's interests? Include an explanation of how nude dancing could be considered "speech."
7. Discuss whether Nazi Germany could have gone as far as it did if a similar First Amendment had been present in Germany.
8. Should all schools, public and parochial, receive equal support from the government?
9. Should there be any restrictions on public (i.e., government) employees' freedom of speech? Should it matter if the employee is speaking as a citizen on a matter of public concern? If yes, what would comprise an adequate justification from the employer to treat the employee differently than a regular citizen?
10. Discuss whether the U.S. government is hypocritical when, on the one hand, freedom of religion is guaranteed, but, on the other hand, Christianity is so obviously stated in the words of the Pledge of Allegiance, the fact that clergy are assigned to Congress, and the like.

References

Belz, E. (2010, June 28). "Narrow Loss." *WORLD Magazine*. Retrieved July 21, 2016 from www.worldmag.com/2010/06/narrow_loss

Black's Law Dictionary, 3rd pocket edition. (2006). St. Paul, MN: Thomson/West.

Cohen, H. (2009, October 16). *Freedom of Speech and Press: Exception to the First Amendment*. Washington, DC: Congressional Research Service.

Davis, K. C. (2010, October). "God and Country." *Smithsonian*, pp. 86–96.

Ducat, C. R. (2010). *Constitutional Interpretation*, 9th ed. Belmont, CA: Wadsworth/Cengage Learning.

Dwyer, T. P. (2010, April 9). "The Legal Landscape of Police Employee Free Speech." *PoliceOne.com News*. Retrieved July 21, 2016 from www.policeone.com/legal/articles/2035292-The-legal-landscape-of-police-employee-free-speech/

Gardner, T. J., & Anderson, T. M. (2012). *Criminal Law*, 11th ed. Belmont, CA: Wadsworth Publishing Company.

Garner, G. W. (2009, March). "Surviving the Circus: How Effective Leaders Work Well with the Media." *The Police Chief*, pp. 52–57.

Mayes, S. (2010, March 1). "Clackamas Man Exercises Free Speech Rights by Giving Cops the Finger." *The Oregonian*. Retrieved July 21, 2016 from http://www.oregonlive.com/clackamascounty/index.ssf/2010/02/clackamas_man_exercises_free_s.html

O'Brien, T. (2010, April 16). "*Christian Legal Society v. Martinez*." *Religion and Ethics Newsweekly*. Retrieved July 21, 2016 from http://www.pbs.org/wnet/religionandethics/?p=6109

Shin, A. (2010a, July 26). "Freedom of Photography: Police, Security, Often Clamp Down Despite Public Right." *The Washington Post*, p. B02. Retrieved July 21, 2016 from http://www.washingtonpost.com/wp-dyn/content/article/2010/07/25/AR2010072502795.html

Shin, A. (2010b, June 16). "Traffic Stop Video on YouTube Sparks Debate on Police Use of Md. Wiretap Laws." *The Washington Post*. Retrieved July 21, 2016 from www.washingtonpost.com/wp-dyn/content/article/2010/06/15/AR2010061505556.html

Slocumb, D. J., & Roberts, R. (2010, July 15). "Opposing View on Cops and Cameras: Respect Officers' Rights." *USA Today*. Retrieved July 16, 2016 from http://usatoday30.usatoday.com/news/opinion/editorials/2010-07-15-editorial15_ST1_N.htm

"The Trial of John Peter Zenger." (n.d.). Philadelphia, PA: Independence Hall Association. Retrieved July 21, 2016 from www.ushistory.org/us/7c.asp

Vernon, R., & Wu, F. (2010). "*Humanitarian Law Project v. Holder* (09-89); *Holder v. Humanitarian Law Project* (08-1498)." *Legal Information Institute Bulletin*, Cornell University Law School. Retrieved July 21, 2016 from www.law.cornell.edu/supct/cert/09-89

"Violent Threats." (2008, August 31). *Law Officer*. Retrieved July 21, 2016 from http://lawofficer.com/2008/08/violent-threats/

Cases Cited

Abington School District v. Schempp, 374 U.S. 203 (1963)
Abrams v. United States, 250 U.S. 616 (1919)
Agostini v. Felton, 521 U.S. 203 (1997)
Aguilar v. Felton, 473 U.S. 402 (1985)
American Civil Liberties Union v. Mukasey, 534 F. 3d 181 (2008)
Barnes v. Glen Theatre, 501 U.S. 560 (1991)
Beard v. Banks, 548 U.S. 521 (2006)
Brandenburg v. Ohio, 395 U.S. 444 (1969)
Brown v. Entertainment Merchant's Association, 131 S.Ct. 2729 (2011)
Burwell v. Hobby Lobby, 573 U.S. ___ (2014)
Cantwell v. Connecticut, 310 U.S. 296 (1940)
Chicago v. Morales, 527 U.S. 41 (1999)
Christian Legal Society v. Martinez, 561 U.S. 661 (2010)
Church of Lukumi Babalu Aye v. Hialeah, 508 U.S. 520 (1993)
City of Boerne v. Flores, 521 U.S. 507 (1997)
City of Ladue v. Gilleo, 512 U.S. 43 (1994)
City of San Diego v. Roe, 543 U.S. 77 (2004)
Clark v. Community for Creative Non-Violence, 468 U.S. 288 (1984)
Cohen v. California, 403 U.S. 15 (1971)
Cohen v. Cowles Media Company, 501 U.S. 663 (1991)
Connick v. Myers, 461 U.S. 138 (1983)
Cruz v. Beto, 405 U.S. 319 (1972)

Davis v. Beason, 133 U.S. 333 (1890)
DeJonge v. Oregon, 299 U.S. 353 (1937)
Dennis v. United States, 341 U.S. 494 (1951)
Duryea v. Guarnieri, 564 U.S. 379 (2011)
Employment Division v. Smith, 494 U.S. 872 (1990)
Engle v. Vitale, 370 U.S. 421 (1962)
Everson v. Board of Education, 330 U.S. 1 (1947)
Fogel v. Collins, 531 F.3d 824 (9th Cir. 2008)
Fulwood v. Clemmer, 206 F. Supp. 370 (D.C. Cir. 1962)
Gannett v. DePasquale, 443 U.S. 368 (1979)
Garcetti v. Ceballos, 547 U.S. 410 (2006)
Gertz v. Robert Welch, Inc., 418 U.S. 323 (1974)
Gitlow v. New York, 268 U.S. 652 (1925)
Goldman v. Weinberger, 475 U.S. 503 (1986)
Griffin v. Coughlin, 673 N.E. 2d 98 (1996), *cert. denied*, 519 U.S. 1054 (1997)
Heffron v. International Society for Krishna Consciousness, 452 U.S. 640 (1981)
Holder v. Humanitarian Law Project, 651 U.S. (2010)
Holt v. Hobbs, 574 U.S. ___ (2015)
Hutchinson v. Proxmire, 443 U.S. 111 (1979)
Jacobson v. Massachusetts, 197 U.S. 11 (1905)
Kelley v. Johnson, 425 U.S. 238 (1976)
Konigsberg v. State Bar of California, 366 U.S. 36 (1961)
Kunz v. New York, 340 U.S. 290 (1951)
Lane v. Franks, 573 U.S. ___ (2014)
Lemon v. Kurtzman, 403 U.S. 602 (1971)
Lewis v. City of New Orleans, 415 U.S. 130 (1974)
Lynch v. Donnelly, 465 U.S. 668 (1984)
Lyng v. Northwest Indian Cemetery Protective Association, 485 U.S. 439 (1988)
Madsen v. Women's Health Center, Inc., 512 U.S. 753 (1994)
Marsh v. Chambers, 463 U.S. 783 (1983)
McCreary County v. ACLU, 545 U.S.844 (2005)
McCullen v. Coakley, 573 U.S. ___ (2014)
McIntyre v. Ohio Elections Commission, 514 U.S. 334 (1995)
Miller v. California, 413 U.S. 15 (1973)
Minnesota v. Hershberger, 495 U.S. 901 (1990)
Mukasey v. American Civil Liberties Union, 129 S. Ct. 1032 (2009)
Murray v. Curlett, 374 U.S. 203 (1963)
NAACP v. Alabama, 357 U.S. 449 (1958)
National Socialist Party v. Skokie, 432 U.S. 43 (1977)
Near v. Minnesota, 283 U.S. 697 (1931)
New York Times v. Sullivan, 376 U.S. 254 (1964)
New York v. Zenger, 17 Howell's St. Tr. 675 (1735)
O'Lone v. Estate of Shabazz, 482 U.S. 342 (1987)
Pickering v. Board of Education, 391 U.S. 563 (1968)
Prewitt v. State of Arizona ex rel. Eyman, 315 F. Supp. 793 (D.C. Ariz. 1969)
Prince v. Massachusetts, 321 U.S. 158 (1944)
Procunier v. Martinez, 416 U.S. 396 (1974)
R.A.V. v. City of St. Paul, 505 U.S. 377 (1992)
Reed v. Town of Gilbert, 576 U.S. ___ (2015)
Reno v. American Civil Liberties Union, 521 U.S. 844 (1997)
Reynolds v. United States, 98 U.S. 145 (1879)
Roberts v. United States Jaycees, 468 U.S. 609 (1984)
Rosenberger v. Rector and Visitors of the University of Virginia, 515 U.S. 819 (1995)
Roth v. United States, 354 U.S. 476 (1957)
Schenck v. United States, 249 U.S. 47 (1919)
Shaw v. Murphy, 532 U.S. 223 (2001)
Sheppard v. Maxwell, 384 U.S. 333 (1966)
Smilow v. United States, 465 F.2d 802, vacated on other grounds, 409 U.S. 944 (1972)
Snyder v. Phelps, 562 U.S. 443 (2011)
Spence v. State of Washington, 418 U.S. 405 (1974)
State v. Massey, 229 N.C. 734, 51 S.E.2d 179 (1949)
Stone v. Graham, 449 U.S. 39 (1980)
Street v. New York, 394 U.S. 576 (1969)
Texas v. Johnson, 491 U.S. 397 (1989)
Thornburg v. Abbott, 490 U.S. 401 (1989)
Town of Greece v. Galloway, 572 U.S. ___ (2014)
Turner v. Safley, 482 U.S. 78 (1987)
United States v. Allen, 760 F.2d 447 (1985)
United States v. Alvarez, 567 U.S. ___ (2012)
United States v. American Library Association, 539 U.S. 194 (2003)
United States v. Dickens, 695 F.2d 765, cert denied 460 U.S. 1092 (1983)
United States v. Lee, 455 U.S. 252 (1982)
United States v. O'Brien, 391 U.S. 367 (1968)
United States v. Slabaugh, 852 F.2d 1081 (8th Cir. 1988)
United States v. Starks, 515 F.2d 112 (1975)
United States v. Stevens, 559 U.S. 460 (2010)
Van Orden v. Perry, 545 U.S. 677 (2005)
Virginia v. Black, 538 U.S. 343 (2003)
Wallace v. Jaffree, 472 U.S. 38 (1985)
Warner v. Orange County Dept. of Probation, 827 F. Supp. 261, 267 (S.D.N.Y. 1993)
West Virginia State Board of Education v. Barnette, 319 U.S. 624 (1943)
Wilson v. Swing, 463 F. Supp. 555 (M.D.N.C. 1978)
Wooley v. Maynard, 430 U.S. 705 (1977)
Zobrest v. Catalina Foothills School District, 509 U.S. 1 (1993)
Zurcher v. Stanford Daily, 436 U.S. 547 (1978)

CHAPTER 6

The Second Amendment
The Gun Control Controversy

A well-regulated militia, being necessary to the security of a free state, the right of the people to keep and bear arms shall not be infringed.
—Second Amendment to the U.S. Constitution

The Second Amendment right to bear arms is a hotly debated issue in the United States. Private ownership of firearms in the nation exceeds 200 million, and every year about 4.5 million firearms are sold.

Chapter 6 The Second Amendment: The Gun Control Controversy

Learning Objectives

LO1 Identify who was, historically, included in the militia and what was required of them.

LO2 Summarize the opposing interpretations of the Second Amendment that have clashed over the years.

LO3 Explain the significance of District of Columbia v. Heller (2008).

LO4 Understand the significance of McDonald v. Chicago (2010).

LO5 Describe the provisions of the Brady Act.

LO6 Outline what the Law Enforcement Officers Safety Act (LEOSA) allows and what its three goals are.

Key Terms

castle law	militia	straw purchase
Commerce Clause	Operative Clause	Sunset Clause
demurrer	Prefatory Clause	
dictum	prohibited persons	

Introduction

The Second Amendment protects the "right of the people to keep and bear arms." However, the amendment also begins with a phrase explaining its purpose: that a "well-regulated militia" is "necessary to the security of a free state." At a time when personal freedoms and concerns for self-protection are in political debate with whether more guns mean more safety, the Second Amendment is being subjected to careful scrutiny.

What exactly does this brief but controversial amendment mean? Does this phrase mean that the people are allowed to bear arms only if they are part of a militia or defending this country? Does it mean anyone can possess any gun any time? Can guns be used for national defense but not for self-defense? These questions are part of the ongoing debate over gun control and the Second Amendment.

This chapter begins with a brief historical background on the Second Amendment and a look at how interpretation of this amendment has fueled the debate concerning individual versus state rights in matters of gun control. Then the slow start regarding early case law and the Second Amendment is presented, followed by the *Heller* decision and how this case represented a shift in the Court's interpretation of Second Amendment rights. Next is a discussion of the incorporation of the Second Amendment, making it applicable to the states, and a look at some of the variation in state and local gun laws. Then federal regulations aimed at gun control are examined, followed by a discussion of the association between guns, crime, and violence. Cases governing the police response to gun possession reports are covered next. The chapter concludes with a consideration of the current gun control debate, gun control as a political issue, and whether finding common ground and a compromise is possible.

Historical Background

The Second Amendment, like the rest of the Constitution, was drafted in a time when fear of tyranny from a strong central government was uppermost in new Americans' minds. During the colonial period and the country's earliest years, a permanent army was not possible because of lack of funding and personnel, as well as organizational challenges. In many ways, the colonists were on their own and needed to be prepared, especially with Britain challenging their new country. The result: formation of state militias. A **militia** was a group of citizens who defended their community as emergencies arose. Militias consisted mainly of able-bodied adult male civilians and some professional soldiers when available and necessary. Militias did not encompass the entire national population but did provide necessary protection and a sense of security.

militia an armed group of citizens who defend their community as emergencies arise

If militia members were called to service, they were to bring their own arms and ammunition. The private populace's arms made up the militia's arms. Most states mandated that all male citizens between certain ages, for instance 18 to 45, be members of the militia. States directed that these males were to be armed and taught basic military skills and protocol. In *Federalist Paper Number 46*, James Madison emphasized to citizens they had "the advantage of being armed, which the Americans possess over the people of almost every other nation."

LO1 *During the country's early years, the militia was considered to be the entire adult male populace of a state. They were not simply allowed to keep arms but were at times required to do so by law.*

Some suggest firearms are part of the U.S. fabric. Indeed, the U.S. attitude toward weapons arose from the practical need for the pioneers to protect themselves against any number of threats, as well as the philosophical belief that they needed to protect themselves from political tyranny. Today, however, a divide exists among citizens regarding guns and gun ownership. To many, a gun is a symbol of violence and aggression, but to others it symbolizes self-sufficiency, independence, and personal safety. Such emotional imagery may stand in the way of intelligent debate.

The Debate: Interpreting the Second Amendment

In 1794, the militia was composed of all free male citizens, armed with their own muskets, bayonets, and rifles. Now, the militia is generally considered to consist of National Guard units in every state, armed with government-supplied and government-owned sophisticated modern weaponry. How might the great differences in today's militia from that in 1794 affect the interpretation of the Second Amendment? How citizens answer that question determines on which side of the controversy they stand: do people have a right to bear arms as individuals or only as part of a militia?

Modern-Day Militias in the United States

Confrontations between individuals and government continue to occur in this country involving those some consider the equivalent of modern militia members, only taking a stand for their own freedom. In 1992, at Ruby Ridge in Idaho, the FBI, Bureau of Alcohol, Tobacco, Firearms, and Explosives (ATF), and U.S. marshals were involved in a standoff with an armed family who refused to obey conventional law and stated, "The tyrant's blood shall flow.... Whether we live or die we will not obey you ... war is upon our land." The ensuing shootout, which ended with the deaths of two family members and one law enforcement official, was a hotly debated action.

In 1996, an 81-day standoff occurred between the FBI and the Montana "Freemen," who considered themselves a Christian patriot group. The Freemen claimed land as their own sovereign nation and refused to abide by laws with which they disagreed. The situation was resolved peacefully. However, the subject will no doubt continue to address the tension between the Constitution and individual rights. Some people today feel much like those more than 200 years ago—that the government has become too powerful and that individuals need to reclaim that power, often with the firearms they believe they are entitled to possess.

More recent standoffs between law enforcement and armed militias have occurred in Nevada and Oregon, states where federal agencies own and regulate immense parcels of land: "Those with anti-government views, particularly in western states, often focus on the federal government's land-use policies ... [as a way to feed their] views of a tyrannical federal government out of control" (Williams, 2016).

The Intelligence Project run by the Southern Poverty Law Center (SPLC) identified 988 anti-government "patriot" groups active in the United States in 2015, 276 of which were classified as militias (SPLC, 2016). The remainder were "common-law" courts, publishers, ministries, and other citizens' groups that oppose the "New World Order" and adhere to extreme antigovernment doctrines. The SPLC notes that the antigovernment movement has grown rapidly since 2008 for reasons that include the struggling economy, changes in the U.S. demographics due to immigration, and the election of this country's first African-American president (SPLC, 2016). Amidst these constant societal changes, the need to balance individual rights with those of the government becomes apparent.

Prefatory Clause announces a purpose but does not necessarily restrict the Operative Clause

Operative Clause identifies the action to be taken or prohibited

Balancing Individual and States' Rights

Two opposing interpretations of the Second Amendment have clashed in past decades and have revolved around the phrasing of this amendment into two parts: a Prefatory Clause and an Operative Clause. A **Prefatory Clause** announces a purpose but does not necessarily restrict the Operative Clause. An **Operative Clause** identifies the action to be taken or prohibited. The debate surrounding the Second Amendment centers around the Prefatory Clause and the intentions of the founding fathers.

LO2 *The two opposing interpretations of the Second Amendment involve whether the amendment guarantees individuals' rights to keep and bear arms or whether it guarantees the states freedom from federal government infringement on this right.*

Individual Rights Proponents of "the right to bear arms," including the National Rifle Association (NRA), endorse an individual-rights interpretation that would guarantee that right to all citizens. Individual rights proponents see the amendment as primarily guaranteeing the right of the people, not the states. Although they concede that a state right is embodied within the amendment, that right is a product of the more central individual right. By guaranteeing the arms of the individuals who make up the militia, the Constitution guaranteed the militia's arms. The collective right that preserves the states' militia is guaranteed only if the individual right is first maintained.

The amendment is placed in close proximity to other individual rights, although the states are not expressly mentioned until the Tenth Amendment. Madison's notes state that the amendments were to relate first to private rights. Furthermore, arms were such a pervasive part of colonial life that five state conventions recommended an amendment to guarantee the right to bear arms.

Support for this view may be found in the Los Angeles riots that followed the not-guilty jury verdict in the Rodney King case. Citizens cheered the shopkeepers in Koreatown as they defended their property with weapons. A sobering lesson of the Los Angeles uprising for many people was that the police cannot protect everyone during a citywide emergency. Many gun owners, including a great many handgun owners, cite defense against crime as their main reason for owning a gun.

Likewise, some activist groups argue that an armed citizenry is the best defense against tyranny and that their thinking is in line with those who wrote the Second Amendment. This view, however, has not, until recently, been supported by the courts. The courts throughout history have consistently rejected individual rights view in favor of states' rights interpretation.

States' Rights The legal foundation for much of the federal government's regulatory authority, including firearms, is provided for by the **Commerce Clause** of the U.S. Constitution (Article 1, Section 8, Clause 3). Those favoring a states' rights interpretation see the Second Amendment as protecting and modifying Article 1, Section 8 of the Constitution, which grants Congress the power "to provide for the calling forth of the Militia to execute the laws of the Union." The purpose of the amendment is to "assure the continuation and render possible the effectiveness of such forces" (*United States v. Miller*, 1939). Furthermore, the Second Amendment contains a sort of mini-preamble, clearly proclaiming as its purpose the fostering of a "well-regulated Militia," a purpose extraneous to one allowing individual possession of weapons for use against fellow citizens. Consequently, the courts have consistently interpreted the Second Amendment as allowing states to regulate private gun ownership.

This interpretation is linked to the traditional Whig fear of standing armies. The amendment preserves states' power to defend against foreign and domestic enemies, and it reduces the need for a large standing army, which was seen as inherently contrary to preserving a free, democratic people.

Commerce Clause section of the U.S. Constitution (Article 1, Section 8, Clause 3) that provides the legal foundation for much of the federal government's regulatory authority, including firearms

Case Law Regarding the Second Amendment

Federal regulation of firearms possession was virtually nonexistent for more than 140 years after ratification of the Bill of Rights. The first notable case involving the Second Amendment was *United States v. Cruikshank* (1875), in which the U.S. Supreme Court, responding to a claim of a right to bear arms for a lawful purpose, ruled, "This is not a right granted by the Constitution. . . . The Second Amendment declares that it shall not be infringed; but this, as has been seen, means no more than it shall not be infringed by Congress."

Despite this decision, more than half a century passed before the federal government made an effort to regulate the possession of firearms, mainly because the Court had little reason to interpret the amendment. The National Firearms Act of 1934 was the first such effort at federal regulation. Section 11 of the Act forbade a person "who has not in his possession a stamp-affixed order (from the person requesting the firearm) to ship, carry or deliver any firearm in interstate commerce."

One of the first important rulings on the Second Amendment involved this act. Jack Miller was convicted of violating the National Firearms Act by feloniously transporting a double-barreled, 12-gauge shotgun (having a barrel less than 18 inches) from Oklahoma to Arkansas (*United States v. Miller*, 1939). The district court granted the defense a **demurrer,** a request that a suit be dismissed because although the facts are true, they do not sustain the claim against the defendant. The United States appealed the demurrer and certiorari was granted. The Supreme Court interpreted the Second Amendment as providing for maintaining a militia: "With the obvious purpose to assure the continuation and render possible the effectiveness of such forces [as outlined in Article 1, Section 8 of the Constitution] the declaration and guarantee of the Second Amendment were made. It must be interpreted and applied with that view in mind." Thus the *Miller* Court recognized a state right rather than an individual right to bear arms and that the Second Amendment protects only arms that bear some relation to preserving the militia.

demurrer a request that a suit be dismissed because the facts do not sustain the claim against the defendant

The Court held, "In the absence of any evidence tending to show that possession or use of a shotgun having a barrel of less than 18 inches in length, at this time, has some reasonable relationship to the preservation or efficiency of a well-regulated militia, we cannot say that the Second Amendment guarantees the right to keep and bear such an instrument." Although this decision held that a law prohibiting transportation of unregistered shotguns in interstate commerce was not unconstitutional, any precedent established by *Miller* is debatable because the case dealt with the possession of not just any gun but of a specific type of gun.

The decision was not intended to be a broadly sweeping determination that designated which arms are protected and which are not. The Court also clearly stated its position on individual rights and the Second Amendment: "The right to keep and bear arms is not a right conferred upon the people by the federal constitution. Whatever rights in this respect the people may have depend upon local legislation; the only function of the Second Amendment being to prevent the federal government and the federal government only from infringing on that right."

This position was reiterated later in *Stevens v. United States* (1971), when a federal circuit court held that the Second Amendment applies "only to the right of the state to maintain a militia and not to the individual's right to bear arms, there can be no serious claim to any express constitutional right of an individual to possess a firearm."

A Shift in Interpretation: The Heller Decision

In the 70 years following *Miller*, lower federal and state courts interpreted the Second Amendment in more than 30 cases, and in every case except one, the courts held that the amendment referred to the right to keep and bear arms only in connection with a state militia. The aberrant decision came in *United States v. Emerson* (1999), when U.S. District Judge Sam R. Cummings went against all federal court precedent and restored a domestic abuser's firearms, citing the Second Amendment as guaranteeing the individual's right to keep and bear arms.

The Supreme Court has ruled on the amendment relatively few times compared with contests over other amendments. Until recently, *United States v. Miller* (1939) was the only Supreme Court case to specifically address the Second Amendment's scope. Most of the adjudication has been at the federal district level and has seldom gone beyond the court of appeals. The Supreme Court has repeatedly denied certiorari in cases in which the individual right to bear arms is at issue.

However, in *District of Columbia v. Heller* (2008), the Supreme Court took a stand on the controversy. Dick Heller was a special D.C. police officer who applied to register a handgun he wished to keep at home, but his application was denied. A District of Columbia law bans handgun possession. The law authorizes the police chief to issue one-year licenses but requires residents to keep lawfully owned firearms unloaded and disassembled or bound by a trigger lock or similar device.

Heller sued the city on Second Amendment grounds. The district court dismissed the suit, but the D.C. Circuit reversed, holding that the Second Amendment protects an individual's right to possess firearms and that the city's total ban on handguns, as well as its requirement that firearms in the home be kept nonfunctional even when necessary for self-defense, violated that right. The Supreme Court affirmed, holding:

> The Second Amendment protects an individual right to possess a firearm unconnected with service in a militia, and to use that arm for traditionally lawful purposes, such as self-defense within the home.
>
> The Amendment's Prefatory Clause announces a purpose but does not limit or expand the second part, the Operative Clause. The Operative Clause's text and history demonstrate that it connotes an individual right to keep and bear arms.

Heller was important because it marked the first time the Court had ruled that the Second Amendment protects an individual right to own guns. The Court further explained that the Second Amendment right extends to modern arms that were not in existence at the time of the founding of our country and rejected the idea that only arms useful in warfare and the militia are protected.

In reality, however, the ruling affected only the federal government and Washington, D.C., by virtue of its federal nature, because, at that point, the Second Amendment had not yet been incorporated. *Heller* did, however, open the door to incorporating the amendment.

Incorporation of the Second Amendment

In *Presser v. Illinois* (1886), the Court refused to incorporate the Second Amendment into the Fourteenth Amendment. Herman Presser was part of a citizen militia group of armed ethnic German workers, associated with the Socialist Labor Party. The group had been formed to counter the armed private armies of companies in Chicago. The indictment charged that Presser, on September 24, 1879, "did

---

CASE IN BRIEF

District of Columbia v. Heller (2008)

ISSUE Is the Second Amendment violated by a provision of the D.C. code that bans the possession of functional handguns in the home?

RULING Yes. The Second Amendment protects an individual's right to possess a functional handgun in one's home and to use it for traditionally lawful purposes, regardless of any connection to the militia.

LO3 *The Supreme Court stated in* District of Columbia v. Heller *(2008) that the Second Amendment protects an individual's right to possess a firearm unconnected with service in a militia.*

unlawfully belong to, and did parade and drill in the city of Chicago with an unauthorized body of men with arms, who had associated themselves together as a military company and organization, without having a license from the Governor, and not being a part of, or belonging to, 'the regular organized volunteer militia' of the State of Illinois, or the troops of the United States." A motion to dismiss the indictment was overruled. Presser then pleaded not guilty, and, with both parties having waived a jury trial, the case was tried by the court. In refusing to incorporate the Second Amendment into the Fourteenth Amendment the Court stated:

> We think it clear that the sections under consideration, which only forbid bodies of men to associate together as military organizations, or to drill or parade with arms in cities and towns unless authorized by law, do not infringe the right of the people to keep and bear arms. But a conclusive answer to the contention that this amendment prohibits the legislation in question lies in the fact that the amendment is a limitation only upon the power of congress and the national government, and not upon that of the state.

The Court found Presser guilty and sentenced him to pay a fine of $10.

In **dictum** (the court's side opinion) on a case that involved illegal search and seizure, Justice William Douglas summed up the federal position on gun control (*Adams v. Williams*, 1972): "A powerful lobby dins into the ears of our citizenry that these gun purchases are constitutional rights protected by the Second Amendment. . . . There is under our decisions no reason why stiff state laws governing the purchase and possession of pistols may not be enacted."

The Second Amendment remained unincorporated until 2010, when *McDonald v. Chicago* held that the right of an individual to "keep and bear arms" *is* incorporated by the Due Process Clause of the Fourteenth Amendment and applies to the states. The decision cleared up the uncertainty left in the wake of *Heller* on the scope of gun rights in regard to the states.

After *Heller*, McDonald et al. challenged the City of Chicago and the Village of Oak Park laws that banned almost all handgun possession by private individuals, asserting the ban left them vulnerable to criminals. The Seventh Circuit previously had upheld the constitutionality of the handgun ban and, relying on precedent cases, affirmed that *Heller* explicitly refrained from voicing an opinion on whether the Second Amendment applied to the states. However, the Supreme Court held that "the Fourteenth Amendment incorporates the Second Amendment right, recognized in *Heller*, to keep and bear arms for the purpose of self-defense." The Court reversed and remanded, holding that the right to keep and bear arms is fundamental to our scheme of ordered liberty and that it was clear that the framers of the Fourteenth Amendment deemed such a right as fundamental.

The day the case was decided, Paul Helmke, president of the Brady Campaign to Prevent Gun Violence, issued the following statement:

> We can expect two things as a result of today's decision by the U.S. Supreme Court in *McDonald v. Chicago*: the gun lobby and gun criminals will use it to try to strike down gun laws, and those legal challenges will continue to fail.
>
> We are pleased that the Court reaffirmed its language in *District of Columbia v. Heller* that the Second Amendment individual right to possess guns in the home for self-defense does not prevent our elected

dictum (plural dicta) statements by a court that do not deal with the main issue in the case or an additional discussion by the court

MYTH
The Constitution asserts that the right to own a handgun cannot be limited or restricted in any fashion. A person can own any gun and carry it anywhere in anyway.

FACT
On the contrary, the Court's ruling in *Heller* affirmed that some people can be prohibited from possessing a gun, some places may prohibit guns, and sales of guns may be regulated. The Court emphasized that nothing in the *Heller* opinion casts doubt on these facts.

LO4 In McDonald v. Chicago (2010) the Supreme Court, holding that the right to keep and bear arms was among those fundamental rights necessary to our system of ordered liberty, ruled that the Second Amendment does apply to the states and incorporated it under the Fourteenth Amendment.

> **CASE IN BRIEF**
>
> *McDonald v. Chicago* (2010)
>
> **ISSUE** Is the Second Amendment applicable to the states?
>
> **RULING** Yes. The Fourteenth Amendment's Due Process Clause has long been the vehicle for applying constitutional rights to the states, and because the right to keep and bear arms for self-defense is "fundamental to the Nation's scheme of ordered liberty" and "deeply rooted in this Nation's history and tradition," the right should be applied to the states through it.

representatives from enacting common-sense gun laws to protect our communities from gun violence. We are reassured that the Court has rejected, once again, the gun lobby argument that its "any gun, for anybody, anywhere" agenda is protected by the Constitution. The Court again recognized that the Second Amendment allows for reasonable restrictions on firearms, including who can have them and under what conditions, where they can be taken and what types of firearms are available.

Chicago can amend its gun laws to comply with this ruling while continuing to have strong, comprehensive and Constitutional gun laws, just as Washington, DC, has done. After the *Heller* decision, at least 240 legal challenges have been brought to existing gun laws, nearly all of which have been summarily dismissed. There is nothing in today's decision that should prevent any state or local government from successfully defending, maintaining, or passing, sensible, strong gun laws (Brady Campaign to Prevent Gun Violence, 2010).

Variation in State and Local Gun Laws

In *Heller*, Justice Antonin Scalia, writing for the 5–4 majority, noted, "Like most rights, the right secured by the Second Amendment is not unlimited. . . . Nothing in our opinion should be taken to cast doubt on longstanding prohibitions on the possession of firearms by felons and the mentally ill, or laws forbidding the carrying of firearms in sensitive places such as school and government buildings, or laws imposing conditions and qualifications on the commercial sale of arms." Thus, despite the incorporation of the Second Amendment right to keep and bear arms, *Heller* left open two important questions: (1) what are the limits and contours of the right to own a gun (e.g., types of guns, magazine capacity) and (2) what test or level of scrutiny should be applied when evaluating these laws? It is in the effort to answer these questions that variation among state and local gun laws are identified.

One point of contention in contemporary gun control debate centers on what standard of review a court should use to evaluate laws that impose a burden on a person's Second Amendment right. In *Heller*, the Supreme Court left this unanswered, because the law in question there could not survive any test. For example, in *Gowder v. City of Chicago* (2012), the federal district court analyzed an ordinance under a "text, history, and tradition" approach to explain why the law was unconstitutional. In contrast, the court in *United States v. Decastro* (2012) used an analysis that reserved heightened scrutiny for those laws that substantially burden the right to bear arms. To show when a heightened form of scrutiny is unnecessary, the *Decastro* court explained that a "law that regulates the availability of firearms is not a substantial burden on the right to keep and bear arms if adequate alternatives remain for law-abiding citizens to acquire a firearm for self-defense." In addressing the scrutiny requirement, Judge Diane S. Sykes observed in the now-vacated *Skoien* panel opinion:

> The Second Amendment is no more susceptible to a one-size-fits-all standard of review than any other constitutional right. Gun-control regulations impose varying degrees of burden on Second Amendment rights, and individual assertions of the right will come in many forms. A severe burden on the core Second Amendment right of armed

self-defense should require strong justification. But less severe burdens on the right, laws that merely regulate rather than restrict, and laws that do not implicate the central self-defense concern of the Second Amendment, may be more easily justified. (*United States v. Skoien*, 2009)

States retain the right to impose stricter regulations related to firearms than those required by the federal government. Before looking at federal regulation of firearms, consider first how states differ in their laws pertaining to concealed carry, defense of one's home, and restrictions on the types of firearms legally allowed.

Concealed Carry Laws

States vary in their laws regulating concealed carry, or carrying a concealed weapon (CCW), also called right-to-carry (RTC). Some states have laws that say carrying a concealed weapon is a citizen's basic right. These states allow permits to be easily obtained, provided the gun buyer meets certain background requirements, including not having violated certain laws or been determined to be mentally ill. Some states also require the completion of classroom and range training courses. Other states limit CCW permits to when employment or personal safety justifies it.

These variations in state laws have left circuit courts with the challenge of applying the Second Amendment to contexts outside of the home in an effort to determine if and when a regulation goes too far. The Supreme Court has said that self-defense is central to keeping and bearing arms, but delineating the limits to carrying arms outside of the home, concealed or not, has been particularly difficult, with many inconsistencies across the circuits. For example, in *Peruta v. County of San Diego* (2016), the 9th Circuit has said "that the Second Amendment right to keep and bear arms does not include, in any degree, the right of a member of the general public to carry concealed firearms in public," a decision in line with those from the 2nd, 3rd, 4th, and 10th Circuits. Contrast that with *Moore v. Madigan* (7th Circuit, 2012), where the court struck down a concealed-carry regulatory scheme that was a "blanket prohibition" on carrying a gun in public. Furthermore, courts have not yet settled on the level of scrutiny to be applied to concealed carry cases: some have applied strict scrutiny while others have applied an intermediate level where the regulation must be shown to be substantially related to an important government objective.

Researchers at Johns Hopkins University Center for Gun Policy and Research provide examples reflecting the array of past and present legislation, including a Virginia law limiting people to buying only one handgun per month; a Washington, D.C., law banning most new handgun sales to the public (since relaxed); and a Maryland law prohibiting sales of low-cost, so-called Saturday-night specials. Although some states require licensing handgun owners or registering guns, or both, other states have sought to require the government to issue a permit unless they have a compelling reason not to.

Many states have established "gun-free zones" around schools, hospitals, courthouses, venues for public gatherings, and other "sensitive" areas, with conspicuous signs prohibiting guns on the premises, violation of which is grounds for revocation of an offender's concealed carry permit. How effective such signs are is debatable. It is likely that only law-abiding citizens will adhere to them. Advocates of gun-free zones believe such designations make people feel safer, whereas critics note that those wishing to commit egregious crime such as mass murder actually choose such areas because those inside are disarmed and therefore less able to fight back.

In *United States v. Lopez* (1995), the Supreme Court held 5–4 the federal law banning guns near schools to be unconstitutional, effectively striking down the Gun-Free School Zones Act. Although Justice Department lawyers argued that the law was a legitimate extension of Congress's power to regulate interstate commerce, Chief Justice William H. Rehnquist found the law "has nothing to do with commerce or any sort of enterprise." This overturning of the Gun-Free School Zones Act may not have much practical effect, however, because more than 40 states, exercising their right to pass laws controlling guns, have banned possession of handguns near schools.

Police departments commonly seek restrictions on their officers' off-duty activities. However, when such restrictions impinge on officers' constitutional rights, obvious problems ensue. Such was the case in *Edwards v. City of Goldsboro, N.C.* (1999). In 1995, North Carolina enacted a concealed carry handgun bill that enabled citizens to carry concealed handguns after mandatory training and screening. Sergeant Kenneth Edwards, a 20-year veteran of the City of Goldsboro's police department and a firearms instructor, had completed specific training to teach the concealed carry course. To run his own part-time business, he obtained a business license, scheduled instructional classes to be held during off-duty time at a private location, and submitted a request for off-duty employment.

The police chief, a vocal opponent of the concealed carry law, denied Edwards's request for off-duty employment because of the issues that surround carrying a weapon. Edwards argued that the chief, motivated by personal and political reasons, had issued an illegal order prohibiting the officer's expression and association. The Fourth Circuit Court of Appeals agreed, observing that the court must "balance the interests of the (public employee), as a citizen, in commenting upon matters of public concern, and the interest of the (government), as an employer, in promoting the efficiency and public services it performs through its employees." The Court concluded the balancing test weighed in favor of Edwards: "We cannot discern any legitimate interest of the defendants in preventing a police officer of the city from conducting a concealed handgun safety course for the public that is a creature of state law."

Castle Laws

castle law a legal claim based on English common law that designates one's place of residence (or, in some states, any place legally occupied, such as one's car or place of work) as a place in which one enjoys protection from illegal trespassing and violent attack

Castle laws are passed by states, and not all states have such laws. A **castle law** is a legal claim based on English common law that designates one's place of residence (or, in some states, any place legally occupied, such as one's car or place of work) as a place in which one enjoys protection from illegal trespassing and violent attack. It gives a person the legal right to use deadly force to defend that place ("A man's home is his castle"), and any other innocent persons legally inside it, from violent attack or an intrusion that may lead to violent attack. Legally, use of deadly force that actually results in death may be defended as justifiable homicide.

One state with a castle law is Indiana, which has had a codified Castle Doctrine since 2006. Under this statute, a person is justified in using reasonable force against any other person to protect themselves or a third party from what the person reasonably believes to be the imminent use of unlawful force. Furthermore, a person has no duty to retreat in his or her own home if they reasonably believe that that force, including deadly force, is necessary to prevent serious bodily injury to themselves or a third party or the commission of a forcible felony. Finally, the statute provides that no person in Indiana shall be placed in legal jeopardy of any kind whatsoever for protecting themselves or a third party by reasonable means necessary (Indiana Code (IC) 35-41-3-2). Essentially, this doctrine establishes both a defense against criminal prosecution and immunity from civil liability for the use of force against an intruder in one's own home (Eldridge, 2012).

In March 2012, in the wake of *Barnes v. State* (2011), the Indiana legislature modified the law, making it legal under certain circumstances for a citizen to invoke the Castle Doctrine and use deadly force against anyone, including police officers, who "unlawfully" intrudes into the citizen's home, curtilage, or motor vehicle, again with no duty to retreat. Eldridge (2012) cautions: "Ultimately, the implications of this extension of use of force to 'castle defenders' in the modern era will likely result in more violence exercised by people with less training and the further erosion of respect for the authority of our institutions, officers, courts, and the rule of law."

Some states have "Make My Day" Laws, a nickname referring to the classic line spoken by character Harry Callahan (played by Clint Eastwood) in the 1983 film *Sudden Impact*, "Go ahead, make my day," and first used by Colorado in passing a 1985 statute that protects people against any criminal charge or civil suit if they use force, including deadly force, against an invader of their home.

Other states have "Stand Your Ground" laws, which extend beyond one's home, in contrast to "castle laws," which limit a citizen's right to use deadly force to within their home or business. Florida's "Stand Your Ground" law, passed in 2005, expanded the definition of justifiable self-defense and provided that anyone claiming to feel "threatened" no longer had an obligation to retreat, call police, or avoid use of deadly force. This law was at the center of the murder trial involving the shooting death of 17-year-old Trayvon Martin by block watch-coordinator George Zimmerman. Since it passed in Florida, at least 20 other states have enacted similar laws, intended to protect law-abiding citizens forced to fend off home invaders, muggers, and carjackers. The mere claim of fear provided the legal presumption that use of deadly force was justified.

Gun-control advocates immediately criticized the "Stand Your Ground" law when it was signed in 2005, with the Brady Campaign to Prevent Gun Violence handing out leaflets at the airport to warn visitors about the new law. The communication director for the Brady Campaign called the law unnecessary, claiming, "There are some people in Florida who should be in jail who are not in jail because this new law was passed. It is frightfully dangerous to encourage the most aggressive people in society to take the law into their own hands" (Basu, 2010). The law has also complicated once-routine homicide prosecutions, with one prosecutor stating, "We have been forced to spend significant time and resources litigating for defendants charged with violent crime. The law has the great potential to be misapplied and could well protect violent criminals in specific cases" (Grimm, 2010). Defense attorneys, however, often present the opposite view, stating that the law is fact-specific and can protect people from malicious prosecution (Basu, 2010).

> **MYTH**
> Starter pistols and "air guns" are not firearms and are not subject to federal or state laws.
>
> **FACT**
> Under the Gun Control Act of 1968, 18 USC Section 921 (a)(3), a *firearm* is "any weapon (including a starter gun) which will or is designed to or may be readily converted to expel a projectile by the action of an explosive; the frame or receiver of any such weapon; any firearm muffler or firearm silencer; or any destructive device. Such term does not include an antique firearm." As the ATF notes, a starter pistol is therefore a firearm, but an air gun is not because it uses compressed air, not an explosive agent, to expel a projectile. However, this is not to say state laws do not or cannot regulate or define air guns as firearms.

> **CASE IN BRIEF** ▶
>
> *Caetano v. Massachusetts* (2016)
>
> **ISSUE** Does the Second Amendment protect the right to own a stun gun?
>
> **RULING** Yes. Despite a stun gun not being an arm in existence at the time of the Second Amendment's passing, it is a protected "bearable arm."

Castle laws are significant in many cases involving the Fourth Amendment right to be free from "unreasonable" searches and seizures by law enforcement, as discussed in the following chapters.

In contrast to "castle" and "stand your ground" laws, some states require a person to retreat from the threat before they resort to deadly force. Eighteen "retreat" states have some type of law that does not allow force to be used unless one cannot safely flee or avoid the danger.

Restrictions on Types of Firearms

Although some weapons, such as fully automatic "machine guns" and those altered to be more conducive to criminal activity, such as sawed-off shotguns, have always been illegal for most people to own (law enforcement personnel and licensed collectors being the exception), what exactly constitutes a *weapon* or *firearm* has not been as easy to define. Some jurisdictions have included anything that explodes or projects anything, including paintball guns and bows and arrows, whereas others have sought to be more specific. The definition of "assault rifle" has generated its own share of debate with the Federal Assault Weapons Ban (a provision of the Violent Crime Control and Law Enforcement Act of 1994).

Whether or not something is defined as a "bearable arm" is important because on those designated as such are afforded Second Amendment protection. This designation was at issue in *Caetano v. Massachusetts* (2016). In this case, Jaime Caetano had a stun gun to protect herself from a violent ex-boyfriend. She was arrested for violating a Massachusetts state law that prohibited possession of such a weapon. Caetano was eventually convicted, and the Supreme Judicial Court of Massachusetts upheld the conviction. The court reasoned that because stun guns were not in common use at the time of the Second Amendment's enactment and stun guns were not adaptable to military use, they were not subject to Second Amendment protection. Therefore, the state could ban all arms of this type.

The U.S. Supreme Court vacated the state court's decision, explaining that *Heller* made it clear the Second Amendment applies to arms not in existence at the time of the ratification of the Second Amendment. In addition, *Heller* did not limit Second Amendment protection to arms only useful in war. As the Court stated in *Heller*, "the Second Amendment extends, prima facie, to all instruments that constitute bearable arms, even those that were not in existence at the time of the founding."

Federal Regulation and the Second Amendment

Although until 2010 the Second Amendment was consistently interpreted to protect the states' rights from federal intervention, the federal government passed several gun control laws before then. In 1938, the Federal Firearms Act was passed, requiring dealers shipping firearms across state lines and importers to be licensed by the federal government. In 1967, Congress passed the Omnibus Crime Control and Safe Streets Act, a portion of which made possession of firearms by convicted felons unlawful.

In 1968 after the assassinations of President John F. Kennedy, the Rev. Martin Luther King, Jr., and Senator Robert Kennedy, the Gun Control Act was passed, which banned federal licensees from selling firearms to **prohibited persons,** anyone they knew or had reasonable cause to believe was or had been:

- Under indictment for or convicted of a felony.
- A fugitive.
- A drug user.
- Adjudicated a mental defective or committed to a mental institution.
- Fit into other limited categories.

prohibited persons
individuals to whom, under the Gun Control Act, selling a firearm is forbidden

The Supreme Court has ruled that the federal law that bars gun ownership by convicted felons does not apply to those convicted in foreign courts. In *Small v. United States* (2005), the Court overturned the conviction of a man who bought a gun in Pennsylvania after serving more than three years in a Japanese prison for smuggling guns into that country. Justice Stephen Breyer, writing for the majority, said the phrase "convicted in any court" applies only to convictions in U.S. federal or state courts, not to foreign courts.

Constitutional Law in ACTION

Officer Weltz is sent to take a report of a domestic assault. When he arrives, the victim, Julie Johnson, explains that she and her husband, Jack Johnson, were having an argument over the bills. The husband became upset because he is out of work, and she was mad because he stopped looking for a job. He began drinking a lot of beer, and the argument continued.

During a particularly heated exchange, Jack slapped Julie on her cheek. After slapping Julie, Jack left the house. He was still gone when the officer arrived. Officer Weltz could see a red mark on Julie's cheek, which was slightly swollen.

Officer Weltz's department has started an initiative at prosecuting domestic violence more effectively. Part of this initiative is that the officer is to ask the victim if the abuser or suspect has any guns. If so, the officer is to take them for "safekeeping" in an effort to keep any future abuse from involving the gun. Also, if later convicted of domestic abuse, the abuser would not be able to legally own a firearm because of federal law.

Officer Weltz asks Julie if Jack owns any guns. She says that he owns a hunting rifle and a semiautomatic handgun. She shows them to Officer Weltz, who seizes them for safekeeping under his department policy. He brings them to the station where they are inventoried.

- *Does the taking of the guns for safekeeping violate procedural due process?*
- *Would the length of time for "safekeeping" matter in making your decision?*
- *Do you think anyone can own any gun, or is the government allowed to regulate ownership to some degree?*

The Gun Control Act also required the registration of "destructive devices," including cannons, antitank guns, and bazookas, and prohibited importation of cheap, "junk" handguns, such as the $6 Saturday night special that killed Senator Kennedy.

In 1986, Congress banned the purchase and sale of all fully automatic weapons. All privately owned automatic weapons bought before 1986 were to be registered but would remain in their owners' hands.

The Brady Act

On November 30, 1993, President Bill Clinton signed the Brady Handgun Violence Prevention Act, and on February 28, 1994, the Brady Act went into effect. The law, which aimed to prevent prohibited persons from obtaining handguns, was named in honor of Jim Brady, the press secretary to President Ronald Reagan, who was shot during a 1981 assassination attempt on the President. Despite the endorsement of four former presidents (Nixon, Ford, Carter, and Reagan) and the active support of President Clinton, seven years were required for the Brady Bill to get through Congress and become law.

LO5 *The Brady Act contained the interim provision of a mandatory five-day waiting period on all handgun purchases and required local law enforcement to conduct criminal background checks on all handgun purchasers. This provision was replaced in 1998 by the National Instant Criminal Background Check System (NICS). However, states can, and many do, enact their own longer, waiting periods, and the Brady Act does not prohibit such measures.*

The mandatory waiting period provision of the Brady Act was phased out on November 30, 1998 and replaced with the permanent provision of a mandatory, computerized National Instant Criminal Background Check System (NICS), which provides immediate information for criminal background checks on all firearm purchasers. This new provision allows applicants to receive a nearly instantaneous decision regarding their request to purchase a gun. The issuing law-enforcement agency can contact the FBI by computer and either receive clearance or be denied the permit. Unless federal computer records indicate that a potential purchaser is under indictment or information for, or has been convicted of, a felony; has a dishonorable discharge; has illegal alien status; or possesses any other possible disability that qualifies them as a prohibited person, the purchase may be approved at the time.

The federal government is not empowered to require state or local law enforcement agencies to run background checks on prospective gun buyers. In 1997 the Supreme Court ruled 5–4 in *Printz v. United States* that the background check provision violated the principle of separate state sovereignty. Justice Scalia, writing for the narrow majority, stated, "The federal government may neither issue directives requiring the states to address particular problems, nor command the states' officers, or those of their political subdivisions, to administer or enforce a federal regulatory program. Such commands are fundamentally incompatible with our constitutional system of dual sovereignty."

The constitutionality of the Brady Act continues to be challenged. Some jurisdictions interpret the law differently. For example, the City of Kenneway, Georgia, passed a law in 1982 mandating the head of each household to own at least one firearm and have ammunition to "protect the safety, security and general welfare of the city and its inhabitants." However, because of what others say is an escalating number of deaths and injuries resulting from guns, including those involving youths, other jurisdictions are becoming increasingly strict.

Although acknowledging that any background check is better than no background check, critics of the instant check system say it sacrifices safety for convenience because many centralized records are kept only at the state level, and many more records, such as mental health records, may not be computerized. Also, relevant records may not be identified in time, if at all. To address these concerns, Congress enacted the NICS Improvement Amendments Act of 2007 (NIAA), which strengthened the NICS by increasing the quantity and quality of relevant records from Federal, State, and tribal authorities accessible by the system. Such records include information relating not only to criminal history and criminal dispositions but also to mental illness, restraining orders, and misdemeanor convictions for domestic violence.

In an effort to further connect the dots between mental health records and background checks for gun purchasers, the Department of Health and Human Services modified a privacy rule within the Health Insurance Portability and Accountability Act (HIPPA) in January 2016 to allow certain entities (generally those that make mental health determinations) to disclose directly to NICS information on individuals who are prohibited from possessing a firearm. This rule makes it so that people who have been involuntarily committed to a mental institution, or who are considered by mental health professionals to be a danger to themselves or others, are not given legal clearance to purchase a gun.

Records held by the Social Security Administration (SSA) are also being viewed as relevant to data collection efforts by the NICS. Rule changes have been proposed to mandate the reporting of the approximately 2.7 million people currently receiving disability payments for mental health problems: "A potentially large group within Social Security are people who, in the language of federal gun laws, are unable to manage their own affairs due to 'marked subnormal intelligence, or mental illness, incompetency, condition, or disease'" (Zarembo, 2015). The measure would involve having the SSA report names to NICS under the "mental defective" category, although the agency is still trying to determine how that definition should be applied.

In February 2004, the NICS began to include a review of terrorist watch lists, even though being named on such a list is *not* currently one of the disqualifying criteria under federal gun control laws. The terrorist watch list, formally called the Terrorist Screening Database (TSDB), is an unclassified collection of names maintained by the FBI-led Terrorist Screening Center (TSC) and was added to the NICS so that federal officials could determine if terror suspects might be disqualified from buying a gun on *other* grounds listed in the federal gun control laws. The TSDB is part of a larger initiative called the Terrorist Identities Datamart Environment (TIDE), the U.S. government's central, shared knowledge bank on known and suspected terrorists and international terror groups. TIDE contains both classified and unclassified information (National Counterterrorism Center, 2016).

Lawmakers are proposing legislation at the federal level that would make being named in TIDE one of the disqualifying criteria for gun purchases. However, data indicate that being on a watch list has not, to date, prevented many people from buying guns. FBI statistics show that, between 2004 and 2014, people on terrorist watch lists tried to buy guns 2,233 times and were successful more than 90 percent of the time (Doyle, Ybarra, & Lightman, 2016). In addition, individuals are added to and removed from the watch list all the time, as ongoing federal investigations either reveal or fail to discover any tangible evidence linking a person to terrorism. Yet many of those on the watch list will never commit any overt acts that threaten public safety, and some of those removed from the list were simply not watched long enough. Analysis shows that roughly 16,500 names are removed, on average, from the watch list each year after being determined that they no longer meet the inclusion criteria. However, Omar Mateen, an American-born Muslim who shot and killed 49 people at a gay nightclub in Orlando, Florida on June 12, 2016, had once been on the watch list but was taken off after a 10-month FBI investigation found no evidence of a connection to terrorism (Doyle et al., 2016). Some states have grown increasingly frustrated with Congress's failure to enact stricter background check policies and are, themselves, proposing state-level legislation to prevent gun violence. For example, the governor of Connecticut has declared his intention to sign an executive order that would ban those on government watch lists from buying guns or ammunition and is seeking cooperation from the White House to gain access to those lists (Harris & Lichtblau, 2015).

The Federal Bureau of Investigation (FBI) is overhauling the NICS to increase its effectiveness and efficiency, with improvements to include 24/7 processing of background checks, better notification of local authorities when certain prohibited persons unlawfully attempt to buy a gun, and the hiring of more than 230 additional examiners and other staff to help process these background checks more quickly (The White House, 2016). This new resolve to enhance efforts to keep guns out of the hands of the wrong people comes in the wake of several high-profile incidents in which applications by people who should have been denied gun purchases fell through the cracks of the background check system. One example of such a lapse occurred when Dylann Roof, the 21-year-old accused of murdering nine people in a South Carolina church on June 17, 2015, was able to buy a .45-caliber pistol because information relating to his prior arrest for and admission of possession of narcotics, a drug crime that would have triggered a rejection of his gun purchase, was not properly entered into criminal records databases used for background checks (Nakashima, 2015).

The Violent Crime Control and Law Enforcement Act of 1994

In September 1994, Congress passed and President Clinton signed into law the Violent Crime Control and Law Enforcement Act of 1994. This act banned the manufacture of 19 different semiautomatic guns with multiple assault-weapon features, as well as copies or duplicates of such guns. Such weapons served no legitimate sporting or hunting purpose but are the firearms of choice for terrorists, drug dealers, and gang members. The act also prohibits transfer to or possession of handguns and ammunition by juveniles, prohibits possession of firearms by people who have committed domestic abuse, and provides stiffer penalties for criminals who use firearms to commit federal crimes.

Sunset Clause a set ending time for legislation that is not renewed to prevent old law from remaining on the books

Despite strong support, the ban expired with a **Sunset Clause** (a set ending time for legislation that is not renewed to prevent old law from remaining on the books) in 2004, when after significant debate, Congress did not renew it. That same year, federal legislation was passed, allowing off-duty and retired police officers to carry concealed weapons, another controversial issue.

IN THE NEWS

"Jail Error Led to Charleston Shooting Suspect's Gun Purchase"

By *CBS Interactive, Inc. (Associated Press,* July 14, 2015)

LEXINGTON, S.C.—Both the FBI and a county sheriff's department agency promise to review a series of mistakes that allowed South Carolina church shooting suspect Dylann Roof to get a gun he never should have been allowed to buy.

Lexington County Sheriff Jay Koon told The Associated Press on Monday that a clerk at his jail entered in the incorrect location for Roof's drug arrest in February. That meant an FBI examiner using records from a state database couldn't find the details about the arrest when Roof wanted to buy a gun.

The background check found nothing after three days and Roof was eventually allowed to buy the .45-caliber handgun authorities say was used in the June 17 shooting at Emanuel African Methodist Episcopal Church in Charleston that killed nine people.

The jail discovered mistakes two days after Roof's drug arrest, but the change wasn't corrected in the state police database of arrests. So when an FBI examiner pulled Roof's records in April, she called the wrong agency.

FBI Director James Comey on Friday promised a full review when he said Roof should have never been allowed to buy the gun. The sheriff on Monday also promised he was making changes that would flag discrepancies like the one that appeared to let Roof slip through the cracks. He didn't name the employee who made the error or say if the worker faced any discipline.

The FBI allows a gun sale if it can't give a definitive answer about whether someone can buy the gun after three days, which is what happened in Roof's case. The FBI examiner knew Roof had an arrest record, but couldn't find the documents.

CBS News' Paula Reid reported that federal law bans the sale of a firearm to "an unlawful user of or addicted to any controlled substance."

Roof was arrested in March for possession of Suboxone, a Schedule III prescription drug used to treat addiction to opioids. According to the police report, he had admitted using it. Even if he hadn't been convicted of the crime, the FBI says the admission of drug use should have been enough to trip the background check.

In 2014, the FBI reported about 2 percent of background checks end with the FBI not getting enough information and failing to give an answer. Officials said they do about 58,000 checks on a typical day, handled by about 500 people at a call center.

There were a couple of mistakes that ended up in the criminal records database. State police records of Roof's drug arrest pulled by the AP minutes after he was identified as the church shooting suspect had the drug charge listed as a felony with the arresting agency as Lexington County Sheriff's Office. They have since been corrected. The charge is a misdemeanor and

(Continued)

(Continued)

the arresting agency was the Columbia police department.

Koon, the sheriff, said that when the FBI examiner called his deputies, they pointed out the arrest was by Columbia Police. But the woman doing the FBI background check checked a spreadsheet of law enforcement agencies in Lexington County and it did not include Columbia because it is mostly in neighboring Richland County. The examiner called the police department in West Columbia—where the gun was bought—and found nothing.

Only a very small part of Columbia is in Lexington County, and the city's jurisdiction includes the entire Columbiana Centre mall where Roof was arrested. The officer searched Roof and found a drug doctors use to treat narcotic addiction without a prescription, according to a police report.

That information should have been enough to prevent Roof from buying a gun based on a federal law banning gun sales to anyone who uses or is addicted to a controlled substance, Comey said.

The FBI examiner also said it sent a fax to prosecutors in Lexington County looking for more information about the arrest and the fax was never answered.

A secretary said chief prosecutor Donnie Myers was in court in Saluda County on Monday. He didn't return a phone message.

Last month, a law enforcement source told CBS News' Pat Milton that a .45 caliber gun was found in the car when Roof was arrested during a traffic stop the day after the shooting. Roof purchased the .45 caliber pistol with $400 his father gave him for his birthday, sources said.

Constitutional Law in ACTION

A state law has been passed that forbids a person to carry a gun "ready to use"—loaded, immediately accessible (i.e., easy to reach), and uncased. Police officers are exempted from the law, as is a person on his or her own property (owned or rented), or in his or her home, or in his or her fixed place of business (i.e., does not apply to taxi drivers, delivery drivers, or other mobile offices workers), or on the property of someone who has permitted the person to be there with a ready-to-use gun. Even carrying an unloaded gun in public, if it is uncased and immediately accessible, is prohibited, other than by police and other excepted persons.

- *Is this law constitutional?*
- *Do you think this law proposes a heavy burden on a person's right to possess a gun?*
- *What impact does the fact that this law regulates gun possession outside of one's home have on its constitutionality?*

The Law Enforcement Officers Safety Act

In 2004, the Law Enforcement Officers Safety Act (LEOSA) was enacted. This federal law allows a "qualified law enforcement officer" and a "qualified retired law enforcement officer" to carry a concealed firearm in any jurisdiction in the United States, regardless of any state or local law to the contrary, with two exceptions. Two types of state laws are not overridden by the federal law, those being "the laws of any state that (1) permit private persons or entities to prohibit or restrict the possession of concealed firearms on their property; or (2) prohibit or restrict the possession of firearms on any state or local government property, installation, building, base or park." LEOSA-qualified persons must obey whatever state laws apply on those two points. They are free to disregard all other state and local laws that govern the carrying of concealed firearms.

The International Association of Chiefs of Police (IACP) strongly opposed the legislation, concerned about officer and citizen safety, use of force and firearm-training standards, officer identification and eligibility issues, supervision of retired police, liability, and a firm belief that states and localities should determine who is eligible to carry firearms in their communities.

Since the Act was established, many states and police departments have struggled to comprehend and implement the law, partly because of the unclear language included regarding who is qualified. Some agencies fear that liability could result from issuing a certificate pursuant to federal law (Wethal, 2010).

LO6 *The Law Enforcement Officers Safety Act allowing "qualified" active and retired law enforcement officers to carry concealed weapons anywhere in the United States has three goals: (1) to establish equality between local LEOs and their federal counterparts who already carry nationwide, (2) to create an unpaid homeland security force to help protect the nation, and (3) to allow qualified current and retired LEOs the means to defend themselves and their families against criminals.*

Other Proposed Federal Legislation

With each new legislative session, gun control bills are proposed and killed, new laws are passed and old laws are repealed, making it difficult to provide an accurate and current inventory of all gun-related legislation. When legislation is proposed, it first goes to committee. If approved, it is introduced in the House of Representatives (H.R.) and given a number. If passed by the House, the legislation goes to the Senate (S.) and is given a new number. Its status can be tracked through GovTrack.us.

As discussed, recent legislation has been proposed to curb terrorists' access to firearms. The Denying Firearms and Explosives to Dangerous Terrorists Act of 2009 (H.R.2159), which went nowhere, was reintroduced in 2015 (S. 551) and aims to prohibit those who are on the terror watch list from purchasing firearms. The last hearing was in December 2015 and, as the text goes to press, there have been no new developments.

The Protection of Lawful Commerce in Arms Act of 2005 prohibited lawsuits against gun manufacturers and dealers (and others) for damages resulting from the use of their products. However, these companies can still be sued for negligence and defective products, just like any other consumer manufacturer. Some current presidential candidates have stated they are in favor of repealing the law, and the results of the election could change the status of this act.

In July 2010 a forum was held before the subcommittee on Crime and Terrorism and Home Security on the proposed Gun Show Loophole Closing Act of 2009 (H.R. 2324). A Virginia Tech survivor, Colin Goddard, testified about his experience on April 16, 2007, when he was shot four times. Goddard also showed footage of his undercover investigation of gun shows, highlighting how easy it was to buy guns from unlicensed sellers who collect no tax, complete no paperwork, conduct no background checks, and do not even require buyers to show a driver's license. At the forum, Goddard was joined by Tom Mauser, whose son was killed at Columbine (Colorado) High School with guns bought at a gun show (Castellano, 2012).

Guns, Crime, and Violence

As of 2010, an estimated 300 million firearms were privately owned by civilians in the United States, of which about 100 million were handguns (Agresti & Smith, 2016). Data from the U.S. Department of Justice's Bureau of Justice Statistics indicates that a total of 478,400 fatal and nonfatal violent crimes were committed with a firearm in 2011, and that firearm violence accounted for roughly 70 percent of all homicides from 1993 to 2011 (Planty & Truman, 2013). According to the FBI's *Crime in the United States 2014*, offenders used firearms in 67.9 percent of the nation's murders, 40.3 percent of robberies, and 22.5 percent of aggravated assaults (FBI, 2014a). The Brady Campaign to Prevent Gun Violence (2016b) reports that every day, on average, 298 people are shot in the United States and 90 of them die as a result of gun violence. Furthermore (Brady Campaign to Prevent Gun Violence, 2016a):

- The U.S. firearm homicide rate is 20 times higher than the combined rates of 22 countries that are our peers in wealth and population.
- Firearm homicide is the second leading cause of death (after motor vehicle crashes) for young people ages 1 to 19 in the United States.
- Although guns can and have been used successfully in self-defense in the home, a gun in the home is 22 times more likely to be used to kill or injure in a domestic homicide, suicide, or unintentional shooting than to be used in self-defense.
- Since the Brady Law was initially passed, about 2 million people have been blocked from purchasing a gun as a result of a background check. About half of those were felons.
- Our current background check system applies to only about 60 percent of gun sales, leaving 40 percent (online sales, purchases at gun shows, etc.) without a background check.

The Police Executive Research Forum (PERF) looked at the gun control issue as seen at the local level, which is where the IACP firmly believes it belongs (Wexler, 2010). The PERF conducted two surveys and then held a summit to report and discuss the findings. The main participants were chiefs of police, but also invited to the summit were representatives of the two major gun groups and the Brady Campaign because "you don't make peace with your friends" (Wexler, 2010). Local police linked gun crime most closely to drug and gang issues, with nearly two-thirds of responding agencies identifying these two factors as "very important" in causing their local gun crime.

A survey conducted by Mayors Against Illegal Guns, an association of more than 500 mayors, found that nearly half of the guns that crossed state lines and were used in crimes in 2009 were sold in just 10 states: Georgia, Florida, Virginia, Texas, Indiana, Ohio, Pennsylvania, North Carolina, California, and Arizona. According to the Mayors' report, those states have more relaxed gun laws, suggesting that "criminals and gun traffickers may favor certain states as the sources of guns" (Associated Press, 2010).

Lott, in the best seller *More Guns, Less Crime* (1998), set forth the argument that citizens carrying guns makes us a safer nation. This same argument is presented in *The Bias against Guns* (2003, p. 3), in which Lott asserts, after examining how crime rates change over time in relation to concealed carry laws: "Gun control disarmed law-abiding citizens more than criminals, which meant that criminals had less to fear from potential victims. Guns not only make it easier for people to harm others, guns also make it easier for people to protect themselves."

Donohue (2003, p. 399) presents an opposite finding: "Our best, albeit admittedly imperfect, statistical evidence indicates that increases in permit rate growth may lead to slight increases in crime."

Research by Kovandzic and Marvell (2003) found little evidence that increases in the number of citizens with concealed-handgun permits reduce or increase rates of violent crime. Similar findings were reported by the Centers for Disease Control and Prevention (CDC), whose independent task force of public health officials and other scientists reviewed 51 evaluations of gun laws and found insufficient evidence to determine the effectiveness of any of the firearm laws (Hann, Bilukham, Crosby, Fullilove, Liberman, Moscicki, Snyder, Tuma, & Briss, 2003).

Unlike the average citizen, law enforcement officers are well trained in gun safety, yet their training does not exempt them from becoming victims of gun violence. Data from the FBI indicates that of the 51 law enforcement officers feloniously killed in 2014 in the line of duty, most (46) were killed with firearms, and of these, 33 were killed with handguns (FBI, 2014b). Furthermore, 39 of these officers were wearing body armor when they were killed with firearms.

A disturbing trend has emerged in recent years where multiple officers are being shot and killed by a single perpetrator in events called "cluster killings" (Nowicki, 2010). In 2009, such cluster killings included the four officers shot in Seattle, Washington; four in Oakland, California; three in Pittsburgh, Pennsylvania; and two in Crestview, Florida (Long, 2009). More recently, sparked by police shootings of unarmed black men, ambushes on law enforcement have killed officers in Dallas, Texas, and Baton Rouge, Louisiana. People on both sides of the gun-control debate cite statistics such as these to prove their points.

Although courts, including the Supreme Court, support efforts of law enforcement to control guns used in crimes, they have been reluctant to relax search-and-seizure requirements of government in cases merely because they may involve weapons. Because in most states carrying a properly licensed handgun is legal, a report that a person has a handgun, with no additional information regarding criminal activity, may not create reasonable suspicion that a crime is being or will be committed, thus justifying a *Terry* stop.

Another disturbing trend is the increase in the number of people who willfully, in public, attempt to instigate confrontations with the police by openly carrying a gun. Fortunately for officers, these encounters are often recorded.

Constitutional Law in ACTION

Officer Jazinski is called to a local gas station on a report of a man with a gun. The dispatcher tells Jazinski that the caller sees a man putting gas in his car, the man appears very angry, and he has a handgun in a holster on his belt.

The officer arrives and finds the man described by the caller. The man also has a handgun, in a holster, and on his side. By this point, the man has started to argue with others pumping gas.

Officer Jazinski approaches the man, orders him to put his hands up, quickly handcuffs him, and takes the man's gun from his holster. The man is belligerent with the officer but complies with all the orders and eventually calms down.

The man tells Officer Jazinski that he has a permit to carry the handgun. The man also adds that he is in fact angry because he had a bad day at work, and this led to a verbal argument with other customers.

Checks are run and the man is found to have a permit to carry. Your state allows anyone with a permit to carry the handgun concealed or out in the open. The man is in compliance with all applicable laws. There was no crime at the gas station either. He is un-handcuffed and given his gun. He gets into his car and leaves.

- *Are the actions by the officer constitutional?*
- *Is the fact that the man is arguing with customers when the officer arrives important?*
- *What if the man was not arguing with others and was not belligerent when approached by the officer?*

A unanimous Supreme Court ruling in *Florida v. J.L.* (2000) established that "in order for an anonymous tip to be reliable enough to justify police action, even when a firearm is reported, it must do more than simply describe a suspect's appearance and location." Writing for the Court, Justice Ruth Bader Ginsburg stated, "Firearms are dangerous, and extraordinary dangers sometimes justify unusual precautions, [but] an automatic firearms exception to our established reliability analysis would rove too far. Such an exception would enable any person seeking to harass another to set in motion an intrusive, embarrassing police search of the targeted person simply by placing an anonymous call falsely reporting the target's unlawful carriage of a gun."

Likewise, in *Pennsylvania v. D.M.* (2000), the Supreme Court held that an anonymous tip with a physical description and location that a person had a gun was not enough for reasonable suspicion without anything else to cause suspicion.

The Current Gun Control Debate

Both those for and those against gun control effectively argue that any statistical evidence is biased, uses flawed research, is used to prove a specific point, or somehow is used to endorse a political point. The plethora of research provides ample data to be interpreted as people wish, and even elected officials have vastly different views of what the law is and should be. Data regarding most controversial issues are to be carefully scrutinized, which is certainly the case with research associated with firearms.

In Opposition to Gun Control

Various philosophies prevail in the gun control opposition camp. Some focus on the issue of constitutionality and rigorously defend individuals' rights to keep and bear arms, whereas others reflect a more passive resignation, believing such legislation is merely a paper tiger that offers no real bearing on any crime control efforts.

A common argument among gun control opponents is the claim that such laws will only put guns where they do not belong—in criminals' hands. The NRA and other advocacy groups have captured this philosophy about gun control with phrases suggesting "If guns are outlawed, only outlaws will have guns" and "Guns don't kill people, people do." They also note that violent crime has been decreasing.

The founding fathers wrote the Second Amendment to protect citizens' right to defend themselves against oppression, whether at the hands of another individual or those of tyrannical government. The right to keep and bear arms is a critically important constitutionally protected right; therefore, any laws restricting the keeping and bearing of arms in any way are clearly therefore unconstitutional.

In Support of Gun Control

Advocates of gun control often refer to the issue as "crime control"—not "gun control." Historical analysis shows that the amendment was written to protect colonists from England's King George III's military forces and contains nothing that could be construed today as prohibiting gun control.

Many advocates of gun control criticize the ability of some to circumvent the law. The Brady Campaign to Prevent Handgun Violence points out that despite legislation now banning the sale of assault weapons, thousands of these firearms are presently privately owned and for sale at gun shows because of grandfather clauses in the laws.

To counter the argument that violent crime has been decreasing in the country, gun control advocates contend that the decrease may be attributable to many factors other than legislation, including increased numbers of police in the community; implementation of new, more aggressive and more effective police tactics; and the crackdown on illegal drug trafficking.

Gun Control as a Political Issue

Thus far, the judiciary has left most gun control laws to the states to be determined through the political process. Chief Charlie Deane of Prince William County, Virginia, calls the gun issue the "third rail of policing." If politicians touch it, they don't last long (*Guns and Crime*, 2010). This lack of involvement has concerned many leaders in law enforcement. The executive director of PERF, Wexler (2010, p. iii), notes:

> It seems that the United States has become anesthetized to gun violence. While the 1999 Columbine school massacre in Colorado resulted in widespread demands for action to prevent such tragedies from occurring, it seemed that more recent incidents ... no longer prompted many calls for reform, because people no longer expect that any reforms will be made.

Even though violent crime in the United States has declined sharply since the 1990s, our nation still endures far higher homicide rates than do other countries—for example, 46 killings per day in the United States compared with only 8 killings per day in the entire European Union, which has a population 60 percent larger than the United States.

Prospects for reform at the federal level have improved somewhat. In 2009, Washington showed little or no appetite for taking on gun crime issues. Currently, in the wake of the Newtown, Connecticut, school shooting, gun control has become a more prominent topic among legislators and citizens alike. The struggle to find common ground, however, remains a challenge.

Finding Common Ground— Is a Compromise Possible?

Despite all the controversy over gun control, where the courts stand is without question. Gun control by the states is not constitutionally prohibited, and under most circumstances, legislation by the federal government is not prohibited.

The history of the courts suggests that they will defer to the discretion of the states on almost all matters concerning gun control. Thus far, the only actions the courts may find constitutionally offensive are a complete nationwide ban on firearms and acting on reports of gun possession without further evidence.

The controversy over the effectiveness of existing gun control legislation and the need to add to that body of legal work has spread into many different occupational venues, pulling in a variety of advocates and opponents from a wide range of professions. The CDC now keeps statistics on gun-related injuries and deaths. These statistics include types of weapons, ammunition used, whether the weapon was stolen, information when youths are involved, and the relationship between the first person to own the weapon and the victim or assailant. Educators, physicians, the clergy, and community groups are concerned as well.

The past president of the Brady Campaign to Prevent Gun Violence, Helmke, suggested that enforcing the laws on the books isn't the answer and advocated searching for the middle ground: "The Supreme Court said that near-total gun bans like D.C.'s were off the table, but it also said that 'any gun, anywhere, anybody, any time' is also off the table. Justice Scalia said that the right is not unlimited: You can have restrictions on who buys guns, what kind of guns they are, where they take them, how they're sold, where they're stored. That's the middle ground we should be looking at. This isn't Second Amendment trench warfare anymore. It should be about finding out what works" (Police Executive Research Forum, 2010, pp. 32–33 and 35). Helmke suggests that most can agree that illegal trafficking needs to stop and that we need to focus on problem dealers, look at multiple sales, and strengthen the ATF and give it the appropriate resources.

Boston Commissioner Edward Davis notes that the issue is not about taking people's guns. The issue is finding what's reasonable: "I think it's great that the National Shooting Sports Foundation and the NRA are at the table here. We need to continue the conversation with both of these organizations about what can work and what is acceptable. There may have been some aggravation in this discussion today simply because the law enforcement representatives are literally stepping over the bodies in the street. But I think most law enforcement officials aren't on one side or the other of the gun debate. We're looking for reasonability" (Police Executive Research Forum, 2010, p. 33).

Wexler (2010, p. 35) notes in the conclusion of the report that all sides agree on the need for mandatory sentencing for those who make "straw purchases" of guns. A **straw purchase** is when a buyer uses an intermediary (the "straw man") to purchase a firearm(s) from a licensed firearms dealer and then sells the weapon(s) to individuals who cannot legally buy guns themselves, such as felons and the severely mentally retarded. Before a person may purchase a firearm, he or she must provide personal information. Federal law imposes criminal penalties for making a false statement in connection with the purchase. Wexler suggests that enacting mandatory minimums would help break the impasse and get this issue off dead center: "A public debate on such a proposal would bring the issue of violence back into the news. We need to put an end to the apathy regarding the shootings and killings that happen every day in major U.S. cities" (Police Executive Research Forum, 2010, p. 35).

Interestingly, the Supreme Court ruled in 2014 that it is still a violation of the federal law to make a false statement in relation to the purchase of a firearm, even if the original purchaser and the person to whom the gun is sold could both legally possess a firearm. This case, *Abramski v. United States* (2014), involved a legal purchaser of a handgun who falsely stated on the background check form that he was buying the firearm for himself, when in reality he was buying it for his uncle, who also was not prohibited from possessing a firearm.

---

straw purchase an illegal transaction when a buyer uses an intermediary (the "straw man") to purchase a firearm(s) from a licensed firearms dealer and then sells the weapon(s) to individuals who cannot legally buy guns themselves, such as felons and the severely mentally retarded

◀ **CASE IN BRIEF**

Abramski v. United States (2014)

ISSUE Is it a crime to falsely report that one is buying a firearm for themselves when, in reality, the purchase is being made on behalf of another, even if both parties can legally own a firearm?

RULING Yes. The law is meant to collect important information about the final purchaser of a firearm in order to keep guns out of the hands of those who should not possess them. This cannot be done if the records do not reflect the actual person who will have possession of the gun after the purchase.

Summary

Historically, the militia was considered to be the entire adult male populace of a state. They were not simply allowed to keep arms but were at times *required* to do so by law. A central controversy over the Second Amendment is whether people have a right to bear arms as individuals rather than only as part of a militia.

The two opposing interpretations of the Second Amendment involve whether the amendment guarantees individuals' rights to keep and bear arms or whether it guarantees the states freedom from federal government infringement on this right. Judicial decisions over time reveal changes in how the Court has viewed Second Amendment guarantees. In *United States v. Miller* (1939) the court recognized a state right rather than an individual right to bear arms. In 1971 the courts ruled that there was no express right of an individual to keep and bear arms (*Stevens v. United States*). Both decisions have since been reversed.

In a landmark decision, the Supreme Court stated in *District of Columbia v. Heller* (2008) that the Second Amendment protects an individual's right to possess a firearm unconnected with service in a militia. In *McDonald v. Chicago* (2010) the Supreme Court, holding that the right to keep and bear arms was among those fundamental rights necessary to our system of ordered liberty, ruled that the Second Amendment *does* apply to the states and incorporated it under the Fourteenth Amendment.

The Brady Act, passed in 1993, contained the interim provision of a mandatory five-day waiting period on all handgun purchases. This provision was phased out and replaced in 1998 with the permanent provision of an instant, computerized criminal background check of all handgun purchasers. Some states still impose a waiting period on firearms purchases.

The Law Enforcement Officers Safety Act, allowing "qualified" active and retired law enforcement officers to carry concealed weapons anywhere in the United States, has three goals: (1) to establish equality between local LEOs and their federal counterparts who already carry nationwide, (2) to create an unpaid homeland security force to help protect the nation, and (3) to allow qualified current and retired LEOs the means to defend themselves and their families against criminals.

Discussion Questions

1. Should the government control the possession of guns or be able to restrict certain types of firearms? What about large capacity magazines?
2. Does the Brady Act serve a legitimate function?
3. Considering the history behind the drafting of the Second Amendment, can any original interpretations reasonably be used today? If so, how?
4. In Great Britain, police officers do not routinely carry firearms because, among other reasons, firearms are not considered the public threat they are elsewhere. Could this ever occur in the United States?
5. Would having severe penalties for gun violations help reduce gun violence? Should the law make the reward not worth the risk?
6. What makes more sense to you: restricting guns altogether or restricting who has access to guns? In other words, should legislation and enforcement efforts focus on the gun or on the individual?
7. Is a "cooling off" period for gun permits reasonable?
8. Does regulating handguns but not rifles and shotguns make sense?
9. Most "mass casualty" shootings are over quickly, even before police can arrive. In light of this reality, does it make sense to allow citizens to arm themselves? What impact does terrorism have on your response to this question?
10. Rewrite the Second Amendment as though you were asked to address contemporary concerns.

References

Agresti, J. D., & Smith, R. K. (2016, June 13). "Gun Control Facts." *Just Facts*. Retrieved July 23, 2016 from www.justfacts.com/guncontrol.asp

Associated Press. (2010, September 27). "Report: 10 States Sell Half of Imported Crime Guns." *PoliceOne.com News*. Retrieved July 23, 2016 from www.policeone.com/federal-law-enforcement/articles/2719054-Report-10-states-sell-half-of-imported-crime-guns

Basu, K. (2010, August 1). "'Stand Your Ground' Law Put to Test." *Florida Today*, p. A1.

Brady Campaign to Prevent Gun Violence. (2010, June 29). "Statement of Paul Helmke on U.S. Supreme Court Ruling." Washington, DC: Author. Retrieved July 23, 2016 from www.prnewswire.com/news-releases/statement-of-brady-president-paul-helmke-on-second-amendment-ruling-by-us-supreme-court-97309384.html

Brady Campaign to Prevent Gun Violence. (2016a). "About Gun Violence." Wash-ington, DC: Author. Retrieved July 23, 2016 from http://www.bradycampaign.org/about-gun-violence

Brady Campaign to Prevent Gun Violence. (2016b, March). "Gun Deaths Fact Sheet." Washington, DC: Author. Retrieved July 23, 2016 from http://www.bradycampaign.org/sites/default/files/Gun%20Deaths%20Fact%20Sheet_Mar2016.pdf

Castellano, A. (2012, December 20). "Virginia Tech Survivor Colin Goddard Fights Back Against Guns." *ABC News*. Retrieved July 23, 2016, from http://abcnews.go.com/US/virginia-tech-survivor-colin-goddard-fights-back-guns/story?id=18022765#.UZvgH_co5mM

Donohue, J. J., III. (2003, July). "The Final Bullet in the Body of the More Guns, Less Crime Hypothesis." *Criminology and Public Policy*, 2(3), pp. 397–410.

Doyle, M.; Ybarra, M.; & Lightman, D. (2016, June 15). "Terror Watch List Takes Center Stage Among Gun-Control Proposals." *McClatchyDC*. Retrieved July 22, 2016 from http://www.mcclatchydc.com/news/politics-government/congress/article84037982.html

Eldridge, J. (2012, July 20). "The Castle Doctrine and Indiana's Controversial New Law." PoliceOne.com, July 20, 2012. Retrieved July 23, 2016 from https://www.policeone.com/legal/articles/5827610-The-Castle-Doctrine-and-Indianas-controversial-new-law/

Federal Bureau of Investigation. (2014a). *Crime in the United States 2014*. Washington, DC: Author. Retrieved July 23, 2016 from https://ucr.fbi.gov/crime-in-the-u.s/2014/crime-in-the-u.s.-2014/offenses-known-to-law-enforcement/violent-crime

Federal Bureau of Investigation. (2014b). *Law Enforcement Officers Killed and Assaulted, 2014*. Washington, DC: Author. Retrieved July 23, 2016 from https://ucr.fbi.gov/leoka/2014/officers-feloniously-killed

Grimm, F. (2010, August 5). "'Stand Your Ground' Works—For Criminals." *The Miami Herald*. Retrieved July 23, 2016 from http://criminallawbook.com/assets/stand-ground.pdf

Hann, R. A.; Bilukham, O. O.; Crosby, A.; Fullilove, M. T.; Liberman, A.; Moscicki, E. K.; Snyder, S.; Tuma, F.; & Briss, P. (2003, October 3). "First Reports Evaluating the Effectiveness of Strategies for Preventing Violence: Firearms Laws. Findings from the Task Force on Community Preventive Services." *Morbidity and Mortality Weekly Report*, pp. 1–20.

Harris, E. A., & Lichtblau, E. (2015, December 10). "Connecticut to Ban Gun Sales to Those on Federal Terrorism Lists." *New York Times*. Retrieved July 23, 2016 from http://www.nytimes.com/2015/12/11/nyregion/connecticut-to-ban-gun-sales-to-those-on-federal-terrorism-lists.html?_r=0

Kovandzic, T. V., & Marvell, T. B. (2003, July). "Right-to-Carry Concealed Handguns and Violent Crime: Crime Control through Gun Decontrol?" *Criminology and Public Policy*, 2(3), pp. 363–396.

Long, C. (2009, December 12). "Gun Deaths Tried to Fray the Thin Blue Line in '09." *Boston Globe*. Retrieved July 23, 2016 from http://archive.boston.com/news/nation/articles/2009/12/12/number_of_cops_killed_by_gunfire_spikes_in_2009/

Lott, J. R., Jr. (1998). *More Guns, Less Crime: Understanding Crime and Gun Control Laws*. Chicago: University of Chicago Press.

Lott, J. R., Jr. (2003). *The Bias against Guns: Why Almost Everything You've Heard about Gun Control Is Wrong*. Washington, DC: Regnery Publishing, Inc.

Nakashima, E. (2015, July 10). "FBI: Breakdown in Background Check System Allowed Dylann Roof to Buy Gun." *The Washington Post*. Retrieved July 22, 2016 from https://www.washingtonpost.com/world/national-security/fbi-accused-charleston-shooter-should-not-have-been-able-to-buy-gun/2015/07/10/0d09fda0-271f-11e5-b72c-2b7d516e1e0e_story.html

National Counterterrorism Center. (2016, June 30). "Terrorist Identities Datamart Environment (TIDE)." Washington, DC: Author. Retrieved July 22, 2016 from https://www.nctc.gov/docs/tide_fact_sheet.pdf

Nowicki, E. (2010, March). "Cluster Killings of Police Officers." *Law and Order*, p. 6.

Planty, M., & Truman, J. L. (2013). *Firearm Violence, 1993–2011*. Washington, DC: Bureau of Justice Statistics. (NCJ 241730)

Police Executive Research Forum. (2010, May). *Guns and Crime: Breaking New Ground by Focusing on the Local Impact*. Washington, DC: Author.

Southern Poverty Law Center. (2016). "Active Antigovernment Groups in the United States." Montgomery, AL: Author. Retrieved July 21, 2016 from https://www.splcenter.org/active-antigovernment-groups-united-states

Wethal, T. (2010, June). "The Confusion with Concealed Carry." *Law Enforcement Technology*, pp. 30–36.

Wexler, C. (2010, May). "Introduction" (p. iii) and "Conclusion" (p. 35) in *Guns and Crime: Breaking New Ground by Focusing on the Local Impact*. Washington, DC: Police Executive Research Forum.

The White House. (2016, January 4). *FACT SHEET: New Executive Actions to Reduce Gun Violence and Make Our Communities Safer*. Washington, DC: Author. Retrieved July 21, 2016 from https://www.whitehouse.gov/the-press-office/2016/01/04/fact-sheet-new-executive-actions-reduce-gun-violence-and-make-our

Williams, J. (2016, January 26). "The Oregon Militia Standoff, Explained." Vox Media, Inc. Retrieved July 21, 2016 from http://www.vox.com/2016/1/3/10703712/oregon-militia-standoff

Zarembo, A. (2015, July 18). "Obama Pushes to Extend Gun Background Checks to Social Security." *Los Angeles Times*. Retrieved July 22, 2016 from http://www.latimes.com/nation/politics/la-na-gun-law-20150718-story.html

Cases Cited

Abramski v. United States, 573 U.S. ___ (2014)
Adams v. Williams, 407 U.S. 143 (1972)
Barnes v. State, 946 N.E.2d 572 (2011)
Caetano v. Massachusetts, 136 S.Ct. 1027 (2016)
District of Columbia v. Heller, 544 U.S.570 (2008)
Edwards v. City of Goldsboro, N.C., 178 F.3d 231 (4th Cir. 1999)
Florida v. J.L., 529 U.S. 266 (2000)
Gowder v. City of Chicago, District Court, N.D. Illinois, June 19, 2012.
McDonald v. Chicago, 561 U.S. 742 (2010)
Moore v. Madigan, 702 F. 3d 933 (7th Circuit, 2012)
Pennsylvania v. D.M., 529 U.S. 1126 (2000)
Peruta v. County of San Diego (2016)
Presser v. Illinois, 116 U.S. 252 (1886)
Printz v. United States, 521 U.S. 898 (1997)
Small v. United States, 544 U.S. 385 (2005)
Stevens v. United States, 440 F.2d 144 (6th Cir. 1971)
United States v. Cruikshank, 92 U.S. 542 (1875)
United States v. Decastro, 682 F.3d 160 (2012)
United States v. Emerson, 46 F. Supp. 2d 598 (N.D. Texas, 1999)
United States v. Lopez, 514 U.S. 549 (1995)
United States v. Miller, 307 U.S. 174 (1939)
United States v. Skoien, 587 F. 3d 803 (Court of Appeals, 7th Circuit, 2009)

CHAPTER 7

The Fourth Amendment:
An Overview of Constitutional Searches and Seizures

The right of the people to be secure in their persons, houses, papers, and effects, against unreasonable searches and seizures, shall not be violated, and no Warrants shall issue, but upon probable cause, supported by Oath or affirmation, and particularly describing the place to be searched, and the persons or things to be seized.

—Fourth Amendment to the U.S. Constitution

Facts will determine if a stop and frisk has occurred, and the Fourth Amendment will then determine what the police are permitted to do.

Section III The Fourth Amendment: Governing Constitutional Searches and Seizures

Learning Objectives

LO1 *Understand what the Fourth Amendment forbids and requires.*

LO2 *Know who is governed by the Fourth Amendment.*

LO3 *Explain how probable cause relates to searches and arrests.*

LO4 *Identify the one requirement of all search and arrest warrants.*

LO5 *Describe, in the context of the continuum of contacts, the relationship between an officer's actions and the constitutionality of those actions.*

LO6 *Clarify what a stop and what a frisk are and when each is permitted.*

LO7 *Summarize what the Terry decision established.*

LO8 *Outline what the exclusionary rule is, the precedent case for it, and what primary purpose it serves.*

LO9 *Discuss the exceptions to the exclusionary rule.*

Key Terms

articulable facts	furtive conduct	reasonable
attenuation doctrine	good faith	reasonableness
bright-line approach	harmless error	Fourth Amendment
case-by-case method	inevitable discovery	approach
consent decree	doctrine	reasonable suspicion
continuum of contacts	litigious	search
conventional Fourth	magistrate	seizure
Amendment	memorandum of	stop
approach	agreement (MOA)	*Terry* stop
exclusionary rule	nightcap(ped) warrant	totality of
frisk	no-knock warrant	circumstances
fruit of the poisonous	probable cause	
tree doctrine		

Introduction

If the First Amendment is considered the cornerstone of U.S. freedom, then the Fourth Amendment must be a building block with which freedom continues to develop. The Fourth Amendment is unique because it speaks not only to that desire but also to a need. A prominent theory of human behavior and motivation was set forth by famed psychologist Abraham H. Maslow (1908–1970). In Maslow's hierarchy of needs (Figure 7.1), the need for *security* comes right after the basic physical needs of food, clothing, and shelter (Maslow, 1954).

Although most of us take it for granted, one of the greatest advantages of living in the United States is to be able to live unimpeded by government. A continuing argument in this country, and one the First Amendment permits to be pursued, is whether we, indeed, have "too much" government. More than 200 years after the drafting of the Constitution, governmental controls remain important to Americans.

Governmental controls ensure that citizens can drive to and from their destinations without the fear of being pulled over by an overly zealous police officer who simply does not like the color of their car—or skin. It means that citizens can enjoy the security of their homes without fearing an intrusion by the government

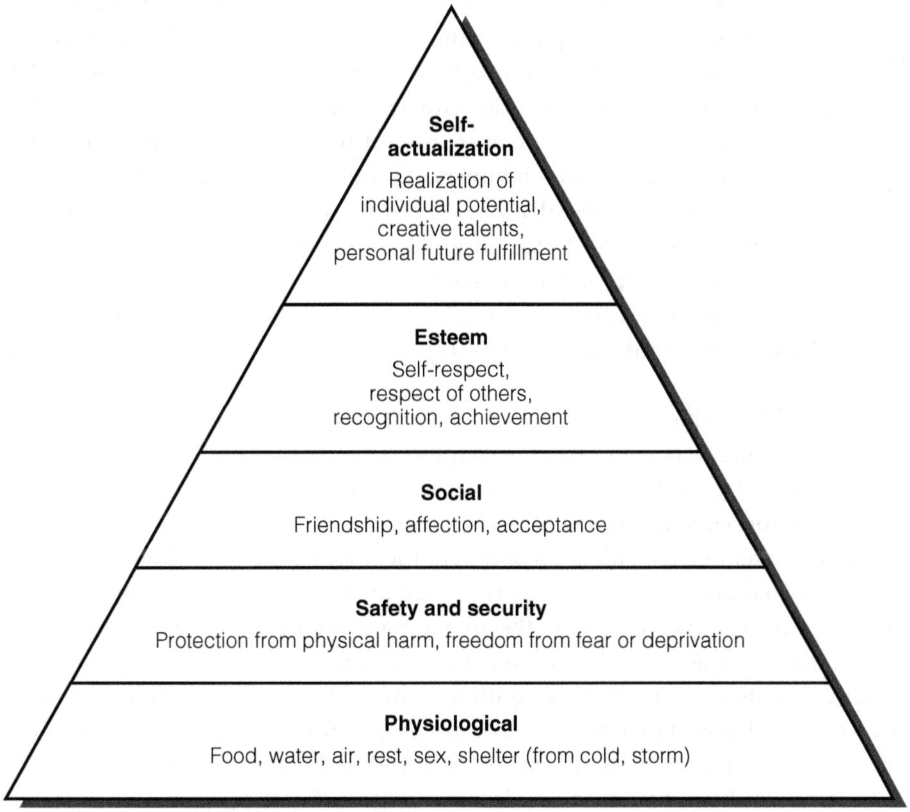

Figure 7.1 Maslow's Hierarchy of Needs

seizing assets, property, or records just because they are engaged in an unpopular line of work.

Of course, this security does not mean the government is barred from carrying out its responsibility. Limited governmental power is necessary for the laws of the country to be enforced and the government's business to be carried out. However, a balance is required for a democracy such as ours to exist—a balance between the government's powers and the people's freedom; that balance is what the law of search and seizure is all about. Because Americans take this freedom seriously, U.S. law has developed to firmly regulate how and when government agents can impose on people.

At the core of restrictions on governmental infringement of citizens' freedom is the Fourth Amendment, which forbids unreasonable search and seizure. These two key words—*search* and *seizure*—are fundamental to understanding the Fourth Amendment. A **search** is an examination of a person, place, or vehicle for contraband or evidence of a crime. A search, by its nature, is an intrusion into someone's privacy and, thus, is strictly regulated by the Fourth Amendment. A **seizure** is a taking by law enforcement or other government agent of contraband, evidence of a crime, or even a person, into custody. It too is regulated by the Fourth Amendment.

search an examination of a person, place, or vehicle for contraband or evidence of a crime

seizure a taking by law enforcement or other government agent of contraband, evidence of a crime, or even a person into custody

Strong opposition to indiscriminate and baseless government searches and seizures was one of the driving forces behind the Revolution. Two practices of England were at the forefront. *Writs of assistance* were used by revenue officers to search ships and other water vessels, as well as homes and businesses, for evidence of smuggled goods or goods on which taxes had not been paid. Government officials could force other citizens to help in the execution of the writs, too. *General warrants* were issued to search homes and other private places for evidence of crimes, especially libel. Both were issued on little or no suspicion and often were "valid" for an indeterminate length of time. Students wishing to further explore several cases that discuss these issues can reference *Frank v. Maryland* (1959), *Henry v. United States* (1959), and *Stanford v. Texas* (1965). A fourth relevant case, *Boyd v. United States* (1886), is discussed later in this chapter.

LO1 The Fourth Amendment forbids unreasonable searches and seizures and requires that any search or arrest warrant be based on probable cause.

Figure 7.2 provides an overview of a Fourth Amendment inquiry and the path to valid searches and seizures. This chapter explains the "yes" responses in the top line of the figure. Chapter 8, lawful seizures, and Chapter 9, lawful searches, explain the consequences of the "no" responses.

This chapter begins with a discussion of the importance of the Fourth Amendment to law enforcement and who is regulated by the Fourth Amendment. Then, it examines the two main clauses of the amendment, the Reasonableness Clause and the Warrant Clause. This discussion is followed by an explanation of search and arrest warrants and a look at the continuum of contacts from a simple encounter to an arrest. This explanation leads to a discussion of the first Fourth Amendment encounter on the continuum, the law of stop and frisk. Next is a discussion of two important results of Fourth Amendment violations by the government: (1) evidence being excluded from court through the exclusionary rule and (2) the officer, the government agent, and perhaps the entire department or agency facing civil liability. The chapter concludes by considering what happens when state law conflicts with constitutional law.

The Importance of the Fourth Amendment to Law Enforcement

The Fourth Amendment governs much of what police officers are legally allowed to do as they "serve and protect" and is so important that three chapters in this text are devoted to it. In addition to its importance to the U.S. scheme of government, the Fourth Amendment provides students of the Constitution with ample opportunity to develop a working understanding of the country's legal system.

The Fourth Amendment has continued to evolve constitutionally, substantively, and procedurally through common and statutory law. It remains the pivotal area of debate in the field for law enforcement and in the courtroom for the prosecution and the defense, as well as in the classroom for students and legal scholars. Each word and phrase within this amendment continues to be reexamined and redefined in the true spirit of the Constitution because constantly changing human interaction and behavior spawns ever unique circumstances that result in government's intrusion into people's lives.

The idea that citizens can enjoy privacy and freedom from government intrusion with regard to themselves, their possessions, their homes, and their businesses is what citizens have come to *expect*, rather than what we consciously *desire*, as was the case more than 200 years ago. The U.S. Constitution has taken the U.S. legal system, its government, and those enjoying the freedom a long way in a comparatively short time. This chapter examines the Fourth Amendment in its entirety and how it affects our lives, considering the rights ensured by the Fourth Amendment and the consequences of government's violations of this law.

Before embarking on the substance of the Fourth Amendment, recall the explanation of *procedural law*. This chapter begins to examine those constitutional amendments that make up the body of procedural law, an entire body of law unto itself. This is the law used to enforce other laws and is known as *criminal procedure*.

In a constitutional democracy, crime control considers both ends and means. The "ends" consists of finding the truth to obtain justice, that is, convicting the guilty *and* exonerating the innocent. The law of criminal procedure seeks this balance. "Criminal law's ultimate ends are dual and conflicting. It must be designed from inception to end, to acquit the innocent as readily, at least, as to convict the guilty. This presents the inescapable dilemma of criminal procedure . . . that the easier it is made to prove guilt, the more difficult it becomes to establish innocence" (Hall, 1942, p. 725).

The Fourth Amendment's prohibition against unreasonable searches and seizures by the police is perhaps the most vital component of criminal procedure because of ample opportunities the U.S. Supreme Court has had to set forth regarding when any government agent may and may not act, as well as when they have an expectation, or duty, to do so.

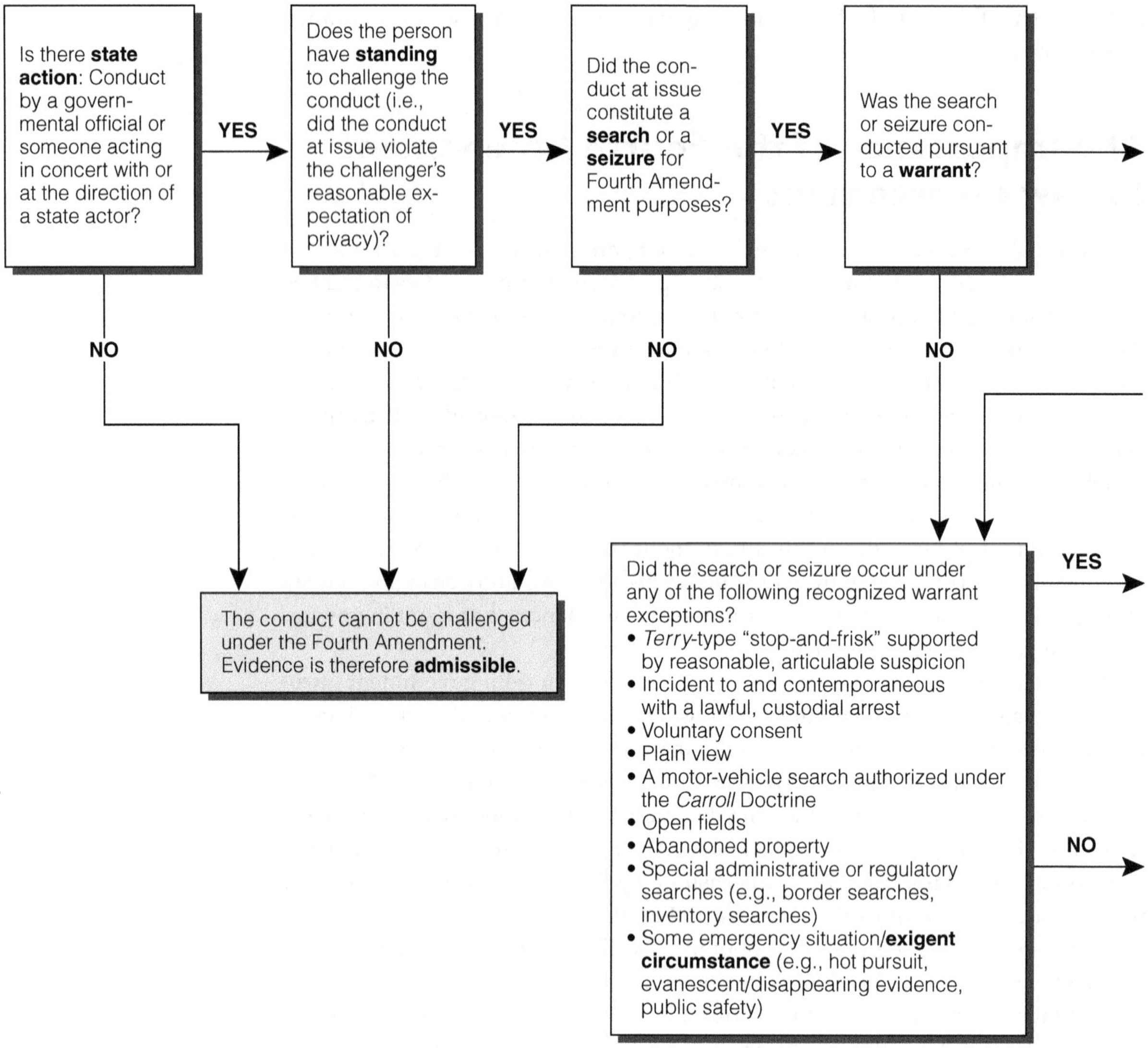

Figure 7.2 Overview of a Fourth Amendment Inquiry

Source: FERDICO/FRADELLA/TOTTEN. *Criminal Procedure for the Criminal Justice Professional*, 10E. © 2009 Wadsworth, a part of Cengage Learning, Inc.

Who Is Regulated by the Fourth Amendment?

As the U.S. Constitution was originally drafted, the Fourth Amendment itself applied to only federal government, but now it is equally applied to state government by the Fourteenth Amendment, as established in *Wolf v. Colorado* (1949). Therefore, any government agent (whether federal, state, county, or municipal) is regulated by the Fourth Amendment.

When most people consider search-and-seizure law, they think of its impact on such agencies as the FBI or local police. Again, any employee of the government

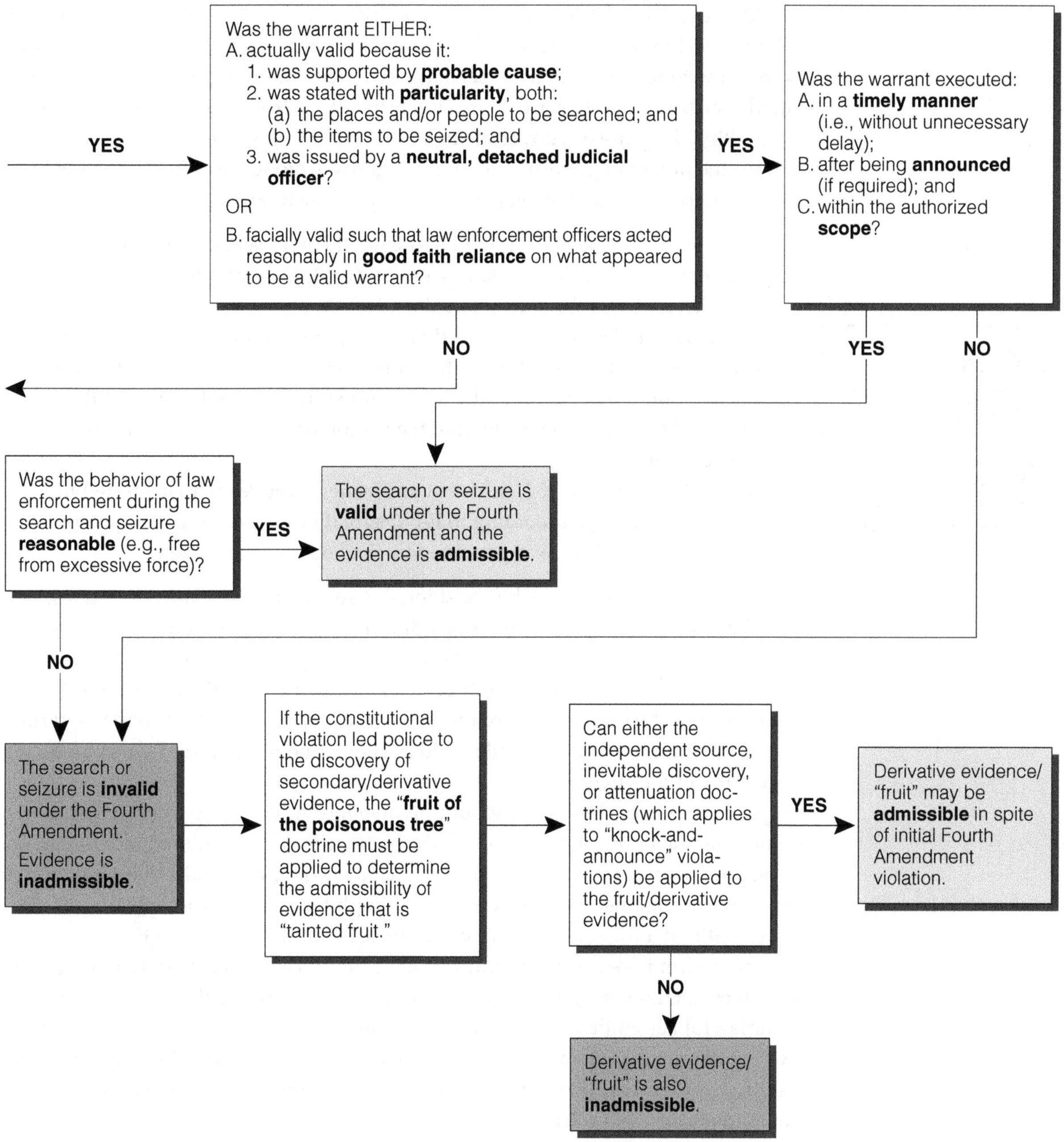

Chapter 7 The Fourth Amendment: An Overview of Constitutional Searches and Seizures **209**

Was the warrant EITHER:
A. actually valid because it:
 1. was supported by **probable cause**;
 2. was stated with **particularity**, both:
  (a) the places and/or people to be searched; and
  (b) the items to be seized; and
 3. was issued by a **neutral, detached judicial officer**?
OR
B. facially valid such that law enforcement officers acted reasonably in **good faith reliance** on what appeared to be a valid warrant?

Was the warrant executed:
A. in a **timely manner** (i.e., without unnecessary delay);
B. after being **announced** (if required); and
C. within the authorized **scope**?

Was the behavior of law enforcement during the search and seizure **reasonable** (e.g., free from excessive force)?

The search or seizure is **valid** under the Fourth Amendment and the evidence is **admissible**.

The search or seizure is **invalid** under the Fourth Amendment. Evidence is **inadmissible**.

If the constitutional violation led police to the discovery of secondary/derivative evidence, the "**fruit of the poisonous tree**" doctrine must be applied to determine the admissibility of evidence that is "tainted fruit."

Can either the independent source, inevitable discovery, or attenuation doctrines (which applies to "knock-and-announce" violations) be applied to the fruit/derivative evidence?

Derivative evidence/ "fruit" may be **admissible** in spite of initial Fourth Amendment violation.

Derivative evidence/ "fruit" is also **inadmissible**.

Figure 7.2 (*Continued*)

at any jurisdictional level is influenced by the constitutional restrictions. This regulation includes all governmental agencies, including but not limited to the Secret Service, the Internal Revenue Service, and the Food and Drug Administration. The Fourth Amendment also regulates state agencies, such as state revenue agencies, county sheriffs and local police, public schools and colleges, and other regulatory bodies as well as local, county, and municipal bodies of government.

LO2 *If a person is an employee of any governmental agency or is an agent of the government in any capacity, that person is bound by the Fourth Amendment. The Fourth Amendment does not apply to private parties.*

Private individuals or agencies are not regulated by the Fourth Amendment. When a rebellious teenager angrily informs his parents that they cannot come into his room without a warrant, he has made an inaccurate statement. Private security guards, such as store detectives, are similarly not controlled by the Fourth Amendment. Why? They are not government agents, and the Constitution was established to limit the power of government and its agents. Among cases involving the issue of searches conducted by private individuals are the following:

- *United States v. Parker* (1994) held that United Parcel Service employees could open, without warrants, packages and inspect their contents whenever a customer insured a package for more than $1,000.
- *United States v. Tapley* (2016) held that a computer repair technician did not act as a government agent when he found some unusual pictures of children on a computer; reported it to the police, who found no violation; and then continued the search on his own of the computer, eventually finding child pornography.
- *United States v. Ross* (1982) held that an airline employee who inspected the defendant's luggage according to FAA regulations was acting in a governmental capacity and, thus, was governed by the Fourth Amendment.

> **MYTH**
> The Fourth Amendment restricts the actions of all U.S. citizens.
>
> **FACT**
> No. Only the government and its agents are subject to the requirements of the Fourth Amendment.

Can a private party ever be considered a government agent? Sometimes, yes. Two factors that are considered when determining whether someone is working as an agent of the government are (1) whether the government (e.g., a law enforcement officer) knows of the search or acquiesces in it and (2) what the intent of the person performing the search is (see *United States v. Walther*, 1981). A certain amount of government knowledge and participation are required when assessing the totality of the circumstances.

An example for discussion would involve individuals who seize evidence of a crime from the home of another—maybe because they were invited into the home, or maybe because they actually broke into the residence. Could that evidence be used in court against the homeowner, although the person who actually seized it did so without a warrant and without permission of the homeowner?

The answer is yes, if the person was not acting as any sort of government agent. This does not, however, make the individual immune from liability for committing an unlawful act while obtaining the information. Similarly, a private store detective could search someone without a warrant or without the other constitutional requirements with which the police need to comply because the Constitution does not regulate private police.

In *United States v. Jacobsen* (1984), the Court held that even when a private person had opened a package and then resealed it, the government agent could expose to view that which had previously been observed by the private person without the exposure constituting an illegal search. In this case, a Federal Express worker came across a package that had been accidentally torn open by a forklift. As per company policy, the worker examined the contents of the damaged package for insurance claims purposes and discovered a white powdery substance. Suspecting it was illegal drugs, the worker summoned management, who contacted the Drug Enforcement Administration (DEA). The responding DEA agents removed a trace of the powder, subjected it to a chemical test, and determined that it was cocaine.

Constitutional Law in ACTION

Sergeant White is investigating a stolen identity ring. This ring uses stolen identities to obtain credit cards, make purchases, and then return items for cash. During surveillance, Sergeant White watches as a member of this ring, Joe Smith, enters a high-end electronics retailer. Believing that Smith is about to commit credit card fraud using a stolen identity, White follows him.

Smith selects two ultra-high-definition televisions and pays for them with a credit card. He begins to push the televisions out to his car. With nothing else to go on other than the fact that Smith used a credit card to purchase the televisions, Sergeant White tells a store security guard to go outside and search Smith for more cards while White watches from inside the store.

The security guard does so and finds several other credit cards in Smith's possession. All of the cards have different names on them. Sergeant White then goes outside and arrests Smith for identity theft.

- In general, would the Constitution regulate the conduct of the security guard?
- Did Sergeant White participate to the degree that this scenario would fall under the Fourth Amendment?
- If the security guard had acted on his own, knowing only that Sergeant White identified Smith as being involved in an identity theft ring, would the guard's actions fall under the Fourth Amendment?

Subsequently, a warrant was obtained to search the place to which the package was addressed, the warrant was executed, and respondents were arrested.

After the respondents were indicted for possessing an illegal substance with intent to distribute, their motion to suppress the evidence on the ground that the warrant was the product of an illegal search and seizure was denied, and they were tried and convicted. The court of appeals reversed, holding that the validity of the warrant depended on the validity of the warrantless test of the white powder, that the testing constituted a significant expansion of the previous private search and that a warrant was required. The Supreme Court, however, granted certiorari and held that the federal agents did not infringe any constitutionally protected privacy interest that had not already been frustrated as the result of private conduct. To the extent that a protected possessory interest was infringed, the infringement was *de minimis* and constitutionally reasonable, thereby reversing the judgment of the appellate court.

What if the private party had agreed to go in and get the item from the house, or the private security guard had agreed to search the person for the police? Then, arguably, this private person, although not employed by the government, has become an agent of the government, and the Fourth Amendment would then apply. Having looked at who is regulated by the Fourth Amendment, consider now the important clauses of this amendment.

◀ **CASE IN BRIEF**

United States v. Jacobsen (1984)

ISSUE Is it a violation of the Fourth Amendment for an employee of a private company to open and inspect the contents of a package?

RULING No. The actions were of a private person, not acting at the direction or with the knowledge of a government official.

The Clauses of the Fourth Amendment

The Fourth Amendment contains two clauses of importance to search-and-seizure issues:

- The Reasonableness Clause: "The right of the people to be secure in their persons, houses, papers and effects, against *unreasonable* searches and seizures shall not be violated."
- The Warrant Clause: "[A]nd no Warrants shall issue but upon *probable cause*, supported by Oath or affirmation, and particularly describing the place to be searched, and the persons or things to be seized."

Two Interpretations

These two clauses have been viewed differently by the Supreme Court. Until the 1960s, the Court used the **conventional Fourth Amendment approach,** viewing the two clauses as intertwined and firmly connected. This interpretation holds that all searches not conducted with both a warrant and probable cause are unreasonable and, therefore, unlawful. Importantly, the protection from government action under this line of thought is that the judge (i.e., neutral and detached magistrate) is involved before the police action takes place.

Since the 1960s, however, the Court has broadened government's power by adopting what has been called the **reasonableness Fourth Amendment approach,** which takes a post-action evaluative approach. This interpretation sees the two clauses as separate, distinct, and addressing two separate situations. Here, the protection against government intrusion is afforded after the police action in that the court will assess whether or not the action was reasonable based on the information the police had at the time. In some instances, searches can be reasonable without either warrants or probable cause.

Justice Scalia stated in *City of Los Angeles v. Patel* (2015):

> The Fourth Amendment provides, in relevant part, that "[t]he right of the people to be secure in their persons, houses, papers, and effects, against unreasonable searches and seizures, shall not be violated, and no Warrants shall issue, but upon probable cause." Grammatically, the two clauses of the Amendment seem to be independent—and directed at entirely different actors. The former tells the executive what it must do when it conducts a search, and the latter tells the judiciary what it must do when it issues a search warrant. But in an effort to guide courts in applying the Search-and-Seizure Clause's indeterminate reasonableness standard, and to maintain coherence in our case law, we have used the Warrant Clause as a guidepost for assessing the reasonableness of a search, and have erected a framework of presumptions applicable to broad categories of searches conducted by executive officials. Our case law has repeatedly recognized, however, that these are mere presumptions, and the only constitutional *requirement* is that a search be reasonable.

When a valid warrant has been issued and, thus, probable cause has been judicially determined, the Supreme Court has continued to find the requirements of the Fourth Amendment satisfied. A great number of cases have developed as the Court has sought to determine under what circumstances searches and seizures are valid without warrants or probable cause.

---

conventional Fourth Amendment approach
viewing the Reasonableness Clause and the Warrant Clause as intertwined and firmly connected

reasonableness Fourth Amendment approach
the Reasonableness Clause and the Warrant Clause are interpreted as separate issues

Critical concepts to understanding the Fourth Amendment are *reasonableness*, *reasonable expectation of privacy*, and *probable cause*. These terms are considered when deciding what the government, including the police, is permitted to do and when. The terms have also been the basis for many court decisions and remain a viable point of argument in criminal cases.

The Constitution was written in general terms to permit the societies it would continue serving to determine what they consider reasonable, rather than creating a cast-in-stone definition. Such foresight enables this body of law to change along with those it serves. Even the courts have struggled with definitions. They, too, desire to keep the door open for case-by-case interpretation. The guidelines provided through court opinions do not provide any more precise definitions of these terms. Nonetheless, an understanding of key terms such as *probable cause* and *reasonable* are often at the heart of the interpretation.

> **MYTH**
> A police officer will always need a warrant to conduct a search.
>
> **FACT**
> The Constitution has been interpreted to allow for warrantless searches under a few, well-delineated exceptions.

Reasonableness

"The touchstone of the Fourth Amendment is reasonableness, and the reasonableness of a search is determined 'by assessing, on the one hand, the degree to which it intrudes upon an individual's privacy and, on the other, the degree to which it is needed for the promotion of legitimate governmental interests'" (*United States v. Knights*, 2001). In other words, the Fourth Amendment prohibits "unreasonable" searches and seizure. The Reasonableness Clause of the Fourth Amendment makes warrantless searches and seizures valid and constitutional when they are sensible.

How would you define *reasonable*? It is a challenge, but the cases that have sought to do so have come up with the same descriptors most of us would: **Reasonable** means sensible, rational, and justifiable. It is one of those terms the framers of the Constitution used to require interpretation and application of a law intended to meet the needs of the people, rather than providing such rigidity that a commonsense application could not be made. Much debate, and much law, has occurred as a result of defining what is reasonable for the government to do. Case definitions for reasonable include:

- "What is reasonable depends upon a variety of considerations and circumstances. It is an elastic term which is of uncertain value in a definition" (*Sussex Land & Live Stock Co. v. Midwest Refining Co.*, 1923).
- "Not extreme. Not arbitrary, capricious or confiscatory" (*Public Service Comm'n v. Havemeyer*, 1936).
- "That which is fair, proper, just, moderate, suitable under the circumstances, fit and appropriate to the end in view, having the faculty of reason, rational, governed by reason not immoderate or excessive, honest, equitable, tolerable" (*Cass v. State*, 1933).

Two approaches have been used to determine reasonableness:

- **Bright-line approach**—Reasonableness is determined by a specific rule applying to all cases.
- **Case-by-case method**—Reasonableness is determined by considering the totality of circumstances in each individual case. This method is most commonly used in U.S. courts.

reasonable sensible, rational, and justifiable

bright-line approach determining the reasonableness of an action according to a specific rule that applies to all cases

case-by-case method determining the reasonableness of an action by considering the totality of circumstances in each case

A key consideration in determining whether a search or seizure is reasonable is the balance between individual rights and the needs of society, as stressed previously. Another consideration is whether a person's reasonable expectation of privacy has been violated by the government.

The essence of the Constitution is to prevent government from being unnecessarily involved in our lives. The Constitution does not provide an absolute right to be free from government intrusion, only unreasonable interference. Along with a right to be secure from other unreasonable government intrusion is a right to privacy, but this debate has not found answers as readily as have those areas police more often find themselves involved with. It is important to understand that *privacy* is multifaceted and that the privacy rights addressed in the First Amendment differ from those protected by the Fourth Amendment. As was discussed in Chapter 5, privacy within the context of the First Amendment has to do with government restriction and regulation of areas considered "private," such as people's personal relationships and choices pertaining to sexual relationships, birth control, abortion, and sexual preference. But *privacy* in the context of the Fourth Amendment is used to help determine if a search has taken place, or whether the government has intruded into an area considered private, and thus protected, in order to look for evidence or contraband. The law surrounding one's reasonable expectation of privacy is discussed in greater detail in Chapter 9.

Probable Cause

In addition to the term *reasonable*, another key term in the Fourth Amendment is *probable cause*.

probable cause exists when facts and circumstances are sufficient in themselves to warrant a person of reasonable caution to believe that an offense has been or is being committed; stronger than reasonable suspicion but less than the quantum of evidence required for conviction

totality of circumstances the principle on which a number of legal assessments are made; is not a mathematical formula for achieving a certain number of factors but rather a sum total of layers of information and the synthesis of what the police have heard, what they know, and what they observe as trained officers, including probable cause, used to assess whether the sum total would lead a reasonable person to believe what the officers concluded

> Probable cause (to arrest) exists when the facts and circumstances within the officers' knowledge and of which they had reasonable trustworthy information are sufficient in themselves to warrant a man of reasonable caution in the belief that an offense has been or is being committed. (*Brinegar v. United States*, 1949)

In *Brinegar*, the Court referenced Chief Justice John Marshall's observation in *Locke v. United States* (1813) that **probable cause** "means less than evidence which would justify condemnation or conviction," then added, "[s]ince Marshall's time, at any rate, it has come to mean more than bare suspicion."

Smith v. United States (1949) defined probable cause as "the sum total of layers of information and the synthesis of what the police have heard, what they know and what they observe as trained officers. We [the Court] weigh not individual layers but the laminated total." This "laminated total," more often referred to as the **totality of circumstances,** is the principle on which a number of legal assessments are made, including probable cause. Totality of circumstances is not a mathematical formula for achieving a certain number of factors; rather, it is looking at what does exist to assess whether the sum total would lead a reasonable person to believe what the officers concluded. The more factors present, generally the more likely a finding of probable cause will be upheld. However, probable cause may also be developed with fewer factors but factors that are strong. In factor assessment, quality and quantity are both important, but if one is lacking, the other can compensate.

Probable cause is evaluated from an objective viewpoint and is extremely fact-dependent, as well as being *contextual*. The same facts in one situation may not provide probable cause in a different situation. The Court has described probable cause as being a "fluid concept—turning on the assessment of probabilities in particular factual contexts—not readily, or even usefully, reduced to a neat set of legal rules" (*Illinois v. Gates*, 1983). Probable cause is stronger than reasonable suspicion and is a concept crucial to understanding when police may or may not act in the course and scope of their duties. It can legally justify searches and arrests with or, in some cases, without warrants and requires the determining question of, "Would a reasonable person believe that a crime was committed and that the individual committed the offense, or that the contraband or evidence is where it is believed to be?"

The terms *reasonable person* and *believe* are challenging to precisely define, especially when time is of the essence to an officer in the field. Probable cause exists when a reasonable person, in the same or similar situation, would believe that a crime probably has been committed and that the person committing the crime or evidence of it will be found in a particular location.

Probable cause must be established *before* a lawful search or arrest can be made. Note that the terms used here are *arrest* and *search*, not *stop* and *frisk*. Facts and evidence obtained after a search or arrest cannot be used to establish probable cause. They can be used, however, to strengthen the case if probable cause was established before the arrest, making the arrest legal. If probable cause is not present, police cannot act; if they do, consequences will ensue. Without probable cause, seized evidence may be inadmissible in court, arrests determined illegal, and officers and others held liable for such illegality, as discussed later in the chapter. Probable cause and its establishment are key elements in motions to suppress in both warrant and warrantless situations.

> **LO3** Probable cause determines when officers may execute lawful searches and arrests with or, in some cases, without a warrant. Probable cause to search means officers reasonably believe that evidence, contraband, or other items sought are where police believe these items to be. Probable cause to arrest means officers reasonably believe that a crime has been committed by the person they seek to arrest.

Sources of Probable Cause

The two basic source categories of probable cause are observational and informational.

Observational Probable Cause Observational probable cause is derived from a government agent's personal experiences—what officers perceive through their own senses of sight, hearing, smell, touch, and taste. Officers' experience, training, and expertise may lend additional credibility in justifying probable cause because such things sharpen one's situational awareness and enhance the senses, thereby enabling officers to assess things an ordinary person might be unable to. Glennon (2008) describes this ability as intuition or a sixth sense. Officers often refer to it as a "gut feeling." Social scientists refer to it as "cognitive dissonance."

The physical actions of an individual may draw the attention of police and lead to probable cause. It is not relevant that the behaviors *might* have innocent explanations (i.e., the conduct is not criminal). Observing **furtive conduct**, that is, questionable, suspicious, or secretive behavior, will understandably raise an officer's suspicion, and although a person's level of nervousness may not be enough by itself, it can play a part in the totality of the circumstances (*United States v. McCarty*, 1988; *United States v. Ingrao*, 1990).

furtive conduct
questionable, suspicious, or secretive behavior

Physical evidence may establish probable cause. In *State v. Heald* (1973), the court ruled that evidence at a burglary scene, including a distinctive tire tread left in the snow, provided sufficient probable cause to arrest when the police approached the suspect vehicle and the driver drove away.

Admissions made to a police officer, verbally or through actions, may provide sufficient observational probable cause or lead to a finding of probable cause under the totality of the circumstances analysis. In *Rawlings v. Kentucky* (1980), a suspect admitted that the contents of her purse (drugs) belonged to her, and the court found this admission to be sufficient probable cause for the police to arrest her. False or implausible answers may also contribute to probable cause, such as occurred in *United States v. Anderson* (1987), when officers stopped a car on a road known to be used by people transporting drugs and found a large amount of cash wrapped in small bundles, secured with rubber bands. The suspects said they had just won the money in Atlantic City, but the officers did not believe the answers fit their questions.

Presence at a crime scene or in a high crime area may also contribute to probable cause, although usually is not sufficient alone. Additional factors that may need to be considered include the specificity of the suspect's or vehicle's description; the size of the area in which the offender might be found, which relates to the length of time that has passed since the crime occurred; and the number of other people or vehicles in the area at the time. However, if the suspect is present at a recent crime, that presence may be sufficient, as was the case in *State v. Mimmovich* (1971), in which officers found the suspects of a burglary in suspiciously close proximity to the burglarized dwelling immediately after it occurred. If suspects were crawling out a window during a suspected burglary, that action could be sufficient.

Association with other known criminals is another factor that may contribute to the finding of probable cause. In *United States v. Di Re* (1948), the Court said that "one who accompanies a criminal to a crime rendezvous cannot be assumed to be a bystander," and that one's presence with others engaged in criminal activity can contribute to a finding of probable cause. However, the fact that someone has been involved in past criminal activity (*Beck v. Ohio*, 1964) or fails to protest his or her arrest is insufficient in itself to infer probable cause to support an arrest.

Informational Probable Cause   Often, officers do not personally witness criminal activity and, consequently, must rely on information provided by others. In fact, seldom do the police actually see the crimes being committed. Usually, other sources help establish informational probable cause and include official sources such as roll call, dispatch, police bulletins, and wanted notices or unofficial sources such as witnesses, victims, and informants. A series of Supreme Court decisions set forth the legal requirements for establishing probable cause when working with informants.

In *Draper v. United States* (1959), a narcotics officer received information from a reliable informant that heroin was being transported on a train by a person the informant described in great detail, including what he would be wearing, even the fact he "walked real fast." The officers set up surveillance and arrested a man matching the description. Heroin and a syringe were found in a search incident to the arrest. The Supreme Court at that time held that information from a reliable informant, corroborated by the police, upheld a determination of probable cause.

Constitutional Law in ACTION

At 4:00 a.m. on a snowy early morning in December, Fred Perkins was sitting in his car with the engine and lights off. Officer Jones, who was patrolling the neighborhood because of recent burglaries in the area, noticed the car because of a city ordinance that prohibits parking on the street between 3:00 a.m. and 6:00 a.m. Also, Jones had not seen any other cars on the road or anyone on foot in the area for over 30 minutes, likely due to the time of night and the falling snow.

Jones pulled up to Perkins' car and got out of her squad car. Perkins exited the vehicle and told Jones that his car broke down as he was passing through the area. Jones asked for identification, and Perkins gave her a state identification card. Jones noticed that Fred lived 25 miles away.

While they talked, Jones noticed a set of footprints in the snow going up the driveway at 3702 Issa Road, and she asked Perkins if he had been visiting anyone. Perkins said he was not visiting anyone in the area. Jones found it strange that someone would use Issa Road, which is a residential side street, to pass through the area, especially given that the freeway was nearby. Also in the driveway were a toolbox, a gas can, and a snow blower, none of which were covered in snow.

Jones placed Perkins in handcuffs and put him in her squad car. Another officer arrived on the scene to stay with Perkins while Jones set off to follow the footprints. The footprints led to the garage of 3702 Issa Road. The service door had been kicked open. Jones knocked on the door to the house and the homeowner, Mr. Stanley, answered. Stanley told Jones that he had come home from work at midnight and locked his garage door. Mr. Stanley also said that the snow blower and gas can were from his garage but that he did not own the toolbox.

- *Did Officer Jones establish probable cause to believe that Fred Perkins had committed a burglary?*

- *In your opinion, what is the most important fact in this situation to support a determination of probable cause?*

- *Would probable cause exist if it had been summer and no footprints were in the snow? If the snow blower, gas can, and tool box were covered in snow? If it were 4:00 p.m. and many people were walking around the area?*

A more stringent set of requirements for using informants in establishing probable cause was later set forth in *Aguilar v. Texas* (1964), when the court devised a two-pronged test. The first prong tested the informant's credibility. Is the person reliable? Is the informant's identity known? Is the informant a law-abiding citizen or a criminal? The second prong tested the informant's basis of knowledge and reliability of the information provided. Is the information accurate? Did the informant personally witness the information given? If not, did the information come from another source? Is the information still believable? What is this informant's track record?

In *Spinelli v. United States* (1969), the Court faced the question of whether probable cause existed to support a search warrant that uncovered evidence to convict

Spinelli of running a gambling operation. This case examined the determination that had deemed an informant reliable despite the absence of facts to support the perceived reliability. Even more important to the decision, the Court continued, was that, "The tip does not contain a sufficient statement of the underlying circumstances from which the informer concluded that Spinelli was running a bookmaking operation. We are not told how the FBI's source received his information—it is not alleged that the informant personally observed Spinelli at work or that he had ever placed a bet with him. Moreover, if the informant came by the information indirectly, he did not explain why his sources were reliable. In the absence of a statement detailing the manner in which the information was gathered, it is especially important that the tip describe the accused's criminal activity in sufficient detail that the magistrate may know that he is relying on something more substantial than a casual rumor circulating in the underworld or an accusation based merely on an individual's general reputation." Thus, *Spinelli* refined how a judge should evaluate the two prongs of *Aguilar* when determining the existence of probable cause stemming from an informant.

This two-pronged approach was abandoned in 1983 in *Illinois v. Gates*, which sharpened up the definition of what constitutes probable cause and the totality of the circumstances to be considered. In this case, a tip from an anonymous informant led to police obtaining and executing a search warrant for drugs in the defendant's home. Justice William Rehnquist held that because "the most basic function of any government is to provide for the security of the individual and of his property," the spirit of the law was better served by determination of the existence of probable cause by consideration of the totality of the circumstances in deciding whether a "reasonable and prudent person" would believe that, in this case, contraband was located in a particular location, thus, indicating criminal activity. Justice Rehnquist noted that "probable cause is a fluid concept—turning on the assessment of probabilities in a particular factual context—not readily, or even usefully reduced to a neat set of legal rules." This totality of circumstances test made establishment of probable cause by use of informants easier for police.

In *United States v. Sokolow* (1989), the Court justified a warrantless investigative stop as reasonable under the Fourth Amendment because, given the totality of the circumstances present, sufficient reasonable suspicion existed. **Reasonable suspicion** is more than an experienced officer's hunch or intuition, and more than mere whim, caprice, or idle curiosity; it is a rational inference taken from specific and articulable facts, and viewed objectively using the totality of the circumstances. **Articulable facts** are descriptions or actions described in clear, distinct statements. Although *Sokolow* dealt with another issue, that of "drug courier profiles," this case demonstrates that the totality of circumstances will be relied on in determining the constitutional justification for intrusion by the police.

In *Florida v. Harris* (2013), the Supreme Court visited the issue of whether an "alert" by drug detection dog could provide probable cause to search a vehicle. In this case, Aldo, a German Shepherd, "alerted" to the driver's door handle of a truck that his handler had stopped for an equipment violation. A subsequent search of the truck produced evidence of methamphetamine manufacturing.

The defendant, Harris, tried to have the evidence suppressed, claiming that the "alert" did not provide probable cause to search for illegal drugs. The trial court

reasonable suspicion more than an experienced officer's hunch or intuition, and more than mere whim, caprice, or idle curiosity; it is a rational inference taken from specific and articulable facts, and viewed objectively using the totality of the circumstances

articulable facts actions described in clear, distinct statements

ruled that probable cause had been developed, Harris entered a plea, but then appealed to the Florida Supreme Court, which determined that a K-9 alert does not provide probable cause to search. The court found that the dog's training and certification in drug detection was not enough and ruled that actual field performance information was required to establish probable cause.

The case ended up before the Supreme Court, where the judgment of the Florida Supreme Court was overturned. In its ruling, the Supreme Court reiterated that probable cause is a fluid concept, based on context and facts, and cannot be "reduced to a neat set of legal rules." The Court wrote:

> In short, a probable-cause hearing focusing on a dog's alert should proceed much like any other. The court should allow the parties to make their best case, consistent with the usual rules of criminal procedure. And the court should then evaluate the proffered evidence to decide what all the circumstances demonstrate. If the State has produced proof from controlled settings that a dog performs reliably in detecting drugs, and the defendant has not contested that showing, then the court should find probable cause. If, in contrast, the defendant has challenged the State's case (by disputing the reliability of the dog overall or of a particular alert), then the court should weigh the competing evidence. In all events, the court should not prescribe, as the Florida Supreme Court did, an inflexible set of evidentiary requirements. The question—similar to every inquiry into probable cause—is whether all the facts surrounding a dog's alert, viewed through the lens of common sense, would make a reasonably prudent person think that a search would reveal contraband or evidence of a crime. A sniff is up to snuff when it meets that test.

The preceding cases help explain the common law development of probable cause and show that the more factual information an officer can articulate, the greater the likelihood the existence of probable cause will be upheld in court. In addition, probable cause is the key determination of whether a judge will grant officers a warrant to search or arrest.

Search and Arrest Warrants

Government agents who have probable cause to believe evidence of a crime is located at a specific place or that an individual is involved in a crime must go before a neutral and detached **magistrate** (judge) and swear under oath who or what they are looking for and where they think it can be found.

In determining whether probable cause for the warrant exists, the reviewing judge must consider the totality of the circumstances. In other words, all the factors submitted are viewed as a whole in considering whether a reasonable person would believe what the officers claim. The warrant must include the reasons for requesting it, the names of the officers who applied for it, names of others who have information to contribute, what or who specifically is being sought, and the signature of the judge issuing it.

As any law enforcement officer will attest, obtaining a warrant is not just a matter of "walking up and getting one." Rather, the officer has the responsibility to provide sufficient data to the judge that the facts provide the necessary probable cause. Because the judge determines whether probable cause exists, the officer

CASE IN BRIEF

Florida v. Harris (2013)

ISSUE Is an alert by a well-trained narcotics detection dog certified to detect illegal contraband sufficient to establish probable cause for the search of a vehicle?

RULING Yes. Probable cause is a fluid concept that takes the totality of the circumstances into account. Each side should put their best case forward, presenting the evidence at hand, to show probable cause does or does not exist.

magistrate a judge

LO4 All warrants are to be based on probable cause.

must argue the probable cause aspect of the case early on. Not every judge will sign a warrant. The officer may be directed to come back with additional information or be told that a warrant will not be issued on the facts presented.

The fact that an *independent judge* determines the existence of probable cause removes this discretionary decision from the officer involved with the case. Court rulings have delineated this independence as one requirement for judges issuing warrants: "An issuing magistrate must meet two tests. He must be neutral and detached, and he must be capable of determining whether probable cause exists for the requested arrest or search" (*Shadwick v. City of Tampa*, 1972). A valid warrant shifts the granting of suppression of evidence to the defendant and provides a shield against officer liability.

With technology that has evolved from hard-wired landlines, pagers and fax machines, and now to cell phones and wireless Internet networks, coordination among police, prosecutors, and judges makes obtaining warrants easier than in the past. Many jurisdictions authorize "telephonic warrants," which occur when a judge grants the warrant over the phone.

Knock-and-Announce Rule

Officers can break a door or window or break a car window to make an arrest or to execute a search warrant if necessary, but the general rule is that law enforcement officers must first knock and announce their authority and purpose before breaking into a dwelling. This requirement is referred to as the *knock-and-announce rule*, the intent of which is to protect human life, prevent the unnecessary destruction of property, and to protect a person's privacy and dignity when faced with a sudden police entrance (*Hudson v. Michigan*, 2006).

The knock-and-announce rule protects citizens' rights, and it can enhance officer safety in executing a warrant. For example, a plainclothes police sergeant executing a search warrant was killed by a suspect who claimed to have fired on someone breaking into his house. Although the police asserted they identified themselves as police, the prosecution was unable to prove beyond a reasonable doubt that the resident was not acting in self-defense.

In *Miller v. United States* (1958) the Court held, "The requirement of prior notice of authority and purpose before forcing entry into a home is deeply rooted in our heritage, and should not be given grudging application.... Every householder, the good and the bad, the guilty and the innocent, is entitled to the protection designed to secure the common interest against unlawful invasion of the home." Because the officers did not give notice before breaking into Miller's home, the subsequent arrest was unlawful and the evidence seized should have been suppressed.

A similar finding occurred in *Wilson v. Arkansas* (1995), when the Court stated, "Given the long-standing common-law endorsement of the practice of announcement, we have little doubt that the framers of the Fourth Amendment thought that the method of an officer's entry into a dwelling was among the factors to be considered in assessing the reasonableness of a search or seizure." Although the Court stated that whether "knock and announce" had occurred would be part of determining the reasonableness of a search, "the Fourth Amendment's flexible requirements of reasonableness should not be read to mandate a rigid rule of announcement that ignores countervailing law enforcement interests."

The question of how long officers must wait after knocking and announcing themselves before forcibly entering has been before the courts. In *United States v. Banks* (2003), the Court determined that a 15-to-20-second wait after knocking and announcing before a forcible entry was sufficient to satisfy the Fourth Amendment. In this case, officers armed with a search warrant arrived at suspected drug dealer Lashawn Banks' apartment and followed standard procedure, knocked loudly on the front door, and stated, "Police search warrant." After waiting 15 to 20 seconds without hearing anything from inside the apartment, police forcibly entered with a battering ram.

Banks, who was just finishing a shower at the time, heard neither the knocks nor the announcement and was standing naked in the hallway outside of his bathroom when police entered his apartment. He was quickly forced to the floor by officers and handcuffed. Police began questioning him and provided underwear for Banks to wear during questioning. After a thorough search of the apartment, police uncovered a significant amount of crack cocaine as well as a firearm.

At the criminal trial, the defense filed a motion to suppress statements made by Banks during questioning on the grounds that the officers failed to wait a reasonable period of time before forcefully entering his residence when executing the search warrant. When the District Court denied this motion, Banks pled guilty, but eventually tried to retract his guilty plea on the advice of a new attorney, who argued that the search was unconstitutional because officers did not wait long enough before breaking down the door and had no evidence that waiting longer would have had negative consequences. A Ninth Circuit Court of Appeals agreed, ruling the search unconstitutional and suppressing the evidence found during it.

The Supreme Court granted certiorari and unanimously reversed the Ninth Circuit Court's decision. Justice David Souter delivered the Court's opinion: "The officers' 15- to 20-second wait before forcible entry satisfied the Fourth Amendment. . . . After 15 to 20 seconds without a response, officers could fairly have suspected that Banks would flush away the cocaine if they remained reticent. . . . This Court's emphasis on totality analysis leads it to reject the government's position that the need to damage property should not be part of the analysis of whether the entry itself was unreasonable." The Court stated that reasonableness must be viewed under the totality of the circumstances, noting that an important fact was not the time that it would have taken Banks to open the door but, rather, the time it would take to destroy the evidence.

An audio or video recording of knock-notice announcements would provide evidence of compliance with the knock notice as well as the exact amount of time that elapsed before the forced entry. Some departments have opted to make this practice a matter of formal policy-directed procedure.

Special Conditions

In certain instances, exigent circumstances may justify an entry by police without first announcing their presences, including when victims or hostages may be inside, when a crime is actually in progress, when evidence or contraband may be destroyed, or when making the officers' presence known would place them in danger. In such instances officers may ask for special conditions to be attached to a warrant, such as making an unannounced entrance or carrying out a search at night.

◀ CASE IN BRIEF

United States v. Banks (2003)

ISSUE After knocking and announcing a search warrant, is 15 to 20 seconds a reasonable amount of time to wait before forcing entry?

RULING Yes. When looking at the totality of the circumstances and the particular exigency facing the officers, waiting 15 to 20 seconds was enough time.

no-knock warrant issued when officers want to make an unannounced entrance because they are afraid evidence might be destroyed or officer safety requires it

If officers want to make an unannounced entrance because they fear evidence might be destroyed or officer safety requires it, they can request a **no-knock warrant.** However, not all states give judges and magistrates authority to issue no-knock warrants. The search warrants for drug busts using bulldozers to crash through the walls of suspected crack houses would have such a provision. Having obtained a pre-authorized no-knock provision, officers may, at the time the warrant is executed, use independent judgment and forego the knock-and-announce requirement, based on facts that exist at the time the warrant is executed, when such facts demonstrate that there is ". . . reasonable suspicion that knocking and announcing their presence, under the particular circumstances, would be dangerous or futile, or that it would inhibit the effective investigation of the crime by, for example, allowing the destruction of evidence" (*Richards v. Wisconsin*, 1997).

In other cases, the illicit activity occurs primarily at night—illegal gambling, for example. In such cases, the officers can ask the judge to include a provision that allows them to execute the warrant at night—a **nightcap(ped) warrant.** All that the officer needs to show is a reasonable suspicion that, to preserve evidence or protect officers, a nighttime search is necessary, a similar standard of proof to the no-knock entry request.

nightcap(ped) warrant issued when officers wish to execute a warrant at night because that is when the suspected illicit activity is primarily occurring

Executing the Warrant

Once signed by a judge, the warrant becomes an order for the police to carry out the search or arrest. Unless special conditions have been included in the warrant, government agents must carry out the warrant during daylight hours and must also identify themselves as officers and state their purpose. The officers may use reasonable force to execute the warrant if they are denied entrance or if no one is home. In *Michigan v. Summers* (1981), the Court ruled that it is constitutional to detain the occupants of a premises during the execution of a search warrant while a proper search is being conducted. Police officers also may refuse to allow people to enter their residence while the police obtain a search warrant. In *Illinois v. McArthur* (2001), the Court held that although preventing a suspect from entering his or her own home constituted a seizure of that person, if the warrant was being obtained as rapidly as possible, such police action was reasonable. The Court explained that exigent circumstances existed and the seizure of the suspect was as brief and unintrusive as possible.

Having discussed how the Fourth Amendment ensures individual freedom by restricting government's power to intrude, consider next when the government is permitted to search and seize and the broad range of contacts that exist.

The Continuum of Contacts

continuum of contacts the almost limitless variations of contacts between the public and the police illustrating how justification for police action increases as their reasons for thinking criminal activity is afoot build

To understand when government can exercise its immense power, begin by analyzing the variety of contacts people and government may have. These contacts can be viewed as existing along a continuum, as shown in Figure 7.3. The **continuum of contacts** represents the almost limitless variations of contacts between the public and the police and illustrates how justification for police action increases as their reasons build for thinking criminal activity is afoot.

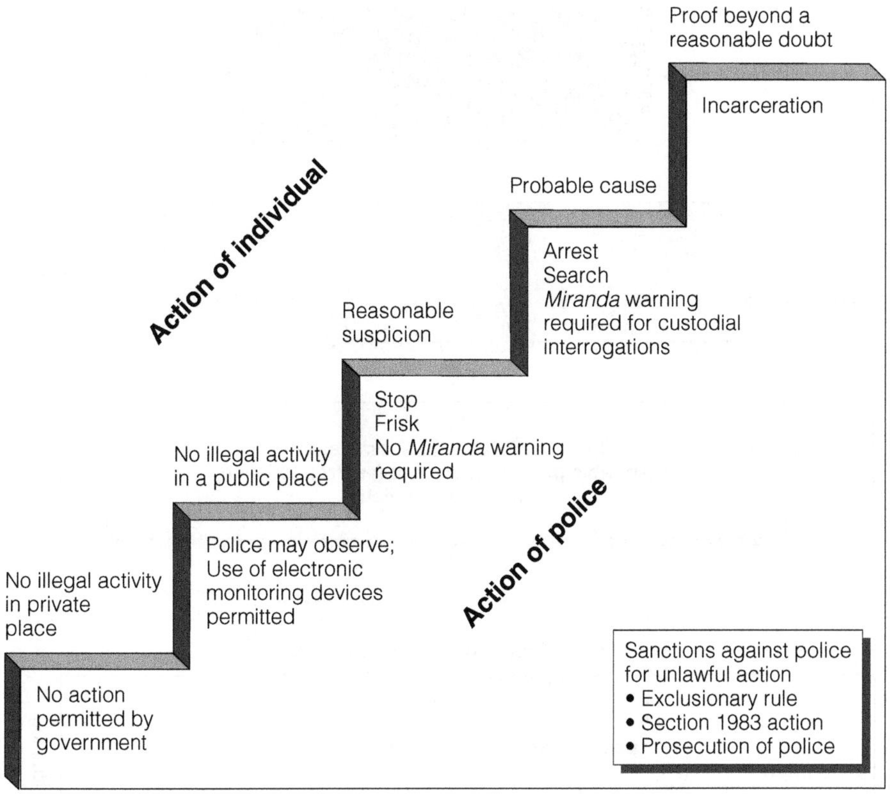

Figure 7.3 The Continuum of Contacts between Individuals and the Police

At one end of the continuum, contact consists of nothing more than an individual and an officer crossing paths and exchanging "hellos." Here, the police are unjustified taking any action. At the other extreme, an individual's conduct leads to sufficient probable cause and justifies police in arresting the person, by force if necessary.

Like any continuum, an infinite number of points exist between the two extremes—a middle ground involving many other daily contacts between the citizenry and the government, in which interactions are not so clearly defined. This realm includes situations when the police or other government agencies are considering, or actually conducting, an investigation, or when an individual or business or other organization is merely suspected of illicit activity. Figure 7.4 illustrates the degree of intrusion on individual liberty and whether the Fourth Amendment is implicated.

Although the intent of the Constitution is to prevent the government from intruding on people's lives when they have done nothing wrong, this freedom, as with all constitutional rights, is not absolute. When police have lawful reason to act, they are expected to do so, and they have the right to do so. The U.S. Supreme Court has clearly stated that police have a responsibility, in fact a duty, to act to prevent crimes and apprehend criminals and has shown continued support for law enforcement. When police are suspicious, they would be foolish to turn their backs

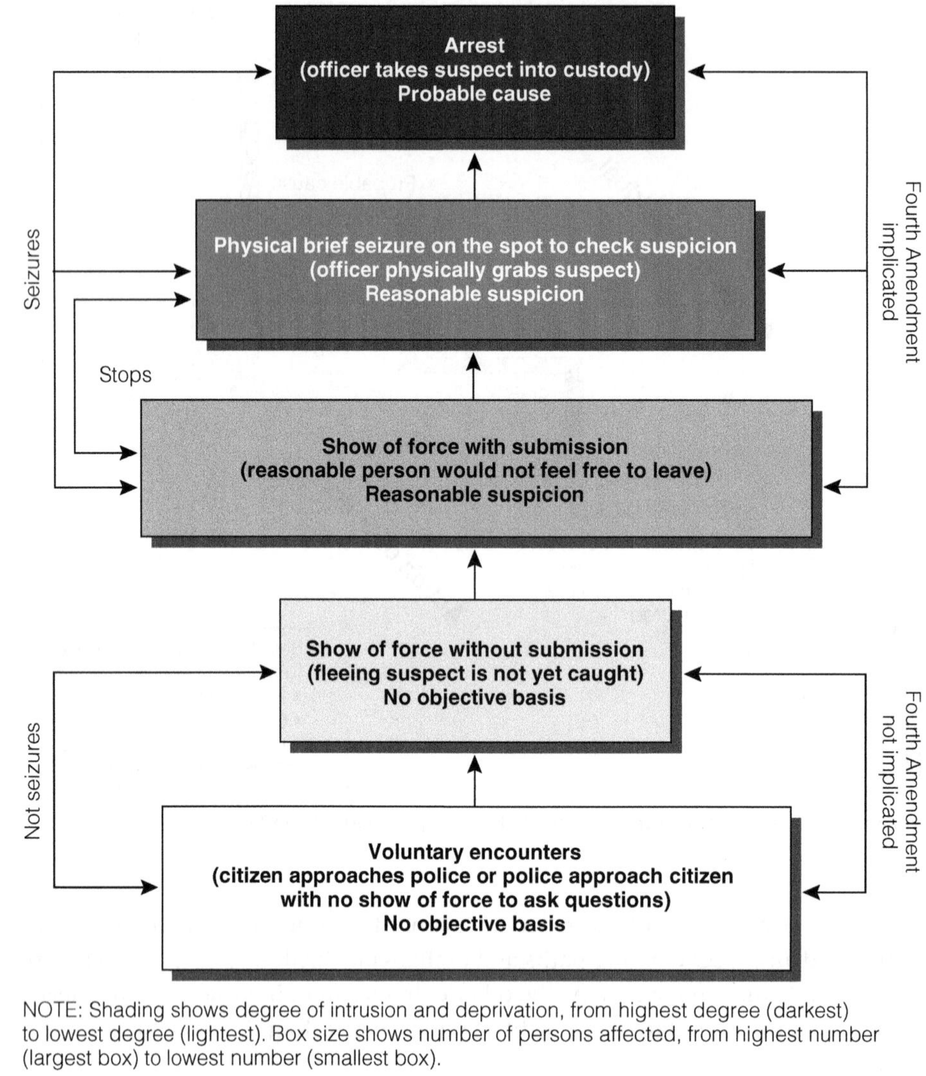

224 Section III The Fourth Amendment: Governing Constitutional Searches and Seizures

```
                    Arrest
         (officer takes suspect into custody)
                 Probable cause
                        ▲
                        │
    Physical brief seizure on the spot to check suspicion
              (officer physically grabs suspect)
                   Reasonable suspicion
                        ▲
                        │
              Show of force with submission
         (reasonable person would not feel free to leave)
                   Reasonable suspicion
                        ▲
                        │
              Show of force without submission
              (fleeing suspect is not yet caught)
                     No objective basis
                        ▲
                        │
                  Voluntary encounters
   (citizen approaches police or police approach citizen
         with no show of force to ask questions)
                   No objective basis
```

Seizures / Stops / Not seizures (left side labels)
Fourth Amendment implicated / Fourth Amendment not implicated (right side labels)

NOTE: Shading shows degree of intrusion and deprivation, from highest degree (darkest) to lowest degree (lightest). Box size shows number of persons affected, from highest number (largest box) to lowest number (smallest box).

Figure 7.4 Seizures and the Fourth Amendment

L05 *As contact between an individual and an officer proceeds upward along the continuum, police acquire increasing justification to seize and search the person, taking away the person's most valued right—freedom. The legal corollary of this progression of contact is that the more intrusive an officer's action becomes, the more justification is required for it to be considered constitutional.*

until they can acquire more information and then return to try to find the person; the suspect would be long gone.

The police officer's job is to decide, often in a split second, where a particular interaction with a suspect falls along the continuum. The system demands that police make a knowledgeable good faith decision in accordance with the Constitution. The Supreme Court has continued to recognize the difficult job police have and that, given a proper understanding of law, they often are able to make good decisions under challenging circumstances. The Constitution continues to give law enforcement the tools they need to carry out their duties in an almost limitless number of situations.

Each step on the continuum builds on the previous one, like building blocks, adding either facts in quantity or quality to allow further government intrusion. Chapter 8 addresses this area further, but when probable cause exits, with or without a warrant, the police will be justified in arresting the person.

As the continuum also shows, searches and seizures cannot be neatly separated. At any point on the continuum of contacts, a situation may escalate to the next level of contact and thus change how the police may or may not be permitted to act. For example, the police may have no authority to act when driving by someone who appears to be merely walking along a public sidewalk, but if the officer sees something in the rearview mirror that causes him or her to become suspicious, the situation could justify a stop and possibly a frisk. Depending on what results from these interactions, if probable cause develops, the stop could escalate to the level of an arrest and then a search incident to that arrest, and it could all happen in a matter of moments.

The law of search and seizure defines what authority government has when interacting with the public and how agents can follow up on their suspicions. This authority begins with an examination of the law of stop and frisk. Chapters 8 and 9 will consider these and other forms of seizures and searches.

The Law of Stop and Frisk

The law of stop and frisk is the first point on the continuum of contacts in which police have constitutional authority to interfere with a person's freedom. Stop-and-frisk law may be more easily understood by examining its purpose: to balance the rights of an individual and the government's need for tools to carry out its job of protecting society from lawbreakers. Police officers should neither be expected to ignore their reasonable suspicions nor be denied the right to ensure their own safety by checking for weapons. The law of stop and frisk balances the rights of the people and the individual during that "in-between time," when probable cause has not yet developed but officers should be expected to respond, at least in a limited way. The understanding that *any* intrusion on a person's freedom involves Fourth Amendment protections, including stops and frisks, is crucial.

LO6 A **stop** *is a brief detention of a person based on specific and articulable facts for the purpose of investigating suspicious activity. A* **frisk** *is a limited pat-down search for weapons for the protection of the officer and others. It is not automatically permitted with a stop but only when the officer suspects the person is armed and dangerous.*

Basic Definitions

The law of stop and frisk gives law enforcement the authority to act in the gray area of the continuum, between the point of no unlawful activity whatsoever and thus no authority for officers to act, and the point of probable cause when they may arrest. This area of law deals not with reasonable belief, but reasonable *suspicion*. If the officers do not have probable cause to arrest, but yet suspect that a person is engaged in illegal activity, what is their recourse?

Although the suspect is not free to go just then, without the investigation producing anything more, he or she will be free to go shortly. A stop differs from an arrest, in that when arrested, a person is not free to go. The Court has held that because this detention is not an arrest (it is a stop), no *Miranda* warning need be given. For this reason, a driver stopped by the police for a traffic violation need not

stop a brief detention of a person, short of an arrest, based on specific and articulable facts for the purpose of investigating suspicious activity

frisk a reasonable, limited pat-down search for weapons for the protection of a government agent and others

be advised of his or her *Miranda* rights—although the driver is not free to go for a short time, he or she will be, so it is not an arrest.

Although the words *stop* and *frisk* do not appear in the Fourth Amendment, the Court has found they are tantamount to a search and seizure of the person, with the only differences being the standard required by the police to act, what they may then do, and the duration. The constitutional requirement of *reasonableness* is required before one is stopped or frisked, just as it is before one is arrested and searched.

Law enforcement officers talk about developing a "sixth sense"—an ability to know that something is not right. What they are really talking about are observational skills officers develop. One deputy police chief describes it as "soft vision"—surveying all that is present while on patrol, paying specific attention to those events the officer is trained to note. Tire tracks in fresh snow, furtive conduct by a pedestrian, a discarded parcel, a door ajar, the attendant at an all-night convenience store not visible—to the average citizen such circumstances mean nothing and probably would not even be noticed. To the trained and experienced eye of the law enforcement professional, however, they mean an opportunity to delve further into what may be criminal activity. Just what can a government agent do in response to such suspicions? The law of stop and frisk permits officers to act on their suspicions rather than to turn away, awaiting that infrequent, obvious crime to be committed before their eyes.

An action such as fleeing from the police will certainly raise the circumspection of law enforcement and contribute heavily in establishing reasonable suspicion. In *Illinois v. Wardlow* (2000), a stop was held lawful when the suspect was in a high-crime area and fled upon seeing the police. The Court held that the individual's flight at the sight of police was enough to provide reasonable suspicion for an investigatory stop. In *United States v. Arvizu* (2002), the Supreme Court reaffirmed that reasonable suspicion (fleeing from the law) may be part of the totality of the circumstances. *Arvizu* also reaffirmed the importance of an officer's training and experience in determining the existence of reasonable suspicion, as the Court

> **MYTH**
> Anytime a person is legally stopped by an officer, that officer has the right to conduct a frisk to discover if that person is concealing any contraband.
>
> **FACT**
> A frisk is a *limited* pat-down search for *weapons* for the protection of the officer and others. It is not automatically permitted with a stop but only when the officer suspects the person is armed and dangerous.

Constitutional Law in ACTION

Sergeant Oldham is driving through an area well known for drug dealing. He has been a police officer for more than 20 years and is well known for his instincts relating to criminal activity. He sees one young man standing on the corner. Sergeant Oldham has a "gut feeling" that the man is dealing crack. Oldham stops his patrol car, gets out, and orders the man to put his hands up. The man complies, but as he does, he drops a baggie containing 10 rocks of crack. He is arrested.

- *What is the required level of suspicion to stop the young man?*
- *Is the officer's "gut feeling" enough to do so?*
- *What facts does the sergeant have to support his action?*

Constitutional Law in ACTION

Sergeant Oldham is driving through an area well known for drug dealing. He has been a police officer for more than 20 years and is well known for his instincts relating to criminal activity. He sees one young man standing on the corner. Sergeant Oldham has a "gut feeling" that the man is dealing crack. Oldham stops his patrol car two blocks away and watches the man for 20 minutes.

During that time, Oldham observes four separate occasions where one person walks up to the man, hands him something, and then the man gives the person something back. The two people then part ways. Sergeant Oldham also sees the man wave and whistle at passing cars. A couple of the cars pull over, the man leans in the driver's window for a minute or so, then walks away and the car leaves.

In his years of experience, Sergeant Oldham believes this man is dealing drugs.

The next time a pedestrian approaches the man, Sergeant Oldham drives his patrol car up to the pair who, upon seeing the officer, start to walk away. Oldham gets out of his squad and orders both of the people to stop. As the man stops and turns around, he drops a baggie containing crack on the sidewalk. The man is arrested.

- *How is this scenario different from the preceding one?*
- *What facts does the sergeant have to support a stop?*
- *What effect does the sergeant's experience have on the outcome?*

---

explained, "This process [of looking at the totality of the circumstances] allows officers to draw on their own experience and specialized training to make inferences from and deductions about the cumulative information available to them that 'might well elude an untrained person.'"

Terry v. Ohio

The landmark case for stop-and-frisk law is *Terry v. Ohio* (1968), which provides a classic example of how a stop-and-frisk situation may arise and how the law deals with it. In this case, the Court addressed the common law enforcement practice of stopping suspects to ask them questions to assess whether they were involved in criminal activity.

Detective Martin McFadden had been a police officer with the Cleveland Police Department for 39 years, and 35 of that as a detective. To untrained eyes, the men Detective McFadden saw outside the jewelry store that day were merely standing there talking, but McFadden sensed more. On the basis of his experience, he suspected they were casing the store, planning to rob it, and possibly were armed. He watched as the two men walked back and forth, looking into the store window, walking to the corner, and then returning to talk to each other. Another man joined them, then went inside the store, returned, and the routine continued.

◀ **CASE IN BRIEF**

Terry v. Ohio (1968)

ISSUE Does an officer violate the Fourth Amendment when he seizes a person and searches that person for weapons on facts that do not rise to the level of probable cause?

RULING No. The Fourth Amendment prohibits unreasonable searches and seizures. Balancing the need for effective law enforcement and the safety of officers, a person may be subjected to a brief detention and a frisk when the objective facts support the belief that a crime is occurring, has occurred, or is about to occur and that the person detained may be armed and dangerous.

When the three men were together outside the store, McFadden approached them, identified himself as a police officer, asked their names and grabbed one of the men, placing him between himself and the other two. He quickly patted down the outer clothing of that man, later identified as John Terry, and felt what could be a gun in Terry's pocket, but he could not remove it. He ordered the three into the store at gunpoint, removed Terry's coat, and took a .38-caliber revolver from the pocket. When he patted down the other men, he found a revolver in the coat of one. Both men were charged with carrying concealed weapons.

The defense lawyers argued the guns had been seized illegally, so could not be used as evidence. The Ohio trial judge found both suspects guilty, and Terry and the other man appealed their conviction to the U.S. Supreme Court. Before this case reached the Supreme Court, the other man died, so the decision refers to only defendant Terry.

The legal issue before the Court was simply phrased: "whether it is always unreasonable for a policeman to seize a person and subject him to a limited search for weapons unless there is probable cause for an arrest." The U.S. Supreme Court upheld the Ohio court verdict, ruling Detective McFadden had acted reasonably because his experience and training supported his suspicion that the three men were planning a robbery; the robbery would probably involve weapons; and nothing occurred to make him think differently. He had to act quickly when he saw the three men gather at the store. In their opinion, the Court stated:

> Each case of this sort will, of course, have to be decided on its own facts. We merely hold today that where a police officer observed unusual conduct which leads him reasonably to conclude in light of his experience that criminal activity may be afoot and that the persons with whom he is dealing may be armed and presently dangerous, where in the course of investigating this behavior he identifies himself as a policeman and makes reasonable inquiries, and where nothing in the initial stages of the encounter serves to dispel his reasonable fear for his own or others' safety, he is entitled for the protection of himself and others in the area to conduct a carefully limited search of the outer clothing of such persons in an attempt to discover weapons which might be used to assault him.

LO7 *The Terry decision established that, in what is termed a **Terry stop**, an officer, with articulable reasonable suspicion that a crime is occurring, has occurred, or is about to occur, may conduct a brief investigatory stop, including a pat down for weapons if the officer has reason to suspect the person is armed and dangerous.*

Therefore, such a search is reasonable under the Fourth Amendment, and any weapons seized may properly be introduced in evidence against the person from whom they were seized.

Guidelines established by *Terry v. Ohio* determining whether a stop or frisk is valid include the following:

Terry stop an officer with articulable reasonable suspicion may conduct a brief investigatory stop, including a pat down for weapons if the officer has reason to suspect the person is armed and dangerous

- Suspicious circumstances, that is, conduct that leads an experienced officer to believe that a crime is about to be committed and that the person about to commit the crime may be armed and dangerous.
- While investigating the behavior, officers identify themselves as police officers and make reasonable inquiries, for example, "What is your name?"
- If officers are still suspicious and suspect the person may be armed and dangerous, they may conduct a limited search of the person's outer clothing to protect themselves and others in the area.

Consider next what are likely consequences of ignoring the constraints on searches and seizures imposed by the Fourth Amendment.

Consequences of Fourth Amendment Violations

When police violate a person's constitutional rights by conducting an unlawful stop and frisk or search and seizure, two serious consequences may occur: (1) the evidence may be excluded from court and (2) internal sanctions as well as civil and criminal liability may be incurred.

The Exclusionary Rule

The exclusionary rule is by far the most frequently used means to address constitutional infractions by the government in criminal cases because of its proximity to, and absolute effect on, searches and seizures found to be unconstitutional due to police misconduct. However, as noted in *United States v. Leon* (1984), "The Fourth Amendment contains no provision expressly precluding the use of evidence obtained in violation of its commands. . . . This [exclusionary] rule thus operates as a judicially created remedy designed to safeguard Fourth Amendment rights generally through its deterrent effect, rather than a personal constitutional right of the person aggrieved."

> **LO8** The **exclusionary rule,** which is judge-made case law promulgated by the Supreme Court to deter law enforcement misconduct, prohibits evidence obtained in violation of a person's constitutional rights from being admissible in court (Weeks v. United States, 1914). The primary purpose underlying the exclusionary rule is to deter government misconduct.

The exclusionary rule helps preserve judicial integrity by preventing judicial agreement in denying a person's Fourth Amendment rights, deters police misconduct by making improperly obtained evidence inadmissible in court, and protects citizens' constitutional "right to privacy." However:

exclusionary rule judge-made case law promulgated by the Supreme Court to deter police or government misconduct

> The exclusionary rule is among the most controversial and the most passionately debated rules of law governing our criminal justice system. It is not hard to understand why this is so. The exclusionary rule is the primary means by which the Constitutional prohibition of unreasonable searches and seizures is currently enforced; thus it is seen by some as the primary protection of personal privacy and security against police arbitrariness and brutality. It is also the basis for judges' decisions to exclude reliable incriminating evidence from the trials of persons accused of crime, and is thus considered by others to be little more than a misguided loophole through which criminals are allowed to escape justice. (Wilson, 1986, p.1)

The exclusionary rule goes back as far as 1886, when the Supreme Court held in *Boyd v. United States* that forced disclosure of papers that evidenced a crime could not be admissible in court:

> The practice had obtained in the colonies of issuing writs of assistance to the revenue officers, empowering them, in their discretion, to search suspected places for smuggled goods, which James Otis pronounced "the worst instrument of arbitrary power, the most destructive of English liberty and the fundamental principles of law, that ever was found in an English law book"; since they placed "the liberty of every man in the hands of every petty officer."

Numerous theories suggest ways the law might respond to unlawful searches and seizures by the police other than preventing evidence, sometimes the only evidence in a case, from getting to a jury. However, the Court has continued to hold that illegally obtained evidence be excluded as the primary means of upholding an individual's constitutional rights.

The exclusionary rule reflects an insistence of U.S. law that the ends do not justify the means. If they did, any means of eliciting evidence would be permissible, including torture. Besides the inherent fact that forced confessions are unreliable, torture is not something the spirit of the United States condones. However, with the United States being pushed to its limits with respect to terrorism, new debate over means of obtaining information has arisen, as was the case regarding the prisoner treatment in Abu Ghraib Prison during the Iraq War.

Some question whether another way can be found to discourage police misconduct without punishing the public. Alternatives that have been considered include having an independent review board in the executive branch; applying a civil tort action against the government; conducting a hearing separate from the main criminal trial but before the same judge or jury; adopting an expanded good faith exception; and adopting of the British system, which admits the evidence but sanctions the officer (del Carmen, 2010). Unquestionably a *cost/benefit analysis* is at play, but as Chief Justice Warren Burger stated in *United States v. Calandra* (1974), "The rule is a judicially created remedy designed to safeguard Fourth Amendment Rights generally through its deterrent effect."

Previous editions of this text noted how firm the Supreme Court had stood in their intolerance toward unreasonable search and seizure by domestic law enforcement, even when evidence that would otherwise convict the guilty is not permitted. This stance is undergoing change, however, and the Court, as recently as in *Davis v. United States* (2011), has begun to move away from the idea that the exclusionary rule is a "self-executing mandate implicit in the Fourth Amendment itself." In other words, it is not automatic. Because of the high societal cost, a balancing of interests must be done. The deterrence benefit must outweigh the cost of lost evidence, which is often trustworthy and reliable. The Court will look at the flagrancy of the violation and the culpability of the officer when balancing the interests. The Court, in *Davis*, reiterated that exclusion is a last resort. "Our cases hold that society must swallow this bitter pill when necessary, but only as a 'last resort.'"

Interestingly, in *Hudson v. Michigan* (2006) the Court specifically ruled that violation of the knock-and-announce rule does not require suppression of the evidence obtained during the ensuing search. In other words, the general rule excluding evidence obtained in violation of the Fourth Amendment does not apply to the knock-and-announce rule. In this case, the Court did refer to alternative remedies such as civil lawsuits or internal discipline but held that the exclusionary rule was too high a social cost for this violation.

Although opponents are many, those who support the exclusionary rule believe the risk far outweighs compromising constitutional ideals. *Weeks v. United States* (1914) and *Mapp v. Ohio* (1961) firmly established the exclusionary rule in criminal procedure.

Weeks v. United States In *Weeks v. United States*, Fremont Weeks was charged with using the mail for illegal gambling purposes after officers searched his home on two different occasions without a warrant. The issue was simply whether illegally obtained evidence is admissible in court, to which the Supreme Court held it was not, stating that the right to be free from unreasonable searches and seizures under the Fourth Amendment applies:

> to all invasions on the part of the government and its employees of the sanctity of a man's home and the privacies of life. It is not the breaking of his doors and the rummaging of his drawers that constitutes the essence of the offense; but it is the invasion of his indefeasible right to personal security, personal liberty and private property.

The *Weeks* Court specifically excluded illegally obtained evidence from use in federal prosecutions. *Mapp v. Ohio* (1961) extended the doctrine, through incorporation, to state proceedings.

Mapp v. Ohio The Fourteenth Amendment forbids states to "deprive any person of life, liberty or property, without due process of law," and after *Weeks*, the question arose as to whether the exclusionary rule should be applied at the state level. Initially, *Wolf v. Colorado* (1949) held that the exclusionary rule was not then applicable at the state level. This precedent was followed for more than a decade. Some evidence was excluded for other reasons, however. For example, *Elkins v. United States* (1960) disallowed the admission of evidence illegally obtained by state officials into federal trials (the silver platter doctrine). In 1961, the *Wolf* precedent was reversed when *Mapp v. Ohio* made the exclusionary rule applicable at the state level.

In *Mapp*, the defendant refused to allow officers without a warrant into her home. The officers had information that a suspect was hiding in her basement and returned three hours later with reinforcements. When Mapp did not respond, officers broke in and searched the home, finding obscene materials. The Supreme Court, overruling *Wolf*, held that "all evidence obtained by searches and seizures in violation of the Constitution are by the same authority inadmissible in a state court." Reversing the trial court, the Supreme Court stated:

> Since the Fourth Amendment's right of privacy has been declared enforceable against the States through the Due Process Clause of the Fourteenth Amendment, it is enforceable against them by the same sanction of exclusion as is used against the Federal government. Were it otherwise, then just as without the *Weeks* rule the assurance against unreasonable searches and seizures would be "a form of words," valueless and undeserving of mention in a perpetual charter of inestimable human liberties, so too, without that rule the freedom from state invasions of privacy would be ephemeral.

Evidence Obtained in a Manner That Shocks the Conscience In *Rochin v. California* (1952), the Court held that searches that "shock the conscience" are a violation of due process, and any evidence so obtained will, therefore, be inadmissible in a court of law. It is important to note that this "shock the conscience" criterion is a different standard under due process than that which was discussed previously. The standard here deals with due process issues that arise from specific acts by officers, not from those enacted by a legislature into law. In *Rochin*, the police took the suspect to the hospital and had his stomach pumped after observing him swallow

◀ **CASE IN BRIEF**

Mapp v. Ohio (1961)

ISSUE May evidence obtained in violation of the Fourth Amendment be used in *state* court?

RULING No. Evidence obtained through a violation of the Fourth Amendment cannot be used in state court, just as it cannot be used in federal court. This provision has been incorporated.

pills. Morphine capsules were recovered in this search, but in invoking the exclusionary rule, the Court stated:

> [T]he proceedings by which this conviction was obtained do more than offend some fastidious squeamishness or private sentimentalism about combating crime too energetically. This is conduct that shocks the conscience. Illegally breaking into the privacy of the petitioner, the struggle to open his mouth and remove what was there, the forcible extraction of his stomach's contents—this course of proceeding by agents of the government to obtain evidence is bound to offend even hardened sensibilities. They are methods too close to the rack and screw to permit constitutional differentiation.

Thus, in *Rochin*, the evidence was excluded as a result of a due process violation, not by the application of the exclusionary rule. At the time of the decision, the exclusionary rule had not yet been applied to the states through *Mapp*.

The exclusionary rule may affect specific illegally obtained evidence, as well as any other evidence obtained as a result of the original illegally obtained evidence. Such evidence is referred to as "fruit of the poisonous tree."

Fruit of the Poisonous Tree *Silverthorne Lumber Co. v. United States* (1920) extended the exclusionary rule delineated in *Weeks* (1914). In this case, a U.S. marshal unlawfully entered and searched the Silverthorne Lumber Company's offices and illegally took books and documents. When the company demanded their return, the government did so, but not before making copies of the documents. These copies were later impounded by the district court and became the basis for a grand jury indictment. A subpoena was then served on the company to produce the originals. When the company refused, it was convicted of contempt of court. The Supreme Court, however, reversed the conviction saying, "The essence of a provision forbidding the acquisition of evidence in a certain way is that not merely evidence so acquired shall not be used before the Court, but that it shall not be used at all." In other words, once the primary source (the "tree") is proved to have been obtained unlawfully, any secondary evidence derived from it (the "fruit") is also inadmissible.

The **fruit of the poisonous tree doctrine** states that evidence obtained as a result of a previous illegality must be excluded from trial. This extension of the exclusionary rule is based on the same rationale as the exclusionary rule itself, that is, to deter illegal police activity and to preserve the integrity of the court. The Supreme Court has, however, permitted such evidence to be used in some proceedings.

In *United States v. Calandra* (1974), the Court ruled that "fruits of illegally seized evidence" could be used as a basis for questions to a witness before a grand jury. In addition, some lower courts have allowed such evidence to be used in sentencing and in probation or parole revocation hearings.

In *Wong Sun v. United States* (1963), the Court held that statements obtained even indirectly as a result of an illegal arrest or search are not admissible in court because they are "tainted fruit of the poisonous tree." In *Wong Sun*, however, the Court also stated that because he voluntarily returned several days after providing what was deemed an inadmissible statement, the subsequent statement had become so *attenuated as to dissipate the taint*. However, a meaningful break in the events must occur, so in *Taylor v. Alabama* (1982) the Court held that even when a

fruit of the poisonous tree doctrine evidence obtained as a result of a previous illegality (a constitutionally invalid search or activity) must be excluded from trial

suspect was read his *Miranda* rights several times after an unlawful arrest before he confessed, the admission was not admissible.

In examining the question of how far to follow the taint of the original violation, the court will consider several factors, including (1) the length of time that passed between the initial violation and the procurement of the secondary evidence, (2) any occurrence of intervening events, and (3) how blatant or deliberate the initial violation was. The totality of these spacial and temporal factors, often referred to as *Brown* factors in reference to the case in which they were delineated, allows the court to assess whether or not the secondary evidence is so far removed from the initial constitutional violation that the "taint" is effectively removed. The dissipation of taint, through time and space, is called the **attenuation doctrine,** and it allows evidence that was obtained after a previous illegality to be introduced in court (*Brown v. Illinois*, 1975). As such, the attenuation doctrine is an exception to the fruit of the poisonous tree doctrine.

attenuation doctrine evidence obtained as a result of a previous illegality may be admissible at trial if it is so far removed, through time and space, from the original violation that any "taint" has dissipated

Recently, in *Utah v. Strieff* (2016), the Supreme Court looked at whether a valid arrest warrant is a sufficient intervening factor to break the connection between a stop lacking reasonable suspicion and the discovery of methamphetamine on the suspect. It ruled that yes, a valid arrest warrant was enough to attenuate (break the connection) between the unconstitutional police conduct and the discovery of the evidence. Exclusion is not warranted when the causal connection is too attenuated. Here, although the time between the events was short, the violation was not deliberate, and the arrest warrant was a strong intervening event.

In this case, Strieff was detained by an officer who was investigating drug dealing from a nearby house. The officer, as conceded by the prosecutor, lacked reasonable suspicion. However, acting on the belief that he did, the officer obtained identification from Strieff and checked him for warrants. In fact, Strieff had an outstanding arrest warrant for a traffic violation. He was arrested and a search incident to arrest produced methamphetamine.

The Court looked at the factors from *Brown* and concluded that the temporal proximity between the unconstitutional stop and the search incident to arrest favors suppressing the evidence. The officer discovered drug contraband on Strieff only minutes after the stop, and precedence supports the idea that a substantial amount of time should elapse between the two events.

In contrast, a second factor—the presence of intervening events—strongly favors the prosecution. The valid arrest warrant, predating the investigation and entirely unconnected with the stop, favors finding sufficient attenuation between the unlawful conduct and the discovery of evidence. The warrant authorized the officer to arrest Strieff, and once the arrest was valid, the search incident to arrest was lawful.

The third factor, blatant or deliberate violation, supports the prosecution. According to the Court, the officer "was at most negligent, but his errors in judgment hardly rise to a purposeful or flagrant violation of Strieff's Fourth Amendment rights."

A strong dissent by Justice Sotomayor explained that the initial unconstitutional police conduct is exactly what the exclusionary rule is meant to deter. Unconstitutional police conduct is just that, and allowing an officer to take advantage of that does not deter this behavior. Justice Kagan also wrote a dissenting opinion in which she offered the position that the unconstitutional stop and the discovery of the arrest warrant were, in fact, too close in time to break the connection between the two. Despite these dissenting opinions, a major takeaway from *Strieff* is that an arrest warrant discovered subsequent to an unconstitutional stop is a strong enough intervening factor to tip the scales in favor of allowing the evidence.

Any assumption about the exclusionary rule that implies the Supreme Court does not support law enforcement is simply not the case. Although the Supreme Court has decided cases that eliminated evidence police obtained illegally, it has also established some commonsense exceptions to the exclusionary rule.

Exceptions to the Exclusionary Rule

The exclusionary rule applies only in criminal trials in which a constitutional right has been violated. Several important exceptions to the exclusionary rule have evolved from common law by the U.S. Supreme Court.

The Inevitable Discovery Doctrine *Nix v. Williams* (1984) resulted in the **inevitable discovery doctrine**. To understand how this doctrine came about, one must backtrack to a previous trial, *Brewer v. Williams* (1977). The trials involved the same case and defendant (Williams) but different prosecutors. The case involved in both trials began on Christmas Eve of 1968, when 10-year-old Pamela Powers disappeared while attending an event at a YMCA with her family in Des Moines, Iowa. Shortly after she was reported missing, a 14-year-old boy reported having been asked by a YMCA resident to hold several doors open for him while the man loaded a bundle from the building into a car. The boy reported seeing two skinny white legs within the bundle.

An arrest warrant was subsequently issued for Robert Williams, a YMCA resident and an escapee from a psychiatric hospital. Williams eventually turned himself in to police in Davenport, Iowa. An agreement was reached through Williams's lawyer that the defendant would be returned by police to Des Moines.

All agreed that Williams would not be interrogated in any way during the 160-mile trip. However, during the drive, knowing that Williams was a psychiatric patient and that he possessed a strong religious faith, one officer said the following to Williams (known as the "Christian Burial Speech"):

> I want to give you something to think about while we're traveling down the road.... Number one, I want you to observe the weather conditions, it's raining, it's sleeting, it's freezing, driving is very treacherous, visibility is poor, it's going to be dark early this evening. They are predicting several inches of snow for tonight, and I feel that you yourself are the only person that knows where this little girl's body is, that you yourself have only been there once, and if you get a snow on top of it, you yourself may be unable to find it. And since we will be going right past the area on the way to Des Moines, I feel that we could stop and locate the body, that the parents of this little girl should be entitled to a Christian burial for the little girl who was snatched away from them on Christmas Eve and murdered. And I feel we should stop and locate it on the way rather than waiting until morning and trying to come back out after a snowstorm and possibly not being able to find it at all.

---

inevitable discovery doctrine exception to exclusionary rule deeming evidence admissible even if seized in violation of the Fourth Amendment when it can be shown that the evidence would have inevitably been discovered through lawful means

LO9 *Among the exceptions to the exclusionary rule are the inevitable discovery doctrine, existence of a valid independent source, harmless error, and good faith.*

The detective told Williams that he did not want an answer, but that he just wanted Williams to think about it as they drove. Williams eventually directed the officers to the little girl's body.

Although the lower courts admitted Williams's damaging statements into evidence, the Supreme Court in *Brewer v. Williams* affirmed the court of appeals' decision that any statements made by Williams could not be admitted against him because the way they were elicited violated his constitutional right to counsel. This case is also discussed in the section dealing with confessions and the right to counsel. The Court said:

> The pressures on state executive and judicial officers charged with the administration of the criminal law are great, especially when the crime is murder and the victim a small child. But it is precisely the predictability of those pressures that makes imperative a resolute loyalty to the guarantees that the Constitution extends to us all.

The Court granted Williams a second trial without his damaging statements being admissible. At this trial (*Nix v. Williams*), the Court allowed the body to be admissible evidence, not because it was found as a result of the improper questioning by the police, but because an independent search party would have eventually discovered it:

> If the government can prove that the evidence would have been obtained inevitably and, therefore, would have been admitted regardless of any overreach by the police, there is no rational basis to keep that evidence from the jury in order to ensure the fairness of the trial proceedings.

Williams was convicted.

Valid Independent Source If evidence that might otherwise fall victim to the exclusionary rule is obtained from a valid, independent source, that evidence can be admitted. In *Segura v. United States* (1984), although evidence discovered during an illegal entry into an apartment was excluded, evidence later found in the apartment while a search with a warrant was being executed was admissible because the warrant was obtained with information totally unconnected with the illegal entry.

In *Murray v. United States* (1988), the Court again held that evidence initially seen during an illegal search but later recovered under a valid warrant would be admissible. In this case, the police initially broke in without a warrant but returned later with a valid warrant not using what they had seen during the initial break-in to support the probable cause in the warrant.

Harmless Error In instances in which the preponderance of evidence suggests the defendant's guilt and the "tainted" or illegal evidence is not critical to proving the case against the defendant, the **harmless error** exception applies. This standard was first set forth by the Court in *Chapman v. California* (1967) when it ruled "that before a federal constitutional error can be held harmless, the court must be able to declare a belief that it was harmless beyond a reasonable doubt." And in *Harrington v. California* (1969), the Court ruled that the evidence should be examined as a whole, and that if overwhelming untainted evidence supported the conviction, or if the error involved a well-established element of the crime, then the error would be considered "harmless."

◀ CASE IN BRIEF

Nix v. Williams (1984)

ISSUE Should evidence be excluded from trial when the suspect gives information in violation of his Sixth Amendment right to counsel that leads to the discovery of that evidence?

RULING No. When the prosecution is able to show that the evidence would have been discovered through lawful means anyway, it is admissible.

harmless error an exception to the exclusionary rule involving the admissibility of involuntary confessions and referring to instances in which the preponderance of evidence suggests the defendant's guilt and the "tainted" or illegal evidence is not critical to proving the case against the defendant

Constitutional Law in ACTION

Sergeant Worrall is on patrol in her squad car when she sees a car being driven the wrong way down a one-way street. After the car turns the corner, Sergeant Worrall turns on her red lights and siren and pulls the car over.

Sergeant Worrall walks up to the driver and thinks it is someone she knows who is a drug dealer. She tells the driver, "Get out of the car." When the driver does, Sergeant Worrall reaches into the driver's jacket pocket and pulls out heroin. She arrests the man.

Before she brings the man to jail, Sergeant Worrall checks to see if the man has any warrants. This is something that is routinely done every time someone is pulled over. The driver is found to have a felony warrant for his arrest.

Later at trial, the driver argues that the heroin should be suppressed under the exclusionary rule. The rationale is that Sergeant Worrall did not have probable cause to search the driver.

- *Should the heroin be excluded from trial? Why or why not?*
- *Would an exception to the exclusionary rule apply? Which one?*
- *What facts are available to show that the heroin would have been inevitably found?*

The reversal of a conviction is no longer automatic when a constitutional violation occurs. As long as the error was harmless, of which the burden is on the prosecution to show beyond a reasonable doubt, the conviction will stand.

In *Arizona v. Fulminante* (1991), the Court ruled that the harmless error doctrine applies to cases involving admissibility of involuntary confessions. In this case, Fulminante was accused of murdering his stepdaughter, but the murder could not be proved. While he was in prison on an unrelated charge, he became friends with another inmate, Sarivola, who later became a paid FBI informant. Sarivola told Fulminante that Fulminante was getting hostile treatment from the other inmates because of the rumor that Fulminante was a child killer. He suggested that if Fulminante would tell him the truth, he would protect him. Fulminante confessed to him. At trial, the defense sought to suppress the confession on the grounds it was coerced. The Court agreed. The prosecution then sought to have the confession admitted under the harmless error doctrine, but the Court ruled the error was not harmless, because the confession was likely to contribute to Fulminante's conviction. The confession was not admitted.

Good Faith Instances in which police officers are not aware they are violating Fourth Amendment principles involve the **good faith** exception. The good faith exception often comes into play when the government is executing arrest or search warrants. If such warrants are later found to be invalid, perhaps because of a typographical error citing the wrong address or apartment number, the evidence obtained while the warrants are executed is still admissible because the officers were acting in "good faith."

CASE IN BRIEF

Arizona v. Fulminante (1991)

ISSUE Does the harmless error doctrine apply to coerced confessions?

RULING Yes. If the conviction would have resulted without the use of the evidence obtained from the coerced confession, the use of that evidence is a "harmless error" and the conviction will stand.

good faith officers are unaware that they are acting in violation of a suspect's constitutional rights

Good faith boils down to whether police followed procedure and who erred (i.e., did a neutral magistrate make a mistake in signing a warrant?). In a dissenting opinion in *Stone v. Powell* (1976), Justice Bryon White argued that the exclusionary rule should not disqualify evidence "seized by an officer acting in the good-faith belief that his conduct comported with existing law. . . . Excluding the evidence can in no way affect his future conduct unless it is to make him less willing to do his duty." Indeed, the salience of the balancing test—weighing the costs to society against the deterrent effect—is especially strong when a court invokes the good faith exception because there can be no benefit to society by allowing evidence of guilt to be wiped away when officers truly believe they are acting in accordance with constitutional procedure.

United States v. Leon (1984) and *Massachusetts v. Sheppard* (1984), two cases decided on the same day, are "arguably the most important cases decided on the exclusionary rule since *Mapp v. Ohio* (1961). They represent a significant, although narrow, exception to that doctrine" (del Carmen, 2010, p.104). In *United States v. Leon* (1984), the Supreme Court specifically addressed the issue of whether the exclusionary rule should be modified so evidence obtained by an officer with a warrant later found to not be based on sufficient probable cause could still be used in court against the defendant at trial. Because no police misconduct occurred, which is what the exclusionary rule seeks to discourage, when an officer lawfully executes a warrant, the possibility that the warrant itself was issued without sufficient probable cause should not withhold valuable evidence from the trial.

The *Leon* case held that the exclusionary rule would be applied to only the following three situations in searches conducted pursuant to a warrant:

- The magistrate abandoned the prescribed detached and neutral role in issuing the warrant.
- The officers were dishonest or reckless in preparing their affidavit or the search warrant.
- The officers could not have harbored an objectively reasonable belief in the existence of probable cause.

Remember that the purpose of having a neutral magistrate is to remove from the police the responsibility of determining probable cause. If the police are acting in good faith on the validity of the warrant (which directs an officer to carry out the warrant), the motivation of the exclusionary rule no longer applies because it is not serving to prevent police misconduct.

Whereas the issue in *Leon* was the failure of the affidavit to establish probable cause, the critical point in *Sheppard*, in contrast, was that although the police did establish probable cause, a typographical error occurred in the warrant (the judge forgot to cross out the words *controlled substance*—an important difference with substantial constitutional implications). Note, however, that *Leon* and *Sheppard* establish a good faith exception only if a warrant has been obtained. The onus is then on the magistrate, not the officer: "In these cases, the Court said that there were objectively reasonable grounds for the officers' mistaken belief that the warrants authorized the searches. . . . The cases are similar . . . in that judges, not the police, made the mistakes. The Court said that the evidence in both cases was admissible because the

◀ **CASE IN BRIEF**

United States v. Leon (1984)

ISSUE Should the exclusionary rule apply to evidence discovered while executing a search warrant that officers reasonably relied upon despite its lack of probable cause?

RULING No. Excluding this evidence would serve no purpose in deterring intentional police misconduct when they reasonably rely upon a search warrant issued by a judge, and therefore, the cost to society would be too great not to allow the evidence into trial.

judge, not the police, erred and the exclusionary rule is designed to control the conduct of the police, not the conduct of judges" (del Carmen, 2010, p. 104).

Whereas the *Leon* case is limited to searches pursuant to a warrant, *Illinois v. Rodriguez* (1990) took this concept a step further by not invoking the exclusionary rule to a search based on an officer's reasonable, albeit mistaken, belief that a third party actually had authority to consent to a search. In *Maryland v. Garrison* (1987), police obtained a warrant to search what they honestly thought was a single apartment unit at a location. However, when the contraband was found in a second apartment there, even though it was not included in the warrant, the evidence was held to be admissible.

In 1995 in *Arizona v. Evans*, the Court continued the trend to broaden instances when objective good faith on the part of a police officer will save a constitutionally defective search: "The exclusionary rule does not require suppression of evidence seized in violation of the Fourth Amendment where the erroneous information resulted from clerical errors of court employees." In this case, officers observed Isaac Evans driving the wrong way on a one-way street. During the traffic stop, officers learned Evans's driver's license had been suspended and an outstanding misdemeanor warrant had been issued for his arrest. While being handcuffed, Evans dropped a hand-rolled cigarette that turned out to be marijuana. More marijuana was found inside Evans's car.

At trial, Evans moved to suppress the evidence as fruit of an unlawful arrest—the arrest warrant for the misdemeanor had been cancelled two weeks before the arrest but had not been entered into the system's database because of a clerical error by a court employee. The Court ruled, however, that because the police whose conduct the exclusionary rule was meant to control did not commit the error, then the exclusionary rule should not apply. In other words, the police had made an "honest mistake."

Herring v. United States (2009) "resolves the lingering question of whether evidence that is the fruit of an erroneous arrest, based on an error in a law enforcement-maintained database, is admissible. The answer is yes. The good faith exception to the exclusionary rule operates to admit unlawfully obtained evidence when officers are acting reasonably and make honest mistakes" (Means & McDonald, 2009, p. 24). The officer in the case knew Bennie Herring, and when Herring was in the vicinity, the officer checked for warrants on him. The warrant clerk advised the officer that the neighboring county had an active arrest warrant for Herring, so the officer pulled him over and arrested him. The search incident to the arrest turned up methamphetamine in Herring's pocket and a pistol in his vehicle. Shortly afterward, the clerk informed the officer that no active arrest warrant existed because it had been recalled five months previously.

In the 5–4 decision, Chief Justice John Roberts wrote the majority opinion adopting the balancing approach to the exclusionary rule, in which the court balances the costs of exclusion of the evidence to the public safety to the deterrent benefit to the police, and concluded that under this balance the exclusionary rule did *not* apply:

1. The fact that a Fourth Amendment violation occurred—that is, a search or arrest was unreasonable—does not necessarily mean that the exclusionary rule applies.
2. The extent to which the exclusionary rule is justified by these deterrence principles varies with the culpability of the law enforcement conduct.

CASE IN BRIEF

Arizona v. Evans (1995)

ISSUE Does the exclusionary rule apply to evidence seized as a result of an inaccurate police record (an arrest warrant)?

RULING No. Court employees, not the police, were responsible for the inaccurate record. The application of the exclusionary rule would have no deterrent effect on the police, which is the objective of the rule.

3. To trigger the exclusionary rule, police conduct must be sufficiently deliberate that exclusion can meaningfully deter it, and sufficiently culpable that such deterrence is worth the price paid by the justice system. As laid out in our cases, the exclusionary rule serves to deter deliberate, reckless, or grossly negligent conduct, or in some circumstances recurring or systemic negligence. The error in this case does not rise to that level.
4. We do not suggest that all recordkeeping errors by the police are immune from the exclusionary rule. In this case, however, the conduct at issue was not so objectively culpable as to require exclusion.

Petitioner's claim that police negligence automatically triggers suppression cannot be squared with the principles underlying the exclusionary rule, as they have been explained in our cases. In light of our repeated holdings that the deterrent effect of suppression must be substantial and outweigh any harm to the justice system, we conclude that when police mistakes are the result of negligence such as that described here, rather than systemic error or reckless disregard of constitutional requirements, any marginal deterrence does not "pay its way." In such a case, the criminal should not go free because the constable has blundered (*Herring v. United States*, 2009).

The *Herring* decision broadens the good faith exception and shifts the analysis to one of "deliberateness and culpability." The Court has continued down this same line of reasoning, looking at the culpability of the officer and what deterrent effect the exclusionary rule would have had in a situation. In *Davis v. United States* (2011), the Court ruled on a case involving a search of a car incident to arrest. Between the time of Davis's 2007 arrest and conviction, and then his appeal in 2010, the law surrounding these searches changed via *Arizona v. Gant* (2009), a case in which the Court refused to apply the exclusionary rule to a situation in which the officers had followed existing law at the time. The application of the rule in this situation would not deter unconstitutional police conduct, and the actions were not deliberate, grossly negligent, or reckless. The Court's determination in *Davis* was that the "harsh sanction" of excluding valuable evidence and subsequent societal costs outweighed any deterrent value.

◀ **CASE IN BRIEF**

Herring v. United States (2009)

ISSUE Does the exclusionary rule apply when a negligent police error leads to evidence used against a defendant?

RULING No. The culpability of the officer should be evaluated along with the deterrent effect of the rule in the particular situation.

Internal Sanctions, Civil Liability, and Criminal Liability

Government wrongdoing can seldom be excused, and severe consequences may result, in addition to having evidence excluded. Administrative liabilities, civil liabilities, and criminal liabilities can be incurred at the local, state, or federal level, as summarized in Table 7.1.

Departments are able to hold their employees accountable under agency rules and regulations. Sanctions ranging from written reprimands to unpaid suspensions to termination are examples of consequences that might befall police officers who violate the Fourth Amendment.

Administrative sanctions are individualized, but a mechanism is available to hold entire organizations accountable if violations are systemic. Enacted in 1994 as part of the Violent Crime Control Act, 42 U.S.C. §14141 authorizes the Department of Justice (DOJ) to investigate and, if warranted, bring a civil lawsuit against a department

Table 7.1 Administrative, Civil, and Criminal Liability

	Federal law	**State law**
Civil liabilities	Title 42 of U.S. Code, Section 1983—Civil Action for Deprivation of Civil Rights	State tort law
	Title 42 of U.S. Code, Section 1985—Conspiracy to Interfere with Civil Rights	
	Title 42 of U.S. Code, Section 1931—Equal Rights under the Law	
Criminal liabilities	Title 18 of U.S. Code, Section 242—Criminal Liability for Deprivation of Civil Rights	State penal code provisions specifically aimed at public officers for crimes like these
	Title 18 of U.S. Code, Section 241—Criminal Liability for Conspiracy to Deprive a Person of Rights	Official oppression
	Title 18 of U.S. Code, Section 246—Violations of Federally Protected Activities	Official misconduct
		Violation of the civil rights of prisoners
		Regular penal code provisions punishing such criminal acts as assault, battery, false arrest, serious bodily injury, and homicide
Administration liabilities	Federal agency rules or guidelines vary from one agency to another	Agency rules or guidelines at the state or local levels vary from one agency to another

Source: DEL CARMEN. *Criminal Procedures*, 7E. © 2007 Wadsworth, a part of Cengage Learning, Inc.

when it has "reasonable cause to believe" that a "pattern or practice" of unconstitutional conduct has occurred. The goal of the law is to eliminate and correct systemic problems within a police department, not address individual occurrences.

This mechanism has been increasingly used by the DOJ under the Obama Administration. Since 2009, the DOJ has investigated more than 20 police agencies, more than twice the number investigated during the five previous years combined (DOJ, 2014). Citizens, civil rights organizations, or high-profile events may lead the DOJ to investigate a department. Often, an agency is targeted because its problems represent nationwide issues (Kelly, Childress, & Rich, 2015). If an investigation leads to a finding of a "pattern or practice" of unconstitutional behavior, the DOJ may file a lawsuit or settle with the organization through a consent decree or a memorandum of agreement. Both serve to change problematic department practices.

A **consent decree** is a court-enforced agreement, with oversight provided by a federal judge. In addition, the court will appoint a monitor to report the organization's compliance quarterly. A **memorandum of agreement (MOA)**, on the other hand, is not judicially enforced but does have an appointed monitor who makes quarterly reports.

Each consent decree and MOA is unique, based on facts and circumstances specific to a department, and each is meant to correct identified actions. Common methods used to make corrections are new policies and procedures, often in the areas of search and seizure. An additional method is the development and implementation of an "early warning system" to identify potential problem officers and take corrective action early through training or counselling. Training and investigating citizen complaints are other common areas these agreements address.

A similar federal law applies to jails and prisons. The Civil Rights of Institutionalized Persons Act, 42 U.S.C. §1997, was passed in 1980, the purposes of which were to reduce acts of abuse and excessive use of force and correct deplorable living

consent decree a court-enforced agreement, with oversight provided by a federal judge and a court-appointed monitor who reports the organization's compliance quarterly

memorandum of agreement (MOA) not judicially enforced but does have an appointed monitor who makes quarterly reports

conditions that amount to constitutional violations. The mechanism is the same as §14141 in that the DOJ investigates an institution to see if there is a "pattern or practice" of violations of prisoner rights.

The effectiveness of consent decrees and MOAs is open for debate. Some scholars and advocates see it as a successful way to reform police organizations. Others see these methods as too expensive. For example, the LAPD consent decree is estimated to have cost $300 million, which is passed on to the taxpayers (Kelly et al., 2015). Police proactivity has seen a decline, another "cost" to the law-abiding taxpayer. Seattle, Washington, for example, has been under a consent decree since 2012 and has seen this reaction by officers to federal oversight. "Cops are human beings," said Ron Smith, president of Seattle's union for rank-and-file officers. "They said, 'Well, when we did those things, that's what got us in trouble. So we won't do those things anymore.'" (Kelly et al., 2015).

Lawsuits against police are an occupational hazard (del Carmen, 2010). U.S. society is **litigious** (prone to suing), and the police are an attractive target because they wield power and are public employees. Widespread public perception that the government has deep pockets can entice some people to pursue legal action when they might not otherwise. Furthermore, if a civil liability suit against the government is won, the plaintiff's lawyer's fees are paid by the defendant, making this avenue of litigation attractive for attorneys as well. Because the entire agency or department or the entire jurisdiction can be sued, some awards are enormous. Consider the following examples:

litigious a tendency toward suing; a belief that most controversies or injurious acts, no matter how minor, should be settled in court

- "U.S. to pay $2 million in Wrongful Terror Attack"
- "66 Bullets Costs County $13 million"
- "New York Will Pay $50 Million in 50,000 Illegal Strip Searches"
- "The City of Los Angeles Agreed to Pay $15 Million to a Man Who Said Police Officers Shot Him in the Head and Chest and Then Framed Him in the Attack"
- "Jury Assesses Damages of $256 Million for Motorist's Collision with Off-Duty Police Officer That Left One Child Dead, One Quadriplegic and One Paralyzed on One Side with a Damaged Brain"
- "Chicago Reaches $18-Million Settlement with Family of Unarmed Woman Shot and Killed by Officer at the Conclusion of an 81-Block Pursuit of the Vehicle in Which She Was Riding" (del Carmen, 2010, pp.444–445).

As in a number of other areas of developing law, issues relating to law enforcement liability will continue to receive attention in the media and the courts. Students and practitioners of the law stay current on these issues.

A Final Consideration: When State Law Conflicts with Constitutional Law

Several cases have examined what happens when state law restrictions exceed the constitutional standard of lawful arrest based on probable cause. In *Atwater v. City of Lago Vista* (2001), the Supreme Court ruled that for federal civil liability purposes and to determine admissibility of evidence under the Fourth Amendment exclusionary rule, state restrictions do not prevail over constitutional standards (Rutledge, 2008). In this case, Gail Atwater was stopped because neither she nor her two children in the front seat were wearing seat belts, in violation of Texas law. The maximum penalty for the offense was a $50 fine. The officer, however, had previously warned her about the violation, so he stopped her truck and arrested her on a misdemeanor. She was transported to the police station and mug shots were taken. Then she was taken before a magistrate, posted bail, and was released.

Atwater filed a federal civil rights suit against the officer and the city claiming that her Fourth Amendment rights had been violated. After lower courts dismissed her suit, she appealed to the U.S. Supreme Court, which affirmed the dismissal, stating, "If an officer has probable cause to believe that an individual has committed even a very minor criminal offense in his presence, he may, without violating the Fourth Amendment, arrest the offender."

In *Virginia v. Moore* (2008), the court broadened police search authority by allowing drug evidence gathered after an arrest that violated state law to be used at trial, "an important search-and-seizure case turning on the constitutional limits of 'probable cause'" (Mears, 2008). In this case, police stopped David Lee Moore for driving his vehicle on a suspended license, a misdemeanor offense. Under Virginia law, the protocol for such incidents was to issue only a citation and a summons to appear in court and then to release the driver. But in this case, the officers arrested Moore and searched him, finding cocaine. Moore was tried on drug charges and convicted. He appealed, arguing that the evidence was obtained in violation of state law, reasoning that the responding officers should have issued a citation under state law, and the Fourth Amendment does not permit search incident to citation. The Supreme Court, however, disagreed with Moore and unanimously upheld the actions of the officers, with Justice Antonin Scalia stating, "The arrest rules that the officers violated were those of state law alone. It is not the province of the Fourth Amendment to enforce state law."

The Court asserted that if Fourth Amendment protections were linked to state law, the law would "vary from place to place and from time to time" causing confusion. Although states can regulate arrests as they desire, their various restrictions do not alter the traditional Fourth Amendment protection:

> In a long line of cases, we have said that when an officer has probable cause to believe a person committed even a minor crime in his presence, the balancing of private and public interests is not in doubt. The arrest is constitutionally reasonable....
>
> States, we said, remained free "to impose higher standards on searches and seizures than required by the Federal Constitution," but regardless of state rules, police could search a lawfully seized vehicle as a matter of federal constitutional law....
>
> State arrest restrictions are more accurately characterized as showing that the State values its interests in forgoing arrests more highly than its interests in making them, ... or as showing that the State places a higher premium on privacy than the Fourth Amendment requires. A State is free to prefer one search-and-seizure policy among the range of constitutionally permissible options, but its choice of a more restrictive option does not render the less restrictive ones unreasonable, and hence unconstitutional ...
>
> We conclude that warrantless arrests for crimes committed in the presence of an arresting officer are reasonable under the Constitution, and that while States are free to regulate such arrests however they desire, state restrictions do not alter the Fourth Amendment's protections. (*Virginia v. Moore*, 2008)

This ruling, in effect, confirmed that as long as probable cause exists to arrest, search incident to arrest is reasonable.

CASE IN BRIEF

Virginia v. Moore (2008)

ISSUE Does the Fourth Amendment prohibit the use of evidence resulting from an arrest based on probable cause but in violation of state law?

RULING No. The Fourth Amendment's protections are not changed by state laws. If that were the case, the Constitution would vary from place to place and time to time. Note that had this case been challenged in state court based solely on state law (and not the federal Constitution), the outcome might have been different.

Summary

The Fourth Amendment forbids unreasonable searches and seizures and requires that any search or arrest warrant be based on probable cause. If a person is an employee of any governmental agency or is an agent of the government in any capacity, that person is bound by the Fourth Amendment. The Fourth Amendment does not apply to private parties.

The reasonableness clause of the Fourth Amendment makes warrantless searches and seizures valid and constitutional when they are sensible. The Constitution does not provide an absolute right to be free from government intrusion, only *unreasonable interference*.

Probable cause determines when officers may execute lawful searches and arrests with, or in some cases, without a warrant. *Probable cause to search* means officers reasonably believe that evidence, contraband, or other items sought are where police believe these items to be. *Probable cause to arrest* means officers reasonably believe that a crime has been committed by the person they seek to arrest. All warrants are to be based on probable cause. When executing a search or arrest warrant, the common law rule is that for an entry into a home to be constitutional, police must first knock and identify themselves and their purpose—the knock-and-announce rule.

A stop is a brief detention of a person based on specific and articulable facts for the purpose of investigating suspicious activity. A frisk is a limited patdown search for weapons for the protection of the government agent and others. It is not automatically permitted with a stop, but only when the agent suspects the person is armed and dangerous. The law of stop and frisk deals with that time frame during which officers follow up on their suspicions but before the time that the requisite probable cause is established to justify an arrest (*Terry v. Ohio*, 1968). The *Terry* decision established that, in what is termed a *Terry* stop, an officer with articulable reasonable suspicion that a crime is occurring, has occurred, or is about to occur, may conduct a brief investigatory stop, including a pat down for weapons if the officer has reason to suspect the person is armed and dangerous.

An unlawful search or seizure can have two serious consequences: (1) the evidence may be excluded from court and (2) internal sanctions as well as civil and criminal liability may be incurred. The exclusionary rule is judge-made case law promulgated by the Supreme Court to deter police misconduct. It prohibits evidence obtained in violation of a person's constitutional rights from being admissible in court (*Weeks v. United States*). The primary purpose underlying the exclusionary rule is deterring government misconduct. *Mapp v. Ohio* made the exclusionary rule applicable at the state level. Evidence obtained in ways that *shock the conscience* will not be admissible in court. Among the exceptions to the exclusionary rule are the inevitable discovery doctrine, existence of a valid independent source, harmless error, and good faith. Government misconduct could also result in departmental discipline against an officer, civil lawsuits, and criminal charges.

Discussion Questions

1. Explain why the Fourth Amendment applies to the federal government and to state, county, and municipal governments.
2. Explain the meaning of search and seizure.
3. How does a stop differ from an arrest?
4. How does a frisk differ from a search?
5. At what point does a stop and frisk develop into a search and seizure?
6. What restrictions does the Fourth Amendment put on private security guards, such as store detectives or private investigators?
7. Explain why people might sue when they feel their rights have been violated. Is there something that makes it so attractive to sue law enforcement? Keep in mind the deep pockets theory.
8. Should a case be dismissed because the one piece of evidence that would surely prove the defendant was guilty was not admitted because of a police error in obtaining it?
9. To protect the public, can government ever really go "too far"?
10. Why should a government agent try to get a warrant whenever possible?

References

del Carmen, R. V. (2010). *Criminal Procedure: Law and Practice*, 7th ed. Belmont, CA: Wadsworth Publishing Company.

Department of Justice. (2014). *Police Reform and Accountability Accomplishments under Attorney General Eric Holder*. Washington, DC: Author. Retrieved June 5, 2016 from https://www.justice.gov/sites/default/files/opa/press-releases/attachments/2014/12/04/spl_police_accomplishments_12.4.14.pdf

Glennon, J. (2008, January 15) "Intuition on the Street." *PoliceOne.com News*. Retrieved May 31, 2013 from www.policeone.com/pc_print.asp?vid=1647830

Hall, J. "Objectives of Federal Criminal Rules Revision." *Yale Law Journal*, 51, p. 725.

Kelly, K.; Childress, S.; & Rich, S. (2015, November 13). "Forced Reforms, Mixed Results." *Washington Post*. Retrieved June 5, 2016, from http://www.washingtonpost.com/sf/investigative/2015/11/13/forced-reforms-mixed-results/

Maslow, A. H. (1954). *Motivation and Personality*. New York: Harper & Row.

Means, R. & McDonald, P. (2009, April). "A Trifecta: Computer Error, Qualified Immunity, Passenger Frisks." *Law and Order*, pp. 24–25.

Mears, B. (2008, April 23). "Supreme Court Broadens Police Searches." *CNN*. Retrieved May 31, 2013 from www.cnn.com/2008/CRIME/04/23/scotus.searches/index.html

Rutledge, D. (2008, June) "Fourth Amendment Supremacy." *Police*, pp. 66–70.

Wilson, B. P. (1986). *Exclusionary Rule*. (NCJ 100738.) Washington, DC: National Institute of Justice, Crime File Study Guide.

Cases Cited

Aguilar v. Texas, 378 U.S. 108 (1964)
Arizona v. Evans, 514 U.S. 1 (1995)
Arizona v. Fulminante, 499 U.S. 279 (1991)
Arizona v. Gant, 556 U.S. 332 (2009)
Atwater v. City of Lago Vista, 532 U.S. 318 (2001)
Beck v. Ohio, 379 U.S. 89 (1964)
Boyd v. United States, 116 U.S. 616 (1886)
Brewer v. Williams, 430 U.S. 387 (1977)
Brinegar v. United States, 338 U.S. 160 (1949)
Brown v. Illinois, 422 U.S. 590 (1975)
Cass v. State, 124 Tex. Crim. 208, 61 S.W.2d 500 (1933)
Chapman v. California, 386 U.S. 18 (1967)
City of Los Angeles v. Patel, 576 U.S. ___ (2015)
Davis v. United States, 564 U.S. 229 (2011)
Draper v. United States, 358 U.S. 307 (1959)
Elkins v. United States, 364 U.S. 206 (1960)
Florida v. Harris (2013)
Frank v. Maryland, 359 U.S. 360 (1959)
Harrington v. California, 395 U.S. 250 (1969)
Henry v. United States, 361 U.S. 98 (1959)
Herring v United States, 555 U.S. 135 (2009)
Hudson v. Michigan, 547 U.S. 586 (2006)
Illinois v. Gates, 462 U.S. 213 (1983)
Illinois v. McArthur, 531 U.S. 326 (2001)
Illinois v. Rodriguez, 497 U.S. 177 (1990)
Illinois v. Wardlow, 528 U.S. 119 (2000)
Locke v. United States, 11 U.S. (7 Cranch) 339 (1813)
Mapp v. Ohio, 367 U.S. 643 (1961)
Maryland v. Garrison, 480 U.S. 79 (1987)
Massachusetts v. Sheppard, 468 U.S. 981 (1984)
Michigan v. Summers, 452 U.S. 692 (1981)
Miller v. United States, 357 U.S. 301 (1958)
Murray v. United States, 487 U.S. 533 (1988)
Nix v. Williams, 467 U.S. 431 (1984)
Public Service Comm'n v. Havemeyer, 296 U.S. 506 (1936)
Rawlings v. Kentucky, 448 U.S. 98 (1980)
Richards v. Wisconsin, 520 U.S. 385 (1997)
Rochin v. California, 342 U.S. 165 (1952)
Segura v. United States, 468 U.S. 796 (1984)
Shadwick v. City of Tampa, 407 U.S. 345 (1972)
Silverthorne Lumber Co. v. United States, 251 U.S. 385 (1920)
Smith v. United States, 337 U.S. 137 (1949)
Spinelli v. United States, 393 U.S. 410 (1969)
Stanford v. Texas, 379 U.S. 476 (1965)
State v. Heald, 307 A.2d 188 (Me. 1973)
State v. Mimmovich, 284 A.2d 282 (Me. 1971)
Stone v. Powell, 428 U.S. 465 (1976)
Sussex Land & Live Stock Co. v. Midwest Refining Co., 294 F. 597 (8th Cir. Wyo. 1923)
Taylor v. Alabama, 457 U.S. 687 (1982)
Terry v. Ohio, 392 U.S. 1 (1968)

United States v. Anderson, 676 F. Supp. 604 (E.D. Pa. 1987)
United States v. Arvizu, 534 U.S. 266 (2002)
United States v. Banks, 540 U.S. 31 (2003)
United States v. Calandra, 414 U.S. 338 (1974)
United States v. Di Re, 332 U.S. 581 (1948)
United States v. Ingrao, 897 F.2d 860 (7th Cir. 1990)
United States v. Jacobsen, 466 U.S. 109 (1984)
United States v. Knights, 534 U.S. 112 (2001)
United States v. Leon, 468 U.S. 897 (1984)
United States v. McCarty, 862 F.2d 143 (7th Cir. 1988)
United States v. Parker, 32 F.3d 395 (8th Cir. 1994)
United States v. Ross, 456 U.S. 798 (1982)
United States v. Sokolow, 490 U.S. 1 (1989)
United States v. Tapley, 1st Circuit Court of Appeals (2016)
United States v. Walther, 652 F.2d 788 (9th Cir. 1981)
Utah v. Strieff, 136 S.Ct. 1001 (2016)
Virginia v. Moore, 553 U.S. 164 (2008)
Weeks v. United States, 232 U.S. 383 (1914)
Wilson v. Arkansas, 514 U.S. 927 (1995)
Wolf v. Colorado, 338 U.S. 25 (1949)
Wong Sun v. United States, 371 U.S. 471 (1963)

CHAPTER 8

Conducting Constitutional Seizures

The Constitution does not guarantee that only the guilty will be arrested. If it did, §1983 would provide a cause of action for every defendant acquitted—indeed, for every suspect released.

—U.S. Supreme Court (*Baker v. McCollan*, 1979)

Being arrested is the ultimate government seizure. Here a woman is arrested after she failed a sobriety test at a DUI checkpoint.

Learning Objectives

LO1 List the elements of a seizure.

LO2 Understand the relationship between seizures, stops, and arrests.

LO3 Explain what factors determine how long a stop may last.

LO4 Know whether the Miranda warning must be given during a traffic stop.

LO5 Identify how arrest is usually defined.

LO6 Clarify when an arrest can legally be made.

LO7 Establish where arrests can be made.

LO8 Describe how much force can be used in making an arrest.

LO9 Recognize what the only justification for use of deadly force is.

LO10 Determine who has immunity from arrests.

Key Terms

arrest	fresh pursuit	hot pursuit
citizen's arrest	functional equivalent	pretext stop
de facto arrest		

Introduction

Chapter 7 painted a broad picture of how the Fourth Amendment influences searches and seizures. The Fourth Amendment's prohibition of unreasonable searches and seizures applies to people, places, and things. The law of seizures refers to government's taking physical control of people or property, and it applies to both stops and arrests.

In *Mendenhall v. United States* (1980), the Supreme Court held "that a person has been 'seized' within the meaning of the Fourth Amendment only if, in view of all the circumstances surrounding the incident, a reasonable person would have believed that he was not free to leave." The *Mendenhall* test provides that a seizure involves more than just the police's intention to seize; it also must include the objective aspect in which a reasonable person would believe that, under such circumstances, they were not free to terminate the encounter and leave as well.

Nearly a decade later the Court defined the "seizure" of a person as "governmental interference with a person's freedom of movement through means intentionally applied" (*Brower v. County of Inyo*, 1989). Shortly thereafter, in *California v. Hodari D.* (1991), the Court held that a person is not considered seized until he or she submits or is physically forced to submit. *Hodari* is important because under federal law, a seizure (arrest or stop) is not made unless the object of the seizure is actually brought under physical control by the officers or the object submits to control. Although this is a requirement under the Constitution, some states do not require that a person submit to or be in the physical control of an officer to be considered "seized."

Taken together, these cases set forth the four elements to any seizure: intending to seize the object (*Brower*), exercising the authority to do so (*Brower*), physically controlling the object of the seizure or the object submitting (*Hodari*), and the objective understanding of what is occurring such that a reasonable person would not feel free to leave (*Mendenhall*).

LO1 *The elements of a seizure are (1) intending to seize an object (including a person), (2) exercising authority to do so, (3) physically controlling the object, and (4) the understanding of what is happening such that a reasonable person would not feel free to leave.*

In this chapter, we address when and how police can seize people and how the Fourth Amendment relates to the seizure of property (contraband or evidence). This topic will be further discussed in Chapter 9, which specifically addresses searches.

This chapter looks at the requirements for the ultimate seizure, a lawful arrest. Perhaps one of the most intrusive and powerful of all government actions is the actual taking into physical custody, or the arresting, of an individual. The police have this unique power, which sets them apart from all other professions. The Constitution seeks to control this power through both a variety of rules and the courts. Although an area of extreme concern for champions of the Constitution, the necessity for the power to arrest is recognized as a power government requires. Recall the "continuum of contacts" discussed in Chapter 7, going from minimal interference through a stop to maximum interference through arrest.

This chapter begins with a look at the intensity and scope of a seizure, how those two elements combine to transform a stop into an arrest, and the constitutional limits to investigatory stops. The remainder of the chapter focuses on the subset of seizures called *arrests*, beginning with some definitions of arrest and a look at when and where arrests may generally be lawfully made. This is followed by an examination of de facto arrests, a review of the knock-and-announce rule, a brief discussion of the community caretaking doctrine, and how events can escalate into an arrest. Next, issues arising from an arrest are examined, including pursuit and the use of force. The chapter concludes with a brief discussion of citizen's arrest, the rights of those in custody, and who is immune from arrest in this country.

Intensity and Scope of a Seizure: Stop and Arrest Compared

Law enforcement involves decisions and discretion. Police officers are charged with investigating suspicious circumstances and have constitutional authority to stop people to investigate even before police can lawfully arrest anyone. What begins as a simple stop of a person merely to investigate the possibility of crime may progress to a frisk and then to an arrest and full-body search, as discussed in Chapter 7.

Table 8.1 Stop versus Arrest

	Stop	Arrest
Justification	Reasonable suspicion	Probable cause
Warrant	None	Preferable
Officer's intent	Investigate suspicious activity	Make a formal charge
Search	Pat down for weapons	Full search for weapons and evidence
Scope	Outer clothing	Area within suspect's immediate control
Record	Minimal (field notes)	Fingerprints, photographs, and booking

Recall the definition of a *stop* given in Chapter 7: a *brief detention* of a person based on specific and articulable facts for the purpose of investigating suspicious activity. During a stop, the infringement on a person's liberty is temporary, and although the suspect is not free to go just then, without the investigation producing anything more, he or she will be free to go shortly. The term *detention* is often used in place of stop, but they are the same thing; they both refer to a seizure that must be justified by *reasonable suspicion* (RS) of criminal activity on the part of the detainee. Under this standard, it is incorrect for officers to speak of having "PC for the stop," because probable cause (PC) is *never* constitutionally required for a stop (*United States v. Sokolow*, 1989). Probable cause is the constitutional requirement for arrest.

Thus, the level of suspicion or proof (i.e., reasonable suspicion or probable cause) will dictate what an officer can and cannot do at a given point. The determination of at what point in time the seizure occurs is important because it sets in motion the protections of the Constitution, with respect to either reasonable suspicion or probable cause. No seizure, no Fourth Amendment requirements.

> **LO2** A seizure need not necessarily be an arrest (it could be a stop), but all arrests are seizures.

A *stop*, therefore, is quite different from an *arrest*, but both are seizures regulated by the Fourth Amendment. The intensity and scope of the seizure transforms a stop into an arrest. Thought of another way, an arrest is always a seizure, but a seizure is not always an arrest (it could be a stop).

The basic differences between a stop and an arrest are summarized in Table 8.1. Keep these basic differences in mind as you read this chapter.

Investigatory Stops

Determining whether the interaction with police constitutes a stop or arrest is crucial because how police proceed with seizing property, such as contraband or evidence, will determine whether it will be admissible as evidence or excluded. The analysis of whether a search of the person and possible seizure of contraband or evidence is constitutional begins with the determination of whether the intervention by police is considered a lawful *stop* or an *arrest*. To those uninformed about the law, these words may seem synonymous; to the criminal justice system, the differences are critical. The *Terry* case, which was introduced in Chapter 7, established that the authority to stop is independent of the power to arrest. A stop is *not* an arrest, but it *is* a seizure within the meaning of the Fourth Amendment and, therefore, requires reasonableness. Whether a stop or an arrest take place, the officer will

Constitutional Law in ACTION

Billy is crossing the street just as a marked squad car stops at the intersection for a stop sign. The officers look at Billy, who panics. Billy turns and runs the other way, down the street. As he is running, he drops a handgun. The officers see this and now give chase. They order Billy to stop over the squad's PA, but he continues to run. Billy trips and falls in a yard a few blocks away, and the officers catch up to him and handcuff him. They retrieve the gun Billy dropped and find out Billy does not have a permit to carry it. They arrest Billy.

- *Does it matter if Billy believes he is not free to leave at the point when the officers look at him as he crosses the street?*
- *In Billy's position, how would you feel?*
- *At what point is Billy seized under the Fourth Amendment?*
- *Why is it important to determine at what point in time Billy was seized?*

need to establish that certain conditions exist to make the action constitutional. In addition, knowing what action took place determines what additional actions an officer may perform, such as searching someone incident to arrest or conducting a frisk (two topics we will discuss later).

Establishing Reasonable Suspicion

For an investigatory stop to be constitutional, the officer must have articulable reasonable suspicion of criminal activity. In other words, the officer has to be able to explain in detail, or articulate, what specifically was suspicious. Using the totality of the circumstances test, officers must have a particularized and objective basis for suspecting the person stopped (*United States v. Cortez*, 1981). In *Cortez*, the Court described reasonable suspicion this way:

> The totality of the circumstances—the whole picture—must be taken into account. Based upon that whole picture the detaining officers must have a particularized and objective basis for suspecting the particular person stopped of criminal activity.... The analysis proceeds with various objective observations, information from police reports, if such are available, and consideration of the modes or patterns of operation of certain kinds of lawbreakers. From these data, a trained officer draws inferences and makes deductions—inferences and deductions that might well elude an untrained person. This process does not deal with hard certainties, but with probabilities. Long before the law of probabilities was articulated as such, practical people formulated certain common-sense conclusions about human behavior; jurors as fact-finders are permitted to do the same—and so are law enforcement officers.

In *United States v. Hensley* (1985), the Court held that the existence of a wanted poster or flyer provided sufficient reasonable suspicion for the police to stop a person, stating, "In an era when criminal suspects are increasingly mobile and increasingly likely to flee across jurisdiction boundaries, this rule is a matter of common sense: It minimizes the volume of information concerning suspects that must be transmitted to other jurisdictions and enables police in one jurisdiction to act promptly in reliance on information from another jurisdiction."

Although the standard is less than probable cause, it must be more than a mere hunch or even a general suspicion and cannot be a "fishing expedition" based on a whim or a "gut feeling things were really wrong" (*United States v. Pavelski*, 1986). Case law has continued to develop this area of criminal procedure.

What if reasonable suspicion is based on the misinterpretation of a law? This was the question the Supreme Court sought to answer in *Heien v. North Carolina* (2014). This case involved a traffic stop made on the basis of a faulty right rear brake light. Believing this was a violation of North Carolina state law, the officer pulled the car over. A subsequent investigation of the driver and the passenger, Heien, found that the two were in possession of over 52 grams of cocaine.

Heien challenged the stop in an attempt to get the cocaine suppressed as evidence. The trial court ruled in favor of the state, but the North Carolina Court of Appeals reversed, finding that, upon closer inspection of the statute, only one brake light is required to be functional under North Carolina law. The state appealed to the North Carolina Supreme Court, which found that the officer's mistake of law was reasonable because a nearby statute required all rear lamps to be in working order. Therefore, the traffic stop was valid.

On appeal to the Supreme Court, Heien again argued that a mistake of the law by an officer cannot support reasonable suspicion. The Supreme Court disagreed. The Fourth Amendment requires reasonableness, and mistakes of fact or law might very well be reasonable. Justice Roberts wrote, "To be reasonable is not to be perfect, and so the Fourth Amendment allows for some mistakes on the part of government officials." He added, "Reasonable suspicion arises from the combination of an officer's understanding of the facts and his understanding of the relevant law. The officer may be reasonably mistaken on either ground. Whether the facts turn out to be not what was thought, or the law turns out to be not what was thought, the result is the same: the facts are outside the scope of the law." In this case, the officer's mistake of law was reasonable.

◀ **CASE IN BRIEF**

Heien v. North Carolina (2014)

ISSUE Does a police officer's mistake of law provide the suspicion required by the Fourth Amendment to justify a traffic stop?

RULING Yes. As long as the mistake of law is reasonable, it can provide reasonable suspicion.

Informants and Anonymous Tips In *Adams v. Williams* (1972), the Court held that information from an informant, and not just personal observation by an officer, may establish the requisite suspicion to make a stop:

> The Fourth Amendment does not require a policeman who lacks the precise level of information necessary for probable cause to arrest to simply shrug his shoulders and allow a crime to occur or a criminal to escape. On the contrary, *Terry* recognized that it may be the essence of good police work to adopt an intermediate response.

In another case, *Alabama v. White* (1990), police received an anonymous tip that Vanessa White would leave a specific apartment at a precise time, travel to a specific motel in a brown Plymouth station wagon with a broken taillight, and possessed cocaine. The police went to the described apartment, saw Vanessa get into the car, and head toward the motel. She was stopped and further investigation revealed she was, in fact, in possession of cocaine.

> **MYTH**
> The police can take tips at face value and act on them.
>
> **FACT**
> No, officers need to corroborate information to eliminate the spectre of jokes or grudges and base their actions on facts.

CASE IN BRIEF

Florida v. J.L. (2000)

ISSUE Is an anonymous tip that a person is carrying a gun illegally, without any more information, enough to establish reasonable suspicion to stop and frisk the person?

RULING No. Officers must have additional facts that support the tip because the anonymous information lacked reliability. Officers should use the tip as a starting point and make additional observations to establish reasonable suspicion.

The Court held that reasonable suspicion had been established, albeit a "close case," and standing alone it would not establish reasonable suspicion. But here, the caller gave "inside information" that showed a "special familiarity" with White's activities. In addition, the police had corroborated some of the anonymous tipster's information, which made the tipster reliable. Importantly, the Court explained that when a tipster tells the truth about some things, he or she is more likely to tell the truth about other things, including criminal behavior.

However, an anonymous tip, with nothing else, has been held to lack sufficient reliability to establish the reasonable suspicion for a *Terry* stop, given the totality of the circumstances. In *Florida v. J.L.* (2000), the Court held that an anonymous call telling police that a young Black male wearing certain clothing at a bus stop had a gun was not enough to be considered reasonable suspicion, and the gun the police found on him was held inadmissible because it was the fruit of an illegal search.

Even though these two cases began with information from an anonymous tip and, on their face, appear similar, they are in fact much different when the details are examined. In *White*, the tipster gave a high level of detail, including predicting White's future actions. *J.L.*, in contrast, involved a "bare-bones" tip that did not include predictive information and which did not allow the police to corroborate the information in order to establish the tipster's credibility, such as how the caller knew that J.L. had a gun or any suggestion of a special familiarity with J.L.

Courts in several states have upheld vehicle stops based on anonymous tips that the driver of a vehicle is drunk. In some jurisdictions, courts have relied on *J.L.* to find that certain vehicle stops of suspected drunk drivers are reasonable, even though the officer does not observe erratic driving when the reported vehicle is located. These courts based their reasoning on a combination of the following factors: (1) the dangers inherent in drunk driving, which kills more than 10,000 people annually, (2) detailed descriptions of the vehicle and driving provided by an eyewitness, (3) the fact that traffic stops are more common and less invasive than pedestrian stops, and (4) the reduced expectation of privacy of motorists driving on public roadways (Rutledge, 2010).

Other jurisdictions have taken the position that the ruling in *J.L.* is absolute, applying to every detention made on the basis of an uncorroborated anonymous tip of erratic driving, finding no difference between an anonymous tip of erratic driving and an anonymous tip that a person is carrying a firearm (Rutledge, 2010). This was the finding by the Virginia Supreme Court in *Harris v. Commonwealth* (2008). The importance of this case lies in recognizing that different state courts have ruled differently on how they treat anonymous tips with respect to forming reasonable suspicion.

The question since *J.L.* has been whether its ruling applies to *every* situation, in particular, cases where the anonymous tip is about a dangerous situation, like drunk driving. The Court wrote in *J.L.* that it would not "speculate about the circumstances under which the danger alleged in an anonymous tip might be so great as to justify a [stop and] search even without a showing of reliability."

The Court recently addressed a tip about a drunk driver in *Navarette v. California* (2014). In this case, a caller reported to 911 that she had been run off the road by a silver Ford F-150 pickup truck and that she suspected the driver was drunk. She was able to provide the license plate number to dispatch. California Highway Patrol

Constitutional Law in ACTION

Jessie waves to Officer Taylor and asks to speak with him, telling the officer that he saw the driver of a blue, older minivan driving while drinking out of a bottle of beer at the corner of 1st Street and Main a few minutes ago. Jessie remembers only the first three digits of the license plate—456. Jessie also adds that the driver was a middle-aged White female. Furthermore, Jessie gives the officer his full name and telephone number in case he needs anything further.

Officer Taylor goes to the area of 1st and Main to look for the minivan and sees what he thinks to be the one Jessie described pull out of the parking lot of the liquor store. Officer Taylor sees the driver is a White middle-aged female and the license plate starts with 456.

After the minivan pulls out on the street, Officer Taylor pulls behind it and signals it to stop. The driver pulls the minivan to the curb and parks. Officer Taylor walks to the driver's window and asks the driver for her license. Officer Taylor observes two open bottles of beer sitting in cup holders, that the driver has bloodshot and watery eyes, and that her breath smells of alcohol. The driver is arrested for DWI and having an open bottle of beer in the car.

- *How is this situation different from J.L.?*
- *What objective facts does the officer have to support an investigatory stop of the car and driver?*
- *Do you think these facts establish reasonable suspicion?*

---

located the truck about 15 minutes later and followed it for five minutes, but did not observe any reckless driving. The officers then pulled the truck over. Officers approached the driver and passenger, who were brothers, and smelled a strong odor of marijuana coming from the truck. Thirty pounds of marijuana was subsequently found in the truck bed. The brothers plead guilty to transporting marijuana.

The case made its way from the California court system to the Supreme Court, where the question presented was whether an officer is required to corroborate anonymous information to establish reliability. In a majority opinion by Justice Thomas, the Court explained that an officer does not need to rely on his or her own observations alone to establish reasonable suspicion but, in fact, can rely on information from another. This information cannot generally stand alone because the veracity of an anonymous caller is mostly unknown. At times, however, an anonymous caller can give enough information to indicate a level of reliability sufficient enough to support reasonable suspicion.

In this case, the caller was run off the road, indicating first-hand knowledge of the incident, which is generally viewed as reliable. The caller also described the truck with some level of detail. In addition, the 911 reporting system contains information that eliminates the possibility for false reports such as recording the call and documenting the cell phone number and location from which the call was made. The truck was also found a short time after the call and in an area suggested by the timeline of events and direction of travel.

> **CASE IN BRIEF**
>
> *Navarette v. California* (2014)
>
> **ISSUE** Does the Fourth Amendment require an officer who receives an anonymous tip regarding a drunken or reckless driver to corroborate dangerous driving before stopping the vehicle?
>
> **RULING** No. So long as the officer is reasonable in believing the anonymous tip contains reliable information, the officer is not required to corroborate it.

The dangerous actions of the driver also factored into the Court's finding that reasonable suspicion existed to stop the truck. Justice Thomas wrote, "The 911 caller in this case reported more than a minor traffic infraction and more than a conclusory allegation of drunk or reckless driving. Instead, she alleged a specific and dangerous result of the driver's conduct: running another car off the highway."

Justice Scalia wrote a dissenting opinion in which he argued that the facts should still have been corroborated to adequately support reasonable suspicion: "The Court's opinion serves up a freedom-destroying cocktail consisting of two parts patent falsity: (1) that anonymous 911 reports of traffic violations are reliable so long as they correctly identify a car and its location, and (2) that a single instance of careless or reckless driving necessarily supports a reasonable suspicion of drunkenness."

The ruling in this case tends to show that the particular situation and how dangerous it is—in this case, drunk driving—will influence whether or not reasonable suspicion is deemed present in the facts.

> **CASE IN BRIEF**
>
> *Illinois v. Wardlow* (2000)
>
> **ISSUE** Does a person's unprovoked flight away from police officers, while in a high-crime area, establish reasonable suspicion to stop the person?
>
> **RULING** Yes. Taken in isolation, a person's mere presence in a high-crime area is insufficient to support a stop. However, when combined with other facts, such as unprovoked flight at the sight of police officers, it will establish reasonable suspicion to stop the person.

Flight from Police In *Illinois v. Wardlow* (2000), the Supreme Court addressed the issue of flight as justification for seizure, determining that reasonable suspicion to chase is *not* automatic when people run. In this case, officers observed William "Sam" Wardlow standing on the sidewalk of an area known for heavy narcotics trafficking, holding an opaque bag. When Wardlow saw the police, he immediately fled. Officers gave chase, caught Wardlow, and conducted a frisk for weapons based on their experience that weapons were commonly present during drug deals. A loaded gun was found in the bag, and Wardlow was arrested for a weapons violation.

Wardlow moved to suppress the weapon, arguing the stop and frisk were unreasonable under the Fourth Amendment. Several appeals eventually brought the case before the Illinois Supreme Court, which viewed Wardlow's flight as nothing more than a refusal to agree to a voluntary conversation, ruling no inference of reasonable suspicion could be drawn from such action, even in a high narcotics-traffic area. The case was appealed to the U.S. Supreme Court, which ruled that Wardlow's presence in a high-crime area was a relevant fact that officers *could* consider in deciding whether they had reasonable suspicion that Wardlow was involved in criminal activity. It also held that unexplained flight, on noticing the police, is a pertinent factor in determining whether reasonable suspicion exists. Justice William H. Rehnquist noted, "Headlong flight—wherever it occurs—is the consummate act of evasion: It is not necessarily indicative of wrongdoing, but it is certainly suggestive of such."

> **MYTH**
> Simply running at the sight of police will not give an officer a legal basis to stop and question you.
>
> **FACT**
> True. But when combined with other facts, there may be enough reasonable suspicion to legally stop you.

Although running away itself may not be enough to cause reasonable suspicion, it is a relevant factor overall. As was the case in *Wardlow* and other cases, additional factors contribute to the totality of the circumstances. Merely refusing to talk to the police, as held in *Florida v. Royer* (1983), is not unlawful behavior, either.

Length of the Stop

Royer also addressed how long a person may be detained: "An investigative detention must be temporary and last no longer than is necessary to effectuate the purpose of the stop. Similarly, the investigative methods employed should be the least intrusive means reasonably available to verify or dispel the officer's suspicion in a short period of time."

This issue was also considered in *United States v. Sharpe* (1985): "In assessing whether a detention is too long in duration to be justified as an investigative stop, we consider it appropriate to examine whether the police diligently pursued a means of investigation that was likely to confirm or dispel their suspicions quickly. . . . The question is not simply whether some other alternative was available, but whether the police acted unreasonably in failing to recognize or pursue it."

In this case, the stop took some 20 minutes. The Court held no rigid specific time limit applied, but rather, considerations factored into what a reasonable amount of time would be are (1) the purpose of the stop, (2) the reasonableness of the time used for the investigation that the officers wish to conduct, and (3) the reasonableness of the means of investigation used by the officer. Because the detention is allowable, although for only a brief period, reasonable force to stop and detain the suspect is also permissible. "A rule of thumb might be that the duration of an investigative detention should normally be measured in minutes, not hours—though in a serious case where circumstances required it, 75 minutes might be reasonable" (Means & McDonald, 2009, p. 24).

The Supreme Court has ruled in past cases that, during a traffic stop, telling the driver to exit a stopped vehicle (*Pennsylvania v. Mimms*, 1977), having a canine "sniff" the exterior of a car for the presence of drugs (*Illinois v. Caballes*, 2005), and asking a few off topic questions (*Arizona v. Johnson*, 2009) are all reasonable actions and do not require additional reasonable suspicion to perform, *as long as they do not prolong the length of the stop*. In *Rodriguez v. United States* (2014), the Court was asked if taking such actions *after* a traffic stop was completed required justification in addition to the reason for the stop.

Dennys Rodriguez was pulled over after an officer saw the vehicle he was driving veer slowly onto the highway shoulder, drive on the shoulder for several seconds, and then jerk back into traffic. Nebraska state law prohibits driving on the shoulder. The officer ran checks on the driver, Rodriguez, and his passenger, and wrote a warning ticket for the driving violation.

After returning all of the identification and vehicle documents, and issuing the warning ticket, the officer asked Rodriguez for consent to search the vehicle. Rodriguez said no, but the officer had Rodriguez and the passenger step away from the vehicle and then walked his K9 partner around the exterior of the vehicle two times. The K9 alerted to the presence of drugs, and a large amount of methamphetamine was found. A total of seven or eight minutes had passed between the time the warning ticket was issued and when the drugs were found.

Rodriguez moved to suppress the evidence based on the fact that the officer did not have reasonable suspicion to prolong the traffic stop. Both the district court and the Eighth Circuit ruled that the seven- to-eight minute extension of the traffic stop was *de minimis*, and therefore was reasonable despite the lack of additional reasonable suspicion.

The Supreme Court disagreed. Extending the stop *after* the time reasonably required to investigate the initial violation supported by reasonable suspicion was unconstitutional. A traffic stop "may last no longer than is necessary" to deal with investigating the initial violation. The stop was constitutional up to the point where

◄ CASE IN BRIEF

Rodriguez v. United States (2014)

ISSUE May an officer extend an already-completed stop for a canine sniff without reasonable suspicion or other lawful justification?

RULING No. Extending a traffic stop beyond the time it takes to investigate the initial violation is only constitutional if additional justification is present. The time allowed for a stop is determined by what the officer is investigating.

LO3 *How long a stop may last depends on factors that indicate the suspect is not detained an unreasonably long time, including the purpose of the stop and the time and means the investigation requires. Extending the stop after the time reasonably needed to deal with the initial violation is unconstitutional.*

the traffic violation investigation concluded (when the warning ticket was issued). The Supreme Court vacated the Eighth Circuit decision and remanded it to determine if independent reasonable suspicion existed to support the dog sniff.

Protective Actions during Stops

Situations may arise in which an officer does not have probable cause to arrest, but the circumstances dictate that the detainee be handcuffed or put in the back seat of a squad car. *Terry* permits officers to take all necessary measures to protect themselves, without turning a stop into an arrest, if the circumstances reasonably support such actions. For example, if the circumstances warrant, officers may draw their weapons, have a reasonable number of backup officers, handcuff individuals, or place them in the back of a squad car without turning the detention into an arrest. If a savvy defense lawyer asserts that any of the preceding actions transforms a *Terry* stop into an arrest, the appropriate officer response is that although the defense's client was not free to go, the client was being detained in such a manner for officer safety reasons while a reasonable investigation into criminal activity was conducted (Scarry, 2009).

A frisk may be an allowable protective action during an investigatory stop, depending on the circumstances. Recall from Chapter 7 that a frisk is a limited pat-down search for weapons for the protection of the government agent and others. The phrase "stop and frisk," as authorized by *Terry*, links the two actions and describes both a seizure and a search, each of which must be justified. The *stop* is justified if there is a reasonable suspicion the person is involved in criminal activity; the *frisk* is justified if there is a reasonable suspicion the detainee may be armed and dangerous.

An officer might have justification for a stop but not for a frisk. For example, if an officer stops a person based on reasonable suspicion that the person was recently involved in an act of indecent exposure, the stop would be justified, but a frisk would likely not be (Rutledge, 2009).

MYTH
If the police put handcuffs on you, you are "arrested."

FACT
Not necessarily. They are many factors that come into play when determining if a person is arrested or not, and being placed in handcuffs is just one of them.

The Controversy over Pedestrian Stops

"Police in major U.S. cities stop and question more than a million people each year—a sharply higher number than just a few years ago. Most are Black and Hispanic men. Most are frisked, and nearly all are innocent of any crime, according to figures gathered by the Associated Press" (Long, 2009). Civil liberties advocates say the stop-and-frisk practice is racist and does not deter crime. Herbert (2010) says the practice has gotten completely out of control, citing statistics from the New York Police Department from 2004 to 2009 when officers stopped pedestrians nearly 3 million times, frisking and otherwise humiliating many of them. More than 90 percent of those stopped and frisked were completely innocent.

Many police departments, on the other hand, maintain such stops are a valuable tool that turns up illegal weapons and drugs and prevents more serious crime. New York Police Commissioner Raymond Kelly contends that stop-and-frisk helped police solve 170 crimes (Rivera & Baker, 2010). The fact that police departments in the precincts with the largest minority populations use this practice to deter drug dealing and violent crime can result in misleading statistics.

Constitutional Law in ACTION

Officer Brown sees David Dwyer driving a car on Main Street. David goes right through a stop sign–controlled intersection without stopping, nearly colliding with another car. Officer Brown pulls Dwyer over. During the stop, the officer has a hard time hearing Dwyer because of the traffic noise, so the officer has Dwyer step out of the car, and the two talk on the side of the road.

While talking to Dwyer, Officer Brown hears a radio call regarding an armed robbery. The description of the car matches Dwyer's, and the location of the robbery occurred at the spot where Dwyer ran the stop sign. The officer handcuffs Dwyer, frisks him for weapons, and has him sit in the squad car, telling Dwyer, "Just sit here for a few minutes while I try and sort this out."

As Dwyer is getting into the squad, he blurts out, "You must know about the weed in my car. It's under the seat." The officer finds a small amount of marijuana under Dwyer's front seat.

After about 10 minutes, the officer learns information that shows it is unlikely Dwyer is the robber. He has Dwyer step from the squad car, un-handcuffs him, and gives him a ticket for not stopping at the intersection and possessing a small amount of marijuana.

- Did Officer Brown arrest Dwyer? Why or why not?
- Was the frisk justified? What facts support your conclusion?

Traffic Stops

Although the operation of a motor vehicle on public roads is considered a privilege, the driver and occupants remain protected by the Constitution. Being stopped by the police for no or insufficient reason is considered unreasonable and, therefore, a constitutional violation of Fourth Amendment rights. *Delaware v. Prouse* (1979) established:

> [E]xcept in those situations in which there is at least clear, articulable, reasonable suspicion that a motorist is unlicensed or that an automobile is not registered, or that either the vehicle or an occupant is otherwise subject to seizure for violation of law, stopping an automobile and detaining the driver in order to check his driver's license and the registration of the automobile are unreasonable under the Fourth Amendment.

Motorists, for example, may be stopped if driving a car with expired license plates or for an equipment violation, such as burned-out turn signals, headlights, or taillights. A vehicle may also be stopped because of erratic driving or if it matches the description of a vehicle seen at or near a crime or coming from the direction of a crime scene. Certainly, an investigatory stop is justified if the driver or occupants of a vehicle are suspected of committing a crime.

A traffic stop for an offense classified as a petty misdemeanor, for example, a relatively minor driving or equipment violation (not defined by the law as crimes) is just that, a *stop*. Therefore, the *Miranda* warning is not required—the person is

◀ **CASE IN BRIEF**

Delaware v. Prouse (1979)

ISSUE Is it constitutional to stop a car to do a random check of the driver's license status when there is no probable cause or reasonable suspicion?

RULING No. A stop in this manner is unreasonable and violates the Fourth Amendment. An officer must at least establish reasonable suspicion that the driver is committing or has committed a crime to make a seizure (i.e., a stop).

LO4 Because a traffic stop is brief and occurs in public, it is not considered an arrest, thus *Miranda* warnings need not be given.

not under arrest and is free to go—as soon as the officer issues the citation. In *Berkemer v. McCarty* (1984), the Supreme Court held, "Persons *temporarily* detained pursuant to [stops made by police for traffic offenses] are not *in custody* for the purposes of *Miranda*. In addition to the detention being brief, it occurs in public." According to the *Berkemer* Court, these factors "mitigate the danger that a person questioned will be induced to speak where he would not otherwise do so freely." *Miranda* is discussed in Chapter 10.

In *Pennsylvania v. Mimms* (1977), two officers on routine patrol observed Mimms driving a vehicle with an expired license plate. The officers stopped Harry Mimms to issue a traffic ticket. One officer approached and asked Mimms to step out of the car and produce his license and vehicle registration. When the driver stood up, the officers noticed a large bulge under Mimms's jacket. Fearing it was a weapon, one officer frisked Mimms and discovered a loaded .38-caliber revolver. Mimms sought to exclude the evidence during trial, arguing it was obtained illegally. The Court, however, sided with the officers, ruling once a police officer has lawfully stopped a vehicle for a traffic violation, he or she may order the driver out of the car, even without suspicion of other criminal activity or threat to the officer's safety. Once the driver is out of the vehicle, if the officer then reasonably believes the driver may be armed and dangerous, the officer may conduct a frisk. The Court, in *Maryland v. Wilson* (1997), extended *Mimms* by stating:

> An officer making a traffic stop may order passengers to get out of the car pending completion of the stop. . . . As a practical matter, the passengers are already stopped by virtue of the stop of the vehicle. The only change in their circumstances which will result from ordering them out of the car is that they will be outside of, rather than inside of, the stopped car. Outside the car, the passengers will be denied access to any possible weapon that might be concealed in the interior of the passenger compartment.

Ordering the driver out of the vehicle is permitted as a safety precaution for the police once a lawful stop of the vehicle has been made. The Court cited statistics showing that 30 percent of officers shot in the line of duty were shot as they approached someone seated in a vehicle. In the case of passengers, the Court again conveyed its safety concern for police personnel by permitting the passengers to be ordered out of the vehicle as well. No explanation need be given.

A question of concern to officers is, when a vehicle is subject to a traffic stop, is a passenger in that vehicle "seized" for the purposes of the Fourth Amendment? In *Brendlin v. California* (2007), the Supreme Court ruled unanimously "yes"—all occupants in a vehicle, not just the driver, are considered seized for the purposes of the Fourth Amendment during a traffic stop. Thus, all occupants may challenge the constitutionality of the stop. In this case, Bruce Brendlin was a passenger in a vehicle stopped for expired registration tabs. Although the officer had determined through dispatch, before making the stop, that the registration renewal was being processed and had observed a valid temporary registration permit properly affixed to the car, the officer decided, nonetheless, to proceed with the stop despite lacking reasonable suspicion to do so.

After approaching the vehicle, the officer recognized the passenger as "one of the Brendlin brothers." Recalling that either Scott or Bruce Brendlin had dropped

---

CASE IN BRIEF ▶

Pennsylvania v. Mimms (1977)

ISSUE May an officer order the driver out of a car during a traffic stop as a matter of course?

RULING Yes. The Court ruled that ordering a driver out of the car, with no additional suspicion than the original stop, is a minimal intrusion and is outweighed by officer safety issues. In *Maryland v. Wilson*, the Court added that passengers may be ordered out of the car as well with no additional suspicion.

CASE IN BRIEF ▶

Brendlin v. California (2007)

ISSUE During a traffic stop, is a passenger of a vehicle seized under the Fourth Amendment?

RULING Yes. The occupants of a car are seized just as the driver is. Therefore, the occupants are able to challenge the constitutionality of a stop.

out of parole supervision, the officer asked Brendlin to identify himself. The officer returned to his squad car, verified that Brendlin was a parole violator with an outstanding no-bail warrant for his arrest and requested backup. Once reinforcements arrived, Brendlin was ordered out of the car at gunpoint and placed under arrest. When police searched Brendlin incident to arrest, they found an orange syringe cap on his person. A pat-down search of the driver revealed syringes and a plastic bag of a green, leafy substance, and she was formally arrested. Officers then searched the car and found tubing, a scale, and other items used to produce methamphetamine.

Charged with possession and manufacture of methamphetamine, Brendlin moved to suppress the evidence obtained in the searches of his person and the car as fruits of an unconstitutional seizure, arguing that the officers lacked probable cause or reasonable suspicion to make the traffic stop. The trial court denied the motion and ruled that the stop was legal, but the California Court of Appeal reversed, holding that Brendlin was seized by the traffic stop, which was unlawful. Reversing, the state supreme court held that suppression was unwarranted because Brendlin, as a passenger, was not seized at the point of the traffic stop. It was only after the officer determined the passenger's arrest warrant status that Brendlin became seized. The case ultimately found its way to the U.S. Supreme Court, which ruled that Brendlin had been illegally seized the moment the vehicle stopped at the side of the road because the stop was illegal. The Court vacated and remanded the case.

In *Arizona v. Johnson* (2009), the Court ruled in favor of an officer who frisked a passenger during a traffic stop. In this case, three members of a gang task force made a stop in a neighborhood associated with the Crips. The stop was based on a license plate check that showed the vehicle's registration had been suspended for an insurance-related violation. The officers had no reason to suspect anyone in the vehicle of criminal activity. The backseat passenger, Lemon Johnson, was wearing a blue bandana and other attire consistent with Crips membership and carrying a scanner in his back pocket. Wanting to question Johnson alone, one officer asked Johnson to step out of the car and, given the Crips' reputation, patted him down for weapons. The pat down revealed the butt of a gun, and Johnson was charged with and convicted of unlawful possession of a weapon.

The Arizona Court of Appeals reversed Johnson's conviction saying that the detention had evolved into a separate, consensual encounter stemming from an unrelated investigation of one of the officers into Johnson's possible gang affiliation. The Arizona Supreme Court denied review. The U.S. Supreme Court reversed this judgment. Justice Ruth Bader Ginsburg, writing for the Court, stated, "When the stop is justified by suspicion (reasonably grounded, but short of probable cause) that criminal activity is afoot, as the [*Terry*] Court explained, the police officer must be in a position to act instantly on reasonable suspicion that the persons temporarily detained are armed and dangerous" (*Arizona v. Johnson*, 2009). The Court analyzed three other Supreme Court cases in its decision: *Pennsylvania v. Mimms*, *Maryland v. Wilson*, and *Brendlin v. California*. The Court stressed that "An officer's inquiries into matters unrelated to the justification of the traffic stop . . . do not convert the encounter into something other than a lawful seizure, so long as those inquiries do not measurably extend the duration of the stop." The Court remanded the case to the lower court to decide the issues consistent with its opinion.

◀ CASE IN BRIEF

Arizona v. Johnson (2009)

ISSUE May an officer frisk a passenger of a car lawfully stopped solely for a traffic violation?

RULING Yes. As long as the traffic stop is valid and the officer develops reasonable suspicion that the passenger is armed and dangerous, the passenger may be frisked.

Thus, if police officers make a lawful stop for a traffic violation, they may order the driver and passengers out of the car under *Mimms* and *Wilson*. If, during such a stop, officers are reasonably suspicious that the situation is dangerous, they may order the driver out of the car and frisk him or her and can order any passengers in the car out and frisk them as well. Furthermore, if a frisk of at least one occupant of a car is permitted, the police may also check the passenger compartment for weapons (*Michigan v. Long*, 1983). *Johnson* allows the frisk of a passenger as long as the stop of the car is legal and reasonable suspicion exists for the passenger being armed and dangerous.

Courts have differed on whether an arrest has actually occurred when the offense for which the party has been stopped constitutes more than a petty violation. Officers have broad discretion in how they deal with traffic law violations and in many instances may cite the driver, issue a summons for a required court appearance, or arrest and jail the defendant. Cases vary across the country regarding at what point the circumstances have crossed from a stop to an arrest with traffic enforcement contacts. The analysis would be the same, whether a stop and frisk has escalated in intensity and scope to an arrest by considering the totality of the circumstances and whether the individual reasonably believed he was not free to go. This situation exemplifies the importance of officers' understanding of the law, how they perceive the circumstances, and how their actions are recorded in their reports and presented during court testimony.

Whren v. United States (1996) addressed the issue of the **pretext stop,** that is, stopping a vehicle to look for evidence of a crime under the justification of a less-serious traffic stop. In *Whren*, plainclothes officers saw a truck wait at a stop sign for an unusually long time, turn suddenly without signaling, and then speed away. The officers stopped the vehicle and, as they approached it, saw the defendant holding bags of crack cocaine. The defendant argued that the police used the traffic stop as a pretext to uncover the drugs. The Court held that as long as probable cause existed to believe a traffic violation occurred, stopping the motorist was reasonable: "Subjective intentions play no role in ordinary, probable-cause Fourth Amendment analysis."

The precise contours of investigatory stops regarding past crimes can be problematic. One of the main purposes of an investigatory stop is to prevent crime. In the situation where a past crime has occurred, that purpose no longer exists. However, the Supreme Court explained in *United States v. Hensley* (1985), mentioned earlier, that the authority to stop a suspect thought to have committed a past crime "promotes the strong government interest in solving crimes and bringing offenders to justice." This is particularly important when the crime is a felony, as in *Hensley*, or involves a threat to public safety. The Court stopped short of stating that it is constitutional to stop someone to investigate any past crime.

Left unanswered is the question of what is allowable when investigating a past misdemeanor. Courts have upheld the reasonableness of stops for misdemeanors committed in the presence of police, but the question has been raised whether it is constitutional to stop a vehicle based on an alleged or suspected misdemeanor *not* committed in police presence. The Ninth Circuit U.S. Court of Appeals became the first federal appellate court to tackle this question in *United States v. Grigg* (2007), and the court's answer was "no" under the facts of this particular case. Incidentally,

pretext stop stopping a vehicle to search for evidence of a crime under the guise of a traffic stop

CASE IN BRIEF ▶

Whren v. United States (1996)

ISSUE Is it unconstitutional to stop a car for a traffic violation when there exists another law enforcement objective?

RULING No. As long as the basis for the original stop was valid, it does not matter if the *real* objective was different.

this has since become the majority rule in the federal circuits, being determined on a case-by-case basis and not on a per se rule disallowing such stops.

The *Grigg* case involved the complaint of a driver who played the car's stereo at an obnoxiously loud volume, in violation of the city's noise ordinance, in a residential neighborhood. The investigating officer who made the stop saw an SKS rifle on the passenger seat, and a frisk revealed that Justin Grigg held concealed brass knuckles. He was arrested for possession of an unregistered automatic weapon.

The trial judge ruled that the stop was a proper *Terry* stop. The Ninth Circuit Court of Appeals, however, ruled that stopping Grigg was not constitutionally proper but did leave open the possibility that other completed misdemeanors might lawfully justify an investigative detention, stating that any decision to stop a vehicle based on a report of a completed misdemeanor "must consider the nature of the misdemeanor offense in question, with particular attention to the potential for ongoing or repeated danger (e.g., drunken or reckless driving), and any risk of escalation (e.g., disorderly conduct, assault, domestic violence). An assessment of the 'public safety' factor should be considered within the totality of the circumstances, when balancing the privacy interests at stake against a *Terry* stop, along with the possibility that the police may have alternative means to identify the suspect or achieve the investigative purpose of the stop" (*United States v. Grigg*, 2007). This same consideration comes in to play when considering roadblocks and checkpoints.

Roadblocks and Checkpoints

A roadblock stops vehicles without suspicion of criminal activity by the person stopped, an action contrary to the commands of the Fourth Amendment. Although the police have a reason for conducting the roadblock, they are checking everyone, rather than a particular individual. The purposes of the roadblock have been considered by courts, as have the means. In *Brown v. Texas* (1979), the Supreme Court created a balancing test:

> The *Brown* balancing test requires that courts evaluating the lawfulness of roadblocks consider three factors: (1) the gravity of the public concerns that are addressed or served by the establishment of the roadblock; (2) the degree to which the roadblock is likely to succeed in serving the public interest; and (3) the severity with which the roadblock interferes with individual liberty.

United States v. Pritchard (1981) held that checkpoints to inspect drivers' licenses and vehicle registrations were constitutionally permissible as long as officers did not stop just one vehicle for this purpose or conduct random checks.

To combat drunken driving, the Michigan State Police established sobriety checkpoints, at which every driver at that location was stopped and checked. In *Michigan Department of State Police v. Sitz* (1990), the police checked drivers at a specific location. They had contact with 126 vehicles, each delayed about 25 seconds, and netted two arrests. When this practice was challenged as violating the Fourth Amendment, the Supreme Court, using the *Brown* balancing test, concurred that sobriety checkpoints are a seizure but one that is reasonable because the "means of intrusion on motorists stopped briefly at sobriety checkpoints is slight." In this

---

MYTH
Drunk driving checkpoints are always illegal.

FACT
Not true. The particular facts of each checkpoint will need to be analyzed to determine its reasonableness. Also, some states have found them unconstitutional under their state constitution.

◀ **CASE IN BRIEF**

Michigan Department of State Police v. Sitz (1990)

ISSUE Does a state highway checkpoint, at which every vehicle is required to stop and the driver's sobriety checked, violate the Fourth Amendment when no individualized suspicion exists?

RULING No. Although such a stop is a seizure under the Fourth Amendment, the initial intrusion at the checkpoint is minimal when balanced against the interests in preventing drunk driving, and carefully established checkpoints are reasonable. Note that further investigation of each driver may require individualized suspicion.

case, the severity of the drunken-driving problem combined with the policies in place to limit intrusiveness garnered the Court's approval.

Conversely, the Supreme Court held in *City of Indianapolis v. Edmond* (2000) that vehicle checkpoints for *drugs* violate the Fourth Amendment. Justice Sandra Day O'Connor, writing for the Court, stated, "We have never approved a checkpoint program whose primary purpose was to detect evidence of ordinary criminal wrongdoing. Rather, our checkpoint cases have recognized only limited exceptions to the general rule that a seizure must be accompanied by some measure of individualized suspicion." The primary difference between drug interdiction checkpoints and other checkpoints is that the primary purpose of drug interdiction checkpoints was to discover evidence of criminal wrongdoing, whereas previously approved checkpoints such as sobriety checkpoints had public safety goals. The Court concluded: "If we were to rest the case at this high level of generality, there would be little check on the ability of the authorities to construct roadblocks for almost any conceivable law enforcement purpose. Without drawing the line at roadblocks designed primarily to serve the general interest in crime control, the Fourth Amendment would do little to prevent such intrusions from becoming a routine part of American life" (*City of Indianapolis v. Edmond*, 2000).

> **CASE IN BRIEF**
>
> *City of Indianapolis v. Edmond* (2000)
>
> **ISSUE** Does a vehicle checkpoint violate the Fourth Amendment when the primary purpose is to detect drugs?
>
> **RULING** Yes. The objective of the checkpoint is to detect evidence of ordinary criminal wrongdoing without any individualized suspicion as a starting point. To be reasonable, the motivations must be more focused and not of a general crime control nature.

Although general checkpoints to check people, even if to check for public safety concerns, for the most part, rendered unconstitutional, the Court reiterated in *Edmond* (2000) that its decision did not change the lawfulness of sobriety or border checkpoints or those involving some individualized suspicion.

Illinois v. Lidster (2004) determined that a roadblock to find a witness to a fatal hit-and-run crash that happened a week before was lawful because it met the balancing tests from both *Brown* and *Sitz*. In *Lidster*, the police stopped traffic at the same time the accident occurred, although a week later, and going the same direction, hoping to find a witness. A driver approaching the checkpoint was arrested for drunk driving after nearly hitting an officer. The arrested driver argued that the checkpoint was unconstitutional pursuant to *Edmond*, but the Court disagreed:

> **CASE IN BRIEF**
>
> *Illinois v. Lidster* (2004)
>
> **ISSUE** Is the Fourth Amendment violated by designing a checkpoint to stop all motorists and ask them about a fatal hit-and-run accident?
>
> **RULING** No. The purpose of the checkpoint is to stop and elicit information about a fatal hit-and-run accident committed by another, not to determine if the vehicle's occupants were committing a crime.

> The concept of individualized suspicion had little role to play . . . the stop's primary law enforcement purpose was *not* to determine whether a vehicle's occupants were committing a crime, but to ask vehicle occupants, as members of the public, for their help in providing information about a crime in all likelihood committed by others. . . . The relevant public concern was grave. . . . Police were investigating a crime that had resulted in a human death.

In addition, the interference with people's liberty was "minimal. . . . Each stop required only a brief wait in line—a very few minutes at most."

Stops at International Borders

The increased awareness of and concern over terrorism and heightened pressures to secure our nation's borders have affected police practices and interpretation of the law. How much protection and to where such protection extends are subjects of continuing legal development, especially during these times of increased vigilance, yet precedent cases continue to be the basis on which future decisions are made.

A series of cases have concluded that checkpoints at or near international borders need no justification to stop all vehicles to check for illegal entrants into the

United States. The Supreme Court has held that the government's compelling interest in protecting the nation's borders alone justifies stopping any vehicle or individual, but stops may not be done on the basis of ethnicity, religion, or the like. Suspects may even be held at international borders longer than would be considered reasonable beyond that point of entry into the United States.

The Supreme Court has also recognized that routine border stops and searches may be carried out at borders and at their **functional equivalent,** meaning being essentially the same or serving the same purpose, for example, airports that receive nonstop flights from foreign countries. Although many international airports are not located directly near a physical border of the United States, they do provide a point of entry for individuals traveling from other countries and are, thus, the *functional equivalent* of a natural geographic border.

In *United States v. Martinez-Fuerte* (1976), the Supreme Court allowed the border patrol to set up permanent or fixed checkpoints on public highways leading to or away from the Mexican border, ruling that these checkpoints are not a violation of the Fourth Amendment.

United States v. Brignoni-Ponce (1975) involved a roving patrol, not a stationary checkpoint. The fixed border crossing was closed at the time because of inclement weather, and the stop of Brignoni-Ponce's vehicle, which led to the discovery of two illegal aliens inside the vehicle, was made by officers on roving patrol after Brignoni-Ponce had driven across the border. The Court stated that border patrol officers could detain and question, as opposed to actually searching, people in a car if reasonable suspicion existed, adding that within 100 miles of an international border, reasonable suspicion was all that was needed (but that merely "looking Mexican" was insufficient cause). If the stop based on reasonable suspicion produced the probable cause for a warrant, any evidence would be admissible. Checkpoints farther than 100 miles from an international border are sometimes also made for other reasons, such as stopping everyone in the name of public safety. This area of law is changing.

United States v. Montoya de Hernandez (1985) involved the holding by U.S. Customs agents of a woman suspected of being a "balloon swallower (a person who ingests a container of narcotics to be expelled later)." The suspect was seized for more than 16 hours while customs agents got a court order to conduct medical tests on her. A rectal examination revealed 88 bags of cocaine. Her detention and subsequent search at the border for that period, although well beyond what would be considered a normal customs search and inspection, was constitutional because the agents reasonably suspected she was smuggling drugs.

United States v. Flores-Montano (2004) held that 37 kilograms of marijuana was admissible when found by customs agents who took apart a vehicle's gas tank. The defendant argued the government needed reasonable suspicion to remove the gas tank, but Chief Justice Rehnquist disagreed: "Government's interest in preventing the entry of unwanted persons and effects is at its zenith at the international border. Congress has always granted the executive plenary authority to conduct routine searches and seizures at the border, without probable cause or a warrant, to regulate the collection of duties and to prevent the introduction of contraband into this country."

Whatever the purpose of a stop, sometimes circumstances dictate that officers detain a suspect for a more thorough investigation.

functional equivalent
essentially the same or serving the same purpose

MYTH
Race can never be a factor in establishing reasonable suspicion.

FACT
Not true. Race can be a factor, but it cannot be the *only* factor.

◀ **CASE IN BRIEF**

United States v. Brignoni-Ponce (1975)

ISSUE Is it contrary to the Fourth Amendment to stop a car, as part of a roving checkpoint near the border, when the sole basis for the stop is the ethnicity of the occupants?

RULING Yes. Because this case involved a roving patrol conducted away from the border checkpoint, the officers needed reasonable suspicion to stop and investigate the occupants.

◀ **CASE IN BRIEF**

United States v. Flores-Montano (2004)

ISSUE Is it constitutional to search, by disassembling a gas tank on a car, at a border checkpoint without any suspicion of illegal activity?

RULING Yes. There is less privacy at the border than in the interior of the country, and a search of this type is reasonable simply by the fact that it happened at the border. The government has a strong interest in protecting the country against the illegal entry of people or things.

Arrests: An Overview

arrest the taking of a person into custody, in the manner authorized by law, to present that person before a magistrate to answer for committing a crime

Most state laws define an **arrest** in general terms as the taking of a person into custody, in the manner authorized by law, to present that person before a magistrate to answer for committing a crime.

The requirement of the Fourth Amendment that searches and seizures be *reasonable* dictates that the physical response by the police must be commensurate with the offense. The general guideline is that a person is under arrest if a reasonable person would believe that, under the existing circumstances and when viewed objectively, there was a restraint on movement that one associates with formal arrest and that the person was, in fact, being detained by the police and not free to go. Subjective, as opposed to objective, beliefs are not considered when determining if an arrest has occurred.

L05 *To arrest is to deprive a person of liberty by legal authority, taking a person into custody for the purpose of holding him or her to answer a criminal charge.*

An arrest may involve actual physical detention or a command, verbal or otherwise, by the officer requiring the suspect to stay. Often this situation results from what began as a simple stop based on reasonable suspicion.

When Arrests May Be Lawfully Made

Generally, lawful arrests can be made in one of three ways.

Officers can usually make a lawful arrest:

- for any crime committed in their presence.
- for any felony if they have probable cause.
- with an arrest warrant.

In the first two instances, a warrant is not required, although they are preferred by the courts and desirable to protect police from lawsuits. An estimated 95 percent of all arrests are made without warrants.

Warrantless Arrests for Crimes Committed in the Presence of an Officer If police officers observe a crime being committed, they have the authority to arrest without a warrant the individual(s) involved in committing the crime. "In the presence of" includes any of the officer's senses, for example, hearing a drug buy going down or smelling the odor of marijuana. The information the officer obtains becomes the probable cause for arrest.

As noted in *State v. Pluth* (1923), the officers must know that a crime is being committed before making the arrest. They cannot merely suspect that someone is about to commit a crime. The crime or the attempt must actually take place in the officer's presence.

Some laws of arrest depend on whether the violation is a misdemeanor or a felony. The difference, specifically defined within a state's criminal code, is a mathematical one: How much time would a person be sentenced to if convicted of that particular offense? Generally, a felony carries a minimum prison sentence of one year.

Officers who come to the crime scene of a misdemeanor after it has been committed are sometimes limited on whether or not they can make an arrest, even though the suspect is still at the scene. In many states, officers must obtain an arrest warrant to make an arrest for a misdemeanor not committed in their presence, despite the Court's ruling in *Atwater v. City of Lago Vista* (2001), when it held: "We simply cannot conclude that the Fourth Amendment, as originally understood, forbade peace officers to arrest without a warrant for misdemeanors. . . ." State criminal procedure statutes define such limitations, and all states have laws or rules of criminal procedure authorizing the arrest of persons for which the offense actually carries no jail or prison time.

However, exceptions do exist. For example, officers may arrest for misdemeanors not committed in their presence if the suspect might flee, might conceal or destroy evidence, or if the incident involves a traffic accident. In some states, such as Minnesota, officers may arrest for some unwitnessed misdemeanors such as domestic assault, driving under the influence of drugs or alcohol, and shoplifting. In fact, in the case of domestic assault, police in Minnesota are mandated to make an arrest if they have probable cause to believe an assault was committed by that person.

Warrantless Arrests Based on Probable Cause The second type of lawful warrantless arrest is an arrest based on probable cause that the suspect has committed a felony. Referring to the previous discussion of probable cause, if a law enforcement officer has sufficient information to reasonably believe, given the totality of the circumstances, that a crime is occurring or has occurred, and that the suspect is the offender, the officer may arrest without a warrant—but *only* for a felony-level crime. As with warrantless crimes committed in the presence of an officer, some

Constitutional Law in ACTION

Officer Jones is called to an address on Main Street regarding a domestic disturbance. He arrives and speaks with Mrs. Kemp. She tells the officer that her husband was upset tonight over Mrs. Kemp losing her job and became so angry that he slapped her in the mouth. This caused a small cut to her lip, a misdemeanor in Officer Jones's state. Mr. Kemp then went to his workshop in the garage.

Officer Jones goes to the workshop and sees Mr. Kemp. Immediately, Mr. Kemp exclaims, "I didn't do anything!" At that time, Officer Jones tells Mr. Kemp he is under arrest for domestic assault (even though the officer was not present when the assault happened). Mr. Kemp is then handcuffed and brought to jail.

- *Is it lawful for the officer to arrest Mr. Kemp for a misdemeanor not committed in his presence?*
- *What if Mr. Kemp had caused his wife to get stitches, making the assault a felony?*
- *Could the officer arrest Mr. Kemp several hours later in a different location?*
- *What does the officer need to arrest Mr. Kemp? In other words, what legal standard must be met before the officer can arrest Mr. Kemp?*

states have statutory exceptions permitting warrantless arrests based on probable cause for certain lesser crimes, such as DWI, domestic assault, and shoplifting.

United States v. Watson (1976) established that an arrest without a warrant made in a public place is valid if it is based on probable cause, even if the arresting officers had time to obtain an arrest warrant. Recall that probable cause can be based on anything an officer becomes aware of through the senses—observational probable cause—or on information provided by others.

In contrast to warrantless arrests for misdemeanors, which must be made as soon as practical, warrantless arrests for felonies based on probable cause do not need to be made immediately. This differentiation is based on the severity of the felony and society's interest in expediting a felon's arrest, as long as sufficient probable cause exists.

> **LO6** *A lawful arrest can be made by an officer for any crime committed in their presence, for any felony if they have probable cause, and with an arrest warrant. Police may, without a warrant, arrest for any crime committed in their presence or for any felony based on probable cause. However, a warrant is preferred by the courts and helps protect the police from lawsuits.*

Arrests with a Warrant A conventional interpretation of the Fourth Amendment requires that to be reasonable, all arrests be made with a warrant based on probable cause. The warrant must name the person making the complaint, the specific offense being charged, the name of the accused, and the basis for the probable cause.

The person making the complaint must swear the facts given are true and sign the complaint. Usually the complaint is made by the investigating police officer. In *Watson* (1976) the Supreme Court held, "Law enforcement officers may find it wise to seek arrest warrants where practicable to do so, and their judgments about probable cause may be more readily accepted where backed by a warrant issued by a magistrate." The Court went on to note, however, "We decline to transform this judicial preference into a constitutional rule when the judgment of the nation and Congress has for so long been to authorize warrantless public arrests on probable cause." The Court further emphasized that requiring a judge to review the facts of every situation and then issue an arrest warrant before officers could act would "constitute an intolerable handicap for legitimate law enforcement."

Where Arrests May Be Made

Arrests may be made in public places without a warrant if probable cause exists, as established in *Watson* (1976). Even if a person retreats to a private place, the warrantless arrest based on probable cause is valid, as explained in *United States v. Santana* (1976).

Payton v. New York (1980) established that police may not enter a private home to make a routine felony arrest unless exigent circumstances exist, such as in hot pursuit, to be discussed shortly. In this case, police gathered evidence sufficient to establish probable cause that Payton had murdered a gas station manager. Without a warrant, they went to his apartment to arrest him. When no one answered the door, they forced it open. Payton was not there, but the police found a .30-caliber shell casing that was used as evidence in Payton's murder conviction. On appeal, the evidence was excluded, with the Supreme Court holding, "In terms that apply equally to seizures of property and to seizures of persons, the Fourth Amendment has drawn a firm line at the entrance to the house. Absent exigent circumstances, that threshold may not reasonably be crossed without a warrant."

> **CASE IN BRIEF** ▶
>
> *Payton v. New York* (1980)
>
> **ISSUE** Does the Fourth Amendment require a warrant to enter a home to make an arrest?
>
> **RULING** Yes. In the absence of exigent circumstances, the police may not enter a home to make a warrantless arrest.

In *Payton*, the Court affirmed the value of having an arrest warrant: "An arrest warrant founded on probable cause implicitly carries with it the limited authority to enter a dwelling in which the suspect lives when there is reason to believe the suspect is within."

May the police enter the home of a third party to arrest a person who is the subject of an arrest warrant? *Steagald v. United States* (1981) examined this question and answered that the police could not. To protect the interests of the third party, a *search* warrant is needed to enter a third party's home. If this were not the case, an arrest warrant would give the police authority to enter *any* home where they believed the suspect might be located.

Indeed, the founding fathers wanted to ensure that a person's home, which receives the highest protection under the Constitution, was free from unreasonable searches or seizures, and the courts have maintained and supported this basic freedom.

> **LO7** Police may make a warrantless arrest based on probable cause in a public place or in a private place that a suspect has retreated to from a public place. Police may not make a nonconsensual, warrantless entry into a home to make a felony arrest of that person or of a guest in the home unless exigent circumstances exist.

The Community Caretaking Doctrine

In many states, police officers are charged with community caretaking functions as well, totally divorced from the detection, investigation, or acquisition of evidence relating to violation of any criminal statute. However, under the "community caretaking doctrine," police officers are allowed, without reasonable suspicion of any criminal activity, to approach and detain citizens for community caretaking purposes (Collins, 2008). This doctrine does not implicate the Fourth Amendment unless it is determined that the person has been seized. As long as there is an objective basis showing that the officer felt the person was in peril or otherwise in need of assistance, then the Fourth Amendment is not yet implicated (because the person is not seized), and the officer has a right to investigate. Once the emergency is over, any further actions on behalf of the officer may constitute a seizure and the Fourth Amendment comes into play. Thus, as long as the interaction is not seen as a seizure, any evidence of wrongdoing is admissible. If, however, the facts of the encounter escalate so that a crime exists, the rules of arrest come into play.

An Arrest or Not? De Facto Arrests

As noted, a simple stop can escalate into an arrest. Sometimes the totality of the circumstances qualifies the seizure as a *detention tantamount to arrest*, also called a **de facto arrest.** This is a situation in which the police take action in a manner that is, in reality, an arrest, but without the requisite probable cause. And any arrest without probable cause is an illegal arrest.

Kaupp v. Texas (2003) illustrates this situation. Police officers were investigating the homicide of a 14-year-old girl and had the confessed killer in custody. The killer implicated a friend, Robert Kaupp. The officers did not have enough corroboration to establish probable cause to get an arrest warrant, so they decided to bring him in and confront him with the evidence. At 3 A.M., three officers were admitted to Kaupp's home by his father. The officers woke Kaupp with a flashlight, handcuffed him, and, without allowing him to get dressed, took him to the station. A statement Kaupp gave them was used to convict him of complicity in the murder. The

de facto arrest a situation in which the police take someone in for questioning in a manner that is, in reality, an arrest, but without the requisite probable cause

◀ CASE IN BRIEF

Kaupp v. Texas (2003)

ISSUE Is a person arrested when officers wake him in the middle of the night, handcuff him, and take him, dressed only in his boxers, to the police station after a visit to a crime scene?

RULING Yes. The officers effectively arrested Kaupp despite a lack of probable cause because the circumstances surrounding his detention and transport to the police station would make a reasonable person believe they were not free to leave.

Supreme Court, however, overturned the conviction, noting that the police lacked probable cause for the de facto arrest, which made it illegal, and as "tainted fruit," the statement was ruled inadmissible.

Another leading case in this area is *Dunaway v. New York* (1979), in which police picked up the defendant based on information that implicated him in a murder. They took him to the police station for questioning. He was never told he was under arrest, but he was not free to leave. Even though he was not booked and, therefore, would have no arrest record, the Supreme Court ruled that the seizure was illegal because the defendant was not free to leave. The seizure was much more than a simple stop and frisk and, as such, should have been based on probable cause. In its ruling, the Court declared, "Hostility to seizures based on mere suspicion was a prime motivation for the adoption of the Fourth Amendment."

Courts will not concern themselves with what the police officer calls the event: a stop, detention, or arrest. What does matter is whether, "by means of physical force or show of authority, (the officer) has in some way restrained the liberty of a citizen" (*Terry v. Ohio*, 1968). In *Michigan v. Chesternut* (1988), the Supreme Court stated it would not formulate an exact definition of what constitutes a seizure, rather the analysis would view the totality of the circumstances to determine whether "a reasonable person would have believed that he was not free to leave."

Because of the implications for the arrestee and the arresting officer, the Court has found itself confronted with determining when police can seize a person and what circumstances constitute a seizure. It need not always be what one might imagine—someone handcuffed in the back of a police car. It might be in the course of a defendant being pursued while taking flight or being in the midst of officers causing the person to think he or she is not free to go. This contention is echoed in *Cupp v. Murphy* (1973): "The detention of the respondent against his will constituted a seizure of his person, and the Fourth Amendment guarantee of freedom from unreasonable searches and seizures is clearly implicated."

fresh pursuit a situation in which police are immediately in pursuit of a suspect and may cross state jurisdictional lines to make an arrest of a felon who committed the felony in the officers' state

Pursuit

Pursuit is a serious, often dangerous police activity that endangers not only the pursuing officers and suspect but also innocent bystanders. The pursuit of a suspect does not necessarily end at a border, as often portrayed in the movies. The terms *fresh pursuit* and *hot pursuit* are used to establish this distinction.

The term **fresh pursuit** explains the circumstances in which officers leave their jurisdiction and enter another to make an arrest of a felon who committed the felony in the officers' jurisdiction and then fled across jurisdictional lines. Many states have adopted the Uniform Act of Fresh Pursuit, which allows police officers of one state to enter another state in fresh pursuit to arrest a suspect who has committed a felony in the state from which the offender is fleeing. Some states require that anyone so arrested be brought immediately before the nearest court. Other states allow the arresting officers to return with their prisoner to their own state. Often, the result of the pursuit will be that the suspect will be charged with crimes in all jurisdictions involved.

MYTH
To be considered "hot pursuit," there needs to be a wild chase on public streets, either in a car or on foot, with an officer hot on the heels of a suspect.

FACT
Not true. In reality, although some type of chase is occurring, hot pursuit does not require an extended "hue and cry in and about the public streets."

Hot pursuit is another issue. In a **hot pursuit** officers are "hot on the tail" of a suspect and, because of the exigencies of the situation, are allowed to forcibly enter constitutionally protected areas, such as a home, without a warrant. Hot pursuit requires that (1) the officers have probable cause that the person committed a serious crime, (2) the arrest is set in motion in a public place, and (3) the pursuit is immediate and continuous. In *Warden v. Hayden* (1967), the Court held that police officers in hot pursuit of an armed robbery suspect but lacking a warrant "acted reasonably when they entered the house and began to search for a man of the description they had been given and for weapons which he had used in the robbery or might use against them. The Fourth Amendment does not require police officers to delay in the course of an investigation if to do so would gravely endanger their lives or the lives of others."

United States v. Santana (1976) established that a hot pursuit justifies forcible entry into an offender's home without a warrant. In this case, the police attempted to arrest the defendant in her doorway when she fled into her house and the police followed. The Court found, "We thus conclude that a suspect may not defeat an arrest that has been set in motion in a public place ... by the expedient of escaping to a private place."

In a ruling favoring police, the Supreme Court in *Scott v. Harris* (2007) ruled that police can put a fleeing motorist at risk of serious injury or death in an attempt to stop the motorist's flight from endangering the lives of innocent motorists and pedestrians. In this case Deputy Timothy Scott was involved in the pursuit of Victor Harris, clocked doing 73 miles per hour (mph) in a 55-mph zone and, when a county deputy activated his flashing lights to try to make a traffic stop, Harris sped off at greater than 85 mph down a two-lane road. Scott pursued and, after being authorized by his supervisor to "take him out," Scott applied his push bumper to the rear of Harris's vehicle, causing Harris to lose control, go off the road, overturn, and crash. The crash left Harris a quadriplegic. Harris filed an excessive force lawsuit under the Fourth Amendment. A videotape of the pursuit clearly contradicted Harris's version of the events and showed Harris forcing drivers off the road, running multiple red lights, and causing several police cars forced to engage in the same hazardous maneuvers to keep up. The Court noted, "What we see on the video more closely resembles a Hollywood-style car chase of the most frightening sort, placing police officers and innocent bystanders alike at great risk of injury." In deciding the case, the Court stated, "A police officer's attempt to terminate a dangerous high-speed car chase that threatens the lives of innocent bystanders does not violate the Fourth Amendment even when it places the fleeing motorist at risk of serious injury or death."

This victory for police clearly showed that two lower courts, which had not seen the video, were wrong to hold that a deputy sheriff who had rammed the suspect's car could be held liable for his actions. This case also illustrates the close relationship between pursuits and use-of-force incidents, which are both regulated by the Fourth Amendment's restrictions on seizures because *Scott* is technically a use-of-force case. Furthermore, it illustrates well the fact that force can be used not only to stop the escape of someone who is dangerous but also to capture someone who, because of the manner in which they are fleeing, poses a threat to innocent bystanders.

---

hot pursuit the period during which an individual is being immediately chased by law enforcement and, because of the exigencies of the situation, officers are allowed to forcibly enter constitutionally protected areas, such as a home, without a warrant

◀ CASE IN BRIEF

Scott v. Harris (2007)

ISSUE Can an officer take actions that place a fleeing motorist at risk of serious injury or death to stop the motorist's flight from endangering the lives of innocent bystanders?

RULING Yes. It is reasonable to use force, even deadly force, to stop a motorist who is driving so recklessly as to put innocent people in jeopardy. It comes down to whether the force is reasonable.

Use of Force

Among events that have startled the United States was the March 3, 1991, event bystander George Holliday happened to videotape and that was seen repeatedly by nearly everyone in this country: the aftermath of a 115-mph chase, in which 26-year-old Rodney King was seen being repeatedly subjected to baton blows by police. The question, as stated by *Time Magazine* in its cover story article on May 11, 1992, after the acquittal of the officers involved and ensuing riots across the country, was, "It seemed impossible that any jury could acquit the four officers who were accused of beating Rodney King. How could anyone discount the brutal vision of King being clubbed and kicked on videotape for 81 unforgettable seconds?"

The debate included accusations of racism and police brutality. It also questioned how much force the police are authorized to use. Legal authority permits reasonable use of force and consequences when that force becomes excessive. Although it has sometimes been the source of misunderstanding, debate, and even outrage, use of force is a component of the law that courts have sought to articulate and, when necessary, hold accountable for their actions those who go too far.

"No other enforcement task is more difficult or demanding personally and professionally than to use force only at the right time, in the right way and for the right reasons" (Means & Seidel, 2010, p. 18). Law enforcement recognizes and accepts five legitimate uses of force, often referred to as the "Rules of Engagement" (Cope & Callanan, 2009):

- Self-defense: a right common to all persons
- Defense of others: a duty assigned to police personnel
- Effectuate an arrest: a vested authority granted by law
- Prevent an escape: a vested authority granted by law
- Overcome resistance: a vested authority granted by law

Police brutality tarnishes the image and reputation of the majority of police personnel who do not engage in such unprofessional behavior. Many officers felt the repercussions of the King incident, as others did after the 1997 assault of Haitian immigrant Abner Louima by at least one New York City police officer. Louima was anally sodomized with a broken broomstick by the officer (three others were acquitted), who threatened to kill Louima if he told anyone.

Police know that what may appear to be excessive use of force is not always the case. At citizens' police academies around the nation, ordinary citizens who want a glimpse into what the law enforcement profession is all about experience firsthand how hard restraining and handcuffing someone who chooses to resist can be. Suspects on intoxicants or those dealing with mental issues sometimes are unaware of police efforts to subdue them, and what may appear brutal is actually a strategic and controlled escalation of the use of force continuum.

The widespread use of video recorders has resulted in police actions, both on the streets and in police stations, being closely scrutinized. People on both sides argue the images only tell part of the story. Emotions aside, at times reasonable force is necessary and authorized by our law. At other times, government agents must be held accountable for wrongdoing. Law enforcement personnel must understand and abide by the law they have sworn to uphold.

What Is Reasonable Force?

Just how much force is acceptable? The easy answer is that which is reasonable. "By law, the police have the authority to use force if necessary to make an arrest, keep the peace or maintain order" (Cole & Smith, 2010, p. 247). A more difficult question surrounds where *necessary* ends and *excessive* starts, and the issue can be divisive: "Research has shown that the greatest use of deadly force by the police is found in communities with high levels of economic inequality and large minority populations" (Cole & Smith, 2010, p. 247). People look to the law for unbiased responses.

Tennessee v. Garner (1985) set standards beyond the broad previous standard of any force to make the arrest. In this case, a 15-year-old boy was shot in the back of the head and killed as he began climbing over a fence after being told to stop by police responding to a prowler call. At the time, Tennessee and many other states had a law referred to as the *fleeing felon rule*, authorizing the use of deadly force to stop *any* fleeing felon. In *Garner*, however, the Supreme Court held, "Unless it is necessary to prevent the escape and the officer has probable cause to believe that the suspect poses a significant threat of death or serious physical injury to the officer or others," deadly force was no longer allowed. Because using deadly force is considered a seizure, *Garner* was the case that began the recognition that the Fourth Amendment should be applied to evaluate uses of force.

The Court provided further guidance in *Graham v. Connor* (1989). The facts of this case were that Dethorne Graham, who was diabetic and in need of orange juice to offset a diabetic reaction, had a friend drive him to a store. Because of the long line, Graham instead rushed back to the car to have his friend take him home. Officers who observed him thought his behavior suspicious and stopped them. In the ensuing interaction with police, during which the officers said he would not explain his behavior, Graham alleged he sustained multiple injuries at the hands of the police and sued.

The Court replaced the "substantive due process test" of whether the officer acted "in good faith" or "maliciously and sadistically" with a new test: "objective reasonableness." The Court held, "The calculus of reasonableness must embody allowance for the fact that police officers are often forced to make split-second judgments—in circumstances that are tense, uncertain and rapidly evolving—about the amount of force that is necessary in a particular situation." The reasonableness of force used must be judged "from the perspective of the officer on the scene rather than with the 20/20 vision of hindsight." This is the "lens" through which the courts will view the force incident and evaluate (1) the severity (dangerousness) of the crime at issue, (2) if there is an immediate threat to the officer or others, and (3) whether or not the suspect is actively resisting or attempting to evade arrest by flight—elements commonly referred to as the "*Graham* factors." The evaluation is done on a case-by-case basis, with the Court considering the specific facts and circumstances of each case. Ultimately, the *Connor* Court did not decide if excessive or reasonable force was used; it decided only on the issue of what the standard should be. The case was vacated and remanded back to the lower court for a decision on whether or not, based on reasonableness, the force was excessive.

The result of these cases is not that police cannot use force but that it must be reasonable under the circumstances. When making an arrest, officers may use that force necessary to gain control of the person: "In a regularly lengthening series of

CASE IN BRIEF
Tennessee v. Garner (1985)

ISSUE Can deadly force be used to apprehend a fleeing, nonviolent felon?

RULING No. Deadly force is not justified when the fleeing felon presents no immediate danger to the officer or to others. A police officer may not seize an unarmed, nondangerous felony suspect through the use of deadly force.

MYTH
The police must always be correct in their assessment of the situation when using force. If they are proven wrong or mistaken later, it will be deemed an excessive use of force.

FACT
Not true. Facts learned after the force incident cannot be used to show the force was excessive or that it was reasonable. One must always use only the facts that the officer had at the moment the force was used.

CASE IN BRIEF
Graham v. Connor (1989)

ISSUE What is the standard for liability in proving excessive force?

RULING The Fourth Amendment provides an explicit textual guarantee to be free from unreasonable searches and seizures. It provides the standard of *reasonableness* for evaluating the use of force (a seizure), deadly or not, against a free citizen.

LO8 *When making an arrest, police officers can use only as much force as is reasonable to overcome resistance and gain compliance. Excessive force may cause the officer to be sued.*

MYTH
Police have to use the least amount of force necessary to achieve their legal objective.

FACT
Not true. All that the law requires is that the officer use "reasonable" force.

decisions, federal courts have held that the Constitution does not require officers to use the least amount of force possible in a given situation. It requires only that the force used be 'reasonable'" (Means & Seidel, 2009, p. 31). The circumstances include when the officer believes deadly force is necessary to prevent the death or serious bodily injury to another.

It is important to note, too, that the force used by an officer must be *intentional* in order to fall under the Fourth Amendment's objective reasonableness test. For example, if an officer is chasing after a suspect and accidentally collides with a woman walking her dog, this is not a use of force situation. Contrast that with the situation where an officer twists the arm of a suspect behind her back to place handcuffs on her and, in doing so, breaks her wrist. This incident is intentional and will be evaluated under the Fourth Amendment.

For force to be deemed reasonable, the transaction underlying the need for force must be a lawful objective: "The cure for most 'force problems' is found in the Fourth Amendment classroom—studying the law of arrest and detention, search and seizure" (Means & Seidel, 2008, p. 27). Officers must know the "core" transaction and what lawful choices are available, because uncertainty about what the law allows regarding the seizing or searching of a suspect or the entrance to protected space leads to officer hesitance and can seriously jeopardize officer safety (Means & Seidel, 2008). Legal environments in which officers operate influence the use of force that is legally permissible:

- Voluntary contact—words of request, invitation, solicitation, cooperation, or just simple conversation—not a seizure; requires no justification. The officer's exact words and body language are critical. No force of any kind is permitted.
- Investigative detention—a limited seizure requiring reasonable suspicion that the individual is involved in criminal activity. If a suspect resists or flees, reasonable force may be used to obtain compliance, including use of restraints.
- Arrest—a seizure requiring probable cause. Allows the use of restraints as well as the involuntary movement of a suspect from one place to another.
- Defense of self or others—force can be used not only when making a seizure but also to protect the officer or another person. Level of force depends on circumstances and can include deadly force if reasonably required to prevent the death or serious bodily injury of the officer or another.

Police often respond to calls that appear routine but end up escalating into an arrest. Such calls may involve a person experiencing a mental health crisis or someone under the influence of drugs or alcohol. "Sometimes, a drastic series of events requires officers to make life-and-death decisions. And when a life is taken, the good ol' American way is to sue the police officers who were called to assist" (Scarry, 2008, p. 72). *Hastings v. Barnes* (2007) illustrates one such situation.

In this case, Todd Hastings called a social services agency saying he was having suicidal thoughts and asked for help. The two responding officers and a reserve officer were told Todd wasn't known to be armed, but when they arrived, Todd appeared nervous and agitated. He tried to slam the door shut and ran into a nearby bedroom. When the officer entered the home they saw Todd grab a Samurai sword with a 20-inch blade and a 21-inch handle. One officer yelled "knife" and all three drew their weapons. They ordered Todd several times to put the sword down. In the hopes of obtaining compliance with their order, one officer pepper-sprayed Todd, who, unfazed by the spray, turned the sword toward the officers and began moving in their direction. The officers, still in the doorway, attempted to retreat but couldn't because it was too crowded. Todd was shot four times and died at the scene.

Todd's brother, Clint Hastings, filed a civil rights lawsuit claiming the officers had violated Todd's Fourth Amendment right to be free from unreasonable searches and seizures and that the officers' unreasonable actions, which ran counter to their training, had escalated, instead of de-escalated, the situation involving a mentally ill person. The officers requested summary judgment, based on qualified immunity, saying their decision to shoot Todd was a measure of self-defense and, therefore, objectively reasonable under the Fourth Amendment. A three-judge panel denied summary judgment, saying:

> Our review of the record convinces us that whether [the officers'] actions unreasonably precipitated their need to use deadly force calls for a jury determination. But viewing the facts in the light most favorable to Hastings, a constitutional violation occurred. Todd was not a criminal suspect. He was a potentially mentally ill/emotionally disturbed individual who was contemplating suicide and had called for help. Rather than attempt to help Todd, [the officers] crowded themselves into Todd's doorway (leaving no room for retreat), issued loud and forceful commands at him and pepper-sprayed him, causing him to become even more distressed. At the time they pepper-sprayed him, Todd was not verbally or physically threatening them. . . . Although Todd had a sword, his stance, at least up until the time he was pepper-sprayed, was defensive, not aggressive, posing no threat to anyone but himself. A reasonable jury could find that under these facts [the officers'] actions unreasonably escalated the situation to the point deadly force was required.

In reaching this decision, the court had relied on the officers' training to establish the unlawfulness of their actions, noting that such training called for officers responding to mentally ill or emotionally disturbed individuals to be calm; attempt to establish a line of communication; not irritate them; not move suddenly, give rapid orders, or shout at them; not enter their comfort or critical zones or crowd them; and not touch them unless necessary.

Officers should be trained in all aspects of use of force, including the law, weapons use, and when different degrees of force are appropriate. Force continuums, such as the one shown in Figure 8.1, provide graphic representation of the gradations of force police officers are trained to use. From the mere presence of an officer to control a situation, to the use of verbal commands, hands, aerosol weapons, batons, or electrical weapons, to the use of deadly force, the police have options available, and all are appropriate to implement when reasonable.

It is important for an officer to understand that he or she may, depending on the facts of the situation, start at any point in the continuum and move up or down within seconds, not necessarily moving through every option.

Ongoing debate exists regarding the effectiveness of force continuums, and many departments are presently moving away from their use. Although such continuums are beneficial in that they provide to those unfamiliar with use-of-force

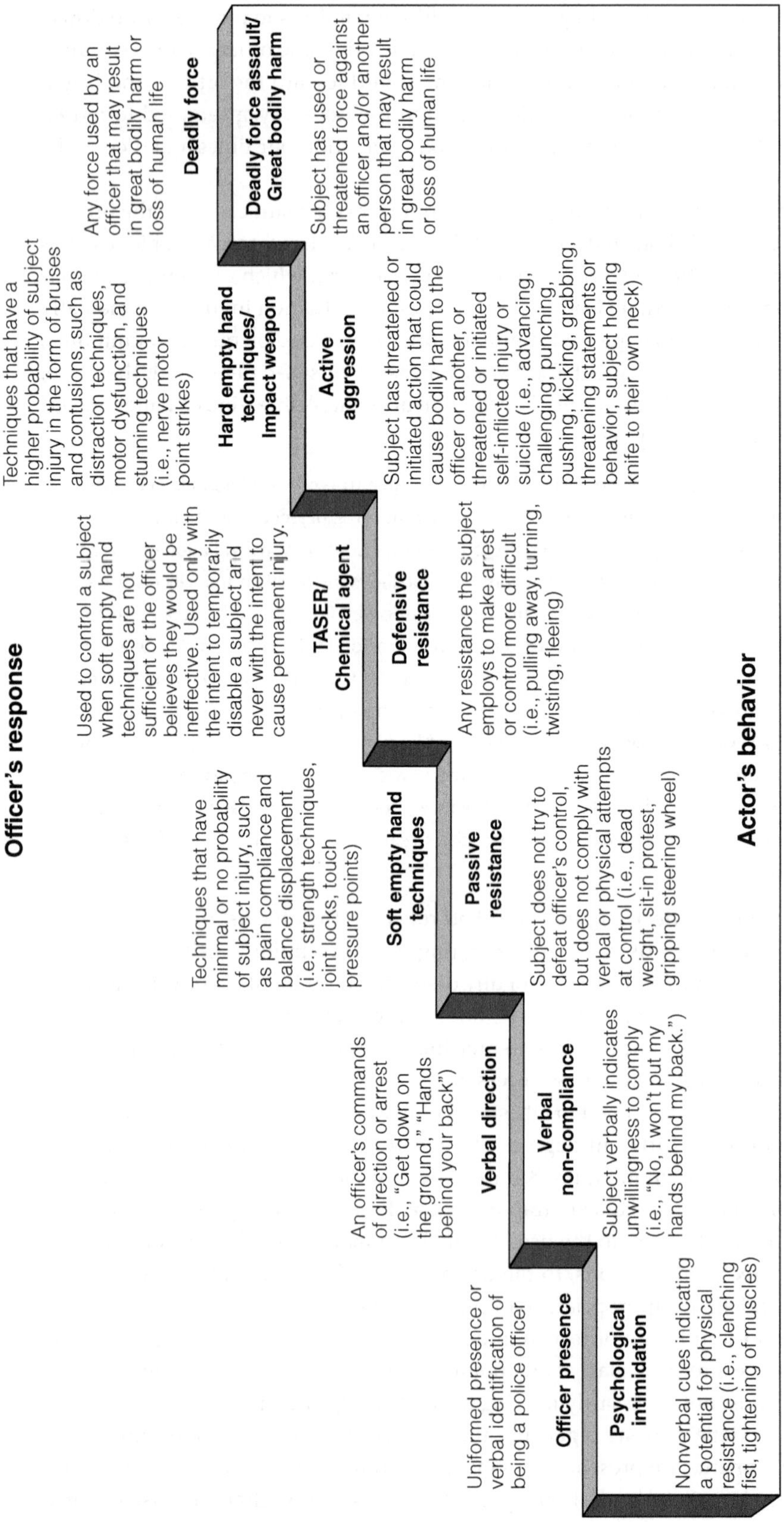

274 Section III The Fourth Amendment: Governing Constitutional Searches and Seizures

Officer's response

Deadly force

Deadly force assault/Great bodily harm

Any force used by an officer that may result in great bodily harm or loss of human life

Subject has used or threatened force against an officer and/or another person that may result in great bodily harm or loss of human life

Hard empty hand techniques/Impact weapon

Active aggression

Techniques that have a higher probability of subject injury in the form of bruises and contusions, such as distraction techniques, motor dysfunction, and stunning techniques (i.e., nerve motor point strikes)

Subject has threatened or initiated action that could cause bodily harm to the officer or another, or threatened or initiated self-inflicted injury or suicide (i.e., advancing, challenging, punching, pushing, kicking, grabbing, threatening statements or behavior, subject holding knife to their own neck)

TASER/Chemical agent

Defensive resistance

Used to control a subject when soft empty hand techniques are not sufficient or the officer believes they would be ineffective. Used only with the intent to temporarily disable a subject and never with the intent to cause permanent injury.

Any resistance the subject employs to make arrest or control more difficult (i.e., pulling away, turning, twisting, fleeing)

Soft empty hand techniques

Passive resistance

Techniques that have minimal or no probability of subject injury, such as pain compliance and balance displacement (i.e., strength techniques, joint locks, touch pressure points)

Subject does not try to defeat officer's control, but does not comply with verbal or physical attempts at control (i.e., dead weight, sit-in protest, gripping steering wheel)

Verbal direction

Verbal non-compliance

An officer's commands of direction or arrest (i.e., "Get down on the ground," "Hands behind your back")

Subject verbally indicates unwillingness to comply (i.e., "No, I won't put my hands behind my back.")

Officer presence

Psychological intimidation

Uniformed presence or verbal identification of being a police officer

Nonverbal cues indicating a potential for physical resistance (i.e., clenching fist, tightening of muscles)

Actor's behavior

NOTE: Subject may enter the continuum at any level. Officer may enter at any level that represents a reasonable response to the perceived threat posed by the subject.

Figure 8.1 Use of Force Continuum

Source: Owatonna (Minnesota) Police Department Use of Force Report

issues a visual representation of escalating and de-escalating events, a hierarchy of force, and the relationships between response levels, they can be (and often are) distorted by plaintiffs in court cases and do not reflect objective reasonableness accurately, particularly the totality of the circumstances. Furthermore, they may lead an officer to believe, incorrectly, that a step-by-step progression is required when, in many cases, events unfold so rapidly (either escalating or de-escalating) that a reasonable force response may require skipping steps along the hierarchy.

De-escalation of force is something all officers should be aware of and which many departments are placing new emphasis on in training. Use-of-force situations are fluid, and the amount of force that is considered reasonable will likely change throughout an encounter. Officers must know how to ratchet down the force response just as effectively as moving up the level of force applied. For example, an officer may be reasonable in using a Taser to place a much larger, combative individual under arrest. However, the use of the Taser may not be reasonable later in the encounter, for example, if the suspect begins to cooperate and the threat decreases.

The Supreme Court has never categorically banned any specific tactic, weapon, technique, or equipment. The closest it has come was in *City of Los Angeles v. Lyons* (1983), which involved the so-called chokehold. Plaintiffs sought an injunction to prohibit its use, alleging unconstitutional excessive force. Federal and appellate courts granted the injunction, ruling the tactic as "unreasonable" when neither death nor serious injury was threatened. By the time the case got to the Supreme Court, the Los Angeles Police Department (LAPD) had modified its policies. The Court reversed the findings of the lower courts, saying there now was no need to consider the matter because use of the challenged tactic was not likely to be repeated. In other words, the case was *moot*.

Use of Less-Lethal Force

The proliferation and use of less-lethal weapons in law enforcement has skyrocketed in the past decade. Weapons as simple as OC sprays and as advanced as electronic muscular disruption devices have rapidly become mainstays in law enforcement arsenals.

A survey by the Police Executive Research Forum (PERF) and the University of South Carolina found that arm-locks and other "empty-hand tactics" are still the most common use of force but have declined significantly (PERF, 2009). Six general categories of less-lethal weapons currently in use are physical restraints (nets, glue), light, acoustics, chemicals (OC or pepper spray), impact projectiles, and electric sources (conducted energy devices [CEDs] or electronic control devices [ECDs]), the TASER® being the most commonly used weapon in this category. A study by PoliceOne asked readers to complete the following sentence: "The last time you deployed a less-lethal weapon, it was a. . . ." Fifty-eight percent responded TASER, followed by OC (28 percent), baton (9 percent), 40 mm (3 percent), and beanbag (2 percent) (Hawkes, 2010).

Scoville (2008, p. 35) cautions, "When a cop uses, or doesn't use, a less-lethal weapon in contemporary America, there can be hell to pay. . . . Perhaps nowhere in contemporary American society does the question of the right tool for the right job come into play more often than in matters of police use of force." In considering less-lethal options, one point is clear: "We always say, 'Never bring a beanbag to a gunfight.' If the suspect has a firearm, in most situations I would think less-lethal weapons are not appropriate" (Basich, 2010, p. 51).

The wide range of less-lethal options and when each might be appropriate are beyond the scope of this text. Only the use of TASER is briefly discussed because debate over its use has found its way into a lower court.

The Use of TASERs

The controversy surrounding the safety of conductive energy devices (CEDs) is also beyond the scope of this text, but the weight of evidence shows clearly that such devices rarely cause death and have probably saved countless lives when a firearm was not needed to achieve the desired results. In a study of risk of injury from five major force options, use of conducted energy weapons (CEW) scored highly on safety for both suspects and officers. The TASER X26 (the most recent model) was the most frequently deployed of the five options against nearly half (48.2 percent) of resistant arrestees. About 1 percent ended up hospitalized, about 12 percent needed minor outpatient treatment, and 42 percent had only minor injuries. There were no fatalities (Force Science Research Center, 2008). Since then numerous other studies have supported the safety of such devices.

In 2009, a lower court ruled for the first time on the constitutionality of the use of TASERs, causing a national stir. In *Bryan v. McPherson* (2009), the 9th Circuit Court of Appeals acknowledged the value in having a tool such as the TASER, saying, "We recognize the important role controlled electric devices like the Taser X26 can play in law enforcement. The ability to defuse a dangerous situation from a distance can obviate the need for more severe, or even deadly, force and thus can help protect police officers, by-standers, and suspects alike. We hold only that the X26 and similar devices constitute an intermediate, significant level of force that must be justified by 'a strong government interest [that] *compels* the employment of such force.'"

Consider, from the official court transcript, the following factual and procedural background:

> Carl Bryan's California Sunday was off to a bad start. The twenty-one-year old, having stayed the night with his younger brother and some cousins in Camarillo, which is in Ventura County, planned to drive his brother back to his parents' home in Coronado, which is in San Diego County. However, Bryan's cousin's girlfriend had accidently taken Bryan's keys to Los Angeles the previous day. Wearing the T-shirt and boxer shorts in which he had slept, Bryan rose early, traveled east with his cousins to Los Angeles, picked up his keys and returned to Camarillo to get his car and brother. He then began driving south towards his parents' home. While traveling on the 405 highway, Bryan and his brother were stopped by a California Highway Patrolman who issued Bryan a speeding ticket. This upset him greatly. He began crying and moping, ultimately removing his T-shirt to wipe his face. Continuing south without further incident, the two finally crossed the Coronado Bridge at about seven-thirty in the morning.
>
> At that point, an already bad morning for Bryan took a turn for the worse. Bryan was stopped at an intersection when Officer McPherson, who was stationed there to enforce seatbelt regulations, stepped in front of his car and signaled to Bryan that he

was not to proceed. Bryan immediately realized that he had mistakenly failed to buckle his seatbelt after his earlier encounter with the police. Officer McPherson approached the passenger window and asked Bryan whether he knew why he had been stopped. Bryan, knowing full well why and becoming increasingly angry at himself, simply stared straight ahead. Officer McPherson requested that Bryan turn down his radio and pull over to the curb. Bryan complied with both requests, but as he pulled his car to the curb, angry with himself over the prospects of another citation, he hit his steering wheel and yelled expletives to himself. Having pulled his car over and placed it in park, Bryan stepped out of his car.

There is no dispute that Bryan was agitated, standing outside his car, yelling gibberish and hitting his thighs, clad only in his boxer shorts and tennis shoes. It is also undisputed that Bryan did not verbally threaten Officer McPherson and, according to Officer McPherson, was standing twenty to twenty-five feet away and not attempting to flee. Officer McPherson testified that he told Bryan to remain in the car, while Bryan testified that he did not hear Officer McPherson tell him to do so. The one material dispute concerns whether Bryan made any movement toward the officer. Officer McPherson testified that Bryan took "one step" toward him, but Bryan says he did not take any step, and the physical evidence indicates that Bryan was actually facing away from Officer McPherson. Without giving any warning, Officer McPherson shot Bryan with his taser gun. One of the taser probes embedded in the side of Bryan's upper left arm. The electrical current immobilized him whereupon he fell face first into the ground, fracturing four teeth and suffering facial contusions. Bryan's morning ended with his arrest and yet another drive—this time by ambulance and to a hospital for treatment.

One of the ECD probes in Bryan's arm required surgical removal in the emergency room. Brave and O'Linn (2010, p. 12) note, "The case was decided based on a motion for summary judgment, thus the court was required to use a 'perceptual lens' that presumes that the plaintiff's facts are true." Applying the standards set forth in *Graham v. Connor*, the court found that the officer's use of the Taser under the given circumstances was not a reasonable use of force because Bryan neither posed an immediate threat to the safety of the officer, himself or others, nor attempted to evade or resist at the time the ECD was deployed. Additional circumstances of the case included the facts that Bryan was stopped for a seat belt violation and was not a dangerous felon or considered a flight risk; he was standing 15 to 25 feet away from the officer and was not advancing on McPherson. The court concluded that Bryan was, at most, a disturbed and upset young man, not an immediately threatening one, and that the officer should have considered less-intrusive alternatives and tactics for effecting the arrest, such as waiting for approaching backup (Brave & O'Linn, 2010). As Means and McDonald (2010, p. 55) note, "This case is only controlling law in the Ninth Circuit. However, it provides judicial guidance on law enforcement's use of electronic control devices, particularly in the context of excessive force allegations."

Recently, the 4th Circuit Court of Appeals made a decision that will impact law enforcement officers' use of a CED in that circuit. *Armstrong v. Village of Pinehurst* (2016) is a case that involved Ronald Armstrong, a very large man who had run from a hospital where he was being treated for paranoid schizophrenia and bipolar disorder. His sister brought him to the hospital because he had not taken his medication for five days and had been poking holes in his skin "to let the air out."

Officers located Armstrong walking in traffic and talked him out of the road. At that point, he began to eat grass and dandelions and put cigarettes out on his tongue.

The officers soon learned Armstrong had an involuntary commitment order signed by a doctor authorizing them to take him into custody. Importantly, the order noted that Armstrong was only a danger to himself. As officers approached with two hospital security guards, Armstrong wrapped his body around a signpost. In an effort to dislodge Armstrong, one officer applied his Taser in "drive stun" mode, which is used as pain compliance technique, and viewed as a lesser use of force than a Taser in "dart mode." It took five applications of the Taser before the officers and security guards could get Armstrong off the post and secure him. He had to be handcuffed and his legs shackled because he was kicking at the officers. After the scuffle, Armstrong was discovered to have stopped breathing and he later died at the hospital. It is unclear what caused the death.

Looking at the *Graham* factors, the 4th Circuit stated, "The government's interest in seizing Armstrong was to prevent a mentally ill man from harming himself. The justification for the seizure, therefore, does not vindicate any degree of force that risks substantial harm to the subject." The court went on to declare, "Where, during the course of seizing an out-numbered mentally ill individual who is a danger only to himself, police officers choose to deploy a taser in the face of stationary and non-violent resistance to being handcuffed, those officers use unreasonably excessive force. While qualified immunity shields the officers in this case from liability, law enforcement officers should now be on notice that such taser use violates the Fourth Amendment." Thus, through this ruling, it is now unreasonable force in the 4th Circuit to use a Taser as a pain compliance tool ("drive stun" mode) against a subject only resisting through non-violence, unless the officer can show that an immediate danger is present.

There is a dissenting opinion in this case. Although the judge agreed with the majority's grant of qualified immunity to the officers, the judge was critical of the fact that the majority "launches into an extended discussion on the merits of an excessive force claim." The judge believed that the majority went too far in analyzing the case when they didn't need to, and went against *Graham* by not allowing for the tense, rapidly evolving situation the officers faced. The dissenting judge wrote:

> My fine colleagues in the majority have done as good a job as can be expected given the circumstances. But the very exemplary quality of the effort serves to illustrate the perils of the enterprise. The majority notes "that different seizures present different risks of danger," but fails to recognize that the spectrum of risk presented cannot be easily sketched by an appellate court. It is hard to disagree with the majority's highly generalized assertion that Taser use is unwarranted "where an unrestrained arrestee, though resistant, presents no serious safety threat." But of course, what conduct qualifies as "resistant," and what rises to the level of a "serious safety threat" is once again dependent on the actual and infinitely variable facts and circumstances that confront officers on their beat.

Use of Deadly Force

Use of deadly force is restricted to cases of self-defense or to save the life of another. Deadly force is "that force which a reasonable person would consider likely to cause death or serious bodily harm. Its use may be justified only under conditions of extreme necessity, when all lesser means have failed or cannot reasonably be employed" (10 C.F.R. § 1047.7). As discussed, the "fleeing felon" rule that allowed police officers to shoot any felon attempting an escape is no longer permissible (*Tennessee v. Garner*, 1985):

> The use of deadly force to prevent the escape of all felony suspects, whatever the circumstances, is constitutionally unreasonable. It is not better that all felony suspects die than that they escape. Where the suspect poses no immediate threat to the officer and no threat to others, the harm resulting from failing to apprehend him does not justify the use of deadly force to do so.

LO9 *The only justification for use of deadly force is self-defense or protecting the lives of others.*

As Justice Bryon White set forth, even deadly force can be exercised in preventing the escape (i.e., "arresting") of an individual but "only if the officer has probable cause to believe that the suspect poses a significant threat of death or serious physical injury to the officer or others." Thus, no longer can one be shot with justification merely because he or she is a fleeing felon.

It is critical to understand that in any use of force situation, deadly or not, the general principle is that the more intrusive the seizure (the higher level of force), the stronger the government interest should be (why the force is being applied). This makes sense because "deadly force is unmatched"; there must be a strong interest at stake to use it.

Garner is important for several reasons. To start, it was the first case to use the Fourth Amendment as the standard for a force situation, emphasizing that deadly force is a seizure under the Constitution. Second, the Court recognized that in order to use deadly force when a suspect is fleeing an officer, facts must exist that rise to the level of probable cause in order to believe that the suspect poses a "significant threat of death or serious physical injury to the officer or others." Standing alone, the fact that a felon is fleeing the officer does not authorize deadly force. Additionally, when probable cause exists to believe that a person has committed a crime threatening or inflicting serious physical harm, deadly force may be used to prevent the escape of that person. The Court also added the importance of the officer warning a person that deadly force is about to be used. However, there is one caveat to this: It must be "feasible" for the officer to do so. Officers have to make split-second decisions, and mandating a warning be given in every situation is not a practical expectation.

For many years, courts interpreted *Garner* as setting the standard for deadly force. In reality, though, deadly force is just a type of force. It is subject to the same standard as lesser forms of force. In short, deadly force is evaluated under the rule set forth in *Graham v. Connor*.

Recall the case of *Scott v. Harris* (2007) presented earlier in the chapter in which Harris, fleeing from police at very high speeds, was left paralyzed after crashing his car because of a push maneuver Deputy Scott had applied to Harris's vehicle. Harris sued Scott for excessive force, claiming deadly force was unreasonable in that situation. In a shift from lower court interpretation of the law surrounding deadly force, the Supreme Court stated the issue was not whether the actions of the officer put a person at risk of serious harm or death, but whether or not the force was reasonable. In explaining this further, the Court pointed out that the decision in *Garner* was an application of the reasonableness test. Writing for the majority, Justice Antonin Scalia stated that *Garner* did not establish a "magical on/off switch that triggers rigid preconditions whenever an officer's actions constitute 'deadly force.'" Ultimately, like any other use of force evaluation, force must be reasonable. "[I]n the end we must still slosh our way through the factbound morass of 'reasonableness.'" In every use of force encounter, facts are what determine reasonableness.

Putting It All Together

Before leaving the discussion of use of force, it is important for students to understand how a person's status (e.g., "free," pre-trial, or convicted and incarcerated) dictates how courts will evaluate the force used against them and what test will be applied, as shown in Table 8.2.

Evaluating force used on a pre-trial detainee is done under the Fifth Amendment Due Process Clause for federal officials or the Fourteenth Amendment's Due Process Clause for state and local officials. A pre-trial detainee is a person who is in custody, such as in jail awaiting trial, and has not yet been convicted or sentenced to punishment. In *Kingsley v. Hendrickson* (2015), the Supreme Court was asked if, in order to prove excessive, a plaintiff must show only that the force was deliberate and objectively unreasonable. The Court held that yes, in order to prove excessive force in a pre-trial circumstance, "a pretrial detainee must show only that the force purposely or knowingly used against him was objectively unreasonable."

Constitutional Law in ACTION

Trooper Williams was part of a DWI enforcement detail. He was transporting an arrestee to face a judge for charging. As the trooper approached the courtroom, the doors suddenly burst open and an unarmed detention officer ran out, yelling, "He's got a gun! He's got a gun!" Trooper Williams immediately pulled his gun as the detention officer ran past.

Following on the heels of the detention officer came Anderson. The trooper saw Anderson running full speed at him with his hands clasped together. Anderson was about 20 feet from the trooper and closing fast. Unknown to Trooper Williams, Anderson was another arrestee detained as part of the DWI enforcement and was in handcuffs. Believing Anderson had a gun, Trooper Williams fired his weapon and hit Anderson several times, causing serious injuries.

Additional troopers arrived and entered the courtroom and subdued a second person. It was quickly determined that Anderson was not the man with the gun that the detention officer was running from. The man from whom the detention officer was running was, instead, the second man still inside the courtroom.

- *Using the Graham factors, was Trooper Williams' use of force reasonable? What facts are important in making this determination?*
- *Is it relevant that Anderson turned out not to be the man with the gun?*
- *Does it matter that shooting a gun at another is considered deadly force?*

Table 8.2 Use of Force Standards

Status of the person receiving the force		Test used by the court and the origin of the test	Use of force: what the plaintiff must show to establish a constitutional violation

Free	*Not Seized* under the Fourth Amendment	Shocks the conscience
		■ Due Process Clause
		    □ Fourteenth Amendment for state and local officers
		    □ Fifth Amendment for federal officers
			Outrageous conduct intended to injure and not related to a government interest, such as arrest, that can be said to *shock the contemporary conscience.*

	Seized under the Fourth Amendment	Objective reasonableness ■ Fourth Amendment	The force knowingly or purposely used was *objectively unreasonable* in light of the totality of the circumstances, including whether the suspect was an immediate threat, if the suspect was actively resisting or evading arrest, and the dangerousness of the crime.

Pre-Trial Detainee		Objective reasonableness
		■ Due Process Clause
		    □ Fourteenth Amendment for state and local officers
		    □ Fifth Amendment for federal officers
			The force knowingly or purposely used was *objectively unreasonable* from the perspective of a reasonable officer on the scene.

Convicted, Sentenced, Incarcerated		Cruel and unusual punishment ■ Eighth Amendment	Malicious and sadistic force used only to cause harm rather than a good faith effort to maintain or restore order.

The Court has not, to date, ruled if the Fourth Amendment applies to use-of-force situations in the pre-trial detainee setting.

Citizen's Arrest

Not all arrests are made by government agents. Common law has held that anyone witnessing certain crimes may make a **citizen's arrest** and then turn that individual over to the authorities. Most states now address this by statute. Although use of force is often not addressed in these statutes, anyone may lawfully use reasonable force to repel an assault, including when making a citizen's arrest. The law of citizen's arrest is what private security officers use. Because of this law, the Fourth Amendment, or any constitutional restraints for that matter, do not bind them.

citizen's arrest the detention by a nongovernment agent of one accused of an illegal act

Any private citizen making a citizen's arrest, however, will be liable if the arresting citizen violates any civil or criminal laws when so doing or does not follow the requirements of the applicable code pertaining to citizen's arrest. Problems that arise in this area include excessive force by individuals making a citizen's arrest, which has been the case in a number of incidents with, for example, bar bouncers who excessively detain someone who has been placed under a citizen's arrest. Most state statutes do not specify whether a private person making an arrest can use force and whether such a person can call for assistance from others, as the police can.

Most statutes state that the arrestee must be *immediately* turned over to law enforcement. In some cases, a suspect has sued the arresting party for offenses that include false imprisonment and assault. A person who makes a citizen's arrest must use caution, for his or her own safety and to carry out the arrest without committing a crime or becoming open to civil liability. This type of situation is why an increasing number of states are licensing private security personnel and mandating training, and most professional security operations have extensive training to avoid such problems.

Constitutional Law in ACTION

Mack and his former girlfriend, Angie, went to the casino together. After spending some time gambling, the two went to the bar and began to talk. Mack explained how he wanted to get back together, but Angie told him she just wanted to remain friends. The two began to argue and she got up to return to the casino alone.

Mack followed her and tried to continue the discussion. Angie repeatedly told him to leave her alone—to the point where other patrons and employees began to notice their interaction. Finally, security approached Mack and told him he needed to leave.

Mack began walking out with security behind him. At the entrance he stopped, turned around, and tried to come back inside. The security guards again told him to leave, adding that now he was trespassing and was not allowed to come back for two weeks.

One hour later, Mack returned looking for Angie. The security guards told him that he was under arrest for trespassing and phoned the police to come get Mack. The guards took Mack by the arm and attempted to handcuff him while they waited for the police. Mack pushed one guard in the chest and then balled his hands into fists, taking a boxer's stance. Another security guard tackled Mack and then handcuffed him.

As a result of the tackle, Mack hurt his shoulder. He sued the security guards for battery. The guards defended their actions under a state statute that allows a private person to make a citizen's arrest when a person commits a crime in their presence, and to do so using reasonable force.

- *What facts are important to determine if the guards used reasonable force as allowed by the statute?*

- *Should the guards be held liable for the injury to Mack's shoulder? Why or why not?*

- *Would your opinion change if, instead of just tackling Mack, the security guards punched and kicked him while Mack was on the ground?*

Immunity from Arrest

Certain classifications of people have immunity from arrest because of federal or state statutes. Many states have granted their legislators immunity from civil lawsuits. Some states even give legislators immunity from traffic arrests on their way to sessions, as is the case with federal legislators as well. However, a legislator facing criminal charges has no such immunity.

When a witness is subpoenaed to testify in another state, that person will not be subject to arrest for a crime committed in that state before his entrance into that state to testify (but is not immune for arrest for a crime committed while in the state to testify). Such witnesses are also granted a reasonable time to leave the state after testifying without being subject to arrest. Both forms of immunity discussed are matters of public policy, so as not to interfere with the legal process.

LO10 *Foreign diplomats, including ambassadors, ministers, their assistants and attachés, and their families and servants, have complete immunity from arrest. Foreign consuls and their deputies as well as some legislators and out-of-state witnesses may also have limited immunity.*

Summary

The elements of a seizure are (1) intending to seize an object (including a person), (2) exercising authority to do so, (3) physically controlling the object, and (4) the understanding of what is happening such that a reasonable person would not feel free to leave. A seizure need not necessarily be an arrest, but all arrests are seizures.

The *Terry* case established that the authority to stop and frisk is independent of the power to arrest. A stop is not an arrest, but it *is* a seizure within the meaning of the Fourth Amendment and, therefore, requires reasonableness. How long a stop may last depends on factors that indicate the suspect was not detained an unreasonably long time, including the purpose of the stop and the time and means the investigation required. Extending the stop after the time reasonably needed to deal with the initial violation is unconstitutional.

Officers may stop motorists for violations of the law, which may include equipment violations, erratic driving, or invalid vehicle registration, as well as when an occupant inside the vehicle is suspected of having committed a crime. Because a traffic stop is brief and occurs in public, it is not considered an arrest, thus *Miranda* warnings need not be given.

To arrest is to deprive a person of liberty by legal authority, taking the person into custody for the purpose of holding him or her to answer a criminal charge. Police may, without a warrant, make a lawful arrest for any crime committed in their presence. Police may, without a warrant, make a lawful arrest for an unwitnessed felony based on probable cause. Police may make a warrantless arrest based on probable cause in a public place or in a private place that a suspect has retreated to from a public place. Police may not make a nonconsensual, warrantless entry into a home to make a felony arrest of that person or of a guest in the home unless exigent circumstances exist.

When making an arrest, police officers can use only as much force as is reasonable to overcome resistance and gain compliance. Excessive force may cause the officer to be sued. The only justification for use of deadly force is self-defense or protecting the lives of others.

Foreign diplomats, including ambassadors, ministers, their assistants and attachés, and their families and servants, have complete immunity from arrest. Foreign consuls and their deputies as well as some legislators and out-of-state witnesses may also have limited immunity.

Discussion Questions

1. Explain what factors are important in determining whether a person is considered "arrested."
2. Identify the difference between a stop and an arrest.
3. Why might states authorize probable cause arrests for certain unwitnessed misdemeanors?
4. How much force can be used by an officer when executing an arrest? How is it determined?
5. When determining whether a stop or an arrest is lawful, how is the term *reasonable* determined? And do the subject's subjective feelings enter the analysis of determining reasonableness?
6. How does the entertainment industry portray arrest situations? Do you think this portrayal is generally realistic?
7. Do you know anyone who has been arrested? If so, what did they have to say about it?
8. Should anyone be immune from arrest, for example, foreign diplomats?
9. Should police officers who are doing their best to enforce the law ever be punished in any way if they are acting in "good faith"?
10. Under what circumstances is someone other than a law enforcement official authorized to make an arrest?

References

Basich, M. (2010, March). "Not Going for the Kill." *Police*, pp. 44–51.

Brave, M., & O'Linn, M. K. (2010, February). "*Bryan v. McPherson*—A New Standard for the Use of Electronic Control Devices?" *The Police Chief*, pp. 12–13.

Cole, G. F., & Smith, C. E. (2010). *The American System of Criminal Justice*, 12th ed. Belmont, CA: Wadsworth/Cengage Learning.

Collins, J. M. (2008, February). "Community Caretaking Doctrine." *The Police Chief*, pp. 10–11.

Cope, C. J., & Callanan, J. (2009, June 13). "Understanding the Objectively Reasonable Standard 'Overcoming Resistance' (Part One)." *LawOfficer.com*. Retrieved July 26, 2016 from http://lawofficer.com/2009/06/understanding-the-objectively-reasonable-standard-overcome-resistance-part-one/

Force Science Research Center. (2008, July 18). "New Study Ranks Risks of Injury from 5 Major Force Options." *Force Science News*, #102.

Hawkes, A. (2010, February 16). "Keeping Your Less Lethal Options Open." *PoliceOne.com News*. Retrieved July 26, 2016 from https://www.policeone.com/less-lethal/articles/2001750-Keeping-your-less-lethal-options-open/

Herbert, B. (2010, March 2). "Watching Certain People." *The New York Times*. Retrieved July 26, 2016 from www.nytimes.com/2010/03/02/opinion/02herbert.html?_r=0

Long, C. (2009, October 9). "Police 'Stop-and-Frisk' Technique Drawing Criticism." *PoliceOne.com News*. Retrieved July 25, 2016 from https://www.policeone.com/patrol-issues/articles/1952830-Police-stop-and-frisk-technique-drawing-criticism/

Means, R., & McDonald, P. (2009, November). "How Long Is Too Long during a *Terry* Stop?" *Law and Order*, pp. 22–24.

Means, R., & McDonald, P. (2010, April). "TASER and the 9th Circuit Decision." *Law and Order*, pp. 52–56.

Means, R., & Seidel, G. (2008, December). "Assessing Legal Validity of the Core Transaction." *Law and Order*, pp. 24–27.

Means, R., & Seidel, G. (2009, February). "Maintaining Proportionality and Managing Force Escalations." *Law and Order*, pp. 31–32.

Means, R., & Seidel, G. (2010, March–April). "Keys to Winning with Use of Force: A Four-Step Plan." *Tactical Response*, pp. 18–20.

Police Executive Research Forum. (2009, December). "Survey by PERF and University of South Carolina Shows Rapid Increase in CED Employments." *Subject to Debate*, pp. 1, 6. Retrieved July 26, 2016 from http://www.policeforum.org/assets/docs/Subject_to_Debate/Debate2009/debate_2009_dec.pdf

Rivera, R., & Baker, A. (2010, July 16). "Police Cite Help from Stop-and-Frisk Data in 170 Cases." *The New York Times*. Retrieved July 26, 2016 from www.nytimes.com/2010/07/17/nyregion/17frisk.html?_r=1&pagewanted=print

Rutledge, D. (2009, April). "Updating Weapons Frisks." *Police*, pp. 66–69.

Rutledge, D. (2010, January). "Beware of False Headlines." *Police*, pp. 64–67.

Scarry, L. (2008, January). "Escalating Events May Violate Fourth Amendment." *Law Officer Magazine*, pp. 72–75.

Scarry, L. (2009, May). "Less than Probable Cause: Protective Actions in *Terry* Stops." *Law Officer Magazine*, pp. 26–29.

Scoville, D. (2008, December). "Damned If You Do, Dammed If You Don't." *Police*, pp. 34–41.

Cases Cited

Adams v. Williams, 407 U.S. 143 (1972)
Alabama v. White, 496 U.S. 325 (1990)
Arizona v. Johnson, 555 U.S. 323 (2009)
Armstrong v. Village of Pinehurst (2016)
Atwater v. City of Lago Vista, 532 U.S. 318 (2001)
Baker v. McCollan, 443 U.S. 137 (1979)
Berkemer v. McCarty, 468 U.S. 420 (1984)
Brendlin v. California, 551 U.S. 249 (2007)
Brower v. County of Inyo, 489 U.S. 593 (1989)
Brown v. Texas, 443 U.S. 47 (1979)
Bryan v. McPherson, Case No. 08-55622 (9th Cir. [CA] 2009)
California v. Hodari D., 499 U.S. 621 (1991)
City of Indianapolis v. Edmond, 531 U.S. 32 (2000)
City of Los Angeles v. Lyons, 461 U.S. 95 (1983)
Cupp v. Murphy, 412 U.S. 291 (1973)
Delaware v. Prouse, 440 U.S. 648 (1979)
Dunaway v. New York, 442 U.S. 200 (1979)
Florida v. J.L., 529 U.S. 266 (2000)
Florida v. Royer, 460 U.S. 491 (1983)
Graham v. Connor, 490 U.S. 386 (1989)
Harris v. Commonwealth, No. 2320-06-2, 2008 WL 301334 (February 5, 2008)

Hastings v. Barnes, No. 04-5144, 2007 U.S. App. Lexis 24446 (10th Cir. 2007)
Heien v. North Carolina, 574 U.S. ___ (2014)
Illinois v. Cabellas, 543 U.S. 405 (2005)
Illinois v. Lidster, 540 U.S. 419 (2004)
Illinois v. Wardlow, 528 U.S. 119 (2000)
Kaupp v. Texas, 538 U.S. 626 (2003)
Kingsley v. Hendrickson, 135 S.Ct.1039 (2015)
Maryland v. Wilson, 519 U.S. 408 (1997)
Mendenhall v. United States, 446 U.S. 544 (1980)
Michigan v. Chesternut, 486 U.S. 567 (1988)
Michigan v. Long, 463 U.S. 1032 (1983)
Michigan Department of State Police v. Sitz, 496 U.S. 444 (1990)
Navarette v. California, 572 U.S. ___ (2014)
Payton v. New York, 445 U.S. 573 (1980)
Pennsylvania v. Mimms, 434 U.S. 106 (1977)
Rodriguez v. United States, 575 U.S. ___ (2015)
Scott v. Harris, 550 U.S. 372 (2007)
State v. Pluth, 157 Minn. 145, 195 N.W. 789 (1923)
Steagald v. United States, 451 U.S. 204 (1981)
Tennessee v. Garner, 471 U.S. 1 (1985)
Terry v. Ohio, 392 U.S. 1 (1968)
United States v. Brignoni-Ponce, 422 U.S. 873 (1975)
United States v. Cortez, 449 U.S. 411 (1981)
United States v. Flores-Montano, 541 U.S. 149 (2004)
United States v. Grigg, No. 06-30368, 2007 WL 2379615 (9th Cir. 2007)
United States v. Hensley, 469 U.S. 221 (1985)
United States v. Martinez-Fuerte, 428 U.S. 543 (1976)
United States v. Montoya de Hernandez, 473 U.S. 531 (1985)
United States v. Pavelski, 789 F.2d 485 (7th Cir. 1986)
United States v. Pritchard, 645 F.2d 854 (10th Cir. 1981)
United States v. Santana, 427 U.S. 38 (1976)
United States v. Sharpe, 470 U.S. 675 (1985)
United States v. Sokolow, 490 U.S. 1 (1989)
United States v. Watson, 423 U.S. 411 (1976)
Warden v. Hayden, 387 U.S. 294 (1967)
Whren v. United States, 517 U.S. 806 (1996)

CHAPTER 9

Conducting Constitutional Searches

It is unreasonable for a police officer to look for an elephant in a matchbox.

—Legal maxim

Constitutional law is living and changes over time, and the law governing legal searches is no exception. Rapid advances in technology are challenging the law in unprecedented ways and changing how we think about privacy.

Chapter 9 Conducting Constitutional Searches

Learning Objectives

LO1 *Understand what constitutes a "search" under the Fourth Amendment.*

LO2 *Explain the limitations placed on searches with a warrant.*

LO3 *List the exceptions to the warrant requirement that have been established.*

LO4 *Identify when a vehicle can be legally searched without a warrant and the precedent case.*

LO5 *Clarify what constitutes an exigent circumstance.*

LO6 *Summarize how a reasonable expectation of privacy and the trespass doctrine relate to searches of open fields, abandoned property, and public places.*

LO7 *Grasp whether jail and prison inmates, probationers, and parolees have full Fourth Amendment protection.*

LO8 *Describe how electronic surveillance is governed by the Fourth Amendment and what relationship exists between electronic surveillance and one's reasonable expectations of privacy.*

Key Terms

administrative warrant	plain feel	reasonable expectation
contemporaneous	plain touch	of privacy
contraband	plain view	remoteness
curtilage	protective sweep	voluntariness test
exigent circumstances	qualified immunity	waiver test
penumbra		wingspan

Introduction

Promulgating law and enforcing it are awesome responsibilities that have never been taken lightly. The consequences of good or bad law are enormous, as are the consequences of good or bad law enforcement. Herein lies the criticality of the Fourth Amendment for those who make the law, enforce it, and ultimately benefit from its protection.

By now you should have begun to see how search and seizure, although two separate actions, overlap greatly. In this area of police work, where one search or seizure under specific circumstances may not be considered "constitutional," under other circumstances that same search or seizure may be allowed. For instance, an exception might apply to the situation, or a different fact may be present that now justifies the action. There is such overlap in this area that often, where one circumstance does not get you what you need, another will. This also demonstrates how fact-specific search-and-seizure analysis under the Fourth Amendment must be.

This chapter begins with the basic tenets of Fourth Amendment search analysis and an explanation of the constitutional scope of searches. Next is a discussion of searches with warrants and the seven general exceptions to this requirement. This is followed by a look at border searches and "special needs" searches. The chapter concludes with a discussion of how the Fourth Amendment has been applied to the electronic era, including electronic surveillance, and how privacy interests are being affected by expanding technology.

Tenets of Fourth Amendment Search Analysis

Prior to 1967, courts took a property-based approach to defining a search and when constitutional protections were implicated, holding that only when the government physically intruded into "persons, houses, papers, and effects," in an effort to obtain information, did a search occur. The case illustrating this principle is *Olmstead v. United States* (1928), in which the Supreme Court determined that a search did not take place when government agents wiretapped telephone lines *outside* the suspect's home and office. Because there was no physical trespass into a constitutionally protected area and there was not a taking of tangible items, no search was said to have occurred, and the commands of the Fourth Amendment did not apply.

But in 1967, the definition of what constituted a search changed when, in *Katz v. United States*, the Court explained that the Constitution protects people, not places. In *Katz*, the defendant had been convicted of gambling violations, and the evidence against him was a conversation heard by FBI agents using an electronic device attached to the public phone booth Katz was calling from. Katz argued that even a public phone booth is a constitutionally protected area because the user expects privacy and that evidence collected electronically was a violation of the right to privacy of the person using the phone booth. The Supreme Court agreed, holding that any form of electronic surveillance (including recording phone calls) that violates a *reasonable expectation of privacy* constitutes a search. No actual physical trespass is required by the government: "The Fourth Amendment protects people not places.... Wherever a man may be, he is entitled to know that he will remain free from unreasonable searches and seizures." The Court's opinion continued:

> The government stresses the fact that the telephone booth from which the petitioner made his call was constructed partly of glass, so that he was as visible after he entered it as he would have been if he had remained outside. But what he sought to exclude when he entered the booth was not the intruding eye, it was the uninvited ear. He did not shed his right to do so simply because he made his calls from a place where he might be seen. No less than an individual in a business office, in a friend's apartment or in a taxicab, a person in a telephone booth may rely upon the protection of the Fourth Amendment. One who occupies it, shuts the door behind him, and pays the toll that permits him to place a call, is surely entitled to assume that the words he utters into the mouthpiece will not be broadcast to the world. To read the Constitution more narrowly is to ignore the vital role that the public telephone has come to play in private communication.

CASE IN BRIEF

Katz v. United States (1967)

ISSUE Does it violate the Fourth Amendment to listen to a private telephone conversation despite the fact that no physical intrusion into the area occurs?

RULING Yes. When a person exhibits an actual, subjective expectation that his actions will be private, and those actions are ones that society sees as reasonable, it is considered a search when the government intrudes on that, whether or not a physical trespass occurs.

In *Katz*, Justice John Marshall Harlan II offered a concurring opinion that set a two-part test for defining a **reasonable expectation of privacy**: "First that a person ha[s] exhibited an actual (subjective) expectation of privacy and, second, that the expectation be one that society is prepared to recognize as 'reasonable.'" Both elements—a subjective *intention* to keep something private and an objectively reasonable *expectation* of privacy—are needed for there to be a reasonable expectation of privacy and, thus, implicate the Fourth Amendment. A reasonable expectation of privacy is an implied right that often falls within the **penumbra** (shadow) of other specified rights.

Although according to Justice Harlan's concurrence, a search always has some reference to "place," *Katz* revised Fourth Amendment search analysis by articulating that such scrutiny should address *privacy* rather than *property*, and holding that such intrusion into people's lives does violate an expectation of privacy; therefore, in *Katz*, even though government agents did not physically go onto someone's private property, a search had, indeed, occurred. This Court-created *reasonable expectation of privacy doctrine* remained the dominant view of what defined a search for the next 45 years and was extended from electronic eavesdropping to searches of people, their luggage (including briefcases, purses, and backpacks), where they live, and even their bodies. Searches of homes (*Payton v. New York*, 1980), hotel rooms (*Stoner v. California*, 1964), and businesses (*Maryland v. Macon*, 1985), as well as methods used to obtain evidence from a person's body, such as urine testing (*Skinner v. Railway Labor Executives' Association*, 1989) or the surgical removal of a bullet lodged within a person (*Winston v. Lee*, 1985), were all analyzed according to *Katz* and were held to constitute searches under the Fourth Amendment because, in each, the person had a reasonable expectation of privacy. Although the trespass-based approach set in *Olmstead* was commonly believed to have been replaced by the reasonable expectation of privacy analysis derived from *Katz*, this was, in fact, not the case.

In *United States v. Jones* (2012), the Court resurrected the idea that a search still includes the physical intrusion into a protected area, with Justice Antonin Scalia writing, "for most of our history the Fourth Amendment was understood to embody a particular concern for government trespass upon the areas ('persons, houses, papers, and effects') it enumerates. *Katz* did not repudiate that understanding." In *Jones*, police officers had attached a global position system (GPS) device to Jones's vehicle to monitor his movements because they suspected he was involved in drug trafficking. The officers had a search warrant to install and monitor the GPS, but the specifics of the warrant were not followed. The Court did not rule on whether the installation and monitoring of the GPS device was reasonable or not, which was the government's contention, but focused instead on what actions constitute a "search" under the Fourth Amendment and remanded the case for further proceedings.

In his opinion, Justice Scalia made it clear that both the trespass definition and the *Katz* definition were valid tests for defining a "search" under the Fourth Amendment: "The *Katz* reasonable-expectation-of-privacy test has been *added to*, not *substituted for*, the common-law trespassory test." Justice Sonia Sotomayor's concurrence further noted: "*Katz*'s reasonable-expectation-of-privacy test augmented, but did not displace or diminish, the common-law trespassory test that preceded it. . . . The trespassory

reasonable expectation of privacy a situation in which (1) a person has exhibited an actual (subjective) expectation of privacy and (2) that expectation is one that society is prepared to recognize as reasonable

penumbra a type of shadow in astronomy with the principle extending to the idea that certain constitutional rights are implied within other constitutional rights

◄ CASE IN BRIEF

United States v. Jones (2012)

ISSUE Is it considered a search when the police attach a GPS device to a suspect's vehicle?

RULING Yes. When the police physically trespass on "persons, places, houses, or effects" in an effort to gather information, it is a search under the Fourth Amendment. The physical trespass notion supplements the reasonable expectation of privacy doctrine.

test applied in the majority's opinion reflects an irreducible constitutional minimum: When the Government physically invades personal property to gather information, a search occurs." Simply put, *Katz* never replaced the trespass definition of a search, it merely supplemented it.

There is certainly overlap between the trespass and privacy doctrines. For example, if an officer kicks down a resident's front door and goes inside, both tests have been applied (a physical intrusion as well as a breach of privacy). If, on the other hand, an officer points a thermal imaging device at a home in an effort to gather information, they have invaded the resident's privacy but not physically trespassed. Therefore, when analyzing a search issue today, you must be prepared to make two inquiries: First, did the government physically intrude on a person, house, paper, or effect to gather information? Second, was there a reasonable expectation of privacy in the area that the government infringed on? If the answer to either question is "yes," it can safely be stated that a search implicating the Fourth Amendment has occurred.

> **LO1** *Jones resurrected the aspect of a physical intrusion or trespass in determining whether a "search" has occurred. The reasonable expectation of privacy and the physical trespass in an effort to gather information are both valid analyses that need to be performed to determine if a search has occurred.*

All Fourth Amendment cases begin with the conceptual question: Have the fundamental constitutional rules been met? The fundamental constitutional rules are (1) there must be governmental action; (2) the person making the challenge must have standing, that is, the conduct either violates the challenger's *reasonable expectation of privacy* or their property rights have been *physically intruded on* in an effort to gather information; and (3) *general searches* are unlawful and restrict government from going beyond what is necessary. An understanding of these three concepts, combined with the ability to analyze search-and-seizure issues, will allow an educated response when someone asks, "Can the government *do* that?" The Constitution ensures the people's rights by *limiting* governmental power. Therefore, people enjoy the right to be free from unreasonable searches and seizures by the government because government is allowed to carry out these intrusive acts only under limited and specific circumstances.

The Scope of Searches

Unrestrained general searches offend our sense of justice today, just as they did when the Constitution was drafted. Limited searches conducted in accordance with established constitutional guidelines serve society's needs while protecting the individual. No matter under what authority a search is conducted, one general principle is crucial: *All searches must be limited in scope.* General searches are unconstitutional and never legal.

In *Marron v. United States* (1927) the Supreme Court stated, "The requirement that the warrants shall particularly describe the things to be seized makes general searches under them impossible and prevents the seizure of one thing under a warrant describing another. As to what is to be taken, nothing is left to the discretion of the officer executing the warrant."

> **MYTH** If the police have a search warrant for your house, they can look for anything, anywhere.
>
> **FACT** Not true. The search warrant must specify where the officers may search and what items they are looking for.

The legal maxim at the beginning of this chapter refers to narrowing the scope of a search. Looking for "an elephant in a matchbox" suggests that searching for a stolen 50-inch LCD television in a dresser drawer would be unreasonable. However, police officers may include in the warrant affidavit that they wish to search for receipts as well as documents of title or ownership in addition to the actual items sought. This stipulation allows them to search in much smaller places.

Although the Fourth Amendment generally does not restrict private citizens' actions, it does apply to all government workers. This restriction includes federal, state, county, and local governmental bodies. Just as the FBI, state police, county sheriff, and local police are bound by the Fourth Amendment, so are the Internal Revenue Service (IRS), the Postal Service, fire inspectors, local building officials, and code enforcement officials.

Searches with a Warrant

In striving to limit governmental power, the Fourth Amendment begins with the assumption that searches should be conducted with a warrant. In keeping with the assumption that people have the right to be free from unreasonable searches and seizures, the use of a warrant provides a presumption of reasonableness. However, in situations in which it is unreasonable to expect privacy or there has been no physical intrusion into a protected space on the part of the government, there is no "search" to justify and, consequently, no warrant is needed. Subsequent decisions by the Supreme Court have developed legitimate exceptions to the warrant requirement, but law enforcement may prefer to search with a warrant because the burden is on the government agent to articulate probable cause in a warrantless search, whereas a magistrate declares within a warrant that probable cause has already been judicially acknowledged.

As explained in Chapter 7, government agents who have probable cause to believe evidence of a crime is located at a specific place should go before a neutral judge and swear under oath what they are looking for and where they think it can be found so the judge can issue a search warrant. The Fourth Amendment requires that all searches conducted with a warrant be "based upon probable cause supported by oath and affirmation, and particularly describing the place to be searched and the persons or things to be seized." See Figure 9.1 for a sample warrant.

The framers of the Constitution no doubt chose those words carefully to prohibit the general searches they found so abhorrent under British rule. Although they recognized that the government would have a legitimate interest in enforcing law, including executing searches, the framers limited the scope of any search to only what was necessary and, thus, balanced society's needs with those of the individual.

Illinois v. McArthur (2001) dealt with whether an officer could refuse to allow a resident to enter his home without a police officer until a search warrant could be obtained. Police officers had probable cause to believe Charles McArthur had hidden marijuana in his home. They knocked on his door and requested consent to search the premises, but McArthur refused. The investigating officers told McArthur he was to stay outside his home and could not reenter unless accompanied by a police officer while they obtained a search warrant, which took about two hours. When the warrant was issued, they entered his home and found drug paraphernalia and marijuana, and they arrested him. He was charged with misdemeanor possession of those items. At trial he moved to suppress the evidence as "fruit" of an unlawful police seizure. The Court recognized that the circumstances

SEARCH WARRANT 2-1

STATE OF MINNESOTA, COUNTY OF __Hennepin__   __District__   COURT
TO: __SGT William Johnson and Officers under his Control,__
_____ (A) PEACE OFFICER(S) OF THE STATE OF MINNESOTA.
  WHEREAS, __SGT William Johnson__ has this day on oath, made application to the said Court applying for issuance of a search warrant to search the following described (premises):

__The address of 2119 4th St S, Minneapolis, MN, and any storage units,__
__including but not limited to garages and storage sheds,__
located in the city of __Minneapolis__, county of __Hennepin__ STATE OF MINNESOTA
for the following described property and things:

Firearms, including semi-automatic and revolver style handguns, ammunition, holsters, black ski masks, black jackets, wallets, black sweat shirts, black jeans, black boots, duct tape, masks, gloves, checks/documents from the Good Deal Family Foods, a store located at 2600 1st St N, Minneapolis, MN.

  WHEREAS, the application and supporting affidavit of _____SGT. William Johnson_____ was duly presented and read by the Court, and being fully advised in the premises.
  NOW, THEREFORE, the Court finds that probable cause exists for the issuance of a search warrant upon the following grounds:
  1. The property above-described was stolen or embezzled.
  2. The property above-described was used as a means of committing a crime.
  3. The possession of the property above-described constitutes a crime.
  4. ~~The property above-described is in the possession of a person with intent to use such property as a means of committing a crime.~~
  5. The property above-described constitutes evidence which tends to show a crime has been committed, or tends to show that a particular person has committed a crime.
  The Court further finds that probable cause exists to believe that the above-described property and things are at: __2119 4th St S, Minneapolis, MN, and any storage units, including but not limited to garages and storage sheds.__

  The Court further finds that a nighttime search is necessary to prevent the loss, destruction, or removal of the objects of said search.
  The Court further finds that the entry without announcement of authority and purpose is necessary to prevent the loss, destruction, or removal of the objects and to protect the safety of the peace officers.
  NOW, THEREFORE, YOU, _____SGT William Johnson and officers under his Control,_____

THE PEACE OFFICER(S) AFORESAID, ARE HEREBY COMMANDED TO ENTER WITHOUT ANNOUNCEMENT OF AUTHORITY AND PURPOSE IN THE DAYTIME OR NIGHTTIME TO SEARCH THE DESCRIBED PREMISES: __2119 4th St S, Minneapolis, MN, and any storage units, including but not limited to garages and storage sheds,__ FOR THE ABOVE-DESCRIBED PROPERTY AND THINGS, AND TO SEIZE SAID PROPERTY AND THINGS AND TO RETAIN THEM IN CUSTODY SUBJECT TO COURT ORDER AND ACCORDING TO LAW.

BY THE COURT:

Dated __8-18__, 20 __16__   _____
JUDGE OF HENNEPIN COUNTY DISTRICT COURT

COURT–WHITE COPY • PROS. ATTY.–YELLOW COPY • PEACE OFFICER–PINK COPY • PREMISES/PERSON–GOLD COPY

Figure 9.1 Sample Warrant

in this case were exigent and tailored to that exigency, being as limited in time and as unobtrusive as possible. In reaching its decision, the Court balanced both privacy and law enforcement concerns and determined that the intrusion was reasonable.

Executing the Warrant

As discussed in Chapter 7, the warrant must be executed in a timely manner, that is, without unnecessary delay; after being announced (if required); and without the use of excessive force. Recall the knock-and-announce case of *United States v. Banks* (2003), in which the Court continued to take a case-by-case "totality of the circumstances" approach to deciding the constitutionality of police searches.

The Knock-and-Announce Rule Revisited

In searches with a warrant, the common law rule is that for an entry into a home to be constitutional, police must first knock and identify themselves and their purpose—the knock-and-announce rule introduced in Chapter 7. However, factors that necessitate entry without complying with the general rule will not automatically cause the search to be deemed unreasonable. Exceptions are to be considered on a case-by-case basis, considering the totality of the circumstances. For example, exigent circumstances such as hot pursuit, discussed shortly, allow officers to forcibly enter constitutionally protected areas. In addition, in some instances officers know in advance that they wish to enter without following the knock-and-announce rule because they fear the suspect may harm them or others or may destroy evidence.

In such cases they may request a no-knock warrant to permit them to enter without first announcing themselves. They can, for example, break down a door or enter through a window to force entry into fortified crack houses that have barricaded doors and windows, alarms, and other protection. A no-knock warrant affords officers the element of surprise and is justified when either officer or citizen safety or the destruction of evidence is a concern. A safety trend is the development of specially trained entry teams to assist in executing such dangerous warrant services.

In *Hudson v. Michigan* (2006), the Court held 5–4 that a violation of the knock-and-announce rule does not automatically invoke the exclusionary rule, if deterrence of police misconduct outweighs the social costs. This case involved a minor drug arrest in Detroit with officers executing a search warrant at Booker Hudson's residence. The officers shouted "Police, search warrant," as they approached the residence but did not knock. Three to five seconds later they opened the door and entered the house. When they searched Hudson, the police found five rocks of crack cocaine in Hudson's pants pocket and a loaded gun in the chair in which Hudson was sitting, as well as additional cocaine at other places in the house.

At trial, Hudson moved to suppress the seized evidence because police had not waited to enter. The trial court agreed, but the Michigan Court of Appeals reversed. Hudson was retried, convicted, and appealed again. The Michigan Supreme Court upheld his conviction, after which he appealed to the U.S. Supreme Court, which also upheld the conviction. In an opinion clearly supporting law enforcement, Justice Scalia explained the balance of interests:

> The social costs to be weighed against deterrence are considerable here. In addition to the grave adverse consequence that excluding relevant incriminating evidence always entails—the risk of releasing dangerous criminals—imposing such a massive remedy

◀ **CASE IN BRIEF**

Illinois v. McArthur (2001)

ISSUE Does it violate the Fourth Amendment to temporarily seize a person and restrain him from entering his home while officers are obtaining a search warrant?

RULING No. In this case, the officers had a valid reason for not allowing McArthur to enter his home; they feared he would destroy the drugs if allowed to enter. Also, the seizure was short in duration when balanced against the legitimate needs of the police.

◀ **CASE IN BRIEF**

Hudson v. Michigan (2006)

ISSUE Does the exclusionary rule apply when officers violate the knock-and-announce rule when executing a search warrant?

RULING No. The knock-and-announce rule is intended to promote privacy and safety and limit property damage. It was not intended to suppress evidence obtained by virtue of a search warrant.

would generate a constant flood of alleged failures to observe the rule, and claims that any asserted justification for a no-knock entry had inadequate support. Another consequence would be police officers' refraining from timely entry after knocking and announcing, producing preventable violence against the officers in some cases and the destruction of evidence in others. Next to these social costs are the deterrence benefits. The value of deterrence depends on the strength of the incentive to commit the forbidden act. That incentive is minimal here, where ignoring knock-and-announce can realistically be expected to achieve nothing but the prevention of evidence destruction and avoidance of life-threatening resistance, dangers which suspend the requirement when there is "reasonable suspicion" that they exist.... Massive deterrence is hardly necessary. Contrary to Hudson's argument that without suppression there will be no deterrence, many forms of police misconduct are deterred by civil-rights suits, and by the consequences of increasing professionalism of police forces, including a new emphasis on internal police discipline.

Detention during a Search

Cases that deal with search warrant issues have also assessed what actions during the execution of a warrant are acceptable. *Michigan v. Summers* (1981) established that a search with a warrant includes limited authority to detain the occupants of the premises during the search. In this case, officers arriving at George Summers's residence to execute a lawful search warrant for narcotics encountered Summers leaving his house. Officers detained Summers inside the house while they carried out their search. After locating narcotics and confirming that Summers owned the house, the police arrested him, searched his person, and found heroin in his coat pocket. Summers was charged with possession of heroin but moved to suppress the evidence as fruit of an illegal search in violation of the Fourth Amendment. The trial judge granted the motion and quashed the information, and both the Michigan Court of Appeals and the Michigan Supreme Court affirmed. The U.S. Supreme Court, however, granted certiorari and reversed, ruling that because it was lawful to require Summers to reenter and to remain in the house until evidence establishing probable cause to arrest him was found, his arrest and the search incident thereto were constitutionally permissible.

In *Muehler v. Mena* (2005), the Court determined that the use of handcuffs to secure (seize) the occupants of a residence during the execution of a search warrant was constitutional. Under *Summers*, the seizure of the occupants pursuant to a search warrant is categorical, requiring no additional proof of wrongdoing, and the use of handcuffs is reasonable if the facts permit. (As with any use of force, handcuffing must be reasonable.) Under the facts of this case, the Court determined the use of handcuffs was reasonable because the officers were searching for weapons and violent gang members on the premises.

Another more recent case related to *Summers* is *Bailey v. United States* (2013). In this case, officers saw Bailey leave his apartment where they were planning to execute a search warrant for a gun. Officers stopped and detained Bailey about a mile from the apartment. Evidence was found as a result of the seizure of Bailey and was later used to connect him to the apartment, where a gun and drugs were found.

CASE IN BRIEF ▶

Michigan v. Summers (1981)

ISSUE Is it constitutional to detain members of a residence during the execution of a search warrant?

RULING Yes. Officers have a legitimate justification in detaining the occupants of a residence being searched because of the needs to prevent flight of the occupants if evidence is found, ensure the safety of those searching, and facilitate an orderly search. Detaining the occupants is a minimal intrusion when balanced against these justifications.

CASE IN BRIEF ▶

Muehler v. Mena (2005)

ISSUE Is it reasonable to detain a person in handcuffs at the site where a search warrant is being executed merely because that person is present during its execution?

RULING Yes. Detaining someone at the site of a search warrant's execution is reasonable without any additional basis. Simply by virtue of their presence at the location, they may be seized and detained under *Summers*. Under the facts of this case—multiple people present, weapons being the object of the warrant, and violent gang members associated with the residence—handcuffing in addition to the detention is reasonable.

Constitutional Law in ACTION

Officer Jackson and other officers are on their way to execute a search warrant at a house for illegal drugs at 2 P.M. They are driving marked police cars and are all in police uniforms. The house is a small, one-story house. The search warrant does not allow for a no-knock entry.

As the officers arrive, they approach the front of the house and see someone peek out the front window. As they get to the front porch the officers hear someone shouting, "It's the police!" Then footsteps are heard running around the inside of the house.

Although the search warrant does not provide for a no-knock entry, Officer Jackson rushes to the front door and kicks it open without knocking and announcing himself. The front door is damaged.

All the officers enter the house and detain the three occupants. Drugs, a scale, and money are found on the kitchen table. The three people are arrested and brought to jail.

The arrestees challenge the fact that the search warrant did not allow for a no-knock entry, and the officers ignored that and forced entry with no announcement. The police argue that exigent circumstances existed to dispense with the rule and allowed them to enter as they did.

- *What facts point to the belief that the occupants might destroy any drugs before police could seize them?*
- *What is the level of "proof" required that this possibility exists?*
- *Should the need to secure evidence outweigh someone's privacy interest in their own home?*

The Supreme Court ruled that seizing someone out of the immediate vicinity of the location of the search warrant is unconstitutional. The Court observed that none of the three reasons delineated in *Summers* for detaining someone at the scene of a search warrant applied to a seizure outside of the immediate vicinity of the search warrant. As such, any detention so far removed must have an independent basis, other than a detention under *Summers*, to be constitutional.

Conducting the Search

After officers have obtained their search warrant and gained entrance, they can search only areas in which they reasonably believe the specified items might be found.

If the warrant states only one specific item is being sought, the search must end once it is located. Sometimes government agents come across items not specifically named in the warrant but similar enough to justify those items being seized as well. For example, if officers were executing a search warrant that specified televisions, DVD players, MP3 players, and stereos and came across a room filled with televisions, DVD players, stereos, and *video cameras*, they could seize the video cameras as evidence, even though not specified in the warrant because they are similar to the other items.

CASE IN BRIEF

Bailey v. United States (2013)

ISSUE Is it reasonable to seize a person beyond the immediate vicinity of where a search warrant is being executed, to conduct the search safely?

RULING No. Once an individual has left the immediate vicinity of the search warrant, the police must have independent reasons under the Fourth Amendment to seize and detain that person.

LO2 *Searches conducted with a search warrant must be limited to the specific area and specific items described in the warrant.*

CASE IN BRIEF ▶

Groh v. Ramirez (2004)

ISSUE Is it a violation of the Fourth Amendment to execute a search warrant that does not particularly describe the things to be seized, even if they are described in the affidavit?

RULING Yes. The Constitution clearly requires the particular description of the items to be seized in the warrant. This search warrant was facially invalid, and any reasonable officer would know this.

qualified immunity exemption of a public official from civil liability for actions performed during the course of his or her job unless they violated a "clearly established" constitutional or statutory right of which a reasonable person would have known

contraband anything that is illegal for people to own or have in their possession, for example, child pornography, illegal drugs, or illegal weapons

MYTH
All searches require a warrant.

FACT
Not true. There are many exceptions to the warrant requirement.

Groh v. Ramirez (2004) illustrates the importance of paying attention to the details of the warrant before searching. In this case Officer Jeff Groh obtained a warrant to search the Ramirez residence for weapons. Both affidavit and application contained a particular description of the items to be seized, but the warrant itself did not contain such a description as required by the Fourth Amendment. The section in the warrant that was to contain a list of items to be seized instead described the place to be searched. The warrant was signed by a judge.

A civil action alleging a Fourth Amendment violation was brought by Joseph Ramirez against Groh. The district court ruled that no constitutional violation took place and that Groh retained **"qualified immunity,"** meaning he was legally immune while doing his job unless he violated a "clearly established" constitutional right of which a reasonable person would have known. A Ninth Circuit Court of Appeals panel, however, reversed, and the Supreme Court agreed that a constitutional violation had occurred and that the warrant was invalid because it did not meet the Fourth Amendment requirement that a warrant particularly describe the persons or things to be seized. Even though a judge had approved a complete warrant, Ramirez did not know what the search was after. Thus, Groh did not have qualified immunity from suit.

The recent case of *Messerschmidt v. Millender* (2012) is important here because it shows facts contrary to *Groh*. In this case the Court ruled that officers were entitled to qualified immunity with regard to the warrant because, unlike *Groh* in which the items to be seized listed, "nonsensical[ly]," the house instead of the weapons and even a cursory reading of the search warrant would have alerted any reasonable officer to that error and the realization that the warrant was invalid, the search warrant in *Messerschmidt* was not so facially invalid. It would have required a careful reading and comparison to the affidavit. In addition, the warrant was reviewed by a superior officer, a deputy district attorney, and the magistrate. No reasonable officer would have seen any deficiency in the warrant.

The government can seize any contraband or other evidence of a crime found during a search with a warrant, even though it was not specified. **Contraband** includes anything that is illegal for people to own or have in their possession, such as illegal drugs or illegal weapons. The contraband does not need to be described in the warrant or be related to the crime described in the warrant. The lawful discovery of additional evidence could lead to additional charges, as discussed under the plain view doctrine.

Searches without a Warrant

The Fourth Amendment prefers a warrant because it necessitates judicial review of government action. Thus, the presumption exists that a warrantless search is unreasonable, unlawful, and, therefore, invokes the exclusionary rule, with the resulting evidence not permitted in court. However, as explained in *Kentucky v. King* (2011), "the text of the Fourth Amendment does not specify when a search warrant must be obtained." Reasonableness itself dictates that action may become necessary before the government obtains a warrant signed by a judge. Such practical matters as time, emergency circumstances, the probable destruction of evidence, or escape of a criminal have resulted in legitimate exceptions being made to the general requirement of a warrant. Just as a warrant may be challenged, warrantless searches may also be challenged. The most frequent challenges are that the officer did not establish probable cause or that there was sufficient time to obtain a warrant. Nonetheless, through the development of case law, the Supreme Court has defined the following searches without a warrant to be reasonable under Fourth Amendment guidelines.

Because the preceding have been recognized as lawful exceptions to the warrant requirement, evidence obtained in these circumstances is admissible in court (*Marshall v. Barlow's Inc.*, 1978; *Michigan v. Tucker*, 1974).

LO3 *Exceptions to the warrant requirement include:*
- *Consent search*
- *Frisks for officer safety*
- *Plain feel and plain view*
- *Incident to arrest*
- *Automobile exceptions*
- *Exigent (emergency) circumstances*
- *Open fields, abandoned property, and public places*

Searches with Consent

If an individual gives *voluntary consent* for the police to search his or her person or property, the police may do so without a warrant, and any evidence found will be admissible in court. A consent search must be limited to the area specified by the person granting the permission. Although consent makes searching convenient, the downside is the person may revoke consent at any time. Interestingly, the Court has never required police to tell people they have a right to refuse to consent, and the police do not have to tell motorists they are free to go before asking for consent to search (*Ohio v. Robinette*, 1996). See Figure 9.2 for a waiver and consent to search form.

WAIVER AND CONSENT TO SEARCH

The undersigned _____
residing at _____
_____ hereby authorizes the following
named St. Paul Police Officers _____
to search the _____

_____
(insert description of place or auto, lic. number, etc.)

owned by/or in possession of the undersigned.

I do hereby waive any and all objections that may be made by me to said search and declare that this waiver and consent is freely and voluntarily given of my own free will and accord.

Signed _____ day of _____ 20 ____ at _____ PM   AM

        Signed _____

    Witnessed _____

Figure 9.2 Waiver and Consent to Search Form

Government agents may conduct a search without a warrant if they are given permission by someone with authority to do so. Usually, the only person who can give consent is the person whose constitutional rights might be threatened by a search. This person is said to have *standing*, that is, the right to object to the unreasonableness of a search because of a reasonable expectation of privacy. Fourth Amendment rights are specific to the person and may not be raised on behalf of someone else or in some abstract, theoretical way. Standing, in constitutional law, must involve a case or controversy.

Consent to search an individual must be given by that individual. Consent to search any property must be given by the actual owner or, as set forth in *United States v. Matlock* (1974), by a person in charge of that property. If more than one person owns or occupies a building, only one needs to give permission. Thus, if two people share an apartment, all that is required is the consent from one of them (*Wright v. United States*, 1938). However, consent may be given for only those areas commonly used, not private space of one or the other. Even spouses do not have totality in area of consent if one area is considered to be off-limits to one party.

In some instances, someone else can give a valid consent. For example, in *Matlock* the Supreme Court held that if a person has common authority over the premises of items to be searched, this individual could provide government officials with a valid consent "as against the absent, nonconsenting person with whom that authority is shared." Examples of relationships where third-party consent may be valid include:

- Parent/Child—A parent's consent to search premises owned by the parent will generally be effective against a child living on those premises. However, if the child uses a given area of the premises exclusively, has sectioned it off, has furnished it with his or her own furniture, pays rent or has otherwise established an expectation of privacy, the parent may not consent to a search of that area occupied by the child.
- Employer/Employee—In general, an employer may consent to a search of any part of the employer's premises used by an employee (e.g., employees' lockers can be searched with the employer's consent). Recent cases have held that a computer's contents are *not* shielded by employees' right to privacy.
- Host/Guest—The host, owner, or primary occupant of the premises may consent to a search of the premises. Any evidence found would be admissible against the guest.
- Spouses—If two people, such as husband and wife, have equal rights to occupy and use premises, either may give consent to a search.

CASE IN BRIEF

Georgia v. Randolph (2006)

ISSUE Does the consent to search given by one physically present co-occupant prevail over the refusal of consent by another physically present co-occupant?

RULING No. If more than one occupant is physically present, the refusal of any of them prevails over the consent of the others.

The Supreme Court decision in *Georgia v. Randolph* (2006) affirmed some prior rulings regarding third-party consent but created a new holding that overturns existing rules in many jurisdictions. In this case, Mrs. Randolph called police about marital problems caused by her husband's cocaine use, saying he had drugs in the house. When police arrived, Mr. Randolph refused consent to search, but Mrs. Randolph consented and led the police to the evidence. The state supreme court ruled the wife's consent invalid against her husband's objections, and the state appealed. The U.S. Supreme Court affirmed the state ruling that suppressed the evidence. The Court emphasized that in all its previous cases, the co-occupant against whom the evidence was used was not present to object. When both occupants are present and one objects, the other cannot "override" the co-occupant's refusal: "A warrantless search of a shared dwelling for evidence over the express refusal of consent by a physically present resident cannot be justified as reasonable."

In 2014 the Court addressed a similar question as in *Randolph*, but with a twist. In *Fernandez v. California* (2014), police arrived at Fernandez's apartment door because they suspected him of a recent robbery. Importantly, before the officers knocked on the door, they heard screaming and fighting coming from that building. The door was answered by Fernandez's girlfriend. She appeared to have been crying, had a bump on her nose, and blood on her shirt and hand. At that point, Fernandez appeared at the door, refusing to allow officers into the apartment. Believing that he had assaulted his girlfriend, the officers arrested him. He was also identified by the robbery victim and subsequently booked. About one hour later, the detectives returned and asked the girlfriend for consent to search the apartment, which she gave. Inside, the officers found a knife and the clothing used in the robbery, as well as gang paraphernalia and a sawed off shotgun. Fernandez was later found guilty of several crimes and sentenced to prison.

Fernandez appealed the case after the trial court and appeals court each refused to suppress the evidence. Claiming that the rule of *Randolph* applied to his case, Fernandez stated that he was initially present and objected to the officers entering the apartment; and that his objection should remain in effect until he withdraws it and gives consent; and, if he was considered not present, it was because officers took him to jail, and therefore his absence should not matter.

As to his absence, the police had probable cause to arrest Fernandez and remove him from the apartment; therefore, his absence was the result of an objectively reasonable action. The Supreme Court found that "an occupant who is absent due to a lawful detention or arrest stands in the same shoes as an occupant who is absent for any other reason." The Court then tuned to the argument that Fernandez's initial objection should remain in effect indefinitely. The Court found that this would produce a "plethora of practical problems," including which officers are bound by the objection and the need to determine at what point in time, if any, the objecting party still holds common authority.

The court has allowed, as reasonable, third-party consent searches in which an *apparent authority* existed. In *Illinois v. Rodriguez* (1990), officers did not have an arrest or search warrant, but gained entry to an apartment with the assistance of Gail Fischer, who represented that the apartment was "our[s]" and that she had clothes and furniture there. Fischer unlocked the door with her key and gave the officers permission to enter, where they were able to seize evidence of illegal drugs left in plain view and arrest the other occupant of the apartment, Edward Rodriquez, for possession of the illegal drugs. The trial court granted Rodriquez's motion to suppress the seized evidence, holding that at the time she consented to the entry Fischer did not have common authority because she had moved out of the apartment. The Supreme Court, however, reversed the lower court's decision, arguing that there was no Fourth Amendment violation if the police *reasonably believed* at the time of their entry that the third party possessed the authority to consent. Thus, the Fourth Amendment's reasonable search requirement is satisfied when police conduct a warrantless search of a person's home based on the apparently

CASE IN BRIEF

Fernandez v. California (2014)

ISSUE Can a co-occupant override a previous objection to a police search when the objector is no longer present due to an arrest?

RULING Yes. The arrest, and therefore absence, of the initial objecting party can be overridden with valid consent from a co-occupant obtained at a later time.

CASE IN BRIEF

Illinois v. Rodriguez (1990)

ISSUE Is the consent to search valid when police reasonably believe that the person granting such consent has authority to do so, even when they, in fact, do not?

RULING Yes. If it is reasonable to believe that the person has common authority over the premises such that he or she could give consent, the consent is valid.

authorized consent of another and the person is later shown to not have authority to grant such a search, as long as it is reasonable for the officers to believe that the person had authority to grant the search, based on the totality of the circumstances.

Examples of instances when individuals *cannot* give valid consent to search include:

- Landlord/Tenant—A landlord, even though the legal owner, has no authority to offer consent to a search of a tenant's premises or a seizure of the tenant's property, including children living at home but paying rent to their parent.
- Hotel Employee/Hotel Guest—The Supreme Court extended the principles governing a landlord's consent to a search of tenant's premises to include consent searches of hotel and motel rooms allowed by hotel or motel employees.

In such instances, only the tenant or hotel guest can give consent. The consent must be free and voluntary. The Supreme Court ruling in *State v. Barlow, Jr.* (1974) stated, "It is a well-established rule in the federal courts that a consent search is unreasonable under the Fourth Amendment if the consent was induced by deceit, trickery or misrepresentation of the officials making the search."

A request for permission to search must not be stated in a threatening way. It must not imply that anyone who does not give consent will be considered as having something to hide. Failure to give consent cannot be used to establish probable cause. No display of weapons or force should accompany a request to search. In *Weeds v. United States* (1921), police confronted the defendant with drawn guns and a riot gun and said they would get a warrant if they needed. The Court said consent given under these conditions was not free and voluntary. Likewise, in *People v. Loria* (1961) the police threatened to kick down the door of the defendant's apartment if he did not let them in. The court said consent was not free and voluntary.

Usually, the government should not request to search at night. In *Monroe v. Pape* (1961) Justice Felix Frankfurter stated, "Modern totalitarianisms have been a stark reminder, but did not newly teach, that the kicked-in door is the symbol of a rule of fear and violence fatal to institutions founded on respect for the integrity of man.... Searches of the dwelling houses were the special object of this universal condemnation of officer intrusion. Nighttime search was the evil in its most obnoxious form." Again, unusual circumstances may require such a search.

Florida v. Jimeno (1991) held that consent can justify a warrantless search of a container in a vehicle if the police reasonably believe the suspect's consent includes allowing them to open closed containers. This analysis uses the "reasonableness" line of argument, and, as discussed, what one person considers reasonable may not be how another would interpret it. *Jimeno* determined that when a person gives consent to search a car, consent is being provided to search everything therein, unless specifically restricted.

Courts typically justify the consent exception by two separate tests: (1) the **voluntariness test**—the consent was obtained without coercion or promises and was, therefore, reasonable and (2) the **waiver test**—citizens may consent to waive their Fourth Amendment rights. The voluntariness test considers the totality of circumstances to determine whether the consent was given freely and truly voluntarily. Factors such as the age and education level of the person giving consent, the length of the encounter, and where the encounter took place are considered as part of the totality of circumstances.

MYTH
If you do not consent to a search, you must have something to hide, and that can be used against you.

FACT
Not true. If you decline to consent to a search, that cannot be used to support probable cause.

voluntariness test a determination as to whether one willingly and knowingly relinquished his or her constitutional rights; considers the totality of circumstances to determine whether consent was given freely and truly voluntarily

CASE IN BRIEF

Florida v. Jimeno (1991)

ISSUE When consent is given to search a vehicle, does that consent extend to closed containers found inside the vehicle?

RULING Yes, as long as the container could be reasonably understood to be included within the scope of person's consent.

waiver test citizens may waive their rights, but only if they do so voluntarily, knowingly, and intentionally

Consent may be revoked at any point. For example, in *State v. Lewis* (1992) a state trooper pulled a defendant over for drunken driving. The trooper offered to drive the defendant home, and the man, after accepting, went to his vehicle to retrieve a carry-on bag. The trooper asked permission to check the carry-on bag for guns, and the defendant granted it. Inside the bag the trooper found two large brown bags that smelled of marijuana, so he asked permission to check the bags, but the defendant refused. The trooper opened the bags anyway and found marijuana. The court found this search violated the defendant's Fourth Amendment right to privacy.

Although consent may be revoked at any time, if contraband was found before the revocation of consent, probable cause to arrest that person may then exist and a search incident to arrest could ensue, or the police might cease their search, secure the property, detain those present, and seek a warrant.

Even when police have an alternative justification for a search, such as a warrant, they may ask for consent to establish "another layer of validation" for their actions. And they may ask for this consent even if the subject is in custody, is in handcuffs, or has been stopped for a traffic violation and is not free to go (Means & McDonald, 2010).

Frisks

The elements of stop-and-frisk law were discussed in Chapter 7, and frisks as a protective action taken during a lawful stop were examined in Chapter 8, but frisks are important to include here as a crucial exception to the warrant requirement for a legal search. Recall that if officers have a reasonable suspicion based on specific and articulable facts that an individual is involved in criminal activity, the officers may make a brief investigatory stop. If the officers reasonably suspect the person is presently armed and dangerous, a limited pat down of the detainee's outer clothing may be conducted without a warrant (*Terry v. Ohio*, 1968). A frisk is allowed for the investigating officer's safety:

> When an officer is justified in believing that the individual whose suspicious behavior he is investigating at close range is armed and presently dangerous to the officer or to others, it would appear to be clearly unreasonable to deny the officer the power to take necessary measures to determine whether the person is in fact carrying a weapon and to neutralize the threat of physical harm. (*Terry v. Ohio*)

Factors contributing to the decision to frisk someone might include a suspect who flees, a bulge in the suspect's clothing, a suspect's hand concealed in a pocket, being in a known high-crime area, and when the suspected crime would likely involve a weapon. Whether the frisk is lawful is based on the totality of the circumstances, usually not one factor alone.

Anything that reasonably feels like a weapon may then be removed and used as evidence against the person if it is contraband or other evidence (*Terry v. Ohio*). If an officer has specific information about where a weapon is on a person, the officer may reach directly for it (*Adams v. Williams*, 1972). Similarly, a vehicle's passenger compartment can be searched if that vehicle is stopped and the person is detained but not arrested. Such a search would have to remain limited to the area where a weapon could be, and it would have to be done with the belief that, as in a frisk situation, the person is presently armed and dangerous (*Michigan v. Long*, 1983). Recall from Chapter 8 that passengers in a vehicle can be frisked if they are believed to be armed and dangerous (*Arizona v. Johnson*, 2009). Plain feel is also considered acceptable in a frisk.

Plain Feel and Plain Touch

The Supreme Court ruled in 1993 that police do not need a warrant to seize narcotics detected while frisking a suspect for concealed weapons, as long as the narcotics are instantly recognizable by **plain feel** or **plain touch.** The Court's unanimous opinion was the first time the Court authorized a warrantless pat-down-type frisk to go beyond a protective search for weapons.

In the precedent plain feel case, *Minnesota v. Dickerson* (1993), two police officers saw Timothy Dickerson leaving a known crack house and then, on seeing the officers, stop abruptly and walk quickly in the opposite direction. The officers decided to stop Dickerson and investigate further. They did so, and as one officer testified later in court: "As I pat-searched the front of his body, I felt a lump—a small lump—in the front pocket. I examined it with my fingers and slid it, and it felt to be a lump of crack cocaine in cellophane. I never thought the lump was a weapon." Dickerson was arrested and convicted on that evidence.

When the case was appealed to the Minnesota Supreme Court, however, the conviction was reversed. The court held that the sense of touch is much less reliable than the sense of sight and that it is far more intrusive into the personal privacy that is the core of the Fourth Amendment. The decision was granted review by the U.S. Supreme Court, which upheld the ruling of the Minnesota Supreme Court because the officer did not immediately recognize the object as contraband. However, the Court did support "plain touch" or "plain feel" in frisk situations if contraband is plainly felt by the officer. It held that, when conducting a frisk, if officers feel something they believe to be contraband, rather than being able to seize just weapons as previously set forth in *Terry v. Ohio*, it can be lawfully seized because the situation then escalates to probable cause. As the Court stated in *Minnesota v. Dickerson*, "The (officer's) sense of touch, grounded in experience and training, is as reliable as perceptions from the other senses. Plain feel, therefore, is no different than plain view."

In *Dickerson*, the officer exceeded the scope of a lawful *Terry frisk* by "squeezing, sliding and manipulating" the object to determine whether it was contraband, rather than just "patting down," as authorized by *Terry*. These actions effectively transformed a frisk, based on reasonable suspicion, into a search, which requires probable cause. However, stressing the importance of the ability to *immediately identify* something as contraband, the Court stated in *Dickerson*, "If the officer, while staying within the narrow limits of a frisk for weapons, feels what he has probable cause to believe is a weapon, contraband or evidence, the officer may expand the search or seize the object." *Dickerson* exemplifies how cases create law. Even though the evidence was held inadmissible in this case, the Court created a new "plain touch" doctrine, which holds the force of law, even though Congress never addressed it, because the Supreme Court deemed it law.

If the officer had testified that what he touched did not feel like a weapon, but it was apparent to him, given the totality of the circumstances, including his training and experience, that the object was narcotics, evidence, or other contraband,

---

plain feel items felt during a lawful stop and frisk may be retrieved if the officer reasonably believes the items are contraband and can instantly recognize them as such

plain touch same as plain feel

CASE IN BRIEF

Minnesota v. Dickerson (1993)

ISSUE May an officer seize evidence found while conducting a pat frisk for weapons?

RULING Yes. First, the frisk and stop must both be based on reasonable suspicion. Then any subsequent finding and seizing of contraband is constitutional as long as, during the pat down, the object is "immediately apparent" to the officer as contraband.

the evidence probably would have been admissible if the initial stop and the frisk were lawful. However, an officer may not simply feel or otherwise manipulate the luggage of a traveler with no other justification (*Bond v. United States*, 2000), for the same reason an officer could not just walk up to someone and frisk that person with no justification. The action would be unconstitutional because it violates a reasonable expectation of privacy.

Technology is enabling officers to conduct pat downs without physically touching a subject. A device resembling a blow dryer emits an ultrasound beam that penetrates clothing and soft material and reflects a return beam off hard objects—those made of metal, glass, or plastic. The more ultrasound reflected back to the detector, the greater the return signal. The device allows officers the reasonable suspicion to conduct a more intensive search and can alert officers to any concealed weapons. What the future holds will undoubtedly continue to challenge the reasonableness clause of the Fourth Amendment.

Plain View Evidence

The courts recognize that expecting police officers to either ignore or delay acting on something illegal that they see would be unreasonable. When officers have a right to be where they are, anything they observe in plain view is not the product of a search, may be seized, and is admissible in court.

Means and McDonald (2009a, p. 26) note, "Law enforcement officers commonly use the phrase 'it was in plain view' to explain how an officer located an item. Many officers believe that using that phrase in that way is equivalent to saying that the 'plain view doctrine' applies. In fact, there are two fundamentally different principles involved. The physical sighting of an item, while it may have been plainly visible, is only one aspect of the multifaceted plain view doctrine."

Plain view must meet three criteria: (1) the officer is lawfully present at the place from which the evidence can be plainly viewed; (2) the officer has a lawful right of access to the object; and (3) the object's incriminating character is immediately apparent (*Horton v. California*, 1990). Plain view really comes down to the Court's second criteria in *Horton*: does the officer have legal access to the item to seize it? For example, an officer walking on the sidewalk observes an open garage door and inside the garage she sees a dozen marijuana plants. She meets the first criteria (lawfully present) and the third criteria (immediately recognizable), but on these scant facts, there is no constitutional access (a warrant would be needed to get access). If she had been inside the home instead, perhaps taking a theft report from the owner when she saw the marijuana plants in the kitchen, then she would have legal access and fulfill all three criteria.

Lower courts have allowed seizures based on "plain smell" and "plain hearing," sensory observations that are analogous to the plain view doctrine (Ferdico, 2009). In *United States v. Haley* (1982), the Court held that odor was sufficient to "bring the contents into plain view."

Until 1990 discovery of plain view evidence was also a requirement to be "inadvertent." This requirement was overturned in *Horton v. California* (1990), which held that the inadvertence rule gave no added protection to individuals and, therefore, eliminated it as a requirement.

plain view unconcealed evidence that officers see while engaged in a lawful activity may be seized and is admissible in court

◀ CASE IN BRIEF

Horton v. California (1990)

ISSUE If the discover of plain view evidence was not inadvertent, is it still admissible?

RULING Yes. Although inadvertence is often a condition of plain view evidence, it is not necessary. The initial intrusion into the individual's privacy provides the scope of the search, as well as the authorization for the initial search, and inadvertency adds nothing to the protection of a person's Fourth Amendment rights.

MYTH
For plain view to apply, the officers must accidently or inadvertently see the contraband.

FACT
Not true. As long as the officers are where they can legally be, recognize the item as contraband or evidence, and have lawful access to it, they can seize it.

CASE IN BRIEF ▶

Kyllo v. United States (2001)

ISSUE Is it a search under the Fourth Amendment to aim a thermal-imaging device at a home to gather information?

RULING Yes. It is a search governed by the Fourth Amendment when the police employ a device not in use by the general public to discover information about the interior of a private home that would be known otherwise only by a physical intrusion.

In *Coolidge v. New Hampshire* (1971) the Court ruled:

> What the "plain view" cases have in common is that the police officer in each of them had a prior justification for an intrusion in the course of which he came ... across a piece of evidence incriminating the accused. The doctrine serves to supplement the prior justification—whether it be a warrant for another object, hot pursuit, search incident to lawful arrest or some other legitimate reason for being present unconnected with a search directed against the accused—and permits the warrantless seizure. Of course, the extension of the original justification is legitimate only where it is immediately apparent to the police that they have evidence before them.

For instance, if a government official is invited into a person's home, and the officer sees illegal drugs on the table, the drugs can be seized. Likewise, an officer carrying out a legal act, such as executing a traffic stop or search warrant, may seize any contraband discovered. Similarly, contraband such as marijuana fields can be legally observed from an airplane over private property without a search warrant. (How privacy expectations and issues of trespass or physical intrusion relate to searches of open fields, abandoned property, and some public places is discussed shortly.)

Even what is considered to be in plain view is in flux. Technology is having an impact on this area of Fourth Amendment law as well, with thermal-imaging devices being used to scan buildings for excessive heat generated, for example, by high-intensity lights used for growing marijuana indoors. Most federal courts that have considered this issue have ruled that use of thermal-imaging devices was *not* a search within the meaning of the Fourth Amendment and, therefore, did not require a warrant (*United States v. Pinson*, 1994). However, in *Kyllo v. United States* (2001) the Supreme Court again addressed the issue of whether a search warrant was required for police to scan a home from the street and compare that infrared image to other neighboring buildings, ultimately using the results as probable cause to apply for a search warrant.

In this case, Danny Lee Kyllo's home was scanned by police from the street and the results used to apply for a warrant. The Supreme Court reversed its position in a 5–4 decision, holding that such an act by the police *is* considered a search under the Fourth Amendment and requires a warrant. The effects of this decision may affect law enforcement even further. Because the Court questioned the use of technology when gathering information about the building's interior from the outside, future cases are likely to challenge law enforcement's use of any technology-aided efforts when intruding upon a reasonable expectation of privacy. Heretofore, observations from a public place have been held reasonable, and the courts have also ruled that officers may use visual "enhancements" such as flashlights and binoculars. But *Kyllo* has challenged this idea when such tools as infrared-imaging equipment are used to look "inside" a home. The Court's apparently bright-line rule is that use of thermal imagers directed at a home constitutes a search requiring a warrant or, at least, probable cause. However, the Court also noted that for a technological scan to be in violation of the Fourth Amendment, the device must not be in general public use without explaining what constitutes "general public use." This leaves open a challenge regarding whether or not thermal imaging is in "general public use." For example, a portable infrared camera has been developed to detect moisture accumulation, targeted for use by roofing, insulation, and electrical contractors. Clearly, there is growing potential for such devices to be accessible to the general public.

Imagine the framers of the Constitution reading *Kyllo v. United States*. Although the concept of such technology could not have been imagined at the time the Constitution was drafted, it still serves as the basis for determining when government has gone too far and to secure the people's rights. *Kyllo* also exemplifies how the law of criminal procedure can change. Future cases may well continue to shape the area of warrantless search law.

Searches Incident to Lawful Arrest

After a person has lawfully been taken into custody by a police officer, U.S. law recognizes the necessity of permitting a complete search. First, officer safety requires that any weapon on or near the defendant be located. Second, any evidence or other contraband should be recovered. Although a full search is permissible incident to lawful arrest, how far can such a search go? The more intrusive or extreme a search, the greater the necessity must be before a judge will authorize it.

Assume during this discussion that all arrests are legal; if not, the exclusionary rule would prevent any evidence obtained during the search from being used in court. If an arrest is legal, what kind of search can be conducted? The precedent case is *Chimel v. California* (1969), in which police had an arrest warrant for Ted Chimel before they thoroughly searched his home. However, the evidence found during the search was declared inadmissible. The Supreme Court said:

> When an arrest is made, it is reasonable for the arresting officer to search the person arrested to remove any weapons that the latter might seek to use to resist arrest or effect an escape.
>
> It is entirely reasonable for the arresting officer to search for and seize any evidence on the arrestee's person in order to prevent its concealment or destruction and the area from within which the arrestee might gain possession of a weapon or destructible evidence.

The key phrases in this statement are *the arrestee's person* and *the area from within which the arrestee might gain possession*. The Court described this area as within the person's immediate control—meaning within the person's reach (also defined as the person's **wingspan**). The fact that the suspect is handcuffed does not restrict the scope of the search. The area remains as if the suspect was not handcuffed because the belief that the suspect could access a weapon or hidden contraband that had been within reach is reasonable. This is an area scholars are watching closely, with the current speculation being that searches of the area around an arrestee might eventually be limited by the Court for the same reasons articulated in *Arizona v. Gant* (2009), discussed shortly, especially if the person is secured in handcuffs.

The issue of *contemporaneousness* is important when discussing searches incidental to a lawful arrest. In *James v. Louisiana* (1965), the defendant was arrested for a drug offense, taken to his home, well away from the arrest site, and searched. The Supreme Court held the resulting evidence was not admissible because a search "can be incident to an arrest only if it is substantially **contemporaneous** with the arrest and is confined to the immediate vicinity of the arrest" [emphasis added].

◀ **CASE IN BRIEF**

Chimel v. California (1969)

ISSUE What is the permissible scope of a search incident to arrest?

RULING A valid, custodial arrest allows an officer to search the arrestee and the area immediately surrounding the arrestee to secure any weapons that could be used or any evidence that might be concealed or destroyed.

wingspan the area within a person's reach or immediate control

contemporaneous a concept that holds a search can be incident to an arrest only if it occurs at the same time as the arrest and is confined to the immediate vicinity of the arrest

In other words, not only must a search incident to arrest be limited to the area within the person's reach via *Chimel* but it must also occur contemporaneously. Case law makes clear that the farther away from the area under the defendant's immediate control, the less likely a search incident to the arrest will be considered lawful.

In 1973, however, the Supreme Court expanded the scope of searches allowed after arrests in *United States v. Robinson*. The case involved a full-scale search of an individual arrested for a moving traffic violation. The officer inspected the contents of a cigarette package found on Willie Robinson and discovered illegal drugs. The drugs were admitted as evidence, with the Court stating:

> It is the fact of the lawful arrest which establishes the authority to search, and we hold that in the case of a lawful custodial arrest a search of the person is not only an exception to the warrant requirement of the Fourth Amendment, but is also a "reasonable" search under that Amendment.

Note that this offense allowed for a full custodial arrest and it was only *after* the arrest that the search became justified. Simply being stopped and issued a speeding ticket does not justify a full-scale search; the search must be incident to an arrest.

Not all states follow this ruling, however. For example, the Hawaiian Supreme Court, based on its state constitution, limits the warrantless search after a custodial arrest to disarming the person if the officers believe the arrestee to be dangerous, and searching for evidence related to the crime for which the person was arrested (*State v. Kaluna*, 1974).

The rule established in *Robinson* was further clarified in *United States v. Chadwick* (1977), when the Court explained that a search incident to arrest was limited to personal property that could be "immediately associated with the arrestee." Thus, anything arrestees have under their immediate control may be searched and seized, even if unrelated to whatever criminal act they are suspected of committing. During a full search of an arrestee, anything on the person's body may be searched and seized if evidentiary or unlawful. This evidence includes a person's wallet or purse, which according to *United States v. Molinaro* (1989) may be seized and gone through at the time of arrest. Even seizures of items from the body, such as hair samples or fingernail clippings, are usually allowed without a warrant incident to arrest if reasonable and painless procedures are used (*Commonwealth v. Tarver*, 1975).

Building on this idea is that a breath test, if conducted in the context of a drunk-driving arrest, may be done as a search incident to arrest. In *Birchfield v. North Dakota* (2016), the Supreme Court examined whether implied consent statutes—state laws that make it a crime to refuse to submit to a test of one's blood alcohol level when arrested on suspicion of drunk driving—are constitutionally valid under the Fourth Amendment. To decide this, the Court needed to determine if breath and blood tests are reasonable searches under the Fourth Amendment, despite the lack of a search warrant.

The Court ruled that these implied consent statutes, as applied to breath tests, are valid because a breath test can be done as a search incident to arrest. In examining both the government's interest in public safety and the privacy interests of the individual, the Court explained that the balance weighs in favor of the government.

CASE IN BRIEF

United States v. Robinson (1973)

ISSUE Does the Fourth Amendment allow for a full search of a person after a custodial arrest, even if the officer does not fear for his safety or believe that evidence might be destroyed?

RULING Yes. All that is required for a full search of a person is a lawful, custodial arrest based on probable cause. No additional justification is required.

CASE IN BRIEF

Birchfield v. North Dakota (2016)

ISSUE Under the Fourth Amendment, can a person be compelled to submit to a warrantless breath test by making it a crime to refuse?

RULING Yes. It is a valid search incident to arrest to obtain a sample of one's breath, and failure to submit can be a crime. A blood test, on the other hand, requires a search warrant.

Breath tests are non-invasive and do not supply any more information than the breath sample itself, and the government interest of combatting drunk driving is important. Compelling a blood test, on the other hand, is not reasonable under the Fourth Amendment, because such a test is much more intrusive, and the personal information detailed by the sample can be great. Therefore, a blood test requires a search warrant.

Not all property immediately associated with the arrestee may be searched incident to arrest. In 2014, the Court addressed a split in the circuit courts as to where and how cell phones fit into the "search incident to arrest" scheme. *Riley v. California* (2014) decided that cell phones are "different" and are not subject to the same search incident to arrest rules as other personal items.

Riley was pulled over for a driving with expired license registration. The car was to be impounded because Riley had a suspended license and an inventory search was completed. The inventory yielded two guns, one of which was later tied to a shooting of a rival gang member. The officers arrested Riley after finding the guns and a search incident to arrest produced Riley's cell phone, which was in his pocket. The officers looked at its contents and found pictures and videos tying Riley to a street gang and to the car used in the shooting. All this was introduced at trial to help convict him. Both the trial court and appeals court ruled that the search of the cell phone was valid as incident to arrest.

The Supreme Court ruled differently. It noted that a search incident to arrest is based on the government interests of preserving evidence and protecting the officer, neither of which are present in regard to a cell phone's digital data. Importantly, a cell phone contains vast amounts of private data, from pictures and videos, to bank statements and medical records. The Court stated that cell phone searches are very different than "the brief physical search considered in *Robinson*." The data on a cell phone has a quality that does not mirror that of the "physical realities" that are implicated in search of a person, and the intrusion on one's private affairs is not so limited.

The Court held that a search of the data on a cell phone will not be valid if done as a search incident to arrest, and generally a search warrant is needed to access its contents. "Our holding, of course, is not that the information on a cell phone is immune from search; it is instead that a warrant is generally required before such a search, even when a cell phone is seized incident to arrest."

Even when a full body search may be lawful, police might still be found to have gone too far. This area of law is still being shaped. Since the *Chimel* and *Robinson* cases, state courts have not always been willing to condone full-body searches for all offenses and have found some unreasonable. When the offense is petty, such as a traffic offense or other offenses routinely handled by citation rather than formal booking, some courts have held that police cannot conduct full-body searches.

The issue of **remoteness** may also determine whether a search is unreasonable. In *Chadwick,* the Court held that the search of seized luggage or other personal belongings not immediately associated with the arrestee's body or under his or her immediate control will not be allowed if that search is remote in time and place from the arrest and no emergency exists; in other words, the search and arrest must be contemporaneous.

◀ CASE IN BRIEF

Riley v. California (2014)

ISSUE Is a cell phone subject to a search incident to arrest, just as any other personal item on an arrestee?

RULING No. A cell phone and its digital contents are very different from traditional items that can be searched incident to arrest. A cell phone often contains large amounts of private data, making the data different from that contained in a purse or a wallet. Accessing this information does not further the government interests of a search incident to arrest.

remoteness regarding the unreasonableness and unlawfulness of searches of seized luggage or other personal belongings not immediately associated with the arrestee's body or under his or her immediate control

In *Chadwick*, federal narcotics agents had probable cause to arrest the defendants and seize a footlocker they had placed in the trunk of a car. An hour and a half after the arrest, the agents opened the footlocker and found marijuana. The Supreme Court stated:

> The potential dangers lurking in all custodial arrests make warrantless searches of items within the "immediate control" area reasonable without requiring the arresting officer to calculate the probability that weapons or destructible evidence may be involved.... However, warrantless searches of luggage or other property seized at the time of an arrest cannot be justified as incident to that arrest either if the search is remote in time and place from the arrest ... or no exigency exists. Once law enforcement officers have reduced luggage or other personal property not immediately associated with the person of the arrestee to their exclusive control, and there is no longer any danger that the arrestee might gain access to the property to seize a weapon or destroy evidence, a search of that property is no longer an incident of the arrest.

The *Chadwick* Court did, however, include in their opinion that a warrantless search might be reasonable if some emergency situation existed, stating, "Of course, there may be other justifications for a warrantless search of luggage taken from a suspect at the time of his arrest; for example, if officers have reason to believe their luggage contains some immediately dangerous instrumentality, such as explosives, it would be foolhardy to transport it to the station house without opening the luggage and disarming the weapon."

Maryland v. Buie (1990) allowed a limited **protective sweep** by officers during an arrest in a home for the officers' safety (to determine whether anyone else was present). The Court held:

protective sweep a limited search made in conjunction with an in-home arrest when the searching officer possesses a reasonable belief based on specific and articulable facts that the area to be swept harbors an individual posing a danger to those on the arrest scene

> The Fourth Amendment permits a properly limited protective sweep in conjunction with an in-home arrest when the searching officer possesses a reasonable belief based on specific and articulable facts that the area to be swept harbors an individual posing a danger to those on the arrest scene....
>
> We should emphasize that such a protective sweep, aimed at protecting the arresting officers, if justified by the circumstances, is nevertheless not a full search of the premises, but may extend only to cursory inspection of those spaces where a person may be found.

Thus the two additional options to *Chimel*, as determined in *Buie*, for protective searches incident to in-home arrests are:

- *Without any suspicion* that anyone dangerous is hiding in the home, arresting officers can, nevertheless, look into immediately adjoining spaces large enough to conceal a potential assailant, from which an attack could be immediately launched.
- *With reasonable suspicion* that someone in the home might endanger officers during the arrest or as they exit the property, officers can conduct a "protective" sweep of the entire premises, again looking into any areas where a person could be concealed (Rutledge, 2009a).

In other words, if the search incident to an in-home arrest expands beyond the rooms immediately adjacent to the location where the arrest is occurring, to include spaces on other levels of the home, officers must be able to articulate in their reports and in their testimony a reasonable suspicion that a potential attacker was concealed within the home (Rutledge, 2009a).

Use of Force in Searching an Arrested Person When government agents search a person incident to arrest, they may use reasonable force to protect themselves, as well as to prevent escape or the destruction or concealment of evidence, as discussed in Chapter 8. This permission does not apply to the more invasive body searches for evidence, but to using reasonable force to control the situation, including stopping the person from destroying or hiding evidence that has been, for example, put into his or her mouth to be swallowed is allowed. In *Salas v. State* (1971), when a police officer applied a chokehold on the suspect, forcing him to spit drugs out of his mouth, the court allowed the drugs to be admitted as evidence. The *reasonableness* of the police action determines the lawfulness of it.

Searching People Other Than the Arrested Person When a person is arrested while with someone else, the associate might be logically assumed to have weapons or contraband. However, searches of people who accompany an arrestee must be supported by an independent basis; in other words, the officer must develop reasonable suspicion or probable cause specific to the companion. A search is not justified simply because "you were with Arrestee X, so now I can search you, too." Such searches are limited to a frisk when the officer reasonably believes the companion may be dangerous or might destroy evidence, and then only if that person was in the immediate area of the arrest (*United States v. Simmons*, 1977). Logically, the area under the companion's immediate control may also be searched (*United States v. Lucas*, 1990).

Searching the Vehicle of an Arrested Person The landmark case for the warrantless search of a vehicle incident to an arrest is *New York v. Belton* (1981). This decision was considered a "bright-line rule" for police searches of a vehicle following the arrest of a driver or passenger (Rutledge, 2009c, p. 68). In this case, the Supreme Court said:

> When a policeman has made a lawful custodial arrest of the occupant of an automobile, he may, as a contemporaneous incident of that arrest, search the passenger compartment of that automobile.
>
> It follows from this conclusion that the police may also examine the contents of any containers found within the passenger compartment, for if the passenger compartment is within reach of the arrestee, so also will containers in it be within his reach.

The Court further defined a "container" as any object that can hold another object, including "closed or open glove compartments, consoles or other receptacles located anywhere within the passenger compartments, as well as luggage, boxes, bags, clothing and the like." The Court added that only the vehicle's interior can be searched incident to arrest, *not* the trunk.

The traditional interpretation that, for three decades, supported the bright-line rule under *Belton* has since been narrowed. In *Arizona v. Gant* (2009), the Supreme Court reduced law enforcement's authority to search the passenger compartment of a vehicle incident to arrest. In this case Rodney Gant was arrested in his driveway,

CASE IN BRIEF

Arizona v. Gant (2009)

ISSUE Does the Fourth Amendment allow an automatic search of the passenger compartment of a car incident to the arrest of a recent occupant?

RULING No. Only if the arrestee is unsecured and within reaching distance or it is reasonable to believe there is evidence of the crime of arrest in the car may the passenger compartment be searched incident to arrest.

after parking and exiting his vehicle, for driving with a suspended license. After getting out of his car, Gant was arrested immediately, handcuffed, and placed into the back of a patrol car. Officers then returned to search his vehicle incident to the arrest and found a gun and a bag of cocaine in a jacket in the backseat. Gant was charged with and convicted of possession of narcotics for sale and possession of drug paraphernalia. He appealed on the basis that the warrantless search of his vehicle was a Fourth Amendment violation. The Arizona Supreme Court agreed that the warrantless search of Gant's vehicle was unreasonable because the scene was secure since Gant was in custody and unable to pose a threat to the officers or to destroy evidence. The U.S. Supreme Court affirmed this decision.

Gant provides an excellent example of why police officers must understand the rationale behind why they are permitted to perform certain actions: "The *Gant* decision changes the landscape dramatically with regard to an officer's authority to conduct a warrantless search of a vehicle incident to arrest as a matter of routine. In short, the bright-line rule allowing automatic searches of vehicles incident to the arrest of an occupant [*New York v. Belton*, 1981] has been narrowed to allow such a search only if the officer has a reasonable belief that the arrestee can gain access to the vehicle or that evidence of the crime of arrest will be found in the vehicle" (Judge, 2009, p. 12). Basically, the right to search a vehicle incident to the arrest of one of its occupants (via *Belton*) is no longer automatic (via *Gant*).

In *Gant*, the Court rejected a broad reading of *Belton*, relying instead on parameters set forth in *Chimel* and explaining: "Construing *Belton* broadly to allow vehicle searches incident to any arrest would serve no purpose except to provide a police entitlement, and it is anathema to the Fourth Amendment to permit a warrantless search on that basis." Using the *Chimel* rationale, the Court held that police are authorized to search a vehicle incident to a recent occupant's arrest *only* when the arrestee is unsecured and within reaching distance of the passenger compartment at the time of the search. The second circumstance under which officers are justified to search a vehicle incident to arrest is when it is reasonable to believe that evidence relevant to crime for which the occupant was arrested might be found in the vehicle. This second circumstance, established in *Thornton v. United States* (2004), did not apply in *Gant* because he was arrested for driving on a suspended driver's license, and it was unreasonable to believe that any evidence related to that offense would be found inside the vehicle. *Gant* does, however, leave open other search doctrines that may apply instead of searches incident to arrest. Many of the other exceptions continue to apply, as do probation and parole searches (Wallentine, 2009).

Justification to conduct a search incident to arrest of a vehicle is not present when the vehicle has been stopped for a traffic violation and the driver merely issued a citation, as was the case in *Knowles v. Iowa* (1998). Patrick Knowles was stopped for speeding (43 mph in a 25-mph zone). Although Iowa law allowed the officer the option of arrest, he chose instead to issue a citation and, subsequently, conducted a full search of the vehicle without Knowles's consent. The search produced a bag of marijuana and a pipe, and Knowles was arrested and charged with violating Iowa's controlled substances law.

Although Iowa law stated that issuance of a citation in lieu of an arrest "does not affect the officer's authority to conduct an otherwise lawful search," the U.S. Supreme Court effectively struck down the law as unconstitutional, finding that it

Constitutional Law in ACTION

Officer Singh is patrolling the neighborhood in his squad car. He sees a car run through a red stoplight without even slowing down, so he follows the car and pulls it over for the traffic violation.

Officer Singh talks with the driver, who hands the officer his driver's license. Officer Singh walks back to his squad and checks the driver's license status on the squad computer. When the status comes back as valid, the officer is notified that the driver has a felony warrant.

Officer Singh returns to the car and arrests the driver for the outstanding warrant. The officer handcuffs the driver and conducts a search of the driver incident to arrest, not finding any contraband or evidence. Officer Singh has the driver sit in the back of the squad car and then returns to the driver's car.

The officer then conducts a search of the vehicle incident to arrest and searches the entire passenger compartment, locating a stolen handgun under the driver's seat.

- *Was the search of the car incident to arrest valid?*
- *Did the search meet the criteria set forth in Gant?*
- *Would the result be different if the driver had been arrested for robbing a convenience store that happened an hour before?*

---

violated the Fourth Amendment. *Knowles v. Iowa* made clear that only a lawful custodial arrest justifies a warrantless search incident to arrest. Merely having probable cause to arrest, or issuing a citation when an actual arrest does not occur, does not justify a search.

The issue of when an officer may proceed with a vehicle search incident to arrest of a recent occupant was addressed in *Thornton v. United States* (2004). In this case, Thornton pulled his vehicle over, got out, and was then arrested. The officer proceeded to search his car and found a gun. Thornton claimed the search was unconstitutional because he was arrested outside the car. The Court held the fact that he had exited the car made no difference because it was still considered to have been under his control. A summary of allowed police actions regarding searches of stopped vehicles and their occupants is given in Table 9.1.

The Automobile Exception

A *seizure* occurs whenever a vehicle is stopped, and so Fourth Amendment prohibitions against unreasonable search and seizure apply. Automobiles and other vehicles may need to be searched without a warrant. The initial basis for allowing such a search was because of their *mobility*. This so-called automobile exception has arisen because it would be considered unreasonable for law enforcement officers to expect suspects to voluntarily remain in place while the officers returned to the station to prepare the warrant application and then find a judge to sign it. Detaining suspects for as long as it would take to secure a warrant would also be

CASE IN BRIEF

Knowles v. Iowa (1998)

ISSUE Is a search of a vehicle incident to arrest by virtue of a traffic citation valid under the Fourth Amendment?

RULING No. The issuance of a traffic citation does not concern the same issues, such as detecting a hidden weapon or preserving evidence that may be destroyed, that exist in a full custodial arrest situation.

Table 9.1 Summary of Allowed Police Actions Regarding Searches of Stopped Vehicles and Their Occupants

Action—Under most circumstances, officers may	Precedent case
Order both the driver and any passengers out of a vehicle	*Pennsylvania v. Mimms* (1977) *Maryland v. Wilson* (1997)
Perform a pat down of a driver and any passengers on a reasonable suspicion they may be armed and dangerous	*Terry v. Ohio* (1968)
Conduct a "*Terry* pat down" of the passenger compartment of the vehicle on a reasonable suspicion that an occupant is dangerous and may gain immediate control of a weapon	*Michigan v. Long* (1983)
Conduct a pat down of passengers in a vehicle stopped for a traffic violation, even if the passenger was being questioned on a matter unrelated to the traffic stop	*Arizona v. Johnson* (2009)
Conduct a full search of the passenger compartment, including any containers therein, pursuant to a custodial arrest *only* if the officer has a reasonable belief that the arrestee can gain access to the vehicle or that evidence of the crime of arrest will be found in the vehicle	*Arizona v. Gant* (2009)

unreasonable. This exception, like the others, is not difficult to understand if the underlying reason for it is kept in mind. The automobile exception, as it stands today, simply states that if a government agent has probable cause to believe the vehicle contains contraband or evidence of a crime, no warrant is needed.

The precedent for a warrantless search of automobiles came from *Carroll v. United States* (1925). During Prohibition in the 1920s, among the 1,500 agents pursuing bootleggers were two federal agents posing as buyers in a Michigan honky-tonk. Two bootleggers, George Carroll and John Kiro, were somewhat suspicious. They said they had to go get the liquor and would return in about an hour. They called later to say they could not return until the next day, but they never appeared.

The agents resumed surveillance of a section of road between Grand Rapids and Detroit known to be used by bootleggers. Within a week after their unsuccessful buy, the agents recognized Carroll and Kiro driving by. They gave chase, but lost them. Two months later they again recognized Carroll's car, pursued it, and overtook it. The agents were familiar with Carroll's car, recognized Carroll and Kiro in the automobile, and believed the automobile contained bootleg liquor. A search revealed 68 bottles of whiskey and gin, most behind the seats' upholstery, where the padding had been removed. The contraband was seized and the two men arrested.

Carroll and Kiro were charged with and convicted of transporting intoxicating liquor. Carroll's appeal, taken to the U.S. Supreme Court, resulted in a landmark decision defining the rights and limitations for warrantless searches of vehicles:

> If the search and seizure without a warrant are made upon probable cause, that is, upon a belief, reasonably arising out of circumstances known to the seizing officer, that an automobile or other vehicle contains that which by law is subject to seizure and destruction, the search and seizure are valid.

Over the past several decades, the courts have modified their approach from the original rationale set forth in *Carroll*, with the

---

CASE IN BRIEF

Carroll v. United States (1925)

ISSUE Is it constitutional to search a motor vehicle without a search warrant but with probable cause?

RULING Yes. A motor vehicle on the public roads may be searched with probable cause, and there is no requirement to get a search warrant.

LO4 *Carroll v. United States (1925)* established that vehicles can be searched without a warrant, provided (1) there is probable cause to believe the vehicle's contents violate the law and (2) the vehicle would be gone before a search warrant could be obtained.

second requirement—exigency produced by a vehicle's mobility—falling by the wayside. Beginning with *Chambers v. Maroney* (1970), the emphasis by the courts has been on the existence of probable cause, with no requirement that an exigency exists. In *Chambers*, the car had been stopped and driven to the police station where it was searched. The Court held that a vehicle may be searched without a warrant if probable cause is present, and that if probable cause exists for a search at the scene, it also exists if the search is done at a different location later. In other words, it was constitutional to perform a delayed search as well.

With mobility or exigency no longer a requirement, all that is presently necessary for a warrantless search of a vehicle to be valid is that law enforcement officers have probable cause to believe the vehicle contains contraband or evidence. Recall from Chapter 7 that *probable cause to search* means officers reasonably believe, based on the totality of the circumstances, that evidence, contraband, or other items sought are where police believe these items to be. In *Maryland v. Dyson* (1999), the Court again supported its previous decisions regarding motor vehicle searches by allowing police to search without a warrant when probable cause exists. In this case, Kevin Dyson was stopped by a deputy sheriff who had received a reliable tip, including the make, model, color, and license plate of a vehicle suspected of transporting a sizeable amount of cocaine. Dyson argued the evidence should have been suppressed because there was no exigency to the search and no warrant was obtained to search the vehicle. The Court relied on *Carroll v. United States* (1925) in reaffirming the existence of the motor vehicle exception to the warrant requirement when probable cause exists, adding that exigency need not exist.

If police have legally stopped a vehicle and have probable cause to believe the vehicle contains contraband, they can conduct a thorough search of the vehicle, including the trunk and any closed packages or containers found in the vehicle or the trunk. However, the scope of the search must be reasonable and limited to what the officer has probable cause to look for. For example, if the officer has probable cause to believe the vehicle contains a stolen television, it is not reasonable to search the glove box or a purse inside the vehicle. In *United States v. Ross* (1982), the Court held that when a police officer has probable cause to believe evidence of a crime is concealed in an automobile, the officer may conduct a "search as broad as one that could be authorized by a magistrate issuing a warrant. . . . If probable cause justifies the search of a lawfully stopped vehicle, it justifies the search of every part of the vehicle and its contents that may conceal the object of the search."

In *California v. Acevedo* (1991), the Court held that if police officers have probable cause to believe a container in an automobile holds contraband or evidence of a crime, a warrantless search of the container is justified, even if probable cause to search the entire vehicle for that same evidence or contraband has not been established. *Acevedo* was an attempt to reconcile discrepancies in previous contradictory rules governing searches of closed containers in vehicles that had, for years, confused courts and police officers and impeded effective law enforcement:

> Until today, this Court has drawn a curious line between the search of an automobile that coincidentally turns up a container and the search of a container that coincidentally turns up in an automobile. The protections of the Fourth Amendment must not turn on such coincidences. We therefore interpret *Carroll* as providing one rule to govern all

◀ CASE IN BRIEF

Maryland v. Dyson (1999)

ISSUE Does the Fourth Amendment require probable cause and the existence of an exigency to search a car without a warrant?

RULING No. All that is required to search a car is probable cause to believe that it contains evidence or contraband. An exigency is not necessary.

automobile searches. The police may search an automobile and the containers within it where they have probable cause to believe contraband or evidence is contained.

Wyoming v. Houghton (1999) extended the scope of such searches to include the personal effects of passengers in the vehicle, again within the limits of reasonableness. The Court noted that the government interest in effective law enforcement would be substantially impaired without the ability to search passengers' belongings because (1) a passenger may have an interest in concealing evidence of criminal activity in collusion with the driver and (2) a criminal may hide contraband in a passenger's belongings as readily as in other containers in the car.

In *Illinois v. Caballes* (2005), the Court held that having a police narcotics-detection dog simply walk around a vehicle that had been stopped for speeding is not unconstitutional. In this case, the fact that the suspect was stopped only for a traffic violation did not prevent another officer from having the dog walk around the car, and the dog's alert of narcotics provided sufficient probable cause to then search it.

Inventory Searches of Impounded Vehicles Police officers can legally tow and impound vehicles for many reasons, including vehicles involved in accidents, parked in a tow-away zone, or abandoned on a highway. When the police impound a vehicle for a legitimate reason, they may lawfully conduct an inventory search. Because the vehicle is now in police custody, officers have a duty to ensure personal property is accounted for. If contraband or evidence is found, it will be admissible in court. Although inventory searches are more administrative than a traditional Fourth Amendment search for something illegal, these searches still meet the reasonableness requirement.

The precedent case on inventory search is *South Dakota v. Opperman* (1976). Donald Opperman's illegally parked car was towed to the city impound lot and inventoried. During the routine inventory, a bag of marijuana was found in the unlocked glove compartment. The Supreme Court concluded that the inventory was not unreasonable under the Fourth Amendment, noting:

> These procedures [inventory of impounded vehicles] developed in response to three distinct needs: the protection of the owner's property while it remains in police custody; the protection of the police against claims or disputes over lost or stolen property; and the protection of the police from potential danger. The practice has been viewed as essential to respond to incidents of theft or vandalism. In addition, police frequently attempt to determine whether a vehicle has been stolen and thereafter abandoned.

Inventory searches are generally accepted as standard procedure for many departments. However, if evidence from a routine inventory search is to be admissible in court, the inventory must be just that: routine. Police cannot decide that some vehicles will be searched when impounded, whereas others are not. Routine inventory searches have been held reasonable; checking only certain vehicles has not. Officers from departments that usually do not conduct inventory searches cannot decide to inventory one particular vehicle.

Two Supreme Court cases illustrate the importance of having standard procedures for conducting inventory searches. In *Colorado v. Bertine* (1987), the Court upheld as lawful the Boulder Police Department's standard inventory policy, stating, "Nothing prohibits the exercise of police discretion to impound a vehicle . . . so long as

CASE IN BRIEF ▶

Wyoming v. Houghton (1999)

ISSUE Does it violate the Fourth Amendment to search a passenger's belongings located in the car when the officer has probable cause to believe the car contains contraband?

RULING No. Officers with probable cause to search a car for contraband may search belongings belonging to the occupants of the car as well.

CASE IN BRIEF ▶

South Dakota v. Opperman (1976)

ISSUE Is it constitutional to conduct an inventory of a vehicle's contents when that vehicle is lawfully impounded by the police?

RULING Yes. It is reasonable to conduct an inventory "search" of a car when lawfully impounded because it is done for purposes other than investigating criminal conduct.

that discretion is exercised according to standard criteria and on the basis of something other than suspicion of evidence of criminal activity." The Court's ruling also extended the permissible scope of inventory searches of vehicles to include opening and examining closed containers within the vehicle *if* the police agency has a standard procedure or established routine for such activity. In the absence of such a policy, such a search would violate the Fourth Amendment.

In *Florida v. Wells* (1990), Martin Wells had given the Florida Highway Patrol permission to open his impounded car's trunk. Police found a locked suitcase, which, on being opened, revealed a considerable amount of marijuana. Wells moved to suppress the marijuana on the grounds it was seized in violation of the Fourth Amendment. The Court held that *Colorado v. Bertine* required police agencies to have a policy mandating either that all containers be opened during such searches or that no containers be opened, leaving no room for officer discretion. Noting the absence of any such Florida Highway Patrol policy, the Court ruled, "The instant search was insufficiently regulated to satisfy the Fourth Amendment. Requiring standardized criteria or established routine as to such openings prevents individual police officers from having so much latitude that inventory searches are turned into a ruse for a general rummaging in order to discover incriminating evidence."

Exigent Circumstances

Yet another circumstance in which lawful warrantless searches can be made is if **exigent** (emergency) **circumstances** exist. The courts have recognized that sometimes situations will arise that reasonably require immediate action before evidence may be destroyed. Police officers who have established probable cause that evidence is likely to be at a certain place and who do not have time to get a search warrant may conduct a warrantless search. However, there must be extenuating (exigent) circumstances, such as preventing the imminent destruction of evidence; hot pursuit of a dangerous offender; preventing the escape of someone sought to be detained or arrested in public; public safety or community caretaking concerns; and rescue and emergency aid efforts (*Minnesota v. Olson*, 1990).

exigent circumstances
emergency situations

L05 *Exigent circumstances include danger of physical harm to an officer or others, danger of destruction of evidence, driving while intoxicated, hot-pursuit situations, and individuals requiring "rescuing," for example, unconscious individuals.*

Imminent Destruction of Evidence In *Schmerber v. California* (1966), the Court recognized that, under particular facts, officers might need to search for, or seize, evidence before a warrant can be secured. In this situation, there must be a reasonable belief that evidence or contraband might be removed or destroyed if the officers, with no time to secure a warrant, do not act quickly.

Schmerber was arrested for drunk driving after he was involved in an accident. He was then taken to a hospital to be treated for injuries, where an officer ordered a doctor to take a blood sample from Schmerber to determine the driver's blood alcohol content (BAC). The blood draw occurred despite Schmerber's objections and advice from his lawyer.

The Court recognized that, in this case, time had already passed from when the accident occurred and when Schmerber was brought to the hospital. Taking more time to secure a search warrant would have allowed the evidence to disappear

◀ CASE IN BRIEF

Schmerber v. California (1966)

ISSUE Is the Fourth Amendment violated when the police draw blood from a suspect without a search warrant?

RULING No. On the specific facts of this case, it was reasonable to draw blood without a search warrant because it was reasonable to believe the BAC would dissipate and the evidence would be lost.

because the percentage of alcohol in the body will begin to diminish after drinking stops and the body begins to eliminate it from the system. The Court stated the warrantless search in this case was reasonable because the officer "might reasonably have believed that he was confronted with an emergency, in which the delay necessary to obtain a warrant, under the circumstances, threatened 'the destruction of evidence.'"

In 2013, the Supreme Court revisited the issue of the destruction of evidence in drunk driving cases. In *Missouri v. McNeely*, the Court was confronted with the question of whether the natural dissipation of alcohol in the blood system automatically meets the exigent circumstance requirement and allows the police to force a blood draw. The Court ruled that each situation must be determined on its own facts to determine whether or not the situation qualifies as an exigent circumstance.

Some courts have ruled that if the officers themselves create the exigency, the exigent circumstance exception to the warrant requirement will not apply. This creates a quandary, however, because an officer knocking at the door may be construed as creating an exigency in and of itself. The Supreme Court addressed the problem of police-created exigency in *Kentucky v. King* (2011), a case in which officers pursued into an apartment building a suspect who had sold crack cocaine in an undercover buy. Having lost sight of the suspect briefly, the officers believed he had entered an apartment from which a strong odor of marijuana was coming. Officers pounded on the door and loudly identified themselves as police. A commotion and movement was heard inside, and officers believed that the occupants were destroying the drugs (evidence), so they forced entry. They discovered cash, drugs, and paraphernalia in the apartment, even though the initial suspect was not inside. The Kentucky Supreme Court ruled that the entry was unlawful because the police had created the exigency when they pounded on the door and announced their presence. The Supreme Court reversed, stated that as long as the police do not create the exigency by "means of an actual or threatened violation of the Fourth Amendment," the exigent circumstances rule applies.

It is important to understand that the exigency limits the scope of the warrantless search or seizure. For example, once officers secure evidence that is about to be destroyed, any further searching is prohibited because the exigency is over. There is no "free reign" to search at will, and any further searching requires a warrant.

Hot Pursuit Recall from Chapter 8 that hot pursuit involves pursuit of a suspect into a place that typically holds a reasonable expectation of privacy, such as one's home. *Warden v. Hayden* (1967), presented in Chapter 8, is a good example of a hot pursuit case. Another relevant case is *Welsh v. Wisconsin* (1984), in which a lone witness observed a car that was being driven erratically and that eventually swerved off the road, coming to a stop in a field without causing damage to any person or property. Ignoring the witness's advice to wait for help, the driver (Edward Welsh) walked away from the scene. The police arrived a few minutes later and were told by the witness that the driver was either drunk or sick. After checking the car's registration, the police, without obtaining a warrant, proceeded to Welsh's nearby home, arriving at about 9 P.M. Welsh's stepdaughter answered the door and allowed the police inside, where they found Welsh lying naked in bed. Welsh was

CASE IN BRIEF ▶

Missouri v. McNeely (2013)

ISSUE Is there a per se rule allowing for warrantless blood draw in all drunk driving cases?

RULING No. Each case must be decided on its own facts. Whether or not an exigent circumstance exists and the blood needs to be drawn without a warrant will be determined on a case-by-case basis.

CASE IN BRIEF ▶

Kentucky v. King (2011)

ISSUE Does the exigent circumstance exception to prevent the destruction of evidence apply when police cause the situation in which evidence might be destroyed by simply knocking on the door and announcing their presence?

RULING Yes. As long as the police act without violating or threaten to violate the Fourth Amendment, exigent circumstances apply. Whether or not the police should foresee that their acts will cause the destruction of evidence is immaterial.

arrested for driving a motor vehicle while under the influence of an intoxicant in violation of a Wisconsin statute, a nonjailable first offense at that time. At trial, the state argued that the warrantless arrest was justified because of exigent circumstances, including "hot pursuit" of a suspect, the need to prevent physical harm to the offender and the public, and the need to prevent destruction of evidence. The case eventually went before the Supreme Court. In delivering the opinion of the Court, Justice William Brennan stated:

> *Payton v. New York* held that, absent probable cause and exigent circumstances, warrantless arrests in the home are prohibited by the Fourth Amendment. But the Court in that case explicitly refused "to consider the sort of emergency or dangerous situation, described in our cases as 'exigent circumstances,' that would justify a warrantless entry into a home for the purpose of either arrest or search." Certiorari was granted in this case to decide at least one aspect of the unresolved question: whether, and if so under what circumstances, the Fourth Amendment prohibits the police from making a warrantless night entry of a person's home in order to arrest him for a nonjailable traffic offense. . . .
>
> [In the case before us] the petitioner was arrested in the privacy of his own bedroom for a noncriminal, traffic offense. The State attempts to justify the arrest by relying on the hot-pursuit doctrine, on the threat to public safety and on the need to preserve evidence of the petitioner's blood-alcohol level. On the facts of this case, however, the claim of hot pursuit is unconvincing because there was no immediate or continuous pursuit of the petitioner from the scene of a crime. Moreover, because the petitioner had already arrived home, and had abandoned his car at the scene of the accident, there was little remaining threat to the public safety. Hence, the only potential emergency claimed by the State was the need to ascertain the petitioner's blood-alcohol level.
>
> Even assuming, however, that the underlying facts would support a finding of this exigent circumstance, mere similarity to other cases involving the imminent destruction of evidence is not sufficient. The State of Wisconsin has chosen to classify the first offense for driving while intoxicated as a noncriminal, civil forfeiture offense for which no imprisonment is possible. . . . Given this expression of the State's interest, a warrantless home arrest cannot be upheld simply because evidence of the petitioner's blood-alcohol level might have dissipated while the police obtained a warrant. To allow a warrantless home entry on these facts would be to approve unreasonable police behavior that the principles of the Fourth Amendment will not sanction.

Thus, for the purpose of this discussion, a critical point about the *Welsh* decision was how the Court emphasized that hot pursuit must be "immediate and continuous" from the crime scene and must be in response to a serious crime.

The states and federal circuits are currently split as to what offenses the hot pursuit doctrine applies. In *Stanton v. Sims* (2013), the Court reaffirmed the principle that hot pursuit has never been limited only to felony situations, clarifying the issue slightly. As the law stands now, the crime for which the hot pursuit is occurring must be more than a nonjailable misdemeanor, as in *Welsh*, but the felony committed in *United States v. Santana* (1976)—possession of heroin with intent to distribute—is sufficient.

CASE IN BRIEF

Welsh v. Wisconsin (1984)

ISSUE Does the Fourth Amendment allow a warrantless entry into a home to arrest someone for a nonjailable offense?

RULING No. To justify the application of the exigent circumstance entry without a warrant, the offense must be serious. Here, the offense in question (at the time) did not allow for jail time as punishment.

Constitutional Law in ACTION

While on patrol, Officer Santiago is dispatched to a local convenience store. The dispatcher tells the officer that someone is calling 911 stating the store is being robbed by a 25-year-old white male, wearing blue jeans and a red T-shirt with writing on it. The suspect has a bald head, is wearing sunglasses, and is acting like he has a gun.

As Officer Santiago arrives in the store parking lot, a man matching the description of the robber runs out from inside the store. The man looks in the direction of the police car and then turns and runs the other way. Officer Santiago runs after him.

Officer Santiago chases the man for two blocks and then loses sight of the robber as the robber rounds a corner of an apartment building. An elderly man points to the front door of the building and tells the officer the running man went inside. Officer Santiago goes inside, and just as she does, she sees a man wearing a red shirt go into apartment number 1. She runs to the door, which is now shut, and sees the sunglasses the robber was wearing on the floor outside apartment number 1.

The door is unlocked and Officer Santiago enters into the apartment, yelling "Police!" as she does. She sees the robber in the hallway attempting to change his shirt. Officer Santiago arrests the robber. During the arrest, Officer Santiago sees a gun on the floor and a pile of cash next to it. She seizes the items.

In court the robber seeks to have the gun and the money against him excluded from evidence as being the product of an illegal search.

- *Is the entry into the apartment constitutional? If so, under what exception to the warrant requirement?*
- *What does the officer need to show for that exception to apply?*
- *What about the additional evidence found in the apartment? Can that be seized? Why or why not?*

CASE IN BRIEF

Brigham City, Utah v. Stuart (2006)

ISSUE May police enter a home without a warrant when they reasonably believe that an occupant is seriously injured or in imminent danger?

RULING Yes. The role of an officer is to not only render first aid but also prevent violence and restore order. If the facts of the situation lead to a reasonable belief that someone is in need of help, the police may enter without a warrant.

The Emergency Aid Doctrine In *Brigham City, Utah v. Stuart* (2006) the Supreme Court unanimously held that police may make a warrantless entry into a home if there is "an objective basis for belief that an exigency or emergency exists." In this case, police responding to a loud party complaint at 3:00 A.M. encountered under-aged drinking outside and saw, through a window, a fight occurring inside the home, during which a juvenile assaulted an adult, who was spitting blood.

With intent to stop the assault, police entered the back door and yelled, "Police!" but were not heard over the noise. Three Utah courts agreed the Fourth Amendment required the police knock first to request entry because they did not have a warrant and the circumstances were not sufficient to be considered exigent. The Supreme Court, however, reversed, holding that "police may enter a home without a warrant when they have an objectively reasonable basis for believing that an occupant is seriously injured or immediately threatened with injury." Thus, the actual nature of the injuries is irrelevant. Chief Justice John Roberts, writing for the Court, stated, "Under these circumstances, there was no violation of the Fourth

Amendment's knock-and-announce rule. Furthermore, once the announcement was made, the officers were free to enter; it would serve no purpose to require them to stand dumbly at the door awaiting a response while those within brawled on, oblivious to their presence."

Included in the "danger-to-life" category are individuals suspected of being armed and dangerous, thereby posing a threat to officers or others. In *Ryburn v. Huff* (2012), officers were engaged in a discussion with Mrs. Huff outside her home. When the officers asked whether there were any guns inside the home, Mrs. Huff immediately turned and ran inside her house, and the officers, fearing she might be attempting to access a weapon, followed her inside. The Huffs brought action against the officers, alleging the police entry into their home without a warrant was a violation of the Huffs' Fourth Amendment rights. The Court, however, determined that officer safety concerns prompted the entry and concluded that "a police officer could have reasonably believed that he was justified in making a warrantless entry to ensure that no one inside the house had a gun after Mrs. Huff ran into the house without answering the question of whether anyone had a weapon." In short, the officers had acted constitutionally. The Court further cautioned lower courts not to second-guess officers on the scene about the particular danger present or to evaluate facts in isolation but rather to use the totality of the circumstances and view facts collectively.

Also included in the danger-to-life category are individuals who are found unconscious. If police officers come across an unconscious person, they are obligated to search the person's pockets or purse for identification and for any possible medical information. If they discover evidence of criminal activity or contraband during this search, they may seize it. For example, in *Vause v. United States* (1931), two officers came upon an unconscious man on a public street. Unable to rouse him, they called for an ambulance and then searched his pockets for identification. During this search, they found 15 cellophane packets that contained narcotics. The Court affirmed the reasonableness of the search: "the search of one found in an unconscious condition is both legally permissible and highly necessary."

Open Fields, Abandoned Property, and Public Places

Considering that a crucial tenet in Fourth Amendment search analysis is the existence of a reasonable expectation of privacy, what happens in instances when someone, known or unknown, abandons property? For example, if a person throws something out of a car window while traveling on a freeway, has he or she forfeited any expectation of privacy? What about a tenant who abandons an apartment or discontinues payment on a storage space and never returns to claim the property inside? What about garbage placed curbside to be transported to a dump and then combined with the trash of others throughout the process? Finally, what about something left in an open field so as to be seen by anyone passing by?

This area of search and seizure does not fit neatly in any of the other exceptions to needing a search warrant. It might be considered a natural extension of the plain view doctrine. In effect, however, the courts have dealt with this area by extending the doctrine that anything held out to the public is not protected by the Fourth Amendment because no reasonable expectation of privacy or physical trespass exists.

LO6 *If there is no reasonable expectation of privacy or no physical trespass, Fourth Amendment protections do not apply.*

CASE IN BRIEF

Hester v. United States (1924)

ISSUE Does the Fourth Amendment protect "open fields" such that an officer needs a warrant to view or enter them?

RULING No. The protection of the Fourth Amendment is not extended to "open fields." There is an important distinction between open fields and homes, with the latter being affording Fourth Amendment protection.

The precedent case for search and seizure of abandoned property and open fields is *Hester v. United States* (1924). In this case, the police were investigating bootlegging operations and went to the home of Hester's father. As they came to the house, they saw a man identified as Henderson drive up to the house. The officers hid and saw Hester come out and give Henderson a bottle. The police sounded an alarm, and Hester ran to a car parked nearby and removed a gallon jug; then he and Henderson ran across an open field.

One officer chased them. Hester dropped his jug, which broke, but retained about half its contents. Henderson threw his bottle away. Officers found another broken jar that contained some liquid outside the house. The officers determined the jars contained illegal whiskey. They seized the evidence, even though they had no search or arrest warrants. Hester was convicted of concealing "distilled spirits," but on appeal, he said the officers conducted an illegal search and seizure. The Supreme Court disagreed, stating:

> It is obvious that even if there had been a trespass, the above testimony was not obtained by an illegal search or seizure. The defendant's own acts, and those of his associates, disclosed the jug, the jar and the bottle—and there was no seizure in the sense of the law when the officers examined the contents of each after it had been abandoned.

The Court went on to state, "The special protection accorded by the Fourth Amendment to the people in their 'persons, houses, papers and effects,' is not extended to the open fields." This exception includes property disposed of in such a manner as to relinquish ordinary property rights.

The "open fields" doctrine holds that land beyond that normally associated with use of that land, that is, undeveloped land, can be searched without a warrant. In *Oliver v. United States* (1984), the Court extended *Hester* by holding that "No Trespassing" signs do not bar the public from viewing open fields; therefore, the owner should have no expectation of privacy and the Fourth Amendment does not apply. In this case, officers, responding to a tip that marijuana was being grown in an open field adjacent to a residence, conducted a warrantless search of the field, which was surrounded by a fence with a "No Trespassing" sign affixed, and found the contraband.

CASE IN BRIEF

Oliver v. United States (1984)

ISSUE Is there a reasonable expectation of privacy when a property owner posts "No Trespassing" signs, installs fences around the property, and has a locked gate at the entrance?

RULING No. The "open fields" doctrine applies. Open fields are accessible to anyone, unlike a home, and the methods employed by the property owner do not prevent the viewing of the open fields. Establishing a subjective expectation of privacy is only part of the equation.

The Court held that because open fields are accessible to the public and the police in ways that a home, office, or commercial structure would not be, and because fences and "No Trespassing" signs do not effectively bar the public from viewing open fields, the asserted expectation of privacy in open fields is not one that society recognizes as reasonable. Furthermore, measures taken to protect privacy, such as planting marijuana on secluded land and placing fences, locked gates, and "No Trespassing" signs around the property, do not establish a reasonable expectation of privacy required by the Fourth Amendment. The overriding consideration is not whether the individual chose to conceal "private" activity, but whether the government's intrusion infringed on the personal and societal values protected by the Fourth Amendment. Although the government's intrusion on an open field is a trespass at common law, it is not a search in the constitutional sense. The open fields concept is a federal one, and some states hold that "No Trespassing" signs do, in fact, establish a right of privacy requiring a warrant.

Curtilage is the term used to describe that portion of property generally associated with the common use of land, such as buildings, sheds, and fenced-in areas. It also includes the property around a home or dwelling directly associated with the use of that property. Because there is a reasonable expectation of privacy within the curtilage, it is protected by the Fourth Amendment.

The concept of curtilage evolved in the Supreme Court's attempt to ascertain just how far beyond one's house the reasonable expectation of privacy extended. Inside such areas, the open fields doctrine does not apply. A warrant would be needed to search within the curtilage. In *California v. Ciraolo* (1986), the Court held that police looking from the air into a suspect's backyard does not violate the Fourth Amendment because, although part of the curtilage, it is open to public view from the air. The following year, in *United States v. Dunn* (1987), the Court upheld the warrantless search of a barn that was not part of the curtilage on the same grounds.

In 2013 the Supreme Court decided the case of *Florida v. Jardines*. After receiving a "tip" that Jardines was growing marijuana in his house, officers approached the front porch of the home with a drug-sniffing dog. The dog sniffed the front door and alerted to the presence of drugs. The officers used this alert to obtain a search warrant. The warrant was executed, and marijuana plants were seized from inside the house. Jardines argued in court that the use of the drug-sniffing dog at the front door was an unreasonable search under the Fourth Amendment.

The Supreme Court agreed, ruling that the officers had physically intruded on the curtilage of the house—a constitutionally protected area—when they used the dog to gather information, which amounted to a search under the Fourth Amendment. Officers needed a warrant or some exception to that requirement to conduct this search constitutionally. They had neither. Consequently, the search was unconstitutional, and the marijuana was excluded from evidence.

The Court explained that, in general, a visitor or even an officer may intrude on the curtilage of a home but that the constitutionality of that intrusion depended on what purpose they had for being there. In the Court's opinion, Justice Scalia wrote:

> [A] police officer not armed with a warrant may approach a home and knock, precisely because that is "no more than any private citizen might do" (*Kentucky v. King*, 2011).
>
> But introducing a trained police dog to explore the area around the home in hopes of discovering incriminating evidence is something else. There is no customary invitation to do *that*. An invitation to engage in canine forensic investigation assuredly does not inhere in the very act of hanging a knocker. To find a visitor knocking on the door is routine (even if sometimes unwelcome); to spot that same visitor exploring the front path with a metal detector, or marching his bloodhound into the garden before saying hello and asking permission, would inspire most if us to—well, call the police.

In essence, *Jardines* applied the *Jones* test of physical intrusion for searches involving curtilage.

After a person has discarded or abandoned property, he or she maintains no reasonable expectation of privacy. Thus, something thrown from a car, discarded during a chase, or even disposed of as garbage (once off the curtilage) becomes abandoned property that police may inspect without a warrant. In *California v. Greenwood* (1988), the Supreme Court held that a warrantless search and seizure of trash left curbside for collection in an area accessible by the public, outside of

curtilage the portion of property generally associated with the common use of land

◀ CASE IN BRIEF

Florida v. Jardines (2013)

ISSUE Is it a search to bring a drug-sniffing dog onto the front porch of a homeowner in an effort to gather information?

RULING Yes. Physically intruding on the porch is an intrusion on the curtilage of a house, which is a constitutionally protected area. Because the officers were there to gather information, it is a search under the Fourth Amendment.

the curtilage, does not violate a person's Fourth Amendment rights because there should be no expectation of privacy. Some states, however, have declared searching through trash a violation of their state constitution. In most states, garbage searches remain a standard technique for investigators, particularly narcotics investigators.

"Dumpster diving" or "trash pulls" are methods for obtaining incriminating evidence that often provide legal grounds to obtain a search warrant of a home. To obtain such a warrant, officers must have probable cause to believe there is a pattern of ongoing criminal activity; therefore, depending on the jurisdiction, a single trash pull may be insufficient to establish probable cause. To ensure the constitutionality of the tactic, officers should either conduct multiple trash pulls to establish probable cause for a search warrant or use other investigative techniques to acquire evidence to corroborate what was found in a trash pull (Sanchez & Rubin, 2010).

As technology expands, so too does the discussion surrounding whether discarded property retains a reasonable expectation of privacy. A series of cases has dealt with a person's privacy interest in "abandoned" DNA evidence left on items such as empty soda cans and cigarette butts. One particular case, *United States v. Davis* (2009), provides an informative analysis of a defendant's privacy interests in his DNA and whether law enforcement was justified in collecting such "abandoned" DNA and entering it into Combined DNA Index System (CODIS), the federal DNA database maintained by the FBI, for no apparent reason. In this case, Davis's blood was taken from clothes he was wearing while shot. The hospital where he was treated had placed his clothing in a bag, and Davis never attempted to reclaim these items. The court's opinion is 101 pages long; the following excerpt provides relevant legal analysis relating this case to others dealing with the issue of "abandoned" DNA:

> It is well established that the warrantless search of abandoned property is not unreasonable and therefore does not violate the Fourth Amendment. See, e.g., *California v. Greenwood*, 486 U.S. 35 (1988) (no reasonable expectation of privacy in bagged garbage placed on curb outside curtilage of home for municipal collection);...The determination of whether property is abandoned is based on an objective analysis of act and intent....
>
> [A]bandonment is a problematic concept when applied to DNA because it implies a volitional act of relinquishment that is absent in this case. As one recent commentator has framed the issue: "Do we intend to renounce our actual expectations of privacy with respect to genetic material when we shed our DNA? *The volition that is implied in abandonment is simply unrealistic here.*" Elizabeth E. Joh, Reclaiming "Abandoned" DNA: The Fourth Amendment and Genetic Privacy, 100 Nw. U. L. Rev. 857, 867 (2006) (emphasis added).
>
> Nonetheless, the abandonment analysis in *Greenwood* has been applied to uphold against Fourth Amendment challenge "covert involuntary DNA sampling," a process in which police collect DNA—not from crime scenes—but from known persons who are suspected of crimes, for whom police do not have probable cause to seek a warrant to take a sample directly from them. Joh, *Reclaiming "Abandoned" DNA*, ... (coining new term for this investigative technique to eliminate the implication of volition when DNA is shed without one's knowledge or consent). Thus, instead of taking a sample directly from the targeted individual's body, which would clearly implicate the Fourth Amendment, police obtain discarded or "abandoned" items that are likely to contain the

target's DNA, such as cigarette butts, coffee cups or chewing gum. *See, e.g., Commonwealth v. Bly*, 448 Mass. 473, 862 N.E.2d 341, 356–57 (2007) (suspect connected to murder by DNA analysis of water bottle and cigarette butts he left behind after interview with police); *State v. Wickline*, 232 Neb. 329, 440 N.W.2d 249, 253 (1989) (police not required to obtain warrant to test cigarettes defendant left at police station because he "abandoned these items and sufficiently exposed them to the officer and the public to defeat his claim to Fourth Amendment protection"); *State v. Athan*, 160 Wash.2d 354, 158 P.3d 27 (2007) (no constitutional violation where police addressed phony class-action mailing to suspect in cold rape case and obtained suspect's DNA from saliva on return envelope: "The analysis of DNA obtained without forcible compulsion and analyzed by the government for comparison to evidence found at a crime scene is not a search under the Fourth Amendment.").

Davis had moved to have the DNA evidence suppressed, arguing it was collected unconstitutionally. However, in the end, the Maryland District Court judge chose to treat the DNA evidence as "abandoned," ruling, "There was certainly no blatant or flagrant police action in deliberate disregard of the Defendant's rights that would warrant the remedy of suppression. Accordingly, the Court will, by separate order, deny the Defendant's motion." The Supreme Court, however, has yet to weigh in on the issue of abandoned DNA and privacy rights.

Border Searches

Border searches are vital to U.S. national security. As discussed in Chapter 9, routine searches of persons, belongings, and vehicles at international borders are reasonable under the Fourth Amendment because the Constitution does not require even a hint of suspicion of criminal activity (*Boyd v. United States*, 1886; *Carroll v. United States*, 1925; *United States v. Ramsey*, 1977). Because of the compelling state interest in stopping the flow of illegal immigrants, prohibited goods, and contraband into the country, the courts have recognized that Fourth Amendment protections do not apply at immigration borders, especially at points of entry. Immigration and border agents need no amount of certainty, be it reasonable suspicion or probable cause, to conduct a search at the border, regardless of whether the person being searched is a citizen or noncitizen (del Carmen, 2010).

The same justification that allows searches for no reason at the border is relied on to permit searches with only reasonable suspicion beyond the border but close enough to be considered equivalent. The Supreme Court held in *United States v. Montoya de Hernandez* (1985) that routine searches at a U.S. international border require no objective justification, probable cause, or warrant. In *Quinones-Ruiz v. United States* (1994) the Court stated, "The border search exception applies equally to persons entering or exiting the country."

Regarding a person's *reasonable expectation of privacy*, the Supreme Court has ruled, "A 'search' occurs when an expectation of privacy that society is prepared to consider reasonable is infringed" (*United States v. Jacobsen*, 1984). A more recent case, *Bond v. United States* (2000), involved a border patrol agent's physical manipulation of a bus passenger's carry-on luggage. The agent had boarded the bus to check the passengers' immigration status and to locate illegal drugs by squeezing

◀ CASE IN BRIEF

Bond v. United States (2000)

ISSUE Is the physical manipulation of a person's luggage an unreasonable search?

RULING Yes. A person's luggage is an "effect" under the Fourth Amendment. Physically manipulating it to ascertain its contents is a search because it violates the reasonable expectation of privacy in the luggage and its contents.

the soft luggage some passengers had placed in the overhead storage space above their seats. When the agent squeezed the canvas bag above Bond's seat he noticed that it contained a "brick-like" object. Bond admitted the bag was his and consented to its search, which revealed a "brick" of methamphetamine.

Bond was indicted for federal drug charges but moved to suppress the drugs, arguing that the agent had conducted an illegal search when he squeezed the bag. The Supreme Court reversed the District Court and Court of Appeals when it held, "A reasonable expectation of privacy exists when the person's subjective expectation is objectively reasonable." According to the Court, a traveler's personal luggage is an "effect" protected by the Fourth Amendment. Because Bond used an opaque bag and placed it directly above his seat, he expressed a subjective expectation of privacy in his bag. Furthermore, his expectation of privacy was objectively reasonable because "[w]hen a bus passenger places a bag in an overhead bin, he expects that other passengers or bus employees may move it for one reason or another. Thus, a bus passenger clearly expects that his bag may be handled. He does not expect that other passengers or bus employees will, as a matter of course, feel the bag in an exploratory manner." The agent's manipulation of the bag was an infringement of Bond's reasonable expectation of privacy and constituted a search. This decision directly affects federal and state law enforcement officers' ability to enforce drug laws against those carrying large amounts of narcotics on public transportation.

The complexity of U.S. society has generated an incredible amount of case law pertaining to the Fourth Amendment. What some regard as loopholes that allow the guilty to go free, others see as stringent government control to ensure that either overzealousness or simple error will not result in the innocent being convicted.

The Supreme Court has also recognized that routine border searches may be carried out not only at borders but also at their functional equivalent (as discussed in Chapter 8), meaning being essentially the same or serving the same purpose, for example, airports that receive nonstop flights from foreign countries. People at airports are increasingly being stopped because they fit a drug courier profile. This profile, developed by the Drug Enforcement Administration (DEA), includes the following characteristics: (1) arriving from a source city, (2) little or no luggage or large quantity of empty suitcases, (3) rapid turnaround on airplane trip, (4) use of assumed name, (5) possession of large amount of cash, (6) cash purchase of ticket, and (7) nervous appearance.

This method is well illustrated in *United States v. Sokolow* (1989), which held that use of a drug courier profile to make an investigative stop was legal. In this case, officers used a profile to detain Andrew Sokolow. A drug-detecting dog indicated the presence of narcotics in one of Sokolow's bags. The officers arrested Sokolow and obtained a search warrant for the bag. They found no narcotics but did find documents that indicated involvement in drug trafficking. A second search with the drug-detecting dog turned up narcotics in a second bag that belonged to Sokolow.

At trial, the defense objected to the legality of the investigative stop, but the Court held that the totality of circumstances in the case—the "fit" with numerous criteria for the drug courier profile—established a reasonable suspicion that the suspect was transporting illegal drugs, which made the investigative stop without a warrant valid.

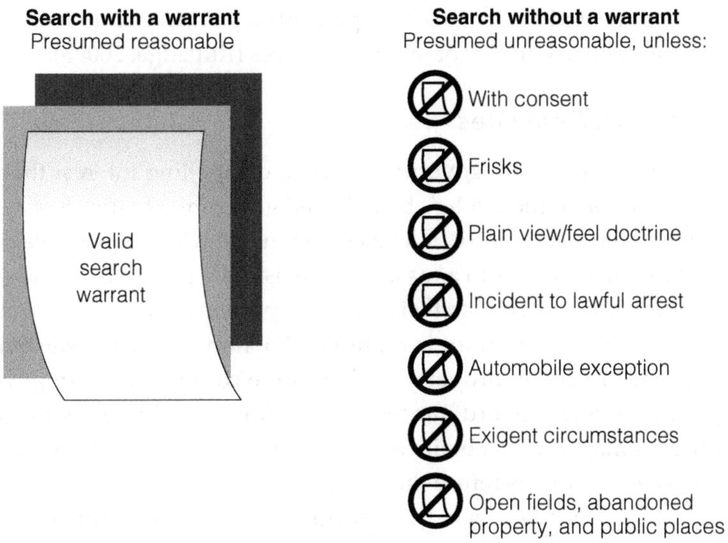

Search with a warrant
Presumed reasonable

Valid search warrant

Search without a warrant
Presumed unreasonable, unless:

- With consent
- Frisks
- Plain view/feel doctrine
- Incident to lawful arrest
- Automobile exception
- Exigent circumstances
- Open fields, abandoned property, and public places

Figure 9.3 Constitutional Analysis of Search and Seizure

A profile of a terrorist has also been developed on the basis of the characteristics of the September 11, 2001, hijackers. All were males from the Middle East who spoke Arabic and were in their twenties. Is special attention to individuals who fit this profile constitutional?

The farther a person gets from the border, however, the more traditional search-and-seizure requirements come back into play. In *Almeida-Sanchez v. United States* (1973), the Supreme Court held that a vehicle search 25 air miles from the Mexican border required a warrant because it was not at the border or its functional equivalent. In *United States v. Ortiz* (1975), the Supreme Court held that the Fourth Amendment prevented border patrol officers from conducting warrantless, suspicionless searches of private vehicles that were removed from the border or its functional equivalent.

Roaming border patrol agents may stop individuals or cars away from the actual border only if they have the traditional reasonable suspicion. Similar to the authorized use of roadblocks elsewhere, border agents can establish roadblocks that stop cars in a certain pattern (every car, every other car, every fifth car, etc.). However, searches may only be conducted according to the traditional rules that apply to vehicles, such as probable cause to believe contraband is present and the like.

Figure 9.3 summarizes when searches are "reasonable" and, therefore, constitutional.

Special Needs Searches

One category of exceptions to the exclusionary rule is "special needs" searches, limited searches that the court considers reasonable because societal needs are thought to outweigh the individual's normal expectation of privacy. Such searches include prison, probation, and parole searches; drug testing for certain occupations; administrative searches of closely regulated businesses; and community caretaking searches. The court has also said that the special need of public school officials to maintain discipline and safety at school presents a justification to relax the usual probable cause standard under some circumstances (Rutledge, 2009b).

Administrative Searches

In certain circumstances, the government has a compelling interest that justifies warrantless searches for the public's benefit, and government officials may conduct a search pursuant to a regulatory or legislative scheme without probable cause or a warrant if the search adheres to a reasonable legislative standard. Certain strongly regulated businesses may be searched during inspections without a warrant. Other times, an administrative warrant is required. An **administrative warrant** allows civil inspections of private property to determine compliance with government rules, regulations, and city ordinances such as fire or building codes. Administrative warrants may also be obtained so government agents can conduct routine inspections when occupants refuse their entry.

Administrative searches were first recognized in *Camara v. Municipal Court of the City and County of San Francisco* (1967), when the Court stated that searches not related to investigating criminal wrongdoing are still regulated by the Fourth Amendment and must be reasonable. The need of the search must be balanced against the intrusion. These types of "administrative" searches allow limited discretion on the part of the searcher and have standardized procedures. Administrative searches also do not necessarily focus on the individual but on the administration of the program or law at hand. The Court uses a balancing test to determine what is reasonable or not (based on the justification offered), given the context of the search.

In *United States v. Biswell* (1972), the Supreme Court reversed a court of appeals ruling that disallowed a warrantless search of a gun shop's locked storeroom, which netted illegal firearms. The Court stated that such inspections pertaining to the sale of illegal firearms are justified and that limited threats such as this inspection to the gun dealer's expectation of privacy are reasonable, adding, "When a dealer chooses to engage in this type of pervasively regulated business and to accept a federal license, he does so with the knowledge that his business records, firearms and ammunition will be subject to effective inspection."

However, in *Marshall v. Barlow's Inc.* (1978) the Court asserted that government inspectors should not be given unlimited authority and found that Occupational Safety and Health Administration (OSHA) employees would not be permitted to simply wander within a business looking for whatever wrongs they might find because to do so would be an unreasonable intrusion into the owner's Fourth Amendment rights.

Public School Searches

Although most searches of students in public schools are conducted by school officials (government agents), those in the criminal justice systems should know the laws related to such searches. The Supreme Court held in *New Jersey v. T.L.O.* (1985) that in a public school, education officials may search a student (including purses, backpacks, or other containers) or student lockers without a warrant or probable cause if there is reasonable suspicion to suspect contraband is present at the point

---

administrative warrant allows civil inspections of private property to determine compliance with government rules, regulations, and city ordinances such as fire or building codes; may also be obtained so government agents can conduct routine inspections when occupants refuse their entry

MYTH
Any search by a government official requires probable cause.

FACT
Not necessarily. Administrative searches, like those in a public school that are based on something other than evidence gathering, can be conducted with less than probable cause.

to be searched. The justification here is the responsibility of public school officials to maintain a safe environment for students. This responsibility would not apply to adult students, dorm rooms, or private schools. The Constitution applies to government officials, which public school personnel are, and not to private school officials.

Safford Unified School District v. Redding (2009) addressed the constitutionality of a strip search of a 13-year-old student, Savana Redding, an eighth-grade student at Bedford Middle School, suspected of furnishing prescription-strength ibuprofen and an over-the-counter drug to other students. The principal at the Arizona school called the young girl into his office and confronted her with the accusation, which she denied. A search of her backpack revealed no pills, so the principal took her to the nurse's office where she was searched by female employees who also found no drugs. Then the women required the student to pull her undergarments away from her body to search for any pills, but none were found.

The student filed a federal civil rights lawsuit against the school and those who searched her alleging a violation of her Fourth Amendment rights and requested a summary judgment, which dismissed the case. After appeals were denied, the case found its way to the Supreme Court, which ruled that the invasive scope of the strip search violated the student's right against unreasonable searches because there was no evidence indicating that pills might be found in her underwear and the items being sought were not particularly dangerous:

> Non-dangerous school contraband does not raise the specter of stashes in intimate places, and there is no evidence in the record of any general practice among Safford Middle School students of hiding that sort of thing in their underwear.... In sum, what was missing from the suspected facts that pointed to the student was any indication of danger to other students from the power of the drugs or their quantity and any reason to suppose that she was carrying pills in her underwear. We think that the combination of these deficiencies was fatal to holding the search reasonable. (*Safford Unified School District v. Redding*, 2009)

The *Redding* opinion leaves intact the *T.L.O.* standard allowing schools to search students on reasonable suspicion, as opposed to the higher probable cause standard, but the Court ruled that the strip search of Redding went too far: "*T.L.O.* requires that a search be both 'justified at its inception' and 'permissible in its scope,' considering the age and gender of the student and the nature of the suspected infraction" (Means & McDonald, 2009b, p. 83). In this case the search of Redding's backpack and outer clothing was reasonable, but the degree of intrusion involved in removing her clothing and exposing her body was unreasonable, especially in view of the fact that officials were seeking only a small quantity of a common medication that posed essentially no threat to the school.

Jail, Prison, Probation, and Parole Searches

A surprise to some people is that prisoners have constitutional rights. However, the rights prisoners have are limited. In *Hudson v. Palmer* (1984) the Supreme Court stated:

> While prisoners enjoy many protections of the Constitution that are not fundamentally inconsistent with imprisonment itself or incompatible with the objectives of

◀ **CASE IN BRIEF**

Safford Unified School District v. Redding (2009)

ISSUE Does it violate the Fourth Amendment to search a 13-year-old girl's underwear for drugs she was suspected of possessing?

RULING Yes. The search is unconstitutional based on the level of intrusion, the girl's age, and the nature of the suspected infraction.

> **MYTH**
> All citizens share the same level of constitutional rights.
>
> **FACT**
> This is false. Those in prison or on probation or parole have "diminished rights" under the Constitution due to their correctional status.

incarceration, imprisonment carries with it the circumscription or loss of many rights as being necessary to accommodate the institutional needs and objectives of prison facilities, particularly internal security and safety. It would be impossible to accomplish the prison objectives of preventing the introduction of weapons, drugs and other contraband into the premises if inmates retained a right of privacy in their cells.

Searches are a reasonable part of prison life among inmates who have little expectation of privacy, but how searches are carried out can conceivably challenge the reasonableness clause of the Fourth Amendment.

In *Moore v. People* (1970), the court ruled that searches conducted by correctional personnel "are not unreasonable as long as they are not for the purpose of harassing or humiliating the inmate in a cruel or unusual manner." Likewise, in *Bell v. Wolfish* (1979) the Supreme Court ruled that unannounced cell searches or shakedowns did not require warrants, were not a violation of inmates' Fourth Amendment rights, and were justified by a correctional facility's need to maintain order. More recently, in *Florence v. Board of Chosen Freeholders of the County of Burlington* (2012), the Court held that strip searches of those entering the jail's general population are constitutional, regardless of the underlying offense or without regard to reasonable suspicion the person might be carrying a concealed weapon.

Suspects to be jailed are subject to a warrantless search, a search that serves two purposes. First, it protects the prisoner's personal property in that the property is all listed and then held in a safe place until the prisoner is released. Second, it protects officers and other prisoners and helps ensure that no weapons or illegal drugs will be taken into the jail.

This rationale underlying this administrative search is different than a search incident to arrest and, therefore, the scope may be quite different. This idea was expressed by Chief Justice Warren E. Burger when he wrote in *Illinois v. Lafayette* (1983), "Police conduct that would be impractical or unreasonable—or embarrassingly intrusive—on the street can more readily—and privately—be performed at the station. For example, the interests supporting a search incident to arrest would hardly justify disrobing an arrestee on the street, but the practical necessities of routine jail administration may even justify taking a prisoner's clothes before confining him, although that step would be rare."

Furthermore, it does not matter that the inventory search is not contemporaneous with an arrest. In *United States v. Edwards* (1974) the Court stated, "Once the accused is lawfully arrested and is in custody, the effects in his possession at the place of detention that were subject to search at the time and place of his arrest may lawfully be searched and seized without a warrant even though a substantial period of time has elapsed between the arrest and subsequent administrative processing, on the one hand, and the taking of the property for use as evidence, on the other."

In *Maryland v. King* (2013), the Supreme Court ruled as constitutional a Maryland law that required the collection of DNA from all people arrested for serious crimes. The DNA identification process was likened to that of fingerprinting or photographing the arrestee, both legitimate booking processes. The Court noted that because the arrestee is already in custody based on probable cause, the need for a warrant is "greatly diminished." The search will be evaluated with reference to "reasonableness" and not individualized suspicion. The majority opinion stressed that the important government interest in identifying arrestees greatly outweighed the minimal intrusion of a "cheek swab" to obtain the sample.

The dissent, written by Justice Scalia, strongly criticized the identification rationale, pointing to the length of time it takes to process a DNA sample for identification. Scalia argued that the real motive behind the Maryland statute authorizing the collection of DNA was not to identify the arrestee but to gather evidence. And this, he wrote, is unconstitutional because it is a search without any individualized suspicion. Those types of searches are only constitutional in narrow situations unrelated to "ordinary crime-solving."

Although courts have generally allowed intrusion, within broad limits, into inmates' privacy, some court rulings have extended the degree of privacy to which inmates are permitted. Two cases, *Turner v. Safley* (1987) and *Jordan v. Gardner* (1993), illustrate the conflict among court decisions regarding inmates' constitutional right to privacy. In *Turner*, the Supreme Court ruled in favor of the administrator-defendant and upheld the correctional policy allowing cross-gender searches: "When a prison regulation impinges on inmates' constitutional rights, the regulation is valid if it is reasonably related to legitimate penological interests." In *Jordan*, however, the circuit court sided with the inmate-plaintiff, holding that female inmates subjected to unclothed body searches by male officers had, in fact, been subjected to an unconstitutional search.

Searches are conducted on visitors, correctional officers, and other corrections personnel because these individuals may smuggle contraband to inmates. The obvious need for prison security is paramount, but courts expect it to be accomplished by lawful, reasonable means.

Not all people convicted of crimes are sent to prison. The majority of those incarcerated are returned to society, most often under some degree of supervision for a determined length of time, while on either probation or parole. *Probation* refers to a situation in which the punishment of a convicted offender is conditionally suspended. The offender must remain in the community and under the supervision of a probation officer, who is usually a court-appointed official. *Parole* refers to release from prison of a convict before the expiration of the prison term on condition that the parolee's activities be restricted (as of residence, occupation, type of associates) and that he or she report regularly to an officer.

More than 4.7 million adults were under community supervision at year end in 2014, the majority of whom (82 percent) were probationers (Kaeble, Glaze, Tsoutis, & Minton, 2016). People on probation or parole are protected by the Constitution; however, what is reasonable for them is considered to be different than that for the general population. Convicted criminals do *not* lose their rights entirely. They are limited, to be sure, but not entirely forfeited. The Court in *Morrissey v. Brewer* (1972) asserted, "It is always true of probationers (as we have said it to be true of parolees) that they do not enjoy the absolute liberty to which every citizen is entitled, but only . . . conditional liberty properly dependent on observation of special (probation) restrictions." Whether one considers any sentencing to accomplish rehabilitation or retribution, government obviously has a vested interest in being involved.

◀ **CASE IN BRIEF**

Maryland v. King (2013)

ISSUE Is it a constitutional search to gather DNA evidence during the booking process from a person arrested for a serious offense?

RULING Yes. Like fingerprinting and photographing an arrestee, DNA collection is an important and legitimate aspect of a booking procedure.

LO7 *Jail and prison inmates, probationers, and parolees have limited Fourth Amendment rights because while under supervision, they should not expect the degree of privacy enjoyed by law-abiding citizens.*

> **CASE IN BRIEF** ▶
>
> *Griffin v. Wisconsin* (1987)
>
> **ISSUE** Is it constitutional for a probation officer to search a probationer's house without a search warrant and with less than probable cause?
>
> **RULING** Yes. The probationer had agreed to a condition of probation that allowed the search of his house, and the law regulating probationers and such searches is reasonable, even though based on less than probable cause.

Several cases have followed *Morrissey* (which confirmed due process during parole revocation hearings) and further defined to what extent the Constitution protects these individuals from unreasonable government intrusions. In *Griffin v. Wisconsin* (1987), the Supreme Court held that a probationer's residence could be searched by a probation officer if there were reasonable grounds to believe contraband was present. Joseph Griffin was on probation under the jurisdiction of the Wisconsin Department of Health and Social Services, which had a policy permitting, upon approval by a supervisor, a probation officer to search a client's home without a warrant if there were reasonable grounds to believe contraband was present. Such a search was conducted after probation officers learned from police that there "were or might be" guns in Griffin's apartment. During the search, a handgun was found, and he was charged accordingly.

Acknowledging that people on probation have constitutional rights, including protection by the Fourth Amendment, the Supreme Court affirmed that government actions must be reasonable. Recognizing the "special needs beyond normal law enforcement," the Court said that the usual requirements of a warrant based upon probable cause were not necessary because to so require would "interfere with the operation of the probation system." The Court did not say a warrantless search could be conducted without cause, but that when there was a state policy allowing a search based on reasonable grounds, the search was reasonable under the Fourth Amendment.

> **CASE IN BRIEF** ▶
>
> *United States v. Knights* (2001)
>
> **ISSUE** May a police officer search a probationer's house without a search warrant?
>
> **RULING** Yes. The probationer agreed to a condition of his probation allowing a search of his home, along with the fact that reasonable suspicion existed, and together the search by the officer is constitutional.

In *United States v. Knights* (2001), the Supreme Court addressed the constitutionality of whether a police officer could search a probationer's home without probable cause or reasonable suspicion; however, the police said they had reasonable suspicion at the time but did not obtain a warrant because they knew that Mark Knights had signed a probation agreement in which he consented to searches at any time. Thus, the Court did not have to deal with suspicionless searches because that was not the case here.

The Court determined that searching Knights's home without a warrant, but with reasonable suspicion, was reasonable under the Fourth Amendment because of the government's interest in regulating and monitoring probationers' behavior. This case, along with *Griffin*, makes clear that individuals on parole or probation have a lesser reasonable expectation of privacy.

In *Knights* the Court stated, "The reasonableness of a search is determined by assessing, on the one hand, the degree to which it intrudes upon an individual's privacy, and, on the other hand, the degree to which it is needed for the promotion of legitimate government interest." Here, the Court clearly balanced the government's interests and those of the individual. *Griffin* and *Knights* differ because there was a procedural rule in *Griffin*, and the search was conducted by a probation officer. In *Knights* such a search was conducted by the police and was based on a condition of his probation. Both cases involved searches based on reasonable grounds.

Courts have found that required drug testing of people on parole or probation for drug offenses is reasonable as in *United States v. Leonard* (1991). In *United States v. Thomas* (1984), a parole officer was permitted to require the client to remove his jacket to show fresh needle marks, with a subsequent search of his clothing netting drugs that were admissible as evidence. However, both searches were also based on a recognition that such searches were conditions of parole.

In *Samson v. California* (2006), the Court sought to further define what rights those on parole, as differentiated from probation, have by holding, "The Fourth Amendment does not prohibit a police officer from conducting a suspicionless search of a parolee." In this case, an officer searched a parolee only because of his status of being on parole, in contradiction to state law requiring the individual "agree in writing to be subject to search or seizure by a parole officer or other peace officer . . . with or without a search warrant and with or without cause." Methamphetamine was found, Donald Curtis Samson was charged and convicted, and his claim of a Fourth Amendment violation was rejected by the trial court. Samson appealed to the Supreme Court.

Writing for the Court, Justice Clarence Thomas explained how the law sought to balance the interests of the individual and government: "Examining the totality of the circumstances, petitioner did not have an expectation of privacy that society would recognize as legitimate. The state's interests, by contrast, are substantial." Further articulating the state's overwhelming interest in supervising parolees, Justice Thomas continued, "Parolees, who are on the continuum of state-imposed punishments, have fewer expectations of privacy than probationers, because parole is more akin to imprisonment than probation is. . . . The essence of parole is release from prison, before the completion of sentence, on the condition that the prisoner abides by certain rules during the balance of the sentence. . . . The extent and reach of those conditions demonstrate that parolees have severely diminished privacy expectations by virtue of their status alone."

◀ **CASE IN BRIEF**
Samson v. California (2006)

ISSUE Does it violate the Fourth Amendment to have a state law that allows a parolee to be searched by a peace officer at any time, with or without suspicion?

RULING No. Under these circumstances the search is constitutional because, when balancing the interests for the effective supervision of parolees and the intrusiveness on the individual's rights, albeit diminished, the balance is in favor of the government interests.

Searches of Public Employee Work Areas

Although employees, no matter where they work, have a degree of interest in retaining some privacy, it is lessened in the public workplace context. Because of this, noninvestigatory work-related searches, or searches related to investigation of employee misconduct, require only reasonableness.

O'Conner v. Ortega (1987) addressed the issue of when public agency employees have legitimate privacy interests in their work areas as well as the circumstances under which work place searches are reasonable, stating that this issue must be approached case by case. In *O'Conner* during an investigation into suspected work-related conduct, the employer searched Magno Ortega's desk and file cabinets and seized his private property. Ortega filed a petition for summary judgment claiming his Fourth Amendment rights had been violated. The district court found the search to be reasonable because there was a need to secure state property. The court of appeals reversed in part and remanded the case to the district court. When the case found its way to the Supreme Court, it, too, reversed and remanded.

The Court agreed that Ortega's desk and file cabinets were protected by the Fourth Amendment, however: "Government searches to retrieve work-related materials or to investigate violations of work-place rules—searches of a sort that are regarded as reasonable and normal in the private employer context—do not violate the Fourth Amendment in the public agency environment" (Wilson, 2008, p. 12). In its opinion the Court stated:

> Government offices are provided to employees for the sole purpose of facilitating the work of an agency. The employee may avoid exposing personal belongings at work by simply leaving them at home.

◀ **CASE IN BRIEF**
O'Conner v. Ortega (1987)

ISSUE Does a public employee have a reasonable expectation of privacy in their workspace? What is the standard for a search when a public employee has a reasonable expectation of privacy?

RULING Yes. A public employee can exhibit a reasonable expectation of privacy in a workspace. A public employer may conduct a search of the workspace with less than probable cause and without a warrant if it is for a work-related purpose, justified by the need for an efficient and orderly operation. The search needs to be supported by reasonable grounds, and the scope must be related to the object of the search and not overly intrusive.

In sum, we conclude that the "special needs, beyond the normal need for law enforcement make the . . . probable-cause requirement impracticable," for legitimate work-related, noninvestigatory intrusions as well as investigations of work-related misconduct. A standard of reasonableness will neither unduly burden the efforts of government employers to ensure the efficient and proper operation of the workplace, nor authorize arbitrary intrusions upon the privacy of public employees. We hold, therefore, that public employer intrusions on the constitutionally protected privacy interests of government employees for noninvestigatory, work-related purposes, as well as for investigations of work-related misconduct, should be judged by the standard of reasonableness under all the circumstances. Under this reasonableness standard, both the inception and the scope of the intrusion must be reasonable:

"Determining the reasonableness of any search involves a twofold inquiry: first, one must consider 'whether the . . . action was justified at its inception,' *Terry v. Ohio*. . . ; second, one must determine whether the search as actually conducted 'was reasonably related in scope to the circumstances which justified the interference in the first place,' *New Jersey v. T. L. O.*"

The issue of public employee privacy becomes even more complex when an electronic component is introduced. Desktop or laptop computers, mobile digital terminals in police cars, cell phones, pagers, tablets, and other products are frequently issued to law enforcement departments to perform their official duties. The courts have generally "lagged far behind" in applying yesterday's legal rules to today's technological innovations (Rutledge, 2010, p. 74). The Supreme Court has made a limited attempt to give constitutional guidance on the issue of whether police managers violate an officer's privacy rights by auditing his or her text messages sent during duty hours over a department-issued electronic paging device—the issue addressed in *City of Ontario v. Quon* (2010).

In this case, SWAT sergeant Jeff Quon, employed by the Ontario (California) Police Department, signed a written statement in 2000 acknowledging that he had read and understood the department's "Computer Usage, Internet and E-mail Policy." This policy stated that the city "reserves the right to monitor and log all network activity including e-mail and Internet use, without notice. Users should have no expectation of privacy or confidentiality when using these resources." An audit of on-duty texting revealed that Quon was using the pager for personal messaging during work hours. In one month he sent or received 456 messages while on duty, of which no more than 57 were work-related. Quon was disciplined, after which he sued the department claiming a violation of his Fourth Amendment rights.

The jury found that the employer conducted the audit for work-related purpose—to determine the need for a new service agreement (satisfying the first part of the *Ortega* test that the search was "justified at its inception"—and the audit was reasonable (satisfying the second part of the *Ortega* test that the search was "reasonable in scope"). Thus, the trial court dismissed Quon's Fourth Amendment claim. The Ninth Circuit Court of Appeals reversed, and the city took its appeal to the Supreme Court, which granted certiorari.

In a 9–0 decision, the Court reversed and remanded, holding, "Because the search of Quon's text messages was reasonable, the petitioners did not violate respondents' Fourth Amendment rights, and the Ninth Circuit erred by concluding otherwise." In writing for the majority, Justice Anthony Kennedy stated,

CASE IN BRIEF

City of Ontario v. Quon (2010)

ISSUE Does a government employer need to use the least intrusive means to search an employee's text messages?

RULING No. All that is required is that the search be reasonable. To be so, it must be justified at its inception (motivated by a legitimate work-related purpose) and the scope limited to locating the information sought and not overly intrusive.

"The Court must proceed with care when considering the whole concept of privacy expectations in communications made on electronic equipment owned by a government employer. The judiciary risks error by elaborating too fully on the Fourth Amendment implications of emerging technology before its role in society has become clear."

This same caution applies to the evolution of technology involving electronic surveillance of private individuals.

Electronic Surveillance, Privacy Interests, and the Fourth Amendment

The issue of electronics and technology bring to the forefront the fact that, to determine whether or not a search has occurred, there sometimes needs to be more than the "physical intrusion" test. There must also be an analysis regarding whether a violation of a reasonable expectation of privacy occurred. The issue of electronic privacy is a burgeoning area of law, with little precedent to rely on other than cases that can be used by analogy. But as with other issues regarding privacy concerns, the case must first be assessed like any other constitutional question: *Is the government involved?*

If so, it must then be determined if a reasonable expectation of privacy exists to implicate the Fourth Amendment when a search occurs. To do this, it must be shown that (1) the person has a subjective view that the material is private and (2) there exists an objective view that the expectation of privacy is reasonable by society's standards. Recall, this is the two-part standard introduced at the beginning of the chapter as derived from *Katz v. United States* (1967), the landmark case in the area of electronic surveillance and the issue of the expectation of privacy.

In *United States v. Karo* (1984), the Court held a warrantless search unconstitutional when the police monitored a homing device (beeper) in a can of material used to make illegal drugs when it was taken into the defendant's home. It is worth noting that the initial placement of the beeper was constitutional because it was put into the container with consent of the original owner and then transferred to the defendant. Where the action turned into an unconstitutional search was when officers monitored the device once inside the defendant's home to obtain information that would not otherwise have been available through visual surveillance.

However, *Karo* case needs to be contrasted with situations in which the police put such a device on or in a car to monitor its location on a public road, under which circumstances the Court has determined the police were merely supplementing their sensory faculties, and there is no reasonable expectation of privacy when driving a car on a public road (*United States v. Knotts*, 1983). The Fourth Amendment also governs *how* electronic equipment is attached or inserted into the place or thing monitored (*United States v. Jones*, 2012).

An interesting recent case that applies the Fourth Amendment with the tracking of an individual is *Grady v. North Carolina* (2015), in which the Supreme Court ruled that the placement of tracking device on a sex offender was a search under the Fourth Amendment. The lower court had determined that it was not, in fact, a search because

LO8 *Electronic surveillance is a form of search and seizure and, as such, is governed by the Fourth Amendment. The Fourth Amendment does not limit the use of electronic equipment that merely enhances the officers' senses but does not interfere with a person's reasonable expectation of privacy. Lights, photography from aircraft, and telescopes fall within this area.*

of the civil nature of the monitoring program. The Court ruled that because, as in *Jones*, the government had physically intruded on Grady's body in order to obtain information, a search had occurred, regardless of the civil nature. The Court, however, did not rule on the constitutionality of the monitoring program, only that it was a search.

The Supreme Court has ruled that the expectation of privacy does not exist when someone voluntarily converses with someone else—the "unreliable ear" exception. The lower courts have held that this expectation does not exist when someone converses in public because others may hear—the "uninvited ear" exception. For instance, a warrant is not required for an undercover officer to converse with suspects and use what they say in court.

Wiretapping created sufficient concern about the government eavesdropping on phone conversations that Congress passed the Wiretap Act of the Omnibus Crime Control and Safe Streets Act of 1968, which prohibits the interception of phone conversations unless one party to the conversation consents or when authorized by a court of competent jurisdiction, with the interception remaining under the control and supervision of the authorizing court. *Interception* is defined within this federal statute as "aural or other acquisition of the contents of any wire, electronic or oral communication through the use of any electronic, mechanical, or other device." Subsequent legislation has brought cell phones within this definition.

The Wiretap Act requires warrants for electronic surveillance and requires states to adopt similar legislation. Beyond calling for judicial supervision of all aspects of electronic surveillance, the Wiretap Act established specific procedures to apply for, issue, and execute court orders to intercept wire or oral communications. The application for such a warrant, or wiretap order, must be detailed and include why less-intrusive means are not practical and show that other investigative means have been attempted (but does not require that *all* other methods be exhausted). The judge who authorizes the wiretap must find probable cause that the suspect has committed or is committing one of a number of specified crimes within the statute and that other means of investigation will not be effective. The order will then be effective for only a specific period, usually no more than 30 days, and the recordings made must be provided to the judge who issued the order, who has control over them.

Following passage of the Wiretap Act, a series of cases and legislation evolved that sought to come to grips with this complex, powerful new area of obtaining evidence. During the 1960s, case law sought to define what uses of technology would be considered "reasonable." In *Osborn v. United States* (1966), undercover federal agents with a warrant taped a conversation using a hidden recorder in an attempt to prove that labor leader Jimmy Hoffa's lawyer was bribing a juror. The evidence was admitted on the basis that the electronic device was used in "precise and discriminate circumstances" set forth in the warrant.

In *Berger v. New York* (1967), the Court held that a Fourth Amendment search does occur when electronic devices are used to capture conversations and that using such devices must be limited, ruling that a "two month surveillance period was the equivalent of a series of intrusions, searches and seizures pursuant to a single showing of probable cause." Warrants may be issued for such a redundant period, but beyond that, they must be reviewed or extended.

United States v. White (1970) held that "the Constitution does not prohibit a government agent from using an electronic device to record a telephone conversation between two parties with the consent of one party to the conversation." In some states, as long as there is one-party consent, a wiretap is not a Fourth Amendment issue.

According to the Pen Register Act, a warrant is not required for use of a device to trace telephone calls (called a trap and trace device for *incoming* numbers) or devices that record what phone numbers were called from a specific phone (known as pen registers that record *outgoing* numbers) because actual conversations are not being monitored. Indeed, the Supreme Court has ruled that using a pen register to obtain numbers dialed from a phone does not constitute a search and, therefore, does not require a warrant (*Smith v. Maryland*, 1979). A warrant could be required, however, to install such devices, and some state courts still view the use of such devices as "unreasonable interception of private communication." Likewise, because cordless and cellular phones use radio waves that anyone can receive, the courts have ruled that police may use randomly intercepted cordless and cellular phone conversations as a basis for obtaining a search warrant (*United States v. Smith*, 1992).

The Electronic Communications Privacy Act

If government is not involved, the Fourth Amendment may not apply, but government does have sufficient enough interest in ensuring people's privacy from others such that federal legislation has been passed. Analogous to U.S. Postal Regulations that restrict who can take another's mail to read, Congress enacted the Electronic Communications Privacy Act (ECPA) (Title 18 of the U.S. Code) in 1986.

The Title I statute of the ECPA addresses the interception of electronic transmissions, which amended the Wiretap Act from addressing only wire and oral communications. Title II of the ECPA (the "Stored Communications Act," or SCA) specifies what and how law enforcement can access *stored* electronic information from network service providers, such as Internet and cell phone companies, and provides criminal penalties for nongovernment persons who violate the act through intrusion into the privacy of others. The Pen Register Act is also considered part of this federal law. In essence, the law regulates when and what electronic communications can be monitored, recorded, or read by a third party. The statute makes it a crime to do these things without authorization provided for under the law, or a specific exception to the ECPA.

The ECPA has since been amended by a series of acts, including the 1994 Act "Communications Assistance to Law Enforcement," the USA PATRIOT Act in 2001, and the USA PATRIOT Act reauthorization act in 2006, demonstrating the never-ending attempt by Congress to keep pace with technology, an effort many contend will never be achieved. The House has passed the Email Privacy Act, a bill that amends the search warrant requirement, and the bill sits before the Senate as this text goes to press. Unlike the current law, the proposed change would require law enforcement to obtain a search warrant to obtain information held by a third party, such as a storage or service provider, regardless of how long the data has been stored. Under current law, access to communications data stored by a third party requires a search warrant if that data has been stored for 180 days or less. If more than 180 days have elapsed, law enforcement needs only a subpoena to retrieve the data.

The issue of whether e-mail, texts, posts on social media, and other cell phone information retained by cellular service companies, subscriber information held by Internet providers, and other forms of electronic communiqués can legally be viewed without the permission of those actually sending and receiving them is finding its way to the courts. To date, the courts have ruled fairly consistently that when a third party (e.g., AOL, Facebook, Verizon) has the data and holds it for business purposes, the individual user loses any reasonable expectation of privacy regarding that information and cannot challenge its seizure or search. But this is beginning to change.

Much of the impetus for such change pertains to the type of data itself, meaning that the more detailed, or "private," the data becomes, the more likely a reasonable expectation of privacy exists. Also considered is how the third party obtains the data; not all data is considered to be voluntarily conveyed to a third party. The following list of cases shows the evolving debate as to what degree a privacy expectation exists in this area, if at all, and if it does exist, what information it covers:

- *United States v. Conner* (6th Cir. 2013) in which the court held no expectation of privacy exists in peer-to-peer sharing services because files on a personal computer are expressly made available for download by the public, including law enforcement.
- *United States v. Graham* (Dist Ct MD 2012) in which the court stated no expectation in privacy exists in historical cell site location records because the information is voluntarily conveyed to the cell providers.
- *In re: Application for Telephone Information Needed for a Criminal Investigation* (2015), the court explained that not all information obtained by a cell phone provider, specifically location data, was *voluntarily* conveyed to a third party, and thus a reasonable expectation of privacy exists in that information.
- *United States v. Warshak* (6th Cir. 2010) in which the court affirmed there is an expectation of privacy in e-mails and to compel a third party to disclose them requires a search warrant based on probable cause even if the third party has the ability or right to view them:

  Given the fundamental similarities between email and traditional forms of communication, it would defy common sense to afford emails lesser Fourth Amendment protection [under the SCA]. . . . It only stands to reason that, if government agents compel an ISP to surrender the contents of a subscriber's emails, those agents have thereby conducted a Fourth Amendment search, which necessitates compliance with the warrant requirement absent some exception.

- *United States v. Perrine* (2008) in which the court said subscriber information given to the Internet provider is not protected by the Fourth Amendment.
- *Guest v. Leis* (2001) in which the court said the sender of an e-mail would lose the reasonable expectation of privacy in an e-mail already received by the recipient.
- *United States v. Andrus* (2007), a case about third-party consent searches, with the court holding that, based on the parent paying for Internet access and having unrestricted access to the room, the parent could consent to the search of an adult child's computer.

- *Konop v. Hawaiian Airlines, Inc.* (2002), which involved unauthorized access to information on Robert Konop's secure website, and in which a federal court held that the statute applied only to data being transmitted, not stored. Konop, a pilot for Hawaiian Airlines, maintained a website where he posted bulletins critical of his employer, its officers, and the incumbent union, Air Line Pilots Association (ALPA). Many of Konop's criticisms were about his opposition to labor concessions that Hawaiian sought from ALPA. Because ALPA supported giving management concessions to the existing collective bargaining agreement, Konop encouraged others via his website to consider alternative union representation. Konop controlled access to his secure website by requiring visitors to log in with a user name and password. However, officers of the airline gained unauthorized access to the site and suspended Konop in retaliation for the content of his posts. Konop filed suit alleging Hawaiian Airlines violated the Wiretap Act and the Stored Communications Act by viewing his secure website under false pretenses.

In addressing *Konop*, the Ninth Circuit Court, having previously identified the intersection between the Wiretap Act and the Store Communications Act as "a complex, often convoluted area of the law" (*United States v. Smith*, 1998), held that the unauthorized access and review of the contents of a password-protected website can constitute violations of both the Wiretap Act and the SCA:

> It is perfectly clear that the framers of the Wiretap Act's current definition of "electronic communication" understood that term to include communications in transit and storage alike.... It makes no more sense that a private message expressed in a digitized voice recording stored in a voice mailbox should be protected from interception, but the same words expressed in an e-mail stored in an electronic post office pending delivery should not. We conclude that it would be equally senseless to hold that Konop's messages to his fellow pilots would have been protected from interception had he recorded them and delivered them through a secure voice bulletin board accessible by telephone, but not when he set them down in electronic text and delivered them through a secure web server accessible by a personal computer. We hold that the Wiretap Act protects electronic communications from interception when stored to the same extent as when in transit.

Another federal court in *United States v. Councilman* (2005), which involved a company scanning people's e-mails for business research, interpreted the statute to apply to e-mail either being transmitted or temporarily stored en route to the intended recipient. Future cases will likely again address whether stored data falls within the statute.

The issue of whether employers can inspect employee computer use rests on whether the company has a policy in place addressing this issue. Questions regarding whether an employee using company equipment on company time has any expectation of privacy is most easily addressed by well-drafted policies that provide the employees' consent to have their company equipment monitored.

This area of law has become increasingly complex and confusing. Technology is outpacing the law, which is slow to catch up, both in the area of statutes and case law. Judges attempt to interpret statutes that were passed decades ago and were based on then-current technology, like a landline. It is often difficult to apply those laws to modern technology, such as a cell phone or cloud computing. Another problem is which statute is applicable: the Wiretap Act because a communication is in transit, or the SCA because the communication is stored? This seems like a simple question, but it is not. Both acts have different standards and requirements, especially for law enforcement.

Balancing Security Concerns with Privacy Interests

Since the terrorist attacks of September 11, 2001, security concerns have increasingly conflicted with privacy concerns. For example, judges across the country are divided over rising global positioning system (GPS) surveillance practices. While new technologies, such as automated license-plate readers in squad cars and facial recognition computer programs linked to an increasing number of surveillance cameras, make police surveillance easier and cheaper, such tools necessarily raise questions and concerns about privacy rights and how much intrusion should be allowed in the name of national security (Savage, 2010).

> **MYTH**
> A search warrant is needed to gather your cell phone records.
>
> **FACT**
> Not true. All that is needed (under most circumstances) is an order or subpoena from a judge stating "specific and articulable facts" that show the information sought relates to an investigation.

IN THE NEWS

"Microsoft Suit Over Secret Government Searches May Signal Emboldened Tech Industry"

By Del Quentin Wilber—Contact Reporter (*Los Angeles Times*, April 14, 2016)

Microsoft Corp. on Thursday sued the Justice Department to overturn a federal law that prevents the technology giant from telling thousands of customers when their information has been sought by federal agents.

The lawsuit represents the latest salvo in the fight between technology companies and law enforcement agencies over the privacy of customer data, a fight most recently waged by Apple Inc. over the FBI's effort to unlock a terrorist's iPhone.

It also highlights the complex legal issues emerging in federal probes of terrorism and other crimes in the age of cloud computing, which allows consumers and businesses to store vast amounts of personal information on remote servers.

At issue in Microsoft's suit, filed in the U.S. District Court in Seattle, is a 1986 law that permits federal judges to bar companies from telling customers that the government is seeking their information. Under the statute, the prohibition is allowed when the government has "reason to believe" disclosure would hinder its investigation.

(Continued)

Microsoft contends the law is being abused, and violates its 1st Amendment right to free speech and its customers' 4th Amendment rights to be protected from unreasonable searches and seizures.

"Microsoft brings this case because its customers have a right to know when the government obtains a warrant to read their emails, and because Microsoft has a right to tell them," the suit reads.

Nearly half of the 5,624 federal demands for customer information that Microsoft has received in the last 18 months have been accompanied by secrecy orders, in many cases for unlimited periods of time, the company said.

The government has "exploited the transition to cloud computing as a means of expanding its power to conduct secret investigations," the lawsuit says. "As individuals have moved their most sensitive information to the cloud, the government has increasingly adopted the tactic of obtaining the private digital documents of cloud customers not from the customers themselves, but through legal processes directed at online cloud providers."

Emily Pierce, a Justice Department spokesperson, declined to comment.

Brad Smith, Microsoft's chief legal officer, said in a blog post that "it's becoming routine for the U.S. government to issue orders that require email providers to keep these types of legal demands secret. We believe that this goes too far and we are asking the courts to address the situation."

The suit comes just weeks after the Justice Department dropped its effort to compel Apple to write software to help it unlock the iPhone used by Syed Rizwan Farook, who along with his wife launched a Dec. 2 attack in San Bernardino that left 14 dead and many others wounded.

The FBI could not unlock the encrypted phone and won an order from a federal judge requiring Apple to write the necessary code to help it gain access to the device. Apple vigorously sought to overturn that ruling and had been joined by a number of technology companies in its court battle. The Justice Department dropped the case when an unidentified third party managed to successfully unlock the phone.

The FBI has not publicly disclosed what was contained on Farook's iPhone, but a source familiar with the investigation confirmed a CBS News account that investigators had not recovered anything significant.

Meanwhile, the Justice Department is seeking to overturn another judge's ruling that blocked its efforts to compel Apple to unlock an iPhone in a New York drug case.

Whereas those disputes were about the government's right to force Apple to help it retrieve data, Microsoft is seeking permission to alert customers to such government requests.

Though Microsoft has taken aim at the government before, the latest move could reflect a new confidence in the tech industry to challenge court orders in the wake of the San Bernardino dispute. Some in Silicon Valley had feared the public would turn against Apple for not helping access cellphone data belonging to a mass shooter. But public opinion polls showed a significant divide.

In the suit, Microsoft noted that not long ago people and businesses stored their most sensitive information in filing cabinets and drawers, and later, on hard drives in their homes or offices. When the government conducted raids to obtain such information, the owners of that data and information almost always were aware that the searches had taken place.

With the recent massive migration of data to the cloud and servers in others' possession, the government has increasingly relied on the Electronic Communications Privacy Act to gag Microsoft and other companies from disclosing information about the warrants. In many instances, the gag orders last for "unreasonably long (or even unlimited) periods of time," Microsoft wrote.

(Continued)

(Continued)

> Microsoft's complaint is reminiscent of another dispute between the federal government and Twitter, the giant social media company. Twitter is suing the Justice Department for the right to disclose the precise number of national security letters it receives from the FBI and the number of orders it receives from the ultra-secret Foreign Intelligence Surveillance Court.
>
> The Justice Department told Twitter that such data were classified and could not be released. The company argued in its October 2014 lawsuit that such a prohibition forces it to either "engage in speech that has been preapproved by government officials or else to refrain from speaking altogether."
>
> Twitter took the legal action, which remains ongoing, about eight months after five other technology companies, including Microsoft, Google Inc. and Facebook reached a compromise permitting them to publish rough estimates of the number of such requests.
>
> *Staff Writer Paresh Dave in Los Angeles contributed to this report.*

The area of electronic surveillance and expectations of privacy offers additional support for the enduring quality of the Constitution. The explosive development of technology continues to present challenges to which the Fourth Amendment can respond. The incredible increase in the use of computers in our society will surely challenge existing law in this area. Although the computer age presents search-and-seizure issues that Benjamin Franklin and Thomas Jefferson could never have dreamed of, the document they helped draft remains responsive. Telephones, pagers, cellular technology, and the Internet all present areas that continue to be further defined by case law.

Summary

Jones resurrected the aspect of a physical intrusion or trespass in determining whether a "search" has occurred. The reasonable expectation of privacy and the use of physical trespass in an effort to gather information are both valid analyses that need to be performed to determine if a search has occurred. All searches must be limited in scope. General searches are unconstitutional and never legal.

Searches conducted with a warrant must be limited to the specific area and specific items described in the warrant. Although warrantless searches are presumed unreasonable, exceptions to the warrant requirement include the following: (1) with consent; (2) frisking for officer safety; (3) plain feel and plain view evidence; (4) incident to lawful, custodial arrest; (5) automobile exceptions; (6) exigent (emergency) circumstances; and (7) open fields, abandoned property, and public places.

In the first exception, consent searches, the consent to search must be voluntary. The search must be limited to the area specified by the person granting permission. The person may revoke the consent at any time. In the second exception, stop-and-frisk situations, if a frisk is authorized by the circumstances of an investigative stop, only a limited pat down of the detainee's outer clothing for the officer's safety is authorized. In the third exception, plain feel and plain view, if, in the lawful course of a frisk, officers feel something that training and experience causes them to believe is contraband, that develops the probable cause required to expand the search and seize the object—plain feel and plain touch. In addition, unconcealed evidence that officers see while engaged in a lawful activity may be seized and is admissible in court—plain view.

In the fourth exception, searches incidental to a lawful, custodial arrest, the search must be contemporaneous and must be limited to the area within the person's reach (*Chimel*). A search incident to lawful arrest allows seizure of property or containers not immediately connected with the arrestee's body, but under his or her immediate control, including backpacks, briefcases, luggage, or other packages. In the fifth exception, the automobile exception, *Carroll v. United States* (1925) established that vehicles can be searched without a warrant provided (1) there is probable cause to believe the vehicle's contents violate the law and (2) the vehicle would be gone before a search warrant could be obtained. The Court has since limited the requirement to search a car based on probable cause only and has eliminated the mobility aspect. The sixth exception, exigent circumstances, includes danger of physical harm to officers or another person, danger of destruction of evidence, driving while intoxicated, hot-pursuit situations, and individuals requiring "rescuing." The seventh exception, open fields, abandoned property, and public places, involves the lack of expectation of privacy and lack of physical trespass; therefore, the Fourth Amendment protection does not apply.

The Court has ruled that routine border searches and searches at international airports are reasonable under the Fourth Amendment. Jail and prison inmates, probationers, and parolees have limited Fourth Amendment rights because while under supervision, they should not expect the degree of privacy enjoyed by law-abiding citizens.

Electronic surveillance is a form of search and seizure and, as such, is governed by the Fourth Amendment. For a search to have occurred, government agents need not physically go onto someone's property. Information obtained whenever there is a reasonable expectation of privacy constitutes a search. The Fourth Amendment does not limit the use of electronic equipment that merely enhances officers' senses but does not interfere with a person's reasonable expectation of privacy. Lights, photography from aircraft, and telescopes fall within this area. To obtain an electronic-surveillance warrant, probable cause that a person is engaging in particular communications must be established by the court, and normal investigative procedures must have already been tried.

Discussion Questions

1. What are the two tests for determining whether or not a search has occurred?
2. What scenarios work best with the "reasonable expectation of privacy" doctrine? How about the "physical intrusion" test?
3. Provide your own definition of *reasonable*.
4. Discuss the advantages to obtaining a warrant.
5. Why are searches of homes different from searches of motor vehicles?
6. Give your own definition of *reasonable expectation of privacy*.
7. Do you think the U.S. Supreme Court has been supportive of law enforcement through its rulings in cases involving the Fourth Amendment?
8. Draft a scenario in which an innocent, routine interaction between a citizen in a public place and the police could result in a continuing escalation through reasonable suspicion to probable cause, and what the results to each party would be.
9. Is the exclusionary rule effective in limiting potential abuse of the Fourth Amendment by police when searching? Could another means be more effective?
10. How do you think the Fourth Amendment will be held to apply to e-mail and other data transmitted over the Internet?

References

del Carmen, R. V. (2010). *Criminal Procedure Law and Practice*, 8th ed. Belmont, CA: Wadsworth/Cengage Learning.

Ferdico, J. N. (2009). *Criminal Procedure for the Criminal Justice Professional*, 10th ed. Belmont, CA: Cengage/Wadsworth Learning.

Joh, E. E. (2006). "Reclaiming 'Abandoned' DNA: The Fourth Amendment and Genetic Privacy." *Northwestern University Law Review*, 100, p. 857, 2006 (UC Davis Legal Studies Research Paper No. 40). Retrieved August 14, 2016 from http://ssrn.com/abstract=702571

Judge, L. A. (2009, June). "Bye-Bye Belton? Supreme Court Decision Shifts Authority for Vehicle Searches from Automatic to Manual." *The Police Chief*, pp. 12–13.

Kaeble, D.; Glaze, L.; Tsoutis, A.; & Minton, T. (2016, January 21). *Correctional Populations in the United States, 2014*. Washington, DC: Bureau of Justice Statistics. (NCJ 249513) Retrieved August 13, 2016 from http://www.bjs.gov/content/pub/pdf/cpus14.pdf

Means, R., & McDonald, P. (2009a, May). "Police Law Myths, Part 1." *Law and Order*, pp. 26–29.

Means, R., & McDonald, P. (2009b, October). "Supreme Court 2008–2009, The Final Wrap." *Law and Order*, pp. 80–83.

Means, R., & McDonald, P. (2010, June). "Myth of Custody and Consent." *Law and Order*, pp. 12–14.

Rutledge, D. (2009a, November). "In-Home Arrest Searches." *Police*, pp. 66–69.

Rutledge, D. (2009b, October). "Public School Searches: 'Special Needs' Require Special Rules." *Police*, pp. 80–81.

Rutledge, D. (2009c, June). "Vehicle Searches Incident to Arrest." *Police*, pp. 68–71.

Rutledge, D. (2010, September). "Electronic Privacy on the Job." *Police*, pp. 74–77.

Sanchez, A. J., & Rubin, J. K. (2010, June). "The Use of Garbage to Establish Probable Cause for Granting Valid Search Warrants." *The Police Chief*, pp. 12–13.

Savage, C. (2010, August 13). "Judges Divided over Rising GPS Surveillance." *The New York Times*. Retrieved August 14, 2016 from http://www.nytimes.com/2010/08/14/us/14gps.html?_r=0

Wallentine, K. (2009, November 11). "PoliceOne Analysis: *12 Supreme Court Cases Affecting Cops.*" *PoliceOne.com News*. Retrieved August 14, 2016 from http://www.policeone.com/legal/articles/1964272-PoliceOne-Analysis-12-Supreme-Court-cases-affecting-cops/

Wilson, K. (2008, August). "When Does an Employer's Search of Employee Work Areas Violate Privacy Rights?" *The Police Chief*, pp. 12–13.

Cases Cited

Adams v. Williams, 407 U.S. 143 (1972)
Almeida-Sanchez v. United States, 413 U.S. 266 (1973)
Arizona v. Gant, 556 U.S. 332 (2009)
Arizona v. Johnson, 555 U.S. 323 (2009)
Bailey v. United States, 133 S.Ct. 1031 (2013)
Bell v. Wolfish, 441 U.S. 520 (1979)
Berger v. New York, 388 U.S. 41 (1967)
Birchfield v. North Dakota, 579 U.S. ___ (2016)
Bond v. United States, 529 U.S. 334 (2000)
Boyd v. United States, 116 U.S. 616 (1886)
Brigham City, Utah v. Stuart, 547 U.S. 398 (2006)
California v. Acevedo, 500 U.S. 565 (1991)
California v. Ciraolo, 476 U.S. 207 (1986)
California v. Greenwood, 486 U.S. 35 (1988)
Camara v. Municipal Court of the City and County of San Francisco, 387 U.S. 523 (1967)
Carroll v. United States, 267 U.S. 132 (1925)
Chambers v. Maroney, 399 U.S. 42 (1970)
Chimel v. California, 395 U.S. 752 (1969)
City of Ontario v. Quon, 560 U.S. 746 (2010)
Colorado v. Bertine, 479 U.S. 367 (1987)
Commonwealth v. Bly, 448 Mass. 473, 862 N.E.2d 341 (2007)
Commonwealth v. Tarver, 345 N.E.2d 671 (Mass. 1975)
Coolidge v. New Hampshire, 403 U.S. 443 (1971)
Fernandez v. California, 571 U.S. ___ (2014)
Florence v. Board of Chosen Freeholders of the County of Burlington, 132 S.Ct. 1510 (2012)
Florida v. Jardines, 569 U.S. 1 (2013)
Florida v. Jimeno, 500 U.S. 248 (1991)
Florida v. Wells, 495 U.S. 1 (1990)
Georgia v. Randolph, 547 U.S. 103 (2006)
Grady v. North Carolina, 135 S. Ct. 1368 (2015)
Griffin v. Wisconsin, 483 U.S. 868 (1987)
Groh v. Ramirez, 540 U.S. 551 (2004)
Guest v. Leis, 255 F.3d 325 (6th Cir. 2001)
Hester v. United States, 265 U.S. 57 (1924)
Horton v. California, 496 U.S. 128 (1990)
Hudson v. Michigan, 547 U.S. 586 (2006)
Hudson v. Palmer, 468 U.S. 517 (1984)
Illinois v. Caballes, 543 U.S. 405 (2005)
Illinois v. Lafayette, 462 U.S. 640 (1983)
Illinois v. McArthur, 531 U.S. 326 (2001)
Illinois v. Rodriguez, 497 U.S. 177 (1990)
In Re: Application for Telephone Information Needed for a Criminal Investigation, Case No. 15-XR-90304-HRL-1(LHK), United States District Court, N.D. California, San Jose Division (July 29, 2015)
James v. Louisiana, 382 U.S. 36 (1965)
Jordan v. Gardner, 986 F.2d 1521 (9th Cir. 1993)
Katz v. United States, 389 U.S. 347 (1967)
Kentucky v. King, 131 S. Ct. 1849 (2011)
Knowles v. Iowa, 525 U.S. 113 (1998)
Konop v. Hawaiian Airlines, Inc., 302 F.3d 868 (9th Cir. 2002)
Kyllo v. United States, 533 U.S. 27 (2001)
Marron v. United States, 275 U.S. 192 (1927)
Marshall v. Barlow's Inc., 436 U.S. 307 (1978)
Maryland v. Buie, 494 U.S. 325 (1990)
Maryland v. Dyson, 527 U.S. 465 (1999)
Maryland v. King, 569 U.S. ___ (2013)
Maryland v. Macon, 472 U.S. 463 (1985)
Maryland v. Wilson, 519 U.S. 408 (1997)
Messerschmidt v. Millender, 132 S.Ct. 1235 (2012)
Michigan v. Long, 463 U.S. 1032 (1983)
Michigan v. Summers, 452 U.S. 692 (1981)
Michigan v. Tucker, 417 U.S. 433 (1974)
Minnesota v. Dickerson, 508 U.S. 366 (1993)
Minnesota v. Olson, 495 U.S. 91 (1990)
Missouri v. McNeely, 133 S.Ct. 832 (2013)
Monroe v. Pape, 365 U.S. 167 (1961)
Moore v. People, 171 Colo. 338, 467 P.2d 50 (1970)
Morrissey v. Brewer, 408 U.S. 471 (1972)
Muehler v. Mena, 544 U.S. 93 (2005)
New Jersey v. T.L.O., 469 U.S. 325 (1985)
New York v. Belton, 453 U.S. 454 (1981)
O'Conner v. Ortega, 480 U.S. 709 (1987)
Ohio v. Robinette, 519 U.S. 33 (1996)
Oliver v. United States, 466 U.S. 170 (1984)
Olmstead v. United States, 277 U.S. 438 (1928)
Osborn v. United States, 385 U.S. 323 (1966)
Payton v. New York, 445 U.S. 573 (1980)
Pennsylvania v. Mimms, 434 U.S. 106 (1997)
People v. Loria, 10 N.Y.2d 368 (1961)
Quinones-Ruiz v. United States, 864 F. Supp. 983 (S.D. Cal. 1994)
Riley v. California, 573 U.S. ___ (2014)
Ryburn v. Huff, 132 S.Ct. 987 (2012)
Safford Unified School District v. Redding, 557 U.S. 364 (2009)
Salas v. State, 246 So.2d 621 (Fla. Dist. Ct. App. 1971)
Samson v. California, 547 U.S. 843 (2006)
Schmerber v. California, 384 U.S. 757 (1966)
Skinner v. Railway Labor Executives' Association, 489 U.S. 602 (1989)
Smith v. Maryland, 442 U.S. 735 (1979)
South Dakota v. Opperman, 428 U.S. 364 (1976)
Stanton v. Sims, 571 U.S. ___ (2013)
State v. Athan, 160 Wash. 2d 354, 158 P.3d 27 (2007)
State v. Barlow, Jr., 320 A.2d 895 (Me. 1974)
State v. Kaluna, 55 Hawaii 361, 520 P.2d 51 (1974)
State v. Lewis, 611 A.2d 69 (Me. 1992)
State v. Wickline, 232 Neb. 329, 440 N.W.2d 249 (1989)
Stoner v. California, 376 U.S. 483 (1964)

Terry v. Ohio, 392 U.S. 1 (1968)
Thornton v. United States, 541 U.S. 615 (2004)
Turner v. Safley, 482 U.S. 78 (1987)
United States v. Andrus, 483 F.3d 711 (10th Cir. 2007)
United States v. Banks, 540 U.S. 31 (2003)
United States v. Biswell, 406 U.S. 311 (1972)
United States v. Chadwick, 433 U.S. 1 (1977)
United States v. Conner (6th Cir. 2013)
United States v. Councilman, 418 F.3d 67 (1st Cir. 2005)
United States v. Davis, 657 F. Supp. 2d. 630 (D. Md. 2009)
United States v. Dunn, 818 F.2d 742 (10th Cir. 1987)
United States v. Edwards, 415 U.S. 800 (1974)
United States v. Graham, 846 F. Supp. 2d 384 (Dist. Court, D. Maryland 2012)
United States v. Haley, 669 F.2d 201 (4th Cir. 1982)
United States v. Jacobsen, 466 U.S. 109 (1984)
United States v. Jones, 565 U.S. 945 (2012)
United States v. Karo, 468 U.S. 705 (1984)
United States v. Knights, 534 U.S. 112 (2001)
United States v. Knotts, 460 U.S. 276 (1983)
United States v. Leonard, 931 F.2d 463 (CA8 1991)
United States v. Lucas, 898 F.2d 606 (1990)
United States v. Matlock, 415 U.S. 164 (1974)
United States v. Molinaro, 877 F.2d 1341 (7th Cir. 1989)
United States v. Montoya de Hernandez, 473 U.S. 531 (1985)
United States v. Ortiz, 422 U.S. 891 (1975)
United States v. Perrine, 518 F.3d 1196 (2008)
United States v. Pinson, 24 F.3d 1056 (8th Cir. 1994)
United States v. Ramsey, 431 U.S. 606 (1977)
United States v. Robinson, 414 U.S. 218 (1973)
United States v. Ross, 456 U.S. 798 (1982)
United States v. Santana, 427 U.S. 38 (1976)
United States v. Simmons, 567 F.2d 314 (7th Cir. 1977)
United States v. Smith, 978 F.2d 171 (5th Cir. 1992)
United States v. Smith, 155 F.3d 1051 (9th Cir. 1998)
United States v. Sokolow, 490 U.S. 1 (1989)
United States v. Thomas, 729 F.2d 120 (1984)
United States v. Warshak, 631 F.3d 266 (2010)
United States v. White, 401 U.S. 745 (1970)
Vause v. United States, 53 F.2d 346 (1931)
Warden v. Hayden, 387 U.S. 294 (1967)
Weeds v. United States, 255 U.S. 109 (1921)
Welsh v. Wisconsin, 466 U.S. 740 (1984)
Winston v. Lee, 470 U.S. 753 (1985)
Wright v. United States, 302 U.S. 583 (1938)
Wyoming v. Houghton, 526 U.S. 295 (1999)

CHAPTER 10

The Fifth Amendment
Obtaining Information Legally

No person . . . shall be compelled in any criminal case to be a witness against himself; nor be deprived of life, liberty, or property, without due process of law.

—Fifth Amendment to the U.S. Constitution

The law of criminal procedure, dictated by due process, requires each step made by police to be in accordance with the Constitution. This includes the interrogation of criminal suspects. Here, an officer reads the *Miranda* warning to a suspect prior to custodial interrogation, informing the suspect of her constitutional right against self-incrimination and to have an attorney present during questioning.

Learning Objectives

LO1 Understand what the Fifth Amendment prohibits the government from doing and what the amendment guarantees.

LO2 List the factors that determine the voluntariness of a confession.

LO3 Identify the primary modern case for analyzing confessions.

LO4 Name the four warnings that are included in Miranda.

LO5 Explain when the Miranda warning must be given.

LO6 Grasp what constitutes a valid waiver of Miranda rights.

LO7 Enumerate what rights in addition to due process are guaranteed by the Fifth Amendment.

Key Terms

beachheading	harmless error doctrine	public safety exception
custodial interrogation	incrimination	rebut
double jeopardy	indictment	USA PATRIOT Act
eminent domain	interrogation	waiver
entrapment	invoke	
grand jury	just compensation	

Introduction

Although each amendment to the Constitution is unique, the Fifth Amendment is particularly intriguing. On the one hand, it is among the best-known amendments, thanks to movies and television. Everyone knows about "the right to remain silent." On the other hand, the Fifth Amendment is filled with other rights of which many people are not aware. For example, the Fifth Amendment explicitly states that the federal government may not deprive any individual of life, liberty, or property without the *due process of law*. The Fourteenth Amendment extends this requirement of due process and equal protection to the states.

The world revolves around communication. However, even as electronic and technological advancements continue to expand, most of the work the government does is done by communicating with people the old-fashioned way—by talking with them. Interviewing remains an important skill for investigators, as does understanding the rights of the individuals with whom they are talking.

Most of this chapter is devoted to the Fifth Amendment rights of individuals when the government is asking them questions. This area of procedural law is vitally important to both sides because so much of law enforcement involves asking people questions. Does the person have to respond? What if he or she does not? Can the police force someone to talk? What if the police do force a person to talk? Exactly what does it mean when a defendant declares his or her Fifth Amendment rights in the courtroom?

What the government can do with the information it acquires usually is determined by who acquired the data and, if it was the government, how its agents obtained the information. The Constitution recognized that government is capable of letting the ends justify the means. Indeed, the framers of the Constitution had seen confessions forced through atrocious means. That sort of excessive, intensive government conduct is what compelled the framers to forge both a new government and its framework, which continues to define the basics of today's governmental authority. The framers' goal was to limit governmental power to ensure freedom for the people. Those who put so much careful thought into developing a document capable of lasting as the world around it changed could have had absolutely no idea how complex crime would become.

Technological developments have only increased the challenges of determining how and when government agents can obtain information. Although technology has been addressed elsewhere in this text, the acquisition of information is an important means by which the Constitution may control potential government misconduct.

This chapter introduces the different means by which the government acquires information and the laws that apply. Because a confession by the accused provides the prosecution with powerful evidence, having such an admission rejected by the court for failing to meet necessary legal requirements can be devastating. What other proof can be as damning as an accused person proclaiming, "I did it"? Although this area of law is admittedly complex, the basic guidelines are consistent with the spirit of the Constitution, based on fairness and due process.

This chapter begins with a discussion of the government's need to know certain information and how the Fifth Amendment governs this need to know, including an explanation of two key clauses—the prohibition against self-incrimination and the guarantee of due process. Next, the law surrounding confessions and the well-known *Miranda* decision are explored, including the public safety exception to *Miranda*. This is followed by discussion of entrapment. Other provisions of the Fifth Amendment are then examined, as well as how this amendment affects the field of corrections. The chapter concludes with a discussion of the USA PATRIOT Act.

Government's Need to Know

A debate as old as any government has been, "What does the government need to know, and what are the limits by which it is acquired?" In 1790, George Washington's friend and contributor to *The Federalist Papers*, John Jay, wrote, "Let it be remembered that civil liberty consists not in a right to every man to do just what he pleases, but it consists in an equal right to all citizens to have, enjoy, and do, in peace, security and without molestation, whatever the equal and constitutional laws of the country admit to be consistent with the public good."

Enforcing the law depends to a great degree on government agents' ability to obtain confessions from those suspected of committing crimes or knowing who did. The balance lies in doing this within the boundaries of the Constitution.

The Right Against Compelled Self-Incrimination

The Fifth Amendment states: "No person shall . . . be compelled in any criminal case to be a witness against himself." **Incrimination** is the act of accusing, implicating, or identifying someone as having been involved in a crime or other wrongdoing. Self-incrimination, therefore, is when someone identifies themselves as having committed a wrong. The self-incrimination clause of the Fifth Amendment was made applicable to state governments in *Malloy v. Hogan* (1964).

The right to not be compelled to testify against oneself is what most people think of when they hear about someone's Fifth Amendment rights. It is critical to understand that the Fifth Amendment protects against testimonial evidence, not physical evidence. Such testimonial evidence obtained through incriminating statements is what people commonly think of when they talk about the "right to remain silent." The Fifth Amendment's protection against compelled self-incrimination means that the government cannot force a person to answer a question (i.e., provide testimonial evidence) when the answer will indicate the person's guilt in a criminal matter. This Fifth Amendment right applies to everyone at all times. "Unless an individual has been formally granted immunity or there are other extraordinary circumstances, no one has to answer police questions that call for incriminating information. They may simply walk away or otherwise decline to answer" (Means & McDonald, 2010c, p. 16).

A person must explicitly **invoke**, or unambiguously assert, his or her right to silence in the face of voluntary police questioning for that right to be enforced, according to the Supreme Court's decision in *Salinas v. Texas* (2013). Salinas voluntarily went with detectives to the police station and answered questions about a double murder. When specifically asked by the police about shotgun shells found at the scene and if they would match his shotgun, Salinas became quiet and did not answer. His silence was used against him at his trial by the prosecutors to show the jury that Salinas was guilty of the murders.

The Supreme Court did not rule on whether or not a defendant's pre-custody silence could be used at trial, as was the original issue, but focused instead on the lack of the right being invoked. In a plurality opinion, Justice Alito explained that mere silence is not enough to assert the right against compelled self-incrimination (by choosing to remain silent) in a pre-custodial setting. "A suspect who stands mute has not done enough to put police on notice that he is relying on his Fifth Amendment privilege."

Notice is important because it gives the court a "contemporaneous record establishing the witness' reasons for refusing to answer" when later evaluating a Fifth Amendment claim. It also allows the government to be aware that a person is relying on the privilege so it can argue why the statements are not self-incriminating.

---

incrimination the act of accusing, implicating, or identifying someone as having been involved in a crime or other wrongdoing

invoke to unambiguously assert or exercise a right

MYTH
The Fifth Amendment does not apply to DNA evidence.

FACT
This is true. The Fifth Amendment protects against compelled *testimony*. Testimony is verbal in nature and does not include physical evidence such as DNA, blood, hair, or your physical appearance.

Precedent shows that a defendant does not normally invoke the right against compelled self-incrimination by simply remaining silent. There are only two exceptions to when the Fifth Amendment right to silence is not required to be invoked: (1) when a defendant is on trial, he or she does not need to take the stand to invoke the right, and (2) if the person is coerced into not invoking the right.

Do these rights include the right to refuse to provide identification to the police during a routine law enforcement *Terry* stop? In *Hiibel v. Nevada* (2004), the Supreme Court said no. This case involved the refusal of a stopped motorist to provide proper identification on request. The refusal and conviction was held to be constitutional and not a denial of Fifth Amendment rights against self-incrimination because, in an on-the-street encounter such as this, compelling someone to identify themself poses no risk to that person of incriminating themself.

Recall that the Fifth Amendment right to be free from compelled self-incrimination applies to everyone at all times; this includes public employees, such as police officers. Two previous cases involved the Fifth Amendment and circumstances when public duty and individual rights conflicted. *Garrity v. New Jersey* (1967) and *Gardner v. Broderick* (1968) are frequently referenced as standing for the proposition that public employees may not be forced to choose between retaining their public employment and exercising their right against compelled self-incrimination (Kruger, 2009). In *Garrity*, police officers were being investigated for "ticket fixing." The officers were told they could refuse to answer questions, but if they did, they could be fired. The Supreme Court ruled that the choice between self-incrimination and losing their job was unconstitutional. It wrote in the opinion that taking a statement under such circumstances was coercive, and "the protection of the individual under the Fourteenth Amendment against coerced statements prohibits use in subsequent criminal proceedings of statements obtained under threat of removal from office, and that it extends to all, whether they are policemen or other members of our body politic."

In *Gardner*, an officer was fired after he refused to sign a waiver forfeiting his right against self-incrimination during grand jury testimony relating to the officer's criminal conduct. The Court ruled that firing an officer for refusing to waive his constitutional rights was coercive and violated the Fifth Amendment. Both of these cases stand for the proposition that an officer can be required to give a statement relating to his or her duties and can face discipline if he or she refuses. However, the statement given, if compelled, cannot be used in any criminal proceeding against him or her.

In *Kansas v. Cheever* (2013), the Court was asked to determine if statements made by a murder suspect during a court-ordered psychiatric examination could be used against him at trial. After a night of cooking and smoking methamphetamine with friends, Cheever had shot and killed a local sheriff. As part of his defense, Cheever claimed that, because he was under the influence of meth at the time of the killing, he was unable to form the mental state of premeditation that was required by the statute. An expert witness for the defense testified that Cheever had suffered brain damage due to long-term meth use and was intoxicated when he shot and killed the sheriff. A previous court in a different proceeding had ordered Cheever to undergo a psychiatric examination. The doctor who examined Cheever testified

---

MYTH
The Fifth Amendment protects a person from self-incrimination.

FACT
This is partly true. The Fifth Amendment protects you from being compelled to testify against yourself, otherwise known as self-incrimination. You cannot be forced to testify against yourself. However, it does not mean you cannot inadvertently give an officer information to use against you or admit to a crime.

◀ **CASE IN BRIEF**

Garrity v. New Jersey (1967)

ISSUE Does the threat of losing one's job for refusing to answer questions during a criminal investigation amount to coercion?

RULING Yes. Being in this situation does not allow a person to make a decision freely. Police officers and other public employees hold the same constitutional rights as every other citizen.

◀ **CASE IN BRIEF**

Kansas v. Cheever (2013)

ISSUE Does it violate the Fifth Amendment to use statements from a court-ordered psychiatric examination to rebut defendant-introduced testimony about his mental state at the time of the crime?

RULING No. The prosecution is not prohibited from presenting evidence to rebut that presented by the defendant. To do so would allow only the defendant to give his version of the story and prevent the jury from hearing both sides.

rebut refute through the presentation of contrary evidence

and provided information obtained from that exam to **rebut**, or refute through the presentation of contrary evidence, Cheever's claim that he had shot the sheriff because he was under the influence of meth. The trial court allowed the testimony, and Cheever was found guilty, but the Kansas Supreme Court vacated the conviction because Cheever had not waived his Fifth Amendment protection.

The Supreme Court reversed, ruling that when a defendant offers evidence of his mental state through an expert who examined him, the prosecutor may also use information learned through an examination, even if it had been court ordered, that is, compelled, to rebut the defendant's claims. Not allowing the prosecution to do so "would undermine the adversarial process, allowing a defendant to provide the jury, through an expert operating as proxy, with a one-sided and potentially inaccurate view of his mental state at the time of the alleged crime."

LO1 *The Fifth Amendment prohibits the government from forcing someone to be a witness against him- or herself through compelled self-incrimination. The Fifth Amendment also guarantees that the government cannot deprive a person of life, liberty, or property without due process of law.*

It is important to understand that Cheever himself brought the statements regarding his mental examinations into evidence by calling forth the expert witness. The outcome likely would have been different had Cheever not initiated his own mental examination nor attempted to introduce the psychiatric evidence at trial and, instead, the prosecutor had introduced the compelled statements (see *Estelle v. Smith*, 1981).

Due Process of Law

In addition to prohibiting compelled self-incrimination, the Fifth Amendment also states, "No person shall . . . be deprived of life, liberty or property, without due process of law." Due process, which was discussed in depth in Chapter 4, is such an important concept of U.S. law that no precise definition accurately suits it, although the concept is simple: basic fairness must remain part of the process. It is the *right to hear and the right to be heard*. It is specifically identified in the Fifth Amendment as a Constitutional right.

The 1950s and 1960s have been called the era of the "due process revolution" in the United States because, during that time, public sentiment demanded that government be held accountable and that the rights under the Constitution be applied equally to all. Government conduct in general was critically evaluated, and police conduct especially was brought into the public's eye more than ever before. *How* the police were allowed to carry out their work as well as *who* the defendant was were considered to a much greater degree. For example, police actions that would "shock the conscience" were found to violate due process (*Rochin v. California*, 1952).

CASE IN BRIEF

Rochin v. California (1952)

ISSUE Is it a violation of due process to pump the stomach of a suspect against their consent to obtain evidence?

RULING Yes. Such conduct by the officers "shocked the conscience" to such a degree that due process was violated. Note that this case was decided before the exclusionary rule was made applicable to the states. Today, this decision would most likely be based on that rather than due process.

In *Rochin*, Justice Felix Frankfurter stated, "Due process of law, as a historic and generative principle, precludes defining, and thereby confining these standards of conduct more precisely than to say that convictions cannot be brought about by methods that offend 'a sense of justice.'" In this case, three deputy sheriffs acted on a tip and entered Antonio Rochin's home through an unlocked door, forced open the second floor bedroom door, and saw Rochin put two capsules into his mouth. The deputies tried to extract them but could not, so they took him to the hospital and had his stomach pumped. Two morphine capsules were recovered and used as evidence against Rochin. In overturning the conviction, Justice Frankfurter said, "This course of proceeding by agents of government to obtain evidence is bound to offend even hardened sensibilities. They are methods too close to the rack and the screw to permit constitutional differentiation."

The due process issue in *Rochin* involved an executive action (i.e., action by the police), not a legislative action. As a result, the test for the constitutionality of that action is different. In *Rochin*, the Court applied the "shocks the conscience" test, whereas in cases involving the legislative realm, the test is generally one of strict scrutiny or rational basis (sometimes an intermediate test is employed).

Also found to violate due process were laws, or lack thereof, that did not provide juveniles with fairness in the legal system (*In re Gault*, 1967). In this case, a 15-year-old boy on probation was taken into custody at night for allegedly making obscene phone calls to a neighbor. His parents were not notified. When Mrs. Gault came home and found him missing, she went to the detention home and was told there would be a hearing the next day. At that hearing, a general allegation of "delinquency" was made, with no specific facts stated. The complaining neighbor was not present, no one was sworn in, no attorney was present, and no record was made of the proceeding. At a second hearing with the same circumstances, the judge sentenced the boy to a state industrial school until age 21—a six-year sentence for which an adult would receive a fine. The Supreme Court overruled this conviction on the grounds that Gault was deprived of his procedural due process rights, as stated by Justice Abe Fortas: "Where a person, infant or adult, can be seized by the State, charged and convicted for violating a state criminal law, and then ordered by the State to be confined for six years, I think the Constitution requires that he be tried in accordance with the guarantees of all provisions of the Bill of Rights made applicable to the States by the Fourteenth Amendment."

◀ **CASE IN BRIEF**

In re Gault (1967)

ISSUE Was the process used to commit Gault to the juvenile facility in accord with the commands of the Fourteenth Amendment's due process clause?

RULING No. In this case, due process was violated. The Court found that inadequate notice of charges, failure to notify Gault's parents, and no protection against self-incrimination, among other things, all played a role in the violation.

The Fifth Amendment and Confessions

There are two ways to evaluate a confession's constitutionality: under the due process voluntariness standard and under *Miranda*. Both are viable because one may be applicable when the other is not (e.g., the *Fulminante* case, as discussed shortly). Keep these two standards in mind as you read this section. Whether examined by using a due process analysis or as a strict Fifth Amendment interpretation, this area of law has been the subject of continued judicial examination and has produced a great deal of litigation in an effort to apply constitutional limits. The primary question is: "When will confessions be admissible as evidence in court?"

Justice Frankfurter, in *Culombe v. Connecticut* (1961), stated, "Despite modern advances in the technology of crime detection, offenses frequently occur about which things cannot be made to speak. And where there cannot be found innocent human witnesses to such offenses, nothing remains—if police investigation is not to be balked before it has fairly begun—but to seek out possibly guilty witnesses and ask them questions, witnesses, that is, who are suspected of knowing something about the offense precisely because they are suspected of implication in it." Approximately 80 percent of criminal cases are solved by less than a full confession, and a study on the success rate of current police interrogation techniques indicated that police interrogations produce at least some incriminating information in 45 to 65 percent of cases (O'Connor & Maher, 2009).

Early common law permitted confessions to be obtained by any manner, including force or the threat of force. This practice continues in some countries and, unfortunately, has been documented in the more recent past in the United States. Wrongdoing by the U.S. military to elicit information from prisoners during wartime, especially regarding terrorism, has spawned new debate about whether the ends can justify the means. Regardless of the motivation, the reliability of such admissions is to be questioned. By the middle of the eighteenth century, English courts began to limit the admissibility of confessions. The courts increasingly questioned whether the confession was voluntary or provided under improper pressure by the authorities. Thus, although the need for interrogations by law enforcement is acknowledged, not all confessions will be admissible in court.

Voluntariness of Confessions

The exclusionary rule prohibits use of confessions obtained in violation of a person's constitutional rights and those otherwise coerced and which are, thus, inherently unreliable. Recalling that the judge-made common law exclusionary rule seeks to hold government accountable for misconduct by prohibiting illegally obtained evidence from being admitted into evidence, an understanding of what is legally or illegally obtained information is crucial. To demonstrate that a confession was made voluntarily, many police departments tape- or video-record interrogations.

CASE IN BRIEF

Brown v. Mississippi (1936)

ISSUE Does it violate due process, and thus make a confession involuntary, to use physical torture as a means to obtain the confession?

RULING Yes. The method used offends the principles of justice rooted in the traditions of our people. A confession obtained by these means is not voluntary and cannot be used in court. This case was decided before the Fifth Amendment was applicable to the states.

The first confession case decided by the Supreme Court was *Brown v. Mississippi* (1936), when the Court held that confessions obtained through brutality and torture by law enforcement officials are violations of due process rights. In this case, Ed Brown was accused of murder, and when he denied the accusation, a deputy sheriff and another hung Brown from a tree, where he continued to insist on his innocence. He was then tied to the tree and whipped, but still he maintained his innocence. Several days later, Brown was again beaten by the deputy and was told he would continue to receive beatings until he confessed. Finally, Brown confessed.

Two other suspects were also taken to that jail and accused of the murder. They were made to strip, were laid over chairs, and were beaten with a leather strap with a buckle. They also finally confessed. The next day, the three were taken to the sheriff where they confessed to the murder. At the trial, which began the next day, the defendants said their confessions were false, obtained through torture. Although rope marks were clearly visible and none of the participants denied that beatings had taken place, the defendants were convicted and sentenced to death.

The Supreme Court held the confessions inadmissible, finding them void for violating the defendants' Fourteenth Amendment due process rights and noting that coerced confessions are simply not reliable: "The trial . . . is a mere pretense where the state authorities have contrived a conviction resting solely upon confessions obtained by violence. . . . It would be difficult to conceive of methods more revolting to the sense of justice than those taken to procure the confessions of these petitioners, and the use of the confessions thus obtained as the basis for conviction and sentence was a clear denial of due process."

In *Fikes v. Alabama* (1957), the Supreme Court summarized the standard of that time as "whether the totality of the circumstances that preceded the confessions deprived the defendant of his power of resistance." This standard has been termed the *due process voluntariness test*, and just as consent for an officer to search must be given freely, suspects must make any admission voluntarily. A coerced confession has little credibility. Such a standard requires case-by-case analysis. In a highly publicized murder case in Minnesota, the accused confessed but later recanted his confession. In a letter to a news reporter, he wrote the following explanation of why an innocent person confined in a cell totally alone might confess:

> I got to the point where I didn't care. I just wanted to get the pain over with. I don't believe people understand what it's like to watch your life fall apart and not even have someone to talk to. . . .
>
> Try imagining sitting in a room the size of your bathroom with no window, not knowing when that door will open or what your family is doing outside it. Then picture that for a year. . . .
>
> I thought I was saving my family from more harm. . . . In my twisted thinking at the time I felt I was doing an honorable thing for the people I love more than myself. . . .
>
> They told me many times in many different ways how much better things would be if I cooperated with them. I don't know if I did it [confessed] hoping things would get better or if I just didn't care. . . . I would of sold my soul to the devil not to hear that door bang again, locking me in for another 23 hours by myself.

> **LO2** *Voluntariness of a confession is determined by (1) the police conduct involved and (2) conduct sufficient to overcome the will of the suspect given the characteristics of the accused.*

The courts have identified two factors in assessing the voluntariness of a confession.

Police Conduct Police conduct will only be considered coercive if it has the effect of overbearing one's will. That is, the key factor in judging police conduct is: Was it overbearing to the point of making the confession involuntary? In *Rogers v. Richmond* (1961), Justice Frankfurter stated that involuntary confessions are "excluded not because such confessions are unlikely to be true, but because the methods used to extract them offend an underlying principle in the enforcement of our criminal law; that ours is an accusatorial and not an inquisitorial system—a system in which the state must establish guilt by evidence independently and freely secured and may not by coercion prove its charge against an accused out of his own mouth." A seminal case illustrating the "police conduct" aspect of coerced confessions is *Colorado v. Connelly* (1986), a case in which Connelly heard the "voice of God," and it told him to confess. The state court ruled the confession involuntary. The Supreme Court, however, overruled and said Connelly's confession was, in fact, voluntary because under the law, it is the police conduct that is scrutinized as to whether it was overbearing.

The following conduct is considered to be among those that violate due process (Ferdico, Fradella, & Totten, 2009, pp. 642–646):

- Threats of violence (*Arizona v. Fulminante*, 1991; *Beecher v. Alabama*, 1967)
- Confinement under shockingly inhumane conditions (*United States v. Koch*, 1977)

- Interrogation after lengthy, unnecessary delays in obtaining a statement between arrest and presentment before a neutral magistrate (*McNabb v. United States*, 1943; *Mallory v. United States*, 1957; *Corley v. United States*, 2009)
- Continued interrogation of an injured and depressed suspect in a hospital intensive-care unit (*Mincey v. Arizona*, 1978)
- Deprivation of food, drink, and sleep (*Greenwold v. Wisconsin*, 1968)

Not all actions by police, even those that may not seem "fair," have been found to violate constitutional rights. The following examples of police actions have been found to *not* violate due process (Ferdico et al., 2009, pp. 664–665):

- Promises of leniency (*United States v. Guarno*, 1987)
- Encouraging a suspect to cooperate (*United States v. Ballard*, 1978)
- Promises of psychological treatment (*United States v. McClinton*, 1992)
- Appeal to religious beliefs (*Welch v. Butler*, 1988)
- Trickery and deceit (*Frazier v. Cupp*, 1969; *People v. McNeil*, 2000; *State v. Schumacher*, 2001; *United States v. Bell*, 2004)

> **harmless error doctrine**
> involves the admissibility of involuntary confessions: if no harm resulted, the confession should be admissible

Arizona v. Fulminante (1991) established that cases involving the admissibility of involuntary confessions could apply the **harmless error doctrine**: If no harm resulted, the confession should be admissible. A key question in this case was whether Fulminante's confession was coerced. In this case, Fulminante was in prison for one crime but was also suspected of having committed murder. A fellow inmate offered to protect Fulminante if he would tell him the truth about the murder, which he did. This inmate later became a state's witness and disclosed Fulminante's confession. The Court ruled that the confession was indeed coerced and, therefore, involuntary. Because it was a key factor in his conviction, the error was not harmless, and the conviction was reversed.

Characteristics of the Accused In addition to police conduct, courts will also consider characteristics of the accused when assessing whether a confession was voluntary. Taking a "totality of the circumstances" approach, factors such as the defendant's age, education and intelligence levels, emotional problems or mental illness, and physical condition (including intoxication) will be considered in determining whether a confession was voluntary, but if it has not been coerced, a confession is presumed to have been voluntarily provided.

A Standard for Voluntariness

In *Haynes v. Washington* (1963), the Supreme Court held that the Fourteenth Amendment due process voluntariness test required examining the totality of the circumstances surrounding each confession. Was the admission truly voluntary? Were the individual's constitutional guarantees protected? Was the good of the people balanced with the government and the accused's freedoms? As with all constitutional cases, the balance was delicate because the final result would vitally affect all concerned, not only in the case at hand but also in all future matters that would depend

IN THE NEWS

"Judge Overturns Conviction of Nephew in 'Making a Murderer'"

By Amy Forliti and Doug Glass (*Associated Press*, August 12, 2016)

MADISON, Wis. (AP) — A judge on Friday overturned the conviction of a Wisconsin man found guilty of helping his uncle kill a woman in a case profiled in the Netflix series "Making a Murderer," ruling that investigators coerced a confession using deceptive tactics.

U.S. Magistrate William Duffin in Milwaukee ordered Brendan Dassey freed within 90 days unless prosecutors decide to retry him. The state Department of Justice, which handled the case, declined to comment Friday. The state could also appeal Duffin's ruling.

Dassey's case burst into the public's consciousness with the popularity of the "Making a Murderer" series that debuted in December. The filmmakers cast doubt on the legal process used to convict Dassey and his uncle Steven Avery in the death of Teresa Halbach, and their work sparked national interest and conjecture. Authorities involved in the case have called the 10-hour series biased, while the filmmakers have stood by their work.

Dassey confessed to helping Avery carry out the rape and killing of Halbach, but his attorneys argued that his constitutional rights were violated throughout the investigation. Dassey didn't testify at his uncle's trial and his confession wasn't presented as evidence there. Both men are serving life sentences.

Duffin said in his ruling that investigators made false promises to Dassey by assuring him "he had nothing to worry about."

"These repeated false promises, when considered in conjunction with all relevant factors, most especially Dassey's age, intellectual deficits, and the absence of a supportive adult, rendered Dassey's confession involuntary under the Fifth and Fourteenth Amendments (of the U.S. Constitution)," Duffin wrote.

Dassey, who is now 26, was 16 when Halbach, a photographer, was killed in 2005 after she went to the Avery family auto salvage yard to take pictures of some vehicles. Court papers describe Dassey as a slow learner with poor grades, with difficulty understanding some aspects of language and expressing himself verbally. He was also described as extremely introverted and poor at picking up on communications such as body language and tone.

Dassey was convicted of first-degree intentional homicide, second-degree sexual assault, and mutilation of a corpse in Halbach's killing. Avery was tried and convicted separately in the homicide.

Avery made headlines in 2003 when he was released from prison after spending 18 years behind bars for a rape he didn't commit. After being freed, he had a $36 million lawsuit pending against public officials when Halbach disappeared on Halloween 2005.

Friday's ruling came after Dassey's appeal was rejected by state courts. The judge said that

(*Continued*)

(Continued)

> Dassey's confession to police in 2006 was "so clearly involuntary" that a state appeals court ruling to the contrary was an unreasonable application of established federal law.
>
> "The court does not reach this conclusion lightly," Duffin wrote.
>
> The investigators did not have any ill motive, the judge wrote, but rather "an intentional and concerted effort to trick Dassey into confessing."
>
> The error was not harmless because Dassey's confession was the entirety of the case against him, the judge said.
>
> Laura Nirider, one of Dassey's attorneys, said he thought that if he told investigators what they wanted to hear, he'd get to go back to school.
>
> "This is justice for that 16-year-old kid . . . who we all saw being bullied into giving a statement that was completely untrue," she said.
>
> Dassey, who has been incarcerated for 10 years, is in shock and wants to go home, she said. If prosecutors decide to bring a new trial, the confession would not be usable, she said.
>
> A brother who has acted as a Halbach family spokesman did not immediately respond to phone messages and an email.
>
> Kathleen Zellner, an attorney for Avery, said in a statement that Avery was thrilled for his nephew. Avery is pursuing his own appeal.
>
> "We know when an unbiased court reviews all of the new evidence we have, Steven will have his conviction overturned as well," Zellner said.
>
> Joe Friedberg, a defense attorney in Minnesota who was not involved in the case but is familiar with it and participated in a forum on it with Avery's first defense attorney, said he doesn't believe the decision will have any bearing on Avery's case.
>
> "The kid's confession was not entered into evidence against Avery, and I don't think it impacted Avery's trial at all," Friedberg said.
>
> Netflix last month announced that new episodes of "Making a Murderer" were in production to follow appeals by both Avery and Dassey.
>
> "As we have done for the past 10 years, we will continue to document the story as it unfolds, and follow it wherever it may lead," filmmakers Laura Ricciardi and Moira Demos said in a written statement following Friday's ruling.
>
> ———
>
> Associated Press writers Amy Forliti and Doug Glass contributed from Minneapolis.

on the outcome. This case-by-case analysis was becoming cumbersome, with the stakes too high to not have some better standard by which to judge whether the confession was voluntary.

The next year saw a move away from case-by-case voluntariness analyses and the forging of a standard. Two cases decided that year, *Massiah v. United States* (1964) and *Escobedo v. Illinois* (1964) (discussed in Chapter 11), considered a single occurrence: "When the process shifts from investigatory to accusatory—when its focus is on the accused and its purpose is to elicit a confession . . . the accused must be permitted to consult with his lawyer" (*Escobedo*). The court saw interrogation to elicit a confession as a critical stage in the judicial process. However, if a suspect refuses to make a written statement without a lawyer present but does make an oral confession, that confession has been held as admissible (*Connecticut v. Barrett*, 1987).

False Confessions

Research on false confessions has produced mixed results. Some researchers conclude that the problem with false confessions is pandemic; others say false confessions are rare. Despite speculation and debate over the actual percentage of false confessions, the fact remains that they do occur.

Some research suggests that the risk of false confessions is higher among the mentally impaired and juveniles (O'Connor & Maher, 2009). More than 90 percent of juveniles questioned by the police waive their *Miranda* rights and seek the assistance of a lawyer. O'Connor and Maher (2009, p. 72) identify three types of false confessions:

- Voluntary confessions—Those in which people claim responsibility for crimes they did not commit without prompting from police.
- Compliant confessions—Cases in which the suspect acquiesces to escape from a stressful situation, to avoid punishment, or to gain a promised or implied reward.
- Internalized false confessions—Those in which innocent but vulnerable suspects, exposed to highly suggestive interrogation techniques, come to confess as well as to believe they committed the crime in question.

At the heart of many cases examining confessions is the landmark *Miranda* decision.

Miranda v. Arizona

Miranda v. Arizona (1966) is perhaps the best-known law enforcement case ever decided. This case, because of its notoriety, has arguably done more to teach constitutional law to the general population than any other source. Most television and movie watchers can recite the requirements set forth by Chief Justice Earl Warren in this pivotal case and understand that the purpose of the warning is to let those accused know they do have rights and to protect themselves.

Miranda is not without critics. The National Center for Policy Analysis says that because of *Miranda* "substantial numbers of criminal convictions are lost each year" and suggests that "*Miranda* may be the single most damaging blow to the nation's crime fighting ability in the past half century." Indeed, decades before *Miranda* the courts were grappling with the need to balance protection of individual freedom and society's need to solve crime, as Justice Robert H. Jackson stated in a concurring opinion in *Watts v. Indiana* (1949): "The suspect neither had nor was advised of his right to get counsel. This presents a real dilemma in a free society. To subject one without counsel to questioning which may and is intended to convict him, is a real peril to individual freedom. To bring in a lawyer means a real peril to solution of the crime, because, under our adversary system, he deems that his sole duty is to protect his client—guilty or innocent—and that in such a capacity he owes no duty whatever to help society solve its crime problem."

◀ **CASE IN BRIEF**

Miranda v. Arizona (1966)

ISSUE Does it violate the Constitution to interrogate a suspect in custody without first advising of them about the right to counsel and the protection against self-incrimination?

RULING Yes. Custodial interrogations are done in a police-dominated atmosphere such that the questioning is inherently coercive and intimidating. To limit that, the suspect must be advised of certain rights.

> **L03** Miranda *remains the precedent case referred to by courts analyzing confession issues.*

The important *Miranda* case is discussed in detail because of its historical review of this area of law, the strong position the Chief Justice took in his opinion, and the equally strong dissents.

The Case

Ernesto Miranda was a poor 23-year-old with only a ninth-grade education. He was arrested at his home for rape and was taken to the police station, where the complaining witness identified him. Within two hours, he signed a written confession. Miranda was never informed of his right to consult with an attorney, to have an attorney present during questioning, or of his right not to be compelled to incriminate himself. Although the confession was not admitted, he was convicted and sentenced to 20 to 30 years in prison. (*An interesting side note*: Miranda was paroled in 1975. On release he hung around bars in a rough part of Phoenix. On New Year's Eve 1976, he was fatally stabbed in a bar fight. When police arrived they apprehended a suspect and advised him, ironically, of his *Miranda* rights. The suspect exercised those rights and made no statement. No charges were ever filed in Miranda's stabbing death.)

The legal issue in *Miranda* was whether the police must inform a suspect who is the subject of custodial interrogation of his constitutional rights concerning self-incrimination and counsel before questioning. Chief Justice Warren wrote:

> We hold that when an individual is taken into custody or otherwise deprived of his freedom by the authorities and is subject to questioning, the privilege against self-incrimination is jeopardized. Procedural safeguards must be employed.... He must be warned prior to any questioning that he has a right to remain silent, that anything he says can be used against him in a court of law, that he has the right to the presence of an attorney, and that if he cannot afford an attorney one will be appointed for him prior to any questioning if he so desires.

Miranda extended the *Escobedo* decision and shifted the area of inquiry to the Fifth Amendment. *Escobedo* brought the right to counsel to the police station before trial; *Miranda* brought the right to counsel into the street if an interrogation is to take place. *Miranda* also changed the analysis of the Fifth Amendment protection against self-incrimination from a totality of the circumstances test for voluntariness to whether those subjected to a custodial interrogation by police were advised of their rights. However, it must be noted that both tests still exist, and *Miranda* has not completely displaced the due process/voluntariness standard. When a *Miranda* violation cannot be used to support an attack, voluntariness still can.

> **L04** *The Constitution requires that I inform you that:*
> - *You have the right to remain silent.*
> - *Anything you say can and will be used against you in court.*
> - *You have the right to talk to a lawyer now and have him present now or at any time during questioning.*
> - *If you cannot afford a lawyer, one will be appointed for you without cost.*

The *Miranda* Warning

Miranda took the unique step of actually directing police officers to tell individuals they had in custody, before questioning them, four specific warnings. The *Miranda* warning itself may be read from a printed card or recited from memory and must include the wording shown in the learning objective.

The Wording

After more than four decades, state and federal courts continue to litigate the adequacy of dozens of variations of the particular wording used by officers and continue to be reversed by the Supreme Court (Rutledge, 2010b). *California v. Prysock* (1981) was the first Supreme Court case to address this issue. In 1978, Randall Prysock brutally murdered a woman. On the evening of the murder Prysock, a minor, was arrested and brought to a substation of the Tulare County Sheriff's Department and advised of his *Miranda* rights. He declined to talk and, because he was a minor, his parents were notified. His parents arrived, and after meeting with them, Prysock decided to answer police questions and was advised of his constitutional rights. The advising officer told Prysock that he had the "right to talk to a lawyer before you are questioned, to have him with you while you are being questioned, and all during questioning." Prysock waived his rights, confessed, was convicted, and was sentenced to life in prison.

The California Court of Appeals reversed the conviction, ruling that the *Miranda* warning was defective because the officer did not follow the "Standard" order for covering the four components of the warning and varied from the usual language used to describe the right to counsel. The court said that "the rigidity of the *Miranda* rules is the decision's greatest strength." On appeal the Supreme Court reversed the California ruling, holding that the warning was not faulty: "This Court has never indicated that the 'rigidity' of *Miranda* extends to the precise formulation of the warnings given a criminal defendant. *Miranda* itself indicated that no talismanic incantation was required to satisfy its strictures. It is clear that the police in this case fully conveyed to the defendant his rights as required by *Miranda*. The Court of Appeal erred in holding that the warnings were inadequate simply because of the order in which they were given."

A second key Supreme Court case addressing the wording of the *Miranda* warning was *Duckworth v. Eagan* (1989). In this case the Court held that the *Miranda* warning does not need to be given verbatim—word for word—as stated in *Miranda v. Arizona*. What is required is that suspects' rights as set forth in *Miranda* are clearly conveyed. As stated in *Anderson v. State* (1969), the question is "whether the words used by the officer, in view of the age, intelligence, and demeanor of the individual being interrogated, convey a clear understanding of all *Miranda* rights."

The most recent ruling on the wording of the *Miranda* warnings is *Florida v. Powell* (2010). In this case, a Florida state court convicted Kevin Powell of being a felon in possession of a firearm and sentenced him to 10 years in prison. Powell appealed on the grounds that his admission should have been suppressed because the officer did not specifically tell him he had the "right to have a lawyer present during questioning." The state appeals court ruled in favor of Powell, agreeing that the statement should have been suppressed, and the Florida Supreme Court upheld this ruling. Florida then appealed to the Supreme Court, which reversed citing prior decision that no exact wording is required to satisfy *Miranda*: "The four warnings *Miranda* requires are invariable, but this Court has not dictated the words in which the essential information must be conveyed. Our decisions in *Prysock* and *Duckworth* inform our judgment here. We reach the same conclusion; the two warnings reasonably conveyed Powell's right to have an attorney present, not only at the outset of interrogation, but at all times."

CASE IN BRIEF

California v. Prysock (1981)

ISSUE Is a Miranda warning valid if the words used by the officer are not "a virtual incantation of the precise language contained in the *Miranda* opinion"?

RULING Yes. The Supreme Court wrote that there is not a required "talismanic incantation." What matters is the content of the warning, not the specific words used to convey the rights protected by the warning.

MYTH
If an officer does not recite the Miranda warning exactly as set forth by the Court in the *Miranda* decision, it is invalid and any statements made by the suspect must be suppressed.

FACT
What matters is the content of the warning, not the specific words used to convey the rights protected by the warning.

Constitutional Law in ACTION

Erik was arrested for kidnapping and assaulting a six-year-old boy. After his arrest he was brought to the precinct to be interrogated. While there, a child abuse detective told the suspect, "Erik, you are probably better off just keeping your mouth shut when I ask you anything. But, if you don't, you have the right to an attorney and to have one present during questioning. Also, if you can't afford one, an attorney will be provided for you. I will use anything you tell me against you in court."

The detective did not have a printed card with the *Miranda* warnings. Erik chose to answer questions that incriminated himself.

- *Did the officer's warning adequately convey the protections of Miranda?*
- *Does it matter what words the officer chose?*
- *What problems may arise with using an officer's own words to convey the Miranda warning rather than reading them off of a printed card?*

How an officer provides the warnings becomes a tactical decision. Some officers may prefer to not read from a card. At times, an officer may think delivering the warnings as stated directly on most *Miranda* cards could be too harsh, such as with younger suspects, and they may opt to recite a "soft" *Miranda* warning. The issue is whether all four warnings are adequately conveyed to the suspect. Any officer could become flustered on the witness stand when told by defense counsel to recite verbatim what was said. Could officers say with certainty they were able to remember the exact words months, maybe years, later in court? Many officers find the routine of reading from the card will permit them to state this procedure in court and read from the card on the stand if so requested.

Premature *Miranda* Warnings

"You are under arrest. You have the right to remain silent." These two sentences are routinely stated by police and, to many citizens, are considered to go hand in hand. However, it is a myth that the words "you are under arrest" must always be followed immediately by the phrase "you have the right to remain silent." They are, in fact, two distinctly separate declarations and should often *not* be used together (Means & McDonald, 2010a).

In *Oregon v. Elstad* (1985), the Supreme Court acknowledged, "*Miranda* warnings may inhibit persons from giving information," an experience every law enforcement officer has had. FBI statistics show that the national clearance rate for violent crimes plunged 28 percent after the *Miranda* decision and has never recovered. These statistics are a caution to officers to not give unnecessary or premature *Miranda* warnings, lest they risk the needless loss of a potential confession (Rutledge, 2009a). Indeed, "*Mirandizing* too soon can be a mistake" (Rutledge, 2009b, p. 60).

The Supreme Court has never held that *Miranda* warnings are required simply because a person is in custody or simply because a person not in custody is interrogated. The need for a warning is triggered by "the interaction of custody *and* official interrogation" (*Illinois v. Perkins*, 1990). Thus, "To ensure admissibility of statements, give *Miranda* warnings just before commencement of apparent custodial police interrogation—not sooner" (Rutledge, 2009b, p. 63).

When the Miranda Warning Must Be Given

"*Miranda* warnings are triggered by a simple formula: Custody + Interrogation = The requirement for *Miranda* warnings" (Petrocelli, 2010, p. 18). The *Miranda* decision defined *interrogation* as "questioning initiated by law enforcement officers after a person has been taken into custody or otherwise deprived of his freedom of action in a significant way." The Court has defined **custodial interrogation** as "questioning initiated by law enforcement officers after a person has been taken into custody or otherwise deprived of his freedom of action in any significant way," adding, "This is what we meant in *Escobedo* when we spoke of an investigation which had focused on an accused" (*Oregon v. Mathiason*, 1977).

custodial interrogation questioning by law enforcement officers after a person has been taken into custody or otherwise deprived of freedom of action in any significant way

Custody   Different nuances in different cases may make determining whether the person was actually *in custody* an issue. Even being handcuffed in a squad car may be a *stop* and not an *arrest*, but the difference can be a thin line. When in doubt, an officer should advise the person of his or her rights; however, this procedure becomes a matter of circumstances and officer discretion. The real problem comes when an officer is not aware of the law and neglects to act accordingly. Confusion over whether a person is *in* custody may be clarified by making two basic inquiries:

1. Has the person been told by police that he or she is under arrest?
2. Has the person been deprived of freedom to the degree one associates with formal arrest, based on a totality of the circumstances?

L05 *The Miranda warning must be given to a suspect interrogated in police custody, that is, when the suspect is not free to leave.*

Here is a fine-line difference of which officers should be aware. In a Fourth Amendment context, for seizure purposes, a person must be deprived of freedom in a significant way so that he or she does not feel reasonably free to leave the situation. However, in a Fifth Amendment context, the question used to define when custody occurs for *Miranda* becomes whether the person considers themselves not free to leave to the point that one would associate the situation with formal arrest. In other words, if the police will not allow the person to leave to the degree that one reasonably associates with a formal arrest, that person is in custody for *Miranda* purposes, even if the police have not said, "You're under arrest." This circumstance echoes the statement of the court in *California v. Beheler* (1983) that, for the purpose of *Miranda*, the ultimate determinant of whether a person is "in custody" is "whether the suspect has been subjected to a formal arrest or to equivalent restraints on his freedom of movement."

Suspect under Arrest   An arrested person is in custody and must be given the *Miranda* warning if he or she is to be questioned by police. All detentions may not require the *Miranda* warning. Even if a person is the suspect of a crime and being questioned, unless the interrogation is done while the suspect is in custody or

> **MYTH**
> The police cannot ask you any questions once you are under arrest unless they read you *Miranda*.
>
> **FACT**
> This is false. Routine booking questions such as name, birth date, or address are not considered investigatory in nature and are unlikely to produce incriminating statements.

deprived of freedom in any significant way, the *Miranda* warning need not be given (*Beckwith v. United States,* 1976). This decision was echoed in *Berkemer v. McCarty* (1984) when the Court held, "The . . . noncoercive aspect of ordinary traffic stops prompts us to hold that persons temporarily detained pursuant to such stops are not 'in custody' for the purposes of *Miranda*." In addition, *Pennsylvania v. Muniz* (1990) established that police may ask routine questions of individuals suspected of driving under the influence of alcohol or drugs and ask them to perform certain tests without giving them the *Miranda* warning. Police may also videotape the responses given.

Suspect at the Police Station If police direct a suspect to come to the police station for questioning or take the suspect there, this atmosphere is coercive and the *Miranda* warning is required. If, however, the suspect voluntarily comes to the station, no warning is required. As noted in *Miranda*, "There is no requirement that police stop a person who enters a police station and states that he wishes to confess to a crime, or a person who calls the police to offer a confession or any other statement he desires to make. Volunteered statements of any kind are not barred by the Fifth Amendment and their admissibility is not affected by our holding today." This circumstance occurred in *Oregon v. Mathiason* (1977), when Mathiason voluntarily came to the police station and was not read *Miranda* before providing self-incriminating statements. The Supreme Court said:

> Any interview of one suspected of a crime by a police officer will have coercive aspects to it, simply by virtue of the fact that the police officer is part of a law enforcement system which may ultimately cause the suspect to be charged with a crime. But police officers are not required to administer *Miranda* warnings to everyone whom they question. Nor is the requirement of warnings to be imposed simply because the questioning takes place in the station house, or because the questioned person is one whom the police suspect. *Miranda* warnings are required only where there has been such a restriction on a person's freedom as to render him "in custody." It was that sort of coercive environment to which *Miranda* by its terms was made applicable, and to which it is limited.

Through the Court's opinion, clarifications have been made to avoid ambiguities.

The same is usually true of questioning a suspect in a police car. If the suspect is told to get into the car, it is usually a custodial situation, especially if the person cannot get out of the car or will not be let out if he or she asks.

If, on the other hand, someone flags down a police car and makes a voluntary confession of a crime he or she just committed, no *Miranda* warning is required. If the officer did not ask any questions of the suspect, no *Miranda* is necessary, and the warning is not required if the person just walks up to an officer and is not in custody and confesses (*United States v. Jonas,* 1986; *United States v. Wright,* 1993).

Suspect is in Custody for Another Offense When a suspect is already in custody for another offense, it would seem the *Miranda* warning must be given before any questioning begins. However, this can be a thorny area because the type of custody is not always clear. For example, in *Howes v. Fields* (2012), the Court said that just because someone is in prison and in custody (in that context), they are not in custody *per se* for Miranda purposes. In the *Howes* decision, the Court quoted

---

CASE IN BRIEF

Oregon v. Mathiason (1977)

ISSUE Is a suspect automatically considered in custody for *Miranda* purposes if the questioning takes place at the police station?

RULING No. Mathiason came to the station on his own after being contacted by telephone, and he was told he was not under arrest and could leave at any time. In fact, he left after 30 minutes of questioning. He was never in custody.

Illinois v. Perkins (1990) and held, "we 'rejected the argument that *Miranda* warnings are required whenever a suspect is in custody in a technical sense.'. . . "

Other Factors Indicating a Custodial Situation Most kinds of physical restraint place the situation within the *Miranda* requirement. As found in *People v. Shivers* (1967), if a police officer holds a gun on a person, that person is in custody and not free to leave. If, however, the suspect also has a gun, he or she would unlikely be considered in custody (*Yates v. United States*, 1967). Consider, for purposes of illustration, this nonexhaustive list used recently by the Eighth Circuit in *United States v. Muhlenbruch* (2011) to determine whether custody existed under *Miranda*:

- whether the suspect was informed that he was free to leave and that answering was voluntary;
- whether the suspect possessed freedom of movement;
- whether the suspect initiated contact or voluntarily acquiesced;
- whether strong-arm tactics or strategies were employed;
- whether the atmosphere was police-dominated;
- whether the suspect was placed under arrest at the end of questioning.

Interrogation The second element that must be present to trigger *Miranda* is interrogation. Interrogation is commonly thought of as the formal, systemic, often intensive questioning by law enforcement of a person suspected of criminal activity. The purpose of interrogation is to elicit evidence or other information relevant to a crime that incriminates the provider of the information as the perpetrator of the illegal action. As already discussed, when such information is provided voluntarily, as with spontaneous statements, no *Miranda* warning is required because the communication was not the product of an interrogation or express questioning by the police: "Confessions remain a proper element in law enforcement. Any statement given freely and voluntarily without any compelling influences is, of course, admissible in evidence. . . . Volunteered statements of any kind are not barred by the Fifth Amendment and their admissibility is not affected by our holding today" (*Miranda v. Arizona*, 1966).

In *Rhode Island v. Innis* (1980), the Supreme Court further clarified what is meant by interrogation. In this case, a taxicab driver had been robbed by a man wielding a sawed-off shotgun. Shortly after the robbery, the victim identified a picture of Thomas Innis as that of the assailant. A patrolman in Providence, Rhode Island, spotted Innis, who was unarmed, on the street, arrested him, and advised him of his rights under *Miranda v. Arizona*. When other police officers arrived at the arrest scene, Innis was twice again advised of his *Miranda* rights, and he stated that he understood his rights and wanted to speak with a lawyer. Innis was then placed in a police car to be driven to the central station in the company of three officers, who were instructed not to question Innis or intimidate him in any way.

While en route to the station, two of the officers engaged in a conversation between themselves concerning the missing shotgun. One of the officers stated that there were "a lot of handicapped children running around in this area" because a school for such children was located nearby, and "God forbid one of them might find a weapon with shells and they might hurt themselves." Innis interrupted the conversation, stating that the officers should turn the car around so he could show

◀ **CASE IN BRIEF**

Rhode Island v. Innis (1980)

ISSUE Is it interrogation for officers to converse in front of an arrestee when that conversation results in the arrestee incriminating himself?

RULING No. An interrogation occurs only when the words or actions by the police, other than routine booking questions, are such that the police should know they are reasonably likely to elicit an incriminating response from the suspect.

them where the gun was located. On returning to the scene of the arrest where a search for the shotgun was in progress, Innis was again advised of his *Miranda* rights, replied that he understood those rights but that he "wanted to get the gun out of the way because of the kids in the area in the school" and then led the police to the shotgun.

Before trial on charges of kidnapping, robbery, and murder of another taxicab driver, the trial court denied Innis's motion to suppress the shotgun and the statements he had made to the police regarding its discovery, and Innis was subsequently convicted. The Rhode Island Supreme Court set aside the conviction and held that Innis was entitled to a new trial, concluding that Innis had invoked his *Miranda* right to counsel and that, contrary to *Miranda*'s mandate that, in the absence of counsel, all custodial interrogation then cease, the police officers in the vehicle had "interrogated" Innis without a valid waiver of his right to counsel. The case went to the Supreme Court to decide the issue of whether Innis was interrogated in violation of the standards promulgated in the *Miranda* opinion. The Court held that, no, Innis had not been interrogated and set forth the following definition of interrogation:

> We conclude that the *Miranda* safeguards come into play whenever a person in custody is subjected to either express questioning or its functional equivalent. That is to say, the term "interrogation" under *Miranda* refers not only to express questioning, but also to any words or actions on the part of the police (other than those normally attendant to arrest and custody) that the police should know are reasonably likely to elicit an incriminating response from the suspect. The latter portion of this definition focuses primarily upon the perceptions of the suspect, rather than the intent of the police. This focus reflects the fact that the *Miranda* safeguards were designed to vest a suspect in custody with an added measure of protection against coercive police practices, without regard to objective proof of the underlying intent of the police. A practice that the police should know is reasonably likely to evoke an incriminating response from a suspect thus amounts to interrogation. But, since the police surely cannot be held accountable for the unforeseeable results of their words or actions, the definition of interrogation can extend only to words or actions on the part of police officers that they should have known were reasonably likely to elicit an incriminating response.

The Court concluded:

> The case thus boils down to whether, in the context of a brief conversation, the officers should have known that the respondent would suddenly be moved to make a self-incriminating response. Given the fact that the entire conversation appears to have consisted of no more than a few offhand remarks, we cannot say that the officers should have known that it was reasonably likely that Innis would so respond. . . . It is our view, therefore, that the respondent was not subjected by the police to words or actions that the police should have known were reasonably likely to elicit an incriminating response from him.

The case was vacated and remanded.

Thus, via *Innis*, the Court set forth the definition of an **interrogation** as the formal, systemic, express questioning by law enforcement of a person suspected of criminal activity, as well as the functional equivalent of express questioning (any

interrogation the formal, systemic, express questioning by law enforcement of a person suspected of criminal activity, as well as the functional equivalent of express questioning (any words or actions by the police, other than those normally attendant to arrest and custody, that the police should know are reasonably likely to elicit an incriminating response from the suspect)

words or actions on the part of the police, other than those normally attendant to arrest and custody, that the police should know are reasonably likely to elicit an incriminating response from the suspect). Absent this second trigger, *Miranda* is not required.

Waiving and Invoking the Rights

A **waiver** is a purposeful, voluntary giving up of a known right. Suspects must know and understand their constitutional rights to legally waive them. The Supreme Court in *Miranda* set forth that a statement will be admissible only if the government meets its "heavy burden" of demonstrating "that the defendant knowingly and intelligently waived his privilege against self-incrimination and his right to retained or appointed counsel." In other words, to waive *Miranda*, a person must do so voluntarily (i.e., without pressure), knowingly, and intelligently (i.e., understanding what the right is and what the consequences of waiving it are). These stipulations were further clarified in *Colorado v. Connelly* (1986), when the Court made it clear that a waiver must be shown to have occurred by a preponderance of the evidence. Silence alone, however, is not a waiver.

The Supreme Court in *Tague v. Louisiana* (1980) reemphasized that the government has the "heavy burden" of showing the person was competent to relinquish these rights, meaning the police must always

> **waiver** a purposeful and voluntary giving up of a known right

> **LO6** If after hearing a police officer read the Miranda warning, suspects remain silent, this silence alone is not a waiver. To waive their rights, suspects must show (1) that they understand their rights and (2) conduct indicative of a waiver, such as agreeing to voluntarily answer questions without a lawyer present.

Constitutional Law in ACTION

Officer Lee is on patrol near an interstate highway. He is checking for drivers violating the speed limit with his radar. He sees a car approaching at a high rate of speed, and his radar shows it is traveling 20 mph over the posted speed limit. He follows the car and pulls it over.

The car has two people in it, a driver and a passenger. The officer sees an open bottle of beer in between the driver and passenger. The officer also finds out that both people have arrest warrants. He places the two under arrest, puts them in his squad car, and returns to the car he pulled over to recover the beer and conduct an inventory search before he tows it from the interstate.

While in the squad car, the two talk back and forth about how they have a stolen gun hidden under the dashboard. The two do not know that the officer's squad camera is recording their conversation. At no time does the officer ask the two any questions.

The car is towed and the two people are brought to jail. Later, the officer listens to the recording and hears the conversation about the gun. He obtains a search warrant for the car and locates the stolen gun. The two are charged with having a stolen gun. The recorded conversation is introduced at trial and is used to convict the two.

- *Are the two in custody?*
- *Does Miranda apply? Why or why not?*

consider suspects' competency to understand and waive their rights. People who are under the influence of alcohol or other drugs, are physically injured, are in shock, or are very young or very old may have difficulty understanding the situation. Also, suspects may rescind the waiver at any point in the interrogation. People must possess sufficient competence to understand they are waiving a crucial constitutional right.

The flip side of a waiver, or relinquishing of rights, is an invocation, or a stated intent to exercise a given right. As noted, if after hearing a police officer read the *Miranda* warning the suspect remains silent, this silence is not a waiver, but neither is it a clear statement that a person intends to invoke their right to remain silent. Paradoxically, a suspect who wishes to exercise, or **invoke**, his or her right to remain silent must first speak up and unambiguously state that desire (*Berghuis v. Thompkins*, 2010). It is important to recognize the two distinct rights a suspect may invoke under *Miranda*: the right to remain silent and the right to counsel. Although a waiver applies to both, these two rights are distinct when invoked, and the police have different rules to follow depending on which right is invoked.

Thus, waiving and invoking rights are separate but related concepts that often go hand in hand. Keep the distinctions in mind as you read the following discussion because it goes back and forth between waiver cases and invocation cases. The point to remember is that individuals must unambiguously invoke their rights, just as they must voluntarily, knowingly, and intelligently waive their rights. But if they do not expressly and unambiguously invoke a right, they might nonetheless waive it by their conduct and the surrounding circumstances.

Right to Remain Silent At any time during questioning, the defendant may choose to exercise or invoke the right to remain silent. *Michigan v. Mosley* (1975) involved a case in which the defendant had invoked his right to remain silent and then was questioned about a different case. Richard Mosley was arrested in Detroit for robberies, was Mirandized, and said he would not talk about the robberies. No questioning took place. Two hours later a homicide detective told Mosley he wanted to talk about a murder. After a new set of *Miranda* warnings, Mosley waived his rights and made incriminating statements. The Supreme Court ruled that the admission was admissible: "Under the *Mosley* rule, a suspect who has invoked only his right to silence can be re-approached to seek a waiver on a different case" (Rutledge, 2010c, p. 66). Technically, it does not matter if the questioning involves the same or different cases. What matters, in what has since been dubbed the *Mosley analysis*, is that the "right to remain silent was scrupulously honored." Here, the passage of two hours, the different crime inquired about, and the different detective asking questions are all factors in showing the right was scrupulously honored.

Colorado v. Spring (1987) established that a waiver of *Miranda* rights is valid, even though the suspect thought the questioning was going to be about a minor crime, but the police changed their line of questioning to inquire about a more serious crime. At this point the suspect could invoke his right to silence.

Patterson v. Illinois (1988) established that a waiver includes waiving both the right against self-incrimination and the right to counsel. There is often confusion about what constitutes a valid waiver and what constitutes an invocation of those

CASE IN BRIEF

Michigan v. Mosley (1975)

ISSUE Once the right to remain silent is invoked by a suspect under *Miranda*, may the police approach the suspect and question him again later?

RULING Yes, the invocation of the right to silence is not permanent. As long as the right of the suspect to stop the questioning was "scrupulously honored" by the police and ceased immediately, they may re-approach after a "cooling off" period.

rights, especially when the suspect is ambiguous. One case that helped better define when a suspect has waived his or her *Miranda* rights was *Berghuis v. Thompkins* (2010), which involved the habeas corpus appeal of a defendant convicted in the shooting of two people outside a Michigan mall. The perpetrator, Van Chester Thompkins, was arrested in Ohio a year after the shooting and was interviewed there by two local Michigan officers. Thompkins was advised of his *Miranda* rights but refused to sign the waiver form. He indicated, however, that he understood his rights. During a three-hour taped interview, Thompkins said little, giving one-word answers to questions. The Supreme Court held that Thompkins had, indeed, waived his Fifth Amendment right against self-incrimination by responding to the question and that if a suspect wants to assert either his right to counsel or his right to silence, it is up to him to do so unequivocally and unambiguously: "A suspect who has received and understood his *Miranda* rights waives the right to remain silent by making an uncoerced statement to police."

This decision has made obtaining a waiver of *Miranda* rights easier: "A binding invocation of the right to silence now requires the suspect to make an unambiguous statement asserting that he does not want to talk to law enforcement or that he wants to remain silent. . . . The Supreme Court's 'clarifications' have somewhat tightened the requirements for invoking *Miranda* rights and loosened *Miranda* waiver requirements—both positions that favor law enforcement" (Means & McDonald, 2010b, p. 19).

Although police and prosecutors have hailed the *Berghuis* decision as a triumph for justice, and defense attorneys have denounced it as an unjust "retreat" from standard protocol established in *Miranda*, some scholars contend that the decision merely reaffirmed a principle established three decades previously in *North Carolina v. Butler* (1979), a right-to-counsel case in which the Supreme Court first recognized that a defendant's *implied* waiver was sufficient to make his statements admissible under *Miranda* (Rutledge, 2010a).

CASE IN BRIEF

Berghuis v. Thompkins (2010)

ISSUE Does a valid *Miranda* waiver need to be explicit?

RULING No. All that needs to be shown is that the suspect made a voluntary choice to speak and that it was done "with a full awareness [knowingly and intelligently] of both the nature of the right being abandoned and the consequences of the decision to abandon it."

Constitutional Law in ACTION

Grant is arrested for punching his wife in the nose during an argument. While he is sitting handcuffed in the back of a squad car, the officer reads Grant his *Miranda* rights.

After the rights are read, the officer asks Grant some questions about the incident. Grant sits there, silently, and occasionally nods his head in response to the officer's question. After about 10 minutes of this, Grant says, "I don't know if I should talk to you after all."

The officer asks Grant some more questions, and Grant answers these questions in great detail, despite his statement about not knowing if he should "talk" to the officer. These answers are later used to convict Grant for domestic assault.

- Was Grant's statement ambiguous?
- Does the fact that Grant was initially silent show he invoked his right to silence? Why or why not?

CASE IN BRIEF

North Carolina v. Butler (1979)

ISSUE Does a waiver need to be explicit to be valid?

RULING No. A combination of silence, an understanding of rights, and conduct can indicate a valid waiver.

Right to Counsel In *Butler*, Willie Butler, who was under arrest for certain crimes and had been advised of his rights under *Miranda v. Arizona*, made incriminating statements to the arresting officers. His motion to suppress evidence of these statements on the ground that he had not waived his right to assistance of counsel at the time the statements were made was denied by a North Carolina trial court, and he was subsequently convicted. The North Carolina Supreme Court reversed, holding that *Miranda* requires that no statement of a person under custodial interrogation may be admitted in evidence against him unless, at the time the statement was made, he explicitly waived the right to the presence of a lawyer.

The case was reviewed by the U.S. Supreme Court, which vacated and remanded, holding: "An explicit statement of waiver is not invariably necessary to support a finding that the defendant waived the right to counsel guaranteed by the *Miranda* case. The question of waiver must be determined on the particular facts and circumstances surrounding the case, and there is no reason in a case such as this for a *per se* rule, such as that of the North Carolina Supreme Court. By creating an inflexible rule that no implicit waiver can ever suffice, that court has gone beyond the requirements of federal organic law, and thus its judgment cannot stand, since a state court can neither add to nor subtract from the mandates of the United States Constitution." Thus, the U.S. Supreme Court held in *Butler* that, "in at least some cases, waiver can be clearly inferred from the actions and words of the person interrogated." Since that decision some lower courts have allowed implied waivers but others have not.

In *Edwards v. Arizona* (1981), the Supreme Court held that after a person has been given his or her *Miranda* warnings and then invokes his or her right to have legal counsel, the suspect cannot be re-approached, either by the same or different officers, and cannot be questioned further until a lawyer is made available. *Edwards* refers to the *Miranda* right to counsel only, and the *Edwards* decision has since been modified under *Shatzer*.

CASE IN BRIEF

Maryland v. Shatzer (2010)

ISSUE Does the *Edwards* rule extend the ban on questioning indefinitely, or may officers re-approach a suspect for questioning despite a request for counsel at a previous point in time?

RULING It does not extend indefinitely. As long as there is a break in custody of 14 days, officers may re-approach the suspect despite the initial request for counsel.

In *Maryland v. Shatzer* (2010), the Court effectively set an expiration date on the right-to-counsel invocation by announcing a new "14-day break-in-custody" rule. This ruling changed *Miranda* protocol under *Edwards* by allowing police the authority to initiate contact with a suspect who had previously asserted the right to counsel if at least 14 days had passed since the original invocation of that right. Before this ruling, the police were allowed contact with the suspect only if (1) the suspect initiated further communication or (2) counsel was made available. *Shatzer* changed this and added to conditions 1 and 2 the provision that after a 14-day break in custody, the *Edwards* rule expires and officers can re-approach.

In 2003, a detective questioned Michael Blaine Shatzer, who was in prison for a prior conviction, about allegations Shatzer had sexually abused his own son. Shatzer invoked his *Miranda* right to have counsel present during interrogation, so the detective terminated the interview. Shatzer was released back into the general prison population, and the investigation was closed.

Another detective reopened the investigation in 2006 and attempted to interrogate Shatzer, who was still incarcerated. Shatzer waived his *Miranda* rights and made inculpatory statements, which the trial court refused to suppress, reasoning that *Edwards v. Arizona* did not apply because Shatzer had experienced a break in *Miranda* custody before the 2006 interrogation. Shatzer was convicted of sexual child abuse. The Court of Appeals of Maryland reversed, holding that the mere passage of time does not end the *Edwards* protections, and that, assuming a break-in-custody exception to *Edwards* existed, Shatzer's release back into the general prison population did not constitute such a break. The Supreme Court, however, disagreed:

> Shatzer's release back into the general prison population constitutes a break in *Miranda* custody. Lawful imprisonment imposed upon conviction does not create the coercive pressures produced by investigative custody that justify *Edwards*. When previously incarcerated suspects are released back into the general prison population, they return to their accustomed surroundings and daily routine—they regain the degree of control they had over their lives before the attempted interrogation. Their continued detention is relatively disconnected from their prior unwillingness to cooperate in an investigation. The "inherently compelling pressures" of custodial interrogation ended when Shatzer returned to his normal life.

Thus, as long as 14 days have passed and the suspect has been out of *Miranda*, or police, custody for that time, having returned to his or her "normal" life, the suspect can be re-approached without violating *Edwards*.

In *Arizona v. Roberson* (1988), Ronald Roberson was arrested for burglary and read his *Miranda* rights. He said he wanted a lawyer, so no questions were asked. Three days later a different officer, unaware of the prior invocation of counsel, approached Roberson, who was still in custody, about a different burglary and read Roberson his *Miranda* rights, but this time Roberson waived his rights and provided a statement on the case. The Supreme Court suppressed, saying before starting an interrogation officers were obligated to learn about previous invocations. After a

Constitutional Law in ACTION

Billy is arrested for burglary of his neighbor's house. He is brought to the police station and read the *Miranda warning*. He is then asked by the detective if he would answer some questions regarding the burglary. Billy says that he wants to get a lawyer first. All questioning stops, and Billy is later released pending charges.

Two months pass, and the detective investigating the case has some new evidence. Billy's DNA has been recovered from a soda can that was taken from the neighbor's refrigerator and opened, with some of its contents consumed.

The detective finds Billy at home and arrests him. Billy is brought to the station house and is again read the *Miranda warning*. This time, Billy answers the detective's questions about the burglary. Billy's responses to the second interrogation are later used to convict him of burglary.

- *Was Billy in custody?*
- *How does Billy's previous arrest affect the detective's ability to question him?*
- *Could the detective re-approach Billy and ask him questions? Why or why not?*

defendant invokes the right to counsel, police may not interrogate him, even about a different crime, unless the command of *Shatzer* has been followed.

In *Minnick v. Mississippi* (1990), Robert Minnick escaped from a Mississippi jail and was captured by the FBI in California. After being Mirandized, Minnick asserted his right to counsel and an attorney was appointed. Minnick and the attorney met several times over the next three days before Mississippi officers arrived to question him. He waived his rights and made incriminating statements. The Supreme Court suppressed, saying that merely having a court-appointed attorney does not satisfy the *Edwards* requirement that the attorney be physically present during any subsequent custodial interrogation by any officers on any case.

In *Davis v. United States* (1994), after a fatal attack by one sailor on another with a pool cue over a pool game, the police arrested Robert Davis and questioned him after advising him of his *Miranda* rights. After one and a half hours of talking to the police Davis said, "Maybe I should talk to a lawyer," but then said, "No, I don't want a lawyer," so the questioning continued. Finding that the statement was not an unambiguous invocation of the right to counsel, the Supreme Court upheld admission of Davis's statements and unanimously affirmed his conviction and sentence: "We decline to adopt a rule requiring officers to ask clarifying questions. If the suspect's statement is not an unambiguous or unequivocal request for counsel, the officers have no obligation to stop questioning him."

> **CASE IN BRIEF**
>
> *Davis v. United States* (1994)
>
> **ISSUE** Does an ambiguous request for an attorney under *Miranda* require police to immediately stop questioning the suspect?
>
> **RULING** No. Any request for an attorney must be clear and unequivocal.

Interestingly, some states do require clarification questions under their state constitutions. In Minnesota, for example, suspects are afforded one further level of protection. Where a suspect's request is "equivocal or ambiguous" but "subject to a construction that the accused is requesting counsel, all further questioning must stop except that narrow question designed to 'clarify' the accused's true desires respecting counsel may continue" (*State v. Robinson*, 1988).

Specific language that does not require questioning to stop includes:

- "I just don't think that I should say anything." (*Burket v. Angelone*, 2000)
- "I don't got nothing to say." (*United States v. Banks*, 2003)
- "Could I call my lawyer?" (*Dormire v. Wilkinson*, 2001)

Beachheading or "Question First"

Sometimes suspects will make self-incriminating statements before police can advise them of their *Miranda* protections. In sharp contrast to these uncoerced, spontaneous confessions are those unconstitutionally elicited statements derived from **beachheading,** or a deliberate "end run" around *Miranda*. Purposely withholding *Miranda* warnings until after a confession is obtained and then giving *Miranda* to re-ask the question has been found by the Supreme Court to be improper.

Oregon v. Elstad (1985) established that if police obtain a voluntary admission from a suspect without first advising the suspect of the right to remain silent, a confession made after the *Miranda* warning is given will be admissible: "Absent deliberately coercive or improper tactics in obtaining the initial statement, the mere fact that a suspect has made an unwarned admission does not warrant a presumption of compulsion. A subsequent administration of *Miranda* warnings to a suspect who has given a voluntary but unwarned statement ordinarily should suffice to remove the conditions that precluded admission of the earlier statement."

beachheading the unconstitutional approach of purposely withholding the *Miranda* warnings until after a confession is obtained and then giving *Miranda* to re-ask the question

In contrast, when police deliberately "beachhead" or withhold *Miranda* in an attempt to elicit a confession first, as was the case in *Missouri v. Seibert* (2004), it will be seen as a violation of a suspect's rights. In this case, Patrice Seibert was arrested as a suspect in a fatal arson and taken into custody but was not read her rights under *Miranda*. At the police station, an officer questioned her for 30 to 40 minutes and obtained a verbal confession to the crime. The officer then gave Seibert a 20-minute break, returned to give her *Miranda* warnings and obtained a signed waiver. He resumed questioning, confronting Seibert with her pre-warning statements and getting her to repeat the information. Seibert moved to suppress both her pre-warning and post-warning statements. The officer testified that he made a *conscious decision* to withhold *Miranda* warnings and question first, then give the warnings and then repeat the question until he got the answer previously given. The district court suppressed the pre-warning statement but admitted the post-warning one, and Seibert was convicted of second-degree murder. The Missouri Court of Appeals affirmed, finding the case indistinguishable from *Oregon v. Elstad*, in which the Supreme Court held that a suspect's unwarned inculpatory statement made during a brief exchange at his house did not make a later, fully warned inculpatory statement inadmissible.

In reversing, the state supreme court held that because the interrogation was nearly continuous, the second statement, which was clearly the product of the invalid first statement, should be suppressed, and distinguished *Elstad* on the ground that the warnings had not intentionally been withheld there. The U.S. Supreme Court affirmed, noting that the objective of a question-first approach is to render *Miranda* warnings ineffective by waiting to give them until after the suspect has already confessed and emphasizing that a critical difference between the two cases was that in *Elstad*, the failure to preliminarily provide the *Miranda* warning was a "good faith" mistake, not a conscious decision. Thus in *Seibert*, the Court, in a 5–4 vote, rejected the two-step questioning tactic as a deliberate way to sidestep *Miranda*:

> *Elstad* does not authorize admission of a confession repeated under the question-first strategy. The contrast between *Elstad* and this case reveals relevant facts bearing on whether midstream *Miranda* warnings could be effective to accomplish their object.... In *Elstad*, the station house questioning could sensibly be seen as a distinct experience from a short conversation at home, and thus the *Miranda* warnings could have made sense as presenting a genuine choice whether to follow up on the earlier admission. Here, however, the unwarned interrogation was conducted in the station house, and the questioning was systematic, exhaustive and managed with psychological skill. The warned phase proceeded after only a 15- to 20-minute pause, in the same place and with the same officer, who did not advise Seibert that her prior statement could not be used against her. These circumstances challenge the comprehensibility and efficacy of the *Miranda* warnings to the point that a reasonable person in the suspect's shoes could not have understood them to convey a message that she retained a choice about continuing to talk....
>
> That the interrogating officer relied on respondent's pre-warning statement to obtain the post-warning one used at trial shows the temptations for abuse inherent in the two-step technique. Reference to the pre-warning statement was an implicit, and false, suggestion that the mere repetition of the earlier statement was not independently incriminating. The *Miranda* rule would be frustrated were the police permitted to undermine its meaning and effect. (*Missouri v. Seibert*, 2004)

◀ CASE IN BRIEF

Missouri v. Seibert (2004)

ISSUE When police intentionally fail to give a *Miranda* warning to a suspect, is a subsequent statement that was Mirandized and repeats the initial statement admissible in court?

RULING No. Under the facts of this case, failing to warn was part of a police strategy to undermine the protections of *Miranda*.

Miranda Survives a Challenge—Dickerson v. United States

CASE IN BRIEF

Dickerson v. United States (2000)

ISSUE May Congress pass a law that effectively overturns the *Miranda* decision?

RULING No. Congress cannot pass a law that supersedes a Supreme Court decision that interprets and applies the U.S. Constitution.

If a feature movie were made about the Fifth Amendment right against self-incrimination, it would undoubtedly be based on *Dickerson v. United States* (2000). The case has everything: history, Congress versus the Supreme Court, police versus criminals, good versus evil, the quest for truth and justice, heated exchanges between Supreme Court Justices, *and* it provides a comprehensive review of how this area of criminal procedure developed and why. The entire legal community anxiously awaited the opinion of the Court as to whether *Miranda* would remain the law.

The drama unfolded the morning of June 27, 2000, when Chief Justice William H. Rehnquist himself delivered the opinion of the Court, which he had written, as had Chief Justice Warren with *Miranda.* Tension was thick, but *Miranda* was upheld by a 7–2 vote, with Rehnquist, an outspoken critic of *Miranda* for nearly 30 years, siding with the majority. In this case, Charles Dickerson was indicted for bank robbery using a firearm. He moved to suppress his statement made to the FBI based on their not advising him of his rights per *Miranda* before being interrogated. The government relied on a federal law, Section 3501 of the Omnibus Crime Control and Safe Streets Act of 1968, which stated that the admissibility of statements should turn only on whether they were voluntarily made, and not only on whether the *Miranda* warning had been given. The case had two major issues: (1) whether *Miranda* would remain in effect when a federal statute did not require it and (2) whether Congress could enact a law contrary to that which the Supreme Court had declared to be the constitutional requirement.

Proving again that the various laws are not isolated unto themselves but rely on one another, the Supreme Court returned to a case discussed previously—*Marbury v. Madison* (1803)—to address whether Congress could supercede the Supreme Court. In using a precedent set nearly 200 years ago, Chief Justice Rehnquist repeated what was determined by *Marbury*: "*Miranda*, being a constitutional decision of this Court, may not be in effect overruled by an Act of Congress. . . . The law is clear as to whether Congress has constitutional authority to do so. This Court has supervisory authority over the federal courts to prescribe binding rules of evidence and procedure."

The second issue, whether *Miranda* would remain good law, is discussed in great detail that reviews the history of Fifth Amendment self-incrimination law. The federal statute in issue returned to a totality of the circumstances to determine whether the statement was voluntary and not strictly requiring the *Miranda* warnings be given. This action, in effect, was a return to what cases before *Miranda* held. The Court found, "*Stare decisis* weighs heavily against overruling it now. Even in constitutional cases, *stare decisis* carries such persuasive force that the Court has always required a departure from precedent to be supported by some special justification. . . . There is no such justification here. *Miranda* has become embedded in routine police practice to the point where the warnings have become part of our national culture." The opinion went on to state, "Experience suggests that [this federal statute's] totality-of-the-circumstances test is more difficult than *Miranda* for officers to conform to, and for courts to apply consistently. The requirement that *Miranda* warnings be given does not dispense with the voluntariness inquiry, but cases in which a defendant can make a colorable argument that a self-incriminating statement was compelled despite officers' adherence to *Miranda* are rare." In sharp dissent, Justices Clarence Thomas and Antonin Scalia accused their colleagues of dismissing previous rulings in which *Miranda*'s constitutional underpinnings were questioned. "Since there is in fact no other principle that can reconcile today's judgment with the post-*Miranda* cases that the court refuses to abandon," wrote Scalia, "what today's decision will stand for, whether the Justices can bring themselves to say it or not, is the power of the Supreme Court to write a prophylactic, extra-constitutional Constitution, binding on Congress and the states." Another law that could be deemed to have become "part of our national culture" in the sense *Miranda* has is difficult to imagine. Finding a better example of how U.S. law does what it was intended to so well is also difficult, yet not without controversy.

Miranda, The Right against Self-Incrimination, and Impeached Testimony

Although the Constitution contains provisions to protect the accused from forced self-incrimination, our justice system also entitles a criminal defendant to testify on his or her own behalf. One noteworthy Fifth Amendment case—*Harris v. New York* (1971)—examined when, if ever, a suspect's statements obtained in violation of *Miranda* could be used at trial. In this case, Viven Harris was arrested after he made two separate heroin sales to an undercover police officer. Before being given the *Miranda* warning, Harris stated that he had made both sales at the request of the officer, a statement that was *not* admitted into evidence at the trial. However, Harris later took the stand in his own defense and testified under oath that he did not make the first sale and that the second sale was not of heroin but merely baking powder in an attempt to defraud the buyer. Harris's initial statement was then used by the prosecution in an effort to impeach Harris's credibility. The question before the court was: Did the prosecution's use of Harris's postarrest statement violate his Fifth Amendment rights guaranteed by the *Miranda* decision?

◀ **CASE IN BRIEF**

Harris v. New York (1971)

ISSUE May a statement in violation of *Miranda* be used to impeach the defendant's testimony?

RULING Yes. As long as the statement is voluntary, the statement may be used to impeach the credibility of the defendant. The statement may not, however, be considered *evidence*.

The Supreme Court answered, "No," noting that although *Miranda* barred the prosecution from making its case with statements the accused made while in custody before having or effectively waiving counsel, it did not follow from *Miranda* that evidence inadmissible against an accused in the prosecution's case in chief is barred for all purposes, provided of course that the trustworthiness of the evidence satisfies legal standards. Chief Justice Warren Burger said, "Every criminal defendant is privileged to testify in his own defense, or to refuse to do so. But that privilege cannot be construed to include the right to commit perjury. . . . The shield provided by *Miranda* cannot be perverted into a license to use perjury by way of a defense, free from the risk of confrontation with prior inconsistent utterances. We hold, therefore, that petitioner's credibility was appropriately impeached by use of his previous conflicting statements."

Miranda Issues Continue

Miranda issues are certainly not over. In *Chavez v. Martinez* (2003), the Supreme Court ruled that violating the *Miranda* decision does not subject law enforcement to civil liability if any statements so obtained are not used against the plaintiff in court. The core Fifth Amendment privilege against self-incrimination does not come into play until trial.

When *Miranda* Warnings Generally Are Not Required

Because the Fifth Amendment guarantees apply only to testimonial evidence, not physical evidence, *Miranda* warnings are *not* required before collecting nontestimonial evidence such as fingerprints, blood, urine, and handwriting samples, nor must they precede the performance of field sobriety tests and the reciting of the alphabet. The "routine booking question" exception allows obtaining biographical information needed to complete an arrest report, and the emergency room exception allows custodial questioning without warnings and waivers where information is needed to neutralize an immediate threat to officer or public safety (Petrocelli, 2010).

Although the *Miranda* decision appears to provide a bright-line rule, case law has continued to guide when the warnings must be given and when they need not. Several instances in which *Miranda* warnings are not normally required include (del Carmen, 2010, p. 372):

- When the officer asks no questions
- During general on-the-scene questioning
- When the statement is volunteered
- When asking a suspect routine identification questions
- When questioning witnesses who are not suspects
- In stop-and-frisk cases
- When asking routine questions of drunken-driving suspects and videotaping the proceedings
- During line-ups, showups, or photographic identifications
- When the statement is made to a private person
- When the suspect appears before a grand jury
- When there is a threat to public safety
- When an undercover officer poses as an inmate and asks questions

Brief questioning in stores, restaurants, parks, hospitals, and other public places is generally considered noncustodial unless the subject is not free to leave. Here again, as explained previously in the chapter, *custody* has different definitions when viewed in different contexts (i.e., under the Fourth Amendment versus Fifth Amendment-*Miranda*). A person can be seized (i.e., detained) under the Fourth Amendment but not be in custody for *Miranda*. Under *Miranda*, the test is whether a person is not free to leave to the point that one would associate the situation with formal arrest. Thus the question is, "If the person tried to leave, would the police stop that person?"

Likewise, brief questioning, such as in stop-and-frisk cases and general questioning at a crime scene, is not a custodial situation. Law enforcement officers are allowed to briefly detain witnesses at a crime scene for questioning without *Miranda* warnings. Citizen witnesses directed by an officer not to leave a crime scene are unlikely to consider themselves in custody, and a court unlikely would so consider them (*Arnold v. United States*, 1967).

Another exception to interrogation in the absence of a *Miranda* warning is questioning done by a private security officer. Remember, the Constitution exists to regulate the *government's* authority. The regulations set forth by the Constitution apply to government agents, not to private individuals. In *State v. Spencer* (1987), the Minnesota Supreme Court relied on the *Miranda* Court that the Fifth Amendment applies only to government agents, and not private security personnel, no matter how much they may look like public police.

This stipulation means private security personnel are not bound by constitutional restraints and thus are not required to advise suspects of their Miranda rights. This does not mean, however, that they will not be held accountable for wrongful acts, including crimes or civil wrongs. Case law continues to recognize the clear differentiation between public police and private security.

The Public Safety Exception

An important exception to the *Miranda* requirement involves public safety. The precedent case occurred in 1984 in *New York v. Quarles*, when the Supreme Court ruled on the public safety exception to the *Miranda* warning requirement.

In this case, a young woman stopped two police officers and told them she had been raped. She described the rapist and said he had just entered a nearby supermarket, armed with a gun. The officers located the suspect, Benjamin Quarles, and ordered him to stop. Quarles ran, and the officers momentarily lost sight of him. When Quarles was apprehended and frisked, he was wearing an empty shoulder holster. One officer asked Quarles where the gun was, and Quarles nodded toward some cartons, saying, "The gun is over there." The officer retrieved the gun, arrested Quarles, and read him his rights. Quarles waived his rights to an attorney and answered questions.

At the trial, the court ruled, pursuant to *Miranda*, that the statement "the gun is over there" and the discovery of the gun as a result were inadmissible. The U.S. Supreme Court, in reviewing the case, ruled that if *Miranda* warnings had deterred the response to the officer's question, the result would have been more than the loss of evidence. As long as the gun was concealed in the store, it was a danger to the public safety: "The need for answers to questions in a situation posing a threat to the public safety outweighs the need for the prophylactic rule protecting the Fifth Amendment's privilege against self-incrimination."

The Court ruled that in this case, the need to have the suspect talk took precedence over the requirement to read the defendant his rights. As the Court noted, the material factor in applying this **public safety exception** is whether a public threat could be removed by the suspect's statement. In this case, the officer asked the question only to ensure his, and public, safety. He then gave the *Miranda* warning before continuing questioning.

Table 10.1 contains a brief history of key cases related to the law of confessions.

Consequences of a *Miranda* Violation

Except in certain circumstances, such as when impeachment or public safety is involved, a statement made under a *Miranda* violation cannot be used in court. However, unlike Fourth Amendment violations, in which fruit-of-the-poisonous-tree applies, violations in the area of *Miranda* do not restrict the use of evidence gleaned from a statement made in the absence of *Miranda*. For example,

◀ CASE IN BRIEF

New York v. Quarles (1984)

ISSUE Are statements made in response to questioning by police and while in custody admissible in court if no *Miranda* warning was given?

RULING Yes. If the situation involves an overriding concern for public safety and the questions are reasonably prompted because of a public safety concern, *Miranda* need not be given before asking questions.

public safety exception allows officers to question suspects without first giving the *Miranda* warning if the information sought sufficiently affects the officers' and the public's safety

Table 10.1 A Brief History of Cases Pertaining to the Law of Confessions

Brown v. Mississippi (1936): Confessions obtained by the government through physical coercion violate the Due Process Clause of the Fourteenth Amendment and are inadmissible.
Rogers v. Richmond (1961): Coercion, either physical or psychological, violates the Due Process Clause, rendering any resulting confessions inadmissible. "Ours is an accusatorial and not an inquisitorial system."
Escobedo v. Illinois (1964): "When the process shifts from investigatory to accusatory—when its focus is on the accused and its purpose is to elicit a confession . . . the accused must be permitted to consult with his lawyer." In determining whether a confession would be admissible, the *Escobedo* Court moved from a due process analysis to a Sixth Amendment right to have a lawyer present and that the suspect must be advised of this.
Miranda v. Arizona (1966): Unless the government has provided the warnings advising the suspect of his or her Fifth Amendment rights, and that individual has provided a valid waiver, statements will not be admissible.
Harris v. New York (1971): The privilege to testify in one's own defense cannot be construed to include the right to commit perjury. The shield provided by *Miranda* cannot be perverted into a license to use perjury by way of a defense.
Michigan v. Mosley (1975): A suspect who has invoked only his or her right to silence can be re-approached to seek a waiver on the same or a different case as long as the right to remain silent is scrupulously honored.
North Carolina v. Butler (1979): An explicit statement of waiver is not invariably necessary to support a finding that the defendant waived the right to counsel guaranteed by the *Miranda* case. The waiver can be inferred from the actions and words of the person interrogated.
Rhode Island v. Innis (1980): An *interrogation* refers not only to express questioning but also to any words or actions by the police (other than those normally attendant to arrest and custody) that the police should know are reasonably likely to elicit an incriminating response from the suspect.
Edwards v. Arizona (1981): After a person has been given his or her *Miranda* warnings and then invokes his or her right to remain silent and to have legal counsel, that person cannot be questioned further until a lawyer is made available. (Modified by *Shatzer* [2010]; see later.)
Berkemer v. McCarty (1984): Roadside questioning of a motorist during a routine traffic stop is not a custodial interrogation, so no *Miranda* warning is required; however, any custodial interrogations, including those resulting from misdemeanor traffic offenses, do require *Miranda*.
New York v. Quarles (1984): This case created the "public safety exception" to the *Miranda* rule. When public safety necessitates immediate action by police, failure to provide the warnings will not render a statement inadmissible.
Oregon v. Elstad (1985): If police obtain a voluntary admission from a suspect without first advising the suspect of the right to remain silent, a confession made after the *Miranda* warning is given will be admissible.
Arizona v. Roberson (1988): After a defendant invokes the right to counsel, police may not interrogate him or her, even about a different crime.
Minnick v. Mississippi (1990): After a defendant requests a lawyer, the lawyer must be present at all subsequent interrogations, even if the individual had consulted with counsel.
Dickerson v. United States (2000): *Miranda* stands rather than a return to the totality of the circumstances test.
Missouri v. Seibert (2004): The two-step questioning tactic of purposely withholding *Miranda* warnings until after a confession is obtained and then giving *Miranda* to re-ask the question is unconstitutional.
United States v. Patane (2004): A *Miranda* violation does not require the suppression of the "physical fruits" of the statement, only the non-use of the actual statement. Any evidence derived from the non-useable statement can be used in court.
Maryland v. Shatzer (2010): This case set a new "14-day break-in-custody" rule, granting police the authority to initiate contact with a suspect who had previously asserted the right to counsel, without violating *Edwards*, if at least 14 days had passed since the original invocation of that right.
Florida v. Powell (2010): No exact wording is required to satisfy *Miranda*.
Berghuis v. Thompkins (2010): A suspect who has received and understood his or her *Miranda* rights waives the right to remain silent by making an un-coerced statement to police.

in *United States v. Patane* (2004), the Court ruled that a *Miranda* violation does not require the suppression of the "physical fruits" of the statement, only the non-use of the actual statement. Any evidence derived from the non-useable statement can be used in court. In other words, the fruit-of-the-poisonous-tree doctrine does not apply to *Miranda* violations.

Fifth Amendment *Miranda* Implications of Using Informants

Many crimes are solved not because officers stumble on crimes in progress but because they get information from a number of sources that help them learn who may have been involved. An informant is any person who gives government agencies information about criminal activity. Informants remain an important source of information.

The use of informants is interesting for several reasons. An issue is whether incriminating statements made to a third party, who happens to be or becomes a police informant, can be used against that person. In the case of *Illinois v. Perkins* (1990), the police put an undercover officer in jail with the suspect in hopes of eliciting incriminating information from the suspect. The Supreme Court held that undercover police agents do not have to administer *Miranda* warnings to incarcerated suspects before soliciting incriminating information from them. *Miranda* does not apply in this situation because there was no custodial interrogation (not a police-dominated atmosphere) that would necessitate reading the warnings. The Court further recognized a limitation to *Miranda*, noting that compulsion is "determined from the perspective of the suspect."

◀ **CASE IN BRIEF**

Illinois v. Perkins (1990)

ISSUE Does an undercover officer need to give *Miranda* to a suspect to whom he is asking questions?

RULING No. If the suspect is unaware that he is talking to an officer, neither the "police-dominated atmosphere" nor the compulsion to speak exists.

Entrapment

Due process remains the underpinning of every component of a legal case. Unconscionable or otherwise illegal behavior by the police brings about constitutional issues. Entrapment falls into this category and may be used as a defense to a criminal charge.

Entrapment is discussed here because, although it can be included in any chapter concerning people's rights, the concept of government going too far is what the study of entrapment is about. As with the issues raised in *Miranda*, government going "too far" is not good for either the government or those it serves.

Entrapment, like the *Miranda* rule, is a subject the public believes it is well versed on because of a heavy diet of television police shows. These dramas often depict officers setting up radar in obviously inconspicuous locations and then being assertively informed by the citizens tagged that the police method is a clear case of entrapment. If only it were so easy.

Entrapment is "an action by the police (or a government agent) persuading a person to commit a crime that the person would not otherwise have committed." Another definition is provided in *Sorrells v. United States* (1932): "Entrapment is the conception and planning of an offense by an officer and his procurement of its commission by one who would not have perpetrated it except for the trickery, persuasion or fraud of the officer." At the same time, however, the Supreme Court noted, "Society is at war with the criminal classes, and the courts have uniformly held that in waging this warfare the forces of prevention and detection may use traps, decoys and deception to obtain evidence of the commission of crime. Nonetheless, when police officers encourage others to engage in criminal activity, this should not be viewed lightly. Such encouragement might, in fact, cause normally law-abiding citizens to commit crime."

Even when the defendant admits to committing the crime, he or she may argue that the law enforcement agents themselves brought the crime about. As noted by Justice Frankfurter in *Sherman v. United States* (1958), "The power of government is abused and directed to an end for which it was not constituted when employed to promote rather than detect crime and bring about the downfall of those who, left to themselves, might well have obeyed the law. Human nature is weak enough and sufficiently beset by temptations without government adding to them and generating crime."

If a private person not connected with law enforcement induces someone to commit a crime, no defense of entrapment can be used. The more involved a third

MYTH
If an officer forgets to read you *Miranda*, you cannot be charged and are free.

FACT
This is false. If *Miranda* applies and is not read to you, you can still be arrested and charged and the only thing affected by the non-*Miranda* statement is that it cannot be used as evidence against you. It can, however, be used to impeach (discredit) your testimony, and the "fruits" of the statement are generally admissible as evidence. Any other evidence derived from the non-*Miranda* statement can also be used against you.

entrapment the act of government officials or agents (usually police) inducing a person to commit a crime that the person would not have otherwise committed

MYTH
If you ask, an officer needs to tell you that he or she is a police officer, otherwise it is entrapment.

FACT
This is false. An officer does not need to disclose whether he or she is an officer.

party is with the police, as an informant or otherwise, however, the greater the argument that the individual is an *agent* of the police, which brings in constitutional consideration.

Whether entrapment exists may be determined by *subject* analysis—asking: "Was the suspect predisposed to commit the crime, or was he an unwary innocent party?" (*Hampton v. United States*, 1976). This is the viewpoint taken by the Supreme Court. Entrapment may also be determined by *objective* analysis—asking: "Was an innocent person induced by the police to commit a crime they never would have otherwise?" (*Sherman v. United States*, 1958). This type of analysis has been adopted by some states.

Lopez v. United States (1963) involved an IRS agent investigating tax irregularities at German Lopez's restaurant when Lopez made an unsolicited offer to pay a cash bribe for the agent's approval of phony records. The agent pretended to play along, reported the attempted bribe to his superiors, and wore a wire to his next meeting with Lopez, obtaining evidence regarding the bribe. Lopez claimed entrapment, but the Supreme Court disagreed saying that the agent had merely afforded an opportunity for a continuing course of criminal conduct by a willing criminal, without overbearing inducements (Rutledge, 2008).

CASE IN BRIEF

Jacobson v. United States (1992)

ISSUE Is it entrapment for the government to contact the defendant multiple times during 26 months, disguised as fictitious organizations selling child pornography, to get the defendant to purchase some?

RULING Yes. The acts of the government were such that they designed and implanted the criminal act in the defendant's mind to the point he was not independently predisposed to commit the crime.

The leading case in entrapment is *Jacobson v. United States* (1992), in which the defendant ordered child pornography, which was not illegal at that time. However, a law was subsequently passed making it illegal, and when a postal inspector found Keith Jacobson's name on a mailing list, he was sent a letter from a fictitious group concocted by law enforcement. In his application for membership, Jacobson stated he was opposed to pedophilia but enjoyed sexual material showing preteen sexual photos. For more than two years, a group of government agencies contacted him through different fictitious organizations, and one postal inspector pretended to be a "pen pal" and began communicating with Jacobson. Eventually, Jacobson placed an order through one of these groups, which was not filled. Still later he ordered a magazine from yet another fake catalogue they sent him, and when it was delivered he was arrested.

The Supreme Court held that Jacobson was entrapped because, they argued, the government did so much as to "implant" in his mind the desire to commit the crime: "Where the Government has induced an individual to break the law and the defense of entrapment is an issue, the prosecution must prove beyond a reasonable doubt that the defendant was predisposed to commit the criminal act prior to first being approached by Government agents."

As stated by the Court in *Sorrells*, "Government agents may not originate a criminal design, implant in an innocent person's mind the disposition to commit a criminal act, then induce commission of the crime so that the Government may prosecute." No entrapment was found when government agents supplied one of the necessary ingredients for manufacturing a prohibited drug (*United States v. Russell*, 1973) or when they supplied heroin to a suspect predisposed to selling heroin (*Hampton v. United States*, 1976).

Other Rights Guaranteed by the Fifth Amendment

The Fifth Amendment is unique in that it covers such an array of legal areas that apply to both criminal and civil law. This broad range reflects the framers of the Constitution's awareness of the power government has over all aspects of people's lives and how that power needs to be regulated. The Fifth Amendment contains a number of seemingly unrelated elements. Some pertain more to criminal law and others to civil law. Some apply only to the federal government, whereas others apply to the states as well. Although this text addresses law as it pertains to criminal justice, to fully appreciate this amendment, it needs to be considered in total. The right of a person to not be a witness against himself or herself is the component this amendment is best known for, but other important rights are also delineated.

> **LO7** In addition to the right to not incriminate oneself, the Fifth Amendment also guarantees:
> - The right to a grand jury indictment.
> - The prohibition against double jeopardy.
> - The right to receive just compensation when government takes private property.

The Right to a Grand Jury

The Fifth Amendment states, "No person shall be held to answer for a capital or otherwise infamous crime, unless on a presentment or indictment of a Grand Jury, except in cases arising in the land or naval forces, or in the Militia, when in actual service in time of War or public danger." A **grand jury** is a group of citizens who determine whether sufficient evidence exists to send an accused to trial. Today, the primary job of a grand jury is to determine whether sufficient evidence exists to hand down an **indictment** (send an individual accused of a crime on to trial to be prosecuted).

Like many other aspects of U.S. law, the concept of a grand jury has a rich history, deriving its name from the French meaning "large." Over centuries of evolution, dating back to medieval England, grand juries served two purposes: (1) to investigate a variety of crimes, including official misconduct, as an arm of the king's rule, and (2) to ensure that innocent citizens were not wrongfully prosecuted. Both purposes were understandably important to those drafting the Constitution because of their attitude toward the country they had left.

A trial jury (sometimes referred to as a petit jury) differs from a grand jury in a number of ways. A trial jury most often comprises 12 jurors, whereas grand juries have 16 to 23 jurors. A trial jury needs a unanimous vote to convict, whereas a grand jury needs only 12 votes to indict. A jury composed of the defendant's "peers" is not required for a grand jury, and a grand jury may investigate misconduct, whereas a trial jury can address only what is brought before it. The jurors in a trial court hear only one case, whereas those on a grand jury hear numerous cases during their assignment. The outcome of a grand jury is to indict or not, whereas a trial jury convicts or acquits. Another major difference is a grand jury is not open to the public, and the prosecutor appears to maintain control during the proceedings. In fact, the accused has no right to counsel or to present evidence. Rather than determining guilt or innocence, a grand jury determines only whether the government has enough evidence, whether it will be admissible or not at trial, to justify the matter proceeding to trial. One reason for the secrecy is that if the grand jury returns a "no bill of indictment," the case will not proceed and no one will know the person was involved, at least in theory. In grand jury proceedings, although the rights of a suspect are minimal, the government, in effect, is actually on trial, or at least must convince the jury it has a case. Table 10.2 summarizes the differences between a grand jury and a trial jury.

grand jury a group of citizens who determine whether sufficient evidence exists to send an accused to trial

indictment a formal accusation of a defendant, usually by a grand jury, that sends the defendant on to trial for prosecution

Table 10.2 Grand Juries and Trial (Petit) Juries Compared

Grand jury	Trial jury (also known as petit jury)
1. Usually composed of 16 to 23 members, with 12 votes required for an indictment	1. Usually consists of 12 members, with a unanimous vote required for conviction
2. Choice usually determined by state law, with "jury of peers" not a consideration	2. Usually chosen from voter registration list and driver's license rolls, with "jury of peers" a consideration
3. Does not determine guilt or innocence; function is to return indictment or conduct investigations of reported criminality	3. Decides guilt or innocence and, in some states, determines punishment
4. Retains the same membership for one month, six months or one year; may return several indictments during that period	4. A different jury for every case
5. Hands down indictments based on probable cause	5. Convicts on the basis of evidence of guilt beyond a reasonable doubt
6. May initiate investigations of misconduct	6. Cannot initiate investigations of misconduct

Source: DEL CARMEN. *Criminal Procedure*, 8E. © 2010 Wadsworth, a part of Cengage Learning, Inc.

The right to a grand jury is the only unincorporated clause of the Fifth Amendment (*Hurtado v. California*, 1884). Even though the Supreme Court has not held the Grand Jury Clause of the Fifth Amendment to be sufficiently essential to the U.S. system of justice to incorporate it under the Fourteenth Amendment Due Process Clause, most states have chosen to use the grand jury process themselves. Depending on the state, prosecutors may be required, or may elect, to have a grand jury evaluate their case. In the states that do not require a grand jury, the prosecutor must convince a judge that sufficient evidence exists to justify a trial. In the other states, a grand jury must indict the defendant for a trial to proceed.

Grand juries have immense power. Nevertheless, debate on the grand jury system's viability continues for several reasons. Only the prosecutor is present during the proceedings, no defendants are permitted to have their lawyers present, everything occurring during the process is kept secret, and evidence that may be inadmissible at trial is permitted. Despite these factors, grand juries are beneficial to the judicial process. The historical roots of the grand jury are noble and are still serving to deflect arbitrary government prosecution. A grand jury provides a step by which, at least in spirit, the innocent are protected. This process also attempts to avoid political or popular pressure on the prosecution in particularly notorious or otherwise sensitive cases.

Critics assert, however, that the system is too one-sided in favor of the prosecution, and the entire process is contrary to the openness the rest of the criminal justice system demands. Either way, grand juries provide the citizenry with an opportunity for involvement, even in cases that proceed no further, thus removing complete authority over criminal cases from the government, including the prosecution. Notably, England abandoned the grand jury process in 1933.

Double Jeopardy

double jeopardy a prohibition against the government from trying someone twice for the same offense

The prohibition against **double jeopardy** prevents the government from trying someone twice in the same jurisdiction for the same offense. The Double Jeopardy Clause has been incorporated into the Fourteenth Amendment's Due Process Clause and, thus, applies to the states. Its purpose was explained by Supreme

Court Justice Hugo Black in *Green v. United States* (1957): "The underlying idea, one that is deeply ingrained in at least the AngloAmerican system of jurisprudence, is that the State with all its resources and power should not be allowed to make repeated attempts to convict an individual for an alleged offense, thereby subjecting him to embarrassment, expense and ordeal and compelling him to live in a continuing state of anxiety and insecurity, as well as enhancing the possibility that even though innocent he may be found guilty."

The Double Jeopardy Clause will apply only when the defendant has been in *jeopardy*. Although many definitions of what this means are abound, the Court has made it quite clear what jeopardy means in the constitutional sense with a bright line rule: a defendant has not been placed in jeopardy until the jury has been sworn and empaneled. This rule was recently an issue in *Martinez v. Illinois* (2014). The Court unambiguously explained: "There are few if any rules of criminal procedure clearer than the rule that" when a jury is empaneled and sworn, double jeopardy has attached.

Double jeopardy prohibits the following: a second prosecution for the same offense after acquittal, a second prosecution for the same offense after conviction, and more than one punishment for the same offense (*North Carolina v. Pearce*, 1969). Determining what is a "same offense" has been a point of debate for the Supreme Court. Over the years, the Court has gone back and forth on this issue, overruling itself more than once. The current test for the "same offense" is the *Blockburger* test, which came out of a 1932 case, *Blockburger v. United States*. The Blockburger test compares the elements of each statute to determine whether a defendant has been prosecuted or convicted twice for the same offense. It is another bright line the Court has drawn and is easy to follow. If the words used in the statutes in question are identical, it is the same offense. If the words are different, they are not the same offense and double jeopardy will not apply. However, there is one important point about determining the same offense: If one of the statutes is a "lesser included offense," the two are considered the same offense.

In addition to determining if the offense is the same, it must also be determined if a defendant's jeopardy has ended in such a manner that a retrial is prohibited. An acquittal is such a manner because it is a finding by the jury or the court that the prosecution's evidence cannot support a conviction of the defendant on the charge faced.

Interestingly, when a judge makes a mistake and directs a verdict midtrial for a defendant, that decision is considered an acquittal for double jeopardy purposes. In *Evans v. Michigan* (2013), after the prosecution rested its case in an arson trial, the judge believed that there was an element of the statute that the prosecution did not prove and, thus, directed a verdict in favor of defendant Evans. However, it was later ascertained that the disproven element of the statute was not required at all. The judge had, in fact, erred. Nonetheless, because the Court had handed down an acquittal based on a determination of the defendant's factual guilt or innocence, it was a valid conclusion to the proceedings and barred a retrial of Evans.

In *Sattazahn v. Pennsylvania* (2003), the Supreme Court held that there is no double jeopardy when one is sentenced to death at a retrial after receiving a life sentence at the original trial when the jury deadlocked during the sentencing phase. *United States v. Lara* (2004) held that Billy Jo Lara, an American Indian who pleaded

> **MYTH**
> A person can never be tried twice for the same offense because of "double jeopardy."
>
> **FACT**
> Not true. The Double Jeopardy Clause only prohibits the government from trying a defendant for the same offense, in the same jurisdiction, more than once under particular facts. Examples where double jeopardy does *not* exist are if the jury acquits the defendant and a mistrial is declared because of prosecutor misconduct, or if the charge is dismissed after the jury is seated.

guilty to assaulting a police officer in the Spirit Tribe Tribal Court, could be tried again in federal court because the courts represented two different jurisdictions. *Seling v. Young* (2001) held that an act considered civil that results in confinement, in this case the civil confinement of a sex offender, does not create double jeopardy to prevent a subsequent criminal trial.

A system of fairness cannot permit inexhaustible resources to be used to continue retrying a defendant. However, this amendment has important nuances. What *is not* considered double jeopardy? A defendant may be tried again when a jury is unable to reach a verdict resulting in a mistrial or when a mistrial is declared for other reasons. In 2012, the Court decided *Blueford v. Arkansas*, in which it ruled that the report of a foreperson is not a final decision regarding acquittal and, therefore, the defendant can be retried in the situation in which a mistrial is declared as a result of a hung jury.

A case may be appealed to a higher court by either side, including the prosecution. If an appeals court grants a defendant a new trial, it is not considered double jeopardy. If an offense is both a state *and* a federal offense, the offenses are considered separate and may be tried independently of each other.

Just Compensation

The Fifth Amendment states "nor shall private property be taken for public use, without just compensation." This is known as the Takings Clause and it means, very simply, that the government cannot take a person's property for public use unless it pays fair market value for it, which is the definition of **just compensation**. More often than not, real property (i.e., real estate) is at the heart of the taking. Personal property, such as a car or boat, may be appropriated by the government, too. The Takings Clause protects this type of property as well (see *Horne v. Department of Agriculture*, 2015).

just compensation the requirement that property owners be paid fair market value by the government when government takes their property

Sometimes the government needs to take private property for the public good, such as to build roadways, bridges, or other public improvements. The government can purchase the property outright if the owner is cooperative, but if the owner is unwilling to sell, the government can acquire the property through **eminent domain**. Under this power, the government will bring a condemnation action against the property and pay the owner fair compensation. It is, in essence, a forced sale of the property to the government.

eminent domain the power of the government to take private property for public use, with the owner being paid just compensation for the taking

Just compensation is determined by looking at the fair market value of the property. This is not a highly litigated area in the constitutional sense, but it can be a contentious issue when the two sides have vastly different values attached to the property. The valuation of a property could be decided by a judge or a jury as part of a lawsuit.

There are times when the government's action amounts to a taking but occurs through a process different than eminent domain. Often, these takings are the result of government regulations. In these situations, the government does not admit to actually taking as it does in a condemnation process, and the property owner is required to bring suit, asking a court to find that property was, in fact, taken, and then order the government to pay fair compensation for that taking.

A taking can occur in one of two ways: (1) physical occupation or appropriation of the property, which can result from either a condemnation action or through regulation, or (2) regulating property to such a degree that the owner's use of it is severely restricted or eliminated. If the physical occupation is permanent, a court will find that a *per se* taking has occurred. This means that just the physical occupation alone, without any additional facts, is enough to find a taking has occurred. For example, in *Loretto v. Teleprompter Manhattan CATV Corp.* (1982), the Court found that a taking had occurred when a New York law mandated that building owners allow cable companies to place equipment in their apartment buildings, despite the fact the physical space actually occupied only a very small area.

In addition to permanent physical occupation, a second *per se* taking can occur where a regulation denies *all* economic or beneficial use of the property. In *Lucas v. South Carolina Coastal Council* (1992), the Court determined that a state law aimed at protecting the island from erosion by prohibiting the owner from building, or rebuilding after a natural disaster, rendered these ocean front lots valueless. When all economically beneficial uses that previously existed become prohibited by a regulation, a taking has occurred.

The Court has recognized that government regulation is important and that not every regulation that restricts a property owner's use is a taking. But, as stated in *Pennsylvania Coal Co. v. Mahon* (1922), "if regulation goes too far it will be recognized as a taking."

The Court has struggled to find a "set formula" for determining when a regulation has caused an economic injury to such an extent that it is considered a taking and the government must pay the property owner for the loss. A leading case involving a regulation diminishing property value is *Penn Central Transportation Co. v. New York City* (1977). The Court recognized that, while the "test" for a taking is ad hoc and fact bound, important factors to look at are (1) the economic impact of the regulation on the owner, (2) the extent to which the regulation interferes with the distinct investment-backed expectations, and (3) the character of the government's action.

As long as the government pays fair compensation for the property, there is little the owner can do to prevent the taking of private property. One possible recourse is to argue that the property was not taken for a public use and have the government action stopped by a court order. This is, however, difficult to show for two reasons, both discussed in *Kelo v. New London* (2005). First, the public use requirement is not limited to its literal meaning. In fact, the Court has interpreted it broadly to mean "public purpose." Second, to meet the required public purpose threshold, the government needs to show only that the taking is rationally related to a public purpose. Importantly, the courts will give deference to legislatures in this area: "For more than a century, our public use jurisprudence has wisely eschewed rigid formulas and intrusive scrutiny in favor of affording legislatures broad latitude in determining what public needs justify the use of the takings power" (*Kelo v. New London*, 2005).

The government may not take property from one private person for the *sole* purpose of transferring it to another. However, it may transfer the property to another if the purpose for the taking is, in the end, for a "public purpose."

On an historical note, the Takings Clause was the first component of the Bill of Rights to be incorporated to apply to the states under the Fourteenth Amendment Due Process Clause (*Chicago, Burlington & Quincy Railroad Co. v. Chicago*, 1897).

CASE IN BRIEF

Kelo v. New London (2005)

ISSUE Is the Takings Clause violated when property is taken from private individuals and then sold to a third party?

RULING No. As long as the property is used for a public purpose, the clause is not violated. The property was taken for economic development, and not to simply benefit one group of people.

Constitutional Law in ACTION

The City of Madison has an airport and needs to extend the runways to allow bigger aircraft to land at the airport. The city leaders believe this will bring in tourism, increasing revenue for the city and spurring job and business growth.

Mr. Peterson owns the land where the runway extension is planned. Peterson owns a total of 1000 acres, about 100 of which are needed for the runway expansion. Peterson currently uses the land for farming but has an offer from a developer to buy all of Peterson's property for development into a golf course, homes, and businesses.

- *How can the city obtain Mr. Peterson's land?*
- *What does the city need to do in order to comply with the Takings Clause?*

Now consider that the city already owns the land needed to build the runway but that it borders Mr. Peterson's property in such a way that, once the runway expansion is complete, planes will be landing and taking off right over Peterson's farm. The new runway has made the value of his Peterson's land decline, and the developer has withdrawn his offer.

- *Was this a taking? How would that be determined?*

Instead of planes landing and taking off over Peterson's property, the city has passed an ordinance prohibiting any building or farming on land bordering the airport. This regulation affects 100 acres of Mr. Peterson's property.

- *Is this a taking?*

Fifth Amendment and Corrections

The Fifth Amendment does not arise often in prisoners' rights cases, but it may apply to inmates being questioned about offenses separate from those they are serving time for (recall *Illinois v. Perkins*, 1990, and *Howes v. Fields*, 2012) or to those inmates involved in internal disciplinary proceedings.

Another issue challenged under the Fifth Amendment is compensation for prison labor. Inmates have claimed they are being deprived of property (just wages) without due process. However, the courts have consistently rejected just compensation arguments on grounds of the Fifth, Thirteenth, and Fourteenth Amendments.

A third area involving the Fifth Amendment focuses on disciplinary actions. In *Baxter v. Palmigiano* (1976), the Supreme Court ruled, "Prison disciplinary hearings are not criminal proceedings; but if inmates are compelled in those proceedings to furnish testimonial evidence that might incriminate them in later criminal proceedings, they must be offered 'whatever immunity is required to supplement the privilege' and may not be required 'to waive such immunity.'"

A fourth Fifth Amendment issue involves the Double Jeopardy Clause. Inmates who commit disciplinary infractions may appear before a disciplinary board and be punished and then find themselves facing criminal prosecution for the same offense. The courts have consistently ruled that this circumstance does *not* constitute double jeopardy.

Before leaving the discussion of the Fifth Amendment, consider another controversial area broadening the government's powers to obtain information: the USA PATRIOT Act.

USA PATRIOT Act

An immediate result of the September 11, 2001 (9/11), terrorist attacks on the United States was the unity that occurred among Americans, including politicians, which resulted in swift approval of the Uniting and Strengthening America by Providing Appropriate Tools Required to Intercept and Obstruct Terrorism Act, also known at the **USA PATRIOT Act.** On October 26, 2001, 45 days after the horrific attacks, President George W. Bush signed the act into law. Because it was hastily routed through the process, arguably out of necessity, Congress determined that much of it would expire at the end of 2005, so it could be re-evaluated.

USA PATRIOT Act
legislation that significantly improves the nation's counterterrorism efforts

This comprehensive law spans much of the specific topics this text addresses. And although the USA PATRIOT Act could have easily been discussed in the chapter on the First Amendment for its connection to freedom of speech issues, or fit in the section dealing with the Fourth Amendment because of the numerous privacy and warrant concerns it presents, we have opted to place it in this chapter based on the pervasive and overarching implications this act has had on due process of law, a constitutional guarantee delineated within the Fifth Amendment. Although coming at a time when the country was stunned by the terrorist attacks and joined together in responding, this law has generated controversy because some say it has eliminated the checks and balances that allowed courts to ensure these powers were not abused.

The act gives federal officials greater authority to track and intercept communications for law enforcement and foreign intelligence gathering. It gives the Secretary of the Treasury regulatory powers to combat corruption of U.S. financial institutions for foreign money laundering. It further closes our borders to foreign terrorists and allows us to detain and remove terrorists already in our country. It creates new crimes, new penalties, and new procedural efficiencies for use against domestic and international terrorists. The USA PATRIOT Act significantly improves the nation's counterterrorism efforts by:

- Allowing investigators to use the tools already available to investigate organized crime and drug trafficking.
- Facilitating information sharing and cooperation among government agencies, so they can better "connect the dots."
- Updating the law to reflect new technologies and new threats.
- Increasing the penalties for those who commit or support terrorist crimes.

Elements of the USA PATRIOT Act

The U.S. Department of Justice summarizes on its website the elements of this law as follows.

Allowing Use of Already Available Tools "Many of the tools the Act provides to law enforcement to fight terrorism have been used for decades to fight organized crime and drug dealers, and have been reviewed and approved by the courts." As Sen. Joe Biden (D-DE) explained during the floor debate about the act, "The FBI could get a wiretap to investigate the Mafia, but they could not get one to investigate terrorists. To put it bluntly, that was crazy! What's good for the mob should be good for terrorists" (Congressional Record, 10/25/01) (U.S. Department of Justice, n.d.). Specifically, the act:

- Allows law enforcement to use surveillance against the full range of terrorism-related crimes, including chemical-weapons offenses, the use of weapons of mass destruction, killing Americans abroad, and terrorism financing.
- Allows federal agents to follow sophisticated terrorists trained to evade detection by using "roving wiretaps" that apply to a particular suspect rather than to a particular phone or communications device.
- Allows law enforcement to conduct investigations without tipping off terrorists by use of delayed notification search warrants. Notice is always provided, but a reasonable delay gives law enforcement time to identify the criminal's associates, eliminate immediate threats to communities and coordinate the arrests of multiple individuals without tipping them off beforehand.
- Allows federal agents to ask a court for an order to obtain business records in national security terrorism cases. The government can now ask the Foreign Intelligence Surveillance Court to order production of the same type of records available through grand jury subpoenas if the government demonstrates the records concerned are sought for an authorized investigation to obtain foreign intelligence information not concerning a U.S. citizen or to protect against international terrorism or clandestine intelligence activities (U.S. Department of Justice).

Facilitating Information Sharing and Cooperation among Government Agencies "The Act removed the major legal barriers that prevented the law enforcement, intelligence and national defense communities from talking and coordinating their work to protect the American people and our nation's security. . . . Now police officers, FBI agents, federal prosecutors and intelligence officials can protect our communities by 'connecting the dots' to uncover terrorist plots before they are completed." As Sen. John Edwards (D-NC) said about the PATRIOT Act, "We simply cannot prevail in the battle against terrorism if the right hand of our government has no idea what the left hand is doing" (Press release, 10/26/01, U.S. Department of Justice).

Prosecutors can now share evidence obtained through grand juries with intelligence officials—and intelligence information can now be shared more easily with federal prosecutors. Such sharing of information leads to concrete results. For example, a federal grand jury recently indicted an individual in Florida, Sami al-Arian, for allegedly being the U.S. leader of the Palestinian Islamic Jihad, one of the world's most violent terrorist outfits. Palestinian Islamic Jihad is responsible for murdering more than 100 innocent people.

Updating the Law to Reflect New Technologies and New Threats The United States no longer has to fight a digital-age battle with antique weapons—legal authorities left over from the era of rotary telephones. "When investigating the murder of *Wall Street Journal* reporter Daniel Pearl, for example, law enforcement used one of the act's new authorities to use high-tech means to identify and locate some of the killers" (U.S. Department of Justice).

The act "allows law enforcement officials to obtain a search warrant *anywhere* a terrorist-related activity occurred. . . . [T]errorism investigations often span a number of districts, and officers therefore had to obtain multiple warrants in multiple jurisdictions, creating unnecessary delays. The Act provides that warrants can be obtained in any district in which terrorism-related activities occurred, regardless of where they will be executed" (U.S. Department of Justice).

Increasing Penalties for Those Who Commit or Support Terrorist Crimes "The Act created a new offense that prohibits knowingly harboring persons who have committed or are about to commit a variety of terrorist offenses, such as destruction of aircraft; use of nuclear, chemical or biological weapons; use of weapons of mass destruction; bombing of government property; sabotage of nuclear facilities; and aircraft piracy" (U.S. Department of Justice).

The act enhances the inadequate maximum penalties for various crimes likely to be committed by terrorists including arson, destruction of energy facilities, material support to terrorists and terrorist organizations, and destruction of national-defense materials. It also enhances "a number of conspiracy penalties, including for arson, killings in federal facilities, attacking communications systems, material support to terrorists, sabotage of nuclear facilities and interference with flight crew members" (U.S. Department of Justice). In addition, the act punishes terrorist attacks on mass transit systems and punishes bioterrorists. Finally, it eliminates the statute of limitations for certain terrorism crimes and lengthens them for other such crimes.

The Renewal of the USA PATRIOT Act

Renewal of this legislation has not occurred easily, with debate focusing on national security needs and whether increased government powers are still needed after an immediate threat seems to have passed. Questions have also been raised as to whether the PATRIOT Act needed to be renewed in its entirety.

After an extension from its expiration at the end of 2005, President Bush signed into law the USA PATRIOT Improvement and Reauthorization Act on March 9, 2006, stating, "The law allows our intelligence and law enforcement officials to continue to share information. It allows them to continue to use tools against terrorists that they used against drug dealers and other criminals. It will improve our nation's security while we safeguard the civil liberties of our people. The legislation strengthens the Justice Department so it can better detect and disrupt terrorist threats. And the bill gives law enforcement new tools to combat threats to our citizens from international terrorists to local drug dealers." (The reauthorized PATRIOT Act also includes new tools to combat the manufacture and distribution of methamphetamine.)

Other than two provisions concerning roving wiretaps and "lone-wolf" situations, the revised version of the PATRIOT Act is permanent; it will not expire and will change only if done so through legislation. On May 26, 2011, President Barack Obama extended the act for four more years and amended USA PATRIOT

Improvement and Reauthorization Act of 2005 with provisions concerning roving electronic surveillance orders and requests for the production of business records and other tangible things. The extension also amends the Intelligence Reform and Terrorism Prevention Act of 2004 with a provision revising the definition of an "agent of a foreign power" to include any non-U.S. person who engages in international terrorism or preparatory activities (the "lone-wolf" provision). The USA Patriot Act was renewed again June 2, 2015, which extended it to 2019. Surveillance powers of the National Security Agency (NSA) were curtailed by the bill.

The USA PATRIOT Act and a Changing Society As noted throughout this text, U.S. constitutional law represents the essence of a living law. Although the reasons underlying passage of the USA PATRIOT Act are most unfortunate, the act provides an ideal example of:

- How U.S. law never remains static.
- The legal system's ability to alter its course in response to change.
- An ability to enact change when many criticize how impossible change is to legislate.
- The ability of legislators to come together in a primarily nonpartisan manner when the country requires.
- How, rather than having legislation continue beyond the time it is needed, it must be renewed, necessitating debate and review.

Polls show that most Americans are willing to sacrifice some privacy if it makes them more secure from terrorism. Others contend the risk of an overly intrusive government is no longer as justified as it may have been immediately after 9/11. The debate continues.

Summary

The Fifth Amendment protects against self-incrimination and guarantees citizens due process of law by limiting the federal government's actions: "No person shall . . . be compelled in any criminal case to be a witness against himself" and "No person shall . . . be deprived of life, liberty or property, without due process of law." The Supreme Court has extended the elements of due process through case law beyond the words of the Constitution but in keeping with its spirit. Voluntariness of a confession is determined by (1) the police conduct involved and (2) conduct sufficient to overcome the will of the suspect given the characteristics of the accused.

Miranda remains the precedent case referred to by courts analyzing confession issues. The four warnings included in *Miranda* are (1) you have the constitutional right to remain silent, (2) anything you say can and will be used against you in court, (3) you have the right to talk to a lawyer now and have him/her present now or at any time during questioning, and (4) if you cannot afford a lawyer, one will be appointed for you without cost. The *Miranda* warning must be given to a suspect interrogated in police custody, that is, when the suspect is not free to leave. If after hearing a police officer read the *Miranda* warning, suspects remain silent, this silence alone is not a waiver. To waive their rights, (1) The suspect must show that they understand their rights, and (2) The suspect must show conduct indicative of a waiver, such as agreeing to voluntarily answer questions without a lawyer present.

Private security officers are not required to advise suspects of their *Miranda* rights. The public safety exception allows police officers to question suspects without first giving the *Miranda* warning if the information sought sufficiently affects the officers' and the public's safety. Except in certain circumstances, such as when impeachment or public safety is involved, a statement made under a *Miranda* violation cannot be used in court. However, the suppression of that statement does *not* apply to derivative evidence that flows from it, unlike the Fourth Amendment violations. In other words, the fruit-of-the-poisonous-tree doctrine does not apply to *Miranda* violations.

In addition to the right not to incriminate oneself, the Fifth Amendment also guarantees the right to a grand jury indictment, the prohibition against double jeopardy, and the right to receive just compensation when government takes private property. The right to a grand jury is the only unincorporated clause of the Fifth Amendment.

The USA PATRIOT Act strengthened the ability of the Justice Department and the FBI to monitor suspected terrorists or their associates and significantly improves the nation's counterterrorism efforts.

Discussion Questions

1. Why should government be limited on how and when it asks questions?
2. What two criteria must be met for the *Miranda* warning to be necessary?
3. Does the *Miranda* decision impede police work?
4. Would a different result occur, given exactly the same circumstances of an interrogation, for what a private security officer could do as opposed to what a city police officer must do?
5. Why shouldn't a stop require the *Miranda* warning?
6. Referencing Justice Oliver Wendell Holmes's proposition that it is better that some criminals escape rather than have the government involved in playing an ignoble part, what logic can you see in releasing a suspect who has confessed to a crime under circumstances that prohibit use of that admission, when the police know that person committed the crime? Where is the fairness here?
7. What do you think motivates informants, and should their information be considered reliable?
8. Why would it be wise for an officer to read the *Miranda* rights from a card?
9. Why might trickery, innuendo, or even falsehoods asserted by police during questioning not be Fifth Amendment violations?
10. Considering the USA PATRIOT Act, do you think Americans could ever sacrifice too many rights in exchange for national security?

References

del Carmen, R. V. (2010). *Criminal Procedure: Law and Practice*, 8th ed. Belmont, CA: Wadsworth/Thomson Learning.

Ferdico, J. N.; Fradella, H. F.; & Totten, C. D. (2009). *Criminal Procedure for the Criminal Justice Professional*, 10th ed. Belmont, CA: Wadsworth/Cengage Learning.

Kruger, K. J. (2009, February). "When Public Duty and Individual Rights Collide in Use-of-Force Cases." *The Police Chief*, pp. 12–13.

Means, R., & McDonald, P. (2010a, April). "Custody and Interrogation Myths," *Law and Order*, pp. 16–18.

Means, R., & McDonald, P. (2010b, August). "*Miranda* Revisited." *Law and Order*, pp. 18–19.

Means, R., & McDonald, P. (2010c, March). "Myths: Attachment and Assertion of Interrogation Rights." *Law and Order*, pp. 16–18.

O'Connor, T. P., & Maher, T. M. (2009, October). "False Confessions." *The Police Chief*, pp. 68–76.

Petrocelli, J. (2010, May). "*Miranda* Warning Issues." *Police*, pp. 18–21.

Rutledge, D. (2008, October). "Entrapment." *Police*, pp. 80–83.

Rutledge, D. (2009a, January). "Non-Custodial Stationhouse Interrogations." *Police*, pp. 62–65.

Rutledge, D. (2009b, December). "Premature *Miranda* Warnings." *Police*, pp. 60–63.

Rutledge, D. (2010a). "*Miranda* Invocation and Waiver." *Police*, pp. 72–75.

Rutledge, D. (2010b, April). "*Miranda* Wording." *Police*, pp. 60–61.

Rutledge, D. (2010c, May). "Rewriting the *Edwards* Rule." *Police*, pp. 66–68.

U.S. Department of Justice. (n.d.). "The USA PATRIOT Act: Preserving Life and Liberty." Retrieved August 15, 2016 from https://www.justice.gov/archive/ll/highlights.htm

Cases Cited

Anderson v. State, 253 A.2d 387 (Md. App. 1969)
Arizona v. Fulminante, 499 U.S. 279 (1991)
Arizona v. Roberson, 486 U.S. 675 (1988)
Arnold v. United States, 382 F.2d 4 (9th Cir. 1967)
Baxter v. Palmigiano, 425 U.S. 308 (1976)
Beckwith v. United States, 425 U.S. 341 (1976)
Beecher v. Alabama, 389 U.S. 35 (1967)
Berghuis v. Thompkins, 560 U.S. 370 (2010)
Berkemer v. McCarty, 468 U.S. 420 (1984)
Blockburger v. United States, 284 U.S. 299 (1932)
Blueford v. Arkansas, 566 U.S. ___ (2012)
Brown v. Mississippi, 297 U.S. 278 (1936)
Burket v. Angelone, 208 F.3d 172, 198 (4th Cir. 2000)
California v. Beheler, 463 U.S. 1121 (1983)
California v. Prysock, 451 U.S. 1301 (1981)
Chavez v. Martinez, 538 U.S. 760 (2003)
Chicago, Burlington & Quincy Railroad Co. v. Chicago, 166 U.S. 226 (1897)
Colorado v. Connelly, 479 U.S. 157 (1986)
Colorado v. Spring, 479 U.S. 564 (1987)
Connecticut v. Barrett, 479 U.S. 523 (1987)
Corley v. United States, 556 U.S. 303 (2009)
Culombe v. Connecticut, 367 U.S. 568 (1961)
Davis v. United States, 512 U.S. 452 (1994)
Dickerson v. United States, 530 U.S. 428 (2000)
Dormire v. Wilkinson, 249 F.3d. 801, 805 (8th. Cir. 2001)
Duckworth v. Eagan, 492 U.S. 195 (1989)
Edwards v. Arizona, 451 U.S. 477 (1981)
Escobedo v. Illinois, 378 U.S. 478 (1964)
Estelle v. Smith, 451 U.S. 454 (1981)
Evans v. Michigan, 568 U.S. ___ (2013)
Fikes v. Alabama, 352 U.S. 191 (1957)
Florida v. Powell, 559 U.S. 50 (2010)
Frazier v. Cupp, 394 U.S. 731 (1969)
Gardner v. Broderick, 392 U.S. 273 (1968)
Garrity v. New Jersey, 385 U.S. 493 (1967)
Green v. United States, 355 U.S. 184 (1957)
Greenwold v. Wisconsin, 390 U.S. 519 (1968)
Hampton v. United States, 425 U.S. 484 (1976)
Harris v. New York, 401 U.S. 222 (1971)
Haynes v. Washington, 373 U.S. 503 (1963)
Hiibel v. Nevada, 542 U.S. 177 (2004)
Horne v. Department of Agriculture (2015)
Howes v. Fields, 132 S.Ct. 1181 (2012)
Hurtado v. California, 110 U.S. 516 (1884)
Illinois v. Perkins, 496 U.S. 292 (1990)
In re Gault, 387 U.S. 1 (1967)
Jacobson v. United States, 503 U.S. 540 (1992)
Kansas v. Cheever, 571 U.S. ___ (2013)
Kelo v. New London, 545 U.S. 469 (2005)
Lopez v. United States, 373 U.S. 427 (1963)
Loretto v. Teleprompter Manhattan CATV Corp., 458 U.S. 419 (1982)
Lucas v. South Carolina Coastal Council, 505 U.S. 1003 (1992)
Mallory v. United States, 354 U.S. 449 (1957)

Malloy v. Hogan, 378 U.S. 1 (1964)
Marbury v. Madison, 5 U.S. (1 Cranch) 137 (1803)
Martinez v. Illinois, 572 U.S. ___ (2014)
Maryland v. Shatzer, 559 U.S. 98 (2010)
Massiah v. United States, 377 U.S. 201 (1964)
McNabb v. United States, 318 U.S. 332 (1943)
Michigan v. Mosley, 423 U.S. 96 (1975)
Mincey v. Arizona, 437 U.S. 385 (1978)
Minnick v. Mississippi, 498 U.S. 146 (1990)
Miranda v. Arizona, 384 U.S. 436 (1966)
Missouri v. Seibert, 542 U.S. 600 (2004)
New York v. Quarles, 467 U.S. 649 (1984)
North Carolina v. Butler, 441 U.S. 369 (1979)
North Carolina v. Pearce, 395 U.S. 711 (1969)
Oregon v. Elstad, 470 U.S. 298 (1985)
Oregon v. Mathiason, 429 U.S. 492 (1977)
Patterson v. Illinois, 487 U.S. 285 (1988)
Penn Central Transportation Co. v. New York City,
   42 N.Y.2d 324 (1977)
Pennsylvania Coal Co. v. Mahon, 260 U.S. 393 (1922)
Pennsylvania v. Muniz, 496 U.S. 582 (1990)
People v. McNeil, 711 N.Y.S. 2d 518 (N.Y. App. Div. 2000)
People v. Shivers, 21 N.Y.2d 188 (N.Y. Court of
   Appeals 1967)
Rhode Island v. Innis, 446 U.S. 291 (1980)
Rochin v. California, 342 U.S. 165 (1952)
Rogers v. Richmond, 365 U.S. 534 (1961)

Salinas v. Texas, 570 U.S. ___ (2013)
Sattazahn v. Pennsylvania, 537 U.S. 101 (2003)
Seling v. Young, 531 U.S. 250 (2001)
Sherman v. United States, 356 U.S. 369 (1958)
Sorrells v. United States, 287 U.S. 435 (1932)
State v. Robinson, 427 N.W.2d 217 (Minn.1988)
State v. Schumacher, 37 P.3d 6, 13 (Idaho Ct. App. 2001)
State v. Spencer, 414 N.W.2d 528 (1987)
Tague v. Louisiana, 444 U.S. 469 (1980)
United States v. Ballard, 586 F.2d 1060 (5th Cir. 1978)
United States v. Banks, 540 U.S. 31 (2003)
United States v. Bell, 367 F.3d 452, 461 (5th Cir. 2004)
United States v. Guarno, 819 F.2d 28 (2d Cir. 1987)
United States v. Jonas, 786 F.2d 1019 (11th Cir. 1986)
United States v. Koch, 552 F.2d 1216 (7th Cir. 1977)
United States v. Lara, 541 U.S. 193 (2004)
United States v. McClinton, 982 F.2d 278, 283
   (8th Cir. 1992)
United States v. Muhlenbruch, 634 F. 3d 987 (Court of
   Appeals, 8th Circuit 2011)
United States v. Patane, 542 U.S. 630 (2004)
United States v. Russell, 411 U.S. 423 (1973)
United States v. Wright, 991 F.2d 1182 (4th Cir. 1993)
Watts v. Indiana, 338 U.S. 49 (1949)
Welch v. Butler, 835 F.2d 92 (5th Cir. 1988)
Yates v. United States, 384 F.2d 586 (5th Cir. 1967)

CHAPTER 11

The Sixth Amendment:
Right to Counsel and a Fair Trial

In all criminal prosecutions, the accused shall enjoy the right to a speedy and public trial, by an impartial jury of the State and district wherein the crime shall have been committed. . . and to be informed of the nature and cause of the accusation; to be confronted with the witnesses against him; to have compulsory process for obtaining witnesses in his favor, and to have the Assistance of Counsel for his defence.

—Sixth Amendment to the U.S. Constitution

A defendant meets with his attorney to discuss a defense strategy. The right to counsel is the only Sixth Amendment guarantee that extends beyond the trial.

Learning Objectives

LO1 List the four factors that are considered in determining whether a trial is sufficiently "speedy."

LO2 Identify the two requirements for juries established by the Sixth Amendment.

LO3 Name the guarantee of the Sixth Amendment that extends beyond the trial.

LO4 Explain when the Sixth Amendment right to counsel exists.

LO5 Understand whether there is a Sixth Amendment right to a lawyer during preindictment identification procedures and how the court will view pretrial identification procedures to determine whether they are unconstitutional.

LO6 Clarify through how many appeals the right to counsel may be invoked.

LO7 Summarize what is required if the right to counsel is waived.

LO8 Pinpoint whether juveniles have Sixth Amendment rights.

LO9 Know how the Sixth Amendment affects corrections.

Key Terms

adversarial judicial system	cross-racial identification	preliminary hearing
arraignment	deliberate elicitation	prima facie
array	detainer	pro se
blind lineup	hearsay	showup
Brady rule	indigent	subpoena
compulsory process	jury nullification	testimonial statement
court trial	lineup	venire
critical stage	offense specific	venue
	peremptory challenges	*voir dire*

Introduction

Although the Sixth Amendment is not the most familiar to the public, it deals with the important matter of fairness at trial and the right to a lawyer during the time leading up to and during prosecution. The Sixth Amendment works well with the Fifth Amendment in that it ensures the defendant has access to legal counsel at certain stages before being tried, as well as a fair trial. In its own right, the Sixth

Amendment stands for protecting the individual against the government's unlimited resources. Article III of the Constitution requires that "a trial of all crimes . . . shall be by jury." However, the results of a prolonged trial prepared for and carried out by government lawyers, preceded by the police investigating the crime, are obvious. Without limitations, government could easily defeat the defendant merely by having more personnel, time, and finances. Few criminal defendants have anything remotely close to what the government can muster in terms of legal resources, so the Sixth Amendment strives to balance the contest.

Only a brief review of history is needed to understand why ensuring the right to a *fair* trial was believed necessary. Take, for instance, the *Star Chamber* (2000), created in 1487 by King Henry VII and abolished in 1641, named for the room with stars painted on the ceiling in the royal palace of Westminster, where this court was originally held. The Crown completely controlled this court, which had wide civil and criminal jurisdiction over everyone, including those too powerful to be tried by lesser courts. Under a veil of secrecy, the almost unlimited authority this court enjoyed permitted the government to subject individuals to trials without juries and to impose unreasonable fines and prison sentences, as well as terribly cruel torture to compel self-incrimination or as punishment.

This chapter dissects and examines the numerous clauses of the Sixth Amendment, beginning with the right to a speedy, public trial, in the area where the crime was committed, and before an impartial, representative jury, followed by the rights of being informed of the accusation and confronting witnesses, sometimes through compulsory process. The discussion next turns to the all-important right to counsel, including the right to counsel at critical stages of criminal proceedings and the need for effective assistance of counsel. Next, waiving the right to legal counsel and the right to represent oneself at trial are described. The chapter concludes with brief discussions of juveniles and the Sixth Amendment, and how Sixth Amendment rights relate to corrections.

The Seven Discrete Clauses of the Sixth Amendment

Under the system the founders of the U.S. Constitution fled, there were few, if any, rights pertaining to trials for the accused, if trials were even available. This situation remains a reason many people from other countries continue to seek freedom under the law in the United States. The Sixth Amendment embodies the concept of *due process*. Basic fairness is what it is about, and the Sixth Amendment extends to criminal defendants seven discrete personal liberties.

Speedy and Public Trial

Although few recent cases address speedy or public trials, a speedy, public trial is necessary in a system that places fairness above all else, and an expeditious trial does, indeed, promote fairness. A delayed or prolonged trial is inherently unfair.

A Speedy Trial Beginning with the presumption that a person is innocent until proven guilty, each individual charged with a crime has the right to have this determination made as quickly as possible. The right to a speedy trial does not attach until the defendant is arrested or indicted and then remains in effect through conviction (*Betterman v. Montana*, 2016). This right expires after conviction, because at that point the presumption of innocence is terminated, which is the legal principle at the heart of this clause.

In addition, the more quickly a trial occurs, the more likely witnesses can be located and their memories will be accurate. Also, not knowing for certain a trial's outcome causes undue stress on those involved, and some defendants must remain in jail because they are financially unable to secure bail. The system, too, suffers because of the additional backup expenses incurred by the government, and cases do not necessarily improve with time.

Delay that harms the accused's defense may cause the charges to be dismissed. In *Barker v. Wingo* (1972), the Supreme Court held that this right is not established by delay alone and that the conduct of both the defendant and the prosecution must be weighed. It set forth four factors to be used in deciding whether defendants have not been afforded their right to a speedy trial.

> **LO1** Whether a trial is sufficiently "speedy" is determined by (1) the length of the delay, (2) the reason for the delay, (3) the defendant's assertion of this right, and (4) the harm caused (Barker v. Wingo).

In *Barker*, the defendant was charged with murder and tried five years later after numerous continuances by the prosecution. The Court admitted that ascertaining whether a trial failed to be "speedy enough" to meet the requirement of the Sixth Amendment is a "balancing act." Perhaps the most important issue is whether the defendant was unduly harmed because of the delay.

The sole remedy for the violation of the constitutional right to a speedy trial is dismissal of the case. In *Strunk v. United States* (1973), the Supreme Court explained that this right is different from the others guaranteed by the Sixth Amendment, in that violations of those rights can be cured by affording the defendant a new trial. However, as mentioned above, the uncertainties and stress that result from facing trial are great and influence the choice of remedy. Although viewed as extreme, dismissal is the only way to enforce the underlying rationale of this right.

A Public Trial   The Sixth Amendment also requires a public trial. The United States prides itself on having a justice system open to public scrutiny. In *Press-Enterprise Co. v. Superior Court* (1984) the Court held, "Open trials enhance both the basic fairness of the criminal trial and the appearance of fairness so essential to public confidence in the system."

The right to a public trial is a "double-edged sword," however, in that it involves the defendant's right to a public trial to avoid the obvious wrongdoings possible if conducted in private and pertains to the media's right to make trials public. This area of law requires a balance between the accused's Sixth Amendment rights and the public's First Amendment rights.

Efforts have been made to achieve this balance by the Court through cases that include *Gannett Co. v. DePasquale* (1979), in which the Court held that the Sixth Amendment does not permit the public (including the press) to attend every trial, but it held in *Richmond Newspapers, Inc. v. Virginia* (1980) that the public does have the right to attend trials unless there is a compelling government interest in doing otherwise, for example, in cases of national security. At play is balancing the interests of the government, the public, and the accused.

Although media coverage ensures that trials are public, at times certain trials become so newsworthy as to cause concern that the accused is harmed because of disruption in court or the case being "tried by the media" in the court of public opinion. Closing a trial to the public is often challenged as violating the public's First Amendment rights. However, as ruled in *Estes v. Texas* (1965), if a trial turns into a three-ring circus, losing the dignified atmosphere expected in court proceedings, the defendant can claim a deprivation of due process rights. This area of law continues to be forged, with the rights of the individual and the media, and the limitations placed on access to trials for the benefits of each, being considered in each case.

An Impartial Jury

LO2 *The Sixth Amendment requires an impartial and representative jury.*

The importance of a jury trial is evidenced by the fact that this is the only right that appears in both the Constitution and the Bill of Rights.

The right to a jury trial was incorporated (applied to the states through the Fourteenth Amendment) in *Duncan v. Louisiana* (1968), as discussed in Chapter 4. Recall Gary Duncan was a 19-year-old black man who slapped a white youth on the elbow and was charged with simple battery, a Louisiana misdemeanor that held a maximum punishment of two years in jail and a $300 fine. He was given a 60-day jail term and fined $150 and, although requested, he was not permitted a jury trial.

On review, Justice Byron White, writing for the Supreme Court, stated, "Because we believe that trial by jury in criminal cases is fundamental to the American scheme of justice, we hold that the Fourteenth Amendment guarantees a right of jury trial in all criminal cases which—were they to be tried in a federal court—would come within the Sixth Amendment's guarantee." Reflecting on history, Justice White continued, "The Declaration of Independence stated solemn objections to the King's making 'Judges dependent on his Will alone, for the tenure of their offices, and the amount and payment of their salaries,' to his 'depriving us in many cases, of the benefits of Trial by Jury. . . .'"

An interesting exception to the general rule is that once a right has been held to apply to the states and federal government it must be done so equally. Although a 12-person jury is required in federal court, state trials are not required to have 12 jurors. Also, although federal juries must reach a unanimous vote for a conviction, states require a unanimous vote only in death penalty cases. The U.S. Supreme Court has, however, declared that state courts must have a minimum of six jurors (*Ballew v. Georgia*, 1978). With six jurors, a unanimous verdict must be reached to find the defendant guilty.

The Court has also held that only more serious offenses warrant a jury trial (generally, those whose punishments could exceed jail time of six months). In *Duncan*, the Court stated that "petty crimes" do not require a jury trial, but the Court did not define what a petty crime was, other than to hold that the potential two-year sentence faced by Duncan was not petty. The Court said, "The penalty authorized for a particular crime is of major relevance in determining whether it is a serious one subject to the mandates of the Sixth Amendment." Nowadays, the maximum penalty attached to an offense is the determining factor to decide what is a petty crime. In the Supreme Court's view, it is the most relevant to determine the seriousness of a crime because it indicates the legislature's viewpoint on the severity of the particular crime (*Lewis v. United States*, 1996).

CASE IN BRIEF ▶

Duncan v. Louisiana (1968)

ISSUE Is the denial of a jury trial in a state criminal prosecution, where a sentence of up to two years of imprisonment is possible, a violation of the Sixth and Fourteenth Amendments of the U.S. Constitution?

RULING Yes, because the right to a jury trial is "fundamental to the American scheme of justice."

MYTH
A defendant always has a right to a trial by jury.

FACT
A jury trial is required only in a criminal trial where the judge will impose a sentence of six months or more.

The Supreme Court has since held that a jury trial is not guaranteed when jail time of less than six months is the maximum possibility. The ruling in *Baldwin v. New York* (1970) underscored the principle that some misdemeanors are serious offenses that require a jury to determine a defendant's guilt when facing incarceration. However, when several offenses are tried together and the culmination of sentences is more than six months, a jury is not guaranteed when the offenses are considered petty (*Lewis v. United States*, 1996). States may deviate from this and provide for a jury under their state law or constitution.

Jury Selection Federal and state courts have a system in place to enable them to randomly compile lists of potential jurors. The potential jury is called an **array**. *Taylor v. Louisiana* (1975) established that the jury panel (those considered eligible to serve on a jury) may not be determined to systematically exclude any class of persons because selection of a jury from a cross section of the community is an important component of the Sixth Amendment.

Once the jury panel, called a **venire,** is established, individual jurors must be selected, adhering to the "impartial" and "representative" parameters set forth in the Sixth Amendment. An impartial jury is one not predisposed to prejudice for or against the defendant. Both the prosecution and the defense seek out the most neutral jury during the process of *voir dire,* which is when potential jurors are questioned by both sides to determine their impartiality. A potential juror who is deemed to be biased one way or the other may be removed, or excused, for cause, and there is no limit under the Sixth Amendment to the number of potential jurors who may be removed by this method.

In addition to being impartial, the jury must also be representative, that is, a "fair cross section of the community." In *Glasser v. United States* (1942), the Court stated, "The proper functioning of the jury system and, indeed, our democracy itself, requires that the jury be a 'body truly representative of the community,' and not the organ of any special group or class."

Jury selection has evolved beyond merely seeking impartial, unbiased jurors. During the *voir dire* process, both sides also attempt to exclude jurors who may be detrimental to their case and to retain those who may be beneficial. Jury selection experts have created a science of what to ask and look for during this process, leading to justifiable inquiries about whether it truly is about only impartiality. Although each side has a certain number of **peremptory challenges** they may assert to remove a potential juror for any reason whatsoever, the use (or abuse) of such peremptory dismissals to create a jury unfairly composed of a group likely to find against the defendant has been held a denial of equal protection. For example, in *Strauder v. West Virginia* (1879) the Court held that a black defendant could not be tried before a jury from which all members of his race were purposely excluded. This finding was also established in *Swain v. Alabama* (1965).

Batson v. Kentucky (1986) held that prosecutors' peremptory challenges to exclude from a jury members of the defendant's race based only on racial grounds violates the equal protection rights of both the defendant and the excluded juror. In this case, *voir dire* eliminated all five black potential jurors from the jury hearing James Kirkland Batson's (a black man) case. The Court held that a state denies a black defendant equal protection when it puts him on trial before a jury from which

array list of potential jury members

venire the selected jury panel

voir dire the process of questioning potential jurors to determine their impartiality

peremptory challenges a specific number of allowances given to each side in a case that they may assert to remove a potential juror for any reason whatsoever

MYTH
An attorney can strike a person from a jury for any reason.

FACT
Although an attorney generally need not give a reason for striking someone from a jury under a peremptory challenge, that person cannot be removed based on race or gender.

◄ CASE IN BRIEF

Batson v. Kentucky (1986)

ISSUE Does it violate the Equal Protection Clause to strike jurors through a peremptory challenge because of their race?

RULING Yes. If the facts as determined by the trial court show a prima facie case of purposeful discrimination, and the prosecutor does not provide a neutral explanation, the Equal Protection Clause is violated.

IN THE NEWS

"Attorneys for Man Accused of Killing State Trooper Seek Eligibility of Convicted Felons to Serve on Jury"

By Mark Bowes (*Richmond Times-Dispatch*, May 19, 2016)

The defense team for the man accused of killing Virginia State Police trooper Junius A. Walker in Dinwiddie County three years ago wants felons whose rights were recently restored by the governor to be considered as eligible candidates for jury duty when Russell E. Brown III stands trial in July.

In what may be the first case of its kind in Virginia since Gov. Terry McAuliffe issued a blanket order restoring the rights of 206,000 felons to vote and sit on juries, Brown's capital murder attorneys have filed a motion in Dinwiddie Circuit Court seeking to unseal juror questionnaires sent last fall to a list of potential Dinwiddie jury candidates provided by the Virginia Supreme Court.

"Mr. Brown is entitled to this juror information in light of the recent order by Gov. Terence R. McAuliffe restoring certain civil rights to felons and in order to prepare any Sixth Amendment fair cross-section constitutional challenge to the Dinwiddie County juror selection process," the May 6 motion says.

The responses to the Dinwiddie questionnaires that the defense seeks were reviewed by Dinwiddie jury commissioners for eligibility, and anyone who had a felony conviction and did not previously have their rights restored was excluded from serving on a jury there in 2016, Circuit Court Clerk John B. Chappell Jr. said Thursday.

The juror questionnaires are not public record and are under seal. A court order is required to have them unsealed for review.

The defense attorneys said in their motion that to sufficiently investigate whether felons have been previously excluded from the eligible pool of potential jurors, their client must have access to the juror questionnaires and the responses to those documents.

The defense team said McAuliffe's April 22 order now allows felons to serve on Dinwiddie juries, but newly eligible jurors in that county "were undoubtedly excluded during the eligibility process conducted by jury commissioners during their review of juror questionnaires."

"Absent review of the requested juror information, Mr. Brown will be unable to sufficiently investigate, prepare, and assert a constitutional challenge to the Dinwiddie County juror selection process," the defense team said in its motion.

"Consequently, without disclosure of the requested juror information, Mr. Brown will be denied his independent federal and state constitutional rights to due process, effective assistance of counsel, a fair and impartial jury, and against cruel and unusual punishment."

Chappell said Dinwiddie Circuit Judge Paul W. Cella has agreed to hear the motion, but a court date has not been set.

Several attempts to reach Commonwealth's Attorney Ann Cabell Baskervill for comment were unsuccessful.

The Dinwiddie development has already begun to reverberate in state political circles.

(*Continued*)

(*Continued*)

"We are just beginning to see the scope of the negative unintended consequences created by the governor's executive order," said Matthew Moran, spokesman for House Speaker William J. Howell, R-Stafford.

"The speaker is gravely concerned about how the order could impact cases like this all around the commonwealth. The thought that someone who shot and killed a dedicated state trooper is using the executive order to avoid conviction has to be troubling to anyone who believes in justice."

McAuliffe spokesman Brian Coy said Virginia's jury selection process remains unchanged and felons whose rights were restored who could end up in a jury pool won't affect that.

"Virginia has a jury selection process for a reason, and that is to screen potential jurors for any biases or conflicts of interests that might imperil the impartiality of a case," Coy said.

"That process is unchanged and that serves Virginia well. And the governor's confident that judges, prosecutors and defense attorneys would continue to leverage that process just as they always have, to make sure the juries they're selecting are impartial. None of that has changed."

"There are extra hurdles to clear before an individual would end up actually being in a position that these folks are concerned about," Coy added.

"And that is, they would have to pass several steps in addition to simply being selected (for inclusion into a jury pool). They would have to get through a defense attorney, or the prosecutor and a judge. So I think that is a usual safeguard not only in this case but in every case."

But Del. Jackson H. Miller, R-Manassas, sees the Dinwiddie development as the start of things to come.

"It just goes to show that we have a governor that bases decisions solely for partisan political purposes and not what's right or what consequences could happen to Virginia," said Miller, who formerly served as a police officer in Arlington and Prince William counties.

"We're starting to see things like this, (and) now we can only pray the common sense of the court system prevails, and tosses this request right out," Miller added.

"But after what the governor did, maybe they won't be able to. This is obviously a slap in the face to law enforcement all the way across the commonwealth."

Republican leaders in the General Assembly have threatened to file suit challenging McAuliffe's legal and constitutional authority to issue a blanket order restoring felons' rights.

Charles J. Cooper, a former assistant attorney general under President Ronald Reagan who once was named "Republican lawyer of the year," has been hired to lead the challenge to the governor's order.

A.E. Dick Howard, a professor at the University of Virginia School of Law who is widely considered the top expert on the Virginia Constitution, has backed McAuliffe and says the executive branch has unqualified authority on the matter.

Brown, 31, is charged with six felony counts, including capital murder of a police officer, in the March 7, 2013, slaying of Walker, 63. The trooper was shot in his police cruiser on Interstate 85. Walker had rolled up to Brown's vehicle, which was stopped on the shoulder, to see if Brown needed any help.

Police said that after shooting Walker with a Russian-made .308-caliber semiautomatic rifle and exchanging fire with another trooper, Brown dropped his weapon and fled, disrobing as he ran. He was found hiding naked in the back of a car at a nearby towing company.

Brown's defense team includes Karin Kissiah, Seth Shelley and Shameka Hall of the Virginia Capital Defender's Office, along with Jacqueline Reiner, who is in private practice.

Cella reluctantly granted a defense motion earlier this year to postpone the trial, originally set to begin March 14, because of a delayed report that could potentially affect the outcome. If the new defense motion doesn't cause a further delay, the trial will begin July 11 and could last through Aug. 5.

Brown's attorneys in January filed notice of their intent to introduce evidence that Brown is not guilty by reason of insanity.

members of his race have been purposefully excluded. Because it has become such an oft-used tactic, the term *Batson challenge* has come to mean the act of claiming, based on this decision, that a trial should be invalidated on the basis of peremptory challenges having excluded a cognizable group from the jury, such as excluding on the basis of race or gender alone. Several requirements exist to prove that a strike of a juror is discriminatory:

prima facie production of sufficient evidence to show that the issue is proven in favor of the party making the assertion

(1) a defendant must make a **prima facie** showing, or produce sufficient evidence to show that the issue is proven in favor of the party making the assertion that a peremptory challenge has been exercised on the basis of race
(2) if that showing has been made, the prosecution must offer a race-neutral basis for striking the juror in question
(3) in light of the parties' submissions, the trial court must determine whether the defendant has shown purposeful discrimination

A similar situation existed in *Snyder v. Louisiana* (2008). In the capital murder trial of Allen Snyder, a black man, all five prospective black jurors were dismissed,

Constitutional Law in ACTION

Peter, who was born in Mexico, was arrested and charged for robbing a local jewelry store. During jury selection, only two jurors (Juror #1 and Juror #4) of the 20 members of the jury panel were of Mexican decent. In fact, both jurors have family in the same part of Mexico where Peter was born. It is a very poor part of the country, and residents struggle to make a living. The government used two of its peremptory strikes to remove both of these potential jury members. Peter was found guilty and sentenced to 10 years in prison. Peter raised a *Batson* challenge regarding the only two potential jurors of Mexican descent being stricken.

- *Can Peter make a prima facie showing that the jurors were stricken based on their race?*

Assume that a *prima facie* showing was made. The prosecutor offered the following reasons for striking the two:

- Juror #1 appeared disinterested, did not make eye contact with the attorneys or judge during *voir dire*, and had been arrested, although not convicted, for robbery. The prosecutor believed that Juror #1's disinterested appearance and criminal history would not allow him to be neutral in reaching a decision.
- Juror #4 was interested in the case, made eye contact throughout *voir dire*, and stated that she could remain unbiased even though she has family living in Mexico, a circumstance that would not affect her ability to come to a decision based on the facts. She did add, however, that she often times has difficulty making decisions. The prosecutor believed that Juror #4 would have a hard time making a decision and, given her family history and connection to Mexico, would be unfairly sympathetic to the defendant.

- *Are the reasons the prosecutor gave race-neutral?*

- *Has Peter shown purposeful discrimination based on the race of the jurors?*

resulting in an all-white jury. The Court concluded that the judge acted improperly allowing the peremptory strikes of the black jurors.

Excluding people as jurors based on their profession is also unconstitutional (*Rawlins v. Georgia*, 1906). This determination is the case throughout the legal process—treating people differently or unfairly can be considered a due process violation.

Although the Sixth Amendment guarantees the right to a jury trial for serious crimes, there is no requirement that a person *must* have a trial by jury. Competent individuals may voluntarily elect to waive any of their rights. For example, waiving the right to a speedy trial or foregoing a jury trial altogether is not uncommon for defendants.

For tactical reasons, a person might waive the right to a jury trial and select a **court trial,** having the case heard before only the bench (or judge), without a jury. For example, a defendant asserting only technical legal claims may have more faith in a judge's comprehension of the law. A defendant previously convicted on other charges may not want to risk that information coming before a jury, which he or she thinks might give it more weight than a judge would. Some crimes are sufficiently heinous that public opinion in general could make a jury trial less desirable.

court trial when a case is heard before only the bench (or judge) without a jury

Jury Nullification In addition to the better-known options of a jury to convict, acquit, or be unable to reach agreement, there is the de facto option called *jury nullification*. **Jury nullification** is the hotly debated ability of a jury that believes a defendant to be guilty but acquits that person because they do not feel the circumstances would make a conviction fair or they disagree with the law. Such an action taken by a jury *nullifies*, or invalidates, the law. Opponents of nullification assert that if a jury believes a person guilty, the law should be enforced, whereas proponents say that if a jury does not feel a law is just, jurors need to seek justice.

jury nullification ability of a jury to acquit a defendant even though jurors believe that person is guilty

Why would a jury in effect nullify a law by returning a "not guilty" verdict? Mostly because jurors do not agree with it or think it unjust. Historically, nullification has probably occurred in such cases as when juries did not want to convict people accused of harboring runaway slaves; juries not agreeing with prohibition or drug laws; and, unfortunately, even juries prompted by racism refusing to convict white defendants accused of murdering blacks. A jury may also feel the penalty is too harsh for the circumstances.

Although support for jury nullification can be traced to colonial times, it is not considered a valid option by the courts today. The jury does not have the power to disregard the law as instructed by the judge. In *United States v. Moylan* (1969) the Fourth Circuit Court stated, "To encourage individuals to make their own determinations as to which laws they will obey and which they will permit themselves as a matter of conscience to disobey is to invite chaos. No legal system could long survive if it gave every individual the option of disregarding with impunity any law which by his personal standard was judged morally untenable. Toleration of such conduct would not be democratic, as appellants claim, but inevitably anarchic." Nonetheless, jury nullification remains an issue because trials are emotional, and jurors' verdicts are often based on emotions, not facts. This hazard is one reason why a defendant might seek a bench trial.

Where the Trial Is Held

The trial is required to at least originate where the crime was committed, and the jury is required to be from "the state and district wherein the crime shall have been committed; which district shall have been previously ascertained by law."

venue the geographic area in which a specific case may come to trial, and the area from which the jury is selected

This district is referred to as the **venue** of the trial—its geographic location. Historically, this requirement was included to prevent colonists from being returned to England for trial. However, it has remained to permit the defendant from being removed far from home, or at least from where the offense was committed, which could put that much more burden on the accused.

A defendant may seek a change of venue for several reasons, most often because of publicity or emotion in the community that may affect the trial. Another reason a change of venue may be granted is because a different location is more convenient for the prosecution, defense, and witnesses than the place where the crime occurred, and the interests of justice require a transfer of the trial location (Ferdico, Fradella, & Totten, 2009).

Being Informed of the Accusation

Fairness dictates that those accused know the charges being made against them and in sufficient detail to respond adequately. The Supreme Court has never formally incorporated this segment of the Sixth Amendment to apply to the states; however, knowing what one is charged with is so fundamentally fair that it has always been considered to fall within the Due Process Clause of the Fourteenth Amendment.

The Right to Confront Witnesses

Experience shows that casting blame is always easier when one is not facing the accused. The Confrontation Clause of the Sixth Amendment requires that witnesses be present in court so the defendant can confront them. In *Crawford v. Washington* (2004), the Supreme Court limited the Confrontation Clause to testimonial statements. A **testimonial statement** is "a solemn declaration or affirmation made for the purpose of establishing or proving some fact." In *Davis v. Washington* (2006), the Court further narrowed what the clause applied to and stated that not all those questioned by police are witnesses, and not all questionings by police are subject to the Confrontation Clause. *Davis* further clarified that when police are gathering information for the primary purpose of handling an ongoing emergency and not for the purpose of using it at trial, that information is considered non-testimony and is not subject to the Confrontation Clause. *Davis* did not answer the question, however, of whether or not statements made to individuals other than law enforcement would be treated the same under the Confrontation Clause.

testimonial statement a solemn declaration or affirmation made for the purpose of establishing or proving some fact

CASE IN BRIEF ▶

Michigan v. Bryant (2011)

ISSUE Does it violate the Confrontation Clause to admit a statement from a dying person as evidence, when there is no chance for the defendant to confront the witness?

RULING No. When there is an ongoing emergency, and it is clear from the circumstances that the police questioning is meant to meet the emergency, the statement can be admitted.

Sometimes exigent circumstances are involved in which testimonial evidence is presented in court and the defendant has no opportunity to confront the witness. Such was the case in *Michigan v. Bryant* (2011), in which the victim-witness told police, before he died, who had shot him. The victim's statements were used at trial to convict Bryant. In this decision, the Court noted that an ongoing emergency is only one factor in determining the primary purpose for the questioning and that there may be other situations in which a statement is not obtained for creating evidence to later be used at trial.

Coy v. Iowa (1988) held that a state law allowing closed-circuit television testimony or testimony from behind a screen violated the Sixth Amendment. Although the Supreme Court has voiced strong preference for face-to-face confrontation, issues in this area arise primarily regarding children's testimony and when hearsay evidence may be introduced.

The Supreme Court has supported state laws that seek to protect juvenile victims by permitting child abuse victims, who may be seriously intimidated by an alleged abuser, to testify via one-way closed circuit television (*Maryland v. Craig*, 1990). Here, the system seeks to balance the accused's rights with the children's best interests.

The Court addressed the question it left unanswered in *Davis* of whether or not statements made to non-law enforcement personnel would be testimonial and implicate the Confrontation Clause. In the case of *Ohio v. Clark* (2015), Clark was convicted of abusing his girlfriend's three-year-old son. The child's preschool teacher had discovered the injuries and asked the boy what happened. The child indicated that Clark had caused them, and the teacher reported the abuse, which led to the subsequent arrest and conviction of Clark.

Ohio law does not allow for a three-year-old to testify. However, the statements made to the preschool teacher were allowed into evidence through her testimony and used to convict Clark. He appealed, claiming the introduction of the statements violated the Confrontation Clause because he could not cross-examine the child. The Court ruled that the child's statements were not testimonial in nature because they were not made for the purpose of creating information to be later used at a trial. The statements were made to address an ongoing emergency: the boy had visible injuries and could have been released back to the abuser if not identified. Therefore, the Confrontation Clause was not violated.

The Court did not make a categorical rule that statements made to non-law enforcement personnel are outside of the Sixth Amendment. It did, however, conclude that statements made to someone not principally involved with investigating criminal behavior are less likely to be testimonial in nature.

In *Melendez-Diaz v. Massachusetts* (2009), the Supreme Court looked at whether it was a violation of the Sixth Amendment right of confrontation for a prosecutor to submit a drug test report without the testimony of the scientist who performed the test. In this case Boston police seized several clear plastic bags containing a substance that resembled cocaine during their investigation. They submitted the substance to the laboratory for analysis. The analysts generated "certificates of analysis" and swore to their validity before a notary public as required by Massachusetts law. The Court ruled that the certificates were improperly admitted as evidence against the defendant's right to confront witnesses who testify against him. This case could affect trial strategy and significantly increase the cost of presenting forensic evidence.

Although the Court ruled that the common practice of submitting laboratory reports without testimony was unconstitutional, it also held that a "notice-and-demand" statute, which both put the defendant on notice that the prosecution would submit a chemical drug test report without the testimony of the scientist *and* gave the defendant sufficient time to raise an objection, was constitutional.

Just six months later the Court granted certiorari in *Briscoe v. Virginia* (2010), another case involving the right to confront witnesses. Under Virginia law prosecutors are allowed to present paper reports during their case as long as they produced the analysts responsible for the reports during the defendant's case, *if requested*, shifting the burden to the defendant and creating a waiver of a constitutional right through inaction. Virginia claims that the scheme is constitutional because the defendants are on notice of the charges against them and may still call the forensic analyst as a witness themselves. The Supreme Court vacated and remanded

◀ **CASE IN BRIEF**

Ohio v. Clark (2015)

ISSUE Do a child's out-of-court statements to a teacher in response to questioning about child abuse become testimonial and therefore subject to the Confrontation Clause?

RULING No. The circumstances were such that there was an ongoing emergency and the questioning was not made in an attempt to create information to later be used at a trial.

◀ **CASE IN BRIEF**

Melendez-Diaz v. Massachusetts (2009)

ISSUE Is a lab report considered testimonial evidence for purposes of the Confrontation Clause?

RULING Yes. The report was created specifically for the purpose of being used in court as evidence, and a live witness needs to be able to testify in court as to the veracity of the report.

the case to Virginia for further proceedings. However, in *Bullcoming v. New Mexico* (2011), the Supreme Court took a definitive stand and held that the analyst who made a DWI report must be the one to testify, not simply a representative from the lab or someone else who can testify about how the test was performed.

The Sixth Amendment also excludes hearsay evidence. **Hearsay** is an out-of-court statement used to prove the truth of the matter asserted. Hearsay overlaps with the Sixth Amendment's Confrontation Clause, as we have seen. If the Confrontation Clause does not bar a statement from being presented, the rules of hearsay might. Although many people assume hearsay must originate with a third party, hearsay can actually include statements made by the person testifying, before taking the stand. The problem with hearsay is that the person who supposedly made the statement is not present to be cross-examined. Far too easily, someone can say, "I heard. . . ." This situation is why the general rule is that hearsay evidence is not admissible; however, an entire body of law addresses the exceptions, including when the person who made the original statement is now dead. Similarly, even if the person who allegedly made the statement is present for cross-examination, the defendant may not be able to get that witness to answer if, for example, the witness claims memory loss or invokes a privilege that will not permit them to answer (such as with a doctor/patient, attorney/client, or spousal privilege to not testify against the other). Evidentiary law pertaining to hearsay and exceptions is complex and voluminous.

hearsay an out-of-court statement used to prove the truth of the matter asserted; can include statements made by the person actually testifying, before taking the stand

Compulsory Process

Compulsory process permits a defendant to require favorable witnesses to appear in court, usually by a court-ordered subpoena. A **subpoena** requires an individual to appear in court to testify or to bring documents or other physical evidence to the court. To obtain compulsory process, the defendant must show that the witness's testimony would be relevant, material, favorable to the defendant, and not cumulative (*United States v. Valenzuela-Bernal*, 1982). Subpoenas can be served by an officer of the court, including a sheriff or police officer, or by any other adult who is not a party to the action. Individuals have given many reasons for not wanting to appear in court, but their acceptance by the court is virtually nonexistent.

compulsory process permits a defendant to require witnesses to appear in court, usually under the issuance by the court of a subpoena

subpoena requires an individual to appear in court to testify or to bring documents or other physical evidence to the court

Right to Counsel

Recall, the Fifth Amendment deals with obtaining information, and the Fifth Amendment right to counsel, as derived from the constitutional protection against self-incrimination, applies only during custodial interrogation. The Sixth Amendment, however, is concerned with achieving fair criminal prosecutions, and the Sixth Amendment right to counsel is far broader, attaching at numerous stages to assist the accused in preparing his or her defense.

LO3 *The right to counsel is the only Sixth Amendment guarantee that extends beyond the trial.*

The right to legal counsel has been held applicable at federal and state levels and is an important right because individuals' rights are monitored through attorneys. Legal systems in other countries, including England in the past, did not have such a right, because, at best, a neutral judge would watch out for the defendant's rights. Can one remain neutral when a lawyer's job is to aggressively represent his client? Probably not, and the Sixth Amendment provides an accused with an attorney during trial and at every *critical stage* of the criminal process.

The Role of Counsel   Attorneys seem to be among the most loathed professionals in society—until a person needs one. The general public often misunderstands what attorneys do, should do, and should not do, as well as what they can and cannot do. Among anticipated questions for a defense attorney speaking to any group is, "How can you defend someone you know is guilty?" The answer is quite simple: Everyone has the right to legal representation, and every lawyer has an obligation to do everything legally permissible to see that the client's rights are upheld. Their job is *not* to befriend, support, or get the client off. It is to ensure that those accused are afforded their legal rights and that they understand the process in which they are involved.

This obligation does not mean lawyers can instruct their clients to lie on the witness stand or that attorneys can provide misleading or untruthful information to the opposing counsel. To understand the role of a criminal defense lawyer, keep in mind that the defendant is presumed innocent until proved guilty, and the burden of proving guilt beyond a reasonable doubt lies solely on the prosecutor. To prove a case to this level is difficult.

A basic premise of the **adversarial judicial system** in U.S. law is that justice is best served when both sides to the conflict give their all. If each side is expected to aggressively assert its position, each side must be able to assert its position from similar legal footing. Many societal ills are blamed on the lawyers representing their clients' interests. Because the client remains in charge of making the majority of decisions throughout any legal process, the attorney may not even be in total agreement with the direction the client wants the case to go.

Although representing some accused parties is distasteful to some attorneys, particularly those clients who are "obviously" guilty or are charged with particularly offensive crimes, the defense counsel's role is crucial. Many people do not know what their rights are and, under the pressure of being accused and tried for a crime, cannot be expected to make the best legal decisions for themselves. The lawyer's role is to know his or her client's rights and to ensure that any infractions are dealt with according to the law.

adversarial judicial system a legal system such as that used in the United States, which places one party against another to resolve a legal issue, stipulating that only in an actual conflict will a judicial body hear the case

Development of the Right to Counsel   England's early legal system did not include the assistance of legal counsel to felons because the government was thought likely to prevail. Undoubtedly this circumstance contributed to the colonists' support of the right to counsel, even before the Sixth Amendment guaranteed it. However, even then, the right to an attorney was for only those who could afford it; those who could not went without. This situation changed as the result of the holding in the infamous "Scottsboro Boys" case (*Powell v. Alabama*, 1932), which established the constitutional necessity of having a lawyer. *Powell v. Alabama* involved a group of black youths who fought with a group of whites and threw them off the train they were on. The black youths were also alleged to have raped two white girls. A sheriff's posse arrested the defendants in Scottsboro, Alabama, and the community hostility resulted in their having to be housed in a different city, guarded by a militia that escorted them to the courthouse and back each day for their own protection. Rather than any of these young, illiterate defendants having their own lawyers, the judge appointed "all members of the bar" to render assistance. All the defendants were indicted within a week. Each trial lasted one day and resulted in each defendant being given the death penalty.

> **CASE IN BRIEF**
>
> *Powell v. Alabama* (1932)
>
> **ISSUE** Is due process met when a state does not provide a specific attorney to assist a defendant in a capital case until the day of the trial?
>
> **RULING** No. A defendant in a capital case must be provided an attorney to assist with his defense before the day of the trial to meet the requirements of due process. (This case was decided under due process because the Sixth Amendment right to counsel had not yet been incorporated.)

The U.S. Supreme Court overturned the ruling, holding that the right to assistance by a lawyer is a basic, fundamental right under the Constitution: "In a capital case, where the defendant is unable to employ counsel, and is incapable of making his own defense because of ignorance, feeblemindedness, illiteracy, or the like, it is the duty of the court, whether requested or not, to assign counsel for him as a necessary requisite of due process of law; and that duty is not discharged by an assignment at such a time or under such circumstances as to preclude the giving of effective aid in the preparation and trial of the case."

The Court went on to explain that even intelligent, educated laypeople have little knowledge of "the science of law" and "without counsel, though he may not be guilty . . . [the defendant] faces the danger of conviction because he does not know how to establish his innocence." At the time this case was decided, the Sixth Amendment had not been incorporated; therefore, it was decided under the Due Process Clause of the Fourteenth Amendment. Today it would likely be a Sixth Amendment case.

A series of cases have continued to shape the right to counsel. In *Harris v. South Carolina* (1949), the Supreme Court began to recognize that if a defendant was denied access to an attorney, his or her confession may not have been voluntary. Remember that in determining whether a confession was, indeed, given voluntarily, the court considers the totality of the circumstances to make sure there was due process. *Spano v. New York* (1959) held that there was an absolute right for a defendant to be represented and that a confession was not voluntary if the police ignored a defendant's "reasonable request to contact the attorney he had already retained."

As cases continued to reinforce the right to counsel, *Gideon v. Wainwright* (1963) firmly held that not only was the right to counsel absolute, but also, in all serious cases, **indigent** (poor, unable to afford a lawyer) defendants accused of a felony were to be provided with legal counsel. *Gideon* is considered a monumental case because it truly placed a poor, uneducated defendant against the entire governmental system and its almost unlimited resources. Gideon actually submitted his request to the Supreme Court in his own handwritten appeal. To the surprise of many people, the Court granted certiorari and, an even greater surprise, found in his favor.

indigent poor, unable to afford a lawyer

> **CASE IN BRIEF**
>
> *Gideon v. Wainwright* (1963)
>
> **ISSUE** Must a state court appoint counsel for an indigent defendant in a felony-level case?
>
> **RULING** Yes. Under the Constitution's Sixth Amendment, counsel must be provided when a defendant is charged with a felony.

Justice Hugo Black, in writing the *Gideon* opinion, reflected on the *Powell* opinion, which stated, "The right of one charged with crime to counsel may not be deemed fundamental and essential to fair trials in some countries, but it is in ours. . . . The right to be heard would be, in many cases, of little avail if it did not comprehend the right to be heard by counsel."

The *Gideon* Court clarified the existing confusion over which offenses necessitated counsel be provided. In some states, only death penalty cases invoked the right to an attorney; in other states, only felonies and not misdemeanors invoked that right. In a previous case (*Betts v. Brady*, 1942), the Supreme Court had held that the requirement of providing poor defendants with legal counsel in felony trials did not extend to the states. This decision was overruled in *Gideon*, which held that any indigent defendant accused of a felony, in federal and state court, be provided a lawyer. See Figure 11.1 for a sample statement of indigency.

In 1972 in *Argersinger v. Hamlin*, the Court extended the right to an attorney to defendants accused of misdemeanor offenses. This ruling turned the process somewhat on end, requiring a backward-looking logic in that the judge would need a degree of prescience to know ahead of time, before the actual trial, if he or she would be sentencing the defendant to jail or prison.

FINANCIAL STATEMENT
ELIGIBILITY DETERMINATION FOR INDIGENT DEFENSE SERVICES

Case No. ....

Presumptive Eligibility:
☐ I currently receive the following type(s) of public assistance in _____
                                                                                             City/County

   ☐ AFDC $ _____   ☐ Food Stamps $ _____   ☐ Medicaid _____
   ☐ Supplemental Security Income $ _____   ☐ Other (specify type and amount) _____
   ☐ I currently do not receive public assistance.

Names and addresses of employer(s) for defendant and spouse:
Self _____

Spouse _____

NET INCOME: Self   Spouse
Pay period (weekly, every second week, twice monthly, monthly) .... _____ _____
Net take-home pay (salary/wages, minus deductions required by law) .... $ _____ _____
Other income sources (please specify)—see reverse
_____ $ _____ _____
                                                                                                                                           COURT USE ONLY
                                 TOTAL INCOME $ _____ + _____ = [_____] A

ASSETS:
Cash on hand .... $ _____ _____
Bank accounts at: .... $ _____ _____
Any other assets: (please specify)
                                      with a
_____ value of .... $ _____ _____
Real estate $ _____ $ _____ _____
               Net Value
                                      with net
_____ value of .... $ _____ _____
 Motor   Year and Make
 Vehicles   with net
_____ value of .... $ _____ _____
               Year and Make
Other Personal Property: (describe)
_____ $ _____ _____
                                                                           COURT USE ONLY
                               TOTAL ASSETS $ _____ + _____ = [_____] B

   ┌──────────────────────────────────────┐
   │ Number in household: _____ │
   │ Number of dependents (spouse/children) │
   │ whom you support: _____ │
   └──────────────────────────────────────┘

EXCEPTIONAL EXPENSES (Total Exceptional Expenses of Family)
Medical Expenses (list only unusual and continuing expenses) .... $ _____
Court-ordered support payments/alimony .... $ _____
Child-care payments (e.g., day care) .... $ _____
Other (describe): _____
_____ } $ _____
                                                                           COURT USE ONLY
                           TOTAL EXPENSES $ _____ = [_____] C
      COLUMN "A" plus COLUMN "B" minus COLUMN "C" equals available funds   = [_____]

THIS STATEMENT IS MADE UNDER OATH: ANY FALSE STATEMENT OF A MATERIAL FACT TO ANY QUESTION CONTAINED HEREIN SHALL CONSTITUTE PERJURY UNDER THE PROVISIONS OF §19.2-161 OF THE CODE OF VIRGINIA. THE MAXIMUM PENALTY FOR PERJURY IS CONFINEMENT IN THE PENITENTIARY FOR A PERIOD OF TEN YEARS.

I hereby state that the above information is correct to the best of my knowledge.
Name of defendant (type or print) _____

_____   _____
     Date   Signature
Sworn/affirmed and signed before me this day.

_____   _____   _____
     Date   Signature   Title

FORM DC-333 4/93 (1143-021 5/94)

Figure 11.1 Statement of Indigency

Source: BACIGAL. *Criminal Law and Procedure*, 2E. © 2002 Delmar Learning, a part of Cengage Learning, Inc. Reproduced by permission. www.cengage.com/permissions.

> **MYTH**
> As a criminal defendant, you will be provided an attorney by the state if you want one.
>
> **FACT**
> Not necessarily. You must face the potential of incarceration and meet certain financial requirements for the state to provide an attorney.

Many thought *Argersinger*, if implemented, would bankrupt the state. The Supreme Court countered this fear in *Scott v. Illinois* (1979), which made actual, not potential, punishment the trigger for the right to counsel. In *Halbert v. Michigan* (2005), the Court held that indigent defendants, even after pleading guilty, are entitled to have a lawyer appointed when seeking a direct appeal.

As law pertaining to the constitutional right to counsel was changing, questions were necessarily being raised. One key question was whether there were times *before* trial that could require counsel. The case of young Danny Escobedo answered that question, while setting the stage for others, all of which continued to forge Sixth Amendment law.

In *Escobedo v. Illinois* (1964), the police repeatedly refused to permit Escobedo access to the lawyer he had hired. The lawyer was told he could not see his client, and the police told Escobedo his lawyer did not want to see him. Escobedo was 22 years old, had no prior contact with police, and was kept handcuffed and standing throughout the interrogation, with testimony affirming that Escobedo was exhausted from lack of sleep. Eventually, he admitted to the murder of his brother-in-law. Justice Arthur Goldberg stated, "We hold [that when] the investigation is no longer a general inquiry into an unsolved crime but has begun to focus on a particular suspect, the suspect has been taken into police custody, the police [interrogate], the suspect has requested and been denied an opportunity to consult with his lawyer and the police have not effectively warned him of this absolute constitutional right to remain silent, the accused has been denied the assistance of counsel in violation of the Sixth Amendment to the Constitution as made obligatory upon the states by the Fourteenth Amendment."

These cases present an excellent example of how common law develops. *Powell* established criminal defendants' right to a lawyer at trial, *Gideon* established that indigent defendants must be provided an attorney at trial, and *Escobedo* established that the right to counsel attaches during a criminal investigation when that investigation begins to focus on an individual.

Current Developments Although the Sixth Amendment guarantees every criminal defendant the right to a competent lawyer, many states do not keep that promise. Because more than 80 percent of defendants are unable to pay for their own lawyers, problems with indigent defense reach to the core of the criminal justice system. Now, however, defense lawyers are able to receive assistance from a program called Access to Justice (ATJ) Initiative, aimed at helping low-income individuals receive legal help. When the ATJ was established by the U.S. Department of Justice in March 2010, then-Attorney General Eric Holder stated, "Although they may stand on different sides of an argument and on different sides of a courtroom, the prosecution and defense can and must share the same objective: not victory, but justice" (Shapiro, 2010).

Right to Counsel at Critical Stages of Criminal Proceedings

Through a series of cases, including those discussed, the Supreme Court has held that no one may be imprisoned for any level of crime without legal representation, unless the accused have knowingly and intelligently waived this right (*Faretta v. California*, 1975). Through the additional development of Sixth Amendment law, the

Court deemed the right to an attorney applies to trial proceedings and to every **critical stage** of a criminal proceeding, considered to occur "where substantial rights of a criminal . . . may be affected" (*Mempa v. Rhay*, 1967). In other words, any step during a criminal prosecution in which the accused's rights may be affected by the absence of legal representation is considered a *critical stage*. Another way to view a critical stage is any point in a criminal proceeding, including pre- and post-trial, when the defendant cannot be presumed to make a decision without the advice of a lawyer.

The Sixth Amendment is triggered not by prosecutorial action but by judicial proceeding (Rutledge, 2008). Consider the following Sixth Amendment rules:

- The Sixth Amendment right to counsel attaches with the grand jury indictment or arraignment (or other first judicial appearance) on a complaint or official charge.
- After attachment the defendant can assert the right by hiring a lawyer, requesting one, or accepting appointment by the court.
- If there is any opportunity between attachment and assertion, police can seek a waiver and obtain an admissible statement.
- Following attachment and assertion, no valid waiver can be obtained for police-initiated questioning on that particular case.
- Attachment and assertion as to one offense does not affect questioning on another (except for lesser-included offense) (Rutledge, 2008).

> **LO4** The Sixth Amendment right to legal counsel occurs at every critical stage of a criminal proceeding, including during the investigation, during custodial interrogation and post-indictment interrogation, during post-indictment identification, at arraignment, at hearings, during the trial, and at sentencing.

critical stage any step during a criminal prosecution in which the accused's rights may be affected by the absence of legal representation

Critical Stages during the Criminal Investigation

In criminal investigations that continue after a defendant is charged, the Supreme Court has identified several events as critical stages that require a lawyer, pursuant to Sixth Amendment protection. *Massiah v. United States* (1964), heard the same year as *Escobedo*, held that statements a defendant makes *after* being charged with a crime, being a critical stage and having retained an attorney, would not be admissible if the attorney is not present. In *Massiah*, after Massiah was indicted, federal agents paid his co-defendant to converse with him in the presence of a hidden radio transmitter. Justice Potter Stewart, writing for the Court, stated, "We hold that the petitioner was denied the basic protections of that guarantee when there was used against him at his trial evidence of his own incriminating words, which federal agents had deliberately elicited from him after he had been indicted and in the absence of his counsel."

The well-known *Miranda v. Arizona* case (1966), discussed in the preceding chapter, further clarifies when a person has the right to counsel. In this case, the Supreme Court stipulated four warnings to be given to suspects in custody. Two of these warnings deal with the right to counsel. The *Miranda* warning is meant to safeguard the Fifth Amendment right against self-incrimination and to declare that a person who is questioned while in police custody has a right to an attorney. The right to counsel is extended by the Sixth Amendment to apply to any critical stage during a criminal prosecution.

◀ **CASE IN BRIEF**

Massiah v. United States (1964)

ISSUE Does it violate the Sixth Amendment to use a statement by a defendant made to a government informant after being charged and retaining counsel?

RULING Yes. Once the defendant is charged and obtains an attorney, he cannot be interrogated by government agents without an attorney present.

Miranda invokes both the Fifth Amendment right against self-incrimination and grants the right to counsel as a way to protect an accused's Fifth Amendment rights. The exclusionary rule will prohibit confessions obtained in violation of these rights from being used in court. In comparing the right to counsel under *Miranda* versus *Massiah*, consider the following points:

- *Miranda* applies only if the suspect is in custody; *Massiah* applies either in or out of custody.
- *Miranda* custody arises at arrest or equivalent physical restraint; *Massiah* attaches at the initiation of adversarial proceedings, for example, indictment, arraignment, or preliminary hearing by indictment or first court appearance.
- *Miranda* does not prohibit undercover questioning; *Massiah* allows passive listening, but not active undercover questioning (Rutledge, 2006, p. 72).

Questioning after the arraignment may not occur either, unless an attorney representing the defendant is present. In *Brewer v. Williams* (1977), the Supreme Court affirmed what they held in *Massiah*, requiring legal counsel after indictment by requiring it after the arraignment. *Brewer* deserves more careful analysis because it illustrates how law enforcement officials can stray from the confines of the Constitution in a way that may not be physically abusive but psychologically manipulative in an effort to solve a particularly heinous crime. In this case, although the defendant was not interrogated through the usual question-and-answer method, there was a **deliberate elicitation** of incriminating statements, meaning the method used purposefully, yet covertly, produced similar or identical effects. What occurred was almost the same as interrogation because the desired result was the same, as discussed in Chapter 7 and the Christian Burial Speech. Some may treat the concept of *deliberate elicitation* as synonymous with *functional equivalent*; they are not, however, the same. *Deliberate elicitation* is the standard used by the Court when referring to *Massiah* violations; *functional equivalent* is used for *Miranda* violations.

Brewer v. Williams also shows how multiple legal issues may evolve from one case, including Fifth and Sixth Amendment issues, the use of the exclusionary rule, and the creation of the inevitable discovery doctrine, all of which paint a fascinating legal picture of how the Supreme Court finds itself addressing complex issues, in particularly troubling factual circumstances.

In holding that the Christian Burial Speech was a de facto interrogation carried out in a way that might have been even more successful than a traditional questioning might have been, the Court found it to deliberately elicit incriminating statements to the same degree as a custodial interrogation, rendering any evidentiary statements to be inadmissible. Thus, the defendant's statements that led to the discovery of the victim's body could not be used in the subsequent trial. Although Fifth Amendment *Miranda* issues existed in *Brewer v. Williams*, the Court did not address those and decided the case based, instead, on the Sixth Amendment and *Massiah* violations.

Chief Justice Warren Burger authored a blistering dissent, arguing against the use of the exclusionary rule here, stating, "The result in this case ought to be intolerable in any society which purports to call itself an organized society. It continues the Court—by the narrowest margin—on the much-criticized course of punishing the public for the mistakes and misdeeds of law enforcement officers, instead of

deliberate elicitation the *Massiah* standard that violates the Sixth Amendment by purposefully, yet covertly, drawing out incriminating statements from a suspect whose Sixth Amendment right to counsel has attached but who has not waived the right

punishing the officer directly, if in fact he is guilty of wrongdoing. It mechanically and blindly keeps reliable evidence from juries whether the claimed constitutional violation involves gross police misconduct or honest human error."

Justice was to prevail, however, as described in Chapter 7. When Williams was retried on appeal, with this case captioned as *Nix v. Williams* (1984), the inevitable discovery doctrine was adopted by the Court to allow the evidence of the victim's body to be admitted. Why? Because at the same time the detective was using an illegally obtained statement to locate the body, volunteer searchers were actually approaching the body and, regardless of the admission by Williams, would have inevitably discovered her body.

Herein lies the importance of thoughtful and well-executed work by criminal justice professionals. Can one blame the detective for his motive, when in fact, he testified at the trial, "I was hoping to find out where that little girl was"? A child was abducted on Christmas Eve by an escaped mental patient. Probably the last thing on his mind was what the case was evolving toward, eventually being dissected by the U.S. Supreme Court. This case illustrates the importance of thorough investigations, a working understanding of the Constitution, and effective report-writing skills.

United States v. Henry (1980) established that a defendant's Sixth Amendment right to counsel is violated if police intentionally create a situation likely to result in incriminating statements after indictment. In this case, Henry had been indicted for armed bank robbery. An FBI investigator contacted an informant who was housed in the same cell block with Henry and told the informant to be alert to any incriminating statements made by Henry about the bank robbery. The informant later told the agent that he and Henry had engaged in conversation about the robbery, and those statements were used in trial to convict Henry. Because law enforcement created the situation likely to produce an incriminating statement, which in this case was the conversation with the informant, the Sixth Amendment was violated. This case can be contrasted with *Kuhlman v. Wilson* (1986) in which the informant only listened to the defendant and reported those statements to law enforcement later. The Court stated that it must be shown that law enforcement took some action beyond merely listening to violate the Sixth Amendment.

Rights during Identification

In addition to questioning people, police work involves identifying perpetrators in the course and scope of case preparation, with the ultimate hope of a successful prosecution. *If* a suspect is identified during this phase and *how* it occurs are significant pretrial events, which the Supreme Court has considered in assessing when Sixth Amendment right-to-counsel protection occurs.

Eyewitness testimony is a valuable investigative tool that provides compelling evidence in court. However, such identification is often faulty and is, in fact, the leading cause of wrongful convictions, with more than 75 percent of all convictions overturned by DNA testing having been originally obtained, in part, through eyewitness testimony (Modafferi, Corley, & Perkins, 2009). Two key factors leading to mistaken identification are improper suggestion by the officers and others, and inaccurate perceptions by the witness, the latter factor being difficult to address because it is derived from the average person's lack of training in observation

> **MYTH**
> Eyewitness identification is the best form of evidence possible.
>
> **FACT**
> Maybe, or maybe not. Numerous studies have shown eyewitness identification may not be as reliable as thought. Stress, emotions, and tunnel vision, among other things, impact eyewitness identification.

cross-racial identification suggests that people of one race have difficulty recognizing facial attributes of other races

showup identification technique in which only one individual is shown to the victim or witness

lineup identification technique in which the victim or witness is shown several people, including the suspect

blind lineup one conducted by someone who does not know who the suspect is

compounded by a stressful situation (Modafferi et al., 2009). Inaccurate witness perception may also involve impaired **cross-racial identification,** a situation in which people of one race have difficulty recognizing facial attributes of other races.

Terms applicable to this area of criminal procedure define ways police identify suspects to victims or other witnesses. A **showup** is when only one individual is shown to the victim or witness. A **lineup** occurs when the victim or witness is shown several people, including the suspect. In addition to viewing actual people, either can occur with photos, video, or even audio recordings when the suspect's voice was a factor.

Gaertner and Harrington (2009, p. 130) note, "Highly publicized DNA exoneration cases, most of which involved mistaken eyewitness identifications, have focused public scrutiny on law enforcement procedures and challenged law enforcement practitioners both to re-examine long-standing practices and to implement change that will reduce the likelihood of such misidentification in the future." Two suggested lineup reforms are supported by more than a quarter century of scientific study—blind lineups and sequential lineups. A **blind lineup** is one conducted by someone who does not know who the suspect is and thus, presumably, cannot offer any cues or prompts (whether conscious or subconscious) to the witness as to who the suspect might be. A sequential lineup requires that photos or individuals be viewed one at a time rather than side by side, with the witness required to make a decision about each before viewing the next. This reduces the opportunity to compare those in the lineup and keeps witnesses from picking the person "most similar." Considerable research has been done, but the results are inconclusive (Mecklenburg, Larson, & Bailey, 2008). Those who are not persuaded by the superiority of the sequential blind lineup question the applicability of laboratory research

Constitutional Law in ACTION

Antonio had been arrested because of a parole violation warrant, the result of being charged with a felony domestic assault in which he broke his girlfriend's nose. Antonio hired a private attorney who represented him when he was charged with the felony. The warrant came out after this, and local police picked him up.

While transporting Antonio to jail on the warrant, the officer driving Antonio strikes up a conversation with him. The officer, not intending to elicit any information from Antonio (he didn't even know about the assault charge), begins to talk about his girlfriend and how frustrating she is to him. She is emotional and is always complaining when the deputy goes out with his friends.

Antonio is quiet at first, but then begins to nod in agreement with the officer. Antonio then adds that he has had the same problem with his girlfriend and says, "The last time she complained I just lost it. I knew what I was doing but I couldn't take it anymore. I just popped her in the nose to shut her up."

This statement is used to convict Antonio.

- *Should this statement be allowed in court as evidence?*

- *What situation applies here: the deliberately elicit standard or the functional equivalent standard? Why?*

to the real world, and the legal and practical implementation issues present in the real world. The debate about these proposed changes will continue.

The Supreme Court has primarily held that right to counsel and due process apply to the area of witness identification of a suspect. Because Sixth Amendment protection occurs during critical stages of the criminal proceedings, it makes sense that when someone has been charged with a crime, an identification procedure such as a lineup would necessitate involving the accused's attorney. However, before a suspect has been charged, there is no Sixth Amendment protection of right to counsel. Nonetheless, due process will dictate that any identification process must not be unnecessarily suggestive.

The Supreme Court has decided several important cases that pertain to pretrial, yet post-indictment, identification rights, the two most significant cases being *Wade* and *Gilbert*. Because this stage is critical in the legal proceedings, a lawyer will be appointed if the defendant cannot afford one, with failure of the government to so act causing any resulting evidence to be inadmissible (*United States v. Wade*, 1967). In addition, the Court addressed the inherent unreliability of eyewitness identifications and the potential for prompting in one form or another during the process, surmising that once an identification is made the witness "is not likely to go back on his word later on, so that in practice the issue of identity may . . . for all practical purposes be determined there and then, before the trial" (*Gilbert v. California*, 1967).

An attorney's presence will oversee the fairness of the procedure, including making sure the process is not "so unnecessarily suggestive and conducive to irreparable mistaken identification that he was denied due process of law" (*Stovall v. Denno*, 1967). Thus, constitutional challenges could include a Sixth Amendment right-to-counsel defense or a due process claim.

In *Foster v. California* (1969), a robbery suspect was put in a lineup with two other men, but only Foster was wearing a jacket like the one worn during the robbery, and he was noticeably taller than the others participating in the lineup. Even after speaking in a separate office with only Foster (not the other men in the lineup), the witness still could not identify Foster, but did a week and a half later when viewing a different lineup with four different men. In noting how suggestive these elements were, the Court held that such conditions violate a person's due process rights.

There is no right to counsel *before* someone is charged with a crime. In *Kirby v. Illinois* (1972), the Supreme Court held that the right to legal counsel attaches "at or after the initiation of adversary judicial criminal proceedings—whether by way of formal charge, preliminary hearing, indictment, information or arraignment." Because the initiation of criminal proceedings is the beginning of the adversarial judicial system, anything thereafter is a critical stage. However, events that occur beforehand are *not* considered to be critical stages, so there is not a Sixth Amendment right attached.

This circumstance means that when police conduct a showup by having a victim or witness look at an individual, or conduct a photo lineup during their preliminary investigation before the suspect is charged, that suspect has no right to legal representation. Again, however, police may not make such events unnecessarily suggestive, so documentation needs to occur to address such a concern. Computer programs are now commonly used to generate a photographic

> **LO5** In the Wade-Gilbert rule, the Supreme Court held that pretrial lineups conducted after charging (postindictment) invoke Sixth Amendment protection and require that the suspect have a lawyer present. However, preindictment identification procedures, or those occurring before a suspect has been formally charged, are not critical stages of criminal proceedings, so there is no Sixth Amendment right to a lawyer.

lineup, wherein specific descriptive parameters similar to those of the suspect (e.g., gender; age; skin color; hair color and length; scars, tattoos, or other distinguishing features; facial hair; height; build, etc.) are entered into the program and used to select other lineup "participants" of similar appearance.

Courts have found that one-person showups are not necessarily unconstitutional because police are expected to occasionally make immediate identifications. The Court has viewed showups as beneficial, allowing for a spontaneous response by a victim while memory is fresh, as long as the police are not unnecessarily suggestive or "aggravate the suggestiveness of the confrontation" (*Johnson v. Dugger*, 1987). Even when an identification procedure is found by a court to be unnecessarily suggestive, the resulting identification may be admissible if the reliability of the witness can be established (Schuck, 2009).

Under Supreme Court guidance, lower courts continue to view identification issues in light of the totality of the circumstances to determine reliability and whether due process rights were infringed on. For example, even when there has been a delay of seven months after the crime in conducting a showup, as was the case in *Neil v. Biggers* (1972), it was not prohibited. In *Biggers*, the Supreme Court set forth five factors courts should consider in determining a witness's reliability:

- The *opportunity of the witness to view the defendant* during the crime (How close was the suspect to the victim? Was there sufficient light to see?)
- The *level of attention* the witness was paying to the defendant
- The *accuracy of any descriptions* of the defendant made by the witness before the identification procedure
- The witness's *level of certainty* in his or her identification (Is the suspect 100 percent certain the suspect committed the crime?)
- The *time* between the crime and confrontation

Even when the suspect has been arrested, the Court has been willing to permit a deviation from the *Wade-Gilbert rule* if there is a danger of a witness dying or becoming otherwise unable to view the suspect, or if the suspect might die. Such was the case in *Stovall v. Denno* (1967), when, after the suspect was alleged to have stabbed a doctor to death and seriously injured the doctor's wife, the suspect was taken to the victim's hospital room, where she identified him before he was permitted to speak with a lawyer. Here, the court held that whether a due process violation occurred depended on the *totality of the circumstances*, with timing being crucial in such a case.

However, in *Perry v. New Hampshire* (2012) the Supreme Court refused to extend the due process analysis to a showup situation that was not created by the police:

> We have not extended pretrial screening for reliability to cases in which the suggestive circumstances were not arranged by law enforcement officers. Petitioner requests that we do so because of the grave risk that mistaken identification will yield a miscarriage of justice. Our decisions, however, turn on the presence of state action and aim to deter police from rigging identification procedures, for example, at a lineup, showup, or photograph array. When no improper law enforcement activity is involved, we hold, it suffices to test reliability through the rights and opportunities generally designed for that purpose, notably, the presence of counsel at postindictment lineups, vigorous cross-examination, protective rules of evidence, and jury instructions on both the fallibility of eyewitness identification and the requirement that guilt be proved beyond a reasonable doubt.

Critical Stages at Hearings, Trials, and Appeals

Legal counsel is required in court at any jurisdictional level for criminal offenses that would result in imprisonment. What about events that occur in court other than an actual trial?

In 1970 in *Coleman v. Alabama*, the Supreme Court held that a **preliminary hearing** is a critical stage of the criminal prosecution and, thus, invokes the right to counsel because it is a formal adversarial proceeding. The preliminary hearing determines whether probable cause exists to believe a crime has been committed and that the defendant committed it. *Moore v. Michigan* (1957) established that a defendant has the right to counsel while submitting a guilty plea to the court. Later, in *Hamilton v. Alabama* (1961) the Court held that an **arraignment,** the hearing at which the defendant is required to enter a plea, is a critical stage under the Sixth Amendment.

In the 1986 case of *Michigan v. Jackson*, Robert Bernard Jackson requested appointment of counsel at his arraignment on a murder charge. But before he had a chance to consult with counsel, police officers, after advising him of his *Miranda* rights, questioned Jackson and obtained a confession. Jackson was convicted over his defense attorney's objection to the admission of the confessions in evidence. The Michigan Supreme Court held that the confession was improperly obtained in violation of the Sixth Amendment. The Supreme Court agreed that the confession should have been suppressed, citing the *Edwards* decision (discussed in Chapter 10) and noting that the reasoning behind *Edwards*—that once a suspect has invoked his right to counsel, police may not initiate interrogation until counsel has been made available to the suspect—applied with even greater force to this case: "The assertion of the right to counsel is no less significant, and the need for additional safeguards no less clear, when that assertion is made at an arraignment and when the basis for it is the Sixth Amendment."

Thus, the *Jackson* rule established that once the accused has invoked his or her right to counsel, police may not question the accused without that attorney being present, even if the accused agrees to waive the right to have their attorney present during that particular session of questioning. Under *Jackson* it follows that any waiver of that right is presumed to be invalid because it was not made with the advice of counsel, and any evidence obtained through interrogation after the invocation of the right to counsel is inadmissible.

The *Jackson* rule, which the Court later described as a "wholesale importation of the *Edwards* rule into the Sixth Amendment," is a prophylactic rule established to prevent police from badgering an accused for inculpatory information once the right to counsel has been invoked. The *Jackson* Court decided that a request for counsel at an arraignment should be treated as an invocation of the Sixth Amendment right to counsel "at every critical stage of the prosecution."

Nearly a quarter of a century later, however, the Supreme Court issued a decision in *Montejo v. Louisiana* (2009) that overruled *Jackson*. In this case Jesse Jay Montejo was sentenced to death for murder and robbery. He was read his rights and admitted to shooting the victim during a robbery. At the preliminary hearing, the judge ordered a public defender be appointed to Montejo, but before he met with his court-appointed attorney, Montejo accompanied officers to where he indicated he had thrown the weapon into the lake. During the drive, Montejo also wrote

preliminary hearing a critical stage of criminal proceedings when it is determined if probable cause exists to believe a crime has been committed and that the defendant committed it

arraignment usually the first court appearance by a defendant during which the accused is advised of his or her rights, advised of the charges, and given the opportunity to enter a plea

Constitutional Law in ACTION

Mr. Hooper had parked his car in his driveway and was walking to the front door of his house. As he neared the door he saw that it was damaged and standing open. Just then, a man came running out of the house and collided with Hooper, who was already calling police on his cell phone.

The man and Hooper both fell to the ground. Hooper had a few seconds to stare into the man's face before the man got up and ran. Hooper told police what he had observed: a 20- to 25-year-old man, wearing a white t-shirt and blue jeans, with a goatee and brown eyes. The man also had a tattoo on his left cheek.

Officers were already in the area and heard the burglary call. The dispatcher told officers the description of the suspect. Within a minute the officers spotted a person matching the description two blocks from Mr. Hooper's house. The man was not hard to spot because it was 10:00 P.M. and there was no one else out in this residential neighborhood.

Mr. Hooper walked over to where the police had stopped the man. The police had the man step from the back of the police car and stand 15 feet from Mr. Hooper. The man was in handcuffs and one officer stood next to him.

The other officer stood next to Mr. Hooper and said, "This is the only guy around, and we were in the area within seconds of you calling." Mr. Hooper identified the man police stopped as the burglar.

- *Was this show-up unnecessarily suggestive? Why or why not?*
- *Do you think Mr. Hooper was able to accurately identify the burglar?*
- *Do you think stress or emotions play a role in accurate memory recall?*

CASE IN BRIEF

Montejo v. Louisiana (2009)

ISSUE Is a waiver to the Sixth Amendment right to counsel invalid simply because the right has attached?

RULING No. Overruling the holding in *Jackson*, the Supreme Court stated that *Miranda*, *Edwards*, and *Minnick* provide the necessary protections to a defendant, whether waiving or invoking the right to counsel under the Sixth Amendment.

a letter of apology to the victim's widow. On his return he met with his attorney, who was incensed that his client had been interrogated in his absence and that the letter was admitted into evidence. Montejo was convicted and sentenced to death.

The Louisiana Supreme Court upheld the conviction noting that in Louisiana, as in many other states, lawyers are automatically assigned to indigent defendants, removing any question of whether Montejo specifically "requested" counsel at his arraignment. The court explained that Montejo waived his Sixth Amendment right to counsel by remaining mute and not acknowledging the appointed counsel. According to the court, something beyond "mute acquiescence" is required to trigger Sixth Amendment protection. The Supreme Court, however, followed a different line of reasoning to reach a similar conclusion, arguing that the *Jackson* framework was unworkable in jurisdictions that appoint counsel regardless of a defendant's request. The Court stated that the protections afforded under *Miranda*, *Edwards*, and *Minnick v. Mississippi* (1990), a case introduced in Chapter 10, were sufficient to protect a defendant's Sixth Amendment rights from police badgering that might elicit culpable evidence.

In its 5–4 ruling the Court affirmed Montejo's conviction stating, "*Jackson* deters law enforcement officers from even trying to obtain voluntary confessions. When the marginal benefits of the *Jackson* rule are weighed against its substantial costs to the truth-seeking process and the criminal justice system, we readily conclude that the rule does not pay its way. *Michigan v. Jackson* should be and is now overruled." Thus, under *Montejo*, police officers may now attempt to obtain a waiver and an admission from a suspect without violating the Sixth Amendment, even after the suspect has been indicted or has made his or her first court appearance on the case *and* either obtained an attorney or has asked for one (Rutledge, 2009).

Douglas v. California (1963) held that the first appeal, a right itself, necessitated counsel. This right extends to only the first appeal and no further.

During the trial itself, both sides must abide by the rules of fairness. The first due process case regarding a trial was *Mooney v. Holohan* (1935), which held that deliberate use of perjured testimony by the prosecutor and deliberate nondisclosure of evidence that would have impeached the perjury violated due process. This holding was reiterated almost 30 years later in *Brady v. Maryland* (1963), which established the rules for "discovery," making unconstitutional "trial by ambush," where the defense learns the identity of prosecution witnesses when they walk down the courtroom aisle.

> **LO6** Any hearing or trial through the first appeal of right invokes the Sixth Amendment right to counsel, but the right does not extend to any additional appeals.

Brady involved a defendant who admitted participating in a murder but claimed his companion did the killing. Before trial, John Brady's lawyer asked the prosecutor to allow him to examine the companion's statements. The prosecutor complied but withheld the statement in which the companion admitted doing the killing. The defense did not learn of this withheld exculpatory evidence until after Brady was convicted and sentenced. On appeal the Supreme Court reversed Brady's conviction saying, "The suppression by the prosecution of evidence favorable to an accused upon request violates due process where the evidence is material either to guilt or to punishment, irrespective of the good faith or bad faith of the prosecution." This holding is called the **Brady rule.**

In *Texas v. Cobb* (2001), the Court asserted that the right of counsel applies only to *charged* offenses. In this case, Raymond Levi Cobb was charged with burglary, at which time his Sixth Amendment rights attached. Later, however, while Cobb was awaiting trial, the police questioned Cobb about the murder of a mother and her child that occurred during the burglary. Cobb waived his *Miranda* rights and confessed to the murders. Cobb's defense was that his Sixth Amendment rights were violated because he was awaiting trial and should not even have been talked to without his lawyer present, whether he waived his rights or not.

The Supreme Court disagreed, relying on *McNeil v. Wisconsin* (1991), holding that the Sixth Amendment is "offense specific," applying only to the offense charged. Even if another crime arises out of that course of conduct, if the additional crime has even one separate element, it is considered an entirely new set of circumstances for Sixth Amendment purposes. The Court also referred to *Blockburger v. United States* (1932), which held that when the "same act or transaction constitutes a violation of two distinct statutory provisions, the test to be applied to determine whether there are two offenses or only one . . . is whether each provision requires proof of a fact which the other does not."

An example would be a suspect indicted for unlawful possession of a firearm used for a robbery but not yet charged with the offense. The "closely related" doctrine would have prevented officers from getting a statement or conducting a

◀ **CASE IN BRIEF**

Brady v. Maryland (1963)

ISSUE Does it violate the Constitution to withhold evidence from the defense?

RULING Yes. When the evidence is favorable to the defendant and is material to the determination of guilt or innocence, it violates due process to withhold that evidence, regardless that it is done with good or bad faith.

Brady rule the suppression by the prosecution of evidence favorable to an accused on request violates due process when the evidence is material either to guilt or to punishment, irrespective of the good faith or bad faith of the prosecution

Constitutional Law in ACTION

Billy was in jail awaiting trial after being charged with distributing marijuana. During his time in jail, he asked several inmates if they knew anyone who would "take care" of the witnesses who were to testify against him. These inmates went to prison officials, who in turn notified the police.

After hearing this, the police put a paid informant in the cell with Billy. The informant was told not to ask Billy anything about his marijuana dealing, but he was free to inquire all he wanted about Billy wanting someone to "take care" of the witnesses.

The informant stayed with Billy for five days in the cell. Billy asked several times if the informant knew anyone he could hire. The informant finally said he did, and Billy went so far as to give the informant names and addresses and have his girlfriend deposit money into the informant's bank account.

Billy was later charged with conspiracy to commit murder and witness tampering based on the informant's information. Billy moved to have the evidence suppressed claiming violation of his Sixth Amendment right to counsel. The court denied this because the informant asked Billy about these related crimes *before* he was charged with them (he had been charged only with distributing marijuana at that point), and the right to counsel had not yet attached.

- When did the right to counsel attach in each crime?
- What effect does the timing of each charge have on whether or not police can question Billy?
- Think back to Miranda. Does it come into play in this scenario?

CASE IN BRIEF

Texas v. Cobb (2001)

ISSUE Does the Sixth Amendment right to counsel attach only to the crime charged and not to related but uncharged crimes?

RULING Yes. The right to counsel under the Sixth Amendment is offense specific.

offense specific the Sixth Amendment right to counsel applies only to the specific charges for which the defendant has been indicted or arraigned

lineup without the suspect's lawyer present. In *Texas v. Cobb*, however, the Supreme Court rejected the closely related doctrine and ruled that the Sixth Amendment right to counsel is "**offense specific**," that is, it applies only to the specific charges for which the defendant has been indicted or arraigned. This is in contrast to the Fifth Amendment right to counsel, which is not offense specific and, once invoked, means that all questioning must stop.

The courts have determined that sentencing is also a critical stage in the criminal justice process. *Townsend v. Burke* (1948) held that a convicted offender has a right to counsel at the time of sentencing.

Table 11.1 summarizes the major Supreme Court cases granting the right to counsel throughout the critical stages of the criminal justice process.

Even when statements are not admissible regarding the charged offense because the person's Sixth Amendment rights were violated, they are still admissible to impeach the witness, meaning to prove that person committed perjury. In *Michigan v. Harvey* (1990), Chief Justice William H. Rehnquist stated, "If a defendant exercises his right to testify on his own behalf, he assumes a reciprocal 'obligation to speak truthfully and accurately' and we have consistently rejected arguments that would allow a defendant to turn the illegal method by which evidence in the Government's possession was obtained to his own advantage, and provide himself with a shield against contradiction of his untruths."

Table 11.1 Key Cases Regarding Right to Counsel

Stage in criminal justice process	Case	When suspect or defendant has a constitutional right to counsel
Investigation	*Escobedo v. Illinois* (1964)	During any police interrogation and when the suspect requests counsel. The case can be read broadly, as applied to any custodial interrogation, or narrowly, as limited to when the suspect is the focus of investigation *and* when the suspect requests counsel before interrogation. Both interpretations are supported by the language in the opinion.
	Miranda v. Arizona (1966)	During any custodial interrogation to secure privilege against self-incrimination
Pretrial	*Massiah v. United States* (1964)	Once adversary proceedings have begun against defendant
	Brewer v. Williams (1977)	Reaffirmed, once adversary proceedings have begun against defendant
	United States v. Wade (1967)	During pretrial postindictment lineup for identification
	Moore v. Illinois (1977)	During in-court identification at preliminary hearing following criminal complaint
	Coleman v. Alabama (1970)	During the preliminary hearing
	Missouri v. Frye (2012)	During the plea bargaining process
	Moore v. Michigan (1957)	When submitting a guilty plea to the court
	Hamilton v. Alabama (1961)	During the arraignment
Trial	*Powell v. Alabama* (1932)	During a trial in a state capital case
	Gideon v. Wainwright (1963)	During a trial of an indigent defendant charged with a noncapital felony
	Argersinger v. Hamlin (1972)	During a trial when the defendant might be imprisoned, whether for a felony or a misdemeanor
	In re Gault (1967)	During juvenile delinquency adjudication that may lead to commitment to a state institution
Sentencing	*Townsend v. Burke* (1948)	At the time of sentencing
Posttrial	*Douglas v. California* (1963)	During first appeal after conviction

More recently, in *Kansas v. Ventris* (2009), the Court held that self-incriminating statements obtained in the absence of a knowing and voluntary waiver of the Sixth Amendment right to counsel were admissible at trial for the purpose of impeaching a defendant's testimony. In this case, while Donnie Ventris was in jail awaiting trial on charges of aggravated robbery and aggravated battery, he made incriminating statements to his cellmate, who had been approached by the prosecution to keep his "ear open" for such evidence. The cellmate later testified as to Ventris's incriminating statements, and Ventris was convicted. Ventris then appealed, claiming this testimony violated his Sixth Amendment right to counsel. Although the district court's decision was affirmed by the court of appeals, it was reversed by the supreme court of Kansas, which held that "[w]ithout a knowing and voluntary waiver of the right to counsel, the admission of the defendant's uncounseled statements to an undercover informant who is secretly acting as a State agent violates the defendant's Sixth Amendment rights." It must be noted that the cellmate had prompted Ventris to talk by stating to Ventris that he appeared to have "something more serious weighing on his mind." Hence, the incriminating statement was deliberately elicited. Had the cellmate just kept an "ear open" as he was told, passive listening would have not been a violation.

The U.S. Supreme Court, however, reversed and remanded that decision, holding that the informant's testimony, although concededly elicited in violation of the Sixth Amendment, was admissible to challenge and impeach Ventris's inconsistent testimony at trial. The Court reasoned that the interests protected by excluding "tainted evidence" are outweighed by the need to ensure "integrity of the trial process."

◀ **CASE IN BRIEF**

Kansas v. Ventris (2009)

ISSUE May a statement made without a valid waiver to the Sixth Amendment right to counsel be used to impeach a defendant?

RULING Yes. Such a statement made without a valid waiver may be used in court, not as evidence but to impeach the credibility of the defendant.

The Presumption of Effective Counsel

The right to legal counsel means little if the counsel provided is ineffective. *Powell v. Alabama* (1932), discussed previously, was the first ineffective counsel case. Understandably, what constitutes effective counsel can be debated, but the Supreme Court has offered this guidance: "The proper measure of attorney performance remains simply reasonableness under prevailing professional norms. . . . The benchmark for judging any claim of ineffectiveness must be whether counsel's conduct so undermined the proper functioning of the adversarial process that the trial cannot be relied on as having produced a just result" (*Strickland v. Washington*, 1984).

Strickland established a two-prong test to establish a claim of ineffective counsel. Defendants must show (1) the counsel's representation fell below an objective standard of reasonableness and (2) there is a reasonable probability that, but for counsel's unprofessional errors, the result of the proceeding would have been different. *Herring v. New York* (1975) asserted, "The very premise of our adversary system of criminal justice is that partisan advocacy on both sides of a case will promote the ultimate objective that the guilty be convicted and the innocent go free."

United States v. Cronic (1984) held that claims of ineffective counsel must point out specific errors of trial counsel and cannot be based on inferences drawn from the defense counsel's inexperience or lack of time to prepare, the gravity of the charges, accessibility of witnesses to counsel, or the case's complexity. Although inexperience may not suffice as ineffective representation, failure to take normal and routine steps before and during trial could.

Strickland was relied on in *Wiggins v. Smith* (2003), when the Court also held that the trial attorney must thoroughly investigate the life history of a defendant if there is reason to believe it may affect the determination of the death penalty. Sixth Amendment law regarding effective counsel continued to evolve in *Missouri v. Frye* (2012), when the Court held that part of effective assistance of counsel is for the defense attorney to inform the defendant about formal and favorable plea offers. This refinement emphasized the second part of the *Strickland* test, that the defendant must show a reasonable probability they would have accepted the plea offer had they not received the deficient performance of counsel (i.e., the non-informing of the plea offer).

If a lawyer has a conflict of interest by representing another client who would prejudice the other, ineffective assistance of counsel would exist, but merely being dissatisfied with the outcome of a trial is not itself sufficient grounds to make such a claim. (Remember, 50 percent of the parties to a trial are unhappy with the results!) Because the *Strickland* decision places the burden to prove ineffective representation on the claimant, few appeals on such grounds are successful.

Some falsely believe that public defenders assigned to defendants who cannot afford their own lawyers are somehow less effective than private attorneys defendants with money are capable of paying for, or that the more a lawyer costs, the better the representation. Trial lawyers more often respect the skills of those who choose to work as public defenders as well as their commitment to watch out for their clients' rights, regardless of their financial status. As with any other professionals, attorneys are motivated to specialize for a variety of reasons, and remuneration is second to their commitment to defending those in need.

MYTH
If I lose my case, my attorney has provided "ineffective assistance."

FACT
Not necessarily. Mistakes or tactical errors are virtually "unchallengeable." It must be shown that the conduct fell outside of reasonable performance given all of the circumstances.

Public defenders are employed by the government to ensure everyone's Fifth Amendment right to counsel is made available, particularly those who cannot afford their own lawyer. Although many jurisdictions employ their own public defenders, others appoint private practice lawyers who agree to take cases, thus providing these clients with a private practice attorney. This situation occurred in *Gideon v. Wainwright*, in which Abe Fortas, who later became a Justice on the Court, was appointed to represent indigent Clarence Gideon in what became a landmark Sixth Amendment case.

Waiver of Sixth Amendment Right to Legal Counsel

A suspect cannot be forced to deal with an attorney and so may waive this right. In *Johnson v. Zerbst* (1938), the Supreme Court stated, "A waiver is ordinarily an intentional relinquishment or abandonment of a known right or privilege. The determination of whether there has been an intelligent waiver of right to counsel must depend, in each case, upon the particular facts and circumstance surrounding that case, including the background, experience and conduct of the accused" (*Johnson v. Zerbst*). See Figure 11.2 for a sample waiver.

Patterson v. Illinois (1988) held that a valid waiver of *Miranda* rights waives the Fifth Amendment right against self-incrimination and waives the Sixth Amendment right to counsel. The requirements that a waiver be knowing and voluntary remain the same. A court will consider the totality of circumstances regarding how the waiver was obtained and the competency and age of the person, as well as issues of intelligence, health, and ability to understand the language.

For a waiver to be effective, it need not be in writing, but whatever statement is made by the suspect must show there was, in fact, an intentional relinquishment of the known right.

To have the individual sign a waiver of the right to counsel is tactically preferable. Additionally, a court will assess whether the suspect was competent enough to waive any rights, for which the totality of the circumstances surrounding the waiver will be examined, including education, intelligence, physical and mental condition, language issues, and age.

LO7 *A waiver of one's Sixth Amendment right to counsel must be voluntary, knowing, and intelligent.*

The Right to Act as One's Own Counsel

Individuals may appear in court without attorneys, representing themselves, that is, ***pro se***. *Pro se* is Latin meaning "for himself."

With the complexity of the entire legal process, it is difficult to understand how some people think themselves competent to provide their own defense. However, some defendants distrust attorneys in general or otherwise believe they can handle their defense adequately, or perhaps the expense of hiring a lawyer compels some to defend themselves if they do not qualify for legal aid.

Faretta v. California (1975) set forth three conditions to be met before a person could represent him- or herself: (1) awareness of the right to counsel,

pro se appearing in court without an attorney, representing oneself

TRIAL WITHOUT A LAWYER
Va. Code § 19.2-160

CASE NO ....

....
☐ General District Court
☐ Juvenile and Domestic Relations District Court
☐ Circuit Court

.... v. ....

WAIVER OF RIGHT TO BE REPRESENTED BY A LAWYER (CRIMINAL CASE)

I have been advised by a judge of this court of the nature of the charges in the cases pending against me and the potential punishment for the offenses, which includes imprisonment in the penitentiary or confinement in jail. I understand the nature of these charges and the potential punishment for them if I am found to be guilty.

I have been further advised by a judge of this court that I have the following rights to be represented by a lawyer in these cases:

a. I have a right to be represented by a lawyer.

b. If I choose to hire my own lawyer, I will be given a reasonable opportunity to hire, at my expense, a lawyer selected by me. The judge will decide what is a reasonable opportunity to hire a lawyer. If I have not hired a lawyer after such reasonable opportunity, the judge may try the case even though I do not have a lawyer to represent me.

c. If I ask the judge for a lawyer to represent me and the judge decides, after reviewing my sworn financial statement that I am indigent, the judge will select and appoint a lawyer to represent me. However, if I am found to be guilty of an offense, the lawyer's fee as set by the judge within statutory limits will be assessed against me as court costs and I will be required to pay it.

I understand these rights to be represented by a lawyer. I understand the manner in which a lawyer can be of assistance and I understand that, in proceeding without a lawyer, I may be confronted with complicated legal issues. I also understand that I may waive (give up) my rights to be represented by a lawyer.

Understanding my rights to be represented by a lawyer as described above and further understanding the nature of the case and the potential punishment if I am found to be guilty, I waive all of my rights to be represented by a lawyer in these cases, with the further understanding that the cases will be tried without a lawyer either being hired by me or being appointed by the judge for me. I waive these rights of my own choice, voluntarily, of my own free will, without any threats, promises, force or coercion.

_____
ADULT

Upon oral examination, the undersigned judge of this Court finds that the Adult, having been advised of the rights and matters stated above and having understood these rights and matters, thereafter has knowingly, voluntarily and intelligently waived his rights to be represented by a lawyer.

....   _____
DATE   JUDGE

CASE NO ....

Figure 11.2 Waiver of Right to Counsel

Source: BACIGAL. *Criminal Law and Procedure*, 2E. © 2002 Delmar Learning, a part of Cengage Learning, Inc. Reproduced by permission. www.cengage.com/permissions.

(2) a valid waiver of Sixth Amendment rights, and (3) competency. In *Faretta*, the Court held, "To force a lawyer on a defendant can only lead him to believe that the law contrives against him. Moreover, it is not inconceivable that in some rare instances, the defendant might in fact present his case more effectively by conducting his own defense." An accused who represents him- or herself cannot later claim ineffective counsel.

Juveniles and the Sixth Amendment

The juvenile justice system was briefly introduced in Chapter 2. *In re Gault* (1967) was a landmark case in which an important philosophical shift occurred, away from the pure *parens patriae* model, where juveniles had no constitutional right during adjudication, toward a due process model in which juveniles were granted certain constitutional rights, including the rights against self-incrimination, notice of the charges being brought, to confront and cross-examine witnesses, and to have counsel (del Carmen & Trulson, 2006).

Research shows juveniles are not appointed legal counsel in all cases, despite the Supreme Court in *Gault* stating, "We conclude that the Due Process Clause of the Fourteenth Amendment requires that in respect of proceedings to determine delinquency which may result in commitment to an institution in which the juvenile's freedom is curtailed, the child and his parents must be notified of the child's right to be represented by counsel retained by them, or if they are unable to afford counsel, that counsel will be appointed to represent the child." Admittedly, juvenile courts have broad discretion, and such terms as *institutionalization* are not as easily interpreted as are terms in the adult system. *In re Gault* applied Sixth Amendment rights to juveniles, with some areas of application remaining to be addressed by the Court. One may anticipate further direction occurring as the Supreme Court addresses them.

LO8 *In re Gault applied Sixth Amendment rights to juveniles, including the right against self-incrimination, to receive notice of the charges, to confront and cross-examine witnesses, and the right to counsel.*

The Sixth Amendment and Corrections

Like the Fifth Amendment, the Sixth Amendment is not frequently cited in prisoners' rights lawsuits.

Often detainers are filed against inmates who have other criminal charges pending against them, ensuring their appearance before the prosecuting jurisdiction for the next trial once their current sentence is complete. For example, in *Smith v. Hooey* (1969) an inmate in a federal institution had state criminal charges pending against him in Texas. He spent six years trying to get his trial, but the detainer process caused the delay.

Other cases regarding right to counsel involve those on probation. *Mempa v. Rhay* (1967) held that a convicted offender has the right to assistance of counsel at probation revocation hearings in which the sentence has been deferred. *Gagnon v. Scarpelli* (1973) held that probationers and parolees have a constitutionally limited right to counsel on a case-by-case basis at revocation proceedings.

LO9 *For prisoners, cases based on the Sixth Amendment involve the right to a speedy trial and the **detainer** problem.*

detainer document filed against inmates who have other criminal charges pending against them

Summary

The Sixth Amendment requires a speedy and public trial. Whether a trial is sufficiently "speedy" is determined by (1) the length of the delay, (2) the reason for the delay, (3) the defendant's assertion of this right, and (4) the harm caused (*Barker v. Wingo*). The Sixth Amendment also requires that the trial occur in the district in which the crime was committed and that defendants have the right to an impartial and representative jury.

The right to counsel is the only Sixth Amendment guarantee that extends beyond the trial. Denying legal counsel for a defendant at trial is a denial of due process (*Powell v. Alabama*). *Gideon v. Wainwright* established that indigent defendants are to be provided lawyers when faced with a "deprivation of liberty." In 1972 in *Argersinger v. Hamlin*, the Court extended the right to an attorney to defendants accused of misdemeanor offenses. Any time the penalty could include prison, the defendant must have access to a lawyer. When police inquiry has begun to focus on a particular suspect, custodial interrogation at the police station entitles a suspect to legal representation when requested (*Escobedo v. Illinois*).

The Sixth Amendment right to legal counsel occurs at every critical stage of a criminal proceeding, including during the investigation; during custodial interrogation and post-indictment interrogation; during post-indictment identification; at arraignment; at hearings; during the trial; and at sentencing. After a defendant has been charged with a crime and retained an attorney, that attorney must be present during any subsequent questioning. In the *Wade-Gilbert rule*, the Supreme Court held that pretrial lineups conducted after charging (post-indictment) invoke Sixth Amendment protection and require that the suspect have a lawyer. Lineups may not be arranged in such a manner as to make the defendant stand out from the others in any unnecessarily suggestive ways. Preindictment (before being formally charged) identification procedures are *not* critical stages of criminal proceedings, so there is no Sixth Amendment right to a lawyer. The court will view pretrial identification procedures in the totality of circumstances when determining whether they were constitutional. Any hearing or trial through the first appeal invokes the Sixth Amendment right to counsel, but the right does not extend to any additional appeals.

The Sixth Amendment right to counsel presumes counsel is effective. A waiver of one's Sixth Amendment right to counsel must be voluntary, knowing, and intelligent. Individuals may appear in court without attorneys, representing themselves, that is, *pro se*. *In re Gault* applied Sixth Amendment rights to juveniles, including the right against self-incrimination, to receive notice of the charges, to confront and cross-examine witnesses, and the right to counsel. Finally, for prisoners, cases based on the Sixth Amendment involve the right to a speedy trial and the detainer problem.

Discussion Questions

1. Does having a lawyer present during a trial ensure fairness?
2. Why would people want to represent themselves in court *pro se*? Would you think more or less of those representing themselves? Why?
3. Define *deliberately elicit*. When does that standard come into play?
4. When has the line been crossed between a public trial at which the media are present and a "trial by the media"? Could this problem ever justify barring the media from attending trials? Does the media ever have that much influence on the public or jurors?
5. Why would someone choose to be a defense attorney? A prosecutor?
6. Do public defenders provide less effective defense than would a private attorney? What might a private attorney with a wealthy client be capable of that a public defender with an indigent client would not?
7. Why is the adversary system of law a necessity to produce just results?
8. Why could one attorney not represent *both* sides in a trial by providing objective facts?
9. Does the adversary system today encourage, or even demand, that attorneys represent their clients "too vigorously"?
10. What is a *critical stage*? What importance does that point in time have on a defendant's rights?

References

Bacigal, R.J. (1996). *Criminal Law and Procedure: An Introduction*. St. Paul, MN: West Publishing Company.

del Carmen, R.V., & Trulson, C.R. (2006). *Juvenile Justice, The System, Process, and Law*. Belmont, CA: Thomson Wadsworth Publishing.

Ferdico, J.N.; Fradella, H.F.; & Totten, C.D. (2009). *Criminal Procedure for the Criminal Justice Professional*, 10th ed. Belmont, CA: Wadsworth/Cengage Learning.

Gaertner, S., & Harrington, J. (2009, April). "Successful Eyewitness Identification Reform: Ramsey County's Blind Sequential Lineup Protocol." *The Police Chief*, pp. 130–141.

Mecklenburg, S.H.; Larson, M.R.; & Bailey, P.J. (2008, October). "Eye Witness Identification: What Chiefs Need to Know Now." *The Police Chief*, pp. 68–81.

Modafferi, P.A.; Corley, M.; & Perkins, C. (2009, October). "Eyewitness Identification: Views from the Trenches." *The Police Chief*, pp. 78–87.

Rutledge, D. (2006, February). "Right to Counsel." *Police*, pp. 70–72.

Rutledge, D. (2008, August). "Pointing the Right to Counsel." *Police*, pp. 74–75.

Rutledge, D. (2009, August). "Sixth Amendment Waivers." *Police*, pp. 62–64.

Schuck, J. (2009, April 24). "Eyewitness Identifications: Determining the Admissibility." *LawOfficer.com*. Retrieved August 22, 2016 from www.lawofficer.com/article/needs-tags-columns/eyewitness-identifications

Shapiro, A. (2010, February 26). "Justice Department to Launch Indigent Defense Program." *NPR*. Retrieved August 22, 2016 from www.npr.org/templates/story/story.php?storyId=124094017

"Star Chamber, Court of." (2000). *Microsoft Encarta Online Encyclopedia*.

NOTE: *The Runaway Jury* by John Grisham presents a fictionalized look at jury selection and manipulation that may be of interest to you.

Cases Cited

Argersinger v. Hamlin, 407 U.S. 25 (1972)
Baldwin v. New York, 399 U.S. 66 (1970)
Ballew v. Georgia, 435 U.S. 223 (1978)
Barker v. Wingo, 407 U.S. 514 (1972)
Batson v. Kentucky, 476 U.S. 79 (1986)
Betterman v. Montana, 136 S.Ct. 1400 (2016)
Betts v. Brady, 316 U.S. 455 (1942)
Blockburger v. United States, 284 U.S. 299 (1932)
Brady v. Maryland, 373 U.S. 83 (1963)
Brewer v. Williams, 430 U.S. 387 (1977)
Briscoe v. Virginia, 559 U.S. ___ (2010)
Bullcoming v. New Mexico, 564 U.S. 647 (2011)
Coleman v. Alabama, 399 U.S. 1 (1970)
Coy v. Iowa, 487 U.S. 1012 (1988)
Crawford v. Washington, 541 U.S. 36 (2004)
Davis v. Washington, 547 U.S. 813 (2006)
Douglas v. California, 372 U.S. 353 (1963)
Duncan v. Louisiana, 391 U.S. 145 (1968)
Escobedo v. Illinois, 378 U.S. 478 (1964)
Estes v. Texas, 381 U.S. 532 (1965)
Faretta v. California, 422 U.S. 806 (1975)
Foster v. California, 394 U.S. 440 (1969)
Gagnon v. Scarpelli, 411 U.S. 778 (1973)
Gannett Co. v. DePasquale, 442 U.S. 368 (1979)
Gideon v. Wainwright, 372 U.S. 335 (1963)
Gilbert v. California, 388 U.S. 263 (1967)
Glasser v. United States, 315 U.S. 60 (1942)
Halbert v. Michigan, 545 U.S. 605 (2005)
Hamilton v. Alabama, 368 U.S. 52 (1961)
Harris v. South Carolina, 338 U.S. 68 (1949)
Herring v. New York, 422 U.S. 853 (1975)
In re Gault, 387 U.S. 1 (1967)
Johnson v. Dugger, 817 F.2d 726 (11th Cir. 1987)
Johnson v. Zerbst, 304 U.S. 458 (1938)
Kansas v. Ventris, 556 U.S. 586 (2009)
Kirby v. Illinois, 406 U.S. 682 (1972)
Kuhlman v. Wilson, 477 U.S. 436 (1986)
Lewis v. United States, 518 U.S. 322 (1996)
Maryland v. Craig, 497 U.S. 836 (1990)
Massiah v. United States, 377 U.S. 201 (1964)
McNeil v. Wisconsin, 501 U.S. 171 (1991)
Melendez-Diaz v. Massachusetts, 557 U.S. 305 (2009)
Mempa v. Rhay, 389 U.S. 128 (1967)
Michigan v. Bryant, 562 U.S. 131 (2011)
Michigan v. Harvey, 494 U.S. 344 (1990)
Michigan v. Jackson, 475 U.S. 625 (1986)
Minnick v. Mississippi, 498 U.S. 146 (1990)
Miranda v. Arizona, 384 U.S. 436 (1966)
Missouri v. Frye, 566 U.S. ___ (2012)
Montejo v. Louisiana, 556 U.S. 778 (2009)
Mooney v. Holohan, 294 U.S. 103 (1935)
Moore v. Illinois, 434 U.S. 220 (1977)

Moore v. Michigan, 355 U.S. 155 (1957)
Neil v. Biggers, 409 U.S. 188 (1972)
Nix v. Williams, 467 U.S. 431 (1984)
Ohio v. Clark, 576 U.S. 1 (2015)
Patterson v. Illinois, 487 U.S. 285 (1988)
Perry v. New Hampshire, 565 U.S. 1 (2012)
Powell v. Alabama, 287 U.S. 45 (1932)
Press-Enterprise Co. v. Superior Court, 464 U.S. 501 (1984)
Rawlins v. Georgia, 201 U.S. 638 (1906)
Richmond Newspapers, Inc. v. Virginia, 448 U.S. 555 (1980)
Scott v. Illinois, 440 U.S. 367 (1979)
Smith v. Hooey, 393 U.S. 374 (1969)
Snyder v. Louisiana, 552 U.S. 472 (2008)
Spano v. New York, 360 U.S. 315 (1959)
Stovall v. Denno, 388 U.S. 263 (1967)
Strauder v. West Virginia, 100 U.S. 303 (1879)
Strickland v. Washington, 466 U.S. 668 (1984)
Strunk v. United States, 412 U.S. 434 (1973)
Swain v. Alabama, 380 U.S. 202 (1965)
Taylor v. Louisiana, 419 U.S. 522 (1975)
Texas v. Cobb, 532 U.S. 162 (2001)
Townsend v. Burke, 334 U.S. 736 (1948)
United States v. Cronic, 466 U.S. 648 (1984)
United States v. Henry, 447 U.S. 264 (1980)
United States v. Moylan, 417 F.2d 1002 (4th Cir. 1969)
United States v. Valenzuela-Bernal, 458 U.S. 858 (1982)
United States v. Wade, 388 U.S. 218 (1967)
Wiggins v. Smith, 539 U.S. 510 (2003)

CHAPTER 12

The Eighth Amendment
Bail, Fines, and Punishment

Excessive bail shall not be required, nor excessive fines imposed, nor cruel and unusual punishment inflicted.

—Eighth Amendment to the U.S. Constitution

The death penalty is a topic of much controversy, with opponents arguing it is a blatant violation of the Eighth Amendment protection from cruel and unusual punishment. The Supreme Court, however, has held that government-sanctioned execution for specific capital crimes is not, in itself, unconstitutional, although the manner in which it is applied has been extensively examined. Lethal injection, the most common form of execution in the United States, is considered by some to be the only politically correct method of capital punishment. The photo is of San Quentin State Penitentiary, home to California's death chamber.

Learning Objectives

LO1 *Identify what three rights are protected by the Eighth Amendment.*

LO2 *Explain what purposes bail serves.*

LO3 *Describe what may be seized under asset forfeiture laws.*

LO4 *Understand where the meaning of "cruel and unusual punishment" comes from.*

LO5 *Know what the general rule under the Eighth Amendment regarding punishments is.*

LO6 *Clarify whether capital punishment has been found to be constitutional, which precedent cases have determined this, and what is required of proceedings that may involve the death penalty.*

LO7 *Summarize what Eighth Amendment rights prisoners often claim.*

Key Terms

asset forfeiture	compensatory damages	proportionality analysis
bail	corporal punishment	punitive damages
bifurcated trial	preventive detention	ROR
commercial bail		

Introduction

The Eighth Amendment protects three rights, one that applies before trial, and the other two after a person has been convicted of a crime.

LO1 The three rights protected by the Eighth Amendment are
- That excessive bail shall not be required.
- That excessive fines shall not be imposed.
- That cruel and unusual punishment shall not be inflicted.

Not unlike other brief amendments, this particular one has found itself embroiled in controversy because of interpretations about other punishments the government can carry such as fines and, most particularly, about whether the death penalty is cruel and unusual. This chapter challenges you to contemplate your perspective about the death penalty. Who does society deem appropriate to put to death? Should this include the mentally ill, the intellectually disabled, and juveniles? How is this ultimate punishment to be carried out? By electrocution, hanging, or firing squad? In an amendment such as this one, every American is challenged to consider whether the ends do justify the means because why the law exists is as important as how it is enforced.

This area of the law is not the only area the high court has been called on to address regarding the Eighth Amendment. For example, what do the terms *cruel* and *unusual* mean as they relate to bail and fines? How is *excessive* defined? With the U.S. Constitution more than two centuries old, can modern standards even begin to match the framers' original constitutional intent?

This chapter begins with a brief history of punishment, followed by a discussion of bail and fines. Next the issue of what constitutes cruel and unusual punishment is explored, including an in-depth examination of capital punishment. The chapter concludes with a look at how the Eighth Amendment affects corrections.

A Brief History of Punishment

If you found the processes of institutions such as the Star Chamber and the Inquisition revolting, the means by which punishment has been inflicted over the history of the world is, at the least, as horrific. This description applies to medieval tortures we like to think the modern world is incapable of committing as well as to public humiliation, branding, amputation, and a host of other almost unthinkable means of enforcing the law.

Recognizing a need to somehow ensure human rights, the Massachusetts Body of Liberties, enacted in 1641, provided a right to bail and prohibited cruel and inhumane punishment. The idea of being held in prison for an indefinite time without any opportunity for even temporary release was an abhorrent thought to those who knew how restrictive government could be.

The Massachusetts Bay Colony, founded by the Puritans, sought to eliminate such English punishments as cutting off hands and burning at the stake. The Body of Liberties allowed the death penalty for religious offenses such as blasphemy but not for burglary and robbery, which were capital crimes in England. Society itself determined and continues to decide the boundaries of reasonable and unreasonable punishment.

As the colonies considered versions of what was to become the Eighth Amendment, the prohibition on the way things had been done stirred debate, with one representative declaring, "It is sometimes necessary to hang a man, villains often deserve whipping, and perhaps having their ears cut off, but are we in the future to be prevented from inflicting these punishments because they are cruel?" (Monk, n.d., p. 173).

In a sense, the correctional system itself speaks to Eighth Amendment and other constitutional issues overall. Our legal system reflects norms but cannot by design change overnight. We would not want it changed on a whim or as a result of politics. Instead, our criminal justice system is responsive, not reactive, to social changes. In *Trop v. Dulles* (1958), Chief Justice Earl Warren observed, "The basic concept underlying the Eighth Amendment is nothing less than the dignity of man.... The amendment must draw its meaning from the evolving standards of decency that mark the progress of a maturing society."

As has been the case with correctional changes brought on by research, the civil rights movement, and different beliefs in how people should be treated and held accountable, Eighth Amendment law has continued to develop to reflect U.S. beliefs, including the tenets of punishment itself.

> **MYTH**
> Anyone arrested is guaranteed bail.
>
> **FACT**
> Not true. The Eighth Amendment only proscribes excessive bail. It does not guarantee bail is available to everyone.

> **LO2** Bail serves two purposes. First, it helps ensure the appearance of the accused at court proceedings. Second, it maintains the presumption of innocence by allowing individuals not yet convicted of a crime to avoid continued incarceration. The Constitution does not guarantee a right to bail; it only prohibits excessive bail, which it does not define.

bail money or property pledged by a defendant for pretrial release from custody that would be forfeited should the defendant fail to appear at subsequent court proceedings

ROR released on their own recognizance; no bail money is required

Bail

The first part of the Eighth Amendment deals with granting bail to individuals accused of crimes. Bail is actually a verb and a noun, dealing with *pretrial release*. **Bail** is the act of pretrial release of a defendant whose promise to return to trial is secured by some form of collateral, most often money, which is also referred to as *bail*.

Bail allows individuals time to prepare a defense and to continue earning income if employed. Only *excessive* bail is prohibited by the Constitution. Bail itself is not guaranteed, and the Eighth Amendment has never been fully incorporated under the Fourteenth Amendment to apply to the states. Although portions of the Eight Amendment have been incorporated, such as the right to be free from cruel and unusual punishment (*Louisiana ex rel. Francis v. Resweber*, 1947; *Robinson v. California*, 1962), the Court has not, to date, decided whether the Eighth Amendment's prohibition of excessive fines applies to the states through the Fourteenth Amendment's Due Process Clause (*Browning-Ferris Industries v. Kelco Disposal*, 1989). In addition, the Supreme Court has presumed, but not expressly held, that the right against excessive bail is applicable to the states. In *Schilb v. Kuebel* (1971), the Court wrote "the Eighth Amendment's proscription of excessive bail has been assumed to have application to the States through the Fourteenth Amendment." The right to bail has historically been assumed through case law and statutory law rather than a constitutional guarantee.

Bail may be denied in capital cases (those involving the death penalty) and when the accused has threatened possible trial witnesses. Also, the amount of bail does not have to be something the accused can pay. Some poor people cannot afford any bail and must stay in jail, thus generating debate over whether the system caters to those with money while discriminating against those without resources. State law varies on whether juveniles may be eligible for release on bail.

The Evolution of Legislation and Case Law on Bail

Although bail as an option has been determined legislatively and through common law, a progression of federal laws has forged codified bail law. (Note the change in emphasis of this law and who the law is primarily seeking to protect.) The Judiciary Act of 1789 provided for bail in noncapital crimes.

The Bail Reform Act of 1966

The Bail Reform Act of 1966 helped indigent defendants who were unable to post bail in the usual monetary manner. This law was enacted to ensure that poor defendants would not remain in jail only because they could not afford bail, as well as to require judges to consider other ways for defendants to guarantee their return for trial. The Bail Reform Act of 1966 allowed judges to consider the defendant's background, family ties, and prior record in setting bail. Under this comprehensive statute, the primary bail condition was for defendants to be released on their own recognizance, or **ROR,** which means the court trusts them to appear in court when required. Some jurisdictions refer to this bail condition as RPR, released on personal recognizance. No bail money is required. Criteria for ROR vary from state to state but usually include the person's residential stability, a good employment record, and no previous convictions.

The Bail Reform Act of 1984

The Bail Reform Act of 1984 (18 U.S.C. §3141) granted judicial authority to include specific conditions of release for the community's safety. It also eliminated a presumption in favor of pretrial release through the bail process, allowing a court to deny bail for defendants when the prosecution is able to demonstrate, during a hearing, clear and convincing evidence that no conditions will reasonably ensure the community's safety.

The Bail Reform Act requires the federal government to assume that the accused will be released and that the court should seek the least restrictive means of detention plausible. Detention alternatives could include outright release or several other options including bail, electronic monitoring, halfway house placement, collateral property, third-party custody, surrendering one's passport, and imposing travel restrictions.

This act also allowed federal courts to deny bail on the basis of danger to the community or of risk to not appear at trial. Known as **preventive detention,** this practice authorized judges to predict the probability of future criminal conduct by those accused of serious offenses and deny bail on those grounds. It is interesting to note that certain crimes carry a presumption of detention, such as federal crimes of terrorism with a penalty of ten years or more, as well as acts of terrorism that transcend national boundaries (see 18 USC 3142[e][3]).

In *Jackson v. Indiana* (1972), the Supreme Court ruled that the government may detain dangerous defendants who may be incompetent to stand trial, and in *Addington v. Texas* (1979), the Court ruled that the government may detain mentally unstable individuals who present a public danger. However, the Jackson Court made clear that these individuals are no less deserving of due process hearings.

Opponents of preventive detention argue that the accused is being punished without trial and that protecting the community is the job of the police, not the purpose of bail. A few months after passage of the Bail Reform Act, in *United States v. Hazzard* (1984), the Supreme Court held that Congress was justified in denying bail to offenders who represent a danger to the community. The Court also upheld preventive detention in *United States v. Salerno* (1987), stating that pretrial detention under this act did not violate due process or the Eighth Amendment. In this case, the government charged Anthony Salerno with 29 counts of racketeering and conspiracy to commit murder. The Court ruled that because the Bail Reform Act contained many procedural safeguards, the government's interest in protecting the community outweighed the individual's liberty. Strongly dissenting to the *Salerno* majority opinion was Justice Thurgood Marshall, who said:

> It is a fair summary of history to say that the safeguards of liberty have frequently been forged in controversies involving not very nice people. Honoring the presumption of innocence is often difficult; sometimes we must pay substantial social costs as a result of our commitment to the values we espouse. But at the end of the day the presumption

preventive detention the right of judges to consider the potential criminal conduct of those accused of serious offenses and deny bail on those grounds

MYTH
Bail is only in place to assure someone shows up to court.

FACT
Although initially this was the purpose of bail, it has been extended to protecting the community at large from the acts of the defendant.

◀ CASE IN BRIEF

United States v. Salerno (1987)

ISSUE Is pretrial detention under the Bail Reform Act unconstitutional when based on a potential threat to the community?

RULING No. If government meets the heavy burden of demonstrating that someone is potentially dangerous, and if the denial of bail is not punitive, then pretrial detention is constitutional.

of innocence protects the innocent; the shortcuts we take with those whom we believe to be guilty injure only those wrongfully accused and, ultimately, ourselves.

Throughout the world today there are men, women, and children interned indefinitely, awaiting trials that may never come or that may be a mockery of the word, because their governments believe them to be "dangerous." Our Constitution, whose construction began two centuries ago, can shelter us forever from the evils of such unchecked power. Over two hundred years it has slowly, through our efforts, grown more durable, more expansive, and more just. But it cannot protect us if we lack the courage and the self-restraint to protect ourselves.

Nonetheless, several states have incorporated elements of preventive detention into their bail systems, for example, excluding certain crimes from eligibility, including crime control factors in release decisions and limiting the right to bail for defendants previously convicted or for those alleged to have committed crimes while on release.

> **CASE IN BRIEF**
>
> *Stack v. Boyle* (1951)
>
> **ISSUE** Is bail set at a higher level than is necessary to secure the defendant's appearance in court constitutional?
>
> **RULING** No. The amount set for bail to assure appearance must be based on each individual and the facts of the case.

The leading case for bail law is *Stack v. Boyle* (1951), which is interesting for reasons that include the time the case was heard. In *Stack*, the defendants were charged with advocating the violent overthrow of the government during the Cold War, when there was great concern over the threat of communism. In this case, the Supreme Court held that any amount exceeding that necessary to ensure a return to trial violated the Eighth Amendment. Judicial calculation of the appropriate amount would consider such matters as the seriousness of the offense and the corresponding threat to community safety, the government's evidence, the defendant's connection with the community and family, finances, mental condition, criminal record, and any history of failing to appear when released on bail. Justice Fred Vinson stated in the Court's opinion,

> From the passage of the Judiciary Act of 1789, to the present . . . federal law has unequivocally provided that a person arrested for a non-capital offense shall be admitted to bail. This traditional right to freedom before conviction permits the unhampered preparation of a defense, and serves to prevent the infliction of punishment prior to conviction. . . . Unless this right to bail before trial is preserved, the presumption of innocence, secured only after centuries of struggle, would lose its meaning.
>
> The right to release before trial is conditioned upon the accused's giving adequate assurance that he will stand trial and submit to sentence if found guilty. . . . Like the ancient practice of securing the oaths of responsible persons to stand as sureties for the accused, the modern practice of requiring a bail bond or the deposit of a sum of money subject to forfeiture serves as additional assurance of the presence of an accused.

commercial bail using the services of a bail bond person to post a defendant's bail for a fee

In the private bail bonding business, a bail bond provider posts a bond for upward of 10 percent of the bail amount with the court, to be paid if the defendant fails to appear. This process is called **commercial bail**. The bail bond provider will post a person's bond for a fee, in effect making a loan but in a situation that traditional financial institutions may well avoid. If the accused fails to appear in court as ordered, the bail bond provider will often help the police catch the person because the bond company would lose its money. In some states, in fact, bail bond providers and others in the private sector have significant authority to locate "bail jumpers" and bring them before the court.

One issue is who can afford to have bail posted for them or, more importantly, who cannot. This issue is why alternatives have been advocated and accepted, including in appropriate circumstances, release of defendants on their own recognizance if there is sufficient cause to believe their return to court need not be in issue.

The Court specifically held in *Salerno* (1987) that pretrial detention without bail does not violate either due process or the Eighth Amendment rights of a defendant. Therefore, even after *Salerno*, state courts are free to forbid preventive detention of state and local prisoners based on excessive bail provisions in the state constitution or through legislation or case law in that jurisdiction.

Fines

After the accused is convicted of a crime, the Eighth Amendment also prohibits punishment by excessive fines. The question then becomes: What is excessive? For example, should the wealthy be fined at a rate concurrent with their financial status? Should the government not be permitted to punish through high fines, perhaps as an alternative to imprisonment? Until recently, there have been comparatively few cases in this area of constitutional law. Some of these cases have addressed whether there can be excessive fines in civil cases.

The Court has continued to uphold the rule that the Constitution regulates government, and because civil cases are, for the most part, between private parties, the excessive fine prohibition does not apply in the civil area. *Browning-Ferris Industries v. Kelco Disposal* (1989) questioned whether the Eighth Amendment applied to civil punishments as well as criminal punishments. In criminal law, the government is always involved as a party to the case.

In civil lawsuits, the plaintiff usually seeks monetary damages from the defendant to right an alleged wrong. **Compensatory damages** reimburse, or compensate, the plaintiff for actual harm done, such as medical expenses or lost business. Cases that have questioned the amounts awarded have primarily dealt with **punitive damages**, an amount the defendant in a civil case must pay the plaintiff beyond compensatory damages. Punitive damages are meant to be just that, additional punishment to the wrongdoer and a warning to others not to engage in similar conduct.

In *Browning-Ferris Industries*, the Supreme Court ruled that the Eighth Amendment applied to criminal cases and to "direct actions initiated by the government to inflict punishment." Punitive damages in civil cases did not involve government actions, the Court said, so the Eighth Amendment did not apply. The Court noted that although it agreed that punitive damages advance the interest of punishment and deterrence, which are also among the interests advanced by criminal law, it failed to see how this overlap required that the excessive fines clause be applied in cases between private parties.

Asset Forfeiture and the Prohibition against Excessive Fines

An area receiving increasingly significant attention is **asset forfeiture,** the uncompensated government seizure of money and property connected with illegal activity. The use of asset forfeiture by law enforcement has become a means by which a great deal of funding is acquired for prevention programs and equipment. State and federal laws have granted police departments and federal law enforcement the authority to seize and forfeit assets and to receive the proceeds from such activities.

CASE IN BRIEF

Browning-Ferris Industries v. Kelco Disposal (1989)

ISSUE Does the Excessive Fines Clause of the Eighth Amendment apply to a civil-jury award of punitive damages?

RULING No. The Eighth Amendment does not apply to awards in cases between private parties. It restricts only those fines directly imposed by and paid to the government.

compensatory damages reimbursement to the plaintiff for actual harm done, such as medical expenses or lost business

punitive damages fines above and beyond the actual economic loss to punish the defendant in a civil trial

asset forfeiture the seizure by the government, without compensation, of money and property connected with illegal activity

LO3 *Property connected with illegal activity may be forfeited when used as a "conveyance" (including aircraft, ships, and motor vehicles) to transport illicit drugs. Real estate used in association with a crime and money or other negotiable instruments obtained through criminal activity also can be seized, and such seizure is considered a civil sanction by the government.*

The U.S. Marshals Service administers the Department of Justice's Asset Forfeiture Program by managing and disposing of properties seized and forfeited by federal law enforcement agencies and U.S. attorneys nationwide. The three goals of the program are (1) enforcing the law, (2) improving law enforcement cooperation, and (3) enhancing law enforcement through equitable revenue sharing. In 2015, the U.S. Marshals managed $3.1 billion worth of property and assets (U.S. Marshals Service, 2016).

Forfeited assets must be used to further a department's crime-fighting mission. This includes purchasing equipment, paying overtime, improving police facilities, conducting training, building detention facilities, and conducting Drug Abuse Resistance Education (D.A.R.E.) programs. Problems for which forfeiture might be a remedy include illegal drug markets, nuisance properties, street racing, drunk driving, drivers with revoked licenses, and prostitution (Worrall, 2009).

Although forfeiture is considered a civil action initiated by the government and not a criminal action per se, the high court has recognized it as an area subject to the Eighth Amendment because forfeiture "constitutes payment to a sovereign as punishment for some offense . . . and, as such, is subject to the limitations of the Eighth Amendment's Excessive Fines Clause" (*Austin v. United States*, 1993). Other constitutional questions forfeiture law raises are whether it constitutes cruel and unusual punishment, double jeopardy, and a denial of due process.

CASE IN BRIEF

Austin v. United States (1993)

ISSUE Does the Excessive Fines Clause apply to asset forfeitures?

RULING Yes. Because the Eighth Amendment protects against punishment, and forfeiture is a type of punishment, the Excessive Fines Clause applies.

In *Austin*, the defendant pled guilty to selling two grams of cocaine, valued at $200, and the government seized property belonging to him (including his business) that netted a profit to the government of $32,000. The Supreme Court unanimously ruled that the Eighth Amendment prohibition against excessive fines applies to civil forfeiture proceedings against property connected to drug trafficking. The Court explained that the focus is not on whether the action in question is civil or criminal but instead on whether the government action is punishment, holding that the amount seized by the forfeiture must bear some relation to the value of the illegal enterprise under the Eighth Amendment prohibition on excessive fines. A fine is considered a payment to a sovereign for committing an offense. This decision is the first constitutional limitation on the government's power to seize property connected with illegal activity and could result in challenges to seizures related to criminal activity.

In *United States v. Bajakajian* (1998), the Court ruled that a $357,144 forfeiture for failing to report to U.S. Customs that more than $10,000 was being taken out of the country was "grossly disproportionate" to the offense. The Court explained that forfeiture is a payment "in kind" to the government and is, thus, a fine if it is punishment for committing some offense; therefore, the Excessive Fines Clause applies.

The Supreme Court held in *United States v. Ursery* (1996) that forfeiture is not double jeopardy because it is considered a civil sanction rather than an additional criminal action. Due process requires that property not be forfeited without a hearing (*United States v. Good*, 1993), but the Court has also held that forfeiture is constitutional even when the owner is not aware of its criminal use. In *Bennis v. Michigan* (1996), Mrs. Bennis argued it was unconstitutional for the government to seize a car of which she was part owner. Her husband was using it when he was arrested for engaging in prostitution, even though she had no knowledge of the crime. In disallowing her claim, the Court referred to "a long and unbroken line of cases in which this Court has held that an owner's interest in property may be forfeited by reason of the use to which the property is put even though the owner did not know that it was to be put to such use."

In 2000 Congress approved the Civil Asset Forfeiture Reform Act, curbing federal law enforcement agencies' asset forfeiture authority and adding due process protections to ensure that property is not unjustly taken from innocent owners. Shortly before the approval, Rep. Henry J. Hyde (R-IL) commented, "Civil asset forfeiture as allowed in our country today is a throwback to the old Soviet Union, where justice is the justice of the government and the citizen did not have a chance." In forfeiture cases, the government must establish that the property was subject to forfeiture by a "preponderance of the evidence" rather than the original higher standard of "clear and convincing." The statute of limitations is five years.

Cruel and Unusual Punishment

The final clause of the Eighth Amendment forbids punishments that are "cruel and unusual," but it does not say what those punishments are. What is cruel and unusual?

The easy answer, which is also the correct one, is that cruel and unusual punishment depends on what a society believes it to be. Just as our previous definition of law includes the idea that law supports the society's current norms, how a society punishes offenders is also directly related to current acceptable norms.

> **LO4** In Trop v. Dulles (1958), Chief Justice Warren stated that the Cruel and Unusual Punishment Clause "must draw its meaning from the evolving standards of decency that mark the progress of a maturing society."

In *Trop*, the Supreme Court restored a soldier's citizenship he had lost as a result of being found guilty of desertion from the army, finding the punishment too extreme. As Justice Marshall noted in a later case, "A penalty that was permissible at one time in our nation's history is not necessarily permissible today." Thus, common punishments during the 1790s, such as whippings and pillories, are no longer constitutional in the twenty-first century.

Although this text emphasizes U.S. law and the events leading to the formation of current law, it is interesting to observe how other countries and cultures, both past and present, determine punishment. Because law in any society seeks to respond to its present needs, always in flux, the punishments considered appropriate also change. Perhaps the "extremity" of the available punishment forms tends to change, as do the society's overall social feelings.

For example, although Americans are steadfast in their belief that crime must be curtailed "at any price," the caning (whipping) of young American Michael Fay in Singapore in 1994, who was found guilty of damage to property, outraged many. Yet, the crime rate in Singapore is considerably lower than that in the United States. So what is appropriate punishment? It is what a society defines it as.

In *Coker v. Georgia* (1977), the Court held that a "punishment is 'excessive' and unconstitutional if it (1) makes no measurable contribution to acceptable goals of punishment and hence is nothing more than the purposeless and needless imposition of pain and suffering or (2) is grossly out of proportion to the severity of the crime." In seeking a more specific answer to what constitutes cruel and unusual punishment, courts have used three inquiries in assessing constitutionality (Clear, Cole, & Reisig, 2006, p. 109):

- Whether the punishment shocks the general conscience of a civilized society
- Whether the punishment is unnecessarily cruel
- Whether the punishment goes beyond legitimate penal aims

proportionality analysis
in essence, making the punishment fit the crime

The Supreme Court established three criteria for **proportionality analysis** of sentences in *Solem v. Helm* (1983):

> A court's proportionality analysis under the Eighth Amendment should be guided by objective criteria, including (1) the gravity of the offense and the harshness of the penalty; (2) the sentences imposed on other criminals in the same jurisdiction; and (3) the sentences imposed for the commission of the same crime in other jurisdictions.

LO5 *The general rule under the Eighth Amendment is that punishments must be proportional or directly related to the crime committed.*

For example, in *Robinson v. California* (1962), the Supreme Court found "excessive" a 90-day jail term for the crime of being "addicted to the use of narcotics." Robinson was not under the influence of drugs when arrested, and the only evidence against him was the scars and needle marks on his arms. The Court believed the defendant was being punished for the mere status of being an addict, not for actual criminal behavior. Conversely, in *Harmelin v. Michigan* (1991), the Supreme Court upheld a mandatory life sentence without parole for a first-time cocaine conviction.

In *Pulley v. Harris* (1984), the Court held that although many states require proportionality review, nothing in the Court's decisions interpreting the Eighth Amendment requires a state appellate court, before affirming a death penalty, to compare the sentence in that case to penalties imposed in similar cases if the defendant requests such a comparison.

In *Ewing v. California* (2003), the high court considered whether a sentence of 25 years to life imprisonment for felony theft under a "three strikes" sentencing schedule was cruel and unusual. They held 5–4 that California's "three strikes" law did not violate the Eighth Amendment. The Court reached the same result in *Lockyer v. Andrade* (2003).

CASE IN BRIEF

Graham v. Florida (2010)

ISSUE Does sentencing a juvenile to life without parole violate the Eighth Amendment?

RULING Yes. The Eighth Amendment prohibits life without parole for juvenile offenders convicted of a nonhomicide offense.

However, in *Graham v. Florida* (2010), the Supreme Court held that a life sentence, without the chance of parole, for a juvenile convicted of a nonhomicide crime violates the Eighth Amendment clause against cruel and unusual punishment. Terrance Graham was 16 years old when he committed armed burglary and another crime. Under a plea agreement, the Florida trial court sentenced Graham to probation and withheld adjudication of guilt. Subsequently, the trial court found that Graham had violated the terms of his probation by committing additional crimes. The trial court then adjudicated Graham guilty of the previous charges, revoked his probation, and sentenced him to life in prison for the burglary. Because Florida has abolished its parole system, the life sentence left Graham no possibility of release except executive clemency. Graham challenged his sentence under the Eighth Amendment's cruel and unusual punishments clause, but the Florida First District Court of Appeal affirmed. Graham's case was granted certiorari by the Supreme Court, which held:

> The concept of proportionality is central to the Eighth Amendment. Embodied in the Constitution's ban on cruel and unusual punishments is the "precept of justice that punishment for crime should be graduated and proportioned to [the] offense."

In sum, penological theory is not adequate to justify life without parole for juvenile nonhomicide offenders. This determination, the limited culpability of juvenile nonhomicide offenders, and the severity of life without parole sentences all lead to the conclusion that the sentencing practice under consideration is cruel and unusual. This Court now holds that for a juvenile offender who did not commit homicide the Eighth Amendment forbids the sentence of life without parole. This clear line is necessary to prevent the possibility that life without parole sentences will be imposed on juvenile nonhomicide offenders who are not sufficiently culpable to merit that punishment. Because "[t]he age of 18 is the point where society draws the line for many purposes between childhood and adulthood," those who were below that age when the offense was committed may not be sentenced to life without parole for a nonhomicide crime....

A state need not guarantee the offender eventual release, but if it imposes a sentence of life it must provide him or her with some realistic opportunity to obtain release before the end of that term. The judgment of the First District Court of Appeal of Florida was reversed, and the case was remanded for further proceedings not inconsistent with this opinion.

The *Graham* decision was added to in *Miller v. Alabama* (2012) when the Court stated that "mandatory life without parole for those under the age of 18 at the time of their crimes violates the Eighth Amendment's prohibition on 'cruel and unusual punishments.'" Although the Court did not say such a sentence could never be handed down, a state law *mandating* such a sentence in *every* case was unconstitutional. In addition, the Court held in *Montgomery v. Louisiana* (2015) that the rule established in *Miller* is a substantive constitutional rule and is to be applied retroactively, even to cases that have been finalized. As a side note, the *Graham* decision is interesting not only because it involved a categorical ban on life sentence for juveniles convicted of nonhomicides but because the Court also looked at other countries to aid its decision in determining what is constitutional.

The Supreme Court tackled the issue of **corporal punishment** (causing bodily harm) in *Ingraham v. Wright* (1977). James Ingraham, a junior high school student, had been hit more than 20 times with a paddle for disobeying a teacher's order. He required medical attention and missed 11 days of school. The Court held, "The state itself may impose such corporal punishment as is necessary for the proper education of the child for the maintenance of group discipline." Furthermore, the Court stated, "The school child has little need for protection of the Eighth Amendment because the openness of the public school and its Supervision by the community affords significant safeguards against the kinds of abuses from which the Eighth Amendment protects the prisoner." This case is included as an example of the controversy that continues, both in the courtroom and elsewhere, as to what consequences are appropriate in the home, school, and court. This does not, however, preclude various civil causes of action a child or parent could bring in court.

corporal punishment
causing bodily harm through physical force, for example, whipping, flogging, or beating

Punishment Options

Few dispute the necessity of punishment as a means of social control in an ordered society. As Cicero noted in *Pro Milone* (50 B.C.E.), "The greatest incitement to crime is the hope of escaping punishment." The challenge is in determining what the most appropriate and effective punishment might be.

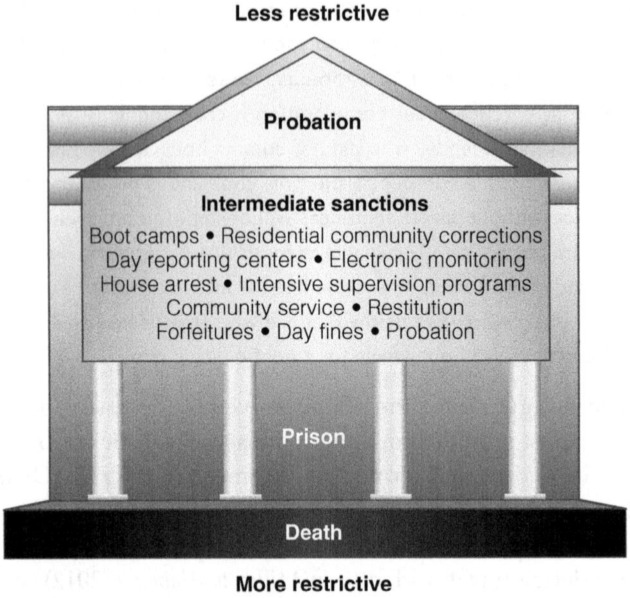

Figure 12.1 The Sentencing Continuum
Source: CARLSON et al. *Corrections in the 21st Century.* © 1999 Wadsworth, a part of Cengage Learning, Inc. Reproduced by permission. www.cengage.com/permissions.

The U.S. criminal justice system continues to work with different ways to meet the goals of punishment, incorporating rehabilitation when possible. Many options are available on the continuum of possibilities, as illustrated in Figure 12.1, including probation, parole, length and types of incarceration, restitution, and new ideas that continue to evolve from the corrections component of the criminal justice system.

Table 12.1 expands on these sentencing options, showing how they relate to the law on the books and the law in action. Of course, particularly heinous crime does not lend itself to the lesser sanctions, but new possibilities continue to present themselves. Not all of these options meet the expectations of the public or politicians. Because new paradigms are not necessarily readily embraced, new correctional concepts are understandably challenged. The real challenge, however, is to honestly inquire whether existing means work and, when they do not, what might. When the prison sanction is selected, the result is often much litigation in this area of Eighth Amendment law that pertains to prisoner treatment.

Physical Forms of Punishment

Modern technology presents several possible treatments for criminals, including Antabuse, a drug used in treating alcoholics by causing nausea and vomiting when alcohol is ingested. Sex offenders have been treated with Depo-Provera, a drug that reduces the sex drive. Use of such drugs and surgical procedures, such as castration and lobotomy, may run counter to the Eighth Amendment's ban on cruel and unusual punishment.

Although other forms of bodily punishment for criminals have disappeared, the death penalty remains in use and is controversial. The Supreme Court has decided

Table 12.1 Sentencing Options

	Law on the books[a]	Law in action
Prison	A correctional facility for housing adults convicted of felony offenses, usually under the control of state government.	More than 1.5 million adults (1,561,500) were incarcerated in either a state or federal prison at year end 2014.[b]
		Males were imprisoned at 5.5 times the rate of females, and females comprised 7.2 percent of the 2014 prison population.[b]
		In 2014, blacks and Hispanics were imprisoned at higher rates than whites in all age groups for both male and female inmates.[b]
Parole	Adults conditionally released to community supervision after serving part of a prison term. The parolee is subject to being returned to prison for rule violations or other offenses.	Nearly 856,900 adults were on parole at year end 2014.[c]
		Twelve percent of parolees in 2014 were women.[c]
		Forty-three percent of parolees in 2014 were white non-Hispanic.[c]
		Nearly one-third (31 percent) of parolees in 2014 were being supervised for a violent offense.[c]
Probation	Punishment for a crime that allows the offender to remain in the community without incarceration but subject to certain conditions.	An estimated 3,864,100 adults were on probation under federal, state, or local jurisdiction at year end 2014.[c]
		More than half (56 percent) of all offenders on probation in 2014 committed a felony, and nearly 1 in 5 (19 percent) were being supervised for a violent offense.[c]
Intermediate Sanctions	A variety of punishments that are more restrictive than traditional probation but less stringent than incarceration.	Much less costly than imprisonment.
		Community service requires offender to perform public service such as street cleaning or hospital volunteer work.
		Electronic monitoring ensures that a probationer does not leave home except to go to work.
Fines	A sum of money to be paid to the government by a convicted person as punishment for an offense.	Often used for misdemeanor offenses.
		Recent research shows that it can be effectively used to punish selected felonies.
Restitution	Requirement that the offender pay to the victim a sum of money to make good the loss.	Most defendants are so poor that they cannot reasonably be expected to make restitution.
Capital Punishment	The use of the death penalty (execution) as the punishment for the commission of a particular crime.	At year end 2013, 2,979 prisoners were on death row.[d]
		Fifty-six percent of death row inmates in 2013 were white.[d]
		Ninety-eight percent of death row inmates in 2013 were male.[d]
		At year end 2013, all 35 states with death penalty statutes, as well as the federal government, authorized lethal injection as a method of execution.[d]

[a] From Neubauer, D.W., & Fradella, H.F. (2014). *America's Courts & the Criminal Justice System*, 11E. Wadsworth, a part of Cengage Learning, Inc. Reproduced by permission. www.cengage.com/permissions.

[b] Carson, E.A, (2015, September). *Prisoners in 2014*. (NCJ 248955.) Washington, DC: U.S. Department of Justice, Bureau of Justice Statistics.

[c] Kaeble, D.; Maruschak, L.M.; & Bonczar, T.P. (2015, November). *Probation and Parole in the United States, 2014*. (NCJ 249057.) Washington, DC: Bureau of Justice Statistics.

[d] Snell, T.L. (2014, December 19). *Capital Punishment, 2013—Statistical Tables*. (NCJ 248448.) Washington, DC: U.S. Department of Justice, Bureau of Justice Statistics.

many cases on the constitutionality of capital punishment. It has also defined the nature of cruel and unusual punishment in noncapital cases. However, the death penalty remains the most debated issue under the Eighth Amendment because it concerns the ultimate issue: life or death.

Capital Punishment

The death penalty dates back centuries. History records many brutal methods of execution, including being buried alive, thrown to wild animals, drawn and quartered, boiled in oil, burned, stoned, drowned, impaled, crucified, pressed to death, smothered, stretched on a rack, disemboweled, beheaded, hanged, or shot. In biblical times, criminals were stoned to death or crucified. The ancient Greeks, in a much more humane fashion, administered poison from the hemlock tree to execute criminals. The Romans, in contrast, used beheading, clubbing, strangling, drawing and quartering, or feeding to the lions. During the Dark Ages, ordeals were devised to serve as both judgment and punishment. These ordeals included being submerged in water or in boiling oil, crushed under huge boulders, or forced to do battle with skilled swordsmen. It was presumed the innocent would survive the ordeal; the guilty would be killed by it. Later, in France, the guillotine became the preferred means of execution.

The death penalty has been an established feature of the U.S. criminal justice system since colonial times, with hanging the preferred method of execution in early years, especially on the frontier. Means of execution evolved as states sought more humane ways of killing their condemned—from hangings to the first electrocution in 1890, the invention of the gas chamber in 1923, the use of the firing squad, and finally, the addition of lethal injection, now the predominant method of execution in the United States. At mid-year 2016, 31 states plus the U.S. military and the federal government authorized the death penalty. The five means of execution currently used in the United States are death by firing squad (used by 1 state), hanging (used by 3 states), gas chamber (3 states), electric chair (7 states), and lethal injection (31 states, the U.S. military, and the federal government) (National Conference of State Legislatures, 2016).

Until the middle of the nineteenth century, the death penalty was the automatic sentence for a convicted murderer. State laws began to draw distinctions between degrees of murder, but the death penalty was still automatic for first-degree murderers. By the early twentieth century, however, state legislatures had given jurors more discretion in sentencing. The jurors were given no guidance by state law in choosing between life and death sentences. Jurors had total discretion in this decision, which could not be reviewed on appeal.

Historically, most criminals facing capital punishment were sentenced under state, not federal, law. Thus, the Eighth Amendment's prohibition against cruel and unusual punishment was not relevant to the overwhelming majority of death penalty cases until the Supreme Court incorporated it to apply to the states in *Robinson v. California* (1962).

Is Capital Punishment Cruel and Unusual?

Of the five means by which the death penalty is carried out in the United States, the Supreme Court has found none of them inherently cruel and unusual, but not without judicial controversy and public dissension. Only hanging has been challenged in federal court and held not to be cruel and unusual (*Campbell v. Blodgett*, 1994), except in the case of a 400-plus pound man because the result of hanging was likely to be decapitation (*Rupe v. Wood*, 1994).

Although today's methods are said to be more civilized, accounts of witnesses to executions raise doubts as to whether progress has been made. Executions by means of poisonous gas and electrocution have occasionally resulted in horrific stories of lingering, painful deaths. For example, during the much publicized 1997 Florida execution of Pedro Medina, who was convicted of killing a police officer, flames shot some 12 inches high from Medina's head while he sat strapped to the state's 74-year-old electric chair, referred to as "Old Sparky." Yet death by such means has not been held to be unconstitutional. Lethal injection is considered by some to be the only politically correct method of capital punishment.

The issue of cruel and unusual punishment has a long history and has given the courts great difficulty in defining it. In *Furman v. Georgia* (1972), the Court's opinion was more than 230 pages. All nine justices wrote separate opinions trying to define the meaning of four words: *cruel and unusual punishment.* In this case, William Furman had broken into a private home in the middle of the night, intending only to burglarize it, although he was carrying a gun. Furman attempted to escape when the homeowner awoke. Furman tripped and his gun discharged, hitting and killing the owner through a closed door. Furman was black; the homeowner was white. Furman was sentenced to death.

In consolidating three other cases with Furman's (all involving white victims and black defendants but having little else in common), the Supreme Court considered the varied public opinions regarding the death penalty. The court ruled that the death penalty *as then administered* in Georgia was cruel and unusual punishment because it was "wantonly and freakishly" imposed. Judges and juries had far too much unguided discretion under current state laws, and the Supreme Court held this led to arbitrary and capricious, or random and unreasonable, death sentences and, thus, violated due process.

In *Furman*, the Supreme Court did not rule the death penalty was unconstitutional in all circumstances. Rather, the Court held that the states had to give judges and juries more guidance in capital sentencing to prevent discretionary use of the death penalty. It held that Georgia's death penalty law, as administered, was invalid.

In effect, the *Furman* case put on hold capital punishment statutes in 37 states, and executions across the country were suspended as a result. In response, about three-fourths of the states and the federal government passed new death penalty laws, in many instances instituting a two-step trial procedure: the first step to determine innocence or guilt and the second step to determine whether to seek the death penalty. Such a two-stage trial is often referred to as a **bifurcated trial.** While reviewing these laws, the Supreme Court finally decided whether the death penalty was inherently cruel and unusual punishment.

Four years after *Furman*, in *Gregg v. Georgia* (1976), the Court sustained a revised Georgia death penalty law by a 7–2 margin, stating, "A punishment is unconstitutionally cruel and unusual only if it violates the evolving levels of decency that define a civilized society. The death penalty today in the United States does not do that—as is proved by public opinion substantially favoring executions, by legislatures enacting death penalty statutes or refusing to repeal them, and by courts willing to sentence hundreds of murderers to death every year." The Court also affirmed the importance of a bifurcated trial.

bifurcated trial a two-step trial for capital cases: the first step is determination of innocence or guilt; the second step, if the defendant is found guilty, is determination of whether to seek the death penalty

L06 Furman v. Georgia (1972) was the landmark case in which the Supreme Court called for a ban on the death penalty in Georgia, ruling its law as it stood was capricious and, hence, cruel and unusual punishment.

In Gregg v. Georgia (1976), the Supreme Court reinstated the Georgia death penalty by sustaining its revised death penalty law. Gregg also held that capital cases require two proceedings: one to determine guilt or innocence and the other to determine the sentence.

In rendering its opinion the Court recognized the significance of public opinion, citing strong public support for the death penalty. The Court noted that three-fourths of state legislatures re-enacted the death penalty after *Furman*; therefore, the death penalty was not "unusual" punishment. In a strong dissent, Justice William Brennan repeated the arguments he had made against the death penalty in *Furman*. Brennan questioned "whether a society for which the dignity of the individual is the supreme value can, without a fundamental inconsistency, follow the practice of deliberately putting some of its members to death. . . . Even the most vile criminal remains a human being possessed of common human dignity." Brennan concluded:

This Court inescapably has the duty, as the ultimate arbiter of the meaning of our Constitution, to say whether, when individuals condemned to death stand before our Bar, "moral concepts" require us to hold that the law has progressed to the point where we should declare that the punishment of death, like punishments on the rack, the screw and the wheel, is no longer morally tolerable in our society.

CASE IN BRIEF ▶

Baze v. Rees (2008)

ISSUE Is the use of the three-drug lethal injection scheme constitutional?

RULING Yes. The lethal injection scheme the state has in place does not violate the Constitutional ban on cruel and unusual punishment because, if performed correctly, it was "humane."

In *Baze v. Rees* (2008), the Court considered the appeal of Ralph Baze and Thomas Bowling, who were sentenced to death in Kentucky. The men argued that executing them by lethal injection would violate the Eighth Amendment prohibition of cruel and unusual punishment. Under court precedent, lethal injection must not inflict "unnecessary pain," and the men's attorneys argued that the chemicals used to kill them carried an unnecessary risk of inflicting pain during the process. The case had nationwide implications because the specific three-drug protocol used for lethal injection in Kentucky was the same as that used by virtually all states authorizing lethal injection. An effective moratorium on executions in the United States took place because certiorari was granted in this case.

In 2008 in a "fragmented" 7–2 decision, with seven justices writing separate decisions, the Supreme Court upheld Kentucky's three-drug protocol for execution by lethal injection. According to Chief Justice John Roberts, in death penalty challenges claiming the method constitutes cruel and unusual punishment, the prisoner must:

1. Show that the method of execution presents a substantial risk of serious harm
2. Identify an alternative that is feasible, readily implemented, and in fact significantly reduces the substantial risk of pain

Only when these conditions of the *Baze* rule have been met will a state's refusal to adopt alternative procedures be considered a violation of the Eighth Amendment. Thus, the focus of the courts is not whether the death penalty itself is constitutional but, rather, whether the manner in which it is carried out is constitutional.

Since *Baze*, lethal injection drugs have become difficult to obtain by states. Anti-death penalty advocates have successfully pressured several manufacturers to refuse to sell the drugs to states for use in executions, forcing states to find other suitable drugs. In the case of *Glossip v. Gross* (2015), prisoners in Oklahoma challenged the state's use of midazolam in its three-drug lethal injection protocol. Midazolam has replaced two drugs that are no longer available in the United

States. In *Glossip*, the prisoners' argument was that the dose of midazolam used by the state violates the prohibition against cruel and unusual punishment because it was not enough to maintain unconsciousness, and therefore would expose the prisoner to a substantial risk of pain when the second and third drugs were administered. However, the prisoners failed to show evidence that this was, in fact, the case. In addition, and as required by *Baze*, the prisoners failed to show that a feasible alternative existed and was available which would present a lesser risk of pain.

Are Lengthy Delays in Execution Cruel and Unusual?

Justices Stephen Breyer and Clarence Thomas have engaged in an unusual public debate over whether long delays in carrying out executions constitute cruel and unusual punishment. Justice Breyer believes the Court should consider this question and dissented when the Court declined to hear arguments in two cases that raised it: *State v. Moore* (2006) and *Knight v. Florida* (1999). Justice Thomas, on the other hand, is indignant that death row inmates could seek to take advantage of what he called "this court's Byzantine death penalty jurisprudence" and then complain when their appeals cause lengthy delays in their executions. Justice Thomas said that, in his view, the question of whether long delays in carrying out death sentences are unconstitutional has been decided, and the answer is no: "I write only to point out that I am unaware of any support in the American Constitutional tradition or in this court's precedent for the proposition that a defendant can avail himself of the panoply of the appellate and collateral procedures and then complain when his execution is delayed." In *Thompson v. McNeil* (2009), the Supreme Court rejected an appeal by convicted murderer William Lee Thompson, who claimed that his 32-year imprisonment caused by his appeals constituted "cruel and unusual punishment."

Who Can Be Executed?

As a general rule, the Supreme Court has upheld the death penalty for murder but not for other crimes. Under the Eighth Amendment, the punishment must be related to the crime, so execution is appropriate only in cases of murder—a life for a life. In many states, new death penalty sentencing systems require judges and juries to consider aggravating factors and mitigating factors in each capital case and to apply the death penalty in only the most heinous cases.

Some such sentencing systems were challenged. For example, in *Maynard v. Cartwright* (1988), the Court held that an Oklahoma statute allowing a jury to impose the death penalty if the murder was "especially heinous, atrocious or cruel" was unconstitutional because it did not sufficiently guide the jury's decision. However, in *Arave v. Creech* (1993), the Court upheld an Idaho law identifying as an aggravating circumstance a murderer who showed "utter disregard for human life."

In 2002 in *Bell v. Cone*, the Supreme Court ruled against Tennessee death row inmate Gary Cone, who claimed his lawyer was incompetent. The Court signaled it will take a narrow view of death row inmates' claims that their lawyers were incompetent. However, because the death penalty is involved, claims will be scrutinized.

A series of cases have addressed the eligibility of individuals found guilty of murder or other "heinous crimes" who might be sentenced to death. This arena is where much of the action on the Eighth Amendment has taken place in the past few years. Issues involve age, race, mental retardation, and mental illness.

Age In *Eddings v. Oklahoma* (1982), the Supreme Court vacated the death sentence of a 16-year-old boy by a 5–4 vote. In *Thompson v. Oklahoma* (1988) the Court held:

> Less blameworthiness should attach to a crime committed by a juvenile than one committed by an adult because inexperience, less education and less intelligence make the juvenile less able to appreciate the consequences of his or her conduct while, at the same time, such conduct is more apt to be influenced by peer pressure. Given this lesser culpability, the retributive purpose of the death penalty is not applicable to a 15-year-old offender. Moreover, since 18 states now prohibit imposing the death sentence on an offender less than 16 years old and another 14 states have abolished the death penalty entirely, it is likely there is a national consensus that imposing the death penalty on a 15-year-old today would offend the conscience of the community.

Unlike *Eddings*, *Stanford v. Kentucky* (1989) held, "In the absence of any historical or modern society consensus against imposing capital punishment on 16- and 17-year-old murderers, such death sentences do not violate the Eighth Amendment."

These cases lead to *Roper v. Simmons* (2005), which held that the Eighth and Fourteenth Amendments will not permit executing anyone under 18 years of age for committing a crime. In this case, Christopher Simmons was 17 years old when he received the death sentence for murdering Shirley Crook while burglarizing her home, and then, with the help of an even younger accomplice, throwing her bound body off a cliff in a park. He appealed on the grounds that the death penalty was cruel and unusual punishment because of his age when he committed the crime. Simmons gave a full confession, even providing a videotaped re-enactment of his crime. In a 5–4 vote, Justice Anthony Kennedy wrote, "When a juvenile offender commits a heinous crime, the State can exact forfeiture of some of the most basic liberties, but the State cannot extinguish his life and his potential to attain a mature understanding of his own humanity," referring to Justice John Paul Stevens's quote regarding evolving standards of decency marking a maturing society.

Justice Kennedy also wrote, "The objective of national consensus here—the rejection of the juvenile death penalty in the majority of states; the infrequency of its use even where it remains on the books; and the consistency in the trend toward abolition of the practice—provides sufficient evidence that today our society views juveniles, in the words . . . used respecting the mentally retarded, as 'categorically less culpable than the average criminal.'"

Race In *McCleskey v. Kemp* (1987), Warren McCleskey presented a thorough statistical study contending that capital punishment in Georgia was filled with racial discrimination. The Court ruled that even if the study was valid, McCleskey had not proved the sentence was the result of racial discrimination.

Just as controversy surrounds whether the criminal justice system in general is biased, cases involving the death penalty raise the issue of bias as well: "The percentage of Blacks who have been executed far exceeds their proportion of

---

CASE IN BRIEF ▶

Roper v. Simmons (2005)

ISSUE Does the execution of a person under the age of 18 violate the Constitution?

RULING Yes. Executing a person under 18 is considered "cruel and unusual" punishment.

the general population. Particularly interesting is that more than 80 percent of the victims of those executed have been White. What makes this finding interesting is that murders, including capital murders, tend to be intraracial. However the death penalty is imposed primarily on the killers of White people, regardless of the race or ethnicity of the offender" (Bohm & Haley, 2007, pp. 329–330). Whether these figures are considered simply factual or disconcerting, the Supreme Court has yet to conclude any constitutional issues are involved.

Intellectual Disability In *Penry v. Lynaugh* (1989), a case involving an intellectually disabled defendant possessing an IQ between 50 and 63 and a mental age of a 6-and-a-half-year-old, the Court held, "Since mentally retarded individuals vary greatly in their mental attributes and thus their limitations, it is not cruel and unusual punishment to impose the death penalty on a retarded defendant who was found competent to stand trial and whose insanity defense was rejected at trial." The defendant's mental state could be considered, but there was no prohibition against executing the mentally ill convicted of a capital offense. (In an interesting side note, just hours before he was to be executed in 1999, Johnny Paul Penry was granted a stay of execution by the U.S. Supreme Court. When told of the stay, his first concern was whether he could still have his last meal of a cheeseburger and French fries. This raises the question, "What is accomplished by executing the intellectually disabled?")

In 2002 the Supreme Court amended its position on capital punishment of the intellectually disabled in *Atkins v. Virginia*, holding that executing the intellectually disabled is cruel and unusual punishment in violation of the Eighth Amendment. The Court recently took on the issue of how "intellectually disabled" is defined so as to determine how states apply *Atkins*. In *Hall v. Florida* (2014), the Court struck down a Florida law which required an IQ score of 70 or lower for a death row inmate to present evidence of intellectual disability. If the IQ score were 71 or higher, as was Hall's, the person was deemed to not be intellectually disabled and subject to execution under *Atkins*. The Court viewed this rule as inflexible to the point of being unconstitutional because it "creates an unacceptable risk that persons with intellectual disability will be executed."

The Mentally Ill Closely related to the question of executing those who are intellectually disabled is the question of forcing a convicted murderer to take drugs to make him sane enough to be executed. The Supreme Court banned execution of the insane in 1986. In *Singleton v. Norris* (2003), the Supreme Court let stand a ruling by a federal appeals court that allowed Arkansas officials to force a convicted murderer to take drugs to make him sane enough to be executed. The Supreme Court held in *Ford v. Wainwright* (1986) that an inmate who became mentally ill while in prison could not be executed.

Appeals

All but one state that has the death penalty require automatic appellate review of death sentences. South Carolina will allow a competent defendant to waive this review. However, there is no such automatic right to have the Supreme Court review every death sentence case, although justices are willing to address many issues having merit.

Because capital punishment is the ultimate sanction a government can inflict, appeals are certain and lengthy. Appeals will be heard by the state courts, and a writ of certiorari may be filed with the Supreme Court. Most capital cases originate in the states, and appeals can be filed directly through the state court system. In addition, the defendants may make indirect or collateral appeals of their sentences through the federal court system by arguing that their constitutional rights have been violated.

Costs of the Death Penalty

Death penalty cases require enormous expenditures on a single defendant. The estimated cost of convicting and executing each offender ranges from $2.5 million to $5 million, a significantly steep price when compared to the less than $1 million spent to house a killer for life without parole (Fagan, 2010). In an era of budget restrictions and tough decisions on how best to allocate limited resources, legislators and taxpayers are directing increased scrutiny toward such costly policies. For example, it is estimated that Florida's death penalty policy costs the state $25 million to $50 million more each year than if it sentenced all murderers to life without parole (Fagan, 2010). Similarly, Indiana taxpayers have spent approximately $37 million more than they would have if the state had sentenced all of the offenders on death row to life without parole instead (Fagan, 2010).

Juries and Capital Punishment Cases

The Supreme Court continues to hear matters pertaining to the death penalty. Whether potential jurors can be excluded because of their objections to the death penalty has been reviewed in several cases, with the *Lockhart v. McCree* (1986) Court determining that jurors whose opposition to the death penalty is so strong that it would prevent or substantially impair the performance of their duties could be removed. In *Morgan v. Illinois* (1992), the Supreme Court held that a prospective juror in a capital case who indicates that if the defendant is found guilty the death penalty should be imposed can be challenged for cause and removed.

In *Simmons v. South Carolina* (1994), the Court held that if the prosecution contends a defendant should be put to death because he is too dangerous to ever return to society, without informing the jury of the option of a sentence of life without parole, this action could be considered a denial of due process.

In June 1999, in *Jones v. United States*, the Supreme Court ruled that juries need not be told the consequences of a deadlock. This case involved the first set of issues to reach the Supreme Court regarding the Federal Death Penalty Act of 1994, which re-established capital punishment at the federal level for a number of crimes. In this case, Louis Jones, Jr., was convicted of kidnapping a woman from an Air Force base, sexually assaulting her, and beating her to death with a tire iron. Jones appealed on the grounds that the jury was not instructed about what would happen if they deadlocked. If they had deadlocked, the judge would have sentenced him to life without parole. Justice Thomas, writing for the majority, believed that telling the jury the consequences of deadlock constitutes "an open invitation for the jury to avoid its responsibility and to disagree." Judge Thomas continued, "In a capital sentencing proceeding, the government has a strong interest in having the jury express the conscience of the community on the ultimate question of life and death. . . . We are of the view that a charge to the jury of the sort proposed by [Jones] might well have the effect of undermining this strong governmental interest."

In *Ring v. Arizona* (2002), the Court ruled that capital punishment can be imposed only by a jury in cases that are tried by the jury. The Court explained that the jury, not the judge, is required to decide, beyond a reasonable doubt, any aggravating factors or any fact that increases the defendant's maximum punishment beyond what is authorized by the jury's guilty verdict. This obligation fulfills the jury's duty as the fact-finder and since *Ring*, the jury is required to make all critical findings in order for the death penalty to be imposed. *Ring* extends the rule from *Apprendi v. New Jersey* (2000), in which the Court stated that any fact that aggravates a sentence must be found as such by a jury. *Ring* made this applicable to death penalty cases. However, in 2004, in *Schriro v. Summerlin*, the Court held that the decision requiring juries, not judges, to impose sentences in capital cases need not be applied retroactively to death row inmates whose sentences already had been affirmed on direct appeal.

This requirement is no longer clearly valid in the wake of the *Hurst* decision. In *Hurst v. Florida* (2016) the Court held that a jury must find each element necessary to impose the death penalty and make a recommendation to the judge. However, the judge is not required to follow the jury's recommendation. This case is important in that it reinforces *Ring*, but it is not "new law" other than that it answers the question about how a judge must handle a jury's recommendation as to a sentence. Alabama also has this system, while other states have a system wherein the judge alone makes the decision, like Montana. Students should be aware that several variations exist.

Continuing Controversy

The death penalty has been and remains extremely controversial, and the debate about the cruel and unusual punishment clause is far from over. It has enjoyed a brief period of prominence, although this prominence may have been achieved at some cost in public perception of the legitimacy of the court's decision-making process. In any event, the court's recent concern with the clause is now seriously threatened by attempts to adopt a more traditional authoritarian approach toward interpreting the clause's language.

Gallup Poll results indicate that the public still supports the death penalty. In October 2015, 61 percent of Americans were in favor of the death penalty as the punishment for murder, the same percentage that supported capital punishment in 2011 (Gallup, 2015). The high point for endorsement for the death penalty was in 1994, when 80 percent of the U.S. public supported it (Saad, 2013). A *Police* magazine survey, to which 2,662 (28 percent) responded, showed that 94 percent of officers supported the death penalty. The primary reason given for favoring the death penalty (96 percent) was that it removed a dangerous person from the population. Another reason given is that capital punishment serves as a powerful deterrent to murder. However, a survey of former and current presidents of the country's top academic criminological societies shows that 88 percent of these experts rejected the notion that the death penalty acts as a deterrent to murder (Death Penalty Information Center, 2016).

Other justifications given for supporting capital punishment are retribution or an eye-for-an-eye morality and fear that violent criminals sentenced to life in prison without parole can actually be paroled ("Officers Support Death Penalty," 2008). To this last reason, Moore (2010, p. 82) recalls the murder of four Lakewood (Washington) police officers gunned down by a convicted killer, Maurice Clemmons, who was serving 108 years in an Arkansas state prison and was granted clemency by then-governor Mike Huckabee: "Twice the government had a chance to keep this man from becoming the mass killer he did; twice it failed to do its job."

How an individual personally responds to such circumstances indicates the emotion that goes into determining what sentences are within our legal confines, with the logical question being whether any particular method serves its purpose. To be sure, debate will continue. The death penalty will be an issue for years to come, with strong advocates and opponents, because at the core of the issue is the question of values.

A modern development affecting the law of criminal procedure is DNA testing, with both prosecutors and defense attorneys putting this compelling evidence to good use. The impact on past cases has proved particularly troubling because of the number of convicted individuals, some awaiting execution, who have since been exonerated through the use of DNA evidence. More than 200 prisoners have been freed since 1989 because of DNA evidence: "Perhaps the worst example . . . occurred in Illinois, where, of 25 prisoners awaiting their fate on death row since 1977, DNA analysis showed a majority could not have committed the murders for which they had been convicted. After the thirteenth prisoner was exonerated, Governor George Ryan in January 2000 announced a moratorium on the death penalty in the state" (Ducat, 2010, p. 583).

The Eighth Amendment and Corrections

Because corrections is an integral component of the criminal justice system, it must be considered along with law enforcement and courts when one learns about the Constitution, as all components are affected by constitutional law. In addition to the rights of those in prison, the study of criminal justice includes consideration of why people are in prison, who makes up prison populations, and whether minorities are disproportionately confined.

The system struggles to understand those who find themselves in prison to better address such issues as prevention, treatment, rehabilitation, and the ever-present question of whether the system is biased. That the statistics reflect a disproportionate number of inmates who are black begs the question of whether the criminal justice system is racist: "The overrepresentation of Blacks in prison is a very heated issue in criminal justice today, and research has not established a consensus on the reasons for that overrepresentation. Currently, however, the weight of the evidence suggests that offense seriousness and prior criminal record generally exert a stronger impact on decisions to imprison than do extralegal factors such as race" (Bohm & Haley, 2007, p. 365). The numbers are a concern, as are the questions of why and how society and the system can best respond.

Due process and equal protection issues are significant concerns in corrections because violations of these rights are unconstitutional. Numbers alone do not provide the answer. Young black and Hispanic males are disproportionately overrepresented in the criminal justice system, and the reasons for this are disputed: "There is no obvious answer. That is one of the reasons recent studies of race and criminal justice find that 'the criminal justice system is neither completely free of racial bias nor systematically racially biased'" (Clear et al., 2006, p. 490). Research, the law, and society as a whole continue to seek enlightenment and provide guidance on such issues of importance to criminal justice.

As with the previous amendments, prisoners have limited constitutional rights, but these rights are not entirely suspended and have been the basis for numerous lawsuits. Eighth Amendment violations are typically divided into two categories: (1) actions against individual prisoners, such as solitary confinement, and (2) institutional conditions to which all inmates are subject. For example, in *Brown v. Plata* (2011) the Supreme Court ruled that adequate medical and mental health care in the California prison system fell below the norms of decency that "inheres in the Eighth Amendment." To remedy this constitutional violation, a three-judge panel, under authority of the Prison Litigation Reform Act (PLRA), ordered that state's prison system to eliminate the overcrowding situation.

The Supreme Court has been called on to determine whether conditions and actions within correctional institutions constitute cruel and unusual punishment in violation of the Eighth Amendment. Courts use two general "frameworks" to evaluate claims of cruel and unusual punishment. In cases that involve conditions of confinement, the standard of deliberate indifference is applied to evaluate the claim. In cases involving use of force, claims are evaluated against a good faith standard.

LO7 *For prisoners, cases based on Eighth Amendment rights involve cruel and unusual punishment, such as overcrowding, solitary confinement, corporal punishment, physical abuse, and the use of force; treatment and rehabilitation; the right not to be treated; and the death penalty.*

Conditions of Confinement and Deliberate Indifference

Conditions and actions relating to confinement are evaluated under the "deliberate indifference" standard, which means that a serious risk to a prisoner is known but that prison officials disregarded that risk. Following are four cases with selected interpretations of the Eighth Amendment as applied to prisoners (Clear & Cole, 2000):

- *Ruiz v. Estelle* (1975) ruled that conditions of confinement in the Texas prison system were unconstitutional.
- *Estelle v. Gamble* (1976) held that deliberate indifference to prisoners' serious medical needs constitutes unnecessary, wanton infliction of pain.
- *Rhodes v. Chapman* (1981) ruled that double-celling and crowding do not necessarily constitute cruel and unusual punishment. The conditions must be shown to involve "wanton and unnecessary infliction of pain" and to be "grossly disproportionate" to the severity of the crime warranting imprisonment.
- *Wilson v. Seiter* (1991) ruled that prisoners must prove prison conditions are objectively cruel and unusual and show they exist because of officials' deliberate indifference.

The issue of second-hand cigarette smoke was addressed in *Helling v. McKinney* (1993). In this case the Court held that the Nevada Department of Prisons "with deliberate indifference, exposed him [McKinney] to levels of ETS [second-hand smoke] that pose an unreasonable risk of serious damage to his future health."

As a result of this case, many correctional facilities have established smoke-free environments or permit smoking only in designated areas or outside. However, many correctional administrators contend that smoking privileges are important in controlling inmate behavior. Not being allowed to smoke may make inmates irritable and aggressive. Ironically, both smokers and nonsmokers claim violation of their Eighth Amendment rights.

Use of Force and Good Faith

When prisoners claim that correctional personnel used force that amounted to cruel and unusual punishment in violation of the Eighth Amendment, the courts will try to determine whether the force was applied in a good faith effort to maintain or restore discipline, or if it was applied maliciously and sadistically in an effort to cause harm.

- *Whitley v. Albers* (1986) held that a prisoner shot in the leg during a riot did not suffer cruel and unusual punishment if the action was taken in good faith to maintain discipline rather than for the mere purpose of causing harm. This case illustrates an important distinction between use of force by prison guards and other correctional staff, in which the actions are judged under the Eighth Amendment, and the force used by police officers, which is a Fourth Amendment issue (Clear & Cole, 2000). The key difference is that, under the Fourth Amendment, the force is used against "free" persons (i.e., those not convicted). (Refer to Chapter 8 and Table 8.2, showing how the "status" of an individual affects how the courts evaluate a use-of-force incident.) In *Albers*, the Court held: "We think the Eighth Amendment, which is specifically concerned with the unnecessary and wanton infliction of pain in penal institutions, serves as the primary source of substantive protection to convicted prisoners in cases such as this one, where the deliberate use of force is challenged as excessive and unjustified."

- The Eighth Amendment standard has also been made applicable to use-of-force incidents in non-riot contexts. In *Hudson v. McMillian* (1992), the Court applied the cruel and unusual punishment test to the force used by prison guards. Inmate Hudson was in an argument with a prison guard named McMillian. While McMillan and several other guards were walking Hudson to a lockdown area, the guards punched and kicked the inmate. The Court said, "Many of the concerns underlying our holding in *Whitley* arise whenever guards use force to keep order. Whether the prison disturbance is a riot or a lesser disruption, corrections officers must balance the need 'to maintain or restore discipline' through force against the risk of injury to inmates." Now, as a result of *Hudson*, whenever a prison official is accused of excessive force in any situation, the test is "whether force was applied in a good-faith effort to maintain or restore discipline, or maliciously and sadistically to cause harm."

Some forms of physical punishment have also been challenged. For example, handcuffing a prison inmate to a post as punishment for bad behavior was found to be cruel and unusual punishment. In *Hope v. Pelzer* (2002), the Court held that

Alabama prisoner Larry Hope did have his Eighth Amendment rights violated when he was handcuffed on two occasions to a hitching post because his behavior was considered disruptive. His arms were held above shoulder level, causing pain and injuries to his arms. Further conduct resulted in Hope spending seven more hours affixed to the post, this time being forced to remain shirtless in the sun. He was provided nothing to drink while at least one guard taunted him about being thirsty. Having previously described cruel and unusual punishment as "unnecessary and wanton pain that is totally without penological justification," the Court held that Hope's Eighth Amendment rights were violated and allowed his civil suit against the guards to move forward.

Other Correctional Issues and the Eighth Amendment

The prisoner management tool of visiting privileges has also been an Eighth Amendment issue. *Overton v. Bazetta* (2003) held it is not cruel and unusual punishment for a prison to suspend visiting privileges for inmates who have failed more than one drug test. Weight lifting in correctional facilities has also been a management tool to help relieve stress for inmates. However, Arizona, Georgia, and North Carolina have banned weight lifting in state prisons and jails, primarily prohibiting use of free weights because they can be used as weapons.

A controversial correctional management tool is the use of chain gangs. Advocates contend that work on a chain gang is appropriate punishment and that it puts criminals to work, giving them the opportunity to make restitution. In addition, the hard work ensures that prison is not pleasant, something society demands. Opponents, however, claim such gangs are a form of cruel and unusual punishment, but courts have not upheld this practice as a violation of the Eighth Amendment.

Summary

The Eighth Amendment protects three rights: a prohibition against excessive bail, excessive fines, and cruel and unusual punishment. Bail serves two purposes. First, it helps ensure the appearance of the accused at court proceedings. Second, it maintains the presumption of innocence by allowing individuals not yet convicted of a crime to avoid continued incarceration. The Constitution does not guarantee a right to bail; it only prohibits excessive bail, which it does not define.

The Bail Reform Act of 1984 established the practice of preventive detention for individuals deemed a threat to society or likely to flee, as well as other options to incarceration. Bail set at a figure higher than an amount reasonably calculated to fulfill its purpose is excessive under the Eighth Amendment (*Stack v. Boyle*, 1951). The excessive bail prohibition has never been formally incorporated to apply to the states under the Fourteenth Amendment, allowing states to deal with it through their constitutions, legislation, and case law. Likewise, the prohibition against excessive fines has not been incorporated, so it does not apply to the states.

One type of fine is asset forfeiture. Property connected with illegal activity may be forfeited when used as a "conveyance" (including aircraft, ships, and motor vehicles) to transport illicit drugs. Real estate used in association with a crime and money, or other negotiable instruments obtained through the criminal activity, also can be seized, and such seizure is considered a civil sanction by the government. The amount seized through asset forfeiture must bear some relation to the value of the illegal enterprise.

In *Trop v. Dulles* (1958), Chief Justice Warren stated that the Cruel and Unusual Punishment Clause "must draw its meaning from the evolving standards of decency that mark the progress of a maturing society." The general rule under the Eighth Amendment is that punishment must be proportional or directly related to the crime committed.

Although capital punishment may appear to be cruel and unusual, the Supreme Court has not held this to be the case. However, in certain instances, the Court has found states to be in violation of its citizens' due process protection. *Furman v. Georgia* (1972) was the landmark case in which the Supreme Court called for a ban on the death penalty in Georgia, ruling its law was capricious and, hence, cruel and unusual punishment. In *Gregg v. Georgia* (1976), the Supreme Court reinstated the Georgia death penalty by sustaining its revised death penalty law. The death penalty itself is not cruel and unusual punishment, but a capital case requires two proceedings: one to determine guilt or innocence and the other to determine the sentence (*Gregg v. Georgia*, 1976). Most states will not consider the death sentence for anyone younger than 15 years of age. In addition, the Supreme Court has prohibited executing intellectually disabled individuals.

For prisoners, cases based on Eighth Amendment rights involve cruel and unusual punishment, such as overcrowding, solitary confinement, corporal punishment, physical abuse, and use of force; treatment and rehabilitation; the right not to be treated; and the death penalty.

Discussion Questions

1. What historical background do you suspect led to the Eighth Amendment being included in the Bill of Rights?
2. If the Bill of Rights does not guarantee the right to bail, how can bail be ensured for those accused of crimes?
3. Explain the basic need for bail.
4. Does the bail system discriminate against the poor?
5. How would you define cruel and unusual punishment? Can you think of any currently lawful punishments you believe are cruel and unusual?
6. Do you support the death penalty? Why or why not? Could you be an executioner or witness to an execution?
7. Should juveniles or intellectually disabled individuals receive life in prison for committing a heinous crime?
8. Should juveniles or intellectually disabled individuals who have committed capital crimes be executed?
9. Does the death penalty deter murder or rape? Why or why not?
10. Should fines be the same for the poor and the wealthy?

References

Bohm, R.M., & Haley, K.N. (2007). *Introduction to Criminal Justice*, 4th ed. New York: McGraw-Hill.

Clear, T.R., & Cole, G.F. (2000). *American Corrections*, 5th ed. Belmont, CA: Wadsworth Publishing Company.

Clear, T.R.; Cole, G.F.; & Reisig, M.D. (2006). *American Corrections*, 7th ed. Belmont, CA: Thomson Wadsworth Publishing.

Death Penalty Information Center. (2016, July 15) "Facts about the Death Penalty." Washington, DC: Author. Retrieved August 24, 2016 from http://www.deathpenaltyinfo.org/documents/FactSheet.pdf

Ducat, C.R. (2010). *Constitutional Interpretation*, 9th ed. Belmont, CA: Wadsworth/Cengage Learning.

Fagan, J.A. (2010). *Capital Punishment: Deterrent Effects and Capital Costs*. New York: Columbia Law School, Center for Crime, Community, and Law.

Gallup. (2015). "Death Penalty." Washington, DC: Author. Retrieved August 24, 2016 from http://www.gallup.com/poll/1606/death-penalty.aspx

Monk, L.R. (n.d.). *The Bill of Rights: A User's Guide*. Alexandria, VA: Close Up Publishing.

Moore, C. (2010, February). "Lives Cut Short." *Law Enforcement Technology*, p. 82.

National Conference of State Legislatures. (2016, August 17)."States and Capital Punishment." Washington, DC: Author. Retrieved August 24, 2016 from http://www.ncsl.org/research/civil-and-criminal-justice/death-penalty.aspx#Methods%20of%20Execution

"Officers Support Death Penalty for Many Murder Cases." (2008, May). *Police*, p. 14.

Saad, L. (2013, January 9). "U.S. Death Penalty Support Stable at 63%." Gallup, Inc. Retrieved August 24, 2016, from www.gallup.com/poll/159770/death-penalty-support-stable.aspx?version=print

U.S. Marshals Service. (2016). "Asset Forfeiture." Washington, DC: Author, Fact Sheet. Retrieved August 24, 2016 from https://www.usmarshals.gov/duties/factsheets/asset_forfeiture.pdf

Worrall, J.L. (2009, March 6). *Asset Forfeiture*. Washington, DC: Center for Problem Oriented Policing.

Cases Cited

Addington v. Texas, 441 U.S. 418 (1979)
Apprendi v. New Jersey, 530 U.S. 466 (2000)
Arave v. Creech, 507 U.S. 463 (1993)
Atkins v. Virginia, 536 U.S. 304 (2002)
Austin v. United States, 509 U.S. 602 (1993)
Baze v. Rees, 553 U.S. 35 (2008)
Bell v. Cone, 535 U.S. 685 (2002)
Bennis v. Michigan, 516 U.S. 442 (1996)
Brown v. Plata, 563 U.S. 493 (2011)
Browning-Ferris Industries v. Kelco Disposal, 472 U.S. 257 (1989)
Campbell v. Blodgett, 978 F.2d 1502 (9th Cir. 1994)
Coker v. Georgia, 433 U.S. 584 (1977)
Eddings v. Oklahoma, 455 U.S. 104 (1982)
Estelle v. Gamble, 429 U.S. 97 (1976)
Ewing v. California, 538 U.S. 11 (2003)
Ford v. Wainwright, 477 U.S. 399 (1986)
Furman v. Georgia, 408 U.S. 238 (1972)
Glossip v. Gross, 136 S.Ct. 20 (2015)
Graham v. Florida, 560 U.S. 48 (2010)
Gregg v. Georgia, 428 U.S. 153 (1976)
Hall v. Florida, 572 U.S. 5 (2014)
Harmelin v. Michigan, 501 U.S. 957 (1991)
Helling v. McKinney, 509 U.S. 25 (1993)
Hope v. Pelzer, 536 U.S. 730 (2002)
Hudson v. McMillian, 503 U.S. 1 (1992)
Hurst v. Florida, 577 U.S. ___ (2016)
Ingraham v. Wright, 430 U.S. 651 (1977)
Jackson v. Indiana, 406 U.S. 715 (1972)
Jones v. United States, 527 U.S. 373 (1999)
Knight v. Florida, 528 U.S. 990 (1999)
Lockhart v. McCree, 476 U.S. 162 (1986)
Lockyer v. Andrade, 538 U.S. 63 (2003)
Louisiana ex rel. Francis v. Resweber, 329 U.S. 459 (1947)
Maynard v. Cartwright, 486 U.S. 356 (1988)
McCleskey v. Kemp, 481 U.S. 279 (1987)
Miller v. Alabama, 567 U.S. ___ (2012)
Montgomery v. Louisiana, 577 U.S. ___ (2015)
Morgan v. Illinois, 504 U.S. 719 (1992)
Overton v. Bazetta, 539 U.S. 126 (2003)
Penry v. Lynaugh, 492 U.S. 302 (1989)
Pulley v. Harris, 465 U.S. 37 (1984)
Rhodes v. Chapman, 452 U.S. 337 (1981)
Ring v. Arizona, 536 U.S. 584 (2002)
Robinson v. California, 370 U.S. 660 (1962)
Roper v. Simmons, 543 U.S. 551 (2005)
Ruiz v. Estelle, 503 F. Supp. 1265 (S.D. Texas, 1975)
Rupe v. Wood, 863 F. Supp. 1307 (W.D. Wash., 1994)
Schilb v. Kuebel, 404 U.S. 357 (1971)
Schriro v. Summerlin, 542 U.S. 348 (2004)
Simmons v. South Carolina, 512 U.S. 154 (1994)
Singleton v. Norris, 124 S.Ct. 74 (2003)

Solem v. Helm, 463 U.S. 277 (1983)
Stack v. Boyle, 342 U.S. 1 (1951)
Stanford v. Kentucky, 492 U.S. 361 (1989)
State v. Moore, 520 U.S. 1176 (2006)
Thompson v. McNeil, 556 U.S. 1114 (2009)
Thompson v. Oklahoma, 487 U.S. 815 (1988)
Trop v. Dulles, 356 U.S. 86 (1958)

United States v. Bajakajian, 524 U.S. 321 (1998)
United States v. Good, 510 U.S. 43 (1993)
United States v. Hazzard, 598 F. Supp. 1442 (N.D.Ill. 1984)
United States v. Salerno, 481 U.S. 739 (1987)
United States v. Ursery, 518 U.S. 267 (1996)
Whitley v. Albers, 475 U.S. 312 (1986)
Wilson v. Seiter, 501 U.S. 294 (1991)

CHAPTER 13

The Remaining Amendments and a Return to the Constitution

We Justices read the Constitution the only way we can: as twentieth-century Americans. The genius of the Constitution rests not in any static meaning it might have had in a world that is dead and gone, but in the adaptability of its great principles to cope with current problems.

—William Brennan, former Supreme Court Justice

Amending the U.S. Constitution is no easy task. For example, the Federal Marriage Amendment has been introduced in Congress multiple times, most recently in 2013, and has repeatedly failed. In fact, the U.S. Supreme Courts has ruled that state laws that ban same-sex marriage are unconstitutional and violate the Fourteenth Amendment (*Obergefell v. Hodges*, 2015).

Learning Objectives

LO1 Describe what the Third Amendment established.

LO2 Explain what was instituted by the Seventh Amendment.

LO3 Define the Ninth Amendment.

LO4 Summarize the Tenth Amendment.

LO5 Identify the amendment that allows the Supreme Court to make other amendments applicable to the states.

Key Terms

delegated powers	federalism	selective incorporation
disenfranchise	reserve powers	suits at common law

Introduction

The amount of material generated by constitutional cases, analysis, and research is astounding. Of course, because the Constitution affects every American's daily life, the fact that so many are intrigued by it should come as no surprise. The USA PATRIOT Act proposed legislation to make flag desecration illegal, and what seems like the continuing sagas of high-powered business people and celebrities running afoul of the law maintain people's interest in the Constitution and the U.S. legal processes. Although the amendments addressed thus far have generated the most attention, in an examination of the Constitution we must look at other amendments as well to understand the document as a whole.

The amendments discussed so far are probably the best-known amendments in the Bill of Rights, and those best suited for students beginning their study of this area of law. To complete your understanding of the Constitution and its amendments, this chapter presents the four remaining amendments of the Bill of Rights, followed by a brief look at the other amendments that have been made to the Constitution. The chapter concludes with a discussion of the various other attempts to pass constitutional amendments.

As you read, keep in mind the analogy of the U.S. Constitution as a framework that provides the basis on which all U.S. law is built. Many subareas of the Constitution can be examined. Those selected for inclusion in this text should help tie together your studies at the basic level, as they themselves help tie together this workable, complex document. Remember, however, that there is much more to this fascinating document than time and space allow in this introductory text.

The Remaining Amendments to the Bill of Rights

Four amendments in the Bill of Rights remain to be discussed: the Third, Seventh, Ninth, and Tenth.

The Third Amendment

No Soldier shall, in time of peace, be quartered in any house, without the consent of the Owner, nor in time of war, but in a manner to be prescribed by law.

LO1 *The Third Amendment prohibits housing soldiers in private homes during peacetime without the owner's consent and during wartime without legal process.*

Although the Third Amendment has never been subjected to Supreme Court review, it holds historical relevance and stands for the general principle that government is to leave people alone without compelling cause. This amendment dates back to colonial times, when England expected the citizenry to feed and shelter British soldiers. Although history, it is history that remains important to the U.S. Constitution as an example of the framers' insistence on curtailing excessive government authority.

The Seventh Amendment

In Suits at common law, where the value in controversy shall exceed twenty dollars, the right of trial by jury shall be preserved, and no fact tried by a jury, shall be otherwise re-examined in any Court of the United States, than according to the rules of the common law.

LO2 *The Seventh Amendment establishes the right to a federal jury trial for all "suits at common law" if the value is more than $20.*

Recall that the Sixth Amendment guaranteed a jury trial for all criminal proceedings. The Seventh Amendment extends this right to civil proceedings involving more than $20, a large sum in 1791, when the Bill of Rights was passed. Incidentally, that amount would convert to roughly $500 in today's economy.

Suits at common law means a legal controversy arising out of civil law rather than criminal law. The difference is easiest to observe in the caption (or title) of the case, which, at the trial court level, would always be the government (e.g., the *city, county,* or *state v.,* or the *United States v.,* the specific defendant in a criminal case). In a civil case, the caption would have the name of one party *v.* the name of the other party. The caption of a case indicates the parties involved. The citation of the case indicates where the judicial opinion could be located. The criminal system ensures the protection of rights everyone enjoys, whereas the civil system ensures rights that one person has against another.

suits at common law
legal controversies arising out of civil law rather than criminal law

The issues involved in civil cases become as complex as those for criminal matters, and because of the complexity of our emerging society, civil cases may be more complex. Although the importance of the outcome in criminal cases is obvious, civil disputes often involve large sums of money, contracts, and other business matters, the ownership of land or other property, the rights to patents, the custody of children, divorces, wills, and an almost endless list of other issues that greatly affect those involved.

MYTH
Criminal cases are, by nature, always more complex than civil cases.

FACT
Civil cases are often as complex, and in some cases *more* complex than criminal cases.

The Seventh Amendment addresses when an individual (not the government or a criminal defendant) is entitled to a *federal* jury trial (not a local or state court). The reasons people would prefer having their cases heard before one court or another, or before a jury or only a judge, are tactical. Some think a federal court is more impartial and, thus, more fair than courts at a local or state level. Some think that a jury would help their cause; others think it would hinder their case. However, both the Constitution and federal law have established what cases federal courts can hear, and different procedures apply at different levels of courts. Where and how a case is handled is just one example of the many decisions attorneys face in best representing their clients.

This amendment was included in the Bill of Rights out of fairness. At issue was the distinction between types of cases in England, which found their way into U.S. law. It was important to differentiate among the types of cases that might be pursued in actions at law or in equity, affecting which court would have jurisdiction over what type of case. A court of law was a court that handled cases in which damages were sought. A court of equity, in contrast, handled suits in which something else was sought, such as specific performance, an injunction, or other special remedies. These terms may sound awkward because they have seldom been used since 1791. However, the Constitution is based on the legal history of those who brought their ideas to the United States, and subsequent courts tend not to change the basic legal concepts too drastically. The challenge has been for the courts to interpret this amendment in a way that serves a practical purpose, while maintaining its historical significance.

The Supreme Court and others have acknowledged that Seventh Amendment analysis is mostly historical, although cases occasionally arise, mostly dealing with whether certain facts warrant a jury trial at all. Today the practical approach to determining whether there is a Seventh Amendment right to a federal jury trial is based on whether a suit involves legal issues similar to issues raised in cases for which federal jury trials were granted by common law. Whether there is a Seventh Amendment right to a federal jury trial is based mainly on historical analysis of common law, in which the rationale used to determine previous cases is used to analyze current-day facts.

In *Thomas v. Union Carbide* (1985), the Court held there was no right to a jury trial when Congress had created other administrative remedies. Conversely, in *Curtis v. Loether* (1974), the Court overturned a lower court's ruling that a black woman was not permitted a jury trial when a white landlord refused to rent to her contrary to the Fair Housing Act. In *Colgrove v. Battin* (1973), the Court said that six-person juries were permissible in federal civil trials. These cases illustrate how common law marches on to carve out further nuances of the system, even in areas presumed to be historically dormant.

The Seventh Amendment is an excellent example of how the framers of the Constitution included both what they considered important to them at the time and what they thought would be important in the future, and how even an amendment may be resurrected when the facts of a modern case demand.

The Ninth Amendment

The enumeration in the Constitution, of certain rights, shall not be construed to deny or disparage others retained by the people.

The Ninth Amendment highlights the founders' beliefs that government's powers are limited by the rights of the people, not the other way around. The Ninth Amendment's significance is also largely historical. Through the Ninth Amendment, the framers addressed concerns that Americans would retain only those rights enumerated in the Constitution. Among those who did not want a Bill of Rights was James Madison. Madison was against an enumerated Bill of Rights, but he argued for the Ninth Amendment to ensure that the Bill of Rights would not, in fact, exclude those rights not listed.

LO3 *The Ninth Amendment established that the rights of U.S. citizens extend beyond those listed in the Constitution.*

The framers made an important statement with the Ninth Amendment, as explained by Supreme Court Justice Potter Stewart in his dissenting opinion in *Griswold v. Connecticut* (1965): "The Ninth Amendment, like its companion the Tenth, which this Court held [in *United States v. Darby*, 1941] 'states but a truism that all is retained which has not been surrendered,' ... was framed by James Madison and adopted by the States simply to make clear that the adoption of the Bill of Rights did not alter the plan that ... the Federal Government was to be a government of express and limited powers, and that all rights and powers not delegated to it were retained by the people and the individual States."

The Ninth Amendment has been referred to on occasion as the forgotten amendment in the Bill of Rights because it is seldom used as a basis for Supreme Court decisions. Some believe that judges have been reluctant to rely on the Ninth Amendment because its language is vague, never defining what specific rights are protected. The Court has referred to the Ninth Amendment in a handful of cases, but the Ninth Amendment has never been the basis of a decision by a majority of the justices. Although the Supreme Court has protected rights not listed in the Bill of Rights, it has not used the Ninth Amendment to do so. This amendment, again, serves as an example of the discussion and interpretations the Constitution continues to generate, particularly by those who assert that the interpretation be made in their own favor.

The Ninth Amendment has also generated significant controversy and much scholarly debate as to what the framers meant and intended with this amendment, serving as an example of how the Constitution does not always provide specific or easy answers.

Although seldom relied on, the Ninth Amendment will remain grounds for the belief that rights not specifically referred to within the Constitution are no less protected. Take a moment to consider all the choices people make during their lifetimes: marriage; raising children; how families are created; what the definition of a family is; where to live, travel, and recreate; the business entered or begun; and, quite literally, every step throughout life. There is no way anyone could list, or the framers of the Constitution could have predicted, what the future would hold. However, through the Ninth Amendment's existence, Americans are assured they will continue to be free to pursue those interests that government does not demonstrate a compelling reason to restrict.

> The makers of our Constitution undertook to secure conditions favorable to the pursuit of happiness. They recognized the significance of man's spiritual nature, of his feelings and his intellect. They knew that only a part of his pain, pleasure and satisfactions of life are to be found in material things. They sought to protect Americans in their beliefs,

their thoughts, their emotions and their sensations. They conferred, as against the Government, the right to be let alone—the most comprehensive of rights and the right most valued by civilized men. (*Olmstead v. United States*, 1928)

The Tenth Amendment

The powers not delegated to the United States by the Constitution, nor prohibited by it to the States, are reserved to the States respectively, or to the people.

LO4 *The Tenth Amendment embodies the principle of* **federalism**, *reserving for the states those powers not granted to the federal government or withheld from the states.*

Under federalism, power is shared by the national government and the states. The U.S. Constitution established a federal system to preserve the existing state governments, while creating a new national government strong enough to deal with the country's problems. A controversial question at the Constitutional Convention was just how much power the national government should have. A primary limit was that the government was one of the enumerated powers, powers specifically listed in the Constitution. However, the Constitution also included an Elastic Clause stating that Congress had the power to make all laws "necessary and proper" to carry out its enumerated powers. The Necessary and Proper Clause became the basis for the implied powers, those powers not specifically listed in the Constitution that are implied by the enumerated powers.

The Necessary and Proper Clause is the final provision (Clause 18) of Article 1, Section 8, the part of the Constitution dealing with the powers of Congress. Recall from Chapter 6 the brief discussion of the Commerce Clause (Article 1, Section 8, Clause 3), another enumerated power provided by the Constitution. The Commerce Clause is often paired with the Necessary and Proper Clause to form the basis of much federal law.

The powers of the national government, both enumerated and implied, are known as the **delegated powers** because they were delegated or entrusted to the national government by the states and the people. The powers kept by the states are known as the **reserve powers.** The Tenth Amendment refers to both types of powers. A primary reserve power is police power, which enables the state to pass laws and regulations that involve the public health, safety, morals, and welfare.

Although the Constitution recognizes both the powers of the states and the federal government, it contains the Supremacy Clause in Article 6, which states that the Constitution of the United States is "the supreme law of the land." The Tenth Amendment attempted to strike a balance between the federal government's power and that of the states, while maintaining individual freedom. That balance has not always been easy to maintain throughout U.S. history. During one such difficult period, only a bloody civil war finally resolved the question of federal versus state power. Since the Civil War, the Supreme Court has worked hard to find the proper balance of the Tenth Amendment.

Madison's version of the Tenth Amendment made clear that any powers not delegated to the federal government belonged to the states or to the people. However, some members of Congress wanted the Tenth Amendment to limit the federal government to those powers specifically listed in the Constitution, just as the Articles of Confederation had done. They wanted the Tenth Amendment to say

federalism a principle whereby power is shared by the national government and the states; the Tenth Amendment provision reserving for the states those powers not granted to the federal government or withheld from the states

delegated powers powers of the national government, both enumerated and implied by legal authority, delegated or entrusted to the national government by the states and the people

reserve powers powers retained by the states

that powers not expressly delegated to the U.S. government were reserved to the states. Madison believed it was impossible to confine a government to the exercise of expressed powers and that there must necessarily be powers by implication.

Unlike the other amendments, the Tenth Amendment does not ensure specific individual rights. Rather, it seeks to ensure to all people that the federal government will not get too powerful. In *Federalist Papers No. 51*, Madison (1788) stated: "In the compound republic of America, the power surrendered by the people is first divided between two distinct governments, and then the portion allotted to each subdivided among distinct and separate departments. Hence a double security arises to the rights of the people. The different governments will control each other, at the same time that each will be controlled by itself."

Historically, the Constitution came to be as a result of fear that federal government might become too powerful. Recognizing the need for a balanced government, a government that could run the nation but leave individualism to the states and their people, the Tenth Amendment sought to strike this balance. The Framers also wanted to ensure government accountability to the citizenry. The necessity for those who legislate to be held accountable to the citizens is removed if state or local officials are forced into implementing federal law because it relieves the federal government from responsibility, both financially and materially from the burdens or inadequacies of the law. The system, thus, was designed such that a state government is responsible to its citizens. In addition, the federal government regulates people, not states. An example of this concept is *Printz*, discussed shortly.

The concept behind the Tenth Amendment was important enough that it was the only amendment agreed on by all the states recommending a Bill of Rights. Like the Ninth Amendment, the Tenth Amendment shows the colonists' concern that specific limitations on the federal government could mean such a government *had* control over all other areas.

The Tenth Amendment's road has been rocky compared with that of other amendments. The question of *what* power federal government has and what goes to the states has challenged the government. Before the Constitution was ratified, the states were sovereign governmental bodies that acted much like separate countries. They issued their own money, set their own tax plans, and interacted with the other states as they saw fit. Although unity had benefits, the concern of "too much" national power had to be addressed before the country could agree on a central constitution. The framers addressed this issue through the Tenth Amendment, together with equal representation in the Senate, which was of particular importance to the smaller states.

Over the years, the federal government became stronger, and although concerns of there being excessive power continue today, a series of Supreme Court cases carved out the role of national government. In 1819 in *McCulloch v. Maryland*, the Court made its strongest assertion of the government's broad national power when it held that Congress had the authority to establish a national bank pursuant to the Necessary and Proper Clause of Article I, Section 8 of the Constitution. Before this decision, the Supremacy Clause of Article VI authorized only specific authority.

The national government's authority and power continued to grow, much to the concern of some. *United States v. Darby* (1941) upheld the Fair Labor Standards Act of 1938, and the limits that the Tenth Amendment was intended to set on expansion of federal authority seemed to have been forgotten.

Like a pendulum, more recent cases have indicated the high court's willingness to reconsider, or at least limit, a never-ending expansion of federal power. A significant case in 1992 involving federal regulations of radioactive waste, *New York v. United States*, resulted in the Court stating, "No matter how powerful the federal interest involved, the Constitution simply does not give Congress the authority to require the states to regulate." The Court, citing *Hodel v. Virginia Surface Mining & Reclamation Assn., Inc.* (1981), emphasized in this case that Congress may not simply "commandee[r] the legislative processes of the States by directly compelling them to enact and enforce a federal regulatory program." The Court added that although Congress has substantial powers to govern, even in areas that affect the state level, "the Constitution has never been understood to confer upon Congress the ability to require the States to govern according to Congress' instructions." This ruling highlights a constitutional boundary for federal legislation: when the federal government goes too far and their legislative intentions transform from ones of encouragement to ones of coercion, the legislation is unconstitutional.

CASE IN BRIEF ▶

United States v. Lopez (1995)

ISSUE Is the 1990 Gun-Free School Zones Act unconstitutional because it exceeds the power of Congress?

RULING Yes. The connection to commerce is too slim for Congress to pass legislation based on the power given to it by the Commerce Clause.

The crucial issue of federalism was addressed in *United States v. Lopez* (1995), a Commerce Clause case in which the Court invalidated an act of Congress for the first time in 50 years, raising important issues of federal versus states' rights. When Congress enacted the Gun-Free School Zones Act of 1990, it made a federal offense of anyone knowingly possessing a firearm in an area the person knows to be a school zone. A 12th-grade student was convicted under this law for carrying a concealed .38-caliber handgun and bullets at school. The Fifth Circuit Court of Appeals reversed the conviction, holding the act was invalid because Congress had exceeded its authority. Chief Justice William H. Rehnquist delivered the Court's opinion, which said, in part:

> To uphold the Government's contentions here, we would have to pile inference upon inference in a matter that would bid fair to convert congressional authority under the Commerce Clause to a general police power of the sort retained by the States.... The broad language in these opinions has suggested the possibility of additional expansion, but we decline here to proceed any further. To do so would require us to conclude that the Constitution's enumeration of powers does not presuppose something not enumerated ... and that there never will be a distinction between what is truly national and what is truly local.

CASE IN BRIEF ▶

Printz v. United States (1997)

ISSUE Can Congress mandate that state and local law enforcement agencies conduct background checks on prospective handgun purchasers?

RULING No. Compelling state and local officials to perform the background checks violates state sovereignty.

In *Printz v. United States* (1997), the Supreme Court struck down that portion of the Brady Bill compelling local law enforcement to perform background checks on applicants for handgun ownership. The Court held the requirement violated "the very principle of separate state sovereignty."

Those studying the Constitution will find it of interest in which direction future cases will call the Tenth Amendment into consideration and how these cases will be decided. Before moving on to amendments that follow the first 10, consider the statement in *West Virginia State Board of Education v. Barnette* (1943), in answer to what makes up the Bill of Rights: "We set up government by consent of the governed, and the Bill of Rights denies those in power any legal opportunity to coerce that consent. Authority here is to be controlled by public opinion, not public opinion by authority."

Although the Ninth and Tenth Amendments are not considered guarantees of specific individual freedoms, some refer to the first eight amendments as the Bill of Rights. However, the Bill of Rights presents a "package" of rights that remain viable because of the balance of the system at the federal and local levels. As eloquently described by Cardozo (1928), "Bills of Rights give assurance to the individual of the preservation of his liberty. They do not define the liberty they promise."

Amendments Beyond the Bill of Rights

The Bill of Rights lays a foundation for individual freedoms, but these freedoms do not stop with the Tenth Amendment. Since 1791, when the first 10 amendments were ratified, until the present, our Constitution has continued to evolve. As proof of the Constitution's ability to respond to the nation's needs, additional amendments have come, and some have gone. Following is a brief overview of the remaining amendments, including those that have been repealed.

The Eleventh Amendment (1795)

The Eleventh Amendment deals with the extent of the judicial power of the United States:

> The Judicial power of the United States shall not be construed to extend to any suit in law or equity, commenced or prosecuted against one of the United States by Citizens of another State, or by Citizens or Subjects of any Foreign State.

This amendment is the only one that deals with the judicial power of the federal government and is actually more an administrative directive. The history of the Eleventh Amendment is noteworthy in that it was introduced the day after the high court ruled in *Chisholm v. Georgia* (1793) that a citizen of one state had the right to sue another state. The ruling does not mean, however, that a citizen cannot sue a local or municipal government or a state *official* in federal court. In *ex parte Young* (1908), the Court held that a state cannot act unconstitutionally, but a state official (as an individual) can act unconstitutionally.

The Thirteenth Amendment (1865)

A key amendment to the Constitution is the Thirteenth Amendment, which abolished slavery, as previously discussed:

> Neither slavery nor involuntary servitude, except as a punishment for crime whereof the party shall have been duly convicted, shall exist within the United States, or any place subject to their jurisdiction.
> Congress shall have power to enforce this article by appropriate legislation.

The Thirteenth Amendment overturned the Supreme Court's *Dred Scott v. Sandford* decision (1857). Using an amendment to overturn a specific Supreme Court decision is rare, dramatic, and a good illustration of the checks and balances in the U.S. government. Closely related to this amendment is the Fourteenth Amendment.

The Fourteenth Amendment (1868)

To review from Chapter 4, the Fourteenth Amendment asserts:

> All persons born or naturalized in the United States, and subject to the jurisdiction thereof, are citizens of the United States and of the State wherein they reside. No State shall make or enforce any law which shall abridge the privileges or immunities of citizens of the United States; nor shall any State deprive any person of life, liberty or property, without due process of law; nor deny to any person within its jurisdiction the equal protection of the laws.

LO5 *The Supreme Court has chosen, through case law and common law, to selectively apply certain amendments to both federal and state governments through* **selective incorporation,** *as stipulated in the Fourteenth Amendment.*

As has been addressed throughout this text, a significant portion of the Bill of Rights amendments has been made to apply to the states as well. Table 13.1 summarizes the cases incorporating provisions of the Bill of Rights into the Due Process Clause of the Fourteenth Amendment, as well as those that remain unincorporated. The Fourteenth Amendment's Due Process Clause and the concept of selective incorporation are especially important in considering individual civil liability issues.

selective incorporation holds that only the provisions of the Bill of Rights that are fundamental to the U.S. legal system are applied to the states through the Due Process Clause of the Fourteenth Amendment

Table 13.1 Cases Incorporating Provisions of the Bill of Rights into the Due Process Clause of the Fourteenth Amendment

First Amendment		
Establishment of religion	*Everson v. Board of Education*	1947
Free exercise of religion	*Cantwell v. Connecticut*	1940
Freedom of speech	*Gitlow v. New York*	1925
Freedom of the press	*Near v. Minnesota*	1931
Freedom to peaceably assemble	*DeJonge v. Oregon*	1937
Freedom to petition government	*Hague v. CIO*	1939
Second Amendment		
Right to keep and bear arms	*McDonald v. Chicago*	2010
Fourth Amendment		
Unreasonable search and seizure	*Wolf v. Colorado*	1949
Exclusionary rule	*Mapp v. Ohio*	1961
Fifth Amendment		
Grand jury	Not Incorporated	
No double jeopardy	*Benton v. Maryland*	1969
No self-incrimination	*Malloy v. Hogan*	1964
Compensation for taking private property	*Chicago, Burlington & Quincy Railroad v. Chicago*	1897
Sixth Amendment		
Speedy trial	*Klopfer v. North Carolina*	1967
Public trial	*In re Oliver*	1948
Impartial jury	*Parker v. Gladden*	1966
Jury trial	*Duncan v. Louisiana*	1968
Venue	Not Incorporated	

Table 13.1 (*Continued*)

Notice	*Cole v. Arkansas*	1948
Confrontation of witnesses	*Pointer v. Texas*	1965
Compulsory process	*Washington v. Texas*	1967
Assistance of counsel	*Powell v. Alabama* (capital cases)	1932
	Gideon v. Wainwright (noncapital felony cases)	1963
	Argersinger v. Hamlin (most misdemeanor cases)	1972
Seventh Amendment		
Jury trial in civil cases	Not Incorporated	
Eighth Amendment		
No excessive bail	*Schilb v. Kuebel* (through *McDonald v. Chicago*, 2010)	1971
No excessive fines	Not Incorporated	
No cruel and unusual punishment	*Robinson v. California*	1962
Ninth Amendment		
"Privacy"*	*Griswold v. Connecticut*	1965

*The word *privacy* does not appear in the Ninth Amendment (nor anywhere in the Constitution), but in *Griswold* several justices viewed the Ninth Amendment as guaranteeing that right.

Source: Adapted from Ferdico, John; Fradella, Henry F.; and Totten, Christopher. *Criminal Procedure for the Criminal Justice Professional*, 11E, 2012. Wadsworth, a part of Cengage Learning, Inc. Reproduced by permission, www.cengage.com/permissions.

Amendments Related to Elections and Structure of Congress

Not all amendments and other portions of the Constitution deal directly with specific rights and liberties. Any successful entity needs basic administrative guidelines to function properly, and these are found in the Constitution as well.

Seven amendments deal in detail with numerous matters related to how the federal government is to be structured and its officials elected. Following is a brief summary of these amendments. The full text of each is presented in Appendix A.

The Twelfth Amendment (1804) established the electoral system by which the President and Vice President are chosen. Given the extreme controversy generated by the 2000 presidential election—with Al Gore winning the popular vote and George W. Bush the electoral college vote and, therefore, the presidency—this system might come under close scrutiny in the future. *Bush v. Gore* (2000) is an apt illustration of the struggle to maintain the balance of power and to determine which branch of government at what level has the power to do what during elections.

The Fourteenth Amendment (1868) established how representatives are apportioned and what their qualifications are.

The Seventeenth Amendment (1913) describes how the U.S. Senate is to be composed, the qualifications required, and how vacancies are to be filled.

The Twentieth Amendment (1933) established that the terms of the President and Vice President end at noon on the 20th day of January and that the terms of senators and representatives end at noon on the 3rd day of January. It also established how often Congress meets and the chain of succession if the President is no longer able to carry out the responsibilities of the office.

> **MYTH**
> The Constitution limits the number of times a person may serve as President of the United States to two four-year terms.
>
> **FACT**
> The two-term limit was not defined until passage of the Twenty-Second Amendment in 1951. Prior to that, Franklin Delano Roosevelt had been the first and only president to serve more than two terms, dying in office several months into his fourth term.

The Twenty-Second Amendment (1951) restricted the term of presidency to two terms.

The Twenty-Third Amendment (1961) gave representation to the district that constitutes the seat of government of the United States—that is, to the District of Columbia.

The Twenty-Fifth Amendment (1967) established procedures for filling vacancies and for actions to take should the President be unable to "discharge the powers and duties" of the office. Considering U.S. Presidents are larger-than-life figures, the unthinkable first occurred when William Harrison died after just one month as President in 1841 and Vice President John Tyler simply took it upon himself to assume the presidency. The Twenty-Fifth Amendment was first proposed after President John F. Kennedy's assassination and provides an official process by which the Vice President may assume power if the President is unable.

The Twenty-Seventh Amendment (1992) states, "No law, varying the compensation for the services of the Senators and Representatives, shall take effect, until an election of Representatives shall have intervened." This amendment's purpose is to prevent Congress from setting its own salary because of the apparent conflict of interest. Nonetheless, Congress has continued to give itself cost-of-living raises, which has not been considered the same as an actual raise. Interestingly, this amendment was first proposed in 1789 by James Madison and was one of the 12 amendments originally proposed to become the Bill of Rights, of which only 10 were ratified. In this case, only six states originally ratified it (later it was discovered Kentucky had ratified the amendment in 1792). The Twenty-Seventh Amendment was ratified in 1992 during a time when public opinion was extremely negative regarding the repeated pay raises Congress gave itself. The issue resurfaced after an undergraduate student had been doing research on the Equal Rights Amendment.

The preceding amendments, along with portions of the Constitution, are important in that they provide the basic administrative and operational bases through which an orderly government will operate. Above all, it remains important to understand that, like a set of directions for any piece of complex machinery, these guidelines provide people with the ability to make something work that would not be possible without such a reference.

Voting Rights

The ability of the Constitution to reflect society's changing needs is well illustrated in the amendments broadening the right to vote, which, initially, was reserved for white males older than 21 years.

The Fifteenth Amendment (1870) required that the right to vote shall not be denied or abridged because of race, color, or previous condition of servitude. In other words, black males were given the vote. The impetus for this amendment was the concern that, despite the passage of the Fourteenth Amendment, states might still try to **disenfranchise**, or deprive, freed slaves of their right to vote. With the power to vote came the political power to protect their freedom. Section 2 of this amendment gives Congress the power to enforce the right by "appropriate legislation."

disenfranchise to deprive a person of a right

The Voting Rights Act (VRA) of 1965, which has been renewed several times, most recently in 2006 for another 25 years, is an example of such legislation and was at the heart of *Shelby County v. Holder* (2013). The VRA was intended to prevent racially motivated voting laws from being enacted in states that historically passed such legislation. Section 5 of the Act directs certain jurisdictions to obtain "preclearance" from either the U.S. Department of Justice or the federal district court before modifying their voting laws, and Section 4 of the Act contains a formula used to determine which state and local jurisdictions come under Section 5. In *Shelby County*, a 5–4 Court held that the coverage formula used in Section 4, and most recently updated in 1975, was unconstitutional, with Chief Justice John Roberts writing that the current system is "based on 40-year-old facts having no logical relationship to the present day." With Section 4 invalidated, Section 5 is effectively without consequence. What the majority opinion emphasized was the fact that the law is no longer tied to current voting discrimination. The conditions that existed when the act was first passed do not exist today and, therefore, do not justify the extreme interference of the federal government into matters concerning local election processes.

The Nineteenth Amendment (1920) required that the right to vote should not be denied on account of sex. Women finally got the vote, 50 years after black males.

The Twenty-Fourth Amendment (1964) requires that the right to vote should not be denied or abridged by reason of failure to pay any poll tax or other tax.

The Twenty-Sixth Amendment (1971) lowered the voting age, giving the vote to U.S. citizens 18 years of age and older.

One area of voting rights that is important to understand is the "one person, one vote" rule. This concept, often litigated under the Equal Protection Clause of the Fourteenth Amendment, stands for the idea that the Constitution mandates that the weight of each vote cast is substantially the same. If one person's vote does not carry the same weight as others, the vote is said to be diluted.

These cases often come up in how legislative voting districts are drawn. What is important is that the ratio of population to elected officials is not disproportionate between districts. The Supreme Court has ruled that in congressional elections, the populations of each district must be as equal as possible to ensure "each vote be given as much weight as any other vote" (*Wesberry v. Sanders*, 1964). But in local and state elections, populations can deviate from this rule and be less than perfect (see *Brown v. Thomson*, 1983), the rationale being that states should be allowed to preserve the integrity of political subdivisions, maintain communities of interest, and create geographic compactness. Differences of less than ten percent are usually acceptable.

In a recent case, *Evenwel v. Abbott* (2016), the issue was what population base of the voting district must be equalized: the total population or that of eligible voters? The Court ruled unanimously that a state may design its legislative districts based on total population and not run afoul of the Equal Protection Clause. The total population method is used by all of the states and many local jurisdictions. In a concurring opinion, Justice Thomas explained that although the total population method is acceptable, there are other constitutional approaches.

Constitutional Law in ACTION

The State of Papagallo is a very diverse state. Many ethnic groups and religions are represented in its communities. Most of these groups came to the State in 1890 after the discovery of oil and a subsequent boom in the economy, and have since stayed for generations. Before 1890, the State had a small population and was primarily composed of whites and blacks.

The State recently enacted a law that allows only those residents with a family history of State residency prior to 1890 to vote in local city and town elections. Anyone, regardless of their ancestry, may vote in statewide elections, provided they meet all other eligible requirements according to State law.

The State has set up the voting districts in the following way: District 1, population 100,000, votes for 1 member of the state legislature; District 2, population 50,000, votes for 1 member of the state legislature; and District 3, population 200,000, votes for 4 members of the state legislature.

- *Does the new state law violate the Fifteenth Amendment? Why or why not?*
- *Does the voting district scheme violate the "one person, one vote" rule? Which district(s), if any, is diluted? How could the districts be drawn to avoid the problem of dilution?*

Taxes

The Sixteenth Amendment (1913) established the federal income tax: "The Congress shall have power to lay and collect taxes on incomes, from whatever source derived, without apportionment among the several States, and without regard to any census or enumeration."

Prohibition

An excellent example of how the Constitution, through the amendment process, can adjust and change to reflect society's wishes is the Eighteenth Amendment (1919), which prohibited the sale and purchase of "intoxicating liquors." This prohibition was ignored by many, with speakeasies opening and gangsters profiting from the illegal sale of liquor. Hundreds of thousands of law enforcement hours and dollars were spent trying to enforce this amendment, but in the end, enforcement was seen as hopeless because it was not what the people wanted. Therefore, the Twenty-First Amendment (1933) was ratified, repealing the "eighteenth article of amendment to the Constitution."

Attempts at Other Amendments

Over the years, various amendments have been proposed espousing different views considered important, such as prohibiting the burning of the U.S. flag, establishing victims' rights, and balancing the federal budget. Although such proposals have been repeatedly defeated, they are likely to be brought up again and serve as yet another example of how change in constitutional law comes about.

California was the first state to pass a victims' rights constitutional amendment in 1982, followed by Florida in 1988. Since then, 30 other states have passed victims' rights constitutional amendments, as shown in Table 13.2.

In 2000, a constitutional amendment failed to win Senate approval, but it was reintroduced in 2003. On June 12, 2003, a Senate subcommittee approved a proposal to amend the Constitution to guarantee rights to crime victims: "Supporters argue that only a constitutional amendment will elevate the rights of crime victims and ensure that judges and prosecutors heed them. Some critics, including the ranking Democrat on the subcommittee, Russell Feingold of Wisconsin, would rather see Congress first try to enact victims' right protections statutorily instead of through a constitutional amendment, which would be more difficult to change later on" (Boyter, 2003, p. 8). Any proposed constitutional amendment requires a two-thirds vote of approval by both the House and Senate. Once the proposed amendment clears Congress, it must then be ratified by at least 38 states to become a constitutional amendment.

In 2003, a proposal to amend the Constitution to prohibit gay marriages was being talked about. Until now, individual states, not the federal government, have been responsible for deciding their own family law and policy. And in light of the Court's recent rulings in same-sex marriage cases, judicial opinion seems to sway in favor of allowing states to continue such legislative independence. Although some

Table 13.2 History of State Victims' Rights Constitutional Amendments

State	Year Passed	Electoral Support (%)	State	Year Passed	Electoral Support (%)
Alabama	1994	80	Nebraska	1997	78
Alaska	1994	87	Nevada	1996	74
Arizona	1990	58	New Jersey	1991	85
California	1982; renewed in 2008	56	New Mexico	1992	68
Colorado	1992	86	North Carolina	1996	78
Connecticut	1996	78	Ohio	1994	77
Florida	1988	90	Oklahoma	1996	91
Idaho	1994	79	Oregon	1999	58
Illinois	1992	77	Rhode Island	1986	*
Indiana	1996	89	South Carolina	1996	89
Kansas	1992	84	Tennessee	1998	89
Louisiana	1998	68	Texas	1989	73
Maryland	1994	92	Utah	1994	68
Michigan	1988	80	Virginia	1996	84
Mississippi	1998	93	Washington	1989	78
Missouri	1992	84	Wisconsin	1993	84

*Passed by Constitutional Convention

Source: Adapted from 2011 National Center for Victims of Crime, www.ncvc.org.

argue that this tradition has resulted in a confusing patchwork of laws, a persuasive argument against such an amendment is that for the first time in our history, an amendment would deny rights to a group of people rather than expand them.

The Process of Amending the Constitution

Article V addresses the process for amending the Constitution. Two methods are possible: (1) both the House and Senate propose an amendment (done through a joint resolution) by a two-thirds majority vote or (2) two-thirds of State legislatures (34) call for a constitutional convention. Of the 27 amendments currently in existence, all have been proposed by Congress, none through a constitutional convention.

Once an amendment is proposed, a letter containing the notice of the amendment proposed and other information is submitted to the governor of each state. Depending on the directions from Congress, the proposal is submitted to the state legislature for a vote or the state will hold a convention. For example, in the Twenty-First Amendment, Congress specified in the text of the amendment that it must be ratified by each state through a state convention, but in the language of the Twentieth Amendment, Congress specified the need for the state legislatures to ratify it.

Congress may also specify a time limit for the ratification process. This occurred in both the Twentieth and Twenty-First Amendments, in which Congress stated the amendment must be ratified within seven years of proposal or it would become inoperative.

Congress does not need to specify a time limit for ratification. In fact, most amendment proposals do not have such language. A case in point: the Twenty-Seventh Amendment was first proposed in 1789 but was not ratified until 1992. Had it been ratified earlier, it would have become known as one of the first dozen amendments, not the twenty-seventh one.

A proposed amendment will become part of the Constitution only if it is ratified by at least three-fourths of the states (38). However, because of the extraordinary importance a basic document such as our Constitution holds, Congress has been, and continues to be, reluctant to make significant changes by adding amendments.

The life of the law has not been logic; it has been experience. The felt necessities of the time, the prevalent moral and political theories . . . even the prejudices which judges share with their fellow men . . . have a good deal in determining the rules by which men should be governed.

—Chief Justice Oliver Wendell Holmes, Jr., U.S. Supreme Court

Summary

Four additional important amendments of the Bill of Rights are the Third, Seventh, Ninth, and Tenth Amendments. The Third Amendment prohibits housing soldiers in private homes during peacetime without the owner's consent and during wartime without legal process. The Seventh Amendment establishes the right to a federal jury trial for all "suits at common law" if the value is more than $20. Cases that involve issues that justify a Seventh Amendment right to a federal jury trial are determined by examining the types of cases heard previously or by a common law analysis. The Ninth Amendment established that the rights of U.S. citizens extend beyond those listed in the Constitution. The right of privacy has been referred to by the Supreme Court and has been used to infer such a right, but the Ninth Amendment does not guarantee this right. The Tenth Amendment embodies the principle of federalism, reserving for the states those powers not granted to the federal government or withheld from the states.

Discussion Questions

1. Discuss why the framers of the Constitution probably thought it necessary to include the Ninth and Tenth Amendments.
2. With reference to Question 1, would only one or the other have been sufficient? If you were to eliminate the Ninth or Tenth Amendment, which would it be and why?
3. Could the United States not have a federal government? What about a much less powerful federal government, and if so, what would this government do?
4. Having come this far in your study of constitutional law, do you think the United States could ever get along without a written constitution?
5. Does the Constitution work as well as it was meant to? Why or why not?
6. Is there any way an internal military dictatorship could take over the present government in the United States and be successful?
7. Is there a present-day concern that the national government is too powerful?
8. If you were to eliminate any portions of the Constitution, which would they be? Why?
9. If you were to propose any new amendments, what would they be?
10. Imagine that a time machine would permit those who conceived the Constitution to be present today. What would they think about how their prescription for freedom has endured the challenges of time? What might they not be pleased with, constitutionally?

References

Boyter, J. (2003, July). "Subcommittee Approves Victims' Rights Amendment." *The Police Chief*, p. 8.

Cardozo, B.N. (1928). *The Paradoxes of Legal Science*. New York: Columbia University Press.

Madison, J. (1788, February 8). "The Structure of the Government Must Furnish the Proper Checks and Balances Between the Different Departments." *Federalist Papers No. 51*. Retrieved August 24, 2016 from https://www.congress.gov/resources/display/content/The+Federalist+Papers#TheFederalistPapers-51

Cases Cited

Argersinger v. Hamlin, 407 U.S. 25 (1972)
Benton v. Maryland, 395 U.S. 784 (1969)
Brown v. Thomson, 462 U.S. 835 (1983)
Bush v. Gore, 531 U.S. 98 (2000)
Cantwell v. Connecticut, 310 U.S. 296 (1940)
Chicago, Burlington & Quincy Railroad v. Chicago, 166 U.S. 226 (1897)
Chisholm v. Georgia, 2 U.S. 419 (1793)
Cole v. Arkansas, 333 U.S. 196 (1948)
Colgrove v. Battin, 413 U.S. 149 (1973)

Curtis v. Loether, 415 U.S. 189 (1974)
DeJonge v. Oregon, 299 U.S. 353 (1937)
Dred Scott v. Sandford, 60 U.S. 393 (1857)
Duncan v. Louisiana, 391 U.S. 145 (1968)
Everson v. Board of Education, 330 U.S. 1 (1947)
Evenwel v. Abbott, 578 U.S. ___ (2016)
ex parte Young, 209 U.S. 123 (1908)
Gideon v. Wainwright, 372 U.S. 335 (1963)
Gitlow v. New York, 268 U.S. 652 (1925)
Griswold v. Connecticut, 381 U.S. 479 (1965)
Hague v. CIO, 307 U.S. 496 (1939)
Hodel v. Virginia Surface Mining & Reclamation Assn., Inc., 452 U.S. 264 (1981)
In re Oliver, 333 U.S. 257 (1948)
Klopfer v. North Carolina, 386 U.S. 213 (1967)
Malloy v. Hogan, 378 U.S. 1 (1964)
Mapp v. Ohio, 367 U.S. 643 (1961)
McCulloch v. Maryland, 17 U.S. (4 Wheat.) 316 (1819)
McDonald v. Chicago, 561 U.S. 742 (2010)

Near v. Minnesota, 283 U.S. 697 (1931)
New York v. United States, 505 U.S. 144 (1992)
Obergefell v. Hodges, 576 U.S. ___ (2015)
Olmstead v. United States, 277 U.S. 438 (1928)
Parker v. Gladden, 385 U.S. 363 (1966)
Pointer v. Texas, 380 U.S. 400 (1965)
Powell v. Alabama, 287 U.S. 45 (1932)
Printz v. United States, 521 U.S. 898 (1997)
Robinson v. California, 370 U.S. 660 (1962)
Shelby County v. Holder, 570 U.S. 2 (2013)
Thomas v. Union Carbide, 473 U.S. 568 (1985)
United States v. Darby, 312 U.S. 100 (1941)
United States v. Lopez, 514 U.S. 549 (1995)
Washington v. Texas, 388 U.S. 14 (1967)
Wesberry v. Sanders, 376 U.S. 1 (1964)
West Virginia State Board of Education v. Barnette, 319 U.S. 624 (1943)
Wolf v. Colorado, 338 U.S. 25 (1949)

Epilogue

An inescapable conclusion to be drawn from studying the history of the U.S. Constitution is that it will not remain static. The people of the United States would not allow that. Americans are demanding of their law, and the fact that the Constitution has the built-in ability to change as demanded by its citizens reflects this important component of the nation's law.

The basic freedoms set forth in the Constitution shall remain because they are the cornerstones on which the United States was built. Freedom of speech and religion, the right to assemble and speak up, and freedom from unreasonable government intrusions will stand the tests of time. But change itself will continue. It has to. As the country and the needs of its people have changed with time, so too will the laws that support this society.

However, the basic mechanisms by which law can change will be maintained. That's what the Constitution is about—providing the predictability that ensures a continuation of the United States' ideals but including the ability to permit law to flow with natural changes brought on by society. But as those who have tried have learned, changing the Constitution is not easy. Nor should it be. Anything as powerful as this document should be altered only when intense scrutiny, evaluation, and input from every stakeholder have been used to weigh the need for change. Although politicians speak of constitutional change as part of their platforms, true scholars understand the importance of maintaining it apolitically. Should the Constitution cater to one side, its effectiveness is lost. Its goal is to serve everyone.

Consider societal desires as a pendulum. On one end of the arc is a conservative perspective; on the other end, a liberal one. These perspectives influence how society perceives its country. It answers such questions as, "Why do people act the way they do?" and "How should society respond?" The perspective a society responds from says a lot about how that society views life at any point in time.

This is illustrated by the two primary schools of thought on the causes of delinquency. The classical theory, developed by Cesare Beccaria, sets forth the concept that people are responsible for their own behavior because they act on their own free will. The positivist theory, developed by Cesare Lombroso, operates on the premise that people's personal and background characteristics are to answer for their behavior, which suggests that these individuals are, in effect, "victims of their society." How you perceive the issues will influence how you will respond. Classicalists would argue for accountability and punishment for delinquent behavior, whereas positivists would argue for treatment. Delinquency trends reflect whether society is leaning more toward a conservative or liberal view at that time.

Similarly, the various laws of governments in the United States (be they municipal, county, state, or federal) will reflect whether society sees itself as being on the more liberal or more conservative side of the pendulum's arc. Prohibition. Marijuana. Flag desecration. Women voting. Slavery. Abortion. Guns. Religion. The laws addressing important social issues reflect how U.S. citizens see themselves and what they think is important at the time. Although change is inevitable, the changes reflect the pendulum's position between conservative and liberal ideals for society at any given moment in history. The pendulum tends to go back and forth, back and forth—which is all the more reason that changes to the Constitution occur only after sincere debate.

What conclusions can be drawn from the pendulum analogy? Simply that change will continue. The ability to adapt to change is what has kept U.S. law so viable, and this viability is what the study of the U.S. Constitution is all about. Begin by considering the complex simplicity on which the Constitution was conceived; it continues to provide stability for one of the most complicated societies to ever develop.

Could we, as a society, operate without a written constitution, as some other societies have? Doubtful. Why can the United Kingdom, for example, operate so efficiently simply on tradition, whereas Americans demand a written document? It is the nature of Americans. It was just this questioning and demanding nature of those who left England that led to the U.S. Constitution in the first place. Citizens want to know why things are the way they are, exactly what is expected of them, and what can be expected of others. "Because your government knows best" would never be an acceptable answer here. The only answer that appeases U.S. citizens' critical nature is that an approach, an issue, or a law is constitutionally permissible. The Constitution is our tradition.

Not everyone agrees with the Constitution in full or in part, and people will continue to challenge it and consider changing it. The document can be changed, but because of the importance of maintaining the premises on which subsequent law will be built, changes to the Constitution will continue to come with great debate and consideration. This is the way it should be. As history has proved, even this great document can change when the people it serves so demand. Fairness. Justice. Due process. Freedom. These ideals are what our Constitution is about.

> *The liberties of our country, the freedoms of our civil Constitution, are worth defending at all hazards; it is our duty to defend them against all attacks. We have received them as a fair inheritance from our worthy ancestors. They purchased them for us with toil and danger and expense of treasure and blood. It will bring a mark of everlasting infamy on the present generation—enlightened as it is—if we should suffer them to be wrested from us by violence without a struggle, or to be cheated out of them by the artifices of designing men.*
>
> **—Samuel Adams**

> *It is the genius of our Constitution that under its shelter of enduring institutions and rooted principles, there is ample room for the rich fertility of American political invention.*
>
> **—Lyndon Johnson**

To live under the American Constitution is the greatest political privilege that was ever accorded to the human race.
—**Calvin Coolidge**

By design, the text comes full circle, asking you to "study the past" because "what is past is prologue." Maybe it was better said by a student in response to the question of whether the United States could rely solely on tradition as some governments do rather than on a written constitution. He stated that the Constitution *is* our tradition. And what law is being promulgated now will become woven into the rich history of the U.S. Constitution and our way of life.

Appendix A

The U.S. Constitution and Amendments

(F.N. Thorpe, ed. *Federal and State Constitutions*, Vol. I, p.3 ff [1909. Retrieved from http://www.archive.org/details/federalstatecons01thoriala]. Text is taken from the Revised Statutes of the United States version, 1878 edition, and has been collated with the facsimile of the original as printed in the original *Journal of the old Congress*.)

Constitution of the United States

We the People of the United States, in Order to form a more perfect Union, establish Justice, insure domestic Tranquility, provide for the common defence, promote the general Welfare, and secure the Blessings of Liberty to ourselves and our Posterity, do ordain and establish this Constitution for the United States of America.

Article I

Section 1. All legislative Powers herein granted shall be vested in a Congress of the United States, which shall consist of a Senate and House of Representatives.

Section 2. The House of Representatives shall be composed of Members chosen every second Year by the People of the several States, and the Electors in each State shall have the Qualifications requisite for Electors of the most numerous Branch of the State Legislature.

No Person shall be a Representative who shall not have attained to the Age of twenty five Years, and been seven Years a Citizen of the United States, and who shall not, when elected, be an Inhabitant of that State in which he shall be chosen.

[Representatives and direct Taxes shall be apportioned among the several States which may be included within this Union, according to their respective Numbers, which shall be determined by adding to the whole Number of free Persons, including those bound to Service for a Term of Years, and excluding Indians not taxed, three fifths of all other Persons.][1] The actual Enumeration shall be made within three Years after the first Meeting of the Congress of the United States, and within every subsequent Term of ten Years, in such Manner as they shall by Law direct. The number of Representatives shall not exceed one for every thirty Thousand, but each State shall have at Least one Representative; and until such enumeration shall be made, the State of New Hampshire shall be entitled to chuse three, Massachusetts eight, Rhode-Island and Providence Plantations one, Connecticut five, New York six, New Jersey four, Pennsylvania eight, Delaware one, Maryland six, Virginia ten, North Carolina five, South Carolina five, and Georgia three.

When vacancies happen in the Representation from any State, the Executive Authority thereof shall issue Writs of Election to fill such Vacancies.

The House of Representatives shall chuse their Speaker and other Officers; and shall have the sole Power of Impeachment.

---

[1]Changed by Section 2 of the Fourteenth Amendment.

Section 3. The Senate of the United States shall be composed of two Senators from each State, [chosen by the Legislature thereof,][2] for six Years; and each Senator shall have one Vote.

Immediately after they shall be assembled in Consequence of the first Election, they shall be divided as equally as may be into three Classes. The Seats of the Senators of the first Class shall be vacated at the Expiration of the second Year, of the second Class at the Expiration of the fourth Year, and of the third Class at the Expiration of the sixth Year, so that one third may be chosen every second Year; [and if Vacancies happen by Resignation, or otherwise, during the Recess of the Legislature of any State, the Executive thereof may make temporary Appointments until the next Meeting of the Legislature, which shall then fill such Vacancies.][3]

No Person shall be a Senator who shall not have attained to the Age of thirty Years, and been nine Years a Citizen of the United States, and who shall not, when elected, be an Inhabitant of that State for which he shall be chosen.

The Vice President of the United States shall be President of the Senate, but shall have no Vote, unless they be equally divided.

The Senate shall chuse their other Officers, and also a President pro tempore, in the Absence of the Vice President, or when he shall exercise the Office of President of the United States.

The Senate shall have the sole Power to try all Impeachments. When sitting for that Purpose, they shall be on Oath or Affirmation. When the President of the United States is tried, the Chief Justice shall preside: And no Person shall be convicted without the Concurrence of two thirds of the Members present.

Judgment in Cases of Impeachment shall not extend further than to removal from Office, and disqualification to hold and enjoy any Office of honor, Trust or Profit under the United States: but the Party convicted shall nevertheless be liable and subject to Indictment, Trial, Judgment and Punishment, according to Law.

Section 4. The Times, Places and Manner of holding Elections for Senators and Representatives, shall be prescribed in each State by the Legislature thereof; but the Congress may at any time by Law make or alter such Regulations, except as to the Places of chusing Senators.

The Congress shall assemble at least once in every Year, and such Meeting shall be [on the first Monday in December,][4] unless they shall by Law appoint a different Day.

Section 5. Each House shall be the Judge of the Elections, Returns and Qualifications of its own Members, and a Majority of each shall constitute a Quorum to do Business; but a smaller Number may adjourn from day to day, and may be authorized to compel the Attendance of absent Members, in such Manner, and under such Penalties as each House may provide.

Each House may determine the Rules of its Proceedings, punish its Members for disorderly Behavior, and, with the Concurrence of two thirds, expel a Member.

Each House shall keep a Journal of its Proceedings, and from time to time publish the same, excepting such Parts as may in their Judgment require Secrecy; and the Yeas and Nays of the Members of either House on any question shall, at the Desire of one fifth of those Present, be entered on the Journal.

Neither House, during the Session of Congress, shall, without the Consent of the other, adjourn for more than three days, nor to any other Place than that in which the two Houses shall be sitting.

Section 6. The Senators and Representatives shall receive a Compensation for their Services, to be ascertained by Law, and paid out of the Treasury of the United States. They shall in all Cases, except Treason, Felony and Breach of the Peace, be privileged from Arrest during their Attendance at the Session of their respective Houses, and in going to and returning from the same; and for any Speech or Debate in either House, they shall not be questioned in any other Place.

No Senator or Representative shall, during the Time for which he was elected, be appointed to any

---

[2]Changed by the Seventeenth Amendment.
[3]Changed by the Seventeenth Amendment.
[4]Changed by Section 2 of the Twentieth Amendment.

civil Office under the Authority of the United States, which shall have been created, or the Emoluments whereof shall have been encreased during such time; and no Person Holding any Office under the United States, shall be a Member of either House during his Continuance in Office.

Section 7. All Bills for raising Revenue shall originate in the House of Representatives; but the Senate may propose or concur with Amendments as on other Bills.

Every Bill which shall have passed the House of Representatives and the Senate, shall, before it becomes a Law, be presented to the President of the United States; If he approves he shall sign it, but if not he shall return it, with his Objections to that House in which it shall have originated, who shall enter the Objections at large on their Journal, and proceed to reconsider it. If after such Reconsideration two thirds of that House shall agree to pass the Bill, it shall be sent, together with the Objections, to the other House, by which it shall likewise be reconsidered, and if approved by two thirds of that House, it shall become a Law. But in all Cases the Votes of both Houses shall be determined by yeas and Nays, and the Names of the Persons voting for against the Bill shall be entered on the Journal of each House respectively. If any Bill shall not be returned by the President within ten Days (Sundays excepted) after it shall have been presented to him, the Same shall be a Law, in like Manner as if he had signed it, unless the Congress by their Adjournment prevent its Return, in which Case it shall not be a Law.

Every Order, Resolution, or Vote to which the Concurrence of the Senate and House of Representatives may be necessary (except on a question of Adjournment) shall be presented to the President of the United States; and before the Same shall take Effect, shall be approved by him, or being disapproved by him, shall be repassed by two thirds of the Senate and House of Representatives, according to the Rules and Limitations prescribed in the Case of a Bill.

Section 8. The Congress shall have Power To lay and collect Taxes, Duties, Imposts and Excises, to pay the Debts and provide for the common Defence and general Welfare of the United States; but all Duties, Imposts and Excises shall be uniform throughout the United States;

To borrow Money on the credit of the United States;

To regulate Commerce with foreign Nations, and among the several States, and with Indian Tribes;

To establish an uniform Rule of Naturalization, and uniform Laws on the subject of Bankruptcies throughout the United States;

To coin Money, regulate the Value thereof, and of foreign Coin, and fix the Standard of Weights and Measures;

To provide for the Punishment of counterfeiting the Securities and current Coin of the United States;

To establish Post Offices and post Roads;

To promote the Progress of Science and useful Arts, by securing for limited Times to Authors and Inventors the exclusive Right to their respective Writings and Discoveries;

To constitute Tribunals inferior to the supreme Court;

To define and punish Piracies and Felonies committed on the high Seas, and Offenses against the Law of Nations;

To declare War, grant Letters of Marque and Reprisal, and make Rules concerning Captures on Land and Water;

To raise and support Armies, but no Appropriation of Money to that Use shall be for a longer Term than two Years;

To provide and maintain a Navy;

To make Rules for the Government and Regulation of the land and naval Forces;

To provide for calling forth the Militia to execute the Laws of the Union, suppress Insurrections and repel Invasions;

To provide for organizing, arming, and disciplining, the Militia, and for governing such Part of them as may be employed in the Service of the United States, reserving to the States respectively, the Appointment of the Officers, and the Authority of training the Militia according to the discipline prescribed by Congress;

To exercise exclusive Legislation in all Cases whatsoever, over such District (not exceeding ten Miles square) as may, by Cession of particular States, and the Acceptance of Congress, become the Seat of the Government of the United States, and to exercise like Authority over all Places purchased by the Consent of the Legislature of the State in which the Same shall be, for the Erection of Forts, Magazines, Arsenals, dock-Yards and other needful Buildings;—And

To make all Laws which shall be necessary and proper for carrying into Execution the foregoing Powers, and all other Powers vested by this Constitution in the Government of the United States, or in any Department or Officer thereof.

Section 9. The Migration or Importation of such Persons as any of the States now existing shall think proper to admit, shall not be prohibited by the Congress prior to the Year one thousand eight hundred and eight, but a Tax or duty may be imposed on such Importation, not exceeding ten dollars for each Person.

The Privilege of the Writ of Habeas Corpus shall not be suspended, unless when in Cases of Rebellion or Invasion the public Safety may require it.

No Bill of Attainder or ex post facto Law shall be passed.

[No Capitation, or other direct, Tax shall be laid, unless in Proportion to the Census or Enumeration herein before directed to be taken.][5]

No Tax or Duty shall be laid on Articles exported from any State.

No Preference shall be given by any Regulation of Commerce or Revenue to the Ports of one State over those of another: nor shall Vessels bound to, or from, one State, be obliged to enter, clear, or pay Duties in another.

No Money shall be drawn from the Treasury, but in Consequence of Appropriations made by Law; and a regular Statement and Account of the Receipts and Expenditures of all public Money shall be published from time to time.

No Title of Nobility shall be granted by the United States: And no Person holding any Office of Profit or Trust under them, shall, without the Consent of the Congress, accept of any present, Emolument, Office, or Title, of any kind whatever, from any King, Prince, or foreign State.

Section 10. No State shall enter into any Treaty, Alliance, or Confederation; grant Letters of Marque and Reprisal; coin Money; emit Bills of Credit; make any Thing but gold and silver Coin a Tender in Payment of Debts; pass any Bill of Attainder, ex post facto Law, or Law impairing the Obligation of Contracts, or grant any Title of Nobility.

No State shall, without the Consent of the Congress, lay any Imposts or Duties on Imports or Exports, except what may be absolutely necessary for executing its inspection Laws: and the net Produce of the Duties and Imposts, laid by any State on Imports or Exports, shall be for the Use of the Treasury of the United States; and all such Laws shall be subject to the Revision and Control of the Congress.

No State shall, without the Consent of Congress, lay any Duty of Tonnage, keep Troops, or Ships of War in time of Peace, enter into any Agreement or Compact with another State, or with a foreign Power, or engage in War, unless actually invaded, or in such imminent Danger as will not admit of delay.

Article II

Section 1. The executive Power shall be vested in a President of the United States of America. He shall hold his Office during their Term of four Years, and, together with the Vice President, chosen for the same Term, be elected, as follows:

Each State shall appoint, in such Manner as the Legislature thereof may direct, a Number of Electors, equal to the whole Number of Senators and Representatives to which the State may be entitled in the Congress: but no Senator or Representative, or Person holding an Office of Trust or Profit under the United States shall be appointed an Elector.

[The Electors shall meet in their respective States, and vote by Ballot for two Persons, of whom one at least shall not be an Inhabitant of the same State with themselves. And they shall make a List of all the Persons voted for, and of the Number of Votes for each; which List they shall sign and certify, and transmit sealed to the Seat of the Government of the United States, directed to the President of the Senate. The President of the Senate shall, in the Presence of the Senate and House of Representatives, open all the Certificates, and the Votes shall then be counted. The Person having the greatest Number of Votes

---

[5]Changed by the Sixteenth Amendment.

shall be the President, if such Number be a Majority of the whole Number of Electors appointed; and if there be more than one who have such Majority, and have an equal Number of Votes, then the House of Representatives shall immediately chuse by Ballot one of them for President, and if no Person have a Majority, then from the five highest on the List the said House shall in like Manner chuse the President. But in chusing the President, the Votes shall be taken by States, the Representation from each State having one Vote; a quorum for this Purpose shall consist of a Member or Members from two thirds of the States, and a Majority of all the States shall be necessary to a Choice. In every Case, after the Choice of the President, the Person having the greatest Number of Votes of the Electors shall be the Vice President. But if there should remain two or more who have equal Votes, the Senate shall chuse from them by Ballot the Vice President.][6]

The Congress may determine the Time of chusing the Electors, and the Day on which they shall give their Votes; which Day shall be the same throughout the United States.

No Person except a natural born Citizen, or a Citizen of the United States, at the time of the Adoption of this Constitution, shall be eligible to the Office of the President; neither shall any person be eligible to that Office who shall not have attained to the Age of thirty five Years, and been fourteen Years a Resident within the United States.

[In Case of the Removal of the President from Office, or of his Death, Resignation, or Inability to discharge the Powers and Duties of the said Office, the Same shall devolve on the Vice President, and the Congress may by Law provide for the Case of Removal, Death, Resignation or Inability, both of the President and Vice President, declaring what Officer shall then act as President, and such Officer shall act accordingly, until the Disability be removed, or a President shall be elected.][7]

The President shall, at stated Times, receive for his Services, a Compensation which shall neither be increased nor diminished during the Period for which he shall have been elected, and he shall not receive within that Period any other Emolument from the United States, or any of them.

Before he enter on the Execution of his Office, he shall take the following Oath or Affirmation:—"I do solemnly swear (or affirm) that I will faithfully execute the Office of President of the United States, and will to the best of my Ability, preserve, protect and defend the Constitution of the United States."

Section 2. The President shall be Commander in Chief of the Army and Navy of the United States, and of the Militia of the several States, when called into the actual Service of the United States; he may require the Opinion, in writing, of the principal Officer in each of the executive Departments, upon any Subject relating to the Duties of their respective Offices, and he shall have Power to grant Reprieves and Pardons for Offenses against the United States, except in Cases of Impeachment.

He shall have Power, by and with the Advice and Consent of the Senate, to make Treaties, provided two thirds of the Senators present concur; and he shall nominate, and by and with the Advice and Consent of the Senate, shall appoint Ambassadors, other public Ministers and Consuls, Judges of the Supreme Court, and all other Officers of the United States, whose Appointments are not herein otherwise provided for, and which shall be established by Law: but the Congress may by Law vest the Appointment of such inferior Officers, as they think proper, in the President alone, in the Courts of Law, or in the Heads of Departments.

The President shall have Power to fill up all Vacancies that may happen during the Recess of the Senate, by granting Commissions which shall expire at the End of their next Session.

Section 3. He shall from time to time give to the Congress Information of the State of the Union, and recommend to their Consideration such Measures as he shall judge necessary and expedient; he may, on extraordinary Occasions, convene both Houses, or either of them, and in Case of Disagreement between them, with Respect to the Time of Adjournment, he may adjourn them to such Time as he shall think proper; he shall receive Ambassadors and other public Ministers; he shall take Care that the Laws

---
[6]Changed by the Twelfth Amendment
[7]Changed by the Twenty-Fifth Amendment.

be faithfully executed, and shall Commission all the Officers of the United States.

Section 4. The President, Vice President and all civil Officers of the United States, shall be removed from Office on Impeachment for, and Conviction of, Treason, Bribery, or other high Crimes and Misdemeanors.

Article III

Section 1. The judicial Power of the United States, shall be vested in one supreme Court, and in such inferior Courts as the Congress may from time to time ordain and establish. The Judges, both of the supreme and inferior Courts, shall hold their Offices during good Behaviour, and shall, at stated Times, receive for their Services, a Compensation, which shall not be diminished during their Continuance in Office.

Section 2. The judicial Power shall extend to all Cases, in Law and Equity, arising under this Constitution, the Laws of the United States, and Treaties made, or which shall be made, under their Authority;—to all Cases affecting Ambassadors, other public Ministers and Consuls:—to all Cases of admiralty and maritime Jurisdiction;—to Controversies to which the United States shall be a Party;—to Controversies between two or more States; [between a State and Citizens of another State;—][8] between Citizens of different States—between Citizens of the same State claiming Lands under Grants of different States, [and between a State, or the Citizens thereof, and foreign States, Citizens or Subjects.][9]

In all Cases affecting Ambassadors, other public Ministers and Consuls, and those in which a State shall be Party, the supreme Court shall have original Jurisdiction. In all the other Cases before mentioned, the supreme Court shall have appellate Jurisdiction, both as to Law and Fact, with such Exceptions, and under such Regulations as the Congress shall make.

The Trial of the Crimes, except in Cases of Impeachment; shall be by Jury; and such Trial shall be held in the State where the said Crimes shall have been committed; but when not committed within any State, the Trial shall be at such Place or Places as the Congress may by Law have directed.

Section 3. Treason against the United States, shall consist only in levying War against them, or in adhering to their Enemies, giving them Aid and Comfort. No Person shall be convicted of Treason unless on the Testimony of two Witnesses to the same overt Act, or on Confession in open Court.

The Congress shall have Power to declare the Punishment of Treason, but no Attainder of Treason shall work Corruption of Blood, or Forfeiture except during the Life of the Person attained.

Article IV

Section 1. Full Faith and Credit shall be given in each State to the public Acts, Records, and judicial Proceedings of every other State, and the Congress may by general Laws prescribe the Manner in which such Acts, Records and Proceedings shall be proved, and the Effect thereof.

Section 2. The Citizens of each State shall be entitled to all Privileges and Immunities of Citizens in the several States.

A Person charged in any State with Treason, Felony, or other Crime, who shall flee from Justice, and be found in another State, shall on Demand of the executive Authority of the State from which he fled, be delivered up, to be removed to the State having Jurisdiction of the Crime.

[No Person held to Service or Labour in one State, under the Laws thereof, escaping into another, shall, in Consequence of any Law or Regulation therein, be discharged from such Service or Labour, but shall be delivered up on Claim of the Party to whom such Service or Labour may be due.][10]

Section 3. New States may be admitted by the Congress into this Union; but no new State shall be formed or erected within the Jurisdiction of any other State; nor any State be formed by the Junction of two or more States, or Parts of States, without the

---

[8]Changed by the Eleventh Amendment.
[9]Changed by the Eleventh Amendment.

[10]Changed by the Thirteenth Amendment.

Consent of the Legislatures of the States concerned as well as of the Congress.

The Congress shall have Power to dispose of and make all needful Rules and Republican respecting the Territory or other Property belonging to the United States; and nothing in this Constitution shall be so construed as to Prejudice any Claims of the United States, or of any particular State.

Section 4. The United States shall guarantee to every State in this Union a Republican Form of Government, and shall protect each of them against Invasion; and on Application of the Legislature, or of the Executive (when the Legislature cannot be convened) against domestic Violence.

Article V

The Congress, whenever two thirds of both Houses shall deem it necessary, shall propose Amendments to this Constitution, or, on the Application of the Legislatures of two thirds of the several States, shall call a Convention for proposing Amendments, which, in either Case, shall be valid to all Intents and Purposes, as Part of this Constitution, when ratified by the Legislatures of three fourths of the several States, or by Conventions in three fourths thereof, as the one or the other Mode of Ratification may be proposed by the Congress; Provided that no Amendment which may be made prior to the Year one thousand eight hundred and eight shall in any Manner affect the first and fourth Clauses in the Ninth Section of the first Article; and that no State, without its Consent, shall be deprived of it's [sic] equal Suffrage in the Senate.

Article VI

All Debts contracted and Engagements entered into, before the Adoption of this Constitution, shall be as valid against the United States under this Constitution, as under the Confederation.

This Constitution, and the Laws of the United States which shall be made in Pursuance thereof; and all Treaties made, or which shall be made, under the Authority of the United States, shall be the supreme Law of the Land; and the Judges in every State shall be bound thereby, any Thing in the Constitution or Laws of any State to the Contrary nowithstanding.

The Senators and Representatives before mentioned, and the Members of the several State Legislatures, and all executive and judicial Officers, both of the United States and of the several States, shall be bound by Oath or Affirmation, to support this Constitution; but no religious Test shall ever be required as a Qualification to any Office or public Trust under the United States.

Article VII

The Ratification of the Conventions of nine States, shall be sufficient for the Establishment of this Constitution between the States so ratifying the Same.

Done in Convention by the Unanimous Consent of the States present the Seventeenth Day of September in the Year of our Lord one thousand seven hundred and Eighty seven and of the Independence of the United States of America the Twelfth In Witness whereof We have hereunto subscribed our Names,

Go. Washington—Presidt. and deputy from Virginia

New Hampshire
John Langdon
Nicholas Gilman

Massachusetts
Nathaniel Gorham
Rufus King

Connecticut
Wm. Saml. Johnson
Roger Sherman

New York
Alexander Hamilton

New Jersey
Wil. Livingston
David Brearley
Wm. Paterson
Jona. Dayton

Pennsylvania
B. Franklin
Thomas Mifflin
Robt. Morris
Geo. Clymer
Thos. FitzSimons
Jared Ingersoll
James Wilson
Gouv. Morris

Delaware
Geo. Read
Gunning Bedford jun
John Dickinson
Richard Bassett
Jaco. Broom

Maryland
James McHenry
Dan of St. Thos. Jenifer
Danl. Carroll

Virginia
John Blair
James Madison, Jr.

North Carolina
Wm. Blount
Richd. Dobbs Spaight
Hu Williamson

South Carolina
J. Rutledge
Charles Cotesworth Pinckney
Charles Pinckney
Pierce Butler

Georgia
William Few
Abr. Baldwin

Attest *William Jackson* Secretary

In Convention Monday September 17th 1787

Present the States of

New Hampshire, Massachusetts, Connecticut, Mr. Hamilton from New York, New Jersey, Pennsylvania, Delaware, Maryland, Virginia, North Carolina, South Carolina and Georgia.

Resolved,
That the preceeding Constitution be laid before the United States in Congress assembled, and that it is the Opinion of this Convention, that it should afterwards be submitted to a Convention of Delegates, chosen in each State by the People thereof, under the Recommendation of its Legislature, for their Assent and Ratification; and that each Convention assenting to, and ratifying the Same, should give Notice thereof to the United States in Congress assembled. Resolved, That it is the Opinion of this Convention, that as soon as the Conventions of nine States shall have ratified this Constitution, the United States in Congress assembled should fix a Day on which Electors should be appointed by the States which shall have ratified the same, and a Day on which the Electors should assemble to vote for the President, and the Time and Place for commencing Proceedings under this Constitution.

That after such Publication the Electors should be appointed, and the Senators and Representatives elected: That the Electors should meet on the Day fixed for the Election of the President, and should transmit their Votes certified, signed, sealed and directed, as the Constitution requires, to the Secretary of the United States in Congress assembled, that the Senators and Representatives should convene at the Time and Place assigned; that the Senators should appoint a President of the Senate, for the sole Purpose of receiving, opening and counting the Votes for President; and, that after he shall be chosen, the Congress, together with the President, should, without Delay, proceed to execute this Constitution.

By the unanimous Order of the Convention
Go. Washington—Presidt.
W. Jackson Secretary.

Amendments to the Constitution of the United States

Amendment I [1791]

Congress shall make no law respecting an establishment of religion, or prohibiting the free exercise thereof; or abridging the freedom of speech, or of the press; or the right of the people peaceably to assembly, and to petition the Government for a redress of grievances.

Amendment II [1791]

A well regulated Militia, being necessary to the security of a free State, the right of the people to keep and bear Arms, shall not be infringed.

Amendment III [1791]

No Soldier shall, in time of peace be quartered in any house, without the consent of the Owner, nor in time of war, but in a manner to be prescribed by law.

Amendment IV [1791]

The right of the people to be secure in their persons, houses, papers, and effects, against unreasonable searches and seizures, shall not be violated, and no Warrants shall issue, but upon probable cause, supported by Oath or affirmation, and particularly describing the place to be searched, and the persons or things to be seized.

Amendment V [1791]

No person shall be held to answer for a capital, or otherwise infamous crime, unless on a presentment or indictment of a Grand Jury, except in cases arising in the land or naval forces, or in the Militia, when in actual service in time of War or public danger; nor shall any person be subject for the same offence to be twice put in jeopardy of life or limb; nor shall be compelled in any criminal case to be a witness against himself, nor be deprived of life, liberty, or property, without due process of law; nor shall private property be taken for public use, without just compensation.

Amendment VI [1791]

In all criminal prosecutions, the accused shall enjoy the right to a speedy and public trial, by an impartial jury of the State and district wherein the crime shall have been committed, which district shall have been previously ascertained by law, and to be informed of the nature and cause of accusation; to be confronted with the witnesses against him; to have compulsory process for obtaining witnesses in his favor, and to have the Assistance of Counsel for his defence.

Amendment VII [1791]

In Suits at common law, where the value in controversy shall exceed twenty dollars, the right of trial by jury shall be preserved, and no fact tried by jury, shall be otherwise re-examined in any Court of the United States, than according to the rules of the common law.

Amendment VIII [1791]

Excessive bail shall not be required, nor excessive fines imposed, nor cruel and unusual punishments inflicted.

Amendment IX [1791]

The enumeration in the Constitution, of certain rights, shall not be construed to deny or disparage others retained by the people.

Amendment X [1791]

The powers not delegated to the United States by the Constitution, nor prohibited by it to the States, are reserved to the States respectively, or to the people.

Amendment XI [1798]

The Judicial power of the United States shall not be construed to extend to any suit in law or equity, commenced or prosecuted against one of the United States by Citizens of another State, or by Citizens or Subjects of any Foreign State.

Amendment XII [1804]

The Electors shall meet in their respective states, and vote by ballot for President and Vice-President, one of whom, at least, shall not be an inhabitant of the same state with themselves; they shall name in their ballots the person voted for as President, and in distinct ballots the person voted for as Vice-President, and they shall make distinct lists of all persons voted for as President, and of all persons voted for as Vice-President, and of the number of votes for each, which lists they shall sign and certify, and transmit sealed to the seat of the government of the United States, directed to the President of the Senate;—The President of the Senate shall, in the presence of the Senate and House of Representatives, open all the certificates and the votes shall then be counted;— The person having the greatest number of votes for President, shall be the President, if such number be a majority of the whole number of Electors appointed; and if no person have such majority, then from the persons having the highest numbers not exceeding three on the list of those voted for as President, the House of Representatives shall choose immediately, by ballot, the President. But in choosing the President, the votes shall be taken by states, the representation from each state having one vote; a quorum for this purpose shall consist of a member or members from two-thirds of the states, and a majority of all states shall be necessary to a choice. And if the House of Representatives shall not choose a President whenever the right of choice shall devolve upon them, before the fourth day of March next following, then the Vice-President shall act as President, as in the case of the death or other constitutional disability of the President.—The person having the greatest number of votes as Vice-President, shall be the Vice-President, if such number be a majority of the whole number of Electors appointed, and if no person have a majority, then from the two highest numbers on the list, the Senate shall choose the Vice-President; a quorum for the purpose shall consist of two-thirds of the whole number of Senators, and a majority of the whole number shall be necessary to a choice. But no person constitutionally ineligible to the office of President shall be eligible to that of Vice-President of the United States.

Amendment XIII [1865]

Section 1. Neither slavery nor involuntary servitude, except as a punishment for crime whereof the party shall have been duly convicted, shall exist within the United States, or any place subject to their jurisdiction.

Section 2. Congress shall have power to enforce this article by appropriate legislation.

Amendment XIV [1868]

Section 1. All persons born or naturalized in the United States, and subject to the jurisdiction thereof, are citizens of the United States and of the State wherein they reside. No State shall make or enforce any law which shall abridge the privileges or immunities of citizens of the United States; nor shall any State deprive any person of life, liberty, or property, without due process of law; nor deny to any person within its jurisdiction the equal protection of the laws.

Section 2. Representatives shall be apportioned among the several States according to their respective numbers, counting the whole number of persons in each State, excluding Indians not taxed. But when the right to vote at any election for the choice of electors for President and Vice President of the United States, Representatives in Congress, the Executive and Judicial officers of a State, or the members of the Legislature thereof, is denied to any of the male inhabitants of such State, being twenty-one years of age, and citizens of the United States, or in any way abridged, except for participation in rebellion, or other crime, the basis of representation therein shall be reduced in the proportion which the number of such male citizens shall bear to the whole number of male citizens twenty-one years of age in such State.

Section 3. No person shall be a Senator or Representative in Congress, or elector of President and Vice President, or hold any office, civil or military, under the United States, or under any State, who having previously taken an oath, as a member of Congress, or as an officer of the United States, or as a member of any State legislature, or as an executive or judicial officer of any State, to support the Constitution of the United States, shall have engaged in insurrection or rebellion against the same, or given aid or comfort to the enemies thereof. But Congress may by a vote of two-thirds of each House, remove such disability.

Section 4. The validity of the public debt of the United States, authorized by law, including debts incurred for payment of pensions and bounties for services in suppressing insurrection or rebellion, shall not be questioned. But neither the United States nor any State shall assume or pay any debt or obligation incurred in aid of insurrection or rebellion against the United States, or any claim for the loss or emancipation of any slave; but all such debts, obligation and claims shall be held illegal and void.

Section 5. The Congress shall have power to enforce, by appropriate legislation, the provisions of this article.

Amendment XV [1870]

Section 1. The right of citizens of the United States to vote shall not be denied or abridged by the United States or by any State on account of race, color, or previous condition of servitude.

Section 2. The Congress shall have power to enforce this article by appropriate legislation.

Amendment XVI [1913]

The Congress shall have power to lay and collect taxes on incomes, from whatever source derived, without apportionment among the several States, and without regard to any census or enumeration.

Amendment XVII [1913]

Section 1. The Senate of the United States shall be composed of two Senators from each State, elected by the people thereof, for six years; and each Senator shall have one vote. The electors in each State shall have the qualifications requisite for electors of the most numerous branch of the State legislatures.

Section 2. When vacancies happen in the representation of any State in the Senate, the executive authority of such State shall issue writs of election to fill such vacancies: provided, that the legislature of any State may empower the executive thereof to make temporary appointments until the people fill the vacancies by election as the legislature may direct.

Section 3. This amendment shall not be so construed as to affect the election or term of any Senator chosen before it becomes valid as part of the Constitution.

Amendment XVIII [1919]

Section 1. After one year from the ratification of this article the manufacture, sale, or transportation of intoxicating liquors within, the importation thereof into, or the exportation thereof from the United States and all territory subject to the jurisdiction thereof for beverage purposes is hereby prohibited.

Section 2. The Congress and the several States shall have concurrent power to enforce this article by appropriate legislation.

Section 3. This article shall be inoperative unless it shall have been ratified as an amendment to the Constitution by the legislatures of the several States, as provided in the Constitution, within seven years from the date of the submission hereof to the States by the Congress.

Amendment XIX [1920]

Section 1. The right of citizens of the United States to vote shall not be denied or abridged by the United States or by any State on account of sex.

Section 2. Congress shall have power to enforce this article by appropriate legislation.

Amendment XX [1933]

Section 1. The terms of the President and Vice President shall end at noon on the 20th day of January, and the terms of Senators and Representatives at noon on the 3rd day of January, of the years in which such terms would have ended if this article had not been ratified; and the terms of their successors shall then begin.

Section 2. The Congress shall assemble at least once in every year, and such meeting shall begin at noon on the 3rd day of January, unless they shall by law appoint a different day.

Section 3. If, at the time fixed for the beginning of the term of the President, the President elect shall have died, the Vice President elect shall become President. If the President shall not have been chosen before the time fixed for the beginning of his term, or if the President elect shall have failed to qualify, then the Vice President elect shall act as President until a President shall have qualified; and the Congress may by law provide for the case wherein neither a President elect nor a Vice President elect shall have qualified, declaring who shall then act as President, or the manner in which one who is to act shall be selected, and such person shall act accordingly until a President or Vice President shall have qualified.

Section 4. The Congress may by law provide for the case of the death of any of the persons from whom the House of Representatives may choose a President whenever the right of choice shall have devolved upon them, and for the case of the death of any of the persons from whom the Senate may choose a Vice President whenever the right of choice shall have devolved upon them.

Section 5. Sections 1 and 2 shall take effect on the 15th day of October following the ratification of this article.

Section 6. This article shall be inoperative unless it shall have been ratified as an amendment to the Constitution by the legislatures of three-fourths of the several States within seven years from the date of its submission.

Amendment XXI [1933]

Section 1. The eighteenth article of amendment to the Constitution of the United States is hereby repealed.

Section 2. The transportation or importation into any State, Territory, or possession of the United States for delivery or use therein of intoxicating liquors, in violation of the laws thereof, is hereby prohibited.

Section 3. This article shall be inoperative unless it shall have been ratified as an amendment to the Constitution by conventions in the several States, as provided in the Constitution, within seven years from the date of the submission hereof to the States by the Congress.

Amendment XXII [1951]

Section 1. No person shall be elected to the office of the President more than twice, and no person who has held the office of President, or acted as President, for more than two years of a term to which some other person was elected President shall be elected to the office of President more than once. But this Article shall not apply to any person holding the office of President when this Article was proposed by the Congress, and shall not prevent any person who may be holding the office of President, or acting as President, during the term within which this Article becomes operative, from holding the office of President or acting as President during the remainder of such term.

Section 2. This article shall be inoperative unless it shall have been ratified as an amendment to the Constitution by the legislatures of three-fourths of the several States within seven years from the date of its submission to the States by the Congress.

Amendment XXIII [1961]

Section 1. The District constituting the seat of Government of the United States shall appoint in such manner as the Congress may direct:

A number of electors of President and Vice President equal to the whole number of Senators and Representatives in Congress to which the District would be entitled if it were a State, but in no event more than the least populous state; they shall be in addition to those appointed by the states, but they shall be considered, for the purposes of the election of President and Vice President, to be electors appointed by a state; and they shall meet in the District and perform such duties as provided by the twelfth article of amendment.

Section 2. The Congress shall have power to enforce this article by appropriate legislation.

Amendment XXIV [1964]

Section 1. The right of citizens of the United States to vote in any primary or other election for President or Vice President, for electors for President or Vice President, or for Senator or Representative in Congress, shall not be denied or abridged by the United States, or any State by reason of failure to pay any poll tax or other tax.

Section 2. The Congress shall have power to enforce this article by appropriate legislation.

Amendment XXV [1967]

Section 1. In case of the removal of the President from office or of his death or resignation, the Vice President shall become President.

Section 2. Whenever there is a vacancy in the office of the Vice President, the President shall nominate a Vice President who shall take office upon confirmation by a majority vote of both Houses of Congress.

Section 3. Whenever the President transmits to the President pro tempore of the Senate and the

Speaker of the House of Representatives his written declaration that he is unable to discharge the powers and duties of his office, and until he transmits to them a written declaration to the contrary, such powers and duties shall be discharged by the Vice President as Acting President.

Section 4. Whenever the Vice President and a majority of either the principal officers of the executive departments or of such other body as Congress may by law provide, transmit to the President pro tempore of the Senate and the Speaker of the House of Representatives their written declaration that the President is unable to discharge the powers and duties of his office, the Vice President shall immediately assume the powers and duties of the office as Acting President.

Thereafter, when the President transmits to the President pro tempore of the Senate and the Speaker of the House of Representatives his written declaration that no inability exists, he shall resume the powers and duties of his office unless the Vice President and a majority of either the principal officers of the executive department or of such other body as Congress may by law provide, transmit within four days to the President pro tempore of the Senate and the Speaker of the House of Representatives their written declaration and the President is unable to discharge the powers and duties of his office. Thereupon Congress shall decide the issue, assembling within forty-eight hours for that purpose if not in session. If the Congress, within twenty-one days after receipt of the latter written declaration, or, if Congress is not in session, within twenty-one days after Congress is required to assemble, determines by two-thirds vote of both Houses that the President is unable to discharge the powers and duties of his office, the Vice President shall continue to discharge the same as Acting President; otherwise, the President shall resume the powers and duties of his office.

Amendment XXVI [1971]

Section 1. The right of citizens of the United States, who are eighteen years of age or older, to vote shall not be denied or abridged by the United States or by any State on account of age.

Section 2. The Congress shall have power to enforce this article by appropriate legislation.

Amendment XXVII [1992]

No law varying the compensation for the services of the Senators and Representatives, shall take effect, until an election of Representatives shall have intervened.

Appendix B

Reading Legal Citations

A legal citation is a standardized way of referring to a specific element in the law. It has three basic parts: a volume number, an abbreviation for the title, and a page or section number. Legal citations are usually followed by the date. Following are examples of legal citations:

- U.S. Supreme Court case: *Horton v. California*, 496 U.S. 128 (1990). This means volume 496 of the *United States Reports* (the official reporter for the U.S. Supreme Court opinions), page 128, decided in 1990.
- Federal law: 42 U.S.C. § 1983. This means title or chapter 42 of the *United States Code*, section 1983.
- Journal: Janice Toran, "Information Disclosure in Civil Actions: The Freedom of Information Act and the Federal Discovery Rules." 49 Geo. Wash. L. Rev. 843, 854–55 (1981). This refers to an article written by Janice Toran that appears in volume 49 of the *George Washington Law Review*, beginning on page 843, and specifically referencing pages 854–855 of the article, which was published in 1981.

If one is researching a state issue, there is usually no need to spend time on another state's law, unless the effort is to persuade a law change by showing how the law has worked in other states. Also, the citation will immediately point out if this is an appellate court case and, thus, what authority it has. This way, the reader will know exactly the position of the case and the level of authority he or she is dealing with. Finally, citing an authority helps avoid the issue of plagiarism and supports what the author is writing.

When string cites or parallel citations are provided, they show where the case can be found in other commercial reporting services. Consider the *Miranda* case citation:

- The simple citation is *Miranda v. Arizona*, 384 U.S. 436 (1966). This shows that the case is found in the official *United States Reports*.
- A string cite for this case would be *Miranda v. Arizona*, 384 U.S. 436, 86 S.Ct. 1602, 16 L.Ed.2d 694 (1966). This shows that in addition to the official *United States Reports*, the case is also in West Publishing Company's *Supreme Court Reporter* (S.Ct.) and the Lawyers Cooperative Publishing Company's *U.S. Supreme Court Reports, Lawyers' Edition* (L.Ed.2d).

A valuable resource to enhance understanding of basic legal citations is www.law.cornell.edu/citation/.

Appendix C

Briefs of *Marbury* and *Miranda*

Brief of *Marbury v. Madison*

Type of Case. This case deals with a petition to the U.S. Supreme Court for a writ of mandamus to compel a government official to deliver a commission, subsequently requiring a determination of whether the Supreme Court may review an act of Congress to determine its constitutionality.

Facts of the Case. Just before President John Adams left office after his defeat by Thomas Jefferson in 1800, Adams made several judicial appointments. Although Adams signed these appointments under the authority granted by Congress, some appointments were not officially made before Adams left office, for no reason other than time pressures. President Jefferson ordered his new Secretary of State, James Madison, to withhold delivery of several commissions made by the previous president, including that of justice of the peace to William Marbury. Marbury, along with several others, petitioned the Supreme Court to require Secretary of State Madison to deliver their commissions.

Legal Issue. Does the Supreme Court have the authority to declare congressional acts unconstitutional?

Holding and Decision. Yes. Because the government of the United States is one of laws, not men, the law needs to be able to remedy wrongs that result from acts of Congress. In this case, the Judiciary Act of 1789 as passed by Congress is unconstitutional.

Because the Constitution limits the Supreme Court's original jurisdiction to only certain areas, giving the Court only appellate jurisdiction in all other areas, the Judiciary Act may not grant the Supreme Court original jurisdiction to issue writs of mandamus. The Constitution limits the rights and powers of the legislature, and the legislature cannot change the Constitution, which itself provides that it is the "supreme law of the land."

If an act of the legislature is repugnant to the Constitution, are courts bound by that law? No. If a law is not in accordance with the U.S. Constitution, the Supreme Court may determine which of the conflicting rules will govern the particular case. If the Constitution is to have the power it was meant to have, it must prevail pursuant to Article 3, Section 2.

The framers meant the Constitution to govern courts as well as Congress. Why else are judges required to take an oath to uphold the U.S. Constitution? The Supreme Court has the authority to review acts of Congress, and in this case, Section 13 of the Judiciary Act of 1789 is unconstitutional.

Rule. Under the Supremacy Clause and Article 3, Section 2 of the U.S. Constitution, the Supreme Court has the authority to review acts of Congress to determine whether they are unconstitutional.

Brief of *Miranda v. Arizona*

Type of Case. This case deals with the issue of whether the police must advise certain criminal suspects who are being questioned of their constitutional right to not speak.

Facts of the Case. After being arrested, the defendant was taken to an interrogation room where he gave a confession to the police. He had not been told of his constitutional right to remain silent or to have a lawyer present because the police assumed he knew about these rights because he had been arrested before.

Legal Issue. Must government agents advise certain suspects of their constitutional Fifth Amendment rights?

Holding and Decision. Yes. Suspects held for interrogation must be clearly informed that they have the right to consult with a lawyer and to have the lawyer with them during interrogation. They must also be advised of their right to remain silent and that anything they state can be used as evidence against them.

If individuals indicate they wish the assistance of counsel before any interrogation occurs, the authorities cannot deny this request. If a person cannot afford legal counsel, it must be provided without cost. Suspects must be advised that they have a right to have legal counsel present during any questioning.

Once the warnings have been given, interrogation must cease at any time before or during questioning if suspects indicate in any way that they wish to remain silent. If the questioning continues, the burden is on the government to demonstrate that the suspect knowingly and intelligently waived the privilege against self-incrimination and the right to retained or appointed counsel.

Rule. When government agents question people in custody, those being questioned must be advised of their specific Fifth Amendment rights dealing with self-incrimination and must knowingly and intelligently waive such privileges.

Appendix D

Citating a Case

Example: Shepard's Citing List: 406 U.S. 340 from *Shepard's United States Reports Citations*

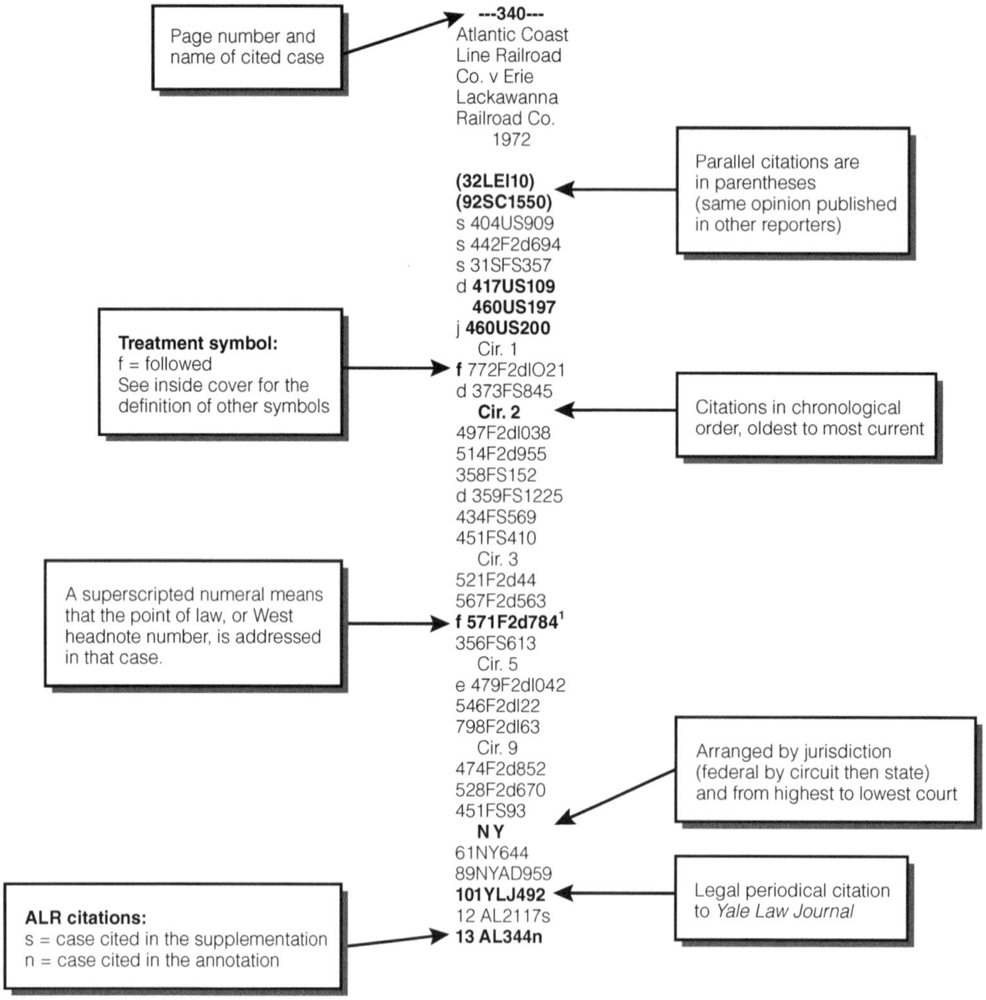

```
---340---
Atlantic Coast
Line Railroad
Co. v Erie
Lackawanna
Railroad Co.
    1972

(32LEl10)
(92SC1550)
s 404US909
s 442F2d694
s 31SFS357
d 417US109
  460US197
j 460US200
   Cir. 1
f 772F2dlO21
d 373FS845
   Cir. 2
 497F2dl038
 514F2d955
 358FS152
d 359FS1225
 434FS569
 451FS410
   Cir. 3
 521F2d44
 567F2d563
f 571F2d784¹
 356FS613
   Cir. 5
e 479F2dl042
 546F2dl22
 798F2dl63
   Cir. 9
 474F2d852
 528F2d670
 451FS93
    N Y
 61NY644
 89NYAD959
101YLJ492
 12 AL2117s
 13 AL344n
```

- Page number and name of cited case
- Parallel citations are in parentheses (same opinion published in other reporters)
- **Treatment symbol:** f = followed. See inside cover for the definition of other symbols
- Citations in chronological order, oldest to most current
- A superscripted numeral means that the point of law, or West headnote number, is addressed in that case.
- Arranged by jurisdiction (federal by circuit then state) and from highest to lowest court
- Legal periodical citation to *Yale Law Journal*
- **ALR citations:** s = case cited in the supplementation. n = case cited in the annotation

Example of Shepard's Citing List
Source: "Tips for Shepardizing Cases." H. Douglas Law Library, Syracuse University College of Law.

Appendix E

Legal Research

Computerized Legal Research

Computerized legal research is now the norm. Nothing has made the law more accessible to *everyone* than the Internet. Although computerized legal research has been in law offices for years, the Internet, along with law-related software, brings more legal sources to homes and offices than ever to allow anyone to locate answers to many legal queries.

Most students and criminal justice professionals use computers for their research. Anyone with basic computer skills has immediate access to a vast array of legal information when studying and working with the law. In a sense, the Internet has truly made the people's law available to them.

The Law on the Web

You might be wondering where and how to start your online legal research. A reasonable starting point, especially for those with only rudimentary legal knowledge, is whatever search engine a person is comfortable with, such as Google, Yahoo, or Bing, although there are many others. The limitation with these is not accessing enough sources but often too many.

In addition to developing a personal/professional reference library, students of the law and those working in the field should become familiar with some of the many Internet sources and databases. Experiment with different ones to find several that work for you, and bookmark them. As you become more interested or reliant on information, it may be worthwhile to subscribe to a source that charges a subscription fee such as LexisNexis and Westlaw.

You might also use a legal search engine such as LawCrawler, which is part of FindLaw. Following are some uniform resource locators (URLs) or addresses to access criminal justice sources on the Web:

American Bar Association	http://www.abanet.org/crimjust/
U.S. Department of Justice, Bureau of Justice Statistics	http://www.ojp.usdoj.gov/bjs
Legal Information Institute at Cornell University	http://www.law.cornell.edu/
National Criminal Justice Association	http://www.ncja.org/
U.S. Supreme Court	http://www.supremecourt.gov/
U.S. Federal Judiciary	http://www.uscourts.gov/
FindLaw	http://www.findlaw.com/
LexisNexis	http://www.lexisnexis.com/default.asp

Information Literacy

Information literacy is the ability to effectively identify an issue, narrow that issue, access appropriate online sites, separate fact from fiction, and present the findings professionally. Once upon a time people learned to navigate a library using the card catalog and the Dewey Decimal System (no doubt ancient or unknown terms to many readers). Times change, as do research methods, but the Internet can bring the law to anyone who knows where to look.

Locating information is only one part of information literacy. Evaluating the validity of the information is also required. How do you tell reliable information from that which is questionable? Most government websites are credible, as are the sites of nationally recognized organizations and associations. Most sites have a page devoted to "About Us." Some sites, such as that of the FBI or the Supreme Court, are obviously credible. If in doubt about a site, go to the "About Us" page to see if you find them credible. Most sites also indicate when specific information was last updated. Determine if that date is acceptable to you.

What's Next?

One exciting development is the online discussion group. Electronic bulletin boards and virtual discussion groups exist for every interest, including law, and profession, including all aspects of criminal justice. Questions can be answered and information shared, literally, at a keystroke.

Another option for discussions is the "blog" (Web log) that anyone can start to encourage rolling conversations about a variety of topics. Blogs are a way to get a variety of perspectives on an even greater variety of topics. Continue developing your information literacy strategy to include these resources, as well as by becoming familiar with the traditional resources.

Regardless of what level of legal information you want to locate, it is important to develop an effective strategy to help you optimize your effort. Increasingly laypeople, students, and professionals find that the Internet is an effective means of accessing legal information and remaining current with ever-changing law.

Steps in Researching a Law of Interest

Most holdings of the Supreme Court are also binding on the states; that is, they have been incorporated by the Fourteenth Amendment, as the Second Amendment was recently. The Fourth Amendment has been incorporated and is binding on the states, so when the Supreme Court makes new law, those in the criminal justice system need to familiarize themselves with it. But they also need to know their own jurisdiction's law, which may be more restrictive than the federal law. The following exercise summarizes the steps that might be taken in researching a new law of interest.

Step 1. Identify the issue (topic) you want to research. This could be a statute (MSS 609.50), a case (*Arizona v. Gant*, 566 U. S. ___ (2009), or a legal concept (frisk). It depends on what you are trying to do: read about a specific case, or learn how a court interprets a statute. You need to know your goal.

> For example, you might select the topic "search incident to arrest in a motor vehicle" to see how Minnesota courts are interpreting it.

Step 2. Identify some research terms or phrases that might be used to reference or discuss your topic. Under "frisk," you might use *"Terry* stop," "protective weapons search," "frisk," or "reasonable suspicion."

> For example, you might choose "search incident to arrest," "automobile," and "occupant."

Step 3. Choose the resources to conduct the research. This will depend on why you are researching a topic. Is it for personal education, such as learning about a topic? Then, *legal periodicals* or *journals* would be helpful, as sometimes these are written more persuasively; that is, the author may be trying to convince the reader of something, rather than just explaining the law.

Another resource to use is *actual case decisions*. You could use these for personal education and if you want the law explained to you objectively without bias.

Two quick things about journal articles: First, know the credentials of the author if possible. This is a question of credibility. Second, journal articles can also lead you to other sources. Cases and other journal articles were likely researched to come up with information in the article.

(Continued)

For example, you might use both sources to get an understanding of how the scholar and the courts are interpreting the case.

Step 4. Decide how to access the resources. Online? A law library with access to Westlaw or LexisNexis? A library with print materials?

You might decide to use scholar.google.com, an excellent free source of court opinions of all levels, federal or state. Type your search topic ("search incident to arrest") into the box and select the "legal opinions and journals" option below the search box. This site also shows how and where each case was cited (important to see if a case has been overruled or limited). This "how cited" feature includes law journals, too. Often, even if courts publish their opinions online, searching for them is difficult. You either need to know the names of the parties or the date the opinion was decided, making searching difficult and tedious.

Step 5. Access your source(s) and search using the terms (or even the case) you have identified.

For example, you might enter "search incident to arrest" and "Arizona v. Gant" into scholar.google.com. In the far left drop-down box, you would select "Minnesota courts." Based on the results you get, you might want to add terms or take them away. Having too many terms can limit the results as much as having too few terms can, especially using the "and" search function.

Step 6. Interpret the results. Pay attention to the cases and what jurisdiction they are from. Make sure they are binding on your jurisdiction, that is, Minnesota State Supreme Court ruling for Minnesota research, not a Wisconsin state court. Also, pay attention to the federal appellate district, which affects the binding nature of the opinion.

Additionally, notice if the opinion is from an appellate level court where opinions become law. Trial level courts don't make the law, they apply it.

Read the opinions using the suggestions given in this text. Pay special attention to the areas where the court gives the rule of law. It is usually a paragraph or two citing cases and language from those cases that tell you what the applicable law is to the case at hand. This is the law the court then uses to make its determination. Look at the other cases mentioned in the opinion. These will give you other resources to use if you want to proceed further.

The results for Minnesota were limited, most likely because the Supreme Court ruling in *Gant* is fairly recent. Four pertinent cases did come up; however, only one of the four was a published opinion:

- *State v. Lussier*, 770 NW 2d (Minnesota Court of Appeals, 2009)—published
- *State v. Iman*—Minnesota Court of Appeals, 2010 (unpublished)
- *State v. Weyaus*—Minnesota Court of Appeals, 2011 (unpublished)
- *State v. Norring*—Minnesota Court of Appeals, 2009 (unpublished)

It appears from these rulings that the Minnesota Court of Appeals is taking a broad view of *Gant*; that is, the court is seeing that "reasonable to believe evidence of the crime of arrest might be found in the vehicle" as a concept holds validity so that as long as facts can be pointed to that in some way, even minimally, evidence might be in the car, in which case it is reasonable to search the car for that evidence under *Gant*.

For example, in *Iman*, the court noted that he was arrested for assault with a deadly weapon (a baseball bat). He had jumped in his vehicle and fled the scene with the bat in the car and was stopped a short time later. These facts point to it being reasonable to believe that evidence of the assault (the bat) was still in the car.

Step 7. Because there are few (and unpublished, at that) opinions, it would be a good idea to see how other courts are interpreting the law. You might go to the federal court of appeals that covers the area you researched because this is the law that applies in Minnesota to cases under the U.S. Constitution.

Doing an "advanced scholar search," you may select the opinions of specific circuit courts. Minnesota is in the Eighth Circuit, and most of the Eighth Circuit cases

(Continued)

were finding probable cause (PC) in situations where it was "reasonable to believe evidence of the crime was in the car." This makes it harder to interpret because it is unclear if they were equating the "reasonable to believe" standard with PC (in which case the search incident to arrest would be irrelevant because the PC would allow the search of the car on its own). Or, did they just find that the evidence rose to that level of suspicion, and thus it was reasonable? Several other cases also found the second reason the Court mentioned in *Gant* to apply; that is, if the arrestee is within reaching distance of the passenger compartment at the time of arrest.

Then try the other federal courts of appeals because they are also interpreting the U.S. Constitution and its relation to the Supreme Court decision (as opposed to state constitutions).

If little or nothing is found, try searching other states within your circuit, and if that doesn't provide enough relevant (but not binding) information, try states around the country. Remember these cases are not binding, they just will give you an idea of how courts are interpreting the new case law.

Glossary

Number in parentheses indicates the chapter in which the term is introduced.

administrative warrant—allows civil inspections of private property to determine compliance with government rules, regulations, and city ordinances such as fire or building codes; may also be obtained so government agents can conduct routine inspections when occupants refuse their entry (9)

adversarial judicial system—a legal system, such as that of the United States, that places one party against another to resolve a legal issue, stipulating that only in an actual conflict will a judicial body hear the case (2)

affirm—agree with a lower court's decision (2)

affirmative action—programs created to spread equal opportunity throughout the diverse American population (4)

amendments—changes to a constitution or bylaws (1)

American dream—the belief that through hard work anyone can have success and ample material possessions (4)

amicus brief—a "friend of the court" brief submitted by a person not a party to the action but interested in the outcome (2)

anti-Federalists—colonists who opposed a strong federal government (1)

appellate jurisdiction—courts authorized to review cases and to either affirm or reverse the actions of a lower court (2)

arraignment—usually the first court appearance by a defendant during which the accused is advised of his or her rights, advised of the charges, and given the opportunity to enter a plea (11)

array—list of potential jury members (11)

arrest—the taking of a person into custody, in the manner authorized by law, to present that person before a magistrate to answer for committing a crime (8)

articulable facts—actions described in clear, distinct statements (7)

asset forfeiture—the seizure by the government, without compensation, of money and property connected with illegal activity (12)

attenuation doctrine—evidence obtained as a result of a previous illegality may be admissible at trial if it is so far removed, through time and space, from the original violation that any "taint" has dissipated (7)

bail—money or property pledged by a defendant for pretrial release from custody that would be forfeited should the defendant fail to appear at subsequent court proceedings (12)

balancing test—a position taken by the appellate courts to balance the needs of society for law and order and for effective law enforcement against the privacy rights of individuals (5)

beachheading—the unconstitutional approach of purposely withholding the Miranda warnings until after a confession is obtained and then giving Miranda to re-ask the question (10)

bifurcated trial—a twostep trial for capital cases: the first step is determination of innocence or guilt; the second step, if the defendant is found guilty, is determination of whether to seek the death penalty (12)

blind lineup—one conducted by someone who does not know who the suspect is (11)

Brady rule—the suppression by the prosecution of evidence favorable to an accused on request violates due process when the evidence is material either to guilt or to punishment, irrespective of the good faith or bad faith of the prosecution (11)

brief—an outline of a legal case that contains the case name and citation, a summary of key facts, the legal issues involved, the court's decision, the reasons for that decision, and any separate opinions or dissents (2)

bright-line approach—determining the reasonableness of an action according to a specific rule that applies to all cases (7)

caption—the title of a case setting forth the parties involved (2)

case law—common law approach, so named because it is based on previous cases; as a term in U.S. law, it is synonymous with common law (2)

case-by-case method—determining the reasonableness of an action by considering the totality of circumstances in each case (7)

castle law—a legal claim based on English common law that designates one's place of residence (or, in some states, any place legally occupied, such as one's car or place of work) as a place in which one enjoys protection from illegal trespassing and violent attack (6)

certiorari—Latin for "to be informed" (3)

citing—using resources and references that track cases so legal researchers can easily determine whether the original holding has been changed through any appeals (2)

citizen's arrest—the detention by a nongovernment agent of one accused of an illegal act (8)

"clear and present danger" test—the test of whether words are so potentially dangerous as to not be protected by the First Amendment (5)

"clear and probable danger" test—the test of whether the gravity of the evil discounted by its improbability justifies an invasion of free speech necessary to avoid any danger (5)

codified law—law specifically set forth in organized, structured codes such as the U.S. criminal code, state statutes, or local ordinances (2)

collective conscience—social solidarity fostered by the shared values of a society (2)

Commerce Clause—section of the U.S. Constitution (Article 1, Section 8, Clause 3) that provides the legal foundation for much of the federal government's regulatory authority, including firearms (6)

commercial bail—using the services of a bail bond person to post a defendant's bail for a fee (12)

common law—early English judge-made law based on custom and tradition; a legal system that, as in the United States, decides present cases on past decisions (2)

comparative law—comparing and contrasting laws to expand understanding of law and legal theory (2)

compensatory damages—reimbursement to the plaintiff for actual harm done, such as medical expenses or lost business (12)

compulsory process—permits a defendant to require witnesses to appear in court, usually under the issuance by the court of a subpoena (11)

concurrent jurisdiction—two or more courts authorized to hear a specific type of case (2)

concurring opinion—one written by a justice who agrees with the holding, but who gives additional or different reasons for voting with the majority (2)

confederation—a union of independent states, in which each state maintains sovereignty (1)

conflict theory—holds that laws are established to keep the dominant class in power, in contrast to the consensus theory (2)

consensus theory—holds that individuals in a society agree on basic values, on what is inherently right and wrong, and that laws express these values (2)

consent decree—a court-enforced agreement, with oversight provided by a federal judge and a court-appointed monitor who reports the organization's compliance quarterly (7)

conservative—decisions that favor the government's interest in prosecuting and punishing offenders over recognition or expansion of rights for individuals (3)

constitution—a system of basic laws and principles that establish the nature, functions, and limits of a government or other institution (1)

constitutionalism—a belief in a government in which power is distributed and limited by a system of laws that must be obeyed by those who rule (1)

contemporaneous—a concept that holds a search can be incident to an arrest only if it occurs at the same time as the arrest and is confined to the immediate vicinity of the arrest (9)

contextual discrimination—describes a situation in which racial minorities are treated more harshly at some points and in some places in the criminal justice system but no differently than whites at other points and in other places (4)

continuum of contacts—the almost limitless variations of contacts between the public and the police illustrating how justification for police action increases as their reasons for thinking criminal activity is afoot build (7)

contraband—anything that is illegal for people to own or have in their possession, for example, child pornography, illegal drugs, or illegal weapons (9)

conventional Fourth Amendment approach—viewing the Reasonableness Clause and the Warrant Clause as intertwined and firmly connected (7)

corporal punishment—causing bodily harm through physical force, for example, whipping, flogging, or beating (12)

court trial—when a case is heard before only the bench (or judge) without a jury (11)

Crime Control Model—emphasizes the "repression of criminal conduct" and holds that the most important function of the criminal justice system is to bring criminal behavior under tight control as efficiently as possible (2)

crimes—acts defined by federal or state statute or local ordinance that are punishable; wrongs against the government and the people it serves (2)

critical stage—any step during a criminal prosecution in which the accused's rights may be affected by the absence of legal representation (11)

cross-racial identification—suggests that people of one race have difficulty recognizing facial attributes of other races (11)

curtilage—the portion of property generally associated with the common use of land (9)

custodial interrogation—questioning by law enforcement officers after a person has been taken into custody or otherwise deprived of freedom of action in any significant way (10)

de facto arrest—a situation in which the police take someone in for questioning in a manner that is, in reality, an arrest, but without the requisite probable cause (8)

delegated powers—powers of the national government, both enumerated and implied by legal authority, delegated or entrusted to the national government by the states and the people (13)

deliberate elicitation—the *Massiah* standard that violates the Sixth Amendment by purposefully, yet covertly, drawing out incriminating statements from a suspect whose Sixth Amendment right to counsel has attached but who has not waived the right (11)

demurrer—a request that a suit be dismissed because the facts do not sustain the claim against the defendant (6)

detainer—document filed against inmates who have other criminal charges pending against them (11)

dictum (plural dicta)—statements by a court that do not deal with the main issue in the case or an additional discussion by the court (2, 6)

discrimination—an action or behavior based on prejudice (4)

disenfranchise—to deprive a person of a right (13)

disparate impact—policies or practices that are not intended to discriminate but, in fact, have a disproportionately negative effect on minorities (4)

disparate treatment—*intentional* acts of employment discrimination based on race, color, religion, sex, and national origin (4)

disparity—a difference, but one that does not necessarily involve discrimination (4)

dissenting opinion—written by a justice who disagrees with the holding and voted against the majority (2)

double jeopardy—a prohibition against the government from trying someone twice for the same offense (10)

due process—provides rules and procedures to ensure fairness to an individual and to prevent arbitrary government actions; the Fifth and Fourteenth Amendments' constitutionally guaranteed right of an accused to hear the charges against him or her and to be heard by the court having jurisdiction over the matter (4)

Due Process Model—emphasizes the rights of the individual, rests on the presumption of innocence, and holds that individual rights are not to be sacrificed for the sake of efficiency (2)

due process of law—prohibits the government from unfairly or arbitrarily denying a citizen his or her fundamental and constitutionally protected rights to life, liberty, and property (4)

eminent domain—the power of the government to take private property for public use, with the owner being paid just compensation for the taking (10)

entrapment—the act of government officials or agents (usually police) inducing a person to commit a crime that the person would not have otherwise committed (10)

equal protection of the law—requires that similarly situated people or classes of people be treated in similar ways under the law (4)

Establishment Clause—clause in the First Amendment that states, "Congress shall make no law respecting an establishment of religion" (5)

exclusionary rule—judgemade case law promulgated by the Supreme Court to deter police or government misconduct (7)

exclusive jurisdiction—courts that can hear only specific cases (2)

exigent circumstances—emergency situations (9)

federalism—a principle whereby power is shared by the national government and the states; the Tenth Amendment provision reserving for the states those powers not granted to the federal government or withheld from the states (13)

Federalists—colonists who favored a strong federal government (1)

Free Exercise Clause—clause in the First Amendment that declares, "Congress shall make no law . . . prohibiting the free exercise [of religion]" (5)

fresh pursuit—a situation in which police are immediately in pursuit of a suspect and may cross state jurisdictional lines to make an arrest of a felon who committed the felony in the officers' state (8)

frisk—a reasonable, limited patdown search for weapons for the protection of a government agent and others (7)

fruit of the poisonous tree doctrine—evidence obtained as a result of a previous illegality (a constitutionally invalid search or activity) must be excluded from trial (7)

functional equivalent—essentially the same or serving the same purpose (8)

furtive conduct—questionable, suspicious, or secretive behavior (7)

general jurisdiction—courts having the ability to hear a wide range of cases (2)

good faith—officers are unaware that they are acting in violation of a suspect's constitutional rights (7)

grand jury—a group of citizens who determine whether sufficient evidence exists to send an accused to trial (10)

Great Compromise—the agreement reached in drafting the U.S. Constitution that gave each state an equal vote in the Senate and a proportionate vote in the House (1)

harmless error—an exception to the exclusionary rule involving the admissibility of involuntary confessions and referring to instances in which the preponderance of evidence suggests the defendant's guilt and the "tainted" or illegal evidence is not critical to proving the case against the defendant (7)

harmless error doctrine—involves the admissibility of involuntary confessions: if no harm resulted, the confession should be admissible (10)

hearsay—an out-of-court statement used to prove the truth of the matter asserted; can include statements made by the person actually testifying, before taking the stand (11)

holding—the rule of law applied to the particular facts of the case and the actual decision (2)

hot pursuit—the period during which an individual is being immediately chased by law enforcement and, because of the exigencies of the situation, officers are allowed to forcibly enter constitutionally protected areas, such as a home, without a warrant (8)

"imminent lawless action" test—a three-part test that the government must meet if certain communication is not to be protected by the First Amendment: (1) the speaker subjectively intended incitement, (2) in context, the words used were likely to produce imminent, lawless action, and (3) the words used by the speaker objectively encouraged and urged incitement; replaced the "clear and present danger" test (5)

implicit bias—the unintentional, subconscious, and automatic sorting and processing of information by the brain which, when combined with a person's history and cultural influences, leads to the formation of associations among groups of people and stereotypes about those groups (4)

incorporation doctrine—holds that those provisions of the Bill of Rights that are fundamental to the American legal system are applied to the states through the Due Process Clause of the Fourteenth Amendment, thereby preventing state or local governments from infringing on people's rights when federal government would not be allowed to (4)

incrimination—the act of accusing, implicating, or identifying someone as having been involved in a crime or other wrongdoing (10)

indictment—a formal accusation of a defendant, usually by a grand jury, that sends the defendant on to trial for prosecution (10)

indigent—poor, unable to afford a lawyer (11)

inevitable discovery doctrine—exception to exclusionary rule deeming evidence admissible even if seized in violation of the Fourth Amendment when it can be shown that the evidence would have inevitably been discovered through lawful means (7)

interrogation—the formal, systemic, express questioning by law enforcement of a person suspected of criminal activity, as well as the functional equivalent of express questioning (any words or actions by the police, other than those normally attendant to arrest and custody, that the police should know are reasonably likely to elicit an incriminating response from the suspect) (10)

invoke—to unambiguously assert or exercise a right (10)

Jim Crow laws—laws that strictly segregated blacks from whites in schools, restaurants, streetcars, hospitals, and cemeteries (4)

judicial activism—allowing judges to interpret the Constitution and its amendments (5)

judicial review—the power of a court to analyze decisions of other government entities and lower courts (3)

jurisdiction—the authority of a legislative body to establish a law, the authority of a particular court to hear certain types of cases, or the authority a law has over a specific group of people (2)

jury nullification—ability of a jury to acquit a defendant even though jurors believe that person is guilty (11)

just compensation—the requirement that property owners be paid fair market value by the government when government takes their property (10)

law—a body of rules promulgated (established) to support the norms of a society, enforced through legal means (i.e., punishment) (1)

legal citation—a standardized way of referring to a specific element in the law (2)

liberal—decisions that are pro–person accused or convicted of a crime, pro–civil liberties or civil rights claimants, pro–indigents, pro–American Indians, and antigovernment (3)

limited jurisdiction—restriction of the types of cases a particular court might hear (2)

lineup—identification technique in which the victim or witness is shown several people, including the suspect (11)

litigious—a tendency toward suing; a belief that most controversies or injurious acts, no matter how minor, should be settled in court (7)

Loyalist—a colonist who did not support the boycott of British goods in the colonies and who still paid allegiance to the British monarchy (1)

magistrate—a judge (7)

memorandum of agreement (MOA)—not judicially enforced but does have an appointed monitor who makes quarterly reports (7)

militia—an armed group of citizens who defend their community as emergencies arise (6)

minutemen—colonial soldiers (1)

mootness—exists when the issues that gave rise to a case have either been resolved or have otherwise disappeared (2)

movant—a party making a motion to the court (4)

nightcap(ped) warrant—issued when officers wish to execute a warrant at night because that is when the suspected illicit activity is primarily occurring (7)

no-knock warrant—issued when officers want to make an unannounced entrance because they are afraid evidence might be destroyed or officer safety requires it (7)

offense specific—the Sixth Amendment right to counsel applies only to the specific charges for which the defendant has been indicted or arraigned (11)

Operative Clause—identifies the action to be taken or prohibited (6)

opinion—a written statement by the court explaining its decision in a given case, usually including the legal issues or points of law involved, a statement of facts, and any precedents on which the decision is based (3)

ordinances—laws or codes established at the local level, that is, the municipal or county level (2)

original jurisdiction—courts authorized to hear cases first, try them and render decisions (2)

Patriot—a colonist who supported the boycott of British goods in the colonies and who owed allegiance to America rather than to the British monarchy (1)

penal codes—criminal codes or laws (2)

penumbra—a type of shadow in astronomy with the principle extending to the idea that certain constitutional rights are implied within other constitutional rights (4)

peremptory challenges—a specific number of allowances given to each side in a case that they may assert to remove a potential juror for any reason whatsoever (11)

petition for certiorari—request that the Supreme Court or a state supreme court review the decision of a lower court (2)

plain feel—items felt during a lawful stop and frisk may be retrieved if the officer reasonably believes the items are contraband and can instantly recognize them as such (9)

plain touch—same as plain feel (9)

plain view—unconcealed evidence that officers see while engaged in a lawful activity may be seized and is admissible in court (9)

pluralism—a society in which numerous distinct ethnic, religious, or cultural groups coexist within one nation, each contributing to the society as a whole (1)

preemption—federal law supersedes state law; if a state law stands as an obstacle to the purposes, objectives, and execution of the federal law, the Supremacy Clause preempts the state law (4)

Prefatory Clause—announces a purpose but does not necessarily restrict the Operative Clause (6)

preferred freedoms approach—a position that stresses that civil liberties are to take precedence over other constitutional values because they are requisite to a democracy (5)

prejudice—a negative attitude regarding a person or thing (4)

preliminary hearing—a critical stage of criminal proceedings when it is determined if probable cause exists to believe a crime has been committed and that the defendant committed it (11)

pretext stop—stopping a vehicle to search for evidence of a crime under the guise of a traffic stop (8)

preventive detention—the right of judges to consider the potential criminal conduct of those accused of serious offenses and deny bail on those grounds (12)

prima facie—production of sufficient evidence to show that the issue is proven in favor of the party making the assertion (11)

prior restraint—a restriction on publishing certain materials prior to a communication occurring (5)

privilege—a claim that is not legally protected (4)

pro se—appearing in court without an attorney, representing oneself (11)

probable cause—exists when facts and circumstances are sufficient in themselves to warrant a person of reasonable caution to believe that an offense has been or is being committed; stronger than reasonable suspicion but less than the quantum of evidence required for conviction (7)

procedural due process—constitutionally guaranteed rights of fairness in how the law is carried out or applied (4)

procedural justice—the idea of being treated fairly during a process or procedure (4)

procedural law—how the law is to be enforced, for example, how and when police can stop people (2)

prohibited persons—individuals to whom, under the Gun Control Act, selling a firearm is forbidden (6)

promulgate—to make law through a legal process (2)

proportionality analysis—in essence, making the punishment fit the crime (12)

protective sweep—a limited search made in conjunction with an in-home arrest when the searching officer possesses a reasonable belief based on specific and articulable facts that the area to be swept harbors an individual posing a danger to those on the arrest scene (9)

public safety exception—allows officers to question suspects without first giving the Miranda warning if the information sought sufficiently affects the officers' and the public's safety (10)

punitive damages—fines above and beyond the actual economic loss to punish the defendant in a civil trial (12)

pure speech—verbal and written methods of communicating or expressing a message (5)

qualified immunity—exemption of a public official from civil liability for actions performed during the course of his or her job unless they violated a "clearly established" constitutional or statutory right of which a reasonable person would have known (9)

racial profiling—the process of using certain racial characteristics, such as skin color, as indicators of criminal activity (4)

ratify—approve a constitutional amendment (1)

"rational basis" test—the standard for analyzing First Amendment claims by prisoners and other constitutional claims as well (5)

reasonable—sensible, rational, and justifiable (7)

reasonable expectation of privacy—a situation in which (1) a person has exhibited an actual (subjective) expectation of privacy and (2) that expectation is one that society is prepared to recognize as reasonable (9)

reasonable suspicion—more than an experienced officer's hunch or intuition, and more than mere whim, caprice, or idle curiosity; it is a rational inference taken from specific and articulable facts, and viewed objectively using the totality of the circumstances (7)

reasonableness Fourth Amendment approach—the Reasonableness Clause and the Warrant Clause are interpreted as separate issues (7)

rebut—refute through the presentation of contrary evidence (10)

recesses—periods when the Supreme Court does not hear cases but considers administrative matters and writes opinions (3)

remand—return a case to the lower court for further action (2)

remoteness—regarding the unreasonableness and unlawfulness of searches of seized luggage or other personal belongings not immediately associated with the arrestee's body or under his or her immediate control (9)

reserve powers—powers retained by the states (13)

reverse—overturn the decision of a lower court (2)

reverse discrimination—giving preferential treatment in hiring and promoting to women and minorities to the detriment of white males (4)

right—a legally protected claim (4)

ripeness doctrine—invoked when a case comes to court too soon, preventing the court from getting prematurely involved in a case that may eventually resolve through other means (2)

ROR—released on their own recognizance; no bail money is required (12)

SAR—(suspicious activity report) an official documentation of observed behavior that may be indicative of intelligence gathering or preoperational planning related to terrorism, criminal, or other illicit intention (4)

search—an examination of a person, place, or vehicle for contraband or evidence of a crime (7)

seizure—a taking by law enforcement or other government agent of contraband, evidence of a crime, or even a person into custody (7)

selective incorporation—holds that only the provisions of the Bill of Rights that are fundamental to the U.S. legal system are applied to the states through the Due Process Clause of the Fourteenth Amendment (13)

showup—identification technique in which only one individual is shown to the victim or witness (11)

sittings—periods during which the Supreme Court hears cases (3)

social contract—a philosophy proposed by French historianphilosopher Montesquieu, whereby free, independent individuals agree to form a society and to give up a portion of their individual freedom to benefit the security of the group (2)

standing—having an actual interest in the matter of dispute (2)

stare decisis—a common law doctrine requiring that precedent set in one case shall be followed in all cases having the same or similar circumstances, thus ensuring consistency in the law; Latin for "let the decision stand" (2)

status offenses—offenses deemed to be illegal when committed by juveniles because of their age, which are not unlawful for adults, such as smoking, drinking, and curfew violations (2)

statutory law—law set forth by legislatures or governing bodies having jurisdiction to make such law (2)

stop—a brief detention of a person, short of an arrest, based on specific and articulable facts for the purpose of investigating suspicious activity (7)

straw purchase—an illegal transaction when a buyer uses an intermediary (the "straw man") to purchase a firearm(s) from a licensed firearms dealer and then sells the weapon(s) to individuals who cannot legally buy guns themselves, such as felons and the severely mentally retarded (6)

strict construction—a rigid interpretation of a law not likely to expand the specifically set forth law of the particular statute, particularly in expanding the intent of that law (3)

strict scrutiny—the legal standard applied to due process analysis of fundamental rights, such as freedom of speech, in which the state must establish it has a compelling government interest that justifies and necessitates the law in question and that the law is narrowly tailored to fit that interest; a high standard and difficult to defend (5)

string cites—additional legal citations showing where a case may be found in commercial reporting services (2)

subpoena—requires an individual to appear in court to testify or to bring documents or other physical evidence to the court (11)

substantive due process—constitutional requirement that laws themselves be fair (4)

substantive law—establishes rules and regulations, as in traffic law (2)

suits at common law—legal controversies arising out of civil law rather than criminal law (13)

summary judgment—a request to the court to review the evidence and, without a trial, reach a decision to dismiss a case against the movant because there is no dispute of material fact that a jury need resolve (4)

Sunset Clause—a set ending time for legislation that is not renewed to prevent old law from remaining on the books (6)

supremacy clause—Constitutional doctrine that federal law will reign when there is conflicting state law (U.S. Const. Art. VI, Paragraph 2) (1)

symbolic speech—a form of speech that expresses an idea or emotion without use of words, such as burning one's draft card, bra or flag, or picketing (5)

Terry **stop**—an officer with articulable reasonable suspicion may conduct a brief investigatory stop, including a pat down for weapons if the officer has reason to suspect the person is armed and dangerous (7)

testimonial statement—a solemn declaration or affirmation made for the purpose of establishing or proving some fact (11)

tort—civil wrong by one individual against another, with the remedy most often being either an order by the court for particular action or compensation (2)

totality of circumstances—the principle on which a number of legal assessments are made; is not a mathematical formula for achieving a certain number of factors but rather a sum total of layers of information and the synthesis of what the police have heard, what they know, and what they observe as trained officers, including probable cause, used to assess whether the sum total would lead a reasonable person to believe what the officers concluded (7)

unenumerated rights—rights not specifically listed in the Bill of Rights (4)

USA PATRIOT Act—legislation that significantly improves the nation's counterterrorism efforts (10)

vacate—set aside or annul a case (2)

venire—the selected jury panel (11)

venue—the geographic area in which a specific case may come to trial, and the area from which the jury is selected (2)

voir dire—the process of questioning potential jurors to determine their impartiality (11)

voluntariness test—a determination as to whether one willingly and knowingly relinquished his or her constitutional rights; considers the totality of circumstances to determine whether consent was given freely and truly voluntarily (9)

waiver—a purposeful and voluntary giving up of a known right (10)

waiver test—citizens may waive their rights, but only if they do so voluntarily, knowingly, and intentionally (9)

wingspan—the area within a person's reach or immediate control (9)

zones of privacy—areas into which the government may not intrude (4)

Case Index

Abington School District v. Schempp, 131
Abramski v. United States, 199
Abrams v. United States, 139
Adamson v. California, 85
Adams v. Williams, 181, 251–252, 301
Adarand Constructors v. Pena, 100
Addington v. Texas, 431
Agostini v. Felton, 131–132
Aguilar v. Felton, 131, 132
Aguilar v. Texas, 217
Alabama v. White, 251–252
Almeida-Sanchez v. United States, 325
American Civil Liberties Union v. Mukasey, 159
Anderson v. Smith, 41
Anderson v. State, 359
Ansonia Board of Education v. Philbrook, 101
Apprendi v. New Jersey, 447
Arave v. Creech, 443
Argersinger v. Hamlin, 406, 419, 465
Arizona v. Evans, 238
Arizona v. Fulminante, 236, 353, 354
Arizona v. Gant, 239, 305, 309–310, 312
Arizona v. Johnson, 255, 259, 302, 312
Arizona v. Roberson, 369, 376
Arizona v. United States, 109
Armstrong v. Village of Pinehurst, 277–278
Arnold v. United States, 374
Atkins v. Virginia, 445
Atwater v. City of Lago Vista, 241, 265
Austin v. United States, 434

Bailey v. United States, 294
Baker v. McCollan, 246
Baldwin v. New York, 397
Ballew v. Georgia, 396
Barker v. Wingo, 395
Barnes v. Glen Theatre, 142
Barnes v. State, 185
Barron v. Mayor and City Council of Baltimore, 83
Batson v. Kentucky, 114, 397, 400
Baxter v. Palmigiano, 384
Baze v. Rees, 442
Beard v. Banks, 169
Beck v. Ohio, 216
Beckwith v. United States, 362
Beecher v. Alabama, 353
Bell v. Cone, 443
Bell v. Wolfish, 328
Bennis v. Michigan, 434–435
Benton v. Maryland, 464
Berger v. New York, 334
Berghuis v. Thompkins, 366, 367, 376
Berkemer v. McCarty, 258, 362, 376
Betterman v. Montana, 395
Betts v. Brady, 406
Birchfield v. North Dakota, 306
Blockburger v. United States, 381, 417
Blueford v. Arkansas, 382
Board of Regents of State Colleges v. Roth, 87
Boddie v. Connecticut, 87
Bond v. United States, 303, 323–324

Bounds v. Smith, 118
Boyd v. United States, 206, 229, 323
Brady v. Maryland, 417
Brandenburg v. Ohio, 149
Brendlin v. California, 258, 259
Brewer v. Williams, 234–235, 410, 419
Brigham City, Utah v. Stuart, 318
Brinegar v. United States, 214
Briscoe v. Virginia, 403
Brower v. County of Inyo, 248
Browning-Ferris Industries v. Kelco Disposal, 430, 433
Brown v. Board of Education of Topeka, 93
Brown v. Entertainment Merchant's Association, 159–160
Brown v. Illinois, 233
Brown v. Mississippi, 352, 376
Brown v. Plata, 449
Brown v. Texas, 261
Brown v. Thomson, 467
Bryan v. McPherson, 276
Bullcoming v. New Mexico, 404
Burket v. Angelone, 370
Burwell v. Hobby Lobby, 136
Bush v. Gore, 77, 465

Caetano v. Massachusetts, 186
California v. Acevedo, 313–314
California v. Beheler, 361
California v. Ciraolo, 321
California v. Greenwood, 321–322
California v. Hodari D., 248
California v. Prysock, 359
Camara v. Municipal Court of the City and County of San Francisco, 326
Campbell v. Blodgett, 440
Cantwell v. Connecticut, 134, 464
Carroll v. United States, 312, 323
Cass v. State, 213
Chambers v. Maroney, 313
Chapman v. California, 235
Chavez v. Martinez, 373–374
Chicago, Burlington & Quincy Railroad Co. v. Chicago, 383, 464
Chicago v. Morales, 164–165
Chimel v. California, 305, 306
Chisholm v. Georgia, 463
Christian Legal Society v. Martinez, 167
Church of Lukumi Babalu Aye v. Hialeah, 136
City and County of San Francisco v. Sheehan, 101
City of Boerne v. Flores, 135, 169
City of Indianapolis v. Edmond, 262
City of Ladue v. Gilleo, 143
City of Los Angeles v. Lyons, 275
City of Los Angeles v. Patel, 212
City of Ontario v. Quon, 332
City of San Diego v. Roe, 158
Clark v. Community for Creative Non-Violence, 152
Clinton v. Jones, 18
Cohen v. California, 147
Cohen v. Cowles Media Company, 163

Coker v. Georgia, 435
Coleman v. Alabama, 415, 419
Cole v. Arkansas, 465
Colgrove v. Battin, 458
Colorado v. Bertine, 314–315
Colorado v. Connelly, 353, 365
Colorado v. Spring, 366
Commonwealth v. Tarver, 306
Connecticut v. Barrett, 356
Connick v. Myers, 156
Coolidge v. New Hampshire, 304
Cooper v. Pate, 117, 118
Corley v. United States, 354
Coy v. Iowa, 402
Crawford v. Washington, 402
Cruz v. Beto, 169
Cruz v. Hauck, 118
Culombe v. Connecticut, 351
Cupp v. Murphy, 268
Curtis v. Loether, 458

Davis v. Beason, 134
Davis v. United States, 230, 239, 370
Davis v. Washington, 402
De Canas v. Bica, 109
DeJonge v. Oregon, 165, 464
Delaware v. Prouse, 257
Dennis v. United States, 149
Dickerson v. United States, 372–373, 376
District of Columbia v. Heller, 180
Dormire v. Wilkinson, 370
Douglas v. California, 417, 419
Draper v. United States, 216
Dred Scott v. Sandford, 81
Duckworth v. Eagan, 359
Dunaway v. New York, 268
Duncan v. Louisiana, 85, 396, 464
Duryea v. Guarnieri, 165

Eddings v. Oklahoma, 444
Edwards v. Arizona, 368, 369, 376
Edwards v. City of Goldsboro, N.C., 184
EEOC v. Abercrombie and Fitch, 100
Elkins v. United States, 231
Employment Division v. Smith, 135
Engle v. Vitale, 131
Escobedo v. Illinois, 356, 376, 408, 419
Estelle v. Gamble, 449
Estelle v. Smith, 350
Estes v. Texas, 396
Evans v. Michigan, 381
Evenwel v. Abbott, 467
Everson v. Board of Education, 130, 464
Ewing v. California, 436
Ex parte Hull, 117
Ex parte McCardle, 61–62

Faretta v. California, 408, 421–422
Fernandez v. California, 299
Fikes v. Alabama, 353
Firefighters Local Union No. 1784 v. Stotts, 96
Fisher v. University of Texas at Austin, 97

506

Case Index

Fletcher v. Peck, 64
Florence v. Board of Chosen Freeholders of the County of Burlington, 328
Florida v. Harris, 218–219
Florida v. Jardines, 321
Florida v. Jimeno, 300
Florida v. J.L., 196, 252
Florida v. Powell, 359, 376
Florida v. Royer, 254
Florida v. Wells, 315
Fogel v. Collins, 151
Ford v. Wainwright, 445
Foster v. California, 413
Frank v. Maryland, 206
Frazier v. Cupp, 354
Fullilove v. Klutznick, 96
Fulwood v. Clemmer, 169
Furman v. Georgia, 441, 442

Gannett Co. v. DePasquale, 395
Gannett v. DePasquale, 163
Garcetti v. Ceballos, 156–157
Gardner v. Broderick, 349
Garrity v. New Jersey, 349
Georgia v. Randolph, 298–299
Gertz v. Robert Welch, Inc., 149
Gibbons v. Ogden, 109
Gideon v. Wainwright, 406, 419, 421, 465
Gilbert v. California, 413
Gitlow v. New York, 139, 148, 464
Glasser v. United States, 397
Glossip v. Gross, 442–443
Goldman v. Weinberger, 137
Goldwater v. Carter, 51
Gowder v. City of Chicago, 182
Grady v. North Carolina, 333–334
Graham v. Connor, 271, 276, 279
Graham v. Florida, 436
Gratz v. Bollinger, 96
Green v. United States, 381
Greenwold v. Wisconsin, 354
Gregg v. Georgia, 441, 442
Griffin v. Coughlin, 138
Griffin v. Wisconsin, 330
Griswold v. Connecticut, 88–89, 459, 465
Groh v. Ramirez, 296
Grutter v. Bollinger, 96–97
Guest v. Leis, 336

Hague v. CIO, 464
Halbert v. Michigan, 408
Hall v. Florida, 445
Hamilton v. Alabama, 415, 419
Hampton v. Mow Sun Wong, 105
Hampton v. United States, 378
Harmelin v. Michigan, 436
Harrington v. California, 235
Harris v. Commonwealth, 252
Harris v. New York, 373, 376
Harris v. South Carolina, 406
Hastings v. Barnes, 272
Haynes v. Washington, 354
Heffron v. International Society for Krishna Consciousness, 137
Heien v. North Carolina, 251
Helling v. McKinney, 449–450
Henry v. United States, 206
Herring v. New York, 420
Herring v. United States, 238, 239
Hester v. United States, 320
Hiibel v. Nevada, 349

Hodel v. Virginia Surface Mining & Reclamation Assn., Inc., 462
Holder v. Humanitarian Law Project, 153
Hollingsworth v. Perry, 103
Holt v. Hobbs, 170
Hope v. Pelzer, 450–451
Horne v. Department of Agriculture, 382
Horton v. California, 303
Howes v. Fields, 362–363, 384
Hudson v. McMillian, 450
Hudson v. Michigan, 220, 230, 293
Hudson v. Palmer, 327–328
Hurst v. Florida, 447
Hurtado v. California, 380
Hutchinson v. Proxmire, 163

Illinois v. Cabellas, 255, 314
Illinois v. Gates, 215, 218
Illinois v. Lafayette, 328
Illinois v. Lidster, 262
Illinois v. McArthur, 222, 291, 293
Illinois v. Perkins, 361, 363, 377, 384
Illinois v. Rodriguez, 238, 299
Illinois v. Wardlow, 226, 254
Ingraham v. Wright, 437
In re Gault, 351, 419, 423
In re Oliver, 464

Jackson v. Indiana, 431
Jacobson v. United States, 378
James v. Louisiana, 305
J.E.B. v. Alabama, 115
Johnson v. Avery, 118
Johnson v. Dugger, 414
Johnson v. Zerbst, 421
Jones v. United States, 119, 446
Jordan v. Gardner, 329

Kansas v. Cheever, 349–350
Kansas v. Ventris, 419
Katz v. United States, 288, 333
Kaupp v. Texas, 267
Kelley v. Johnson, 156
Kelo v. New London, 383
Kentucky v. King, 296, 316, 321
Kingsley v. Hendrickson, 280
Kinsella v. Singleton, 17
Kirby v. Illinois, 413
Klopfer v. North Carolina, 464
Knight v. Florida, 443
Knowles v. Iowa, 310–311
Konigsberg v. State Bar of California, 150
Konop v. Hawaiian Airlines, Inc., 337
Kuhlman v. Wilson, 411
Kyllo v. United States, 304–305

Lane v. Franks, 157, 158
Lemon v. Kurtzman, 131
Lewis v. City of New Orleans, 147
Lewis v. United States, 396, 397
Local 28, Sheet Metal Workers International Association v. EEOC, 96
Lochner v. New York, 88
Locke v. United States, 214
Lockhart v. McCree, 446
Lockyer v. Andrade, 436
Lopez v. United States, 378
Loretto v. Teleprompter Manhattan CATV Corp., 383
Louisiana ex rel. Francis v. Resweber, 430

Lucas v. South Carolina Coastal Council, 383
Lynch v. Donnelly, 134

Madsen v. Women's Health Center, Inc., 154
Mallory v. United States, 354
Malloy v. Hogan, 348, 464
Mapp v. Ohio, 230, 231, 237, 464
Marbury v. Madison, 1, 43, 63, 64, 65, 76, 117, 372
Marron v. United States, 290
Marshall v. Barlow's Inc., 297, 326
Marsh v. Chambers, 133
Martinez v. Illinois, 381
Martin v. Hunter's Lessee, 64, 76
Maryland v. Buie, 308
Maryland v. Craig, 403
Maryland v. Dyson, 313
Maryland v. Garrison, 238
Maryland v. King, 328–329
Maryland v. Macon, 289
Maryland v. Shatzer, 368–369, 376
Maryland v. Wilson, 258, 259
Massachusetts Board of Retirement v. Murgia, 114
Massachusetts v. Sheppard, 237
Massiah v. United States, 356, 409, 419
Mathews v. Eldridge, 87
Maynard v. Cartwright, 443
McCleskey v. Kemp, 444
McClesky v. Kemp, 115
McCreary County v. ACLU, 132
McCullen v. Coakley, 155
McCulloch v. Maryland, 17, 461
McDonald v. Chicago, 86, 181–182, 464
McIntyre v. Ohio Elections Commission, 163
McNabb v. United States, 354
McNeil v. Wisconsin, 417
Melendez-Diaz v. Massachusetts, 403
Mempa v. Rhay, 409, 423
Mendenhall v. United States, 247
Messerschmidt v. Millender, 296
Meyer v. Nebraska, 87, 88
Michigan Department of State Police v. Sitz, 261
Michigan v. Bryant, 402
Michigan v. Chesternut, 268
Michigan v. Harvey, 418
Michigan v. Jackson, 415, 416–417
Michigan v. Long, 260, 302, 312
Michigan v. Mosley, 366, 376
Michigan v. Summers, 222, 294
Michigan v. Tucker, 297
Miller v. Alabama, 437
Miller v. California, 148, 162
Miller v. United States, 220
Mincey v. Arizona, 354
Minnesota v. Carter, 50
Minnesota v. Dickerson, 302
Minnesota v. Hershberger, 137
Minnesota v. Olson, 315
Minnick v. Mississippi, 370, 376, 416
Miranda v. Arizona, 41, 43, 357–377, 409–410, 416, 419
Missouri v. Frye, 419, 420
Missouri v. McNeely, 316
Missouri v. Seibert, 371, 376
Monroe v. Pape, 300
Montejo v. Louisiana, 415, 416
Montgomery v. Louisiana, 437
Mooney v. Holohan, 417
Moore v. City of Albany, 36
Moore v. Madigan, 183
Moore v. Michigan, 415, 419

Moore v. People, 328
Morgan v. Illinois, 446
Morrissey v. Brewer, 329–330
Muehler v. Mena, 294
Mukasey v. American Civil Liberties Union, 159
Murray v. Curlett, 131
Murray v. United States, 235

NAACP v. Alabama, 166
National Park Hospitality Association v. Department of the Interior, 51
National Socialist Party v. Skokie, 151
Navarette v. California, 252–253, 254
Near v. Minnesota, 162, 464
Nebbia v. New York, 90
Neil v. Biggers, 414
New Jersey v. T.L.O., 326–327
New York Times v. Sullivan, 162, 163
New York v. Belton, 309
New York v. Quarles, 375, 376
New York v. United States, 462
New York v. Zenger, 162
Nix v. Williams, 234, 235, 411
Norris v. Alabama, 114
North Carolina v. Butler, 367, 368, 376
North Carolina v. Pearce, 381

Obergefell v. Hodges, 104, 455
O'Conner v. Ortega, 331
Ohio v. Clark, 403
Ohio v. Robinette, 297
Oliver v. United States, 320
Olmstead v. United States, 288
O'Lone v. Estate of Shabazz, 169
Oregon v. Elstad, 360, 370, 371, 376
Oregon v. Mathiason, 361, 362
Osborn v. United States, 334
Overton v. Bazetta, 451

Palko v. Connecticut, 85
Parker v. Gladden, 464
Patterson v. Illinois, 366–367, 421
Payton v. New York, 266, 289, 317
Penn Central Transportation Co. v. New York City, 383
Pennsylvania Coal Co. v. Mahon, 383
Pennsylvania v. D.M., 196
Pennsylvania v. Mimms, 255, 258, 259, 312
Pennsylvania v. Muniz, 362
Penry v. Lynaugh, 445
People v. Loria, 300
People v. McNeil, 354
People v. Shivers, 363
Perry v. New Hampshire, 414
Peruta v. County of San Diego, 183
Pickering v. Board of Education, 156
Plessy v. Ferguson, 85, 93
Plyler v. Doe, 105
Pointer v. Texas, 465
Powell v. Alabama, 405, 419, 420, 465
Press-Enterprise Co. v. Superior Court, 395
Presser v. Illinois, 180–181
Prewitt v. State of Arizona ex rel. Eyman, 168
Prince v. Massachusetts, 137
Printz v. United States, 188, 462
Procunier v. Martinez, 168
Public Service Comm'n v. Havemeyer, 213
Pulley v. Harris, 436

Quinones-Ruiz v. United States, 323

Rakas v. Illinois, 50
R.A.V. v. City of St. Paul, 142
Rawlings v. Kentucky, 216
Rawlins v. Georgia, 401
Reed v. Town of Gilbert, 143
Regents of the University of California v. Bakke, 95
Reno v. American Civil Liberties Union, 159
Reynolds v. United States, 137
Rhode Island v. Innis, 363, 376
Rhodes v. Chapman, 449
Ricci v. Destefano, 99
Richards v. Wisconsin, 222
Richmond Newspapers, Inc. v. Virginia, 88, 395
Riley v. California, 307
Ring v. Arizona, 447
Roberts v. United States Jaycees, 166–167
Robinson v. California, 430, 436, 440, 465
Rochin v. California, 231–232, 350–351
Rodriguez v. United States, 255
Roe v. Wade, 49, 74, 89
Rogers v. Richmond, 353, 376
Roper v. Simmons, 53, 444
Rosenberger v. Rector and Visitors of the University of Virginia, 155
Roth v. United States, 162
Ruffin v. Commonwealth, 117
Ruiz v. Estelle, 449
Rupe v. Wood, 440
Ryburn v. Huff, 319

Safford Unified School District v. Redding, 327
Salas v. State, 309
Salinas v. Texas, 348
Samson v. California, 331
Sattazahn v. Pennsylvania, 381
Schenck v. United States, 148
Schilb v. Kuebel, 430, 465
Schmerber v. California, 315
Schriro v. Summerlin, 447
Schuette v. Coalition to Defend Affirmative Action, 97
Scott v. Harris, 269, 279
Scott v. Illinois, 408
Segura v. United States, 235
Seling v. Young, 382
Shadwick v. City of Tampa, 220
Shapiro v. Thompson, 105
Shaw v. Murphy, 168, 170
Shelby County v. Holder, 467
Sheppard v. Maxwell, 163–164
Sherman v. United States, 377, 378
Silverthorne Lumber Co. v. United States, 232
Simmons v. South Carolina, 446
Singleton v. Norris, 445
Skinner v. Railway Labor Executives' Association, 289
Small v. United States, 187
Smith v. Hooey, 423
Smith v. Maryland, 335
Smith v. United States, 214
Snyder v. Louisiana, 400
Snyder v. Phelps, 154
Solem v. Helm, 436
Sorrells v. United States, 377
South Dakota v. Opperman, 314
Spano v. New York, 406
Spence v. State of Washington, 140
Spinelli v. United States, 217–218
Stack v. Boyle, 432
Stanford v. Kentucky, 444
Stanford v. Texas, 206

Stanton v. Sims, 317
State of Maine v. Jones, 39
State of Washington v. Smith, 41
State v. Barlow, Jr., 300
State v. Heald, 216
State v. Kaluna, 306
State v. Lewis, 301
State v. Massey, 137
State v. Mimmovich, 216
State v. Moore, 443
State v. Pluth, 264
State v. Robinson, 370
State v. Schumacher, 354
State v. Spencer, 375
Steagald v. United States, 267
Stevens v. United States, 179
Stoner v. California, 289
Stone v. Graham, 131
Stone v. Powell, 237
Stovall v. Denno, 413, 414
Strauder v. West Virginia, 114, 397
Street v. New York, 141
Strickland v. Washington, 420
Strunk v. United States, 395
Sugarman v. McDougall, 105
Sussex Land & Live Stock Co. v. Midwest Refining Co., 213
Swain v. Alabama, 114, 397

Tague v. Louisiana, 365–366
Taylor v. Alabama, 232–233
Taylor v. Louisiana, 397
Teague v. Lane, 67
Tennessee v. Garner, 271, 279
Terry v. Ohio, 227–228, 301, 302, 312
Texas v. Cobb, 417, 418
Texas v. Johnson, 141
Thomas v. Union Carbide, 458
Thompson v. McNeil, 443
Thompson v. Oklahoma, 444
Thornburg v. Abbott, 169
Thornton v. United States, 310
Town of Greece v. Galloway, 133
Townsend v. Burke, 418, 419
Trop v. Dulles, 429
Turner v. Safley, 168, 169, 329

United States v. Alvarez, 146
United States v. American Library Association, 159
United States v. Anderson, 216
United States v. Andrus, 336
United States v. Arvizu, 226–227
United States v. Bajakjian, 434
United States v. Ballard, 354
United States v. Banks, 221, 293, 370
United States v. Bell, 354
United States v. Biswell, 326
United States v. Brignoni-Ponce, 109, 263
United States v. Calandra, 230, 232
United States v. Carolene Products Co., 90
United States v. Chadwick, 306
United States v. Conner, 336
United States v. Cortez, 250
United States v. Councilman, 337
United States v. Cronic, 420
United States v. Cruikshank, 178–179
United States v. Darby, 459, 461–462
United States v. Davis, 322
United States v. Decastro, 182
United States v. Di Re, 216

United States v. Dunn, 321
United States v. Edwards, 328
United States v. Emerson, 180
United States v. Flores-Montano, 263
United States v. Good, 434
United States v. Graham, 336
United States v. Grigg, 260–261
United States v. Guarno, 354
United States v. Haley, 303
United States v. Hazzard, 431
United States v. Henry, 411
United States v. Hensley, 250–251, 260
United States v. Ingrao, 215
United States v. Jacobsen, 210, 323
United States v. Jones, 289, 333, 362
United States v. Karo, 333
United States v. Klein, 63
United States v. Knights, 213, 330
United States v. Knotts, 333
United States v. Koch, 353
United States v. Lara, 381–382
United States v. Leon, 229, 237
United States v. Leonard, 330
United States v. Lopez, 118–119, 184, 462
United States v. Lucas, 309
United States v. Martinez-Fuerte, 263
United States v. Matlock, 298
United States v. McCarty, 215
United States v. McClinton, 354
United States v. Miller, 178, 179, 180
United States v. Molinaro, 306
United States v. Montoya de Hernandez, 263, 323
United States v. Moylan, 401
United States v. Muhlenbruch, 363
United States v. O'Brien, 140
United States v. Ortiz, 325
United States v. Paradise, 96

United States v. Parker, 210
United States v. Patane, 376
United States v. Pavelski, 251
United States v. Perrine, 336
United States v. Pinson, 304
United States v. Pritchard, 261
United States v. Ramsey, 323
United States v. Robinson, 306
United States v. Ross, 210, 313
United States v. Russell, 378
United States v. Salerno, 431
United States v. Santana, 266, 269, 317
United States v. Sharpe, 255
United States v. Simmons, 309
United States v. Skoien, 183
United States v. Smith, 39, 335, 337
United States v. Sokolow, 218, 249, 324
United States v. Stevens, 145
United States v. Tapley, 210
United States v. Texas, 107, 109
United States v. Thomas, 330
United States v. Ursery, 434
United States v. Valenzuela-Bernal, 404
United States v. Virginia, 95
United States v. Wade, 413, 419
United States v. Walther, 210
United States v. Warshak, 336
United States v. Watson, 266
United States v. White, 335
United States v. Windsor, 104
United States v. Wright, 362
United Steelworkers of America v. Weber, 96
Utah v. Strieff, 233

Van Orden v. Perry, 132
Vause v. United States, 319
Virginia v. Black, 142

Virginia v. Harris, 67
Virginia v. Moore, 242

Wallace v. Jaffree, 131
Warden v. Hayden, 269, 316
Warner v. Orange County Dept. of Probation, 138
Washington v. Glucksberg, 89
Washington v. Texas, 465
Watts v. Indiana, 357
Weeds v. United States, 300
Weeks v. United States, 229, 230–231
Welch v. Butler, 354
Welsh v. Wisconsin, 316
Wesberry v. Sanders, 467
West Virginia State Board of Education v. Barnette, 133, 134, 462
Whitley v. Albers, 450
Whren v. United States, 260
Wiggins v. Smith, 420
Wilson v. Arkansas, 220
Wilson v. Seiter, 449
Wilson v. Swing, 166
Winston v. Lee, 289
Wolff v. McDonnell, 118
Wolf v. Colorado, 208, 231, 464
Wong Sun v. United States, 232
Wooley v. Maynard, 134
Wright v. United States, 298
Wygant v. Jackson Board of Education, 96
Wyoming v. Houghton, 314

Yates v. United States, 363
Youngstown Sheet & Tube Co. v. Sawyer, 58

Zobrest v. Catalina Foothills School District, 132
Zurcher v. Stanford Daily, 163

Authors Index

Agresti, J. D., 194, 201
Aisch, G., 71, 77
Anderson, T. M., 137, 148, 165, 172
Arkin, W. M., 119, 120, 124
Armento, B. J., 5, 15, 20, 22, 28

Bacigal, R. J., 425
Bailey, P. J., 412, 425
Baker, A., 256, 284
Baker, P., 70, 77
Baldus, D. C., 115, 123
Basich, M., 276, 284
Bass, H. J., 9, 28
Basu, K., 185, 201
Beard, C. A., 12, 28
Beard, M. R., 12, 28
Belz, E., 167, 172
Bilukham, O. O., 195, 201
Bohm, R. M., 445, 448, 453
Boyter, J., 469, 471
Brave, M., 277, 284
Breen, T. H., 7, 28
Briss, P., 195, 201
Brown, R. C., 9, 28
Brunner, B., 95, 123

Callanan, J., 270, 284
Cardozo, B. N., 463, 471
Castellano, A., 194, 201
Childress, S., 240, 241, 244
Christie, B., 108, 123
Clear, T. R., 436, 449, 450, 453
Cohen, A., 172
Cohen, H., 147, 172
Cole, G. F., 271, 284, 436, 449, 450, 453
Collins, J. M., 267, 284
Cope, C. J., 270, 284
Corley, M., 411, 412, 425
Crosby, A., 195, 201

Dasgupta, N., 112, 123
Davis, B., 82, 123
Davis, K. C., 129, 172
del Carmen, Rolando V., 230, 237, 238, 240, 241, 244, 323, 342, 374, 390, 423, 425
DeLone, M., 32, 57
DeSilver, D., 71, 77
Divine, R. A., 7, 28
Donohue, J. J., III., 195, 201
Doyle, M., 189, 190, 201
Ducat, C. R., 63, 78, 95, 96, 123, 149, 155, 172, 448, 453
Dwyer, T. P., 71, 78, 109, 123, 157, 172

Eldridge, J., 185, 201
Engels, F., 32, 57

Fagan, J. A., 446, 453
Farber, D. A., 65, 78
Ferdico, J. N., 303, 353, 354, 390, 402, 425
Fradella, H. F., 353, 354, 390, 402, 425

Fredrickson, G. M., 7, 28
Fridell, L., 112, 123
Frieden, T., 116, 123
Fullilove, M. T., 195, 201

Gaertner, S., 412, 425
Gardner, T. J., 137, 148, 165, 172
Garner, G. W., 164, 172
Garry, L. M., 111, 124
Glaze, L., 329, 342
Glennon, Jim, 215, 244
Goebel, J., Jr., 63, 78
Grimm, F., 185, 201

Haley, K. N., 445, 448, 453
Hall, Jerome, 207, 244
Hann, R. A., 195, 201
Hanson, R. A., 116, 124
Harrington, J., 412, 425
Harris, E. A., 190, 201
Hawkes, A., 275, 284
Herbert, B., 256, 284
Hockenberry, S., 52, 57
Holt, K., 45, 57

Jacoby, J., 11, 28
Joh, E. E., 322, 342
Judge, L. A., 310, 342

Kaeble, D., 329, 342
Keller, J., 71, 77
Kelly, K., 240, 241, 244
Klieman, M., 116, 124
Kornblut, A. E., 107, 123
Kovandzic, T. V., 195, 201
Kowalski, B. R., 113, 123
Krogstad, J. M., 104, 123
Kruger, K. J., 114, 123, 349, 390

LaFountain, R., 45, 57
Lai, K. K. R., 71, 77
Larson, M. R., 412, 425
Lewis, K., 45, 57
Liberman, A., 195, 201
Lichtblau, E., 190, 201
Lightman, D., 189, 190, 201
Liptak, A., 70, 78
Long, C., 195, 201, 256, 284
Lott, J. R., Jr., 195, 201
Lundman, R. J., 113, 123
Lysakowski, M., 106, 123

Madison, J., 461, 471
Maher, T. M., 352, 357, 390
Markon, J., 107, 123
Marvell, T. B., 195, 201
Marx, K., 32, 57
Maslow, Abraham H., 205, 244
Mayes, S., 139, 140, 172
McDonald, Pam, 99, 123, 238, 244, 255, 277, 284, 301, 303, 327, 342, 348, 360, 367, 390

Means, Randy, 99, 123, 238, 244, 255, 270, 272, 277, 284, 301, 303, 327, 342, 348, 360, 367, 390
Mears, Bill, 242, 244
Mecklenburg, S. H., 412, 425
Minton, T., 329, 342
Modafferi, P. A., 411, 412, 425
Monk, L. R., 429, 453
Moore, C., 448, 453
Moscicki, E. K., 195, 201
Moule, J., 92, 93, 123

Nakashima, E., 190, 201
Nash, G. B., 5, 15, 20, 22, 28
Nowicki, E., 195, 202

O'Brien, T., 167, 172
O'Connor, T. P., 352, 357, 390
O'Linn, M. K., 277, 284
Ostrom, B. J., 116, 124
Ostrom, C. W., 116, 124

Packer, H. L., 32, 33, 34, 57
Passel, J. S., 104, 123
Pearsall, A. A., III, 106, 123
Perkins, C., 411, 412, 425
Petrocelli, J., 361, 374, 390
Planty, M., 194, 202
Pope, J., 106, 123
Priest, D., 119, 120, 124
Pulaski, C. A., 115, 123
Puzzanchera, C., 52, 57

Reisig, M. D., 436, 449, 453
Rich, S., 240, 241, 244
Rivera, R., 256, 284
Roberts, R., 161, 172
Robinson, M., 112, 113, 124
Robinson, R. R., 71, 78
Roh, S., 112, 113, 124
Rowan, B., 95, 123
Rubin, J. K., 322, 342
Rutledge, Devallis, 67, 78, 244, 252, 256, 284, 308, 309, 326, 332, 342, 359, 360, 361, 366, 367, 378, 390, 409, 410, 417, 425

Saad, L., 447, 453
Salter, C. L., 5, 15, 20, 22, 28
Sanchez, A. J., 322, 342
Savage, C., 338, 342
Scarry, L., 99, 124, 256, 272, 284
Schauffler, R., 45, 57
Schuck, J., 414, 425
Scoville, D., 275, 284
Seidel, G., 270, 272, 284
Shapiro, R., 408, 425
Shin, A., 160, 161, 172
Slocumb, D. J., 161, 172
Smith, C. E., 68, 69, 70, 78, 271, 284
Smith, R. K., 194, 201
Snyder, S., 195, 201

Solar, M., 111, 124
Spector, E. B., 60, 78
Spohn, C., 32, 57
Strickland, S., 45, 57

Thompson, D. C., 66, 78
Totten, C. D., 353, 354, 390, 402, 425
Trulson, C. R., 423, 425
Truman, J. L., 194, 202
Tsoutis, A., 329, 342
Tuma, F., 195, 201

Vernon, R., 153, 172

Wachtell, M. F., 66, 78
Walker, S., 32, 57, 110, 111, 124
Wallentine, K., 310, 342
Wethal, T., 193, 202
Wexler, C., 106, 124, 194, 197, 199, 202
Wildenthal, B. H., 71, 78
Williams, J., 177, 202
Williams, R. H., 7, 28
Wilson, Bradford P., 229, 244

Wilson, K., 331, 342
Wixson, K. K., 5, 15, 20, 22, 28
Woodworth, G., 115, 123
Worrall, J. L., 434, 453
Wu, F., 153, 172

Ybarra, M., 189, 190, 201
Yourish, K., 71, 77

Zarembo, A., 189, 202

Subject Index

ABC, *This Week*, 107
abortion, 143
Abu Ghraib Prison, 230
Access to Justice (ATJ) Initiative, 408
accusation, being informed of, 402
Adams, John, 63
Adams, Samuel, 8, 474
adjudication hearing, 53
administrative warrant, 326
administrative liability, 240
adversarial judicial system, 49, 405
affirm, defined, 42
affirmative action, 95
affirmative action programs, 95–98
African Americans, in early America, 7, 9
aftercare, 53
age
    and capital punishment, 444
    discrimination based on, 114
    and voting rights, 467
Air Line Pilots Association (ALPA), 337
al-Arian, Sami, 386
Alcoholics Anonymous (AA), and religious freedom, 138
Alien and Sedition Acts of 1798, 152
Alito, Samuel, Jr., 69–71, 86, 98, 167, 348
Alvarez, Xavier, 146–147
amendments, 21
American Bar Association
    Public Education Division, 75
    website of, 493
American Civil Liberties Union, 132, 151
American Colonies
    dissension in, 7–8
    ethnic population of, 5
    timeline of events in, 21–22
American dream, 97
American Indians. *see* Native Americans
American Newspaper Publishers Association, 75
American Revolution, 4, 9, 11
Americans with Disabilities Act of 1990, 101, 114
amicus brief, 50
Amish, religious freedom of, 135
animal cruelty, 136
animal sacrifice, 136
anonymous tips, 251–254
Antabuse, 438
Anthony, Casey, 164
anti-Federalists, 20
anti-Semitism, 129
appeals
    and capital punishment, 445–446
    critical stages at, 415–419
appellate jurisdiction, 44
Areopagitica (John Milton), 162
Arizona immigration law of 2010, 107–109
arraignment, 415
array, 397
arrest, 250
    citizen's, 281
    compared with stop, 248–249

de facto, 267–268
defined, 264
immunity from, 282
knock-and-announce rule and, 220–221, 248
lawful, 264–266
search of vehicle following, 309–311
with warrant, 266
warrantless
    based on probable cause, 265–266
    for crimes committed in the presence of an officer, 264–265
Articles of Confederation, 11–12, 27
articulable facts, 218
assault rifle, 186
assault weapons, 190
Assault Weapons Ban, 186
asset forfeiture, 433–435
Asset Forfeiture Program, 434
assistance of counsel, 465
Associated Press, 191, 256
association, freedom of, 166–167
Association of American Law Schools, 75
atheists, and religious freedom, 138
attenuation doctrine, 233
Attica Prison Riot, 116
Atwater, Gail, 241
automobile exception, 311–315

bail, 430–433
    case law on, 430
    commercial, 432
    legislation, 430
Bail Reform Act of 1966, 430–431
Bail Reform Act of 1984, 431–433
Bakke, Alan, 95
balancing test, 149
Baldwin, Abr., 483
Banks, Lashawn, 221
Bassett, Richard, 482
Batson, James Kirkland, 397
Baylor, Greg, 167
Baze, Ralph, 442
beachheading, 370–371
Beccaria, Cesare, 473
Bedford, Gunning Jr., 482
Belton rule, 273
beyond a reasonable doubt, 39
The Bias against Guns (John Lott), 195
Bible Riots of 1844, 129
Biden, Joe, 386
bifurcated trial, 441
Bill of Rights. *see* U.S. Constitution
Black Codes, 82
Black, Hugo, 85, 138, 381, 406
Blackmun, Harry, 69
Blair, John, 483
blind lineup, 412
Blount, Wm., 483
blue wall of silence, 157
border
    functional equivalent of, 263
    search, 323–325

Bowling, Thomas, 442
Brady Bill. *see* Brady Handgun Violence Prevention Act
Brady Campaign to Prevent Gun Violence, 181–182, 185, 194, 197, 198
Brady Handgun Violence Prevention Act, 118, 188
Brady, James, 118
Brady, John, 417
Brady rule, 417
Braxton, Carter, 11
Brearly, David, 482
Brendlin, Bruce, 258–259
Brendlin, Scott, 258–259
Brennan, William Jr., 69, 141, 317, 442
    freedom of association, 166
Breyer, Stephen, 70, 169, 187, 443
brief, 42
    amicus, 50
Broom, Jaco., 482
Brown, Edmund, 159
Bryan, Carl, 276–277
Bulwer-Lytton, Edward, 161
Bureau of Alcohol, Tobacco, Firearms, and Explosives, 177
    modern day militias and, 177
Burger, Warren E., 22
Bush, George H. W., 69
Bush, George W., 51, 69, 385, 465
Butler, Pierce, 483
Butler, Willie, 368

California Civil Rights Initiative (CCRI), 100
capital punishment, 440–448
    age and, 444
    appeals and, 445–446
    controversy over, 447–448
    costs of, 446
    cruel and unusual punishment and, 440–443
    DNA evidence and, 448
    intellectual disability, 445
    juries and, 446–447
    mental illness and, 445
    mental retardation and, 445
    racial discrimination and, 444–445
    who is executed, 443–445
caption, 41
Cardozo, Benjamin, 85
Carroll, Danl., 482
carrying a concealed weapon (CCW), 183–184
Carter, President Jimmy, 51
case
    briefing of, 42–43
    citing, 44
    hearing of, decisions on, 50–51
    mootness of, 50–51
    path of, to Supreme Court, 62
    ripeness, 51
    standing of, 50
case law, 35
    reading, 41–42

Subject Index

castle laws, 184–186
castration, 438
Catholicism, in early America, 129
cell phone searches, 307
Centers for Disease Control and Prevention (CDC), 195, 198
Central Intelligence Agency, 162
certiorari, 65–67, 119, 132, 151, 166, 179, 211, 221, 403
Chase, Samuel, 67
checkpoints, 261–262
checks and balances, 14, 18
child abuse victim, and right to confront witness, 403
Child Online Protection Act (COPA), 159
child pornography, 159
Christian Burial Speech, 234, 410
Christian Legal Society (CLS), 167
Christmas Day bomb attempt, 119
church, separation from state, 129
Cicero, *Pro Milone*, 437
circumstances
 exigent, 315–319
 totality of, 214
citations, reading, 41
citizen's arrest, 281
citizenship, 83
Citizenship Clause, 83
Civil Asset Forfeiture Reform Act, 435
civil liability, 239–241
civil liability, of police officers, 239
Civil Rights Act of 1964, 93, 95, 100
civil rights movement, 138
Civil War, 37, 81–82, 114, 460
"clear and present danger" test, 148
"clear and probable danger" test, 149
Clemmons, Maurice, 448
Cleveland Police Department, 227
Clinton, Bill, 18, 69, 118, 135, 188, 190
Clymer, Geo., 482
Cobb, Raymond Levi, 417
codified law, 38
Columbine High School (Colorado), shooting at, 194
Combined DNA Index System (CODIS), 322
Commerce Clause, 96, 109, 118, 135, 178
commercial bail, 432
common law, 35
 suits at, 457
community caretaking doctrine, 267
comparative law, 54
compensation for taking private property, 464
compensatory damages, 433
compulsory process, 404, 465
concealed carry gun laws, 183–184
concurring opinion, 42, 51, 74
conduct, furtive, 215
conducted energy devices (CEDs), 275, 276
conducted energy weapons (CEWs), 276
Cone, Gary, 443
conference, 53
confessions
 cases pertaining to, 376
 characteristics of the accused, 354
 false, 357
 police conduct and, 353–354
 voluntariness of, 352–353, 354, 356
conflict theory, 32
Confrontation Clause, 402–404

Congress, 8–12, 14, 16, 130
 structure of, 465–466
Congress of the Confederation, 13
Congressional Medal of Honor, 146
consensus theory, 31–32
consent
 third-party, 298
 voluntariness test of, 300
 waiver test of, 300
consequences of Fourth Amendment violations, 229–241
conservative, defined, 68
constitution
 United States. *see* U.S. Constitution
Constitutional Convention of 1787, 14
 delegates to, 13–15
constitutional law
 beginnings of, 5–6
 changing face of, 53
 historical overview of, 3–26
constitutionalism, 14
constitutionally proscribable, 142
contact, voluntary, 272
contemporaneous, 305
contextual discrimination, 111
continuum of contacts, 225
contraband, 296
Coolidge, Calvin, 475
corporal punishment, 437
corrections
 discrimination in, 116–118
 and Eighth Amendment rights, 448–451
 Fifth Amendment rights and, 384–385
 Religious Freedom Restoration Act (RFRA) 1993, 169
 and Sixth Amendment rights, 423
counsel
 during criminal investigation, 409–411
 at critical stages, 408–419
 development of the right to, 405–408
 effective, presumption of, 420–421
 right to, 368–370, 392–423
  act as one's own, 421, 423
  at critical stages, 408–419
  current developments in, 408
  key cases regarding, 419
  waiver of, 421
 role of, 405
Court of Appeals, 153
Court Statistics Project, 45
court trial, 401
courts, 44–51
 access to, 118
 discrimination in, 104–106
 federal, 47–48
 officers of, 49
 state, 45–47
 system of, 44–51
Crime Control Model, 33
Crime in the United States 2014, 194
crimes, 39, 52
criminal investigation, critical stages during, 409–411
criminal justice, beyond US borders, 53–55
criminal justice system
 crime control versus due process, 32–34
 equal protection in, 110–118
criminal liability, 239–241
criminal liability, of police officers, 239–241
Criminal Police Organization (INTERPOL), 54

criminal procedure, 207
criminal proceedings, critical stages at, 408–419
criminals, 52
critical stage, 408–419
 at appeals, 415–419
 during criminal investigation, 409–411
 at hearings, 415–419
 at trials, 415–419
Crook, Shirley, 444
cross burning, 141–142
cross-racial identification, 412
cruel and unusual punishment, 435–448
Cummings, Sam R., 180
curtilage, 321
custodial interrogation, 363–365
custody
 factors indicating custodial situation, 363
 Miranda warning and, 361–365
 suspect at the police station, 362
 suspect in custody for another offence, 362–363
 suspect under arrest, 361–362

damages
 compensatory, 433
 punitive, 433
Dan of St. Thos. Jenifer, 482
Davis, Edward, 198
Davis, Robert, 370
Dawes, William, 9
Dayton, Jona., 482
de facto arrests, 267–268
Deane, Charlie, 197
death penalty. *see* capital punishment
Declaration of Independence, 10–12, 26
 signers of, 4, 10–11
Defense of Marriage Act (DOMA), 104
delegated powers, 460
deliberate elicitation, 410
delinquent, 53
delinquent acts, 52
demurrer, 179
Department of Homeland Security (DHS), 54, 91
 Immigration and Customs Enforcement (ICE), 106
Department of Justice, Asset Forfeiture Program, 434
Depo-Provera, 438
detainer, 423
detention, 52
 preventive, 431
Dickerson, Charles, 372
Dickerson, Timothy, 302
Dickinson, John, 482
dicta, 43
dictum (dicta), 181
disabilities, discrimination and, 114
disciplinary hearings, due process during, 118
discrimination, 93, 106
 access to court and, 118
 age, 111
 based on religion, 161
 because of sexual orientation, 101
 color and, 95
 contextual, 111
 in corrections, 116–118
 in courts, 114–116
 disabilities and, 114

discrimination (*Continued*)
    disciplinary hearings and, 118
    disparity continuum of, 111
    forms of, 101–104
    gender, 94
    immigration and, 104–107
    against Jews, 129
    in jury selection, 114
    in law enforcement, 111–114
    national origin and, 95
    other forms of, 101–104
    against people with disabilities, 101
    pregnancy policies, 114
    versus prejudice, 92–93
    race and, 93
    racial, 93
    religion and, 95, 98, 124
    residency discrimination, 104
    reverse, 98–100
    in sentencing, 115–116
    sex and, 95, 97
    sexual orientation and, 103
disparate treatment, 99
disparity, 110
    continuum of, 111
disproportionate minority contact (DMC), 111
DNA
    abandoned, 319–232
    collection of from arrested persons, 328
    exoneration and, 412
    familial databases of, 92
DNA evidence, 448
    abandoned DNA, 322–323
    in the United Kingdom, 92
"don't ask/don't tell", 101
double jeopardy, 380, 380–382, 434
Douglas, William, 88–89, 150, 181
draft card burning, 140
driving while Asian ("DWA"), 112
driving while Black ("DWB"), 112
driving while Mexican ("DWM"), 112
Drug Abuse Resistance Education (D.A.R.E.), 434
Drug Enforcement Administration (DEA), 210, 324
drunk driving
    anonymous tips on, 252
    checkpoints for, 261
    destruction of evidence and, 316
due process, 83–92
    and entrapment, 377–378
    enumerated rights and, 84–86
    incorporation and, 84–86
    of law, 83
    privacy rights and, 90–92
    procedural, 84, 86–87
    revolution, 116
    substantive, 84, 87–90
due process clause, 85, 86, 87, 88
    cases incorporating provisions of Bill of Rights into, 464–465
Duncan, Gary, 85, 396
Dyson, Kevin, 313

Eastwood, Clint, 185
Edwards, John, 386
Edwards, Kenneth, 184
Ekas, Robert, 140
elections, 465–466
electoral college, 17
electoral system, 465

electors, 17
Electronic Communications Privacy Act (ECPA), 335–338
    Title I statute of, 335
    Title II statute of, 335
electronic control devices (ECDs), 275
electronic surveillance, 288, 333–335, 340
    privacy and, 333–335, 340
Emancipation Proclamation, 82
emergency aid doctrine, 318–319
End Racial Profiling Act (ERPA) of 2007, 105
entrapment, 377–378
enumerated rights, 84–86
Equal Employment Opportunity Act of 1972, 95
Equal Pay Act of 1963, 95
equal pay for equal work, 94
Equal Protection Clause, 83, 95, 97, 112
equal protection under the law, 79–121
    in criminal justice system, 110–121
    and jury selection, 114
equality, struggle for, 94–110
Escobedo, Danny, 408
Espionage Act (1917), 148
Establishment Clause, 51, 130–133
Establishment Clause (establishment of religion), 464
Establishment Clause of the First Amendment, 130
Euripides, 161
evidence
    admissible, 208–209
    exclusionary rule and, 229–234
    as fruit of the poisonous tree, 232–234
    and good faith exception, 236–239
    and harmless error exception, 235–236
    hearsay, 404
    inadmissible, 208–209
    and inevitable discovery doctrine, 234–235
    obtained in a manner that shocks the conscience, 231–232
    plain view, 303–305
    valid independent source exception and, 235
excessive bail, 430
excessive fines, 430
exclusionary rule, 229–234
    exceptions to, 234–239
    good faith exception, 236–239
    harmless error exception to, 235–236
    valid independent source exception and, 235
exclusive jurisdiction, 44
execution
    and age of prisoner, 444
    lengthy delays in, 443
    lethal injection, 442
exigent circumstances, 315–319
expectation of privacy, 214
expression
    by public employees, 156–159
    symbolic, 140–143
extralegal factors, 110

FAA. *see* Federal Aviation Administration (FAA)
Facebook, 336
Fair Housing Act, 100, 458
Fair Labor Standards Act of 1938, 461–462
false confessions, 357
    compliant confessions, 357
    internalized, 357
    voluntary confessions, 357

familial DNA databases, 92
Fay, Michael, 435
FBI. *see* Federal Bureau of Investigation (FBI)
Federal Assault Weapons Ban, 186
Federal Bureau of Investigation (FBI), 91, 107, 177, 188, 190, 195, 208, 218, 236, 288, 291, 322, 360, 370, 372, 386, 411, 494
    and modern-day militias, 177
federal courts, 47–48
    of appeal, 47
    levels in, 44
    special, 47
Federal Death Penalty Act of 1994, 446
Federal Express, 210
Federal Firearms Act (1938), 186
Federal Gun Control Act of 1968, 186
federal income tax, 468
Federal Judiciary Act of 1789, 61
Federal Labor Relations Authority (FLRA), 119
federal power, check on, 118–121
Federal Rules of Civil Procedure, 40
federalism, 460
    revisited, 119
The Federalist Papers, 20, 76, 163, 347 461
Federalists, 20
Few, William, 483
fighting words, 147
fines, 433–435
firearms
    domestic abuse and, 180
    restrictions on types of, 186
First Continental Congress, 8–9
Fischer, Gail, 299
Fisher, Abigail, 97
FitzSimons, Thos., 482
flag burning, 141
fleeing felon rule, 271, 279
flight from police, seizure and, 254
Fogel, Matthew, 151
Food and Drug Administration, 209
force
    continuum of, 274
    deadly, 278—280
    less-lethal force, 275–276
    reasonable, 271–275
    in searching arrested person, 309
    tasers and, 276–278
    use of, 270–281
Ford, Gerald R., 69
Fort Hood shooting, 119
Fortas, Abe, 351, 421
Fourth Circuit, 154
Frankfurter, Felix, 300, 350, 351, 353, 377
Franklin, Benjamin, 7, 12, 19, 340, 482
Free Exercise Clause, 134–138
free exercise clause (free exercise of religion), 464
free speech, 139
Free Speech Movement, 152
freedom, 126–170
    of assembly, 164–166, 464
    of association, 166–167
    to petition government, 464
    preferred freedoms approach to, 150
    of the press, 161–164, 464
    of religion, 129–138
        corrections and, 161
    of speech, 138–161, 464
    from unreasonable interference by government, 214

French and Indian War, 7
fresh pursuit, 268
frisk, 215, 225. *see also* stop and frisk
    warrantless search and, 301–302
functional equivalent, 263
furtive conduct, 216

Gallup Poll (May 18-22, 2016), immigration and, 106
gender
    discrimination and, 94, 166
    equality and, 100
    in jury selection, 115
genetic material, 322. *see also* DNA
Geneva Convention, 55
Gettysburg Address, 82
Gilman, Nicholas, 482
Ginsburg, Ruth Bader, 69, 70, 72, 167, 196, 259
global positioning systems (GPS), surveillance and, 338
Goddard, Colin, 194
Goldberg, Arthur, 408
good faith exception, 236
Gore, Al, 465
Gorham, Nathaniel, 482
government
    agencies of, and USA PATRIOT Act, 388
    balanced, 461
    continuum of contacts of, 222–225
    delegated powers of, 460
    executive branch of, 14, 17–18
    internal sanctions and, 239–241
    judicial branch of, 14, 18
    judicial power of federal, 463
    legislative branch of, 14, 16–17
    limited, 6
    misconduct of, and exclusionary rule, 229
    need to know of, 347
    powers of, 118–121
    reserve powers of, 460
GPS device, tracking with, 289
Graber, Anthony, 160
Graham, Dethorne, 271
grand jury, 379, 464
    compared with trial jury, 380
    right to, 379–380
Great Compromise, 15
Great Debate (1830), 81
Great Depression, 90
Griffin, Joseph, 330
Grigg, Justin, 261
Groh, Jeff, 296
Guarnieri, Charles, 165
Guide to Law Online, 41
gun control
    balancing individual and states' rights, 177–178
    current debate over, 196–198
    as political issue, 197–198
    possible compromise in, 198–199
    proposed legislation on, 193–194
    Second Amendment and, 174–199
        balancing individual and states' rights, 177–178
Gun Control Act, 187, 188
Gun Control Act of 1968, 186
Gun-Free School Zones Act, 184, 462
gun laws
    castle laws, 184–186
    concealed carry laws, 183–184
    restrictions on types of firearms, 186
    state and local, 182–186
    variations in, 182–186
gun show, 194
guns
    crime and, 194–196
    violence and, 194–196
Guns and Crime (Charlie Deane), 197

Hamilton, Alexander, 15, 20, 76, 93, 482
Hancock, John, 21
Hand, Learned, 149
handguns, 180, 184, 188, 194
Harlan, John Marshall II, 85, 289
harmless error, 235–236
harmless error doctrine, 354
Harris, Vivien, 373
Harrison, William, 466
Hart, John, 11
Hastings, Clint, 273
Hastings College of Law, San Francisco, 167
Hastings, Todd, 272
hate crimes, 141–142
Hayne, Robert, 81
hearings
    critical stages at, 415–419
    disciplinary, 118
    preliminary, 53, 415
hearsay, 404
Helmke, Paul, 181, 198
Henry, Patrick, 3, 8
Herring, Bennie, 238
Holder, Eric H. Jr., 107, 408
holding, 42
Holliday, George, 270
Holmes, Oliver Wendell Jr., 64, 470
Hope, Larry, 451
hot pursuit, 316–317
House of Representatives, 15, 16
Huckabee, Mike, 448
Hughes, Charles Evans, 63
Humanitarian Law Project, 153
Hyde, Henry H., 435

identification
    cross-racial, 412
    rights during, 411–414
Illegal Immigration Reform and Immigrant Responsibility Act of 1996, 106
immigration, 104–106
    Arizona law of 2010, 107–109
    Section 287(g), 106–107
    secure communities, 107
Immigration and Customs Enforcement (ICE), 106
    racial profiling and, 107
Immigration and Nationality Act, 106
"imminent lawless action" test, 149
immunity
    from arrest, 282
    qualified, 296
impartial jury, 396–401, 464
impeached testimony, and *Miranda* warning, 373
"In God We Trust", 134
incorporation, 84–86
incorporation doctrine, 84
incrimination, 348
independent judge, 220
indictment, 379
indigency, statement of, 407
indigent, 406

inevitable discovery doctrine, 234–235
informants, 251–254
    Fifth Amendment and *Miranda* implications regarding, 376–377
information, legal obtaining of, 345–388
Ingersoll, Jared, 482
Ingraham, James, 437
Innis, Thomas, 363
Inquisition, 429
interception, 334
Internal Revenue Service, 209, 291
International Association of Chiefs of Police (IACP), 193
Internet, freedom of speech and, 159–160
interrogation, 361
    and *Miranda* warning, 363–365
inventory search, 314–315
investigatory stop, 249–263
invoke, 348
Iraq War, 230

Jackson, Andrew, 133
Jackson, Robert Bernard, 415
Jackson, Robert H., 58, 357
Jackson rule, 415
Jay, John, 20, 347
Jefferson, Thomas, 7, 10, 15, 21, 63, 93, 130, 161, 340, 490
Jehovah's Witnesses, 134
Jim Crow laws, 93
Joh, Elizabeth E., 322
Johns Hopkins University Center for Gun Policy and Research, 183
Johnson, Andrew, 18
Johnson, Gregory, 141
Johnson, Jeh, 107, 108
Johnson, Lemon, 259
Johnson, Lyndon, 95, 474
Johnson, Wm. Saml., 482
Jones, Louis Jr., 446
Jones, Paula, 18
judgment, summary, 99
judicial activism, 138
judicial review, 63–64
    alternatives to, 65
    controversy over, 65
judicial system, adversarial, 49–50, 405
Judiciary Act of 1789, 430, 432, 490
jurisdiction, 37–38
    appellate, 44
    concurrent, 44
    exclusive, 44
    general, 44
    limited, 44
    original, 44
    of U.S. Supreme Court, 61–63
jurors, peremptory challenges to, 397
jury
    capital punishment and, 446–447
    impartial, 396–401
    voir dire and, 397
jury nullification, 401
jury trial, 464
    in civil cases, 465
    federal, 458
    right to, 458
just compensation, 382–383
justices, U.S. Supreme Court, 68
    conservative, 68
    liberal, 68
Justinian Code, 35

Juvenile Justice and Delinquency Prevention
    Act of 2002, 111
juvenile justice system, 52–53
juveniles, 52
    corrections and, 53
    courts, 52–53
    and death penalty, 446
    law enforcement and, 52
    and Sixth Amendment rights, 423

Kagan, Elena, 70, 72
Kaupp, Robert, 267
Kennedy, Anthony M., 69, 70, 99, 137, 332, 444
Kennedy, John F., 95, 129, 187
Kennedy, Robert, 187
King George III, 7, 9, 197
King Henry VII, 394
King, John, 12
King, Martin Luther, 187
King, Rodney, 160, 270
King, Rufus, 482
King's Bench of Great Britain in 1792, 74
Kiro, John, 312
knock-and-announce rule, 220–221
Knowles, Patrick, 310
Konop, Robert, 337
Ku Klux Klan, 82, 94
Kyllo, Danny Lee, 304

Langdon, John, 482
Lara, Billy Jo, 381
law, 5
    categorizing, 37
    civil, 38–40
    conflicts in, 241–242
    constitutional, 5, 241–242
    continuing need for, 36–37
    criminal, 38–40
    defined, 35
    development of, 35–37
    living, 25
    procedural, 38
    researching, 40–44
law enforcement
    discrimination in, 111–114
    Fourth Amendment and, 207–208
    racial profiling, 112
    racially biased policing, 113
Law Enforcement Officers Safety Act
    (LEOSA), 193
law research, sources for, 40–41
LawCrawler, 493
Lazarus, Emma, 104
Leahy, Patrick, 116
Lee, Richard Henry, 11
legal citations, 41
    reading, 489
legal factors, 110
Legal Information Institute, Cornell
    University
    website of, 493
legal research, 493–496
    computerized, 493–496
    information literacy, 493–494
    law on the web, 493
    steps in researching a law of interest,
        494–496
    what's next, 494
legal system, 31–34
    balancing individual and societal
        rights, 34

components of, 51–53
conflict theory of, 31–32
consensus theory of, 31–32
doctrines governing which cases can be
    heard, 50–51
juvenile justice system, 52–53
overview of, 29–55
purpose of, 31–34
theories about, 31–34
LexisNexis, 493
liberal, defined, 68
Liberation Tigers of Tamil Eelam (LTTE), 153
liberty, 6, 84
Library of Congress Public Services
    division, 41
Lincoln, Abraham, 81
lineup, 412
    blind, 412
litigious, 241
Livingston, Wil., 482
lobotomy, 438
Lombroso, Cesare, 473
Lopez, German, 378
Los Angeles Police Department (LAPD),
    160, 275
    Rodney King and, 160, 270
Louima, Abner, 270
loyalist, 9

Madison, James, 20, 63, 176, 459, 466, 483, 490
magistrate, 219
Magna Carta, 15
    and Bill of Rights, 21
    and U.S. Constitution, 12–13
Make My Day laws, 185
Manifesto of the Communist Party (Marx and
    Engels), 32
Marbury v. Madison (1803), 43, 372, 490
Marbury, William, 63
Marshall, John, 64, 83, 214
Marshall, Thurgood, 69, 431
Martin, Trayvon, 185
Martinez, Leo, 167
Maslow, Abraham H., 205
Maslow's hierarchy of needs, 205
Mason, George, 20
Massachusetts Bay Colony, 6, 429
Massachusetts Body of Liberties, 429
Massachusetts Federalists, 21
Mauser, Tom, 194
Mayors against Illegal Guns, 195
McArthur, Charles, 291
McClesky, Warren, 115
McFadden, Martin, 227
McHenry, James, 482
media coverage, and criminal
    investigations, 164
Medina, Pedro, 441
Memorandums of Agreement (MOAs), 106
mental illness, and capital punishment, 445
mental retardation, and capital
    punishment, 445
Mifflin, Thomas, 482
militia, 176
    modern-day, 177
Miller, Jack, 179
Milton, John, 162
Mimms, Harry, 258
Minnesota Supreme Court, 141
Minnick, Robert, 370
Miranda, Ernesto, 358

Miranda rights, 233
Miranda v. Arizona, 357–378
    brief of the case, 358
    challenge to, by *Dickerson v. United States*,
        372–373
    Miranda violation and, 375–376
    right to counsel, 368–370
    right to remain silent, 366–367
    (text of), 490–491
Miranda warning, 225, 257, 358, 409
    beachheading and, 370–371
    continuing issues around, 373–374
    custody and, 362–363
    entrapment and, 377–378
    informant and, 376–377
    interrogation and, 363–365
    invoking, 365–370
    premature, 360–361
    public safety exception to, 375
    right against self-incrimination and, 373
    right to counsel and, 368–370
    right to remain silent, 366–367
    waiving, 365–370
    when generally not required, 374–375
    when it must be given, 361–365
    wording of, 359–360
Montejo, Jesse Jay, 415
Moore, David Lee, 242
Moore, Roy, 132
mootness, 50–51
More Guns, Less Crime (John Lott), 195
Mormonism, in early America, 129
Morris, Robert, 482
Mosley analysis, 366
Mosley, Richard, 366
movant, 99

Narcotics Anonymous (NA), and religious
    freedom, 138
National Archives website, 10
National Association of Police Organizations
    (NAPO), 119
National Center for State Courts, 116
National Criminal Justice Association, 493
National Firearms Act of 1934, 179
National Fraternal Order of Police
    (FOP), 119
National Instant Check System (NICS), 118
National Instant Criminal Background Check
    System (NICS), 188
National Park Service, 51
National Rifle Association (NRA), 177
national security, free speech and, 153
National Shooting Sports Foundation, 198
Nationwide Suspicious Activity Reporting
    Initiative (NSI), 91
Native Americans, 5
    religious freedom of, 135
needs, Maslow's hierarchy of, 205
New Jersey Plan, 15
New Jersey Turnpike Speeding Survey, 113
New Mexico Penitentiary riot, 116
New York Police Department (NYPD), 160
    stop and frisk, 256
Newtown, CT shooting, 198
nightcap(ped) warrant, 222
Nixon, Richard M., 69, 95, 188
no-knock warrant, 222
nonmovant, 99
notice, 465
nude dancing, 142

Obama administration, 70
Obama, Barack, 70, 72, 387,
obscenity, and freedom of speech, 148
Occupational Safety and Health Administration (OSHA), 326
O'Connor, Sandra Day, 69, 97, 168, 262
offense specific, 418
Office of Juvenile Justice and Delinquency Prevention (OJJDP), 111
Official Secrets Act (Britain), 161
Omnibus Crime Control and Safe Streets Act (1967), 186
open field, search of, 319–323
Operative Clause, 177
opinion, 74–75
　concurring, 42, 74
　dissenting, 42, 74–75
Opperman, Donald, 314
ordinances, 38
original jurisdiction, 44
Ortega, Magno, 331

Packer, Herbert, 32
parole, 53
Partiya Karkeran Kurdistan (PKK), 153
Paterson, Wm., 482
Patriot, 9
peaceful assembly, right to, 164–166
Pearl, Daniel, 387
penal codes, 39
The Pentagon Papers, 162
penumbra, 88, 289
peremptory challenges, 397
petition for certiorari, 47
photograph, right to, 160
physical restraints, 275
Pinckney, Charles, 15, 483
plain feel, 302–303
plain touch, 302–303
plain view, 303
plain view evidence, 303–305
Pledge of Allegiance, 110
Plessy, Homer, 93
pluralism, defined, 5
police
　continuum of contacts with individuals, 222–225
　flight from, 254
　on less-lethal force, 275–276
　Summary of Allowed Police Actions regarding Searches of Stopped Vehicles and their Occupants, 312
Police Chiefs and Sheriffs Speak Out on Local Immigration Enforcement, 105
Police Executive Research Forum (PERF), 105, 194, 275
police officers
　civil liability and, 239–241
　cluster killings of, 195
　criminal liability and, 239–241
　internal sanctions against, 239–241
　misconduct of, and exclusionary rule, 237
PoliceOne, 275
poll tax, 467
Pontiac's Rebellion, 7
Powell, Lewis, 51
powers
　balance of, 18
　federal *versus* state, 18
Powers, Pamela, 234
prayer, in schools, 131

preemption, 108
preferred freedoms approach, 150
prejudice, versus discrimination, 93
preliminary hearing, 53, 415
preponderance of the evidence, 39
President of the United States
　justices, U.S. Supreme Court, 18
　nomination of justices by, 70
press
　freedom of, 161–164
　　balancing with right to fair trial, 163–164
　　prior restraint on, 161
Presser, Herman, 180
pretext stop, 260
preventive detention, 431
The Preview of United States Supreme Court Cases, 72
prior restraint, 161
Prison Litigation Reform Act (PLRA), 449
prisoners
　and Eighth Amendment, 448–449
　rights of, 128, 168–170, 448–449
privacy
　balancing with security, 338–340
　due process and, 90–92
　electronic surveillance and, 333–340
　marital, 89
　reasonable expectation of, 213, 289
pro se, 421
probable cause, 24, 214–215
　to arrest, 215
　as contextual, 215
　informational, 216–219
　observational, 215–216
　to search, 215
　sources of, 215
probation, as sentencing option, 53
procedural due process, 84, 86–87
procedural law, 38, 207
Proclamation of 1763, 7
prohibited persons, and gun control, 187
Prohibition, 433–435
promulgate, 35
property
　abandoned, search of, 319–323
　public and quasi-public, 165
proportionality analysis, 436
Proposition 8, 103
protective sweep, 308
Prysock, Randall, 359
public employees, expression by, 156–159
public places, search of, 319–323
public property, types of, 165
Public Safety Employer-Employee Cooperation Act of 2009, 119–121
public safety exception, to *Miranda* warning, 375
public trial, 395–396
punishment
　brief history of, 429
　capital. *see* capital punishment
　corporal, 437
　cruel and unusual, 435–437
　options for, 437–438
　physical, 438–439
punitive damages, 433
pursuit, 268–269
　fresh, 268
　hot, 269

qualified immunity, 296
Quarles, Benjamin, 375

Quartering Act, 8
quasi-public property, types of, 165
Quon, Jeff, 332

racial discrimination
　capital punishment and, 444–445
　roots of, 93
　in sentencing, 116
racial issues
　equality in twenty-first century, 100
　and voting rights, 466–467
racial profiling, 112–113
Ramirez, Joseph, 296
ratify, defined, 20
rational basis, 168
rational basis test, 168
Read, Geo., 482
Reagan, Ronald, 69, 118, 188
reasonable expectation of privacy, 288, 289
reasonable expectation of privacy doctrine, 289
reasonable suspicion, 228
　establishing, 250–254
reasonableness, 213–214
　bright-line approach, 213
　case-by-case method, 213
　clause of fourth amendment, 213
　Fourth Amendment approach, 212
reasonableness clause, of Fourth Amendment, 212
recesses, 74
Redding, Savana, 327
Rehnquist, William H., 69, 70, 132, 184, 218, 254, 372, 418, 462
released on their own recognizance (ROR), 430
religion, 452
　discrimination on basis of, 101
　free exercise of, 137
　freedom of
　　conduct not protected by, 137
　　and equal access law, 131
　　interpretation of, 138
religious discrimination, 101
Religious Freedom Restoration Act (RFRA) 1993, 135, 169
remand, 42
remoteness, 307
representatives, 465
reserve powers, 460
residency discrimination, 104
Revere, Paul, 7
reverse, defined, 42
reverse discrimination, 98–100
right
　to bear arms, 86, 464
　to counsel, 368–370
　to grand jury, 379–380
　to peaceful assembly, 164–166
　to privacy, 24, 88, 89, 229
　to remain silent, 366–367
　against self-incrimination, 348–350
　　and *Miranda* warning, 373
　to vote, 37
right-to-carry (RTC) gun laws, 183
rights, 117
　balancing individual and societal rights, 128
　Eighth Amendment and, 428
　enumerated, 84–86
　guaranteed by Fifth Amendment, 373

rights (*Continued*)
    during identification, 411–414
    penumbra of, 289
    posttrial, key cases regarding, 419
    pretrial, key cases regarding, 419
    unenumerated, 88, 88–89
ripeness doctrine, 51
roadblocks, 261–262
Roberson, Ronald, 369
Roberts, John G., 69, 70, 103, 153, 238, 318, 442, 467
Robinson, Willie, 306
Romney, Mitt, 129
Ruby Ridge, Idaho, militia, 177
Rules of Engagement, 270
Rutledge, J., 483
Ryan, George, 448

same-sex marriage, 469
Samson, Donald Curtis, 331
San Diego Police Department (SDPD), 158
Santeria, 136
SAR. *see* suspicious activity reporting (SAR)
Saturday-night special, 183
Scalia, Antonin, 69, 100, 142, 182, 242, 279, 289, 373
schools
    firearms in, 182
    parochial, 130
    prayer in, 131
Scott, Timothy, 269
search, 206
    of abandoned property, 319–323
    administrative, 326
    of arrested person, use of force in, 309
    of arrestee's vehicle, 309
    border, 323–325
    conducting, 295–296
    with consent, 297–301
    constitutional, 273–332
    contemporaneousness and, 292
    detention during, 294–295
    executing, 222
    incident to lawful arrest, 305–311
    inventory, of impounded vehicles, 314–315
    of open field, 319–323
    of parolee, 327–331
    of person other than arrestee, 309
    plain feel and, 302–303
    plain touch and, 302–303
    plain view evidence in, 303–305
    of prisoner, 299, 319–322
    of probationer, 322–323
    of public employee work areas, 331–333
    of public places, 319–323
    public school, 326–327
    remoteness in, 295
    scope of, 290–291
    special conditions for, 221–222
    special needs, 325–333
    with suspicion, 308
    tenets of, 288–290
    of vehicle, 309
    of vehicle occupants, 309
    with warrant, 291–293
    wingspan and, 305
    without suspicion, 308
    without warrant, 296–323
search and seizure, 203–242
    constitutional analysis of, 325
    illegal, 181
    unreasonable, 51, 164, 186, 206, 212, 230, 268, 464
search warrant
    automobile exception to, 311–315
    executing, 222, 293
Second Continental Congress, 10
Secret Service, 209
security, 205
    balancing with privacy, 338–340
seizure, 206, 311. *see also* search and seizure
    and community caretaking doctrine, 267
    conducting constitutional, 246–282
    intensity and scope of, 248–249
    invalid, 209
    where arrests may be made, 266–267
selective incorporation, 464
self-incrimination, 464
self-incrimination, right against, 348–350
Senate, 15, 16, 17, 18, 67, 465
sentence, proportionality analysis of, 436
sentencing
    continuum of, 438
    key cases regarding, 419
    options of, 439
    racial discrimination in, 116
sentencing hearing, 53
Sentencing Reform Act (SRA), 115
September 11 attacks. *see* terror attacks of September 11, 2001
Seven Years' War, 7
sexual orientation, discrimination and, 101
Shatzer, Michael Blaine, 368
shepardizing, 43, 492
Shepard's Citations, 43
Sherman, Roger, 482
showup, 414
Silverthorne Lumber Company, 232
Simmons, Christopher, 444
Simpson, O.J., 40
sittings, 73
slavery, 15, 463
    abolition of, 81
    Thirteenth Amendment and, 81–82, 463
    U.S. Constitution and, 15
Smith, Joseph, 129
Smith, Lamar, 116
Smith, William Kennedy, 164
Snyder, Allen, 400
Snyder, Matthew, 154
social contract, 31
Socialist Labor Party, 180
Sokolow, Andrew, 324
Sotomayor, Sonia, 70, 99, 289
Souter, David, 69, 99, 221
Spaight, Richd Dobbs, 483
speech
    balancing test for, 149
    freedom of, 138–161
        and flag burning, 141
        and Internet, 159–160
        restrictions on, 152–155
    imminent lawless action test for, 149
    symbolic, 140–143
speedy trial, 464
Stamp Act, 8
"stand your ground" laws, 186
standing, 50, 103, 208
Star Chamber, 429
stare decisis, 35–36
state action, 208
state courts, 45

intermediate appellate, 47
    levels in, 45
    lower, 45, 47
    State Supreme Courts, 47
state judicial system, 46
state, separation from church, 130
statement, deliberate elicitation of, 410
states, reserve powers of, 460
status offenses, 52
statutory law, 38
Stevens, John Paul, 69, 143, 444
Stevens, Robert, 146
Stewart, Potter, 409, 459
Stockton, Richard, 11
Stolen Valor Act of 2005, 146–147
Stone, Harlan F., 150
stop, 215
    compared with arrest, 249
    defined, 225
    at international border, 262–263
    investigatory, 249–263
    length of, 254–256
    pedestrian, controversy over, 256
    protective actions during, 256
    traffic, 257–261
stop and frisk, 225, 256
    basic definitions, 225–227
    law of, 225–228
Stored Communications Act, 337
straw purchase, 199
Street, Sidney, 141
strict construction, 75
strict scrutiny, 135, 168
string cites, 41
subpoena, 404
substantive due process, 84, 87–90
substantive law, 38
Sudden Impact, 185
suits at common law, 457
summary judgment, 99
Sunset Clause, 190
supremacy clause, 19, 108
surveillance, electronic. *see* electronic surveillance
suspect
    under arrest, 361–362
    being informed of accusation, 402
    in custody for another offence, 362–363
    at the police station, 362
suspicious activity reporting (SAR), 91
    sharing, 92
sweep, protective, 308
Sykes, Diane S., 182
symbolic speech, 140–143

TASER®, 275, 276–278
TASER® X26, 276
taxes, 468
telephonic warrants, 220
Ten Commandments, 133
    in schools, 132
terror attacks of September 11, 2001, 104, 129, 325, 338, 385
terrorism
    counterterrorism command centers in Washington, D.C., area, 119
    and USA PATRIOT Act, 385–388
Terry, John, 227
Terry stop, 195, 228, 252, 256, 261, 349, 494

Subject Index

Third Circuit, 146
Thomas, Clarence, 69–70, 97, 100, 133, 331, 373, 443
    affirmative action and, 97
Thompkins, Van Chester, 367
Thompson, William Lee, 443
Three Mile Island nuclear accident, 161
"three strikes law" (California), 436
Time, 75
Time Magazine, 270
Title I of the Elementary and Secondary Education Act of 1965, 132
Title V of the Rehabilitation Act of 1973, 101
Title VII of the Civil Rights Act, 99
    prohibits intentional acts of employee discrimination, 100
Title IX of the Education Amendments of 1972, 95
tort, 39
totality of circumstances, 214, 300
traffic stops, 112, 257–261. *see also* *Terry* stop
    disparity of, 112
    Miranda warning and, 257
Treaty of Paris, 7
trial
    bifurcated, 441
    compulsory process and, 404
    critical stages at, 415–419
    fair, right to, 392–423
    public, 395–396
    rights of, key cases regarding, 419
    speedy, 394–395
    venue of, 402
trial jury, compared with grand jury, 380
"The Trial of John Peter Zenger", 162
twenty-first century, racial and gender equality in, 100
Tyler, John, 466
Tyson, Mike, 164

unenumerated rights, 88–89
Uniform Act of Fresh Pursuit, 268
Uniform Code of Military Justice, 55
United States, development of, 6–10
unreasonable interference, 214
U.S. Congress, 40
U.S. Constitution, 4, 5, 8, 12, 20, 25, 27, 40, 44, 79, 108, 476–488
    amendment process for, 19
    amendments to, 457–468
        attempts at, 468–470
    analysis of search and seizure, 316
    Article 1 of, 16–17, 460
    Article 2 of, 17–18, 67
    Article 3 of, 18, 44, 61, 490
    Article 4 of, 19
    Article 5 of, 19
    Article 6 of, 19, 460
    balancing meaning of, 142
    beginnings of, 5–6
    Bill of Rights, 4, 17, 19, 37, 80–81, 86, 116, 129, 178, 383, 457–468
        and balance of powers, 21–25
        Magna Carta and, 21
        overview of, 22–25
    certiorari, 97
    commerce clause of, 118, 178, 460
    and Constitutional Convention of 1787, 13–15
    drafting, 15–16
    Eighteenth Amendment to, 468

Eighth Amendment to, 25, 40, 53, 86, 427–451, 465
    corrections and, 448–451
    excessive fines clause of, 433–435
    prisoners' rights and, 449–450
    rights protected by, 428
elastic clause of, 17, 460
Eleventh Amendment to, 463
Fifteenth Amendment to, 37, 466
    racial discrimination and, 94
Fifth Amendment to, 24, 83, 86, 153, 280, 393, 404, 464, 491
    confessions and, 351–357
    consequences of a *Miranda* violation, 375–376
    corrections and, 384–385
    due process and, 350–351
    due process clause, 83–84
    grand jury clause, 379–380
    just compensation, 382–383
    Miranda implications of using informant and, 376–377
    Miranda v. Arizona and, 357–377
    obtaining information legally, 345–388
    protection from double jeopardy, 380–382
    right against self-incrimination and, 348–350
    right to counsel and, 368–370
    rights guaranteed by, 378–383
    rights of prisoners and, 384–385
    USA PATRIOT Act, 385–388
First Amendment to, 23, 51, 74, 88, 126–170, 214, 385, 464
    aid to terrorist groups and, 153
    balancing individual and societal rights, 128
    establishment clause in, 51130–133
    flag burning and, 141
    free exercise clause, 134–138
    freedom of association and, 166–167
    freedom of press and, 161–164
    freedom of religion and, 129–138
    freedom of speech and, 138–161
    pledge of allegiance and, 110
    preferred freedoms approach, 150
    right of freedom of association, 166–167
    right to peaceful assembly and, 164–166
    rights of prisoners and, 168–170
Fourteenth Amendment to, 26, 37, 82–9296, 105, 112, 114, 118, 135, 138, 150, 156, 162, 166, 180–181, 208, 231, 280, 349, 352, 354, 396, 430, 444, 464–465, 494
    double jeopardy clause, 380
    due process clause, 83–86, 181, 402, 406, 423
    equal protection clause, 83, 96, 112
    equal protection under the law and, 79–121
    racial profiling and, 112
    right to privacy and, 88
    selective incorporation and, 464
Fourth Amendment to, 24, 50, 163, 186, 247, 251, 257, 271, 464, 494
    clauses of, 212
    continuum of contacts and, 222–225
    conventional approach to clauses of, 212
    crime and, 163
    electronic surveillance and, 333–340
    exclusionary rule and, 229–239
    importance of, in law enforcement, 207–208

    inquiry of, overview, 208
    interpretations of, 212–213
    persons regulated by, 208–211
    on probable cause, 214–219
    protective sweep, 308
    reasonableness clause of, 213–214
    search and arrest warrants, 219–222
    search and seizure and, 203–242
    stop and frisk, 225–228
    tenets of search analysis, 288–290
    unreasonable searches and, 164
    violations according to, consequences of, 229–239
    warrant clause of, 212
framers of, 461
incorporation doctrine of, 84
influence of Magna Carta on, 12–13
as living law, 25
necessary and proper clause, 460–461
Nineteenth Amendment to, 37, 467
Ninth Amendment to, 25, 89, 458–460, 465
other provisions, 19
overview of, 16–21
ratification of, 20–21
search and, 286–340
Second Amendment to, 8, 23, 71, 86, 174–199, 464, 494
    balancing individual and states' rights, 177–178
    early case law regarding, 178–182
    federal regulation and, 186–194
    gun control controversy and, 182–199
    historical background of, 176
    incorporation of, 180–182
    interpretation of, 176–180
    modern-day militias and, 177
    operative clause of, 177
    prefatory clause of, 177
seizures according to, 246–282
Seventeenth Amendment to, 465
Seventh Amendment to, 457–458, 465
signers of, 10–11
signing of, 19–20
Sixteenth Amendment to, 468
Sixth Amendment to, 24, 85, 392–423, 457, 464
    confrontation clause, 402
    public trial and, 395–396
    and right to counsel, 368–370, 404–408
slavery and, 15
supremacy clause, 461
Supreme Court and, 58–76
as supreme law, 19
Tenth Amendment to, 15, 25, 178, 460–463
Third Amendment to, 8, 24, 86, 457
Thirteenth Amendment to, 37, 81–82, 93, 463
    abolition of slavery and, 81
    ratification of, 80
    slavery and, 81, 93, 463
Twelfth Amendment to, 465
Twentieth Amendment to, 465, 470
Twenty-Fifth Amendment to, 466
Twenty-First Amendment to, 37, 468, 470
Twenty-Fourth Amendment to, 467
Twenty-Second Amendment to, 466
Twenty-Seventh Amendment to, 466, 470
Twenty-Sixth Amendment to, 467
Twenty-Third Amendment to, 466
U.S. Court of Appeals, 47, 119, 151
U.S. Department of Justice, 161, 467
    Bureau of Justice Statistics, 194, 493

U.S. District Courts, 47
U.S. Federal Judiciairy, 493
U.S. Justice Department, 110
U.S. Marshalls Service, asset forfeiture program and, 434
U.S. National Central Bureau, 54
U.S. Postal Regulations, 335
U.S. Supreme Court, 18, 41, 47–48, 58–76, 109, 114, 132, 142, 146, 207, 223, 234, 246, 419, 445
- affirmative action and, 96
- authority for, 60–61
- Burger Court, 69
- certiorari, 65–67
- as check on federal power, 118–119
- conservative, 68
- current, 69–71
- deciding which cases to hear, 65–67
- flag burning, 141
- free exercise clause (freedom of religion) and, 137
- freedom of speech and, 139
- interpretation of the establishment clause, 132
- interpretations of, 84
- judicial review by, 63–67
- jurisdiction of, 61–63
- justices of, 67–73
- liberal, 68
- opinions of, 74–75
- politics and, 68–69
- power of, 75–76
- probable cause and, 109
- procedures of, 73–75
- public opinion of, 60
- recesses of, 74
- Rehnquist Court, 69
- sittings of, 74
- traditions of, 73–75
- Warren Court, 69
- website of, 40, 471

USA PATRIOT Act, 153, 335, 347, 385–388, 456
- changing society and, 388
- information sharing and cooperation among government agencies, 386
- new technologies and threats, 386–387
- penalties and, 387
- renewal of, 387–388
- use of already available tools, 386

vacate, 42
vehicle, impounded, search of, 314–315
venire, 397
Ventris, Donnie, 419
venue, 44, 402, 464
victims' rights amendments, 469
video games, violent, 159
Vietnam War, 138
Vinson, Fred, 432
Violent Crime Control and Law Enforcement Act of 1994, 186, 190
Virginia Military Institute (VMI), 95
Virginia Tech survivor, 194
voir dire, 397
voluntariness
- of confession, 352–354
- standard for, 354, 356

voluntariness test, 300
voluntary contact, 272
voting age, 467
voting rights, 466–467
- extended to Black males, 466
- extended to women, 467, 473
- poll taxes, 467
- voting age, 467

Voting Rights Act, 100, 467

Wade-Gilbert rule, 414
waiver, 365
- of right to counsel, 422
waiver and consent to search form, 297
waiver test, 300
Wall Street Journal, 387
Wardlow, William "Sam", 254
warrant, 208
- administrative, 326
- automobile exception to, 311–315
- executing, 222, 293
- and knock-and-announce rule, 220–221
- nightcap(ped), 222
- sample of, 292
- search with, 291–296
- search without, 296–313
warrant clause, of Fourth Amendment, 212
warrantless search
- emergency aid doctrine and, 318–319
- exigent circumstances and, 315–319
- frisks and, 301–302
- hot pursuit, 316–317
- immanent destruction of evidence, 315–316

Warren Court, 141
Warren, Earl, 69, 357, 429
Washington, D.C., counterterrorism command centers in, 120
Washington, George, 7, 12, 13, 14, 27, 93, 347
Washington Post, 119, 163
weapons, 186
- less-lethal, 275–276
Webster, Daniel, 81
Weeks, Fremont, 230
Wells, Martin, 315
Welsh, Edward, 316
Westboro Baptist Church, 154
Westlaw, 493
White, Byron, 237, 396
Wikipedia, 41
Williams, Robert, 234
Williamson, Hu, 483
Wilson, James, 482
wingspan, 305
Wiretap Act, 334
Wisconsin Department of Health and Social Services, 330
witness, right to confront, 402–404
women's right to vote, 37
World War I, censorship and, 162

yard signs, 142–143
YouTube, 160

Zenger, John Peter, 162
Zimmerman, George, 185
zones of privacy, 89